THE ECOLOGY OF FREEDOM

THE ECOLOGY OF FREEDOM
the emergence and dissolution of hierarchy

MURRAY BOOKCHIN

ak press ೞ   *2005*

Bookchin, Murray
The Ecology of Freedom: The Emergenge and Dissolution of Hierarchy

Library of Congress Control Number 2005923316
ISBN 1-904859-26-7
9781904859260

Published by AK Press

AK Press
674-A 23rd St.
Oakland, CA 94612
USA
www.akpress.org
akpress@akpress.org

AK Press UK
PO Box 12766
Edinburgh, EH8 9YE
Scotland
(0131) 555-5165
www.akuk.com
ak@akedin.demon.co.uk

Cover design by Jacqueline Thaw
Layout by Juliana Spahr
Thanks also to Erika Biddle

Printed in the USA

To Bea, who has added more to my life, done more for me as a human being, and established a sense of decency, care, understanding and kindness than anyone I've ever known. To you, dear Bea, I not only dedicate this book but give it to you with all my love,

Murray, Mar. 1, 1985.

We are enabled to conclude that the lesson which man derives from both the study of Nature and his own history is the permanent presence of a *double tendency*—towards a greater development on the one side of *sociality*, and, on the other side, of a consequent increase in the intensity of life.... This double tendency is a distinctive characteristic of life in general. It is always present, and belongs to life, as one of its attributes, whatever aspects life may take on our planet or elsewhere. And this is not a metaphysical assertion of the "universality of the moral law," or a mere supposition. Without the continual growth of sociality, and consequently of the intensity and variety of sensations, life is impossible.

—Peter Kropotkin, *Ethics*

We are forgetting how to give presents. Violation of the exchange principle has something nonsensical and implausible about it; here and there even children eye the giver suspiciously, as if the gift were merely a trick to sell them brushes or soap. Instead we have charity, administered beneficence, the planned pastering over of society's visible sores. In its organized operations there is no longer room for human impulses, indeed, the gift is necessarily accompanied by humiliation through its distribution, its just allocation, in short, through treatment of the recipient as an object.

—Theodor Adorno, *Minima Moralia*

Ontology as the ground of ethics was the original tenet of philosophy. Their divorce, which is the divorce of the "objective" and "subjective" realms, is the modern destiny. Their reunion can be effected, if at all, only from the "objective" end, that is to say, through a revision of the idea of nature. And it is becoming rather than abiding nature which would hold out any such promise. From the immanent direction of its total evolution there may be elicited a destination of man by whose terms the person, in the act of fulfilling himself, would at the same time realize a concern of universal substance. Hence would result a principle of ethics which is ultimately grounded neither in the autonomy of the self nor in the needs of the community, but in an objective assignment by the nature of things.

—Hans Jonas, *The Phenomenon of Life*

∾ **ACKNOWLEDGMENTS**

I would like to thank the late Angus Cameron of Alfred A. Knopf, Inc., who initially contracted this book three decades ago and continually encouraged me to work on it in the early seventies. I also owe a profound debt to Michael Riordan of Cheshire Books, who zealously saw to its publication in 1982. Dimitri Roussopoulos of Black Rose Books republished the book in 1991 with a new introduction that revises and balances out a number of views that appeared in the 1982 edition. I want to thank Janet Biehl for her suggestions and her role in making the new preface for this 2005 edition more readable. For translating the book and seeing to its publication in Germany, as well as for many suggestions and criticism, I owe an enormous debt to my dear friend Karl-Ludwig Schibel, and to our shared friend Bernd Leineweber of Frankfurt am Main. I owe, also, similar debts to my friends, Amadeo Bertolo and Rossella di Leo, who translated the book into Italian and saw to its publication in Italy.

Many friends and consultants contributed to this book: Richard Merrill, who gave generously of his biological expertise; my children, Debbie and Joseph Bookchin, for the warm atmosphere they provided while the book was being written; Gina Blumenfeld, Daniel Chodorkoff, David Eisen, Linda Goodman, and the book's excellent copy editor, Naomi Steinfeld. I wish to acknowledge the grant I received from the Rabinowitz Foundation for providing part of the means I needed to complete the first four chapters in the early seventies.

I benefited greatly from the work of Max Weber, Paul Radin, and Dorothy Lee for the anthropological sections of this book. The writings of Peter Kropotkin and Karl Marx remain an abiding theoretical tradition to which I am deeply committed. In retrospect, I am less enamored of the Frankfurt School theorists than I was in the past, although their word magic, their defense of reason against mysticism, and their demanding intellectual level remain as inspiring to me today as they were so many years ago.

The Ecology of Freedom is a wayward book that has acquired a life of its own. I cannot refrain from inviting the reader to participate in formulating the changing views it expresses—or should express. Such invitations were commonplace enough for authors to make fifty years or so ago, but they seem to be on their way to oblivion in an age of mass media, where every thought has to be spelled out merely to gain the reader's attention. Hence I will close with the exquisite remarks (all failings of gender aside) of my favorite utopian, William Morris:

> Men fight and lose the battle, and the thing they fought for comes about in spite of their defeat, and when it comes turns out to be not what they want, and other men have to fight for what they meant under another name.

Murray Bookchin
Burlington, Vermont, February 2005
Director Emeritus, Institute for Social Ecology, Plainfield, Vermont
Professor Emeritus, Ramapo College, Mahwah, New Jersey

ʚ PREFACE TO THE 2005 AK PRESS EDITION

The Ecology of Freedom has been in print for nearly thirty years and read by more than 60,000 fairly demanding people in six different languages. Given its challenging depth and scope, it would be of considerable help in understanding its message for the reader to have an ample knowledge of nature philosophy, social history, radical theory, and current political affairs.

Not surprisingly, the book has acquired a life and following of its own and is meant to be read on many different levels. I often lay out premises to which I hope the reader will add themes that merit further elaboration under new social circumstances and possibilities. Moreover the reader is challenged to fill out themes that were only partly developed or hinted at in earlier works. Hence the reader is invited not only to participate with the author on various levels of analysis but in a very real sense to engage in an active authorial role, in which he or she continually raises and strives to answer new questions that continue to emerge in periods of rapid social change. Accordingly, *The Ecology of Freedom* has never been a "final statement" of my views. Indeed, such finality never existed in the works of any serious author, because times are always changing, developing, ebbing, and thereby opening radically new ideological pathways. Yesterday's alleged "final conflicts" actually open new lines of thought that are the opposite of earlier certitudes. Consider only the advances and regressions that were produced by the State, which at one time served the liberatory potentialities of citizenship (as distinguished from the animalistic blood tie) but in later times served the oppressive potentialities of kinship and the mindless dictates of biology in which choice had very little place, if any.

The Ecology of Freedom also draws a sharp line between a simplistic theory of *classificatory* environmentalism and a sophisticated theory of *developmental* social ecology, terms that are filled with many diverse meanings. To most readers, the word *ecology* means little more than what I call "environmentalism"—that is, the habitat in which human beings, other animals, and plants live and interact. By "social ecology," I therefore mean ecology as the dialectical *unfolding* of life-forms from the simple to the complex, or more precisely, from the simple to the diverse. This interpretation is arguably problematical. It can be reasonably claimed that diversity *in itself* does not necessarily yield complexity. But what seems very clear is that without complexity there cannot be diversity. Thus a tendency toward diversity is indispensable to the emergence of our rich cosmos of life-forms—a cosmos that makes up the multitude of "selections" in the geological, biotic, and even subjective universe in which we live. This cosmos also makes up the *human*-made universe, or the "second nature" we are imposing on nonhuman evolution, or "first nature."

I cannot emphasize too strongly that such a two-fold definition of "nature" is one of the most important distinctions I tried to make in this book. Broadly, we must distinguish between a nature that is *self-created* and a nature that is *humanly created.* Ancient philosophy (particularly the work of Plato and Aristotle) danced around this problem when it tried to define the place of God in the universe as craftsman rather than as a thinker. What should be beyond dispute is that by making *humanity* the craftsman who fashioned the universe rather than simply "declared" its existence, rebellious European theologians made human beings into a productive demiurge rather than the source of the mystical "word." In short, a "second nature," was literally *created*, not simply *pronounced.* God became the creation of human beings, not simply a mystical creator.

Social ecology, in turn, is a *philosophy* of evolution, not a mystical restatement of Saint John's apocalypse. Humanity, in turn, is both an extension of ecology's insights into social development, from a biological first nature into society's second nature. *The Ecology of Freedom* tries to *synthesize* these two natures into a third nature. It tries to transform both nonhuman and human-made natures into a more complete nature that is conscious, thinking, and purposeful. This *thinking* nature is ethical and rational, not simply physiological and biochemical, and humanity is the most recent attribute among the many that evolution added over at least two billion years of organic development.

The word *social* in *social ecology* serves the purpose of bringing the highest precepts of libertarian socialism into this concept of an "ecological society"—that is, a society that embodies the highest goals of thinkers like Aristotle, Spinoza, Hegel, Marx, and Kropotkin, to cite the philosophers who have most influenced my thinking.

Social ecology, in effect, is a concept of an ever-developing universe, indeed a vast process of achieving *wholeness* (to the extent that it can *ever* be fully achieved) by means of unity in diversity, with creative potentialities that thematically intertwine two *legacies* or traditions: a legacy of freedom and a legacy of domination. These legacies interact to expand independently and interdependently the landscape of freedom and domination. The legacies educe themes that have been elaborated primarily in the later writings of Marx and Kropotkin as two historical ends. It is thus possible to elaborate an eductive dialectic that can deal with themes like democracy, aesthetics, philosophy, the State, politics and related so-called "superstructural" attributes of social and cultural life as integral parts of life and society, not simply as the offspring of economics that, according to Marx, formed the "base" of social phenomena. A "polymorphous" theory of history, so to speak, supplants the often narrow monism that prevailed among mechanistic Marxists like Friedrich Engels, George Plekhanov, V.I. Lenin, et al., trapping Marx himself in the economistic mid-stage of his own cycle of theoretical development.

In social ecology, democracy, for example, now *becomes an end in itself,* unfolding as a basic theme in the legacy of freedom. Similarly, the State can be explored as a basic component of the legacy of domination, often intertwining with the legacy of freedom, as when it secularized the blood tie into the civic tie qua citizen, then later became an instrument of class rule. The two chapters on these legacies thus form the book's essential structure and unifying orientation—its "double helix," so to speak.

Ernst Bloch, in his critical writings, seemed to find a "principle of hope" in almost every ideology he explored. The times in which I lived for some eighty years allowed for no such generosity. Still, I can single out one theme that will terminate either in an ever-expansive development of human freedom comparable to Marx's ideal of communism or in an era of ongoing crisis and decline in humanity's relationship with the natural world. This book offers no *guarantee of success* in the outcome of human development; only the *possibility* of a *rational* outcome.

In *The Ecology of Freedom,* the simplification of biotic evolution would become the harbinger of a world in dissolution. History, conceived as the overall rational continuum of human affairs, would disappear, and humanity itself would undergo self-dissolution. The disappearance of the organic would find its expression in the steady decline of complexity, in the replacement of meaning, consciousness, agency, and creative causality by complete purposelessness. This disassembly would constitute a conflict more final than the odious prospects of atomization and social breakdown that confronted humanity in the chronic social crises that marked the previous century. It is this that humanity faces in the coming years if the legacy of domination is permitted to unfold at the expense of the legacy of freedom. If we are to avoid this fate and fulfill instead the legacy of freedom's potentiality, we must transcend the ideological limitations of a mystical proletariat, a battle between undefined class interests, and the simplistic aims that bind us to a world long gone. More than ever, we need a clearer vision of humanity's capacity to *think* as well as to act, to confront reality *not only as it is but as it should be* if we are to survive this, the greatest turning point in history.*

Much has happened since *The Ecology of Freedom* was initially published in 1982. In that year much of the utopistic sensibility of the 1960s was still in the air, and environmental movements were springing up throughout the world. Green political organizations were growing, especially in Western Europe and North America. A "principle of hope" still held some sway, as the deep reaction of the 1990s had yet to emerge. Yet I cannot emphasize too strongly that the revolutionary optimism that existed between the Russian Revolution of 1917–18 and the Second World War had been gravely misplaced. Marxism, which regarded the success of revolutionary socialism as an *imminent* certainty, had totally misjudged the future of radicalism in this interwar period. As the myth of working-class hegemony faded with the end of World War II; as the certainty of a victorious world social revolution gave way to an extraordinary expansion of capital; as capitalism itself prospered, such as it had never done in the past—humanity was not living in the dusk of bourgeois society. Rather, capitalism may well have been emerging from its dawn, or at least was still rooted in an early stage of its development. All the estimates of the Left on the decline of bourgeois society *were wrong*—as were the ebullient perspectives that followed in the wake of Red October. We did not know during the interwar period—*nor do we know today*—in what "phase" of capitalism we live. What is now clear is that it would be the height of self-deception to call capitalism today a "moribund," "decaying," or "dying" social system the way we did between 1917 and 1945. Like it or not, capitalism today is robust materially, a fact that the Left must finally face with the utmost candor. And *we still do not know* what forms and features it will have in the years that lie ahead.

But what is reasonably clear to me—and I voice this prognosis with the utmost caution—is that bourgeois society cannot continue its devastation of the ecosphere without destroying the biotic and climatic foundations of its own existence. If society as such is to survive, it must produce a radically new humanity-nature dispensation. That is, we will either create a society that fosters the fecundity of biotic evolution and that makes life an ever-more conscious and creative phenomenon, or produce a world that tears down these ecological elements. This precludes a society that is guided by the maxim of "grow or die"—the immanent bourgeois drive to reduce the

---

* Or as the young Marx so brilliantly put it in his "Contribution to the Critique of Hegel's Philosophy of Law": "It is not enough for thought to strive for realisation, reality must itself strive toward thought." Karl Marx and Frederick Engels, *Collected Works,* vol. 3, *Marx and Engels 1843–1844* (New York: International Publishers, 1975), p. 183.

organic to the inorganic in an ever-competitive frenzy of capital expansion and human exploitation. Capitalism has made social evolution hopelessly incompatible with ecological evolution.

This is the definitive message of *The Ecology of Freedom*. There may be no proletarian revolution, no chronic economic crisis, no world wars, or even an "inevitable final conflict" between classes in the offing. But unless science and technics can contain the pollution and simplification of the planet, there will decidedly be a crisis in the future that strips the biosphere of its very capacity to support complex life-forms. This is one conflict that cannot be placed in doubt—for it blatantly challenges the existence of our species. All the problems explored by *The Ecology of Freedom* converge in the need to create an ecological society based on a new and organic politics called libertarian municipalism, a subject I explored in some detail in my later book *From Urbanization to Cities* (Continuum Books).

Murray Bookchin
Burlington, Vermont, January 30, 2005

∝ TWENTY YEARS LATER . . .
SEEKING A BALANCED VIEWPOINT
introduction to the 1991 edition

Some twenty years ago, I began writing *The Ecology of Freedom* with a very clear purpose in mind: to advance a holistic, socially radical, and theoretically coherent alternative to the largely technocratic, reformist, and single-issue environmental movements that were holding center stage at that time. Thanks to a contract I received from Alfred A. Knopf in 1970 and a modest Rabinowitz Foundation grant, I was able to complete the four opening chapters of this book in 1972. Apart from a few modifications, those chapters remain unaltered from what they were nearly twenty years ago. After various interruptions, I returned to the manuscript as the seventies drew to a close and completed it for publication. In the meantime, the retirement of my original editor at Knopf foreclosed the likelihood that it would be published by that firm, and without ado I turned the manuscript over to a very sympathetic firm, Cheshire Books, which published it in 1982.

I cannot emphasize too strongly that *The Ecology of Freedom* reflects my preoccupation with the rather narrow, pragmatic, often socially neutral environmentalism that held sway two decades ago in a collection of disparate groups. Such environmentalism still, in fact, enjoys preeminence today. These groups continue to focus on specific issues like air and water pollution, toxic waste dumps, the chemicalization of food, and so forth; endeavors, to be sure, that I feel deserve our fullest support. But the views of environmentalists on the causes of, and long-range solutions to, the problems they face seemed—and still seem—to me to be woefully inadequate. Insofar as environmentalists shared a common outlook, it rested on an instrumental, almost engineering approach to solving ecological dislocations. To all appearances, they wanted to adapt the natural world to the needs of the existing society and its exploitative, capitalistic imperatives by way of reforms that minimize harm to human health and well-being. The much-needed goals of formulating a project for radical social change and for cultivating a new sensibility toward the natural world tended to fall outside the orbit of their practical concerns. Lobbying rather than radical politics seemed to embody their social views.

After having been active for decades as an eco-anarchist in fighting pollution, the construction of nuclear power plants, and the chemicalization of food, I decided to write a far-reaching presentation of my views, partly critical and partly reconstructive. In contrast to pragmatic environmentalism, I advanced a comprehensive body of ideas that I call social ecology. For social ecologists, our environmental dislocations are deeply rooted in an irrational, anti-ecological society, a society whose basic problems are irremediable by piecemeal, single-issue reforms. I tried to point out that these problems originate in a hierarchical, class, and today, competitive capitalist system that nourishes a view of the natural world as a mere agglomeration of "resources" for human production and consumption. This social system is especially rapacious. It has projected the domination of human by human into an ideology that "man" is destined to dominate "Nature."

Accordingly, looking back in time to the preliterate "organic society" that existed before hierarchy and capitalism emerged, I explored the nonhierarchical sensibilities, practices, values, and beliefs of egalitarian cultures generally, as well as the social features of organic society, that seemed to be relevant to the development of a radical ecological politics today: the principle of the irreducible minimum, by which organic society guaranteed to everyone the material means of life; its commitment to usufruct rather than the ownership of property; its ethics of complementarity, as distinguished from a morality of command and obedience. All of these principles and values, to my mind, were—and are—desiderata that should find a major place in a future ecological society. I also felt that they had to be integrated with the rationality, science, and in large part the technics of the modern world, redesigned, to be sure, to promote humanity's integration with the nonhuman world. This selective integration could form the overarching practices of an entirely new society and sensibility.

At the same time, I examined organic society's various religious beliefs and cosmologies: its naturalistic rituals, its mythic personalizations of animals and animal spirits, its embodiment of fertility in a Mother Goddess, and its overall animistic outlook. I believed that the Enlightenment's battle against superstition had been long since won in American and European culture, and that no one would mistake me for advocating a revival of animism or Goddess worship. As much as I admired many features of organic cultures, I never believed that we could or should introduce their naïve religious, mythic, or magical beliefs or their cosmologies into the present-day ecology movement. Even in the late seventies, I had unnerving suspicions that one could write on ecology and its spiritual implications, as I did, and easily be mistaken for a spiritualist, and similarly even write on sophisticated organismic forms of thought like dialectics and be misread as a mystic.

But little did I realize that, even as I was writing *The Ecology of Freedom*, new ecologies were in fact emerging, principally in the American Sunbelt, that would seek to do *exactly* what I had tried to avoid. These ecologies began to recycle many beliefs that superficially resemble the kind of ideas I had advanced into a New Age romanticism and produce a mystical ecology that was all but a collection of assorted atavistic religious cults. They now appear under such names as "deep ecology," Earth Goddess worship, and ecological animism, all of which can be generically called "mystical ecology," and they use various New Age ideas, magical rituals, and a wide assortment of religious or quasi-religious practices. Many atavists among these mystical ecologists call for a return to a Neolithic or even Pleistocene "sensibility" and, in extreme cases, literally to prehistoric ways of life. Nearly all of them share a common outlook called "biocentricity," which equates all life-forms—including bacteria and viruses—with one another in terms of their "intrinsic worth." "Biocentrism" is defined in contrast to "anthropocentrism," the largely religious view (as their repeated references to Scriptural texts suggest) that the earth was "created" for human use. Also permeating many mystical ecologies is a preference for "wilderness," as distinguished from humanly altered areas of the planet, and all too often an unfeeling Malthusianism that views famine and disease as "Gaia's" retribution for human intervention into "Nature" as well as for human "overpopulation." Ecofeminism, too, has been transformed from an appreciation of women's historical role in bearing and rearing children into a veneration of women as "closer to nature" than men. Added to this imagery is a belief in an "Earth Goddess" whose worship is expected to transform patriarchal views of women into a theistic "eternal feminine." In short, I began to see a growing array of mystical, romantic, and often downright silly ecologies emerge that now threaten the very integrity of a rational ecology movement. I regard these mystical ecologies as utterly fatuous as they are simply naïve, even when many of them dissociate themselves from the same pragmatic environmentalism of the 1970s that this book criticizes.

Today, attempts to balance reason and technology with organic thinking and spirituality have been virtually subverted by the emergence of mystical, quasi-religious images of nonhuman nature. Indeed, the time when one could use the word "Nature" rather broadly without connoting the crude pantheism of a universal "Oneness" or a strident fetishization of "wilderness" has virtually disappeared. The mischief wrought particularly by "deep ecology," by the misanthropic anti-humanism that extends even to a hatred of the Renaissance, by the unfeeling Malthusianism, and by the often self-contradictory notions structured around "biocentrism"— all have now made ecological politics and philosophy into a highly problematic arena.

This introduction is meant to untangle and dissociate social ecology from these various mystical ecologies, and at the same time retain a critical attitude toward pragmatic environmentalism. More emphatically, I wish to correct any affinity the reader may find between social ecology and the various mystical ecologies that are flourishing today. Despite these new circumstances, which social ecology must confront, I strongly adhere to the ideas *The Ecology of Freedom* advances, nor do I feel any need to modify them, apart from explaining certain metaphors that the mystical ecologists have used in conjunction with social ecologists, albeit for very different purposes. What I wish to do in this introduction is to strike a more *balanced* view of the ideas, interpretations, and data contained in this book. *The Ecology of Freedom* still remains the most comprehensive statement of my ideas and of social ecology generally, and I do not wish to diminish its position in my writings. My work's theoretical arch, if I may call it such, is reared by some nine books, among which *The Ecology of Freedom* may be regarded as the keystone. But I would ask readers of this book to consult some of the other works as well that round out a social ecological perspective, notably *The Rise of Urbanization and Decline of Citizenship*, *Remaking Society*, and *The Philosophy of Social Ecology*.[1] Taken together, these works provide a comprehensive statement of social ecology as it exists today and form a basis for its development in the future.

Lastly, some degree of repetition in preparing this new retrospective introduction is unavoidable. I do not attempt the broad overview of social ecology that appears in the original introduction, a reading of which I regard as indispensable to an understanding of this book, but there are issues that I take up here, like Marxism and ecology, that provide the reader with more detailed explanations of my views. This does not diminish the need to read both introductions: the original, a more elucidatory presentation, and the Black Rose introduction, a more polemical one.

All of my writings are meant to give a coherent view of the social sources of our ecological crisis and to offer an eco-anarchist project to restructure society along rational lines. I use the words *coherent* and *rational* provocatively here, for these terms are anathema to most of the emerging mystical ecologies. Moreover, they are used to challenge a much broader state of mind that has become integrally part of the human condition in the Anglo-American world generally and in many parts of Europe today. Postmodernism, in particular its most vulgar forms, has had a disquieting effect on the need for a coherent and rational body of radical political ideas. With "deconstruction," the claims of reason itself are being dismembered in the name of a passion for "pluralism"—a passion that is understandable in the face of modern totalitarianism but that cannot be justified when it calls any thought-out body of views "logocentric." In this extremely debased form, postmodernism prefixes *logocentric* with adjectives like *white*, *male*, *western*, and *European*, foreclosing all further discussion. I hesitate to predict what new fads are surfacing on college campuses and in the media, even as this introduction is being written.

We are faced with the difficulty that few people seem to know how to build or develop ideas anymore. They promiscuously collect intellectual fragments here and there, like so many dismembered artifacts, drawing upon basically contradictory views and traditions with complete aplomb. Indeed, any serious attempt to rationally discuss the very troubling issues of our time in a coherent manner is often treated as a symptom of psychopathology rather than an earnest effort to make sense of the ideological chaos so prevalent today. Ironically, in its own quixotic way, postmodernism often inadvertently works with a rationality of its own that is nonetheless opaque to itself, and it often strives for the very coherence whose existence it denies to its critics.

The intellectual tendencies that celebrate incoherence, antirationalism, and mysticism are not merely symptoms of a waning intellectuality today. They literally *justify* and *foster* it. The massive shift by many people away from serious concerns with the objective conditions of life—such as institutional forms of domination, the use of technology for exploitative purposes, and the everyday realities of human suffering—toward an introverted subjectivism, with its overwhelming focus on psychology and "hidden" motivations, the rise of the culture industry, and the intellectual anxieties over collegiate issues like academic careers and pedagogical eminence—all testify to a sense of disempowerment in both social and personal life.

That the mystical ecologies are becoming popular today is not a mere intellectual aberration, any more than the popularity of postmodernism. To the contrary, their popularity expresses the inability of millions of people to cope with a harsh and demoralizing reality, to control the increasingly oppressive direction in which society is moving. Hence myths, pagan deities, and "Pleistocene" and "Neolithic" belief-systems together with their priests and priestesses provide a surrogate "reality" into which the naïve acolyte can escape. Indeed, when this preening emphasis on the subjective is clothed in the mystical vapors and inchoate vagaries of fevered imaginations, any recognition of reality is dissolved by beliefs in the mythic. The rational is replaced by the intuitional, and palpable social opponents are replaced by their shadows, to be exorcised by rituals, incantations, and magical gymnastics.

All of these practices are merely socially harmless surrogates for dealing with the authentic problems of our time. Ghosts from a distant past, the products of our ancestors' own imaginations, in turn, are invoked as objects of our reverence in the name of an "earth wisdom" that is actually as ineffectual as we are in our everyday lives. The new surrogate "reality" that is becoming a widespread feature in our time percolates through the mass media and the publishing industry, which are only too eager to nourish, even celebrate the proliferation of wiccan covens, Goddess-worshipping congregations, assorted pantheistic and animistic cults, "wilderness" devotees, and ecofeminist acolytes—to which I can add a new "deep ecology" professoriat that is increasingly prepared to feed a gullible public with "biocentric" pablum.

Perhaps the most compelling real fact that radicals in our era have not adequately faced is the fact that capitalism today has become a *society*, not only an economy. The rivalries, the grow-or-die mentality, and the chaos of the marketplace have percolated from the realms of commerce and industry, which were once largely confined to economic life, into the daily life of familial, personal, sexual, religious, and community relationships. This invasion is reflected by the often unadorned egotism, consumerism, careerism, mutual suspicion, and highly transitory forms of human intercourse, so widespread today. In the decades that followed the end of the Second World War, we have seen a development that has not only produced the anomie of the "lonely crowd;" it has now taken the form of a totally commodified world in which people resemble the very commodities that they produce and consume. Fragmentation has ceased to be a mere malaise and become an ideology, one that conforms with—rather than critiques—the prevailing human condition in the form of a vulgar postmodernism. Present-day antirational ideologies express rather than reject the unthinking and self-seeking "life-world" so frenziedly peopled by the inhabitants of the stock-market floors of the world.

These ideologies, from postmodernism to ecofeminism, serve to subtly enchant the new human commodities with the mental fireworks, amulets, charms, and brightly tinted garments that provide them with a mystical patina to conceal their empty lives. Capitalism has nothing whatever to fear from mystical and "biocentric" ecologies, or their many high-priced artifacts. The bourgeoisie easily guffaws at these absurdities and is only too eager to commodify them into new sources of profit. Indeed, to state the issue bluntly: it is profit, power, and economic expansion that primarily concerns the elites of the existing social order, not the antics or even the protests of dissenters who duel with ghosts instead of institutionalized centers of power, authority, and wealth.

ℭ

My purpose in developing social ecology over the past decades has been a frankly ambitious one: to present a philosophy, a conception of natural and social development, an in-depth analysis of our social and environmental problems, and a radical utopian alternative—to this day, I do not eschew the use of the word *utopian*—to the present social and environmental crisis. It may be helpful here to single out some issues that should be added to the overview I present in the original introduction.

I shall begin by asking: What is humanity's place in natural evolution? This question is not simply an environmental one; it has far-reaching social and philosophical implications. Human beings and human society in varying respects are products of natural evolution; further, human beings are organized anatomically and physiologically by natural evolution to interact with nonhuman nature productively, as creatures that consciously produce their own means of life with tools, machines, and the organized deployment of their very capacity to labor. As Hegel and radical social theorists of the last century emphasized, humanity's interaction or "metabolism" with nonhuman nature not only provides human beings with the means of life; it *defines* them as—one would hope—increasingly conscious and psychologically complex beings. Humanity's emergence from and continuing daily interaction with nonhuman nature is not only the means by which they maintain themselves materially; it is also one of the major ways they become aware of themselves as individuals and as a very unique species. Call them *homo sapiens, homo faber, homo economicus,* or what you will, their very humanness and the kinds of societies they create stem in large measure from their efforts to rework nonhuman nature into a habitat where they can live the "good life" and hopefully contribute fruitfully to the enhancement of natural evolution.

Hence, the question of what place human beings occupy in natural evolution raises some of the most fundamental social issues that radical social theorists confront: the ways in which human labor is used, the role of technics in altering the environment as well as in altering the human spirit, the forms of social relations that human beings develop in dealing with nonhuman nature, and—of paramount importance—the ethics they formulate by which they are guided in interacting with the surrounding world.

I shall be careful in this introduction to avoid using the word "nature" without adding an adjective to qualify it. In fact, the greatest confusion has arisen as a result of the many and often-contradictory meanings imputed to the word throughout the course of Western history and philosophy. (I was no less remiss in this regard than others when *The Ecology of Freedom* was completed a decade ago.) In their inventory of "Some Meanings of 'Nature,'" Arthur O. Lovejoy and George Boas list sixty-six definitions, ranging from "birth" to "matter," and we are then told that their list is "doubtless incomplete."[2] I am no devotee of one-line propositional definitions, but the multiplicity of ways in which the word "nature" has been defined woefully obscures the word's meaning. Judgments about what is "natural" and what is not "natural," indeed about what constitutes the "rights of nature," are a major source of ethical confusion today. This is particularly the case with supporters of "deep ecology," for whom "nature" usually carries the very narrow and particular connotation of "wilderness"—a term that is itself direly in need of explication at a time when human activities have reached directly or indirectly into the most remote areas of the planet so that their impact brings the very notion of "wilderness" into question.

Lest our thinking be frozen by too narrow a notion of "nature" as "primeval wilderness" that a presumably unnatural "humanity" (yet another term that needs clarification) invades and destroys, we must decide what so vague and emotionally highly charged a term means. For in a very broad sense, *everything* is "natural" insofar as it exists—certainly on the subatomic level, be it a plastic table or wolves on the Alaskan tundra. "Nature" defined in this purely materialist sense may be more all-embracing and in its own way more accurate than the narrow or metaphorical uses of the term. But from an *ecological* viewpoint, so sweeping a definition is simply vacuous and lacks that all-important ethical attribute we call *meaning*.

Viewed from a social and ecological standpoint, "nature"—to social ecologists, at least—is not simply everything that "exists." It is an *evolutionary development*, as I emphasize in the body of this book, that should be conceived as an aeons-long process of ever-greater differentiation: from the primal energy pulse that supposedly gave rise to the "Big Bang," to the emergence of subatomic particles and the forces that bind the universe, to the complex elements that are known to us in the periodic table, to the appearance of all the celestial bodies of which we have knowledge, to the combinations of elements into molecules, amino acids, proteins, and so forth—up to or until the emergence of organic and sentient beings on our planet. Nature, in short, is a cumulative evolutionary process from the inanimate to the animate and ultimately the social, however differentiated this process may be.

Following a tradition that may date back to the beginnings of Western philosophy, *nonhuman* nature can be designated "first nature," in juxtaposition to the *social* nature created by human beings, called "second nature." Social ecology is almost alone these days in dealing with these two developments of "nature-as-a-whole" as a highly creative and shared evolution rather than as an oppositional and purely dualistic antinomy. By contrast, mystical ecologies—with their "biocentric" notions—often disdain the problems of humanity and second nature; indeed, they tend to venerate first nature as "wilderness." These ecologies often view the human species as an evolutionary aberration—or worse, as an absolute disaster, a "cancer" on the biosphere.

What we encounter among mystical ecologies is a crude reductionism that ignores the rich differentiations that biotic evolution has produced and sees instead a universal "oneness" and "interconnectedness," that visualizes a "whole" without meaningful differentiations. To this reductionism, social ecology opposes a view of an evolutionary dialectic, of development and emergence, of variety and differentiation, indeed, the phasing of first into second nature as a *shared* and *meaningful* process. The word "nature" is deliberately preserved in the concepts of a first and second *nature* to emphasize that both nonhuman and human nature are the product of natural evolution as a whole—not of a Supernature, be it "immanent," as many mystically oriented ecologies would have us believe, or a vague presence in our midst. Even the most ostensibly secular of "deep ecology" writers tend to exhibit a certain amount of religiosity; by definition, in fact, even the most political acolytes of Goddess-worship are implicitly non-naturalistic, if not explicitly supernaturalistic. The promiscuous use of the word *sacred* to denote natural phenomena in mystical ecologies expresses a belief in the "holiness" of the nonhuman world rather than a sense of wonder. Hence the ease with which these ecologies lend themselves to the sacerdotal and a belief in the divine.

Social ecology, by contrast, contends that if the word *ecology* is used to describe our outlook, it is preposterous to invoke deities, mystical forces to account for the evolution of first nature into second nature. Neither religion nor a spiritualistic vision of experience has any place in an ecological lexicon. Either the term *ecology* applies to natural phenomena *by definition*, or it is a chic metaphor for the disempowered consciousness that fosters mysticism or outright supernaturalism.

Social ecologists use the word *social*, in turn, in a way that is free of the slipshod, often metaphorical confusion that leads to an identification of animal groups, herds, and ecocommunities with *society*. It is basic to social ecology that whereas animals form communities, they do not form societies. Society is the exclusive province of humans, for what distinguishes a human society from an animal community is the existence of social *institutions*. In this respect, social ecology's anarchistic outlook should be distinguished from that of Peter Kropotkin, who not only used the phrase *animal societies* interchangeably with *animal communities* but believed that they stemmed from a "social instinct." Perhaps—but as we shall see, this instinct was by no means social in a human sense; nor does it accord with what we know about the malleability of human society. Community, in short, may be invoked as a necessary condition for sociality of one kind or another, but it is certainly not a sufficient condition for explaining the existence of society.

And indeed, human societies stand in very marked contrast to animal communities. In the first place, animal communities are relatively fixed; some of the most "social" of animals, such as the bee, behave overwhelmingly in response to the way they are genetically "programmed," and their hives are simply large reproductive communities. By contrast, human societies are structured around highly mutable institutions, be they tribal, slave, feudal, or capitalist in form. Societies have to be defended and preserved with a sense of deliberate purpose. Indeed, where animal communities exist with any degree of permanence, their members exhibit little, if any, conscious intentionality. Human societies, by contrast, are not only highly institutionalized and changeable, but they are clothed in *ideologies* that may be altered radically depending upon material and cultural conditions, as the histories of all the great revolutions of the past so dramatically reveal.

⌀

Social ecology's use of the terms *first* and *second nature* gains particular importance when we examine the specifics of the transition from first to second nature. In tracing the natural transitions from first to second nature, or from nonhuman communities to human society, I have been more disposed to adopt Robert Briffault's thesis of prolonged human infantile dependency and maturation—a development that focuses on primate maternal association—than Kropotkin's proto-sociobiological arguments for a genetically imprinted "social instinct," which is actually absent in many advanced animal species, like leopards, and even in primates like the orangutan.

Moreover, *hierarchy*, a strictly social term, is exclusively characteristic of second nature. It refers to institutionalized and highly ideological systems of command and obedience. Etymologically, the word derives from the ancient Greek term meaning "priestly forms of organization." The utmost havoc has been created by anthropomorphically applying the word *hierarchy* to various entities in nonhuman nature. As a social term, *hierarchy* cannot be applied to so-called "dominance-and-submission" relationships among animals, where these truly exist at all. Many allegedly "hierarchical" animal relationships are actually very arbitrary and limited, as I emphasize in the book. They markedly differ in function from one group of individuals to another within the same species. More important, to apply the term to animal communities divests *hierarchy* of its strictly social character.

Still further havoc has been created by applying the word *hierarchy* to humanity's relationship with first nature as a whole, notably by alleging that humanity "dominates" first nature, or indeed, to explain the interrelationships among mineral, geophysical, and inorganic phenomena generally. Such anthropomorphic projections of specifically intrahuman phenomena are utterly unwarranted. Alas, my repeated objections to the extension of anthropomorphic images from the social world to the nonhuman, in this respect, has been of little avail.

Indeed, I have recently been accused of "hierarchical" thinking simply for noting that humanity has been endowed by natural evolution with a degree of intellectuality, a range of expression, a physical flexibility, and a cultural tradition that is unprecedented in the biotic world. My claim that human beings have the potentiality to bring their consciousness to the service of natural evolution in an ecological society has been regarded by "deep ecologists" as self-serving if not arrogant. Social ecologists, let me note, were among the first to elaborate the concept of hierarchy as a part of radical social theory in the 1960s, and it has since become a cliché that underpins, for example, radical feminist views of female oppression as a transclass phenomenon. That people whose ways of thinking are patently anthropomorphic, such as Goddess worshippers, and whose ways of interpreting the nonhuman world are stridently genderized, now level charges of anthropocentricity against social ecology is a curious and intellectually ungracious phenomenon indeed.

To say that human beings are *more advanced* than other life-forms simply connotes the fact that they are more complex, more differentiated, or more fully endowed with certain valuable attributes than others. Let me emphasize that this fact does not in itself mean that humans establish hierarchical relationships with nonhuman nature. Although we may be a highly complex and subjective group of organisms, we are actually more dependent on the phytoplankton in the seas—very simple organisms—that provide us with much of our atmospheric oxygen, than they are dependent on us. Yet no social ecologist would argue that simply by virtue of our complexity and subjectivity, we somehow *command* those indispensable—if simple—oxygen-producing life-forms. I take this question up in more detail later in this introduction; suffice it to say here that the mere existence of *differences*—

including differences of greater or lesser complexity—does not presuppose or imply hierarchy, least of all in relationships between human beings and other life-forms.

As for the cultural evolution of second nature, the opening chapter of *The Ecology of Freedom* draws a sharp distinction between egalitarian organic societies and hierarchical societies. A plausible case can be made for viewing the earliest human communities as egalitarian, in which differentiations along age, gender, and kinship lines were functionally complementary to each, not based on command and obedience. Organic society is notable for its nonhierarchical outlook toward experience, a sensibility that accepts differences in people such as those of age and gender on their own terms, without ranking them in hierarchical status groups. Organic societies usually cast their institutional arrangements along complementary lines, in which differences among individuals form a *pattern* of relationship rather than a system of dominance and submission. Such communities are mutualistic or complementary in that they take responsibility for the well-being of all their members, irrespective of their capabilities. Their members respect each other without exercising judgments that cast people in superordinate and subordinate roles.

By contrast, hierarchical societies are distinctly status-oriented in ways with which we are only too familiar at present. Far too many organic cultures slowly began to organize these differentiations along hierarchical lines. After members of organic societies coalesced into status groups that were often based as much on service as on privilege, their age, gender, and familial ties were soon institutionalized into gerontocracies, patriarchies, and military fraternities. In time, these hierarchical arrangements led to the emergence of social and economic elites—and still later, to economic classes and state bureaucracies. The unity that once marked the emergence of second nature gave way to clashes of interests that sharply pitted human against human, ending the primal but innocent unity of early egalitarian groups.

Hierarchy emerged primarily as an *immanent* development within society that slowly phased humanity from fairly egalitarian relationships into a society institutionalized around command and obedience. The chapter "The Emergence of Hierarchy" traces a logical and anthropologically verified development toward a complex hierarchical society, from gerontocracy, through patricentricity, shamanistic guilds, warrior groups, chiefdoms, and finally to state-like formations, even before classes began to emerge. All of these hierarchical strata interacted in highly complex ways, reworking the biological facts of life, like age and gender, into distinctly institutional forms. Status innovations were permeated by certain honored traditions that had shaped organic society in order to render hierarchy more socially acceptable to dominated people, and eventually to ingrain them as inevitable in the popular mind.

Hierarchy, clearly, has taken many forms that nonetheless share a common feature; they are organized systems of command and obedience. Despite their multiplicity of forms, it is crucial for students of society to fully understand these forms and to eliminate hierarchy per se, not simply replace one form of hierarchy with another. The dialectical unfolding of hierarchy has left in its wake an ages-long detritus of systems of domination involving ethnic, gendered, age, vocational, urban-rural, and many other forms of dominating people, indeed, an elaborate system of rule that economistic "class analyses" and strictly anti-statist approaches do not clearly reveal. If human freedom is to be definitively achieved, this detritus must be exposed and understood in all its complexity and interactions.

It will do us little good to contend that all the evils in the world stem from a monolithic "patriarchy," for example, or that hierarchy will wither away once women or putative "female values" replace "male supremacy" and its "male values." Indeed, hierarchical domination would scarcely be dented if the "revolutionary" call of one leading feminist, Susan Brownmiller, were heeded. "I am not someone who employs the word revolutionary lightly," Brownmiller has written, "but women's total integration into the police forces—and by total I mean 50/50, not less—is a revolutionary goal of the highest importance for the rights of women." One can only pause with astonishment at such a naïve and breathtakingly regressive demand. There is no reason to believe that a gender-integrated police force—or for that matter a gender-integrated army, state bureaucracy, or corporate board of directors (given the very nature of these institutions as inherently hierarchical) would lead to rational and ecological society.

Nor do we gain an understanding of the emergence of patriarchy— more properly, patricentricity, a social orientation that privileges males—to contend, as do many ecofeminists, that hierarchy emerged when a caring, loving, tender "matricentric" village world in the early Neolithic was suddenly swept away by a cavalry invasion of Indo-European patriarchal warriors. That invasions played a role in transforming organic into hierarchical society is a fact I would be the last to deny. But to use invasions almost exclusively to explain this development, as certain ecofeminists do, raises the question of why the invaders themselves were hierarchical. Nor can the emergence of patricentricity be explained by an invasion that presumably occurred in one part of the world while it developed in many remote cultures that could never have had any significant interaction with one another. So simplistic an "explanation" beggars credulity and does violence not only to the ways in which cultures affect one another but runs counter to the historical facts as we know them today. Here, Janet Biehl's examination of ecofeminists' exaggerated accounts of Indo-European or "Kurgan" invasions greatly illuminates these issues.[3]

∾

The complex dialectic of hierarchy in *The Ecology of Freedom* challenges not only the simplifications introduced by mystical and ecofeminist ecologies into the problems of domination but also brings into question the one-sided economistic simplifications that are rooted in traditional Marxian class analyses. I do not wish to diminish the importance of class rule in explaining present-day ecological problems, but class rule must be placed in the much *larger* context of hierarchy and domination as a whole.

If the so-called "materialist conception of history" has made any headway in the environmental movement, it is largely due to the fact that certain Marxists today hold a very elastic notion of Marx's own writings. Marx himself defined *class* in two distinct senses. The first was essentially negative: "In so far as millions of families live under economic conditions that separate their mode of life, their interests and their culture from those of other classes, and puts them in harsh opposition to the latter," he wrote in *The Eighteenth Brumaire of Louis Napoleon,* "they form a class." What makes this definition a negative one is that it crudely presupposes what it is meant to explain. In *The German Ideology,* however, Marx and Engels defined class in a more positive or substantive sense. Here class is seen as originating as a result of a growing division of labor, leading to the patriarchal family, slave society, feudalism, and of course capitalism. It is crucially defined in terms of the ownership of property—be that property women, children, slaves, serfs, capital, or the labor-power of the proletariat that the bourgeoisie buys on the labor market.

Class is thus essentially tied to property, even when property is owned or managed corporately—be it by an elite of free citizens in the ancient world, by feudal lords in the medieval world, or by stockholders in the modern world. Basically, a class nexus is formed by who owns or controls what and whose labor is being exploited economically. If classes can be said to be structured around the ownership and control of property, hierarchies constitute much subtler and more elusive phenomena, based not only on biological facts like age, gender, and kinship differences, for example, but also on social facts like ethnocentricity, bureaucratic control, and national origin. These "facts" are not marked strictly by economic or by exploitative functions. Indeed, the attainment of status and prestige may even involve giving one's property away to the point of sheer destitution, as in the potlatch ceremonies of the Northwest Indians.

Marx elaborated a wealth of social and economic ideas over his huge corpus of writings, but the economistic basis of his social view has proven to be rather simplistic. Nor can the economistic basis of his definition of class be sloughed off by adorning it with all kinds of cultural traits. The subtleties of Marx's notion of alienation and reification, so inspirational to the modern-day neo-Marxist theorists, can never be separated from his overwhelming preoccupation with the labor process and with the commodity as a good produced for exchange—or, more fundamentally, his view of the proletariat's hegemonic role in changing society, a notion that has patently come to grief in our own time.

But the economistic basis of class, especially the control and use of surplus labor, is particularly important in terms of the sweeping historical drama that Marx inherited from the Enlightenment. For it rests squarely on the Marxian notion that first nature is above all a "realm of necessity," of inevitably scarce raw materials, that must be painfully extracted, reworked, and finished into useful things by human labor. Traced back to the biblical myth of "original sin," this drama casts first nature in the role of a "stingy," "intractable," and ungiving domain, one that labor must in some sense "tame" or, at least, endure as a form of "punishment" for the malfeasances of Adam and Eve. Nineteenth-century economics added a fatalistic touch of its own to this theological drama by literally defining itself as the study of scarce resources versus unlimited needs—hence, the contemporary reputation of economics as the "dismal science."

Marxism radically secularized this myth and extended it to encompass the whole tableau of human history. Once classes arose, according to Marx, they acquired their raison d'être because the ultimate historical goal of providing the "good life" for humanity required the domination of first nature. The domination of first nature, in turn, required the mobilization of labor by a privileged, indeed supervisory, class of rulers and exploiters. The exploitation of human beings in the process of production—indeed, the use of human bodies as machines—was thus, for Marx, the earliest technical step toward bringing first nature into the service of humanity, whose liberation was to be definitively completed with the achievement of communism.

Laudable as Marx's ultimate goal may have been, no more plausible apologia for the existence of class or state rule has ever appeared over the course of history, and few have provided better excuses for domination than this one. For what made Marx's version of this dismal drama unique was that he turned it into a heroic epic: once first nature was mastered, dominated, and freely opened to "exploitation," there would be no reason for the continued existence of classes and states. As a result of a proletarian revolution, "humanity" would come into its own as the fulfillment of all its caring, intellectual, and artistic potentialities.

I do not propose to dwell on all the aspects of this simplistic drama. Social ecology's "drama" is fundamentally different from those of both biblical precept and Marxian socialism. First nature is neither stingy nor intractable. Rather, conceived as a *developmental* process—as distinguished from the static, picture-postcard scenic view of "wilderness" that often passes for "nature" in "deep ecology"—it is extraordinarily fecund, marked by an increasing wealth of differentiation, neural complexity, and the formation of diverse ecological niches. To be sure, the planet does contain some places that are unusually inhospitable for life. But first nature can be regarded as a harsh "realm of necessity" mainly in terms of the senseless "needs" it is expected to satisfy. Should these needs become extravagant or utterly irrational, first nature's fecundity might seem to shrink, relative to the needs with which it is burdened. This would clearly be the case if one's interpretation of the "economy of nature" were saddled with the concept of "insatiable wants" that always confront limited resources, a concept that is regrettably implicit in Marx's discussion of needs in volume three of *Capital*. Certainly, among human beings, "needs" are so highly conditioned by society that they must be dealt with as social issues, not simply as matters of geophysics or population numbers. Suffice it to say here that evolution is an ever-differentiating process in which increasingly complex organisms emerge from relatively simple ones—a process in which life, generally speaking, becomes ever more complex, ever more neurally flexible, and increasingly differentiated, despite the tendency of many species to become overly specialized and captive to limited ecological niches.

The view of first nature as intractable or "stingy" thus stands at odds with social ecology's emphasis on the variety and multitude of life-forms we encounter in the fossil record and the world around us. That living things eat or are eaten, that they suffer pain through accidents, as prey, or in struggles for survival—all of which exposes them to selective processes that determine whether they will continue to live or disappear—is not a debatable issue in social ecology's view of first nature. Following very much in the tradition of Peter Kropotkin's *Mutual Aid*, however, social ecology *also* emphasizes that the survival of living beings greatly depends on their ability to be supportive of one another. This "mutual aid," to use Kropotkin's words, and particularly the process of differentiation and the variety of habitats that evolution creates, opens new avenues of biotic development for existing or emerging species. Depending upon the extent to which life-forms develop neurologically, they are capable of making rudimentary choices in adapting to new environments or in actually creating new niches for themselves.

Increasing subjectivity turns organisms into an *active* force in their own evolution, not merely the passive objects of natural selection. Their survival and development now begins to depend upon the rudimentary judgments they make in interacting with and altering their own environments. They begin to make choices—indeed, at times, fairly complex ones—and exhibit a dim form of intentionality that we can properly associate with rudimentary forms of freedom. Looking back over time, it is fair to say that natural evolution is not the narrow, restrictive "realm of necessity" that Marx designated as nature, but rather a highly fecund development that exhibits a striving toward consciousness and freedom, however dim these qualities may seem even in highly complex nonhuman organisms.

I am not making the contention that there are predetermined ends or a *telos* in natural evolution that guides life's development inexorably toward consciousness and freedom. But I would insist that the *potentiality* for achieving consciousness and freedom does exist. The reader is welcome to regard this development as a mere tendency, as a reasonable likelihood, or simply as a blunt fact supported by the fossil record, not as a supposed "law of nature." In any case, a rich tradition exists in Western philosophy that describes a subtle grading of life from fairly simple life-forms to the emergence of complex sentient beings—beings that also *change their environments to meet their own survival needs*. From the minimal notion of organic self-maintenance, I believe that we can plausibly argue that a nisus exists that leads from passive reaction to active interaction, from intentionality to choice, and finally to conceptual thought and foresight. I call this approach to evolution dialectical *naturalism*, in order to distinguish its processual dialectic from the fairly mechanistic "laws" of dialectical materialism advanced by writers like Frederick Engels and from the dialectical idealism of Fichte and Hegel.

Finally, natural evolution has indeed produced beings—human beings—who can act rationally in the world, guided far less by instinct than by a rich intellectuality rooted in conceptual thought and complex forms of symbolic communication. These beings are *of* the biotic world as organisms, mammals, and primates, yet they are also *apart* from it as creatures that produce that vast array of cultural artifacts and associations that we call second nature.

ᴄ℞

Second nature consists largely of the tools that the earliest humans developed over a span of a half-million years or more, the habitats they willfully created for their security and well-being, and the organized social life that they institutionalized as families, then bands, tribes, hierarchies, classes, and the State—and finally, such cultural achievements as philosophy, science, technics, and art. This cultural development is uniquely human. Not only are human societies composed of definable but mutable institutions that have changed radically over the course of social history; they include equally definable but mutable ideologies that rationalize the existence of various institutions, a richly elaborate culture that finds its expression in a wide-ranging symbolic language, and a written historical record—all of which have no precedent in the nonhuman world.

Even more unprecedented is the extent to which second nature changes first nature. Sweeping changes, of immense significance, were often produced, moreover, by aboriginal peoples, albeit on a scale that was greatly exceeded by so-called "industrialized" ones. I shall examine changes made by aboriginal societies at a later point in this introduction. What is important to note for the present is that second nature can be distinguished from first nature not because human beings are less "animalistic" than nonhuman beings, but quite to the contrary, because it is *part of their very animality to seek these changes—as would any living thing if it could.* People change first nature by virtue of their *naturally* endowed capacities to think conceptually, to create extrabiological tools and machines, and to do this with a high degree of collective organization and intentionality that is profoundly different from the behavior and abilities of nonhuman beings. Not only are these unprecedented human survival capacities a product of natural evolution, they open a still newer realm of potentiality—the potentiality to evolve along *social* lines and produce a second nature that profoundly affects the evolution and life-forms of first nature.

Once human society finally emerges as a distinct worldwide phenomenon, it becomes meaningless to speak of ecological issues in strictly biological terms. Indeed, like it or not, nearly every ecological issue is also a social issue. In fact, as we shall see, nearly all our present-day ecological dislocations have their basic sources in social dislocations. Hence my conviction that a serious environmental movement today must be based on *social* ecology if it is to be intellectually consistent, insightful, and environmentally relevant.

I say this provocatively at a time when a huge literature has surfaced that tries to refocus public attention away from social issues and toward socially neutral phenomena like technology *as such*, rather than the social matrix of technics; toward science *as such*, rather than the social abuses of science; and toward reason *as such*, rather than the reduction of reason largely to a means-ends "skill" to be used for instrumental ends. Permeating these rather simplistic efforts to direct public attention away from the social underpinnings of our ecological problems is that same, ubiquitous mysticism and theism that, in an era of social disempowerment, foster a proclivity for supernatural escape. Among ecological radicals, confrontation with the stark problems of the warming of the planet, the thinning of the ozone layer, and other effects of growth produced by capital accumulation is slowly giving way to atavistic celebrations of a mythic Neolithic and Pleistocene. As this rubbish sediments itself into the ecology movement, even confrontation itself is denounced as "divisive" and "disruptive."

Yet rarely have the very *real* divisions and disruptions in second nature been more in need of being confronted than they are today, when the very survival of our biosphere is in question. Nor can we ignore the deep-seated divisions in society that came into existence with hierarchies and classes. One can no longer speak of "humanity" the way one can speak of species of carnivores or herbivores—that is, as groups of fairly uniform biological beings whose individuals are essentially alike. To use such ecumenical words as *humanity, we, people*, and the like in a purely biologistic sense when we discuss social affairs is grossly misleading. Although human beings are certainly mammals no less than bears, wolves, or coyotes, to ignore the hierarchical and class divisions that second nature has produced in their midst is to create the illusion of a commonality that humanity has by no means achieved. This ecumenical view of the human species places young people and old, women and men, poor and rich, exploited and exploiters, people of color and whites *all* on a par that stands completely at odds with social reality. Everyone, in turn, despite the different burdens he or she is obliged to bear, is given the same responsibility for the ills of our planet. Be they starving Ethiopian children or corporate barons, all people are held to be equally culpable in producing present ecological problems. Ecological problems, in effect, are *de-socialized* and restated in genetic, psychological, personal, and purely subjective terms so that they no longer have political or economic content. Not only does this almost conventional approach sidestep the profoundly social roots of present-day ecological dislocations, it *deflects* innumerable people from engaging in a practice that could yield effective social change.

The tendency of mystical ecologists to speak of the ecological crises that "we" or "people" or "humanity" have created easily plays into the hands of a privileged stratum who are only too eager to blame all the human victims of an exploitative society for the social and ecological ills of our time. Political myopia of this kind and the social insensitivity it breeds is worse than naïve; it is blatantly obfuscatory at best and utterly reactionary at worst.

Accordingly, given the emergence of hierarchy and domination, the divisions that beset society are crucially important issues that the modern ecology movement must sternly confront and challenge. I must emphasize that we have to know *how* hierarchy arose if we are to undo it. We must explore the extensive nature of domination in all its ramifications if we are to remove the pathologies of second nature—which we certainly cannot do unless we transcend naive "biocentric" views that equate humans with mosquitoes in terms of a shared "intrinsic worth," whatever that expression may mean. Without a clear insight into the nature of hierarchy and domination, we will not only fail to understand how the social and biotic interact with each other; we will fail to realize that the very *idea* of dominating first nature has its origins in the domination of human by human, and we will lose what little understanding we have of the social origin of our most serious ecological problems.

By the same token, we will grossly distort humanity's potentialities to play a creative role in nonhuman as well as human development. We will deprecate the fact—and such deprecation is already very chic among the theorists of "deep" ecology—that the human capacity to reason conceptually, to fashion tools and devise extraordinary technologies, indeed, to communicate among themselves with a symbolic linguistic repertoire—all can be used for the good of the biosphere, not simply for harming it. What is of *pivotal* importance in determining whether human beings will creatively foster the evolution of first nature or whether they will be highly destructive to nonhuman and human beings alike is precisely the kind of *society* we establish, not only the kind of sensibility we develop.

Which is not to say that in an ecological society the lion will lie down with the lamb or that the biosphere will be sedated into loving quietude with the balm of human kindness. But first nature can indeed be rendered biotically more fecund for nonhuman as well as human life, and the intervention of an ecologically oriented human rationality and technics could foster many evolutionary advances—advances that would diminish the damaging effects of the harmful accidents and chance events that can occur when evolution is left to "Mother Nature" alone. Again, depending upon the kind of society we produce, a new realm of possibility may emerge in which blind necessity can be softened by clear-sighted rationality, and needless suffering can be diminished by human concern and care.

Is this an argument for the belief—imputed by many "biocentric" ecologists to social ecology—that the human species is "superior" to or "higher" than all other life-forms? That humans can "dominate" the biosphere? The use of the words *superior* and *higher* is willfully pejorative when they are applied by "biocentrists" to social ecology. If the terms are used to assert humanity's claim to a "higher rank, station, or authority," to cite the preferred dictionary definition of *superior*, any imputation that social ecology holds such a view is either the result of ignorance or is simply dishonest. For my own part, nowhere in any of my writings do I use the word *superior* to denote humans' relationship to nonhuman beings. That human beings differ significantly from nonhuman beings, however, is a fact that even the most naïve mystics are obliged to acknowledge, short of losing all contact with reality.

Given the constellation of differences that distinguish human from nonhuman life-forms, indeed, differences that have been produced by natural evolution itself, it is fair to say that some species are more flexible than others in their ability to adapt and that they possess more complex nervous systems that endow them with the capability to make more suitable choices from among evolutionary pathways that promote their survival and development. In short, they can be said to be more advanced in dealing with *new* situations than are other, less flexible and less neurologically developed species. But in no sense does it follow that a more *advanced* life-form will or must *dominate* less advanced life-forms. The notion that a more advanced life-form is more "domineering" is a thoroughly anthropomorphic image; it reflects elitist ideologies that justify domination, not relations that necessarily must exist in the natural, or for that matter in the social, world. It is a characteristic instance of the many ideologies of domination that have been projected onto first nature to establish, among other things, command and obedience as *immutable* facts of life. Indeed, one can argue that to the extent that human society becomes more rational, eliminates classes and hierarchies, and undergoes changes in sensibility that are marked by a deep respect for life, the less likely it is that terms like *superior* and *higher* will even have meaning to people, be it in their relationships with one another or in their relationships with other living beings. Indeed, the more fully developed humanity is, its spiritual and intellectual equipment refined by a rational culture, the more sensitive it will become in its view of, and concern for, nonhuman nature.

Because greater reason, science, technology, even knowledge and talent have been historically yoked to the service of hierarchical rule, it seems to follow for many ecologically oriented people that they are antithetical to freedom, care, and an ecological outlook. We quail before words like *technology*, *science*, and *logic* as if they were totally autonomous, reified forces that have an oppressive character in every social context, irrespective of their ethical underpinnings. That animals more advanced than others need not—and actually *do* not—"dominate" less advanced beings seems to totally elude adherents of mystical ecology and its theistic and "deep" offshoots.

☙

Here we arrive at one of the most hotly debated—and at the same time one of the most sophistic—issues in ecological philosophy today: the notion that "intrinsic worth" is equally distributed among all species. Where social ecology sees advances in evolutionary development, "biocentric" proponents of "intrinsic worth" see merely a scattering of morally equatable attributes among species, such that the "rights" of viruses to "self-fulfillment" can be equated with similar "rights" of grizzly bears, or such that the "rights" of grizzly bears can be equated with those of human beings. All, presumably, can be said to possess equal "intrinsic worth." The obfuscations that these "biocentric" illusions and their misanthropic implications have introduced into present-day ecological thinking can hardly be underestimated.

First nature may reasonably be regarded as the *ground* for an ecological ethics or, if you like, as the necessary condition for moral behavior. Social ecology, by conceiving first nature as an evolutionary tendency toward greater subjectivity, sees in the achievement of a rational, self-conscious, and relatively "free nature" the establishment of an ecological society. But as I have often argued, first nature in *itself* is not ethical. "Mother Nature," or whatever gendered kinship tie one may wish to assign to the planet, does not always "know best," as the fossil remains of many remarkable but extinct species attest. In fact, it is doubtful that "she" knows anything at all, as even James Lovelock, the co-artificer of the so-called "Gaia hypothesis," attests. If one notes, for example, the amazing similarity between the stalking behavior of a house-bred cat that has never eaten anything but canned cat-food and that of a lioness on the African plains, one may reasonably question whether even fairly advanced animals "know" much beyond what is imparted to them by their instincts and the rudimentary survival skills that they acquire from the very demanding challenges of eating and risking being eaten. Although the versatility of animal behavior should not be downplayed, whatever most animals learn or "know" is usually limited by simple everyday experience and their relatively restricted forms of communication.

As far as *ethical* issues are concerned, however, no animal or plant species has ever formulated a "social contract" with a mutual recognition of individual rights and duties, however complex their interactions may be. Despite the beliefs of writers like Kropotkin, who saw mutualistic relationships among life-forms as harbingers of ethical behavior, those relationships are not usually conscious ones. Much less do they consist of the conscious responsibilities and the reasoned behavior we call ethical. Indeed, the notion of "intrinsic worth" in nonhuman nature is simply an oxymoron. Human beings may have a deep sense of care, empathy, indeed of love for other life-forms, but for them to regard any ethical principle as *inherent* in first nature is as naïve as the medieval practice of judicially trying and hanging captive wolves for their "criminal" behavior.

For better or worse, human beings are the *sole* ethical agents that exist. Ethics as such literally appeared on the planet with the emergence of human beings in the course of evolution, just as life as such appeared with the emergence of proteins that engaged in metabolic and reproductive activity. Humans—and humans alone—institutionalize their own behavior into relationships that are clearly predicated on acknowledged rights and duties, on rationally justified ethical responsibilities. As I show in this book, human ethical systems have been variously backed up by custom, or traditional forms of behavior; by morals, or behavior conducted by commands; or by reason or logical and conceptual thought.

But even if we grant that these forms of behavior differ considerably, humans have been entirely alone in the world as ethical agents, just as they have been alone in forming mutably institutionalized societies and the ideologies needed to support or change them. First nature is never "cruel" or "kind," "heartless" or "caring," "good" or "bad." Ethics, in effect, was *born* with human society, just as surely as metabolism was born with the emergence of life. The "intrinsic worth" or whatever other kind of value we impute to animals are a product of human artifice that we project upon a world that in fact has no "inherent" values, just as in our fairy tales we project speech and human intentions onto "bad" wolves, "shy" pigs, and "sly" foxes.

The same is true of the "rights" that "biocentrists" attribute to life-forms in the name of "intrinsic worth," not to speak of streams, rocks, forests, mountains, and so forth. "Rights" are never spontaneously generated in first nature; nor is there the least evidence that flora, fauna, and rocks "claim" them, either for themselves or for others. Many animals exhibit care for each other, particularly in maternal-offspring relationships among advanced life-forms. But "Mother Nature" is singularly uncaring taken as a whole and is clearly bereft of ethical obligation. Much as we may want to metaphorically people the world with "immanent" or "transcendental" deities that anthropomorphically reflect our conceptions of *ourselves* and the kinds of communities *we* would like to develop, first nature still remains a realm of ethical vacuity.

This vacuity can only be filled by the rights and obligations that humans consciously deliver to it. Any "worth," "value," and "rights" that exist in first nature are *conferred rights*—rights that human beings alone confer on animals, plants, rocks, streams, and the like. "Rights" cannot be derived from a mystical notion of "intrinsic worth" that simply has no meaning outside of human agency; nor have they ever preceded the appearance of humanity in natural evolution.

Nor can it be argued that the life-forms in first nature are suffused with mutual "respect" for one another. No nonhuman organism "respects" "Mother Nature"—or even knows that "she" exists as anything more than a habitat. In fact, each animal species simply tries to *survive*. It has no evident regard for the "worth," intrinsic or otherwise, of its environment or of the other life-forms that inhabit it. Wolves would devour the last caribou alive if they were hungry, and ungulates would nip away the last remaining patches of vegetation on earth if they required food. We would be hard put to explain the tremendous trail of species extinctions from Cambrian times, some half-billion years ago, up to the Pleistocene Epoch, were it not for the fact that predation as well as geophysical factors drove countless life-forms out of existence with no evidence of mutual "respect," "Earth wisdom," or a sensibility based on "intrinsic worth."

I am not arguing that we should *not* confer rights—possibly even judicial ones, as Justice William O. Douglas tried to do—on nonhuman species, or even on forests, streams, and certain geological formations, for that matter. From a practical standpoint, doing so might be an invaluable way of conserving and expanding ecocommunities that we should preserve for a good many reasons that I need not discuss here. But the fact that a highly perverted society has shown little willingness to respect the nonhuman world should not be used as the basis for defaming the one life-form—human beings—that alone is *capable* of even thinking, discussing, and with the needed social changes, effectively conferring rights on first nature. Whatever rights or other ethical formulations that we develop in an ecological ethics, the fact remains that *we* as a species are the sole ethical agents on the planet who are able to formulate these rights, to confer them, and to see that they are upheld. Whether these rights are formulated and upheld, I must insist, depends overwhelmingly upon the kind of society we create and the sensibility it fosters—not by mystifying a remarkably unknowing or "indifferent" "Mother Nature," or believing in an "Earth Goddess" who has no more reality than the anthropomorphic fables of Mother Goose.

Insofar as human beings alone have an unprecedented capacity to create ethical systems that impart worth to other life-forms, they clearly have a *special worth* in their own right. Insofar as they are capable of being fully conscious of their behavior and its ecological impact. They are extraordinary beings in the biosphere, for no other life-form has this remarkable consciousness. The new misanthropic indulgences that grossly undervalue human beings by claiming that "Gaia" can thrive without them are as stupid as they are despicable. This claim strips organic evolution of any meaning whatever beyond mere survival, of any exultation in the natural emergence of attributes like conceptual thought and symbolic language. By placing the capabilities of human beings and their intellectuality on a par with animal skills for survival, "biocentrists" utterly denigrate that unique species, as well as intellectuality itself. With so limited and reductionist an interpretation of life, one might well wonder why "Gaia" itself should be cherished amidst the cosmic swirl of marvelous galaxies and celestial bodies.

The insidious devaluation of human achievements promoted by mystical ecologies is accompanied by a hatred of all that is specifically human: a hatred of reason, science, art, and technological innovation in almost all its forms. To claim, as one "deep ecologist" has recently done, that the human mind is morally comparable to the "navigational skills of birds, the sonar capability of dolphins, and the intense sociality [!] of ants" is to ignore the fact that the human mind knows more about the specific attributes of these animals than do the animals themselves. Moreover, humans, by virtue of their intellectuality and technical abilities, have the capability of understanding these attributes to the point that they can invent ways to duplicate them and even *surpass* their range. Underlying our "deep ecologist's" judgment—or lack thereof—is a fashionable disdain for the potentialities and creativity of mind, a disdain that has its social roots in an Anglo-American tradition of empiricism, the prevailing mystical Zeitgeist, a privatistic reaction to an increasingly overbearing society, and an emerging temper of self-hatred that is projected onto human life itself with a predictable, compensatory "reverence" for nonhuman nature.

If one grants that ethics is an eminently human creation, that human beings can add a sense of meaning to first nature by virtue of their interpretive powers, that they can confer values as well as create them, then humanity is literally the very *embodiment* of value in nature as a whole. However much "Gaia" might be able to survive without the existence of human beings, such a "Gaia" would have no more ethical meaning or value in the scheme of things than a meteorite. As the embodiment of value, indeed as the very source of value, a human life can no more be placed on a par with the life of a grizzly bear or a wolf than the lives of those admirable animals can be placed on a par with the existence of an inorganic entity like a rock. For with the disappearance of human beings, *value too would disappear*, and the biosphere would be left with no basis for *any* ethical evaluation or discussion of "intrinsic worth," much less ethical agents who can appreciate its wondrous qualities. Hence the exceptional importance of human life, even by comparison with the "noblest" of all other life-forms.

Let me stress once again that in no way does this valuation of human life contradict an ethics of complementarity. An ethics of complementarity opposes any claim that human beings have a "right" to dominate first nature, assuming they could do so in the first place, much less any claim that first nature has been "created" to serve human needs. But such an ethics does place a high premium on a rich diversity of life that makes for *wholeness*, for evolutionary and rational *innovation*, and for a *heterogeneity* of life-forms, if only to make *complementarity* possible. As an ethics that values the emergence of new attributes implicit in life, such as greater flexibility of adaptations to new environments, it gives due recognition to more advanced degrees of sentience, and, if you please, the exercise and joys of mind, self-consciousness, and freedom; but in no sense does it place these attributes of life in any hierarchical system based on command and obedience.

A world reduced to Lynn Margulis's soup of prokaryotic cells or to Starker Leopold's admittedly illusory version of a "primitive" American habitat in Yellowstone Park would indeed be "alive," but it would be little more than that. It would lack humanity's ability to appreciate it, to give it the splendor of meaning, to enrich it with interpretation—indeed, even to create illusions of its "sacredness." In the absence of human beings, reality would be denied the rich sense of wonder so characteristic of mind and a sensibility that could bring mind to the service of fostering the very "interconnectedness" so celebrated by mystical ecologists.

Herein lies the extraordinary value of human life in relation to other forms of life—namely, its ability to *value* phenomena and evolution in any broad ethical sense. If the reader chooses, as our "deep ecologists" do, to respond to my humanistic observations by sneeringly asking, "Who says so?" I can only reply that their very *ability* to ask such questions is evidence of the view I have advanced.

෬

If we are *of* the natural evolution that produced us, yet also *apart* from it, in what ways should we deal with that "apartness"?

Mystical ecologists would like us try to overcome human "apartness" by minimizing or eliminating it altogether. It has become all too fashionable among many mystical ecologists to condemn human intervention into first nature, except to meet the minimal needs of life and survival. We are enjoined to "let nature take its course," to avoid any alteration of first nature except for what is "necessary"—a word that often remains ill-defined—to keep human beings alive and well. Such noninterventionist attitudes are commonly imputed to prehistoric and aboriginal peoples, who presumably lived in total "Oneness" with first nature and the wildlife around them. Taking Aldo Leopold's phrase "not man apart" to its most extreme conclusion, mystical ecologists call for a complete integration to first nature—by "returning to the Pleistocene," as many "biocentrists" demand.

But these calls present us with a host of vexing problems. In the first place, the Pleistocene was not the Paleolithic, (although they are often grouped together for geological convenience); hence we are talking of diverse sensibilities and cultures. It was not until the late Pleistocene that the vocal anatomy of *homo erectus*, a direct ancestor of our species, allowed for speech; before then, any "deep ecologists" who hoped to return to that epoch would have been confined to grunts and growls. Nor was it until the late Paleolithic that human beings like ourselves—*homo sapiens*, who had modern-type anatomies and brains—emerged. The families and communities of the hunting-gathering foragers who lived in the glacial and interglacial periods of the Pleistocene were equipped with little more technology than spears, fire, crude stone scrapers, and the like for hunting animals and cleaning their hides— a technics that would exclude the word processors to which many "deep ecologist" writers are avowedly attached. Disturbingly, we know that *homo erectus*, direct ancestors of our own species who lived in the late Pleistocene, were probably cannibals who ate members of their own species— possibly, but not necessarily, for ritualistic reasons.

These forebears of our species and our own ancestors lived in a climatically turbulent era, marked by advances and retreats of glaciers, wide swings in temperature, and a feast-or-famine diet. Their lives were often very precarious, despite the periodic abundance of game. Nor were they fully equipped with the means to deal with the natural vicissitudes that white middle-class people today take so readily for granted, such as the certainty of warmth in cold weather, adequate shelter, and the ordinary creature comforts to which middle-class people are wedded—leaving all luxuries and pleasures aside. They lacked a written body of knowledge by which a complex tradition of ideas could be handed down; the writing materials with which to express thoughts and reflections that were more complex than those involved in meeting the needs of everyday life; the libraries in which to meditate, research, and gather the wisdom of past ages—in short, the vast array of intellectual and spiritual materials to sensitize their outlook and sensibilities.

It might seem more plausible for "deep ecologists" to call for a return to the *sensibility* of these distant times, rather than an actual physical return. But here too we are besieged by a barrage of unanswered questions. We would want to know what kind of sensibility Pleistocene and Paleolithic hunters had in their dealings with the multitude of animals they encountered in the "Great Age of Mammals," as the two periods have been called. After all, Paleolithic hunter-gatherers developed the stone-tipped spear, the all-important spear-thrower—which made it possible to effectively pierce very tough hides and muscles—and the bow and arrow, which could inflict mortal damage over a sizable distance. The more sophisticated and lethal their hunting kit, the greater an impact these humans must have had on the large mammals of the late Pleistocene and the Paleolithic. If we are to return to the sensibility of these epochs, we would want to know if they really viewed the animals they killed "reverentially," as so many mystical ecologists claim, or if they had a more pragmatic attitude toward them, using magic to propitiate a "bison spirit" or "bear spirit" in rituals before and after kills. We would want to know if they really did feel themselves to be absorbed into an all-encompassing "Oneness" with the animals around them, or whether they had any sense of human self-identity that involved feelings of "apartness" from those animals. We would want to know if they really chose not to intervene in first nature any more than was absolutely necessary, as mystical ecologists believe, or if they significantly altered their surroundings. We would want to know if they really did behave toward wildlife as "tender carnivores" in pursuit of "sacred game," as Paul Shepard's evocative book on hunter-gatherer sensibility is titled, or if they held a more mundane attitude toward animals as means for satisfying their very material as well as subjective needs.

Actually, we will never know with certainty the answers to these questions of sensibility. The outlook that today's mystical ecologists cultivate toward the Pleistocene, the Paleolithic, and the Neolithic is often highly romanticized and certainly does not correspond to many things that we do know about those eras. If I am to examine the nature of aboriginal sensibilities, I must do so as honestly as possible and decide which characterizations *probably* apply better to our ancestors of the distant past. This much is clear: much of the archaeological evidence does not support the ecological-romantic view of early peoples, however unpleasant the data may be. Researchers have argued with good reason, for example, that effective human hunters in the Pleistocene may have played a major role in killing off some, if not most, of the great Pleistocene and Paleolithic mammals. Which is not to deny that others have claimed that climatic changes, with important ecological consequences in the Pleistocene and Paleolithic, are more likely to have ended forever the lives of mammoths, mastodons, woolly rhinoceroses, cave bears, and giant sloths, among others.

The argument that the Pleistocene and Paleolithic animals became extinct solely because changes in climate and temperature caused the flora and fauna on which they thrived to disappear has been seriously challenged by a number of responsible researchers. Paul S. Martin, for one, has championed the view that it was prehistoric hunters who caused the "sudden wave of large-animal extinctions" at the end of the Pleistocene, a wave that "involved at least 200 genera, most of them without phyletic replacement."[4] His largely speculative arguments are based more on the correlation between the extinctions and the appearance of human hunters than on factual evidence. This has led other researchers, like Calvin Martin in his popular *Keepers of the Game*, to contend that in North America large mammals such as the mastodon were often so dependent for subsistence on spruce-fir ecosystems that when those ecosystems began to disappear some eight to ten thousand years ago, the animals could no longer sustain themselves.[5] That a very intelligent mammal like a member of the elephant family would have been limited to such a narrow ecological niche, however, is highly doubtful—and in fact, very recent (1991) evidence from the intestinal remains of a well-preserved mastodon reveals that the animal was quite capable of living on swamp-like vegetation in an ecosystem very different from that of a spruce-fir region. In fact, Calvin Martin to the contrary, mastodons were probably quite capable of flourishing in a variety of "ecological niches." Such evidence throws factual weight on the side of the "overkill," as distinguished from the primarily climatic approach, and supports the view that early hunter-gatherers contributed to or may have exterminated many Pleistocene animals.

After so much has been written by romantics of the last century and mystical ecologists today about the "Oneness" that preliterate peoples felt for the game they hunted, should we be shocked by this conclusion? I believe not—unless we choose to simplify the complex dialectic involved in what we regard as an "ecological sensibility," whether that sensibility applies to prehistoric and aboriginal hunters or to ourselves. Indeed, that early hunters—whose "ecological sensibility" is so revered by mystical ecologists—would try to satisfy their needs *in any way they could* should not surprise us. In fact, these hunters were predatory opportunists, no less than wolves or coyotes, *precisely* because they were very much part of "Nature" (to invoke that much-abused word), just as were all the life-forms around them. Early hunters did not live in Disneyland, where sociable "mice" and gleeful "rabbits" jostle with human visitors in a pseudo-animistic, cartoon-like world.

Another area in dispute is the extent to which preliterate peoples altered the wild environments in which they lived. We know that early hunters were clearly not devout conservers of the original forests, for example. As Stephen J. Pyne emphasizes in his informative study *Fire in America*, "the virgin forest was not encountered in the sixteenth and seventeenth century; it was invented in the late eighteenth and early nineteenth centuries. For this condition Indian fire practices were largely responsible."[6] Hunter-gatherer foragers, in fact, used fire on a global scale to create grasslands for herbivores. The great prairies of the Midwest were literally created by Indian torches, which were systematically applied, long before those lands were expropriated by Europeans. Since humanity's discovery of fire, few forests that we can call "virgin" remain today, however large the girth or height of their individual trees. Great forests of the eighteenth century were often restorations of trees that had been cleared and reduced to parkland and prairies in pre-Columbian times. The "forest primeval" that Longfellow celebrated in his poetry was often made up of trees that European settlers had permitted to come back after Indians had turned the forests and the areas they occupied into parklands. That European settlers permitted the trees to return in order to use them to build ships and homes does not alter the fact that these forests were anything but "primeval," or that Indian communities were anything but reluctant to "tamper" with "Nature."

The wildlife that the grasslands and forests supported were often hunted unrelentingly, sometimes in gross disregard of their dwindling numbers. Long after Paleo-Indians contributed to the extinction of Pleistocene megafauna, their descendants killed elk in "bunches" or groups by hunting down a female "bunch" leader first, then picking off the remaining animals while they haplessly milled around in circles. Countless bison were stampeded off cliffs, corralled in ravines, or otherwise trapped and killed in numbers that seem to have far exceeded what was necessary to meet the needs of their hunters. Large killings were inflicted wherever possible on elk, pronghorns, mountain goats, and caribou.

My point here should be clearly understood: It is *not* my intention to defame aboriginal hunters or to place their behavior on a par with that of lumber companies or the meat-packing industry. No Paleo-Indian and Indian overkills and deforestation compares even remotely to the terrifying ecological devastation and the genocide practiced by Euro-American settlers on the New World and its native people. The greed and exploitation that has destroyed Indian cultures over the past five centuries can in no way be justified morally or culturally. The interaction of European settlers and Native Americans could have opened a new opportunity for a sensitive integration of both cultures, but that opportunity was lost in an orgy of bloodletting and plunder by European settlers, particularly land speculators, railroaders, lumber barons, and capitalist entrepreneurs generally.

But with all due regard to the many remarkable features of Native American cultures, pre-Columbian hunters took a large toll in wildlife, often showing few, if any, concerns for conservation. From such overkills, game animals took years to regenerate. Nor was this regeneration helped by their hunters' fertility rituals, unless we are to naïvely believe, like modern believers in magic, that they served to increase animal fertility. "Thanks to their hunting prowess," observes Alston Chase in his superbly researched and well-written book, *Playing God in Yellowstone,* "the Indians of the Yellowstone region—the Shoshone and their cousins, the Bannock and Lemhi—had eaten themselves out of house and home. When Lewis and Clark first met the Shoshone in 1805, they were starving. Their chief told the explorers that they had 'nothing but berries to eat'"[7]

I will not dwell further on the recorded instances where overkill by aboriginal hunters denuded large areas of wildlife or burned away "primeval" flora—in short, intervened significantly into "primeval" environments long before technology had advanced much further than a Stone Age tool-kit. It is beyond doubt to me—as it is seemingly *not* to many mystical ecologists—that prehistoric and preliterate peoples intervened in first nature as fully as they could and often changed it quite profoundly. Their intervention ranged in scope from overkills of wildlife, to the creation of grasslands, and even to the building of cities like Tenochitlan in Aztec Mexico and terraces in the Andean highlands—all in pre-Columbian times. These are *facts* that are hardly disputed seriously. Apart from the wishful thinking of romantics and mystics, the differences that surround these facts have more to do with the details or scale of the interventions than with the reality of considerable intervention itself.

But I cannot reiterate my point too strongly. Far from seeking to defame aboriginal peoples, I think we must examine the *rationale* for their seeming "insensitivity" to animal life and forests. Hunter-gatherers were living beings like other life-forms, and as any life-form would, they tried to survive by any means possible. At the same time, the needs of these humans were greater and more complex than those of other life-forms. As creatures endowed by natural evolution with highly intelligent minds, they would not only have required animal and vegetable food to meet their immediate needs; they would also have wanted a secure supply of food once they knew how to preserve meat and plants. Owing to their *naturally* endowed intelligence, they would have wanted good clothing, even "luxuries" such as comfortable bedding, sturdy skins for homes, plumage and carved bone amulets, beadlike teeth for ornaments, magical artifacts, an assortment of tools and medicines, and coloring matter for various purposes. That the needs of these humans were greater and more complex than those of other life-forms was due not to any perverse traits but to endowments that stemmed from their evolution as unique animals. These wants, in short, shaped their behavior, as it would have shaped that of *any* nonhuman being. And these wants were a product of an intelligence that had been formed as a result of aeons of evolutionary development, not any demonic or mysterious impulse that is vaguely "unnatural."

Inasmuch as preliterate people were human, moreover, they were capable of reasoning conceptually, of speaking fluently, and of feeling abiding insecurities. Early humanity can hardly be faulted for behaving more intelligently than bears, foxes, and wolves; *natural evolution* endowed them with larger brains and a capacity for making tools and weapons to enhance their powers of survival and for changing their environment to abet their well-being. They had amazing memories, and of extreme importance, they possessed vivid imaginations. They decorated their weapons, painted animals and designs on rocks and caves, engaged in analogic thinking, created myths, and felt passions often incomparably more compelling than any that are discernable in animals.

Yet they were also truly part of "Nature." In the late Pleistocene and early Paleolithic, it was their very "closeness" to first nature, coupled with their emerging second nature, that would have caused them to act in ways that contradict our present-day romanticized notions of their behavior. They were undergoing a major transition from the domain of biological evolution to that of social evolution. As such, they could variously exhibit utter indifference to the pain they inflicted on animals and a strong affinity for them in their rituals—contradictory forms of behavior that occurred almost simultaneously. In these respects, their sensibility was shaped by animalistic as well as cultural needs, indeed by their very "Oneness" with first nature. In turn, their sense of "Oneness" with first nature was shaped by a mental repertoire that could make for what we today would regard as cruelty as well as empathy toward nonhuman life, depending upon the extent to which they identified themselves with it and the kind of society they created, which led to a sense of "apartness" from it—a thoroughly dialectical tension in their outlook.

Allow me to illustrate this point with just one of many examples that can be culled from the anthropological literature. Colin M. Turnbull, a noted anthropologist and the author of an outstanding study of the Ituri forest pygmies in Central Africa, *The Forest People*, celebrates the almost reverential feeling these people genuinely had for their forest habitat. Yet Turnbull was appalled when he discovered that they could be very indifferent to the suffering of captive animals. "The sindula is one of the most prized animals," Turnbull tells us, speaking of a tasty doglike creature that the pygmies had caught in a hunting net. Left in the custody of a pigmy boy Maipe, he continues,

> the youngster, probably not much more than thirteen years old, had speared
> it with his first thrust, pinning the animal to the ground through the fleshy

part of the stomach. But the animal was still very much alive, fighting for freedom. It had already bitten its way through the net, and now it was doubled up, gashing the spear shaft with its sharp teeth. Maipe put another spear into its neck, but it still writhed and fought. Not until a third spear pierced its heart did it give up the struggle.

It was at times like this that I found myself furthest removed from the Pygmies. They stood around in an excited group, pointing at the dying animal and laughing. One boy, about nine years old, threw himself on the ground and curled up in a grotesque heap and imitated the sindula's last convulsions. The men pulled their spears out and joked with one another about being afraid of a little animal like that, and to emphasize his point one of them kicked the torn and bleeding body. Then Maipe's mother came and swept the blood-streaked animal up by its hind legs and threw it over her shoulder into the basket on her back.

At other times I have seen Pygmies singeing feathers off birds that were still alive, explaining that the meat is more tender if death comes slowly. And the hunting dogs, valuable as they are, get kicked around mercilessly from the day they are born to the day they die. I have never seen any attempt at the domestication of any animal or bird apart from the hunting dog. When I talked to the Pygmies about their treatment of animals, they laughed at me and said, "The forest has given us animals for food—should we refuse this gift and starve?" I thought of turkey farms and Thanksgiving, and of the millions of animals reared by our own society with the sole intention of slaughtering them for food.[8]

Behavior of this kind and the sensibility it reveals are by no means peculiar to the Ituri forest pygmies. To torture animals—or men and women captives, in intertribal conflicts—was regarded as routine behavior among a large number of preliterate peoples. Pigs were often beaten to death in Oceania; dogs were grossly maltreated by some Indian peoples, who regarded them as a tasty delicacy, and they were often treated harshly by ordinarily gentle Eskimos, as is attested in many reports over decades. Ethnological accounts of animism and magic tell us, in fact, that for many hunting-gathering cultures, second nature was still so deeply *immersed* in first nature that preliterate people could draw relatively little distinction between themselves and their environments. Not surprisingly, the distinctions between first and second nature were often problematical, with the result that the ability to achieve a clearly defined sense of human self-identity or ego was fairly limited.

൦♋

In short, we cannot resolve the issue of humanity's "apartness" from first nature by trying to eliminate "apartness" in the course of apotheosizing a Pleistocene "Oneness" or imitating a contrived notion of primordial sensibilities. Looking back to the very beginnings of second nature, it should be emphasized that humanity's consciousness of first nature, as distinguished from a consciousness of its specific, narrow ecological niches, *presupposes* that it separate itself from a purely niche-like animal existence. Human beings at some point had to at least *begin* to see first nature generally as an "other" if their self-identity and self-consciousness as human beings were to emerge. Without a sense of contrast between the human and nonhuman, people are limited to the bedrock existence of seeking mere survival, to a way of life so undifferentiated from that of other living things that they know little more than the unmediated confines of their limited ecological community. This way of life is bereft of purpose, meaning, or orientation, apart from what people create in their imagination. And it is a way of life that no human being could endure except by ceasing to think.

Which is to say that, epistemologically at least, differentiation would not exist and the evolution of a human psyche would never get under way. In order for human beings to differentiate themselves in natural evolution, there must be *duality*, such as dualities between self and other and between the human and the nonhuman. Here, duality must not be confused with *dualism*. Today, in fact, the danger that confronts ecological thinking is less a matter of a dualistic sensibility—a dualism that mystical ecologists have criticized to the point of pulverization—but of *reductionism*, an intellectual dissolution of *all* difference into an undefinable "Oneness" that excludes the possibility of creativity and turns a concept like "interconnectedness" into the bonds of a mental and emotional straitjacket. Without otherness, duality, and differentiation, "interconnectedness" dissolves psychological and personal heterogeneity into a "night in which all cows are black," to use one of Hegel's favored aphorisms. The same criticism can be leveled at an ontological reductionism. Without "otherness," duality, and differentiation, all heterogeneity of life-forms would be limited to a deadening homogeneity, and organic evolution could not have occurred. In terms of natural history, the biosphere would indeed still be a "Gaia" covered by Margulis's soup of prokaryotic cells.

Today, to follow a mystical path to "Oneness" is to sink back into the timeless, ahistorical, misty island of the Lotus Eaters, who in Homer's *Odyssey* have no recollection of a past and no vision of a future but vegetate in an unperturbable existence that consists of eating, digesting, and defecating, like animals that live on a strictly day-by-day basis. This is a world that has no sense of "otherness;" no sense of self, no sense of consciousness—

indeed, no sensibility at all beyond the mere maintenance of life, presumably in the bosom of an equally vacuous "cosmic Self." To understand early sensibilities and their development, we must acknowledge that humanity *had* to break with the purely animalistic sensibility—if sensibility it can be called at all—that had confined it to a mere ecological niche, if it was to enter into and know the larger world around it. Human beings had to regard first nature as "other," as they inevitably did, however much romantics of all sorts bemoan the loss of a universal "Oneness" in a golden Pleistocene, Paleolithic, or Neolithic past. Given their naturally endowed potentialities, humans had to go beyond a realm of mere survival into one of creativity and innovation, and satisfy their naturally endowed capacity to adapt environments to meet their own needs—in time, hopefully, along rational and ecological lines.

The terrible psychological upheavals produced by the twentieth century have made us truly wary of social history, of "otherness," of the dualities of separation from nonhuman nature. But "separation" and "otherness" are *human* facts of life, if only because natural evolution has produced a life-form—humanity—whose very specificity is premised on a *conscious* sense of "separation" that can increasingly distinguish human from nonhuman reality. "Otherness" must be conceived of as a *graded* phenomenon, to be sure, one that may result in any of several kinds of society. It may eventuate in very destructive relationships characterized by *opposition*, *domination*, and *antagonism*, as we know today—the results of which stain the social history that lies behind us and possibly the precarious future that lies before us.

But "otherness" may also take the form of *differentiation*, of *articulation*, of *complementarity, as it did in the early history of humanity*. As human beings began to emerge from first nature, possibly in the Pleistocene and certainly in the Paleolithic, their relationship to animals as "others" was largely *complementary*. Hunters know that they are dealing with a nonhuman "other," but as I emphasized in this book many years ago, animism may have been a form of solicitation rather than coercion. Early animism imparted a cooperative impulse to these cultures, despite the fact that animal spirits had to be propitiated. Game, it was assumed, could then be *lured* to "accept" the hunters' spears and arrows, as Paleolithic cave paintings suggest. Even the overkills of the late Pleistocene and early Paleolithic may have arisen not from a sense of the "other" as an opponent or foe, but from a naïve ignorance of the ecological impact these overkills would have on the great Pleistocene megafauna. In this respect, early hunters merely combined the behavior of an ordinary animal predator with that of an increasingly socialized, animistic human being.

After the climatic vicissitudes that marked the Pleistocene Epoch, the environment became more stable for human beings, and with the beginnings of horticulture, when preliterate people settled into permanent village lifeways, early cultures generally seem to have entered into a remarkably balanced relationship with the flora and fauna around them in the Near East and the Americas. Certainly in the Americas, the marvelous abundance of wildlife and many of the magnificent forests reveal that a fair degree of ecological stability marked Indian cultures when whites made contact with new regions of the Americas. Their sense of "otherness" was probably more consciously benign and complementary, based on differentiation rather than opposition. It was rooted in a simple notion of the world as variegated, diversified, and basically ecological. I may add in passing that it is precisely this latter period upon which the second chapter of this book, "The Outlook of Organic Society," focuses, and not only for the Americas but the early Neolithic Near East.

From that very human recognition of their own selves and of natural differences, however, a variegated social history developed, one that included the emergence of hierarchy. Here, the "otherness" of complementarity was often subverted by emerging status groups and slowly gave way to "otherness" based on domination. But the "otherness" of complementarity and the "otherness" of domination existed together and interacted with each other, so that second nature's evolution began to unfold very equivocally. Despite our rightful wariness of the social history of hierarchy and domination, however, ecologically oriented people today cannot ignore the compelling realities of this social history in its entirety—neither its many blemishes nor the many unfulfilled alternatives that it offered for a better world in the past and present, and hopefully, that it will still offer in the future, including reason, science, and technology, with their promise for an ecological society.

Today, we still have to go beyond existing second nature to fulfill the potentiality of combining first and second nature in a new synthesis that I have elsewhere called "free nature." Should this free nature ever come into existence, enriched by the differentiations that mark first and second nature, we could hope to achieve a new sense of "otherness" with first nature that is neither "biocentric" nor "anthropocentric" but complementary—between nonhuman and human—in a richly articulated unity drenched in the sunlight of evolution, not submerged in the darkness of a mythic Pleistocene or a "Gaian" soup of simple unicellular organisms.

∞

Let me to sum up my views quite explicitly. I regard it as a form of ahistorical arrogance, so characteristic of recent times, to look back at preliterate peoples' behavior and cast it in forms that suit modern standards of ecological morality, or respond with pious disappointment to their cruelty or indifference to other living beings. It is a form of modern ahistorical arrogance to expect that they would *not* use their environments up to the hilt or change them as they needed to. What we should properly ask, if we are not to sink into the fatuities of romanticism and mysticism, is not whether humans *should* intervene into nature—for nothing will stop them from trying to fulfill their most basic "natural" potentialities—but *how* they should intervene and toward what *ends*. These are really the profoundly ethical questions that we must ask, and they can only be answered in a *thinking* way—by unscrambling the virtues and vices of humanity's social development, by determining if evolution has any meaningful thrust toward increased subjectivity and consciousness in the great evolutionary parade of life-forms, and by bringing greater mind to bear on the pivotal role of social development in all of these issues.

That many of us, including important thinkers in past generations, have the luxury of questioning hierarchical society's interaction with "Nature," including human nature itself, is the result not of a newly discovered affinity we have with animal life, valid as this affinity may be. It arises mainly from our growing sense of *humanity*, our enlarged sense of humanistic empathy with nonhuman life-forms, not to speak of other human beings. I cannot emphasize too often that no life-forms seem to be capable of sharing our empathic sentiments, except where parental care is involved, and possibly for members of the pack, herd, or band to which they belong. Allowance can also be made for sentiments of affinity that some animals feel for the humans who care for them as pet-owners or shepherds. And to use a word like *empathy* for such cases can only be done in a very anthropomorphic manner, on the dubious assumption that instinct; habit, and conditioned reflexes do not play a major role in forming "empathetic" animal behavior.

As for the sentiments of empathy, care, and concern that humans extend so *broadly* to multitudes of living species, indeed to "Nature" as a whole, let me emphasize again that these sentiments are not to be found in first nature. Animals have no idea of what "Nature" is, any more than did our early ancestors, who were too immersed in it to grasp the natural world as a totality or a vast "otherness," if you will. They could see little beyond their particular ecological niche and the beings that shared it with them. Moreover, if human sensibilities do not draw a distinction between humanity and "Nature," if they do not attain the self-definition, self-consciousness, and self-fulfillment for which people have been equipped by natural evolution, they will always *lack* the empathy, care, aesthetic appreciation, and affinity for first nature that the ecological movement demands of them. Nor could humans have ever become moral agents who can *know* first nature and appreciate it, much less create a free nature that creatively absorbs the best of first and second nature into a realm of social wholeness and ethical complementarity.

The attainment of free nature will involve neither the "re-enchantment," the "redivinization," nor the mystification of "Nature," whether by means of John Muir's inverted Calvinism, Starhawk's magical arts, Gregory Bateson's cybernetics, or "deep" ecology's appeal that we dissolve our "selves" into a "cosmic Self." Nor will free nature be attained by a professoriat, or by essayists, poets, anthropologists, and ecological evangelists who tap out encomiums to hard work and the "simple life" on their word processors. The moral cant that marks the recent reworking of the ecology movement into a wilderness cult, a network of wiccan covens, fervent acolytes of Earth-Goddess religions, and assorted psychotherapeutic encounter groups beggars description. For all their talk about "self-empowerment," theistic "immanence," "care," and "interconnectedness," such mystics actually manage to navigate themselves away from the serious social issues that underlie the present ecological crisis and retreat to strategies of personal "self-transformation" and "enrichment" that are predicated on myths, metaphors, rituals, and "green" consumerism.

A respect and love for first nature has no need for such artifices, artifacts, atavistic practices, or romantic somersaults, much less the growing number of misanthropes whose love of nonhuman life often seems to stem from a detestation of human life. Natural evolution, given its marvelous creativity, its fecundity, its growing subjectivity, and its capacity for innovation, deserves our respect and love for its own attributes. We do not have to create ideological artifacts like deities—female or male—or use magical arts to appreciate first nature as a wondrous phenomenon—including such wonders as the human mind and humanity's capacity to act morally and self-consciously. An appreciation and love of first nature should properly stem from a clear-sighted and aesthetic naturalism, not from a Supernaturalism, with its projection of sovereign humanlike "beings" into the biotic world and its canny use of terms like *immanence* and "earth groundedness." Indeed, whether we truly know and fully appreciate first nature depends very much on having the intellectual and emotional ability *not* to confuse ourselves as human beings with coyotes, bears, or wolves, much less with insensate things like rocks, or rivers, or even more absurdly, with the "cosmos."

Whether this clear-eyed naturalism will become prevalent in the present-day ecology movement is now very much in doubt. One can easily understand and fully appreciate women's resentment of Judeo-Christian patriarchalism, militaristic belief-systems, and the neglect of their identity by a male-oriented world. But for women, or men for that matter, to react to these social and psychological pathologies by adopting a neo-pagan mysticism, an "all-loving" pantheism, or a barely concealed matriarchalism is to replace one body of errors by another, and possibly one social and psychological tyranny by another. Falsehoods and dogmatic beliefs, however benign they may seem at first glance, inevitably imprison the mind and diminish its critical thrust. They presuppose and foster a proclivity for faith, whose arbitrary nature renders their acolytes easily manipulable by assorted New Age gurus, priests, priestesses, witches, and orchestrators of mass culture.

For early hunters themselves, their animistic sensibility was a mixed blessing. Clearly, it featured a cooperative spirit in their relations to animals as "others," and it certainly alerted hunters to the attributes of the animals they stalked. Nevertheless, however much preliterate peoples' animism includes a cooperative dimension, we know today that insofar as it rests on a belief in spirits or a Supernature, it clearly rests on a false image of the natural world. Besides boxing them into inflexible customs and traditions, animism involves an innocent belief in magic that rendered aboriginal peoples very vulnerable to technology, particularly the weaponry, of Europeans who awed them or, with their bullets, bloodily disabused them of the spells with which their shamans had "protected" them.

To believe that animism has any objective reality, as many mystical ecologists suggest, is simply infantile, not unlike the behavior of a child who angrily kicks a stool when he or she falls over it. In view of what we know today about first nature, animistic souls and magical methods have no more basis in objective reality than the visions that many North American Indians traditionally induced in themselves by fasting, self-torture, auto-suggestion, and similar techniques that distort the human sensorium. In a preliterate community, inducing a vision of a guardian spirit by warping one's senses might enhance one's own sense of self-worth, courage, and bravado, thereby making one a better hunter, but these visions tell us no more about the reality of first nature than Castaneda's tales about talking animals. Mythic knowledge and the belief in magic, so important to animism, are a self-delusion—one that is understandable as the beliefs of preliterate peoples, but among modern people they are explicable only as evidence of the extent to which they are removed from reality, indeed, the extent to which they lack authentic "earth wisdom."

Given the growth of ritual as part of the ecology movement and particularly ecofeminism, we would be wise to realize that ritualistic behavior can render people easy to control for many dubious ends. That there are desirable rituals that ease our transitions into different age groups and that prepare us for new responsibilities in life, cement communities, alleviate our sense of loss for the dead, reinforce human solidarity, and even express respect for nonhuman life—all of these are forms of behavior that social ecology readily acknowledges.

But ritualistic behavior must be practiced *knowingly*, indeed, more so today than has ever been the case in the past because the mass media have made us terribly vulnerable to new methods of social control. Our need for all the critical faculties we can muster is heightened by the enormous magnitude of the ecological problems we face. If rituals are used to a point where they foster a noncritical approach to reality or create an illusory substitute for it; if magical trickery becomes a substitute for a rationally explicable kind of causality; if new shamans apply their nostrums to the most intimate areas of life so that it is they, not us, who determine our behavior, the participant can easily become a malleable object rather than an autonomous subject—ironically, I may add, in the name of attaining a "new," "collective," "cosmic," or "ecological" subjectivity. Participants in a ritual of "interconnectedness" who come to believe that that they are "trees," for example, engage in an act of blatant self-deception that may easily diminish their self-identity. The potential damage caused by this loss of ego boundaries is all the more frightening because selfhood is already being weakened and rendered passive by a highly commodified society. Thus, although ritual can be used to alleviate many transitional crises in life, it can also be used very effectively to take over life, to freeze it in manufactured "traditions," and not unlike the Nazi rituals at Nuremberg, indoctrinate and totally subjugate the individual to a new political and psychological tyranny.

The generous utopian ambience that surrounded the ecology movement of the 1960s, with its concern for people as well as the biosphere, is steadily giving way to a dystopian bitterness and misanthropy. Ecology is seriously faced with the danger that it will become mean-spirited and arrogant in its treatment of genuinely denied people. For all their celebrations of "Mother Earth," mystical ecologies generally deal with "her" as though "she" had withered breasts and had lost "her" powers of reproduction. Often knowingly, this tendency in the ecology movement has all but abandoned the commitment of authentic radical movements—socialist and anarchist alike—to human happiness. Radical ecology's earlier confrontational stance toward capitalism and hierarchical society has been increasingly replaced by cries against "technology" and "industrial society"—two very safe, socially neutral targets against which even the bourgeoisie can inveigh in Earth Day celebrations, as long as minimal attention is paid to the social relations in which the mechanization of society is rooted. Radical criticisms of the patently class-biased views of Thomas Malthus are being replaced by anguished cries about the "population problem," as though modern capitalism, given its competitive market economy, would not ravage the planet even if the world's population were reduced to a fraction of its present numbers. The political vigor of the earlier ecology movement is being sapped by religious or quasi-religious cults, an encounter-group mentality of the "personal as political," and mystical vagaries as a substitute for serious reflection and social analyses.

The popularity of "biocentrism," in turn, threatens to trivialize humanity, particularly its capacity for moral agency in "Nature"—ironically, the very intellectual and psychological capacity that is essential to develop a "biocentric" outlook. Aside from the misanthropy that this trivialization nourishes, the eminently ethical demands of "biocentrism" spin on a form of ecological circular reasoning. "Biocentrists" cannot assign human beings an imperative for ethical behavior that they do not assign to all other life-forms, and simultaneously insist that humans are "equal" to other life-forms in terms of "inherent worth." Moreover, even if a "biocentric" society were to emerge, it would be obliged to "intervene" massively in first nature with nearly all the sophisticated technologies it has at its disposal to correct ecological dislocations on a scale that would leave the more purist "deep ecologists" utterly aghast.

The very notion of "equality," as I have argued in chapter 6 in this book, even when applied to human beings alone ignores individual differences in intelligence, talent, age, health, physical infirmity, and the like. Predicated as it is on the notion of justice, "equality" compares poorly indeed with the notion of complementarity, predicated as it is on freedom. A free society in which an ethics of complementarity prevails would make every attempt to compensate for the unavoidable inequalities in physical differences, degrees of intellectuality, and needs among individual human beings. The notion of "equality" is even more inappropriate when it is intended to encompass the nonhuman world as well; differences among species vary far more widely than they do among individual humans. Any form of "equality," including those among humans, that fails to account for differences produced by the "natural inequities" of age, physical capacities, and subjective differences in the nonhuman world would be truly lacking in the empathy that underpins "biocentric" attitudes. "Biocentrism," to put the matter bluntly, is as primitive and unsatisfactory ethically as "anthropocentrism."

Complementarity and *wholeness*, which social ecology substitutes for "biocentricity," "anthropocentricity," "ecocentricity," and other "centricities" that plague us today rest on the notion of "otherness" and the differentiations it presupposes. I have tried to present a fairly nuanced account of the interplay or dialectic between complementarity and conflict in organic society in the opening chapters of this book and, in later chapters, their interplay in ancient, medieval, and capitalist societies, as well as the very important issue of how hierarchy emerged.

❧

But *The Ecology of Freedom* is not only an account of the emergence of hierarchy. As its subtitle indicates, it is also an account of hierarchy's dissolution—not only as a process of realizing an ecological society in the future but in part, at least, as a history of the early uprisings and radical ideas of the dominated strata that sought to undo rule by the elites that oppressed them. In this history there is a very special drama to which the reader's attention should be drawn. I refer to the wealth of historical *alternatives* that oppressed strata formulated and often even brought into being for a time to create free societies for themselves. We must not permit these alternatives to be discarded; far from belonging to the dustbin of history, they should be seen as a treasure trove of discernible institutions, experiences, and experiments, as well as imaginative ideas that never saw the light of day—a treasure that we must eagerly keep alive for the future.

The irreducible minimum, the equality of unequals, and the ethics of complementarity that emerged in organic societies (see chapter 2) are imperishable standards for freedom, albeit standards that must be extended beyond parochial group, band, and tribal bonds. The Greek notions of limit and balance in terms of needs and the Athenian institutions of direct democracy are also imperishable standards, albeit standards that must be divested of patricentricity, slavery, exclusionary forms of citizenship, and the high premium the Greeks placed on the arts of war. Christianity's vision of a universal *humanitas*, for all the defects of the Church, must always be a guiding principle, albeit without any notion of a Supernature to support it. The principle of confederation, so prominent in late medieval cities, as opposed to the nation-state, also belongs to the repertoire of freedom that we can cull from the past, albeit without the patriciates that ruled many cities in the late Middle Ages. It is not atavistic to cull from history the ways in which people developed humanistic lifeways and realistic institutions that could provide workable examples for developing a free society.

To create a society based on differentiation, wholeness, and complementarity, rather than any "centricities" our ideas must be concrete and avoid the diffuseness that is so characteristic of the mystical tendencies in the ecology movement. I have examined in detail what an ecological and rational society might be in a number of my works, including the present one—and I have tried to offer a concrete, almost programmatic project for our times. I have called this project "libertarian municipalism." It is "libertarian" (a term created by nineteenth-century European anarchists, not by contemporary American right-wing proprietarians) in that it advances a new politics of popular control over the material means of life—land, factories, transport, and the like. It is "municipalist" in that it advances a new politics of civic control over public affairs, mainly by means of direct face-to-face citizen assemblies. It is also confederalist, in that it seeks to foster the interdependence of municipalities and their economies on a regional basis—partly to avoid the parochialism of "self-sufficient" communities, which can easily become ingrown and self-aggrandizing; partly to deal with the need to coordinate the operations of these communities in a rational and ecological manner. Policy decisions are initiated, formulated, and decided upon by the citizen assemblies of the municipalities; administrative decisions, subject to careful oversight by the municipalities, are made by mandated, recallable delegates to confederal councils.

Libertarian municipalism, potentially a very significant form of public life today, has a long historical pedigree in cities from the Middle Ages well into the nineteenth century. It was practiced with varying degrees of democracy to countervail emerging centralized nation-states. Libertarian municipalism today seeks to recover and render viable the original Hellenic meaning of the term *politics*—the management of the *polis*'s affairs by means of a truly participatory democratic body of institutions.

The prospect of making such a politics viable today is as plausible as it is necessary. Traditional socialist and anarcho-syndicalist policies of developing a class movement based on proletarian interests that presumably would emerge as a general interest against capitalism have failed beyond any hope of recovery. Capitalism has developed to a level where it has almost completely absorbed the class war envisioned by Marxists and syndicalists. If any general interest can emerge today, it is one that will be shaped by external forces—notably, the ecological limits of an economy that must, by its very nature, "grow or die," thereby endangering the biosphere itself. And if any radical movement for social change and an ecological balance between second and first nature can be achieved, it must be based on a participatory democracy, rooted in a politics of gradual confederalism—the step-by-step formation of civic networks that can ultimately challenge the growing power of the nation-state.

In the vocabulary of past radical movements, this new power would be a "dual" power—a power that, owing to its ability to form a transclass general ecological interest, can face with growing confidence and moral authority the nation-state's monopoly of force. Here the dangers of parochialism that might follow on the heels of decentralization can be reconciled by confederalism. A direct democracy, in turn, avoids the corruptive "politics" produced by political professionalism, bureaucracy, and top-down representative systems of governance. Citizenship, expressed through popular assemblies, can avoid a statist "politics" based on the privatized anonymous "constituent" who exercises no control over his or her social life.

This is not the place to explore the traditions, practices, and prospects associated with libertarian municipalism—the institutions, economies, and interrelationships between civic and confederal bodies, and the new kind of citizen and politics that this system of self-governance involves. The most complete statement of these ideas can be found in my book *The Rise of Urbanization and the Decline of Citizenship.*[9] Suffice it to say here that this political and economic solution to our current problems is also an ecological solution. The private ownership of the planet by elite strata must be brought to an end if we are to survive the afflictions it has imposed on the biotic world, particularly as a result of a society structured around limitless growth. Free nature, in my view, can only begin to emerge when we live in a fully participatory society literally free of privilege and domination. Only then will we be able to rid ourselves of the idea of dominating nature and fulfill our promise for acting as a moral, rational, and creative force in natural as well as social evolution.

ᘓ

Looking over *The Ecology of Freedom* today, I would emphasize the lines I wrote on page 84 that celebrate humanity's capacity to alter the world in a way that combines "a scientific discipline"—ecology—with "the indiscipline of fancy, imagination, and artfulness." The current emphasis by mystical ecologists on nonintervention or minimal intervention by humanity in first nature—the maxim, "let nature take its course"—is completely untenable. Rather, I would ask the reader to consult my quotation of Charles Elton: "The world's future has to be managed, but this management would not be just like a game of chess—[but] more like steering a boat." Today, I would emphasize that while the world cannot be dealt with like a game of chess, it nevertheless does, as Elton points out, have to be "managed." If we do not intervene in the world today for purposes of ecological restoration, the management of wild areas, and reforestation, neither we nor the wildlife we wish to conserve is likely to have any future at all. We have gone beyond a so-called "primeval" world, to a point where the possibility of returning to it is simply excluded. And in many respects we have developed new sensibilities, however marginal they may be today, that are even more advanced than those of our early ancestors.

I would also emphasize my insistence on Hegel's famous maxim, "The True is the Whole" (page 97), and in my insistence on combining our changes of the natural world with the "spontaneity" of first nature. My concern with ecological stability as a function of "unity in diversity" and complexity, however, requires an explanation. The ecological consciousness of the fifties and early sixties, to the extent that there was one, was obliged to advocate ecological stability as a product of crop variety to avoid the use of dangerous pesticides so heavily used in the kind of single-crop monoculture that was—and still is—practiced by agribusiness. Only by playing insect and other animal populations against one another in variegated agricultural situations did it seem possible to reduce or eliminate the use of dangerous chemicals.

Today, my emphasis on diversity and complexity rests on much broader grounds. A diversity of species, in my view, is vitally important because it opens new pathways for the evolution of life. Ecocommunities with more species are usually more complex; they tend to give rise to new, more subjective and more flexible life-forms that in turn open greater evolutionary possibilities. I have discussed this phenomenon, which I call "participatory evolution," in my 1986 essay "Freedom and Necessity in Nature."[10]

I am satisfied that chapter 2, "The Outlook of Organic Society," is substantially sound as it stands today. It is admittedly a polemical chapter, written to countervail the standard image of preliterate cultures as "savage" by emphasizing their benign aspects. I wanted to shatter this ugly image of preliterate peoples and explore more fully the ancestral sources of values like care, nurture, and early humanity's subjectivization or personalization of "Nature." But given the romantic mystification of preliterate societies so very much in vogue today, I should point out that preliterate cultures have—or had—no compunction about intervening significantly in the natural world; indeed, many of their rituals and magical practices were spiritual means to facilitate their acts of intervention. I can only hope that this introduction helps to provide a more balanced account of the Wintu and Hopi Indians, the Ihalmiut Eskimos, and the other preliterate peoples to whom I refer in the book, as active agents in changing first nature.

I would also want to frame my discussion of complementarity in organic society in terms of this introduction's discussion of "otherness." Preliterate people, as they emerged from an awareness of their particular ecological niches into that of a larger sense of first nature, were not oblivious to the fact that the world around them, the game that they hunted, and the plants that they cultivated, may have been highly personalized but were also "other" than human. But this was not initially a view of the "other" as an opponent, much less one that had to be subjugated. It was based on a simple notion of the world as variegated, diversified, and basically ecological, as I have pointed out earlier. While we must carefully advance to a worldview that has a complementary notion of "otherness" rather than a conflictual one, it must have secular and rational underpinnings: a "quasi-animism," if you like, that is based on a respect and appreciation for the continuity of life rather than spirits or the myth of a Supernature.

The most potentially misleading passages in chapter 2 appear on pages 128–129, where I evoke the symbolism of a "Mother Goddess [as] a fertility principle so old in time that its stone remains have even been found in Paleolithic caves and encampments" (page 128). Let me emphasize that nowhere in this passage do I refer to "her" as an *Earth* Goddess or as a *pantheistic* female presence in the world. Nor do I identify "her" with first nature. My characterization of this "Mother Goddess" as the expression of "the fecundity of nature it all its diversity" (page 162) still refers to a fertility principle, not an organized religion with its panoply of priestly corporations. The vegetation goddesses that emerged, as part of full-blown religions with temples often managed by priests, are not equivalent to earlier, generalized fertility principles. These new female agricultural deities, in fact, were easily placed in the service of hierarchy, not organic egalitarian societies. Such goddesses and the priestly elites who gorged on the wealth they accumulated in goddess-oriented temples were no blessing for women, much less for oppressed people who toiled in "her" behalf.

At no point in my discussion did I suggest that we can return to aboriginal lifeways. In fact, I was at pains to warn against any belief that we can—or should—do so. If we are to achieve an ecological society in the future, it will have to be enriched by the insights, knowledge, and data we have acquired as a result of the long history of philosophy, science, technology, and rationality—cleansed of magic, the worship of deities, and primeval religions. Nor can we push our history aside. Rather, we must absorb what is ethically and intellectually valuable in it and discard what is ethically harmful. We should avoid superstition, incipient hierarchy, and a hierarchical sensibility of any kind.

I would want to revise nothing in chapter 3, "The Emergence of Hierarchy." My treatment of the immanent, indeed dialectical *origins* of status relations in early society has stood up beyond my greatest expectations, as recent data indicates. I would only note that all the evidence I could cull gives chronological priority to the emergence of gerontocracies over patriarchies, and that shamans usually played a sinister role in most tribal societies. Attempts by some ecofeminists to recycle my discussion of the development of hierarchy to view patriarchy as the *sole* origin of domination are spurious and self-serving. Indeed, as Janet Biehl has shown so clearly in *Finding Our Way: Rethinking Ecofeminist Politics*, hierarchy assumed such a large variety of forms over time, including forms in which men dominate men, that to single out patriarchy as the exclusive and most abiding source of hierarchy verges on the nonsensical. I was at pains, moreover, to quote E. R. Dodds on page 191 to the effect that the patriarch had enormous power over the male members of the family as well as the female. In patriarchal families both women and men could be dealt with arbitrarily and cruelly, at times even by "matriarchs" like Sarah, who induced Abraham to drive his concubine Hagar and their son Ishmael into the desert. It should be noted that in quoting Max Horkheimer and Theodor Adorno's sentimental passage on page 193 of the book, to the effect that woman is the "image of nature" and a "key stimulus to aggression"—a passage that has found favor with more informed ecofeminists—I strongly qualify their remarks by a footnote that emphasizes women's outstanding role in the early domestic economy around which preliterate society was structured, and its enormous importance in social development.

My distinction between justice and freedom in chapter 6, "Justice—Equal and Exact," is as firmly rooted as ever these days. It is a discussion that acquires special significance in view of "deep ecology's" naïve endeavor to attribute "equality" to all species in a "biocentric democracy." Chapter 7, "The Legacy of Freedom," continues to be as relevant as ever for our time. Gnosticism as an emancipatory ideology is less attractive to me now than it is to many mystics and eco-feminists who, once they learn that the Gnostic "Sophia" was a woman, are ready to embrace unthinkingly all the strictures of this highly dualistic, even sinister religion. I am at pains to note: "Gnosticism must be dealt with very prudently before any of its tendencies are described as a Christian 'heresy.' In its Manichean form, it is simply a different religion, like Islam or Buddhism. In its Ophite form, it is a total, utterly anarchistic, inversion of Christian canon" (page 258). I hold no brook for Gnostic elitism, dualism, or in Marcion's form, its asceticism and amorality (pages 260–261). The point I tried to make in my dialectical treatment of Gnosticism was to elicit its anarchistic and critical thrust, a problem that must be situated in the historical context and development of this religion, not by treating it as an ahistorical and consistent dogma that never underwent any changes in different times and places.

There are no significant changes that I would make in the remaining chapters of the book. That I treated Hebrew transcendentalism unsatisfactorily by failing to emphasize that it sharply distinguished the "eternality" of "Nature" from the "mutability" of society, thereby opening society to the possibility of radical, even revolutionary changes for the first time in history, is a well-deserved criticism. I made this important point only in passing, when I quoted H. and H. A. Frankfort's observation that Hebrew transcendentalism led to a "revolutionary and dynamic teaching" by postulating "a metaphysical significance for [social] history and for man's actions" (page 175). It thereby freed human thought and practice from the unchangeable, indeed necessitarian world of "Nature," its domain of eternal recurrence, and its paralyzing deities. Again, Janet Biehl has provided an invaluable corrective for this omission.[11]

Chapter 11, "The Ambiguities of Freedom," which I regard as the most important in the book, is singularly appropriate today. Its argument for an ecologically oriented rationality, science, and technics could stand rereading by any thoughtful individual. Only one caveat should be noted: my criticisms of Horkheimer and Adorno are too gentle. Despite their word-magic, I do not feel that their ideas have the applicability to our times that so many Frankfurt School admirers would have us believe. *The Dialectic of Enlightenment* is a very enchanting work, but it fares poorly as a defense of reason; nor does it have a clear sense of direction in its treatment of reason. In retrospect, I do not find it accidental that it has been picked up by many postmodernists, together with Adorno's wayward writings, as a precursor of the high-culture nihilism that is very much in vogue today. Chapter 12 deals, of course, with "An Ecological Society," and the "Epilogue" advances the fundamentals of a nature philosophy and a naturalistic ethics. Lest this portion of the book be misunderstood, I point out that we cannot return to an idyllic "Garden of Eden" (page 449) and that reason "must be permitted to stake out its own claim to a libertarian rationality" (page 453). But the reader should be aware that I permitted myself to use many words for strictly evocative purposes, in the hope that I could combine theoretical insights with metaphors that were meant to reach the reader's emotions. My almost animistic remark that "nature is writing its own natural philosophy and ethics" is to be understood as a string of metaphors. "Nature" really does what it does "best"—develop, diversify, and produce increasingly complex phenomena. Despite my quotations from Lynn Margulis's discussion of the active role that life plays in creating its environment, I nowhere accept—and today, I firmly reject—her commitment to a variant of the "Gaia" hypothesis, which sees the planet as a single organism.

In closing, let me restate my plea that the reader examine the original introduction that follows. Despite the fact that it overlaps with the present introduction, within a span of a few pages it provides the essential outlines of social ecology.

The ecology movement will never gain any real influence or have any significant impact on society if it advances a message of despair rather than hope, of a regressive and impossible return to primordial human cultures and sensibilities, rather than a commitment to human progress and to a uniquely *human* empathy for life as a whole. I can easily understand why despair exists among many mystical ecologists—indeed, in the environmental movement generally—over the impact of a grow-or-die capitalistic economy on the biosphere and on the human psyche. While a patronizing, quasi-religious, often misanthropic ecology that denigrates the uniqueness of human beings and the wondrous role they can play in natural evolution may be an understandable response to that economy, it is a denial of humanity's most human potentiality: the ability to change the world for the better and enrich it for virtually all life forms.

We must recover the utopian impulses, the hopefulness, the appreciation of what is good, what is worth rescuing in human civilization, as well as what must be rejected, if the ecology movement is to play a transformative and creative role in human affairs. For without changing society, we will not change the disastrous ecological direction in which capitalism is moving. Spiritualistic movements have been at work in human history for thousands of years. They have doubtless changed the thinking and behavior of many people. But rarely, as the history of all the great world religions attests, have they created an ecologically humanistic society. This kind of society will never be achieved without ideas that confront the material as well as spiritual conditions of life, indeed, of public life as well as private life.

May 20, 1991

---

1. Murray Bookchin, T*he Rise of Urbanization and the Decline of Citizenship* (San Francisco: Sierra Club Books, 1987), published in paperback by Black Rose Books under the title *Urbanization Without Cities* in 1991; *Remaking Society* (Montreal: Black Rose Books, 1989; Boston: South End Press, 1990); and *The Philosophy of Social Ecology: Essays in Dialectical Naturalism* (Montreal: Black Rose Books, 1990); "Thesis on Libertarian Municipalism," *Green Perspectives*, PO Box 111, Burlington, VT 05402.

2. Arthur O. Lovejoy and George Boas, "Some Meanings of 'Nature,'" in *Primitivism and Related Ideas in Antiquity* (Johns Hopkins, 1985; reprinted, New York: Octagon Books, 1965).

3. Janet Biehl, *Finding Our Way: Rethinking Ecofeminist Politics* (Montreal: Black Rose Books, 1991); published in the United States under the title *Rethinking Ecofeminist Politics* (Boston: South End Press, 1991).

4. Paul S. Martin, "Prehistoric Overkill," in *Pleistocene Extinctions: The Search for a Cause*, ed. P S. Martin and H. E. Wright, Jr. (New Haven: Yale University Press, 1967), p. 75.

5. Calvin Martin, *Keepers of the Game: Indian Animal Relationships and the Fur Trade* (Berkeley: University of California Press, 1978), pp. 169–71.

6. Stephen J. Pyne, *Fire in America* (Princeton: Princeton University Press, 1982), p. 71.

7. Alston Chase, *Playing God in Yellowstone: The Destruction of America's First National Park* (New York: Harvest/Harcourt Brace Jovanovich, 1986, 1987), p. 104.

8. Colin M. Turnbull, *The Forest People: A Study of the Pygmies of the Congo* (New York: Clarion/ Simon and Schuster, 1961), pp. 101–102.

9. Bookchin, *The Rise of Urbanization*.

10. Bookchin, "Freedom and Necessity in Nature," *Alternatives* 13 (November 1986); republished in Bookchin, *Philosophy of Social Ecology*.

11. Biehl, *Finding Our Way*, pp. 60–66.

℺   **INTRODUCTION**

This book was written to satisfy the need for a consistently radical social ecology: an ecology of freedom. It had been maturing in my mind since 1952 when I first became acutely conscious of the growing environmental crisis that was to assume such monumental proportions a generation later. In that year, I published a volume-sized article, "The Problems of Chemicals in Food" (later to be republished in book form in Germany as *Lebensgefährliche Lebensmittel*). Owing to my early Marxian intellectual training, the article examined not merely environmental pollution but also its deep-seated social origins. Environmental issues had developed in my mind as social issues, and problems of natural ecology had become problems of "social ecology"—an expression hardly in use at the time.

The subject was never to leave me. In fact, its dimensions were to widen and deepen immensely. By the early sixties, my views could be summarized in a fairly crisp formulation: the very notion of the domination of nature by man stems from the very real domination of human by human. For me, this was a far-reaching reversal of concepts. The many articles and books I published in the years after 1952, beginning with *Our Synthetic Environment* (1963) and continuing with *Toward an Ecological Society* (1980), were largely explorations of this fundamental theme. As one premise led to another, it became clear that a highly coherent project was forming in my work: the need to explain the emergence of social hierarchy and domination and to elucidate the means, sensibility, and practice that could yield a truly harmonious ecological society. My book *Post-Scarcity Anarchism* (1971) pioneered this vision. Composed of essays dating from 1964, it addressed itself more to hierarchy than class, to domination rather than exploitation, to liberatory institutions rather than the mere abolition of the State, to freedom rather than justice, and pleasure rather than happiness. For me, these changing emphases were not mere countercultural rhetoric; they marked a sweeping departure from my earlier commitment to socialist orthodoxies of all forms. I visualized instead a new form of libertarian social ecology—or what Victor Ferkiss, in discussing my social views, so appropriately called "eco-anarchism."

As recently as the sixties, words like hierarchy and domination were rarely used. Traditional radicals, particularly Marxists, still spoke almost exclusively in terms of classes, class analyses, and class-consciousness; their concepts of oppression were primarily confined to *material* exploitation, grinding poverty, and the unjust abuse of labor. Likewise, orthodox anarchists placed most of their emphasis on the State as the ubiquitous source of social coercion.* Just as the emergence of private property became society's "original sin" in Marxian orthodoxy, so the emergence of the State became society's "original sin" in anarchist orthodoxy. Even the early counterculture of the sixties eschewed the use of the term hierarchy and preferred to "Question Authority" without exploring the genesis of authority, its relationship to nature, and its meaning for the creation of a new society.

During these years I also concentrated on how a truly free society, based on ecological principles, could mediate humanity's relationship with nature. As a result, I began to explore the development of a new technology scaled to comprehensible human dimensions. Such a technology would include small solar and wind installations, organic gardens, and the use of local "natural resources" worked by decentralized communities. This view quickly gave rise to another— the need for direct democracy, for urban decentralization, for a high measure of self-sufficiency, for self-empowerment based on communal forms of social life—in short, the nonauthoritarian Commune composed of communes.

As I published these ideas over the years—especially in the decade between the early sixties and early seventies—what began to trouble me was the extent to which people tended to subvert their unity, coherence, and radical focus. Notions like decentralization and human scale, for example, were deftly adopted without reference to solar and wind techniques or bio-agricultural practices that are their material underpinnings. Each segment was permitted to plummet off on its own, while the philosophy that unified them into an integrated whole was permitted to languish. Decentralization entered city planning as a mere stratagem for community design, while alternative technology became a narrow discipline, increasingly

---

* I use the word "orthodox" here and in subsequent pages advisedly. I refer not to the outstanding radical theorists of the nineteenth century—Proudhon, Kropotkin, and Bakunin—but to their followers who often turned their ever-evolving ideas into rigid, sectarian doctrines. As a young Canadian anarchist, David Spanner, put it in a personal conversation, "If Bakunin and Kropotkin devoted as much time to the interpretation of Proudhon as many of our contemporary libertarians do ... I doubt if Bakunin's *God and the State* or Kropotkin's *Mutual Aid* would have ever been written."

confined to the academy and to a new breed of technocrats. In turn, each notion became divorced from a critical analysis of society—from a radical theory of social ecology.

It has become clear to me that it was the *unity* of my views—their ecological holism, not merely their individual components—that gave them a radical thrust. That a society is decentralized, that it uses solar or wind energy, that it is farmed organically, or that it reduces pollution—none of these measures by itself or even in limited combination with others makes an ecological society. Nor do piecemeal steps, however well-intended, even partially resolve problems that have reached a universal, global, and catastrophic character. If anything, partial "solutions" serve merely as cosmetics to conceal the deep-seated nature of the ecological crisis. They thereby deflect public attention and theoretical insight from an adequate understanding of the depth and scope of the necessary changes.

Combined in a coherent whole and supported by a consistently radical practice, however, these views challenge the status quo in a far-reaching manner—in the only manner commensurate with the nature of the crisis. It was precisely this *synthesis* of ideas that I sought to achieve in *The Ecology of Freedom*. And this synthesis had to be rooted in history—in the development of social relations, social institutions, changing technologies and sensibilities, and political structures; only in this way could I hope to establish a sense of genesis, contrast, and continuity that would give real meaning to my views. The reconstructive utopian thinking that followed from my synthesis could then be based on the realities of human experience. What *should* be could become what *must* be, if humanity and the biological complexity on which it rests were to survive. Change and reconstruction could emerge from existing problems rather than wishful thinking and misty vagaries.

෨

My use of the word *hierarchy* in the subtitle of this work is meant to be provocative. There is a strong theoretical need to contrast hierarchy with the more widespread use of the words class and State; careless use of these terms can produce a dangerous simplification of social reality. To use the words hierarchy, class, and State interchangeably, as many social theorists do, is insidious and obscurantist. This practice, in the name of a "classless" or "libertarian" society, could easily conceal the existence of hierarchical relationships and a hierarchical sensibility, both of which—even in the absence of economic exploitation or political coercion—would serve to perpetuate unfreedom.

By hierarchy, I mean the cultural, traditional and psychological systems of obedience and command, not merely the economic and political systems to which the terms class and State most appropriately refer. Accordingly, hierarchy and domination could easily continue to exist in a "classless" or "Stateless" society. I refer to the domination of the young by the old, of women by men, of one ethnic group by another, of "masses" by bureaucrats who profess to speak in their "higher social interests," of countryside by town, and in a more subtle psychological sense, of body by mind, of spirit by a shallow instrumental rationality, and of nature by society and technology. Indeed, classless but hierarchical societies exist today (and they existed more covertly in the past); yet the people who live in them neither enjoy freedom, nor do they exercise control over their lives.

Marx, whose works largely account for this conceptual obfuscation, offered us a fairly explicit definition of class. He had the advantage of developing his theory of class society within a sternly objective economic framework. His widespread acceptance may well reflect the extent to which our own era gives supremacy to economic issues over all other aspects of social life. There is, in fact, a certain elegance and grandeur to the notion that the "history of all hitherto existing society has been the history of class struggles." Put quite simply, a ruling class is a privileged social stratum that owns or controls the means of production and exploits a larger mass of people, the ruled class, which works these productive forces. Class relationships are essentially relationships of production based on ownership of land, tools, machines, and the produce thereof. Exploitation, in turn, is the use of the labor of others to provide for one's own material needs, for luxuries and leisure, and for the accumulation and productive renewal of technology. There the matter of class definition could be said to rest—and with it, Marx's famous method of "class analysis" as the authentic unravelling of the material bases of economic interests, ideologies and culture.

Hierarchy, although it includes Marx's definition of class and even gives rise to class society historically, goes beyond this limited meaning imputed to a largely economic form of stratification. To say this, however, does not define the meaning of the term hierarchy, and I doubt that the word can be encompassed by a formal definition. I view it historically and existentially as a complex system of command and obedience in which elites enjoy varying degrees of control over their subordinates without necessarily exploiting them. Such elites may completely lack any form of material wealth; they may even be dispossessed of it, much as Plato's "guardian" elite was socially powerful but materially poor.

Hierarchy is not merely a social condition; it is also a state of consciousness, a sensibility toward phenomena at every level of personal and social experience. Early preliterate societies ("organic" societies, as I call them) existed in a fairly integrated and unified form based on kinship ties, age groups, and a sexual division of labor.* Their high sense of internal unity and their egalitarian outlook extended not only to each other but to their relationship with nature. People in preliterate cultures viewed themselves not as the "lords of creation" (to borrow a phrase used by Christian millenarians) but as part of the natural world. They were neither above nature nor below it but *within* it.

In organic societies the differences between individuals, age groups, sexes—and between humanity and the natural manifold of living and nonliving phenomena—were seen (to use Hegel's superb phrase) as a "unity of differences" or "unity of diversity," not as hierarchies. Their outlook was distinctly ecological, and from this outlook they almost unconsciously derived a body of values that influenced their behavior toward individuals in their own communities and the world of life. As I contend in the following pages, ecology knows no "king of beasts" and no "lowly creatures" (such terms come from our own hierarchical mentality). Rather it deals with ecosystems in which living things are interdependent and play complementary roles in perpetuating the stability of the natural order.

Gradually, organic societies began to develop less traditional forms of differentiation and stratification. Their primal unity began to break down. The sociopolitical or "civil" sphere of life expanded, giving increasing eminence to the elders and males of the community, who now claimed this sphere as part of the division of tribal labor. Male supremacy over women and children emerged primarily as a result of the male's social functions in the community—functions that were not by any means exclusively economic as Marxian theorists would have us believe. Male cunning in the manipulation of women was to appear later.

_____

* Lest my emphasis on integration and community in "organic societies" be misunderstood, I would like to voice a caveat here. By the term "organic society," I do not mean a society conceived as an organism—a concept I regard as redolent with corporatist and totalitarian notions of social life. For the most part, I use the term to denote a spontaneously formed, non-coercive, and egalitarian society—a "natural" society in the very definite sense that it emerges from innate human needs for association, interdependence, and care. Moreover, I occasionally use the term in a looser sense to describe richly articulated communities that foster human sociability, free expression, and popular control. To avoid misunderstanding, I have reserved the term "ecological society" to characterize the utopistic vision advanced in the closing portions of this book.

Until this phase of history or prehistory, the elders and males rarely exercised socially dominant roles because their civil sphere was simply not very important to the community. Indeed, the civil sphere was markedly counterbalanced by the enormous significance of the woman's "domestic" sphere. Household and childbearing responsibilities were much more important in early organic societies than politics and military affairs. Early society was profoundly different from contemporary society in its structural arrangements and the roles played by different members of the community.

Yet even with the emergence of hierarchy there were still no economic classes or state structures, nor were people materially exploited in a systematic manner. Certain strata, such as the elders and shamans and ultimately the males in general, began to claim privileges for themselves—often merely as matters of prestige based on social recognition rather than material gain. The nature of these privileges, if such they can be called, requires a more sophisticated discussion than it has received to date, and I have tried to examine them carefully in considerable detail. Only later did economic classes and economic exploitation begin to appear, eventually to be followed by the State with its far-reaching bureaucratic and military paraphernalia.

But the dissolution of organic societies into hierarchical, class, and political societies occurred unevenly and erratically, shifting back and forth over long periods of time. We can see this most strikingly in the relationships between men and women—particularly in terms of the values that have been associated with changing social roles. For example, although anthropologists have long assigned an inordinate degree of social eminence to men in highly developed hunting cultures—an eminence they probably never enjoyed in the more primal foraging bands of their ancestors—the supercession of hunting by horticulture, in which gardening was performed mainly by women, probably redressed whatever earlier imbalances may have existed between the sexes. The "aggressive" male hunter and the "passive" female food-gatherer are the theatrically exaggerated images that male anthropologists of a past era inflicted on their "savage" aboriginal subjects, but certainly tensions and vicissitudes in *values*, quite aside from social relationships, must have simmered within primordial hunting and gathering communities. To deny the very existence of the latent attitudinal tensions that must have existed between the male hunter, who had to kill for his food and later make war on his fellow beings, and the female food-gatherer, who foraged for her food and later cultivated it, would make it very difficult to explain why patriarchy and its harshly aggressive outlook ever emerged at all.

Although the changes I have adduced were technological and partially economic—as terms like food-gatherers, hunters, and horticulturists seem to imply—we should not assume that these changes were directly responsible for shifts in sexual status. Given the level of hierarchical difference that emerged in this early period of social life—even in a patricentric community—women were still not abject inferiors of men, nor were the young placed in grim subjugation to the old. Indeed, the appearance of a ranking system that conferred privilege on one stratum over another, notably the old over the young, was in its own way a form of compensation that more often reflected the egalitarian features of organic society rather than the authoritarian features of later societies.

When the number of horticultural communities began to multiply to a point where cultivable land became relatively scarce and warfare increasingly common, the younger warriors began to enjoy a sociopolitical eminence that made them the "big men" of the community, sharing civil power with the elders and shamans. Throughout, matricentric customs, religions, and sensibilities coexisted with patricentric ones, so that the sterner features of patriarchy were often absent during this transitional period. Whether matricentric or patricentric, the older egalitarianism of organic society permeated social life and faded away only slowly, leaving many vestigial remains long after class society had fastened its hold on popular values and sensibilities.

The State, economic classes, and the systematic exploitation of subjugated peoples followed from a more complex and protracted development than radical theorists recognized in their day. Their visions of the origins of class and political societies were instead the *culmination* of an earlier, richly articulated development of society into hierarchical forms. The divisions within organic society increasingly raised the old to supremacy over the young, men to supremacy over women, the shaman and later the priestly corporation to supremacy over lay society, one class to supremacy over another, and State formations to supremacy over society in general.

For the reader imbued with the conventional wisdom of our era, I cannot emphasize too strongly that society in the form of bands, families, clans, tribes, tribal federations, villages, and even municipalities long antedates State formations. The State, with its specialized functionaries, bureaucracies, and armies, emerges quite late in human social development—often well beyond the threshold of history. It remained in sharp conflict with coexisting social structures such as guilds, neighborhoods, popular societies, cooperatives, town meetings, and a wide variety of municipal assemblies.

But the hierarchical organization of all differentia did not end with the structuring of "civil" society into an institutionalized system of obedience and command. In time, hierarchy began to invade less tangible fields of life. Mental activity was given supremacy over physical work, intellectual experience over sensuousness, the "reality principle" over the "pleasure principle," and finally judgment, morality, and spirit were pervaded by an ineffable authoritarianism that was to take its vengeful command over language and the most rudimentary forms of symbolization. The vision of social and natural diversity was altered from an organic sensibility that sees different phenomena as unity in diversity into a hierarchical mentality that ranked the most miniscule phenomena into mutually antagonistic pyramids erected around notions of "inferior" and "superior." And what began as a sensibility has evolved into concrete social fact. Thus, the effort to restore the ecological principle of unity in diversity has become a social effort in its own right—a revolutionary effort that must rearrange sensibility in order to rearrange the real world.

A hierarchical mentality fosters the renunciation of the pleasures of life. It justifies toil, guilt, and sacrifice by the "inferiors," and pleasure and the indulgent gratification of virtually every caprice by their "superiors." The objective history of the social structure becomes internalized as a subjective history of the psychic structure. Heinous as my view may be to modern Freudians, it is not the discipline of *work* but the discipline of *rule* that demands the repression of internal nature. This repression then extends outward to external nature as a mere object of rule and later of exploitation. This mentality permeates our individual psyches in a cumulative form up to the present day—not merely as capitalism but as the vast history of hierarchical society from its inception. Unless we explore this history, which lives actively within us like earlier phases of our individual lives, we will never be free of its hold. We may eliminate social injustice, but we will not achieve social freedom. We may eliminate classes and exploitation, but we will not be spared from the trammels of hierarchy and domination. We may exorcize the spirit of gain and accumulation from our psyches, but we will still be burdened by gnawing guilt, renunciation, and a subtle belief in the "vices" of sensuousness.

ɞ

Another series of distinctions appears in this book—the distinction between morality and ethics and between justice and freedom. Morality—as I use this term—denotes conscious standards of behavior that have not yet been subjected to thorough rational analyses by a community. I have eschewed the use of the word "custom" as a substitute for the word morality because moral criteria for judging behavior do involve *some* kind of explanation and cannot be reduced to the conditioned social reflexes we usually call custom. The Mosaic commandments, like those of other world religions, for example, were justified on theological grounds; they were the sacrosanct words of Yahweh, which we might reasonably challenge today because they are not grounded in reason. Ethics, by contrast, invites rational analyses and, like Kant's "moral imperative," must be justified by intellectual operations, not mere faith. Hence, morality lies somewhere between unthinking custom and rational ethical criteria of right and wrong. Without making these distinctions, it would be difficult to explain the increasingly ethical claims the State has made on its citizens, particularly in eroding the archaic moral codes that supported the patriarch's complete control over his family, and the impediments this authority has placed in the way of politically more expansive societies like the Athenian *polis*.

The distinction between justice and freedom, between formal equality and substantive equality, is even more basic and continually recurs throughout the book. This distinction has rarely been explored even by radical theorists, who often still echo the historical cry of the oppressed for "Justice!" rather than freedom. Worse yet, the two have been used as equivalents (which they decidedly are not). The young Proudhon and later Marx correctly perceived that true freedom presupposes an equality based on a recognition of inequality—the inequality of capacities and needs, of abilities and responsibilities. Mere formal equality, which "justly" rewards each according to his or her contribution to society and sees everyone as "equal in the eyes of the law" and "equal in opportunity," grossly obscures the fact that the young and old, the weak and infirm, the individual with few responsibilities and the one with many (not to speak of the rich and the poor in contemporary society) by no means enjoy genuine equality in a society guided by the rule of equivalence. Indeed, terms like rewards, needs, opportunity, or, for that matter, property—however communally "owned" or collectively operated—require as much investigation as the word law. Unfortunately, the revolutionary tradition did not fully develop these themes and their embodiment in certain terms. Socialism, in most of its forms, gradually degenerated into a demand for "economic justice," thereby merely restating the rule of equivalence as an economic emendation to the juridical and political rule of equivalence established by the bourgeoisie. It is my purpose to thoroughly unscramble these distinctions, to demonstrate how the confusion arose in the first place and how it can be clarified so it no longer burdens the future.

A third contrast that I try to develop in this book is the distinction between happiness and pleasure. Happiness, as defined here, is the mere satisfaction of *need*, of our survival needs for food, shelter, clothing, and material security—in short, our needs as animal organisms. Pleasure, by contrast, is the satisfaction of our *desires*, of our intellectual, esthetic, sensuous and playful "daydreams." The social quest for happiness, which so often seems liberating, tends to occur in ways that shrewdly devalue or repress the quest for pleasure. We can see evidence of this regressive development in many radical ideologies that justify toil and need at the expense of artful work and sensuous joy. That these ideologies denounce the quest for fulfillment of the sensuous as "bourgeois individualism" and "libertinism" hardly requires mention. Yet it is precisely in this utopistic quest for pleasure, I believe, that humanity begins to gain its most sparkling glimpse of emancipation. With this quest carried to the *social* realm, rather than confined to a privatized hedonism, humanity begins to transcend the realm of justice, even of a classless society, and enters into the realm of freedom—a realm conceived, as the full realization of humanity's potentialities in their most creative form.

If I were asked to single out the one underlying contrast that permeates this book, it is the seeming conflict between the "realm of necessity" and the "realm of freedom." Conceptually, this conflict dates back to Aristotle's *Politics*. It involves the "blind" world of "natural" or external nature and the rational world of "human" or internal nature that society must dominate to create the material conditions for freedom—the free time and leisure to allow man to develop his potentialities and powers. This drama is redolent with the conflict between nature and society, woman and man, and body and reason that permeates western images of "civilization." It has underpinned almost every rationalistic account of history; it has been used ideologically to justify domination in virtually every aspect of life. Its apotheosis, ironically, is reached in various socialisms, particularly those of Robert, Owen, Saint-Simon, and in its most sophisticated form, Karl Marx. Marx's image of the "savage who wrestles with nature" is not an expression so much of Enlightenment hubris as it is of Victorian arrogance. Woman, as Theodor Adorno and Max Horkheimer observed, has no stake in this conflict. It is strictly between man and nature. From Aristotle's time to Marx's, the split is regarded as inevitable: the gap between necessity and freedom may be narrowed by technological advances that give man an ever-greater ascendancy over nature, but it can never be bridged. What puzzled a few highly sophisticated Marxists in later years was how the repression and disciplining of external nature could be achieved without repressing and disciplining internal nature: how could "natural" nature be kept in tow without subjugating "human" nature?

My attempt to unravel this puzzle involves an effort to deal with the Victorians' mythic "savage," to investigate external nature and its relationship to internal nature, to give meaning to the world of necessity (nature) in terms of the ability of the world of freedom (society) to colonize and liberate it. My strategy is to reexamine the evolution and meaning of technology in a new ecological light. I will try to ascertain how work ceased to be attractive and playful, and turned into onerous toil. Hence, I am led to a drastic reconsideration of the nature and structure of technics, of work, and of humanity's metabolism with nature.

Here, I would like to emphasize that my views on nature are linked by a fairly unorthodox notion of reason. As Adorno and Horkheimer have emphasized, reason was once perceived as an immanent feature of reality, indeed, as the organizing and motivating principle of the world. It was seen as an inherent force—as the *logos*—that imparted meaning and coherence to reality at all levels of existence. The modern world has abandoned this notion and reduced reason to *rationalization*, that is, to a mere technique for achieving practical ends. *Logos*, in effect, was simply turned into logic. This book tries to recover this notion of an immanent world reason, albeit without the archaic, quasi-theological trappings that render this notion untenable to a more knowledgeable and secular society. In my view, reason exists in nature as the self-organizing attributes of substance; it is the latent subjectivity in the inorganic and organic levels of reality that reveal an inherent striving toward consciousness. In humanity, this subjectivity reveals itself as self-consciousness. I do not claim that my approach is unique; an extensive literature that supports the existence of a seemingly intrinsic *logos* in nature derives mainly from the scientific community itself. What I have tried to do here is to cast my speculations about reason in distinctly historical and ecological terms, free of the theological and mystical proclivities that have so often marred the formulations of a rational nature philosophy. In the closing chapters, I try to explore the interface between nature philosophy and libertarian social theory.

I am also obliged to recover the *authentic* utopian tradition, particularly as expressed by Rabelais, Charles Fourier, and William Morris, from amidst the debris of futurism that conceals it. Futurism, as exemplified by the works of Herman Kahn, merely extrapolates the hideous present into an even more hideous future and thereby effaces the creative, imaginative dimensions of futurity. By contrast, the utopian tradition seeks to permeate necessity with freedom, work with play, even toil with artfulness and festiveness. My contrast between utopianism and futurism forms the basis for a creative, liberatory reconstruction of an ecological society, for a sense of human mission and meaning as nature rendered self-conscious.

This book opens with a Norse myth that depicts how the gods must pay a penalty for seeking the conquest of nature. It ends with a social project for removing that penalty, whose Latin root *poenalis* has given us the word pain. Humanity will become the deities it created in its imagination, albeit as deities *within* nature, not *above* nature—as "supernatural" entities. The title of this book, *The Ecology of Freedom,* is meant to express the *reconciliation* of nature and human society in a new ecological sensibility and a new ecological society—a reharmonization of nature and humanity through a reharmonization of human with human.

ଔ

A dialectical tension pervades this book. Throughout my discussion I often deal with potentialities that have yet to be actualized historically. Expository needs often compel me to treat a certain social condition in embryonic form as though it had already reached fulfillment. My procedure is guided by the need to bring the concept out in full relief, to clarify its complete meaning and implications.

In my descriptions of the historical role of the elders in the formation of hierarchy, for example, some readers might surmise that I believe hierarchy existed at the very outset of human society. The influential role that the elders were to play in forming hierarchies is intermingled with their more modest role at earlier periods of social development, when they actually exercised comparatively little social influence. In this situation I am faced with the need to clarify how the elders constituted the earliest "seeds" of hierarchy. A gerontocracy was probably the first form of hierarchy to exist in society. But, owing to my mode of presentation, some readers might assume that the rule of the old over the young existed during periods of human society when no such rule really existed. Nevertheless, the insecurities that come with age almost certainly existed among the elders, and they eventually used whatever means available to prevail over the young and gain their reverence.

The same expository problem arises when I deal with the shaman's role in the evolution of early hierarchies, with the male's role in relation to women, and so forth. The reader should be mindful that any "fact," firmly stated and apparently complete, is actually the result of a complex process—not a given datum that appears full-blown in a community or society. Much of the dialectical tension that pervades this book arises from the fact that I deal with *processes*, not with cut-and-dried propositions that comfortably succeed each other in stately fashion, like categories in a traditional logic text.

Incipient, potentially hierarchical elites gradually evolve, each phase of their evolution shading into the succeeding one, until the first firm shoots of hierarchy emerge and eventually mature. Their growth is uneven and intermixed. The elders and shamans rely on each other and then compete with each other for social privileges, many of which are attempts to achieve the personal security conferred by a certain measure of influence. Both groups enter into alliances with an emerging warrior caste of young men, finally to form the beginnings of a quasi-political community and an incipient State. Their privileges and powers only then become generalized into institutions that try to exercise command over society as a whole. At other times, however, hierarchical growth may become arrested and even "regress" to a greater parity between age and sex groups. Unless rule was achieved from outside, by conquest, the emergence of hierarchy was not a sudden revolution in human affairs. It was often a long and complex process.

Finally, I would like to emphasize that this book is structured around contrasts between preliterate, nonhierarchical societies—their outlooks, technics, and forms of thinking—and "civilizations" based on hierarchy and domination. Each of the themes touched upon in the second chapter is picked up again in the following chapters and explored in greater detail to clarify the sweeping changes "civilization" introduced in the human condition. What we so often lack in our daily lives and our social sensibilities is a sense of the cleavages and slow gradations by which our society developed in contrast—often in brutal antagonism—to pre-industrial and preliterate cultures. We live so completely immersed in our present that it absorbs all our sensibilities and hence our very capacity to think of alternate social forms. Thus, I will continually return to preliterate sensibilities, which I merely note in chapter 2, to explore their contrasts with later institutions, technics, and forms of thinking in hierarchical societies.

This book does not march to the drumbeat of logical categories, nor are its arguments marshalled into a stately parade of sharply delineated historical eras. I have not written a history of events, each of which follows the other according to the dictates of a prescribed chronology. Anthropology, history, ideologies, even systems of philosophy and reason, inform this book—and with them, digressions and excurses that I feel throw valuable light on the great movement of natural and human development. The more impatient reader may want to leap over passages and pages that he or she finds too discursive or digressive. But this book focuses on a few general ideas that grow according to the erratic and occasionally wayward logic of the organic rather than the strictly analytic. I hope that the reader will also want to grow with this book, to experience it and understand it—critically and querulously, to be sure, but with empathy and sensibility for the living development of freedom it depicts and the dialectic it explores in humanity's conflict with domination.

ᖇ

    Having offered my mea culpas for certain expository problems, I would like to emphatically affirm my conviction that this process-oriented dialectical approach comes much closer to the truth of hierarchical development than a presumably clearer analytical approach so favored by academic logicians. As we look back over many millenia, our thinking and analyses of the past are overly informed by a long historical development that early humanity evidently lacked. We are inclined to project into the past a vast body of social relations, political institutions, economic concepts, moral precepts, and a tremendous corpus of personal and social ideas that people living thousands of years ago had yet to create and conceptualize. What are fully matured actualities to us were, to them, still unformed potentialities. They thought in terms that were basically different from ours. What we now take for granted as part of the "human condition" was simply inconceivable to them. We, in turn, are virtually incapable of dealing with a vast wealth of natural phenomena that were integrally part of their lives. The very structure of our language conspires against an understanding of their outlook.

    Doubtless many "truths" that preliterate peoples held were patently false, a statement that is easily made nowadays. But I will make a case for the notion that their outlook, particularly as applied to their communities' relationship with the natural world, had a basic soundness—one that is particularly relevant for our times. I examine their ecological sensibility and try to show why and how it deteriorated. More importantly, I am eager to determine what can be recovered from that outlook and integrated into our own. No contradiction is created by merging their ecological sensibility with our prevailing analytical one, provided such a merging transcends both sensibilities in a new way of thinking and experiencing. We can no more return to their conceptual "primitivism" than they could have grasped our analytical "sophistication." But perhaps we *can* achieve a way of thinking and experiencing that involves a quasi-animistic respiritization of phenomena—inanimate as well as animate—without abandoning the insights provided by science and analytical reasoning.

    The melding of an organic, process-oriented outlook with an analytical one has been the traditional goal of classical western philosophy from the pre-Socratics to Hegel. Such a philosophy has always been more than an outlook or a mere method for dealing with reality. It has also been what the philosophers call an *ontology*—a description of reality conceived not as mere matter, but as active, self-organizing substance with a striving toward consciousness. Tradition has made this ontological outlook the framework in which thought and matter, subject and object, mind and nature are reconciled on a new spiritized level. Accordingly, I regard this process-oriented view of phenomena as intrinsically ecological in character, and I am very puzzled by the failure of so many dialectically oriented thinkers to see the remarkable compatibility between a dialectical outlook and an ecological one.

My vision of reality as process may also seem flawed to those readers who deny the existence of meaning and the value of humanity in natural development. That I see "progress" in organic and social evolution will doubtlessly be viewed skeptically by a generation that erroneously identifies "progress" with unlimited material growth. I, for one, do not make this identification. Perhaps my problem, if such it can be called, is generational. I still cherish a time that sought to illuminate the course of events, to interpret them, to make them meaningful. "Coherence" is my favorite word; it resolutely guides everything I write and say. Also, this book does not radiate the pessimism so common in environmentalist literature. Just as I believe that the past has meaning, so too do I believe that the future can have meaning. If we cannot be certain that the human estate will advance, we do have the opportunity to choose between utopistic freedom and social immolation. Herein lies the unabashed messianic character of this book, a messianic character that is philosophical and ancestral. The "principle of hope," as Ernst Bloch called it, is part of everything I value—hence my detestation of a futurism so committed to the present that it cancels out futurity itself by denying anything new that is not an extrapolation of the existing society.

I have tried to avoid writing a book that masticates every possible thought that relates to the issues raised in the following pages. I would not want to deliver these thoughts as predigested pap to a passive reader. The dialectical tension I value the most is between the reader of a book and the writer: the hints, the suggestions, the unfinished thoughts and the stimuli that encourage the reader to think for himself or herself. In an era that is so much in flux, it would be arrogant to present finished analyses and recipes; rather, I regard it as the responsibility of a serious work to stimulate dialectical and ecological thinking. For a work that is so "simple," so "clear," so unshared—in a word, so *elitist*—as to require no emendations and modifications, the reader will have to look elsewhere. This book is not an ideological program; it is a stimulus to thought—a coherent body of concepts the reader will have to finish in the privacy of his or her own mind.

1 ✑ THE CONCEPT OF SOCIAL ECOLOGY

The legends of the Norsemen tell of a time when all beings were apportioned their worldly domains: the gods occupied a celestial domain, Asgard, and men lived on the earth, Midgard, below which lay Niffleheim, the dark, icy domain of the giants, dwarfs, and the dead. These domains were linked together by an enormous ash, the World Tree. Its lofty branches reached into the sky, and its roots into the furthermost depths of the earth. Although the World Tree was constantly being gnawed by animals, it remained ever green, renewed by a magic fountain that infused it continually with life.

The gods, who had fashioned this world, presided over a precarious state of tranquility. They had banished their enemies, the giants, to the land of ice. Fenris the wolf was enchained, and the great serpent of the Midgard was held at bay. Despite the lurking dangers, a general peace prevailed, and plenty existed for the gods, men, and all living things. Odin, the god of wisdom, reigned over all the deities; the wisest and strongest, he watched over the battles of men and selected the most heroic of the fallen to feast with him in his great fortress, Valhalla. Thor, the son of Odin, was not only a powerful warrior, the defender of Asgard against the restive giants, but also a deity of order, who saw to the keeping of faith between men and obedience to the treaties. There were gods and goddesses of plenty, of fertility, of love, of law, of the sea and ships, and a multitude of animistic spirits who inhabited all things and beings of the earth.

But the world order began to break down when the gods, greedy for riches, tortured the witch Gullveig, the maker of gold, to compel her to reveal her secrets. Discord now became rampant among the gods and men. The gods began to break their oaths; corruption, treachery, rivalry, and greed began to dominate the world. With the breakdown of the primal unity, the days of the gods and men, of Asgard and Midgard, were numbered. Inexorably, the violation of the world order would lead to Ragnarok—the death of the gods in a great conflict before Valhalla. The gods would go down in a terrible battle with the giants, Fenris the wolf, and the serpent of the Midgard. With the mutual destruction of all the combatants, humanity too would perish, and nothing would remain but bare rock and overflowing oceans in a void of cold and darkness. Having thus disintegrated into its beginnings, however, the world would be renewed, purged of its earlier evils and the corruption that destroyed it. Nor would the new world emerging from the void suffer another catastrophic end, for the second generation of gods and goddesses would learn from the mistakes of their antecedents. The prophetess who recounts the story tells us that humanity thenceforth will "live in joy for as long as one can foresee."

In this Norse cosmography, there seems to be more than the old theme of "eternal recurrence," of a time-sense that spins around perpetual cycles of birth, maturation, death, and rebirth. Rather, one is aware of prophecy infused with historical trauma; the legend belongs to a little-explored area of mythology that might be called "myths of disintegration." Although the Ragnarok legend is known to be quite old, we know very little about when it appeared in the evolution of the Norse sagas. We do know that Christianity, with its bargain of eternal reward, came later to the Norsemen than to any other large ethnic group in western Europe, and its roots were shallow for generations afterward. The heathenism of the north had long made contact with the commerce of the south. During the Viking raids on Europe, the sacred places of the north had become polluted by gold, and the pursuit of riches was dividing kinsman from kinsman. Hierarchies erected by valor were being eroded by systems of privilege based on wealth. The clans and tribes were breaking down; the oaths between men, from which stemmed the unity of their primordial world, were being dishonored, and the magic fountain that kept the World Tree alive was being clogged by the debris of commerce. "Brothers fight and slay one another," laments the prophetess, "children deny their own ancestry ... this is the age of wind, of wolf, until the very day when the world shall be no more."

◌ℛ

What haunts us in such myths of disintegration are not their histories, but their prophecies. Like the Norsemen, and perhaps even more, like the people at the close of the Middle Ages, we sense that our world, too, is breaking down—institutionally, culturally, and physically. Whether we are faced with a new, paradisical era or a catastrophe like the Norse Ragnarok is still unclear, but there can be no lengthy period of compromise between past and future in an ambiguous present. The reconstructive and destructive tendencies in our time are too much at odds with each other to admit of reconciliation. The social horizon presents the starkly conflicting prospects of a harmonized world with an ecological sensibility based on a rich commitment to community, mutual aid, and new technologies, on the one hand, and the terrifying prospect of some sort of thermonuclear disaster on the other. Our world, it would appear, will either undergo revolutionary changes, so far-reaching in character that humanity will totally transform its social relations and its very conception of life, or it will suffer an apocalypse that may well end humanity's tenure on the planet.

The tension between these two prospects has already subverted the morale of the traditional social order. We have entered an era that consists no longer of institutional stabilization but of institutional decay. A widespread alienation is developing toward the forms, the aspirations, the demands, and above all, the institutions of the established order. The most exuberant, theatrical evidence of this alienation occurred in the 1960s, when the "youth revolt" in the early half of the decade exploded into what seemed to be a counterculture. Considerably more than protest and adolescent nihilism marked the period. Almost intuitively, new values of sensuousness, new forms of communal lifestyle, changes in dress, language, music, all borne on the wave of a deep sense of impending social change, infused a sizable section of an entire generation. We still do not know in what sense this wave began to ebb: whether as a historic retreat or as a transformation into a serious project for inner and social development. That the symbols of this movement eventually became the artifacts for a new culture industry does not alter its far-reaching effects. Western society will never be the same again—all the sneers of its academics and its critics of "narcissism" notwithstanding.

What makes this ceaseless movement of deinstitutionalization and delegitimation so significant is that it has found its bedrock in a vast stratum of western society. Alienation permeates not only the poor but also the relatively affluent, not only the young but also their elders, not only the visibly denied but also the seemingly privileged. The prevailing order is beginning to lose the loyalty of social strata that traditionally rallied to its support and in which its roots were firmly planted in past periods.

Crucial as this decay of institutions and values may be, it by no means exhausts the problems that confront the existing society. Intertwined with the social crisis is a crisis that has emerged directly from man's exploitation of the planet.* Established society is faced

* I use the word "man," here, advisedly. The split between humanity and nature has been precisely the work of the male, who, in the memorable lines of Theodor Adorno and Max Horkheimer, "dreamed of acquiring absolute mastery over nature, of converting the cosmos

with a breakdown not only of its values and institutions, but also of its natural environment. This problem is not unique to our times. The dessicated wastelands of the Near East, where the arts of agriculture and urbanism had their beginnings, are evidence of ancient human despoilation, but this example pales before the massive destruction of the environment that has occurred since the days of the Industrial Revolution, and especially since the end of the Second World War. The damage inflicted on the environment by contemporary society encompasses the entire earth. Volumes have been written on the immense losses of productive soil that occur annually on almost every continent of the earth; on the extensive destruction of tree cover in areas vulnerable to erosion; on lethal air-pollution episodes in major urban areas; on the worldwide diffusion of toxic agents from agriculture, industry, and power-producing installations; on the chemicalization of humanity's immediate environment with industrial wastes, pesticide residues, and food additives. The exploitation and pollution of the earth has damaged not only the integrity of the atmosphere, climate, water resources, soil, flora and fauna of specific regions, but also the basic natural cycles on which all living things depend.

Yet modern man's capacity for destruction is quixotic evidence of humanity's capacity for reconstruction. The powerful technological agents we have unleashed against the environment include many of the very agents we require for its reconstruction. The knowledge and physical instruments for promoting a harmonization of humanity with nature and of human with human are largely at hand or could easily be devised. Many of the physical principles used to construct such patently harmful facilities as conventional power plants, energy-consuming vehicles, surface-mining equipment and the like could be directed to the construction of small-scale solar and wind energy devices, efficient means of transportation, and energy-saving shelters. What we crucially lack is the consciousness and sensibility that will help us achieve such eminently desirable goals—a consciousness and sensibility far broader than customarily meant by these terms. Our definitions must include not only the ability to reason logically and respond emotionally in a humanistic fashion; they must also include a fresh awareness of the relatedness between things and an imaginative insight into the possible. On this score, Marx was entirely correct to emphasize that the revolution

into one immense hunting-ground." (*Dialectic of Enlightenment*, New York: Seabury Press, 1972, p. 248). For the words "one immense hunting-ground," I would be disposed to substitute "one immense killing-ground" to describe the male-oriented "civilization" of our era.

required by our time must draw its poetry not from the past but from the future, from the humanistic potentialities that lie on the horizons of social life.

The new consciousness and sensibility cannot be poetic alone; they must also be scientific. Indeed, there is a level at which our consciousness must be neither poetry nor science, but a transcendence of both into a new realm of theory and practice, an artfulness that combines fancy with reason, imagination with logic, vision with technique. We cannot shed our scientific heritage without returning to a rudimentary technology, with its shackles of material insecurity, toil, and renunciation. And we cannot allow ourselves to be imprisoned within a mechanistic outlook and a dehumanizing technology—with its shackles of alienation, competition, and a brute denial of humanity's potentialities. Poetry and imagination must be integrated with science and technology, for we have evolved beyond an innocence that can be nourished exclusively by myths and dreams.

℞

Is there a scientific discipline that allows for the indiscipline of fancy, imagination, and artfulness? Can it encompass problems created by the social and environmental crises of our time? Can it integrate critique with reconstruction, theory with practice, vision with technique?

In almost every period since the Renaissance, a very close link has existed between radical advances in the natural sciences and upheavals in social thought. In the sixteenth and seventeenth centuries, the emerging sciences of astronomy and mechanics, with their liberating visions of a heliocentric world and the unity of local and cosmic motion, found their social counterparts in equally critical and rational social ideologies that challenged religious bigotry and political absolutism. The Enlightenment brought a new appreciation of sensory perception and the claims of human reason to divine a world that had been the ideological monopoly of the clergy. Later, anthropology and evolutionary biology demolished traditional static notions of the human enterprise along with its myths of original creation and history as a theological calling. By enlarging the map and revealing the earthly dynamics of social history, these sciences reinforced the new doctrines of socialism, with its ideal of human progress, that followed the French Revolution.

In view of the enormous dislocations that now confront us, our own era needs a more sweeping and insightful body of knowledge— scientific as well as social—to deal with our problems. Without renouncing the gains of earlier scientific and social theories, we must develop a more rounded critical analysis of our relationship with the natural world. We must seek the foundations for a more reconstructive approach to the grave problems posed by the apparent "contradictions" between nature and society. We can no longer afford to remain captives to the tendency of the more traditional sciences to dissect phenomena and examine their fragments. We must combine them, relate them, and see them in their totality as well as their specificity.

In response to these needs, we have formulated a discipline unique to our age: *social ecology.* The more well-known term "ecology" was coined by Ernst Haeckel a century ago to denote the investigation of the interrelationships between animals, plants, and their inorganic environment. Since Haeckel's day, the term has been expanded to include ecologies of cities, of health, and of the mind. This proliferation of a word into widely disparate areas may seem particularly desirable to an age that fervently seeks some kind of intellectual coherence and unity of perception. But it can also prove to be extremely treacherous. Like such newly arrived words as holism, decentralization, and dialectics, the term ecology runs the peril of merely hanging in the air without any roots, context, or texture. Often it is used as a metaphor, an alluring catchword, that loses the potentially compelling internal logic of its premises.

Accordingly, the radical thrust of these words is easily neutralized. "Holism" evaporates into a mystical sigh, a rhetorical expression for ecological fellowship and community that ends with such in-group greetings and salutations as "holistically yours." What was once a serious philosophical stance has been reduced to environmentalist kitsch. Decentralization commonly means logistical alternatives to gigantism, not the human scale that would make an intimate and direct democracy possible. Ecology fares even worse. All too often it becomes a metaphor, like the word dialectics, for any kind of integration and development.

Perhaps even more troubling, the word in recent years has been identified with a very crude form of natural engineering that might well be called *environmentalism.*

I am mindful that many ecologically oriented individuals use "ecology" and "environmentalism" interchangeably. Here, I would like to draw a semantically convenient distinction. By "environmentalism" I propose to designate a mechanistic, instrumental outlook that sees nature as a passive habitat composed of "objects" such as animals, plants, minerals, and the like that must merely be rendered more serviceable for human use. Given my use of the term, environmentalism tends to reduce nature to a storage bin of "natural resources" or "raw materials." Within this context, very little of a social nature is spared from the environmentalist's vocabulary: cities become "urban resources" and their inhabitants "human resources." If the word *resources* leaps out so frequently from environmentalistic discussions of nature, cities, and people, an issue more important than mere word play is at stake. Environmentalism, as I use this term, tends to view the ecological project for attaining a harmonious relationship between humanity and nature as a truce rather than a lasting equilibrium. The "harmony" of the environmentalist centers around the development of new techniques for plundering the natural world with minimal disruption of the human "habitat." Environmentalism does not question the most basic premise of the present society, notably, that humanity must dominate nature; rather, it seeks to *facilitate* that notion by developing techniques for diminishing the hazards caused by the reckless despoilation of the environment.

To distinguish ecology from environmentalism and from abstract, often obfuscatory definitions of the term, I must return to its original usage and explore its direct relevance to society. Put quite simply, ecology deals with the dynamic balance of nature, with the interdependence of living and nonliving things. Since nature also includes human beings, the science must include humanity's role in the natural world—specifically, the character, form, and structure of humanity's relationship with other species and with the inorganic substrate of the biotic environment. From a critical viewpoint, ecology opens to wide purview the vast disequilibrium that has emerged from humanity's split with the natural world. One of nature's very unique species, *homo sapiens*, has slowly and painstakingly developed from the natural world into a unique social world of its own. As both worlds interact with each other through highly complex phases of evolution, it has become as important to speak of a social ecology as to speak of a natural ecology.

Let me emphasize that the failure to explore these phases of human evolution—which have yielded a succession of hierarchies, classes, cities, and finally states—is to make a mockery of the term social ecology. Unfortunately, the discipline has been beleaguered by self-professed adherents who continually try to collapse all the phases of natural and human development into a universal "oneness" (not wholeness), a yawning "night in which all cows are black," to borrow one of Hegel's caustic phrases. If nothing else, our common use of the word *species* to denote the wealth of life around us should alert us to the fact of *specificity*, of *particularity*—the rich abundance of *differentiated* beings and things that enter into the very subject-matter of natural ecology. To explore these differentia, to examine the phases and interfaces that enter into their making and into humanity's long development from animality to society—a development latent with problems and possibilities—is to make social ecology one of the most powerful disciplines from which to draw our critique of the present social order.

But social ecology provides more than a critique of the split between humanity and nature; it also poses the need to heal them. Indeed, it poses the need to radically transcend them. As E. A. Gutkind pointed out, "the goal of Social Ecology is wholeness, and not mere adding together of innumerable details collected at random and interpreted subjectively and insufficiently." The science deals with social and natural relationships in communities or "ecosystems."* In conceiving them holistically, that is to say, in terms of their mutual interdependence, social ecology seeks to unravel the forms and patterns of interrelationships that give intelligibility to a community, be it natural or social. Holism, here, is the result of a conscious effort to discern how the particulars of a community are arranged, how its "geometry" (as the Greeks might have put it) makes the "whole more than the sum of its parts." Hence, the "wholeness" to which Gutkind refers is not to be mistaken for a spectral "oneness" that yields cosmic dissolution in a structureless nirvana; it is a richly articulated structure with a history and internal logic of its own.

History, in fact, is as important as form or structure. To a large extent, the history of a phenomenon is the phenomenon itself. We are, in a real sense, everything that existed before us and, in turn, we can eventually become vastly more than we are. Surprisingly, very little in the evolution of life-forms has been lost in natural and social evolution, indeed in our very bodies as our embryonic development attests. Evolution lies within us (as well as around us) as parts of the very nature of our beings.

For the present, it suffices to say that wholeness is not a bleak undifferentiated "universality" that involves the reduction of a phenomenon to what it has in common with everything else. Nor is it a celestial, omnipresent "energy" that replaces the vast material differentia of which the natural and social realms are composed. To the contrary, wholeness comprises the variegated structures, the articulations, and the mediations that impart to the whole a rich variety of forms and

---

* The term ecosystem—or ecological system—is often used loosely in many ecological works. Here, I employ it, as in natural ecology, to mean a fairly demarcatable animal-plant community and the abiotic, or nonliving, factors needed to sustain it. I also use it in social ecology to mean a distinct human and natural community, the social as well as organic factors that interrelate to provide the basis for an ecologically rounded and balanced community.

thereby add unique qualitative properties to what a strictly analytic mind often reduces to "innumerable" and "random" details.

ॐ

Terms like wholeness, totality, and even community have perilous nuances for a generation that has known fascism and other totalitarian ideologies. The words evoke images of a "wholeness" achieved through homogenization, standardization, and a repressive coordination of human beings. These fears are reinforced by a "wholeness" that seems to provide an inexorable finality to the course of human history—one that implies a suprahuman, narrowly teleological concept of social law and denies the ability of human will and individual choice to shape the course of social events. Such notions of social law and teleology have been used to achieve a ruthless subjugation of the individual to suprahuman forces beyond human control. Our century has been afflicted by a plethora of totalitarian ideologies that, placing human beings in the service of history, have denied them a place in the service of their own humanity.

Actually, such a totalitarian concept of "wholeness" stands sharply at odds with what ecologists denote by the term. In addition to comprehending its heightened awareness of form and structure, we now come to a very important tenet of ecology: ecological wholeness is not an immutable homogeneity but rather the very opposite—a dynamic *unity of diversity*. In nature, balance and harmony are achieved by ever-changing differentiation, by ever-expanding diversity. Ecological stability, in effect, is a function not of simplicity and homogeneity but of complexity and variety. The capacity of an ecosystem to retain its integrity depends not on the uniformity of the environment but on its diversity.

A striking example of this tenet can be drawn from experiences with ecological strategies for cultivating food. Farmers have repeatedly met with disastrous results because of the conventional emphasis on single-crop approaches to agriculture or *monoculture*, to use a widely accepted term for those endless wheat and corn fields that extend to the horizon in many parts of the world. Without the mixed crops that normally provide both the countervailing forces and mutualistic support that come with mixed populations of plants and animals, the entire agricultural situation in an area has been known to collapse. Benign insects become pests because their natural controls, including birds and small mammals, have been removed. The soil, lacking earthworms, nitrogen-fixing bacteria, and green manure in sufficient quantities, is reduced to mere sand—a mineral medium for absorbing enormous quantities of inorganic nitrogen salts, which were originally supplied more cyclically and timed more appropriately for crop growth in the ecosystem. In reckless disregard for the complexity of nature and for the subtle requirements of plant and animal life, the agricultural situation is crudely simplified; its needs must now be satisfied by highly soluble synthetic fertilizers that percolate into drinking water and by dangerous pesticides that remain as residues in food. A high standard of food cultivation that was once achieved by diversity of crops and animals, one that was free of lasting toxic agents and probably more healthful nutritionally, is now barely approximated by single crops whose main supports are toxic chemicals and highly simple nutrients.

If we assume that the thrust of natural evolution has been toward increasing complexity, that the colonization of the planet by life has been possible only as a result of biotic variety, a prudent rescaling of man's hubris should call for caution in disturbing natural processes. That living things, emerging ages ago from their primal aquatic habitat to colonize the most inhospitable areas of the earth, have created the rich biosphere that now covers it has been possible only because of life's incredible mutability and the enormous legacy of life-forms inherited from its long development. Many of these life-forms, even the most primal and simplest, have never disappeared—however much they have been modified by evolution. The simple algal forms that marked the beginnings of plant life and the simple invertebrates that marked the beginnings of animal life still exist in large numbers. They comprise the preconditions for the existence of more complex organic beings to which they provide sustenance, the sources of decomposition, and even atmospheric oxygen and carbon dioxide. Although they may antedate the "higher" plants and mammals by over a billion years, they interrelate with their more complex descendants in often unravelable ecosystems.

To assume that science commands this vast nexus of organic and inorganic interrelationships in all its details is worse than arrogance: it is sheer stupidity. If unity in diversity forms one of the cardinal tenets of ecology, the wealth of biota that exists in a single acre of soil leads us to still another basic ecological tenet: the need to allow for a high degree of natural spontaneity. The compelling dictum, "respect for nature," has concrete implications. To assume that our knowledge of this complex, richly textured, and perpetually changing natural kaleidoscope of life-forms lends itself to a degree of "mastery" that allows us free rein in manipulating the biosphere is sheer foolishness.

Thus, a considerable amount of leeway must be permitted for natural spontaneity—for the diverse biological forces that yield a variegated ecological situation. "Working with nature" requires that we foster the biotic variety that emerges from a spontaneous development of natural phenomena. I hardly mean that we must surrender ourselves to a mythical "Nature" that is beyond all human comprehension and intervention, a Nature that demands human awe and subservience. Perhaps the most obvious conclusion we can draw from these ecological tenets is Charles Elton's sensitive observation: "The world's future has to be managed, but this management would not be just like a game of chess— [but] more like steering a boat." What ecology, both natural and social, can hope to teach us is the way to find the current and understand the direction of the stream.

What ultimately distinguishes an ecological outlook as uniquely liberatory is the challenge it raises to conventional notions of hierarchy. Let me emphasize, however, that this challenge is implicit: it must be painstakingly elicited from the discipline of ecology, which is permeated by conventional scientistic biases. Ecologists are rarely aware that their science provides strong philosophical underpinnings for a nonhierarchical view of reality. Like many natural scientists, they resist philosophical generalizations as alien to their research and conclusions—a prejudice that is itself a philosophy rooted in the Anglo-American empirical tradition. Moreover, they follow their colleagues in other disciplines and model their notions of science on physics. This prejudice, which goes back to Galileo's day, has led to a widespread acceptance of systems theory in ecological circles. While systems theory has its place in the repertoire of science, it can easily become an all-encompassing, quantitative, reductionist theory of energetics if it acquires preeminence over *qualitative* descriptions of ecosystems, that is, descriptions rooted in organic evolution, variety, and holism. Whatever the merits of systems theory as an account of energy flow through an ecosystem, the primacy it gives to this quantitative aspect of ecosystem analysis fails to recognize life-forms as more than consumers and producers of calories.

Having presented these caveats, I must emphasize that ecosystems cannot be meaningfully described in hierarchical terms. Whether plant-animal communities actually contain "dominant" and "submissive" individuals *within* a species can be argued at great length. But to rank species within an ecosystem, that is to say, *between* species, is anthropomorphism at its crudest. As Allison Jolly has observed:

> The notion of animal hierarchies has a checkered history. Schjelderup-Ebbe, who discovered the pecking-order of hens, enlarged his findings to a Teutonic theory of despotism in the universe. For instance, water eroding

a stone was "dominant" ... Schjelderup-Ebbe called animals' ranking "dominance," and many [research] workers, with an "aha," recognized dominance hierarchies in many vertebrate groups.

If we recognize that every ecosystem can also be viewed as a food web, we can think of it as a circular, interlacing nexus of plant-animal relationships (rather than a stratified pyramid with man at the apex) that includes such widely varying creatures as microorganisms and large mammals. What ordinarily puzzles anyone who sees food-web diagrams for the first time is the impossibility of discerning a point of entry into the nexus. The web can be entered at any point and leads back to its point of departure without any apparent exit. Aside from the energy provided by sunlight (and dissipated by radiation), the system to all appearances is closed. Each species, be it a form of bacteria or deer, is knitted together in a network of interdependence, however indirect the links may be. A predator in the web is also prey, even if the "lowliest" of organisms merely makes it ill or helps to consume it after death.

Nor is predation the sole link that unites one species with another. A resplendent literature now exists that reveals the enormous extent to which symbiotic mutualism is a major factor in fostering ecological stability and organic evolution. That plants and animals continually adapt to unwittingly aid each other (be it by an exchange of biochemical functions that are mutually beneficial or even dramatic instances of physical assistance and succor) has opened an entirely new perspective on the nature of ecosystem stability and development.

The more complex the food-web, the less unstable it will be if one or several species are removed. Hence, enormous significance must be given to interspecific diversity and complexity within the system as a whole. Striking breakdowns will occur in simple ecosystems, such as arctic and desert ones, say, if wolves that control foraging animal populations are exterminated or if a sizable number of reptiles that control rodent populations in arid ecosystems are removed. By contrast, the great variety of biota that populate temperate and tropical ecosystems can afford losses of carnivores or herbivores without suffering major dislocations.

ෙ

Why do terms borrowed from human social hierarchies acquire such remarkable weight when plant-animal relations are described? Do ecosystems really have a "king of the beasts" and "lowly serfs"? Do certain insects "enslave" others? Does one species "exploit" another?

The promiscuous use of these terms in ecology raises many far-reaching issues. That the terms are laden with socially charged values is almost too obvious to warrant extensive discussion. Many individuals exhibit a pathetic gullibility in the way they deal with nature as a dimension of society. A snarling animal is neither "vicious" nor "savage," nor does it "misbehave" or "earn" punishment because it reacts appropriately to certain stimuli. By making such anthropomorphic judgements about natural phenomena, we deny the integrity of nature. Even more sinister is the widespread use of hierarchical terms to provide natural phenomena with "intelligibility" or "order." What this procedure does accomplish is reinforce human social hierarchies by justifying the command of men and women as innate features of the "natural order." Human domination is thereby transcribed into the genetic code as biologically immutable—together with the subordination of the young by the old, women by men, and man by man.

The very promiscuity with which hierarchical terms are used to organize all differentia in nature is inconsistent. A "queen" bee does not know she is a queen. The primary activity of a beehive is reproductive, and its "division of labor," to use a grossly abused phrase, lacks any meaning in a large sexual organ that performs no authentic economic functions. The purpose of the hive is to create more bees. The honey that animals and people acquire from it is a natural largesse; within the ecosystem, bees are adapted more to meeting plant reproductive needs by spreading pollen than to meeting important animal needs. The analogy between a beehive and a society, an analogy social theorists have often found too irresistible to avoid, is a striking commentary on the extent to which our visions of nature are shaped by self-serving social interests.

To deal with so-called insect hierarchies the way we deal with so-called animal hierarchies, or worse, to grossly ignore the very different functions animal communities perform, is analogic reasoning carried to the point of the preposterous. Primates relate to each other in ways that seem to involve "dominance" and "submission" for widely disparate reasons. Yet, terminologically and conceptually, they are placed under the same "hierarchical" rubric as insect "societies"— despite the different forms they assume and their precarious stability. Baboons on the African savannas have been singled out as the most rigid hierarchical troops in the primate world, but this rigidity evaporates once we examine their "ranking order" in a forest habitat. Even on the savannas, it is questionable whether "alpha" males "rule," "control," or "coordinate" relationships within the troop. Arguments can be presented for choosing any one of these words, each of which has a clearly different meaning when it is used in a human social context. Seemingly "patriarchal" primate "harems" can be as loose sexually as brothels, depending on whether a female is in estrus, changes have occurred in the habitat, or the "patriarch" is simply diffident about the whole situation.

Baboons, it is worth noting, are monkeys, despite the presumed similarity of their savanna habitat to that of early hominids. They branched off from the hominoid evolutionary tree more than 20 million years ago. Our closest evolutionary cousins, the great apes, tend to demolish these prejudices about hierarchy completely. Of the four great apes, gibbons have no apparent "ranking" system at all. Chimpanzees, regarded by many primatologists as the most human-like of all apes, form such fluid kinds of "stratification" and (depending upon the ecology of an area, which may be significantly affected by research workers) establish such unstable types of association that the word hierarchy becomes an obstacle to understanding their behavioral characteristics. Orangutans seem to have little of what could be called dominance and submission relations. The mountain gorilla, despite its formidable reputation, exhibits very little "stratification" except for predator challenges and internal aggression.

All these examples help to justify Elise Boulding's complaint that the "primate behavior model" favored by overly hierarchical and patriarchal writers on animal-human parallels "is based more on the baboon, not the gibbon." In contrast to the baboon, observes Boulding, the gibbon is closer to us physically and, one might add, on the primate evolutionary scale. "Our choice of a primate role model is clearly culturally determined," she concludes:

> Who wants to be like the unaggressive, vegetarian, food-sharing gibbons, where father is as much involved in child-rearing as mother is, and where everyone lives in small family groups, with little aggregation beyond that? Much better to match the baboons, who live in large, tightly-knit groups carefully closed against outsider baboons, where everyone knows who is in charge, and where mother looks after the babies while father is out hunting and fishing.

In fact, Boulding concedes too much about the savanna-dwelling primates. Even if the term dominance were stretched to include "queen" bees and "alpha" baboons, *specific* acts of coercion by *individual* animals can hardly be called domination. Acts do not constitute institutions; episodes do not make a history. And highly structured insect behavioral patterns, rooted in instinctual drives, are too inflexible to be regarded as social. Unless hierarchy is to be used in Schjelderup-Ebbe's cosmic sense, dominance and submission must be viewed as *institutionalized* relationships, relationships that living things literally institute or create but which are neither ruthlessly fixed by instinct on the one hand nor idiosyncratic on the other. By this, I mean that they must comprise a clearly *social* structure of coercive and privileged ranks that exist apart from the idiosyncratic individuals who seem to be dominant within a given community, a hierarchy that is guided by a social logic that goes beyond individual interactions or inborn patterns of behavior.*

Such traits are evident enough in human society when we speak of "self-perpetuating" bureaucracies and explore them without considering the individual bureaucrats who compose them. Yet, when we turn to nonhuman primates, what people commonly recognize as hierarchy, status, and domination are precisely the idiosyncratic behaviorisms of individual animals. Mike, Jane van Lawick-Goodall's "alpha" chimpanzee, acquired his "status" by rambunctiously charging upon a group of males while noisily hitting two empty kerosene cans. At which point in her narrative, van Lawick-Goodall wonders, would Mike have become an "alpha" male without the kerosene cans? She replies

---

* An important distinction must be made here between the words *community* and *society*. Animals and even plants certainly form communities; ecosystems would be meaningless without conceiving animals, plants, and their abiotic substrate as a nexus of relationships that range from the intraspecific to the interspecific level. In their interactions, life-forms thus behave "communally" in the sense that they are interdependent in one way or another. Among certain species, particularly primates, this nexus of interdependent relationships may be so closely knit that it approximates a society or, at least, a rudimentary form of sociality. But a society, however deeply it may be rooted in nature, is nevertheless *more* than a community. What makes human societies unique communities is the fact that they are *institutionalized* communities that are highly, often rigidly, structured around clearly manifest forms of responsibility, association and personal relationship in maintaining the material means of life. Although all societies are necessarily communities, many communities are not societies. One may find nascent social elements in animal communities, but only human beings form societies—that is, institutionalized communities. The failure to draw this distinction between animal or plant communities and human societies has produced considerable ideological mischief. Thus, predation within animal communities has been speciously identified with war; individual linkages between animals with hierarchy and domination; even animal foraging and metabolism with labor and economics. All the latter are strictly *social* phenomena. My remarks are not intended to oppose the notion of society to community but to take note of the distinctions between the two that emerge when human society develops beyond the levels of animal and plant communities.

that the animal's use of "manmade objects is probably an indication of superior intelligence." Whether such shadowy distinctions in intelligence rather than aggressiveness, willfulness, or arrogance produce an "alpha" male or not is evidence more of the subtle projection of historically conditioned human values on a primate group than the scientific objectivity that ethology likes to claim for itself.

The seemingly hierarchical traits of many animals are more like variations in the links of a chain than organized stratifications of the kind we find in human societies and institutions. Even the so-called class societies of the Northwest Indians, as we shall see, are chain-like links between individuals rather than the class-like links between strata that early Euro-American invaders so naïvely projected on Indians from their own social world. If acts do not constitute institutions and episodes do not constitute history, individual behavioral traits do not form strata or classes. Social strata are made of sterner stuff. They have a life of their own apart from the personalities who give them substance.

ℭ℞

How is ecology to avoid the analogic reasoning that has made so much of ethology and sociobiology seem like specious projections of human society into nature? Are there any terms that provide a common meaning to unity in diversity, natural spontaneity, and nonhierarchical relations in nature *and* society? In view of the many tenets that appear in natural ecology, why stop with these alone? Why not introduce other, perhaps less savory, ecological notions like predation and aggression into society?

In fact, nearly all of these questions became major issues in social theory in the early part of the century when the so-called Chicago School of urban sociology zealously tried to apply almost every known concept of natural ecology to the development and "physiology" of the city. Robert Park, Ernest Burgess, and Roderick McKenzie, enamored of the new science, actually imposed a stringently biological model on their studies of Chicago with a forcefulness and inspiration that dominated American urban sociology for two generations. Their tenets included ecological succession, spatial distribution, zonal distribution, anaboliccatabolic balances, and even competition and natural selection that could easily have pushed the school toward an insidious form of social Darwinism had it not been for the liberal biases of its founders.

Despite its admirable empirical results, the school was to founder on its metaphoric reductionism. Applied indiscriminately, the categories ceased to be meaningful. When Park compared the emergence of certain specialized municipal utilities to "successional dominance" by "other plant species" that climaxes in a "beech or pine forest," the analogy was patently forced and absurdly contorted. His comparison of ethnic, cultural, occupational, and economic groups to "plant invasions" revealed a lack of theoretical discrimination that reduced human social features to plant ecological features. What Park and his associates lacked was the philosophical equipment for singling out the phases that both unite and separate natural and social phenomena in a developmental continuum. Thus, merely superficial similarity became outright identity—with the unfortunate result that social ecology was repeatedly reduced to natural ecology. The richly mediated evolution of the natural into the social that could have been used to yield a meaningful selection of ecological categories was not part of the school's theoretical equipment.

Whenever we ignore the way human social relationships transcend plant-animal relationships, our views tend to bifurcate in two erroneous directions. Either we succumb to a heavy-handed dualism that harshly separates the natural from the social, or we fall into a crude reductionism that dissolves the one into the other. In either case, we really cease to think out the issues involved. We merely grasp for the least uncomfortable "solution" to a highly complex problem, namely, the need to analyze the phases through which "mute" biological nature increasingly becomes conscious human nature.

What makes unity in diversity in nature more than a suggestive ecological metaphor for unity in diversity in society is the underlying philosophical concept of wholeness. By wholeness, I mean varying levels of actualization, an unfolding of the wealth of particularities, that are latent in an as-yet-undeveloped potentiality. This potentiality may be a newly planted seed, a newly born infant, a newly born community, or a newly born society. When Hegel describes in a famous passage the "unfolding" of human knowledge in biological terms, the fit is almost exact:

> The bud disappears in the bursting-forth of the blossom, and one might say that the former is refuted by the latter; similarly, when the fruit appears, the blossom is shown up in its turn as a false manifestation of the plant, and the fruit now emerges as the truth of it instead. These forms are not just distinguished from one another, they also supplant one another as mutually incompatible. Yet at the same time their fluid nature makes them moments of an organic unity in which they not only do not conflict, but in which each is as necessary as the other; and this mutual necessity alone constitutes the life of the whole.

I have turned to this remarkable passage because Hegel does not mean it to be merely metaphoric. His biological example and his social subject matter converge in ways that transcend both, notably, as similar aspects of a *larger* process. Life itself, as distinguished from the nonliving, emerges from the inorganic latent with all the particularities it has immanently produced from the logic of its most nascent forms of self-organization. So do society as distinguished from biology, humanity as distinguished from animality, and individuality as distinguished from humanity. It is no spiteful manipulation of Hegel's famous maxim, "The True is the whole," to declare that the "whole is the True." One can take this reversal of terms to mean that the true lies in the self-consummation of a *process* through its development, in the flowering of its latent particularities into their fullness or wholeness, just as the potentialities of a child achieve expression in the wealth of experiences and the physical growth that enter into adulthood.

❧

We must not get caught up in direct comparisons between plants, animals, and human beings or between plant-animal ecosystems and human communities. None of these is completely congruent with another. We would be regressing in our views to those of Park, Burgess, and McKenzie, not to mention our current bouquet of sociobiologists, were we lax enough to make this equation. It is not in the particulars of differentiation that plant-animal communities are ecologically united with human communities but rather in their *logic of differentiation*. Wholeness, in fact, is completeness. The dynamic stability of the whole derives from a visible level of completeness in human communities as in climax ecosystems. What unites these modes of wholeness and completeness, however different they are in their specificity and their qualitative distinctness, is the logic of development itself. A climax forest is whole and complete as a result of the same unifying process—the same *dialectic*—that a particular social form is whole and complete.

When wholeness and completeness are viewed as the result of an immanent dialectic within phenomena, we do no more violence to the uniqueness of these phenomena than the principle of gravity does violence to the uniqueness of objects that fall within its "lawfulness." In this sense, the ideal of human roundedness, a product of the rounded community, is the legitimate heir to the ideal of a stabilized nature, a product of the rounded natural environment. Marx tried to root humanity's identity and self-discovery in its productive interaction with nature. But I must add that not only does humanity place its imprint on the natural world and transform it, but also nature places its imprint on the human world and transforms it. To use the language of hierarchy against itself: it is not only we who "tame" nature but also nature that "tames" us.

These turns of phrase should be taken as more than metaphors. Lest it seem that I have rarefied the concept of wholeness into an abstract dialectical principle, let me note that natural ecosystems and human communities interact with each other in very existential ways. Our animal nature is never so distant from our social nature that we can remove ourselves from the organic world outside us and the one within us. From our embryonic development to our layered brain, we partly recapitulate our own natural evolution. We are not so remote from our primate ancestry that we can ignore its physical legacy in our stereoscopic vision, acuity of intelligence, and grasping fingers. We phase into society as individuals in the same way that society, phasing out of nature, comes into itself.

These continuities, to be sure, are obvious enough. What is often less obvious is the extent to which nature itself is a realm of potentiality for the emergence of *social* differentia. Nature is as much a precondition for the *development* of society—not merely its emergence—as technics, labor, language, and mind. And it is a precondition not merely in William Petty's sense—that if labor is the "Father" of wealth, nature is its "Mother." This formula, so dear to Marx, actually slights nature by imparting to it the patriarchal notion of feminine "passivity." The affinities between nature and society are more active than we care to admit. Very specific forms of nature—very specific *ecosystems*—constitute the ground for very specific forms of society. At the risk of using a highly embattled phrase, I might say that a "historical materialism" of natural development could be written that would transform "passive nature"—the "object" of human labor—into "active nature," the creator of human labor. Labor's "metabolism" with nature cuts both ways, so that nature interacts *with* humanity to yield the actualization of their common potentialities in the natural and social worlds.

An interaction of this kind, in which terms like "Father" and "Mother" strike a false note, can be stated very concretely. The recent emphasis on bioregions as frameworks for various human communities provides a strong case for the need to readapt technics and work styles to accord with the requirements and possibilities of particular ecological areas. Bioregional requirements and possibilities place a heavy burden on humanity's claims of sovereignty over nature and autonomy from its needs. If it is true that "men make history" but not under conditions of their own choosing (Marx), it is no less true that history makes society but not under conditions of its own choosing. The hidden dimension that lurks in this word play with Marx's famous formula is the natural history that enters into the making of social history—but as active, concrete, existential nature that emerges from stage to stage of its own evermore complex development in the form of equally complex and dynamic ecosystems. Our ecosystems, in turn, are interlinked in highly dynamic and complex bioregions. How concrete the hidden dimension of social development is—and how much humanity's claims to sovereignty must defer to it—has only recently become evident from our need to design an alternative technology that is as adaptive to a bioregion as it is productive to society. Hence, our concept of wholeness is not a finished tapestry of natural and social relations that we can exhibit to the hungry eyes of sociologists. It is a fecund natural history, ever active and ever changing—the way childhood presses toward and is absorbed into youth, and youth into adulthood.

The need to bring a sense of history into nature is as compelling as the need to bring a sense of history into society. An ecosystem is never a random community of plants and animals that occurs merely by chance. It has potentiality, direction, meaning, and self-realization in its own right. To view an ecosystem as given (a bad habit, which scientism inculcates in its theoretically neutral observer) is as ahistorical and superficial as to view a human community as given. Both have a history that gives intelligibility and order to their internal relationships and directions to their development.

At its inception, human history is largely natural history as well as social—as traditional kinship structures and the sexual division of labor clearly indicate. Whether or not natural history is the "slime," to use Sartre's maladroit term, that clings to humanity and prevents its rational fulfillment will be considered later. For the present, one fact should be made clear: human history can never disengage itself or disembed itself from nature. It will always be embedded in nature, as we shall see— whether we are inclined to call that nature a "slime" or a fecund "mother." What may prove to be the most demanding test of our human genius is the *kind* of nature we will foster—one that is richly organic and complex or one that is inorganic and disastrously simplified.

Humanity's involvement with nature not only runs deep but takes on forms more increasingly subtle than even the most sophisticated theorists could have anticipated. Our knowledge of this involvement is still, as it were, in its "prehistory." To Ernst Bloch, we not only share a common history with nature, all the differences between nature and society aside, but also a common destiny. As he observes:

> Nature in its final manifestation, like history in its final manifestation, lies at the horizon of the future. The more a common technique [*Allianztechnik*]

is attainable instead of one that is external—one that is mediated with the co-productivity [*Mitproduktivität*] of nature—the more we can be sure that the frozen powers of a frozen nature will again be emancipated. Nature is not something that can be consigned to the past. Rather it is the construction-site that has not yet been cleared, the building tools that have not yet been attained in an adequate form for the human house that itself does not yet exist in an adequate form. The ability of problem-laden natural subjectivity to participate in the construction of this house is the objective-utopian correlate of the human-utopian fantasy conceived in concrete terms. Therefore it is certain that the human house stands not only in history and on the ground of human activity; it stands primarily on the ground of a mediated natural subjectivity on the construction site of nature. Nature's conceptual frontier [*Grenzbegriff*] is not the beginning of human history, where nature (which is always present in history and always surrounds it) turns into the site of the human sovereign realm [*regnum hominis*], but rather where it turns into the adequate site [for the adequate human house] as an unalienated mediated good [*und sie unentfremdet aufgeht, als vermitteltes Gut*].

One can take issue with the emphasis Bloch gives to human sovereignty in the interaction with nature and the structural phraseology that infiltrates his brilliant grasp of the organic nature of that interaction. *Das Prinzip Hoffnung* (*The Principle of Hope*) was written in the early 1940s, a grim and embattled period, when such a conceptual framework was totally alien to the antinaturalistic, indeed, militaristic spirit of the times. His insight beggars our hindsight, redolent with its "pop" ecological terminology and its queasy mysticism. In any case, enough has been written about the differences between nature and society. Today, together with Bloch, it would be valuable to shift our emphasis to the commonalities of nature and society, provided we are wary enough to avoid those mindless leaps from the one to the other as though they were not related by the rich phases of development that authentically unite them.

❧

Spontaneity enters into social ecology in much the same way as it enters into natural ecology—as a function of diversity and complexity. Ecosystems are much too variegated to be delivered over completely to what Ernst Bloch called the *regnum hominis* or, at least, to humanity's claim of sovereignty over nature. But we may justly ask if this is any less true of social complexity and history's claims of sovereignty over humanity. Do the self-appointed scientists or "guardians" of society know enough (their normally self-serving views aside) about the complex factors that make for social development to presume to control them? And even after the "adequate form for the human house" has been discovered and given substantiality, how sure can we be of their disinterested sense of service? History is replete with accounts of miscalculation by leaders, parties, factions, "guardians," and "vanguards." If nature is "blind," society is equally "blind" when it presumes to know itself completely, whether as social science, social theory, systems analysis, or even social ecology. Indeed, "World Spirits" from Alexander to Lenin have not always served humanity well. They have exhibited a willful arrogance that has damaged the social environment as disastrously as the arrogance of ordinary men has damaged the natural environment.

Great historical eras of transition reveal that the rising flood of social change must be permitted to find its own level spontaneously. Vanguard organizations have produced repeated catastrophes when they sought to force changes that people and the conditions of their time could not sustain materially, ideologically, or morally. Where forced social changes were not nourished by an educated and informed popular consciousness, they were eventually enforced by terror—and the movements themselves have turned savagely upon and devoured their most cherished humanistic and liberatory ideals. Our own century is closing under the shadow of an event that has totally beclouded the future of humanity, notably the Russian Revolution and its terrifying sequelae. Where the revolution, unforced and easily achieved by the popular movement, ended and Lenin's *coup d'etat* of October, 1917, replaced it can be easily fixed and dated. But how the will of a small cadre, abetted by the demoralization and stupidity of its opponents, turned success into failure in the very name of "success" is more difficult to explain. That the movement would have come to rest had it been left to its own spontaneous popular momentum and self-determination—possibly with gains that might have reinforced more advanced social developments abroad—is perhaps the safest judgment we can make with the hindsight time has given us. Social change, particularly social revolution, tends to find its worst enemies in leaders whose wills supplant the spontaneous movements of the people. Hubris in social evolution is as dangerous as it is in natural evolution and for the same reasons. In both cases, the complexity of a situation, the limitations of time and place, and the prejudices that filter into what often merely *appear* as foresight conceal the multitude of particulars that are truer to reality than any ideological preconceptions and needs.

I do not mean to deny the superadded significance of will, insight, and knowledge that must inform human spontaneity in the social world. In nature, by contrast, spontaneity operates within a more restrictive set of conditions. A natural ecosystem finds its climax in the greatest degree of stability it can attain within its given level of possibilities. We know, of course, that this is not a passive process. But beyond the level and stability an ecosystem can achieve and the apparent striving it exhibits, it reveals no motivation and choice. Its stability, given its potentialities and what Aristotle called its "entelechy," is an end in itself, just as the function of a beehive is to produce bees. A climax ecosystem brings to rest for a time the interrelationships that comprise it. By contrast, the social realm raises the objective possibility of freedom and self-consciousness as the superadded function of stability. The human community, at whatever level it comes to rest, remains incomplete until it achieves uninhibited volition and self-consciousness, or what we call *freedom*—a complete state, I should add, that is actually the point of departure for a new beginning. How much human freedom rests on the stability of the natural ecosystem in which it is always embedded, what it means in a larger philosophical sense beyond mere survival, and what standards it evolves from its shared history with the entire world of life and its own social history are subjects for the rest of this book.

❧

Within this highly complex context of ideas we must now try to transpose the nonhierarchical character of natural ecosystems to society. What renders social ecology so important is that it offers no case whatsoever for hierarchy in nature and society; it decisively challenges the very function of hierarchy as a stabilizing or ordering principle in *both* realms. The association of order as such with hierarchy is ruptured. And this association is ruptured without rupturing the association of nature with society—as sociology, in its well-meaning opposition to sociobiology, has been wont to do. In contrast to sociologists, we do not have to render the social world so supremely autonomous from nature that we are obliged to dissolve the continuum that phases nature into society. In short, we do not have to accept the brute tenets of sociobiology that link us crudely to nature at one extreme or the naïve tenets of sociology that cleave us sharply from nature at the other extreme. Although hierarchy does exist in present-day society, it need not continue—irrespective of its lack of meaning or reality for nature. But the case against hierarchy is not contingent on its uniqueness as a social phenomenon. Because hierarchy threatens the existence of social life today, it *cannot* remain a social fact. Because it threatens the integrity of organic nature, it will not continue to do so, given the harsh verdict of "mute" and "blind" nature.

Our continuity with nonhierarchical nature suggests that a nonhierarchical society is no less random than an ecosystem. That freedom is more than the absence of constraint, that the Anglo-American tradition of mere pluralism and institutional heterogeneity yields substantially less than a social ecosystem—such concepts have been argued with telling effect. In fact, democracy as the apotheosis of social freedom has been sufficiently denatured, as Benjamin R. Barber has emphasized, to yield

> the gradual displacement of participation by representation. Where democracy in its classical form meant quite literally rule by the *demos*, by the *plebes*, by the people themselves, it now often seems to mean little more than elite rule sanctioned (through the device of representation) by the people. Competing elites vie for the support of a public, whose popular sovereignty is reduced to the pathetic right to participate in choosing the tyrant who will rule it.

Perhaps more significantly, the concept of a public sphere, of a body politic, has been literally dematerialized by a seeming heterogeneity—more precisely, an atomization that reaches from the institutional to the personal—that has replaced political coherence with chaos. The displacement of public virtue by personal rights has yielded the subversion not only of a unifying ethical principle that once gave substance to the very notion of a public, but of the very personhood that gave substance to the notion of right.

A broad, frequently raised question remains to be answered: To what extent does nature have a reality of its own that we can legitimately invoke? Assuming that nature really exists, how much do we know about the natural world that is not exclusively social or, to be even more restrictive, the product of our own subjectivity? That nature is all that is nonhuman or, more broadly, nonsocial is a presumption rooted in more than rational discourse. It lies at the heart of an entire theory of knowledge—an epistemology that sharply bifurcates into objectivity and subjectivity. Since the Renaissance, the idea that knowledge lies locked within a mind closeted by its own supranatural limitations and insights has been the foundation for all our doubts about the very existence of a coherent constellation that can even be called nature. This idea is the foundation for an antinaturalistic body of epistemological theories.

The claim of epistemology to adjudicate the validity of knowledge as a formal and abstract inquiry has always been opposed by the claim of history to treat knowledge as a problem of genesis, not merely of knowing in a formal and abstract sense. From this historical standpoint, mental processes do not live a life of their own. Their seemingly autonomous construction of the world is actually inseparable from the way they are constructed *by* the world—a world that is richly historical not only in a social sense but in a natural one as well. I do not mean that nature "knows" things that we do not know, but rather that we are the very "knowingness" of nature, the embodiment of nature's evolution into intellect, mind and self-reflexivity.*

In the abstract world of Cartesian, Lockean, and Kantian epistemology, this proposition is difficult to demonstrate. Renaissance and post-Renaissance epistemology lacks all sense of historicity. If it looks back at all to the history of mind, it does so within a context so overwhelmingly social and from historical levels so far-removed from the biological genesis of mind that it can never make contact with nature. Its very claim to "modernity" has been a systematic unravelling of the interface between nature and mind that Hellenic thought tried to establish. This interface has been replaced by an unbridgeable dualism between mentality and the external world. In Descartes, dualism occurs between soul and body; in Locke, between the perceiving senses and a perceived world; in Kant, between mind and external reality. Thus, the problem of nature's knowingness has traditionally been seen from the knowing end of a long social history rather than from its beginnings. When this history is instead viewed from its origins, mentality and its continuity with nature acquires a decisively different aspect. An authentic epistemology is the physical anthropology of the mind, of the human brain, not the cultural clutter of history that obstructs our view of the brain's genesis in nature and its evolution in society conceived as a unique elaboration of natural phenomena.

In the same vein, I do not wish to accord mind a "sovereignty" over nature that it patently lacks. Nature is a perpetual kaleidoscope of changes and fecundity that resists hard-and-fast categorization. Mind can grasp the *essence* of this change but *never all of its details*. Yet it is precisely in matters of detail that human hubris proves to be most vulnerable. To return to Charles Elton's sensitive metaphors: we have learned to

---

* In fact, natural hierarchy is meaningless in the literal sense of the term because it presupposes a knowingness—an *intellectuality*—that has yet to emerge until the evolution of humanity and society. This knowingness or intellectuality does not suddenly explode in ecosystems with the appearance of humankind. What is antecedent to what exists may contain the potentialities of what will emerge, but those antecedents do not acquire the actualization of these potentialities after they have emerged. That *we* now exist to give the word hierarchy meaning hardly imparts any hierarchical reality to plants and animals that are locked into their own antecedent historical confines. If there is hierarchy in nature, it consists of our vain attempt to establish a sovereignty over nature that we can never really achieve. It also presupposes that we are sufficiently part of nature to render the nonhuman world hierarchical, a notion that dualism is inclined to resist.

navigate our way through the deeper waters of this natural world, but not through the countless and changing reefs that always render our debarkment precarious. It is here, where the details of the shoreline count so tellingly, that we do well not to ignore the currents that experience assures us are safe and that will spare us from the dangers of foundering.

Ultimately, organic knowledge is mobilized insight that seeks to know nature within nature, not to abandon analysis for mysticism or dialectic for intuition. Our own thinking is itself a natural process, albeit deeply conditioned by society and richly textured by social evolution. Our capacity to bring thought into resonance with its organic history (its evolution from the highly reactive organic molecules that form the fundament for the sensitivity of more complex ones, the extravagant cloudburst of life-forms that follows, and the evolution of the nervous system) is part of the knowledge of "knowing" that provides thought with an organic integument as real as the intellectual tools we acquire from society. More than intuition and faith, thought is literally as real as birth and death, when we first begin to know and when we finally cease to know. Hence nature abides in epistemology as surely as a parent abides in its child. What often is mistakenly dismissed as the intuitive phase of knowledge is the truth that our animality gives to our humanity and our embryo stage of development to our adulthood. When we finally divorce these depth phases of our being and thinking from our bodies and our minds, we have done worse than narrow our epistemological claims to Kantian judgements based on a harsh dualism between thought and nature; we have divided our intellects from ourselves, our state of mind from the development of our bodies, our insight from our hindsight, and our understanding from its ancient memories.

∽

In more concrete terms, what tantalizing issues does social ecology raise for our time and our future? In establishing a more advanced interface with nature, will it be possible to achieve a new balance between humanity and nature by sensitively tailoring our agricultural practices, urban areas, and technologies to the natural requirements of a region and its ecosystems? Can we hope to "manage" the natural environment by a drastic decentralization of agriculture, which will make it possible to cultivate land as though it were a garden balanced by diversified fauna and flora? Will these changes require the decentralization of our cities into moderate-sized communities, creating a new balance between town and country? What technology will be required to achieve these goals and avoid the further pollution of the earth? What institutions will be required to create a new public sphere, what social relations to foster a new ecological sensibility, what forms of work to render human practice playful and creative, what sizes and populations of communities to scale life to human dimensions controllable by all? What kind of poetry? Concrete questions—ecological, social, political, and behavioral—rush in like a flood heretofore dammed up by the constraints of traditional ideologies and habits of thought.

The answers we provide to these questions have a direct bearing on whether humanity can survive on the planet. The trends in our time are visibly directed against ecological diversity; in fact, they point toward brute simplification of the entire biosphere. Complex food chains in the soil and on the earth's surface are being ruthlessly undermined by the fatuous application of industrial techniques to agriculture; consequently, soil has been reduced in many areas to a mere sponge for absorbing simple chemical "nutrients." The cultivation of single crops over vast stretches of land is effacing natural, agricultural, and even physiographic variety. Immense urban belts are encroaching unrelentingly on the countryside, replacing flora and fauna with concrete, metal and glass, and enveloping large regions in a haze of atmospheric pollutants. In this mass urban world, human experience itself becomes crude and elemental, subject to brute noisy stimuli and crass bureaucratic manipulation. A national division of labor, standardized along industrial lines, is replacing regional and local variety, reducing entire continents to immense, smoking factories and cities to garish, plastic supermarkets.

Modern society, in effect, is disassembling the biotic complexity achieved by aeons of organic evolution. The great movement of life from fairly simple to increasingly complex forms and relations is being ruthlessly reversed in the direction of an environment that will be able to support only simpler living things. To continue this reversal of biological evolution, to undermine the biotic food-webs on which humanity depends for its means of life, places in question the very survival of the human species. If the reversal of the evolutionary process continues, there is good reason to believe—all control of other toxic agents aside—that the preconditions for complex forms of life will be irreparably destroyed and the earth will be incapable of supporting us as a viable species.

In this confluence of social and ecological crises, we can no longer afford to be unimaginative; we can no longer afford to do without utopian thinking. The crises are too serious and the possibilities too sweeping to be resolved by customary modes of thought—the very sensibilities that produced these crises in the first place. Years ago, the French students in the May–June uprising of 1968 expressed this sharp contrast of alternatives magnificently in their slogan: "Be practical! Do the impossible!" To this demand, the generation that faces the next century can add the more solemn injunction: "If we don't do the impossible, we shall be faced with the unthinkable!"

↝

In the Norse legends, Odin, to obtain wisdom, drinks of the magic fountain that nourishes the World Tree. In return, the god must forfeit one of his eyes. The symbolism, here, is clear: Odin must pay a penalty for acquiring the insight that gives him a measure of control over the natural world and breaches its pristine harmony. But his "wisdom" is that of a one-eyed man. Although he sees the world more acutely, his vision is one-sided. The "wisdom" of Odin involves a renunciation not only of what Josef Weber has called the "primordial bond with nature," but also of the honesty of perception that accords with nature's early unity. Truth achieves exactness, predictability, and above all, manipulability; it becomes science in the customary sense of the term. But science as we know it today is the fragmented one-sided vision of a one-eyed god, whose vantage-point entails domination and antagonism, not coequality and harmony. In the Norse legends, this "wisdom" leads to Ragnarok, the downfall of the gods and the destruction of the tribal world. In our day, this one-sided "wisdom" is laden with the prospects of nuclear immolation and ecological catastrophe.

Humanity has passed through a long history of one-sidedness and of a social condition that has always contained the potential of destruction, despite its creative achievements in technology. The great project of our time must be to open the other eye: to see all-sidedly and wholly, to heal and transcend the cleavage between humanity and nature that came with early wisdom. Nor can we deceive ourselves that the reopened eye will be focused on the visions and myths of primordial peoples, for history has labored over thousands of years to produce entirely new domains of reality that enter into our very humanness. Our capacity for freedom—which includes our capacity for individuality, experience, and desire—runs deeper than that of our distant progenitors. We have established a broader material basis for free time, play, security, perception, and sensuousness—a material potentiality for broader domains of freedom and humanness—than humanity in a primordial bond with nature could possibly achieve.

But we cannot remove our bonds unless we know them. However unconscious its influence may be, a legacy of domination permeates our thinking, values, emotions, indeed our very musculature. History dominates us all the more when we are ignorant of it. The historic unconscious must be made conscious. Cutting across the very legacy of domination is another: the legacy of freedom that lives in the daydreams of humanity, in the great ideals and movements—rebellious, anarchic, and Dionysian— that have welled up in all great eras of social transition. In our own time, these legacies are intertwined like strands and subvert the clear patterns that existed in the past, until the language of freedom becomes interchangeable with that of domination. This confusion has been the tragic fate of modern socialism, a doctrine that has been bled of all its generous ideals. Thus, the past must be dissected in order to exorcise it and to acquire a new integrity of vision. We must reexamine the cleavages that separated humanity from nature, and the splits within the human community that originally produced this cleavage, if the concept of wholeness is to become intelligible and the reopened eye to glimpse a fresh image of freedom.

2 ∝ THE OUTLOOK OF ORGANIC SOCIETY

The notion that man is destined to dominate nature is by no means a universal feature of human culture. If anything, this notion is almost completely alien to the outlook of so-called primitive or preliterate communities. I cannot emphasize too strongly that the concept emerged very gradually from a broader social development: the increasing domination of human by human. The breakdown of primordial equality into hierarchical systems of inequality, the disintegration of early kinship groups into social classes, the dissolution of tribal communities into the city, and finally the usurpation of social administration by the State—all profoundly altered not only social life but also the attitude of people toward each other, humanity's vision of itself, and ultimately its attitude toward the natural world. In many ways, we are still agonized by the problems that emerged with these sweeping changes. Perhaps only by examining the attitudes of certain preliterate peoples can we gauge the extent to which domination shapes the most intimate thoughts and the most minute actions of the individual today.

Until recently, discussions about the outlook of preliterate peoples were complicated by opinions that the logical operations of these peoples were distinctly different from our own. To speak of what was called "primitive mentality" as a "prelogical" phenomenon, to use Levy-Bruhl's unhappy term, or more recently, in the language of mythopoeically oriented mystics, "nonlinear thinking," results from a prejudicial misreading of early social sensibilities. From a formal viewpoint, there is a very real sense in which preliterate people were or are obliged to think in much the same "linear" sense as we are in dealing with the more mundane aspects of life. Whatever their shortcomings as a substitute for wisdom and a world outlook, conventional logical operations are needed for survival. Women gathered plants, men shaped hunting implements, and children contrived games according to logical procedures that were closely akin to our own.

But this formal similarity is not at issue in discussing the preliterate outlook toward society. What is significant about the differences in outlook between ourselves and preliterate peoples is that while the latter think like us in a structural sense, their thinking occurs in a cultural context that is fundamentally different from ours. Although their logical operations may be identical to ours formally, their values differ from ours qualitatively. The further back we go to communities that lack economic classes and a political State—communities that might well be called *organic societies* because of their intense solidarity internally and with the natural world—the greater evidence we find of an outlook toward life that visualized people, things, and relations in terms of their uniqueness rather than their "superiority" or "inferiority." To such communities, individuals and things were not necessarily better or worse than each other; they were simply dissimilar. Each was prized for itself, indeed, for its *unique* traits. The conception of individual autonomy had not yet acquired the fictive "sovereignty" it has achieved today. The world was perceived as a composite of many different parts, each indispensable to its unity and harmony. Individuality, to the extent that it did not conflict with the community interest on which the survival of all depended, was seen more in terms of interdependence than independence. Variety was prized within the larger tapestry of the community—as a priceless ingredient of communal unity.

In the various organic societies where this outlook still prevails, notions such as "equality" and "freedom" do not exist. They are implicit in the very outlook itself. Moreover, because they are not placed in juxtaposition to the concepts of "inequality" and "unfreedom," these notions lack definability. As Dorothy Lee observed in her deeply incisive and sensitive essays on this outlook:

> Equality exists in the very nature of things, as a byproduct of the democratic structure of the culture itself, not as a principle to be applied. In such societies, there is no attempt to achieve the goal of equality, and in fact there is no concept of equality. Often, there is no linguistic mechanism whatever for comparison. What we find is absolute respect for man, for all individuals irrespective of age and sex.[*]

---

[*] See Dorothy Lee, *Freedom and Culture* (Englewood Cliffs, NJ: Prentice-Hall, 1959). Dorothy Lee's essays stand almost alone in the literature on "primitive mentality," and my debt to her material and interpretation is considerable. Although her data and views have become increasingly widespread lately, it is unfortunate that she has received so little mention, not to speak of acknowledgement, among recent journalistic critics of hierarchy.

The absence of coercive and domineering values in organic cultures is perhaps best illustrated by the syntax of the Wintu Indians, a people that Lee studied very closely. She notes that terms commonly expressive of coercion in modern languages are arranged, in Wintu syntax, to denote cooperative behavior instead. A Wintu mother, for example, does not "take" a baby into the shade; she *goes* with it. A chief does not "rule" his people; he *stands* with them. "They never say, and in fact they cannot say, as we do, 'I have a sister,' or a 'son,' or 'husband,'" Lee observes. "*To live with* is the usual way in which they express what we call possession, and they use this term for everything that they respect, so that a man will be said to live with his bow and arrows."

The phrase "to live with" implies not only a deep sense of mutual respect for person and a high regard for individual voluntarism; it also implies a profound sense of unity between the individual and the group. We need not go any further than an examination of American Indian life to find abundant evidence of this fact. The traditional society of the Hopi was geared entirely toward group solidarity. Nearly all the basic tasks of the community, from planting to food preparation, were done cooperatively. Together with the adults, children participated in most of these tasks. At every age level, the individual was charged with a sense of responsibility for the community. So all-pervasive were these group attitudes that Hopi children, placed in schools administered by whites, could be persuaded only with the greatest difficulty to keep score in competitive games.

These strong attitudes of intragroup solidarity were fostered in the earliest days of Hopi childhood and continued through life. They began in infancy with the process of weaning, which emphasized interdependence between Hopi individuals and the group—in marked contrast to the surrounding white culture's emphasis on "independence." Weaning is not merely "a transition from milk to solid foods," observes Dorothy Eggan in a study of Hopi socialization. "It is also a gradual process of achieving independence from the comfort of the mother's body and care, of transferring affections to other persons, and of finding satisfactions within oneself and in the outside world." In this sense, many whites "are never weaned, which has unfortunate consequences in a society where *individual* effort and independence are stressed. The Hopi child, on the other hand, from the day of his birth was being weaned from his biological mother." But this weaning process resulted not from social indifference or maternal neglect. To the contrary, and very characteristically:

Many arms gave him comfort, many faces smiled at him, and from a very early age he was given bits of food which were chewed by various members of the family and placed in his mouth. So for a Hopi, the outside world in which he needed to find satisfaction was never far away.

◌ঽ

From this feeling of unity between the individual and the community emerges a feeling of unity between the community and its environment. Psychologically, people in organic communities must believe that they exercise a greater influence on natural forces than is actually afforded them by their relatively simple technology. Such a belief is fostered by group rituals and magical procedures. Elaborate as these rituals and procedures may be, however, humanity's sense of dependence on the natural world, indeed, on its immediate environment, never disappears. Although this sense of dependence may generate abject fear or an equally abject reverence, there is a point in the development of organic society where it visibly generates a sense of symbiosis, of communal interdependence and cooperation, that tends to transcend raw feelings of terror and awe. Here, people not only propitiate powerful forces or try to manipulate them; their ceremonials help (as they see it) in a creative sense: they aid in multiplying food animals, or in bringing changes in weather and season, or in promoting the fertility of crops. The organic community is conceived to be part of the balance of nature—a forest community or a soil community—in short, a truly ecological community or *ecocommunity* peculiar to its ecosystem, with an active sense of participation in the overall environment and the cycles of nature.

The fine distinction between fear and reverence becomes more evident when we turn to accounts of certain ceremonials among preliterate peoples. Aside from ceremonials and rituals characterized by social functions, such as initiation rites, we encounter others marked by ecological functions. Among the Hopi, major horticultural ceremonies have the role of summoning forth the cycles of the cosmic order, of actualizing the solstices and the different stages in the growth of maize from germination to maturation. Although this order and these stages are known to be predetermined, human ceremonial involvement is an integral part of that predetermination. In contrast to strictly magical procedures, Hopi ceremonies assign a participatory rather than a manipulatory function to humans. People play a complementary role in natural cycles: they facilitate the workings of the cosmic order. Their ceremonies are part of a complex web of life that extends from the germination of corn to the arrival of the solstices. As Dorothy Lee observed,

Every aspect of nature, plants and rocks and animals, colors and cardinal directions and numbers and sex distinctions, the dead and the living, all have a cooperative share in the maintenance of the universal order. Eventually, the effort of each individual, human or not, goes into this huge whole. And here, too, it is every aspect of a person which counts. The entire being of the Hopi individual affects the balance of nature; and as each individual develops his inner potential, so he enhances his participation, so does the entire universe become invigorated.

Contemporary ecological rhetoric tends to blur the wealth of implications that follow from the integration of the individual, community, and environment into a "universal order." Since Lee penned these lines, almost every one of her words have become the cheap coin of the "human potential" movement. Preliterate cultures, in fact, often *begin* with a cosmology consisting of the conclusions that our current bouquet of mystics profess to attain. To organic societies, the puzzling cosmological issue is not life, which exists everywhere and in all things; the puzzle is death, the inexplicably unique condition of nonliving and hence nonbeing. "Soul," in some sense, permeates the entirety of existence; the "dead" matter that science has given us since the Renaissance, as Hans Jonas has so sensitively pointed out, "was yet to be discovered—as indeed its concept, so familiar to us, is anything but obvious." What is most natural to organic societies is an aboundingly fecund, all-encompassing "livingness" that is integral to its knowingness, a world of life that "occupies the whole foreground exposed to man's immediate view. ... Earth, wind, and water—begetting, teeming, nurturing, destroying—are anything but models of 'mere matter."

The direct involvement of humanity with nature is thus not an abstraction, and Dorothy Lee's account of the Hopi ceremonials is not a description of "primitive man's science," as Victorian anthropologists believed. Nature begins *as* life. From the very outset of human consciousness, it enters directly into *consociation* with humanity—not merely harmonization or even balance. Nature as life eats at every repast, succors every new birth, grows with every child, aids every hand that throws a spear or plucks a plant, warms itself at the hearth in the dancing shadows, and sits amidst the councils of the community just as the rustle of the leaves and grasses is part of the air itself—not merely a sound borne on the wind. Ecological ceremonials validate the "citizenship" nature acquires as part of the human environment. "The People" (to use the name that many preliterate communities give to themselves) do not disappear into nature or nature into "the People." But nature is not merely a habitat; it is a *participant* that advises the community with its omens, secures it with its camouflage, leaves it telltale messages in broken twigs and footprints, whispers warnings to it in the wind's voice, nourishes it with a largesse of plants and animals, and in its countless functions and counsels is absorbed into the community's nexus of rights and duties.

What the ecological ceremonial does, in effect, is *socialize* the natural world and complete the involvement of society with nature. Here, the ceremonial, despite its naïvely fictive content, speaks more truthfully to the richly articulated interface between society and nature than concepts that deal with the natural world as a "matrix," "background," or worse, "precondition" for the social world. Indeed, far from dealing with nature as an "It" or a "Thou" (to use Martin Buber's terms), the ceremonial validates nature as *kin*, a blooded, all-important estate that words like *citizen* can never attain. Nature is *named* even before it is deified; it is personified as part of the community before it is raised above it as "supernature." To the pygmies of the Ituri forest, it is "Ndura" and to the settled Bantu villagers the same word strictly designates the forest that the pygmies regard as a veritable entity in itself, active and formative in all its functions.

Hence, the very notion of nature is *always* social at this point in human development—in an ontological sense that the protoplasm of humankind retains an abiding continuity with the protoplasm of nature. To speak in the language of organic society, the blood that flows between the community and nature in the process of being kin is circulated by distinct acts of the community: ceremonials, dances, dramas, songs, decorations, and symbols. The dancers who imitate animals in their gestures or birds in their calls are engaged in more than mere mimesis; they form a communal and choral unity with nature, a unity that edges into the intimate intercourse of sexuality, birth and the interchange of blood. By virtue of a community solidarity that such widely bandied terms as stewardship can hardly convey, organic societies "hear" a nature and "speak" for a nature that will be slowly muffled and muted by the "civilizations" that gain historic ascendency over them. Until then, nature is no silent world or passive environment lacking meaning beyond the dictates of human manipulation. Hence, social ecology has its origins in humanity's initial awareness of its own sociality—not merely as a cognitive dimension of epistemology but as an ontological consociation with the natural world.

❧

I do not mean to deny the old epistemological canon that human beings see nature in social terms, preformed by social categories and interests. But this canon requires further articulation and elaboration. The word social should not sweep us into a deluge of intellectual abstractions that ignore the distinctions between one social form and another. It is easy to see that organic society's harmonized view of nature follows directly from the harmonized relations within the early human community. Just as medieval theology structured the Christian heaven on feudal lines, so people of all ages have projected their social structures onto the natural world. To the Algonquians of the North American forests, beavers lived in clans and lodges of their own, wisely cooperating to promote the well-being of the community. Animals also had their magic, their totem ancestors (the elder brother), and were invigorated by the Manitou, whose spirit nourished the entire cosmos. Accordingly, animals had to be conciliated or else they might refuse to provide humans with skins and meat. The cooperative spirit that formed a basis for the survival of the organic community was an integral part of the outlook of preliterate people toward nature and the interplay between the natural world and the social.

We have yet to find a language that adequately encompasses the quality of this deeply imbedded cooperative spirit. Expressions like "love of nature" or "communism," not to speak of the jargon favored by contemporary sociology, are permeated by the problematical relationships of our own society and mentality. Preliterate humans did not have to "love" nature; they lived in a kinship relationship with it, a relationship more primary than our use of the term *love*. They would not distinguish between our "esthetic" sense on this score and their own functional approach to the natural world, because natural beauty is there to begin with—in the very cradle of the individual's experience. The poetic language that awakens such admiration among whites who encounter the spokesmen for Indian grievances is rarely "poetry" to the speaker; rather, it is an unconscious eloquence that reflects the dignity of Indian life.

So too with other elements of organic society and its values: cooperation is too primary to be adequately expressed in the language of western society. From the outset of life, coercion in dealing with children is so notably rare in most preliterate communities that western observers are often astonished by the gentleness with which so-called primitives deal with the most intractable of their young. Yet in preliterate communities the parents are not "permissive"; they simply respect the personality of their children, much as they do that of the adults in their communities. Until age hierarchies begin to emerge, the everyday behavior of parents fosters an almost unbroken continuity in the lives of the young between the years of childhood and adulthood.

Farley Mowatt, a biologist who lived on the Canadian barrens among the last remnant band of the Ihalmiut Eskimo, noted that if a boy wished to become a hunter, he was not scolded for his presumption or treated with amused condescension. To the contrary, his father seriously fashioned a miniature bow and some arrows that were genuine weapons, not toys. The boy then went out to hunt, encouraged by all the traditional words of good luck that the Ihalmiut accorded an experienced adult. On his return, Mowatt tells us,

> He is greeted as gravely as if he were his father. The whole camp wishes to hear of his hunt, and he can expect the same ridicule at failure, or the same praise if he managed to kill a little bird, which would come upon a full-grown man. So he plays, and learns, under no shadow of parental disapproval, and under no restraint of fear.

The Ihalmiut are not exceptional. The inherently nonauthoritarian relationships Mowatt encountered between Eskimo children and adults is still quite common in surviving organic societies. It extends not only to ties between children and adults but also to the prevailing notions of property, exchange, and leadership. Here again, the terminology of western society fails us. The word *property* connotes an individual appropriation of goods, a personal claim to tools, land, and other resources. Conceived in this loose sense, property is fairly common in organic societies, even in groups that have a very simple, undeveloped technology. By the same token, cooperative work and the sharing of resources on a scale that could be called communistic is also fairly common. On both the productive side of economic life and the consumptive, appropriation of tools, weapons, food, and even clothing may range widely—often idiosyncratically, in western eyes—from the possessive and seemingly individualistic to the most meticulous, often ritualistic, parceling out of a harvest or a hunt among members of a community.

But primary to both of these seemingly contrasting relationships is the practice of *usufruct*, the freedom of individuals in a community to appropriate resources merely by virtue of the fact that they are using them. Such resources belong to the user as long as they are being used. Function, in effect, replaces our hallowed concept of possession— not merely as a loan or even "mutual aid," but as an unconscious emphasis on use itself, on need that is free of psychological entanglements with proprietorship, work, and even reciprocity. The western identification of individuality with ownership and personality with craft—the latter laden with a metaphysics of selfhood as expressed in a crafted object wrested by human powers from an intractable nature— has yet to emerge from the notion of use itself and the guileless enjoyment of needed things. Need, in effect, still orchestrates work to the point where property of any kind, communal or otherwise, has yet to acquire independence from the claims of satisfaction. A collective need subtly orchestrates work, not personal need alone, for the collective claim is implicit in the primacy of usufruct over proprietorship. Hence, even the work performed in one's own dwelling has an underlying collective dimension in the potential availability of its products to the entire community.

Communal property, once property itself has become a category of consciousness, already marks the first step toward private property—just as reciprocity, once it too becomes a category of consciousness, marks the first step toward exchange. Proudhon's celebration of "mutual aid" and contractual federalism, like Marx's celebration of communal property and planned production, mark no appreciable advance over the primal principle of usufruct. Both thinkers were captive to the notion of interest, to the rational satisfaction of egotism.

There may have been a period in humanity's early development when interest had not yet emerged to replace complementarity, the disinterested willingness to pool needed things and needed services. There was a time when Gontran de Poncins, wandering into the most remote reaches of the Arctic, could still encounter "the pure, the true Eskimos, the Eskimos who knew not how to lie"—and hence to manipulate, to calculate, to project a private interest beyond social need. Here, community attained a completeness so exquisite and artless that needed things and services fit together in a lovely mosaic with a haunting personality of its own.

We should not disdain these almost utopian glimpses of humanity's potentialities, with their unsullied qualities for giving and collectivity. Preliterate peoples that still lack an "I" with which to replace a "we" are not (as Levy-Bruhl was to suggest) deficient in individuality as much as they are rich in community. This is a greatness of wealth that can yield a lofty disdain for objects.* Cooperation, at this point, is more than just a

---

* The potlatch ceremonies of the Northwest Coast Indians of America, in fact, no longer clearly reflect the wealth of community that leads to disdain for objects. These "disaccumulation" ceremonies already fetishize the giving qualities from which they may have been derived, but they remain impressive evidence of more innocent forms of usufruct that lacked all connotations of prestige and social recognition.

cement between members of the group; it is an organic melding of identities that, without losing individual uniqueness, retains and fosters the unity of consociation. Contract, forced into this wholeness, serves merely to subvert it—turning an unthinking sense of responsibility into a calculating nexus of aid and an unconscious sense of collectivity into a preening sense of mutuality. As for reciprocity, so often cited as the highest evocation of collectivity, we shall see that it is more significant in forming alliances between groups than in fostering internal solidarity within them.

Usufruct, in short, differs qualitatively from the quid pro quo of reciprocity, exchange, and mutual aid—all of which are trapped within history's demeaning account books with their "just" ratios and their "honest" balance sheets. Caught in this limited sphere of calculation, consociation is always tainted by the rationality of arithmetic. The human spirit can never transcend a quantitative world of "fair dealings" between canny egos whose ideology of interest barely conceals a mean-spirited proclivity for acquisition. To be sure, social forces were to fracture the human collectivity by introducing contractual ties and cultivating the ego's most acquisitive impulses. Insofar as the guileless peoples of organic societies held to the values of usufruct in an *unconscious* manner, they remained terribly vulnerable to the lure, often the harsh imposition, of an emerging contractual world. Rarely is history notable for its capacity to select and preserve the most virtuous traits of humanity. But there is still no reason why hope, reinforced by consciousness and redolent with ancestral memories, may not linger within us as an awareness of what humanity has been in the past and what it can become in the future.

♋

Contractual relations—or more properly, the "treaties" and "oaths" that give specifiable forms to community life—may have served humanity well when compelling need or the perplexities of an increasingly complex social environment placed a premium on a clearly defined system of rights and duties. The more demanding the environment, the more preliterate peoples must explicate the ways in which they are responsible for each other and how they must deal with exogenous factors—particularly nearby communities— that impinge on them. Need now emerges as an ordering and structuring force in institutionalizing the fairly casual, and even pleasurable, aspects of life. Sexual, kinship, reciprocal, federative, and civil areas of the community must acquire greater structure—to deal not only with a more pressing nature but particularly one that includes adjacent communities staking out claims of their own to a common environment. Such claims are internalized by the community itself as a system of sharing. And not only do interests now arise that must be carefully and later meticulously articulated, but, ironically, they also arise from individuals who begin to feel that they carry visibly heavier burdens and responsibilities within the community. These individuals are the nascent "oppressed" (often women) and those we might regard as the nascent "privileged."

Men and women in preliterate communities need each other not only to satisfy their sexual desires but also for the material support they give to each other.* Their marriage establishes a primary division of labor— a sexual division of labor with a sexualized economy as well—that tends to apportion hunting and pastoral tasks to men, including the defense of the community and its relationship to the outsider, and domestic, food-gathering, and horticultural responsibilities to women. By a sexual division of labor, I do not mean merely a biological one, important as the biological dimension may be, but an economy that acquires the very gender of the sex to which it is apportioned. Nor was it necessarily men who formulated the apportionment of the community's material activities between the sexes. More likely than not, in my view, it was women who made this apportionment with a sense of concern over the integrity of their richly hallowed responsibilities and their personal rights. Only later did the emergence of more complex and hierarchical social forms turn their domestic roles against them. This development, as we shall see, was to come from a male envy that must be carefully unravelled.

At a low subsistence level and in a fairly primal community, both divisions of labor are needed for the well-being, if not the survival, of all its members; hence, the sexes treat each other with respect. Indeed, the ability of a man or woman to perform well in this division of labor profoundly influences the choice of a mate and preserves the integrity of a marriage—which is often dissolved by the woman, whose responsibilities in sheltering, feeding, and raising the young visibly outweigh the man's usefulness in discharging these all-important functions. Given

---

* It is not always clear how pressing these sexual desires are from a heterosexual standpoint. My own studies of early sexuality suggest a degree of "polymorphous perversity," to use Freud's perverse formulation, as a *communal* phenomenon—and even more, of bisexuality and homosexuality—that would appall even our own "liberated" age. So ubiquitous is this sexuality that what the anthropologist may discreetly describe as masturbation is, in fact, intercourse with all natural things, particularly animals. Hence, marriage may well involve more economic considerations and social bonds than sexual ones—and sexuality may be latent with a richer animistic meaning than we can ever hope to envision. The sexuality that imbues early technics itself has not yet been fully explored, together with the way it defines work in preliterate society.

the woman's de facto role in the early community's social arrangements, our obsessive preoccupation with "primitive monogamy" seems almost preposterous—if it weren't so plainly ideological and obfuscatory.

The blood-tie and the rights and duties that surround it are embodied in an unspoken oath that comprised the only visible unifying principle of early community life. And this bond initially derives from woman. She alone becomes the very protoplasm of sociality: the ancestress that cements the young into lasting consociation, the source of the blood that flows in their veins, the one who nourishes a commonality of origins, the rearer who produces a mutuality of shared physical and spiritual recognition that extends from infancy to death. She is the instructress in the basic ways of life, the most indisputable personification of community as such, conceived as an intimate familial experience. The young, who first see each other as kin—as common flesh, bone, and blood through their mother—later see each other with an intense sense of identity through her memory, and only faintly in the father, whose physical features they closely resemble.

With the commonality of blood comes the commanding oath that ordains unequivocable support between kin. This support entails not only sharing and devotion but the right to summon an unquestioned retribution on those who injuriously despoil the blood of a kinsperson. Beyond the obvious material needs that must be satisfied for survival itself, the claims of the blood oath provide the first dictates that the primal community encounters. They are the earliest communal reflexes that emerge from human consociation, although deeply laden with mystery. Community, through the blood oath, thus affirms itself with each birth and death. To violate it is to violate the solidarity of the group itself, to challenge its sense of communal mystery. Hence, such violations, be they from within the group or from without, are too heinous to contemplate. Only later will dramatic changes in the most fundamental premises of organic society make kinship and its claims a consciously debatable issue and a subject for ceremonial exploration.*

Mere reflexes, however, are too binding, too defensive, too rigid and self-enclosing to permit any broader social advances. They do not allow for a social solidarity based on conscious alliances, on

---

* Powerful as the *Oresteia* may be psychologically to the modern mind, I would thus regard Aeschylus's trilogy, which deals as much with kinship as it does with mother-right and the claims of citizenship over those of blood-ties, as a haunting Greek ceremonial rather than a well-crafted drama. Only now, perhaps, in our defenseless isolation and monad-like condition as socially alienated beings can we sense the power of the trilogy over an ancient Greek audience that had yet to exorcise the blood oath and tribal custom from their enchanted hold on the human psyche.

further social constructions and elaborations. They constitute an inward retreat into a guardedness and suspicion toward all that is exogenous to the community—a fear of the social horizon that lies beyond the limited terrain staked out by the blood oath. Hence, necessity and time demand that ways be found to place the community in a much larger social matrix. Obligations must be established beyond the confines of the self-enclosed group to claim new rights that will foster survival—in short, a broader system of rights and duties that will bring exogenous groups into the service of the community in periods of misfortune and conflict. Limited by the blood oath, allies are difficult to find; the community, based on association through kinship alone, finds it impossible to recognize itself in other communities that do not share common ancestral lineages. Unless such lineages can be created by intermarriages that recreate the blood oath on its primal terms of shared kinship, new oaths must be devised that, while secondary to blood, can find a comparable tangibility in things. Claude Levi-Strauss's notion to the contrary notwithstanding, women are decidedly not such "things" that men can trade with each other to acquire allies. They are the origins of kinship and sociality—the *arché* of community and its immanent power of solidarity—not little pastries that can be savored and traded away in a Parisian bistro.

Even "things" *as such* do not suffice, for they suggest a system of accounts and ratios that stand at odds with organic society's practice of usufruct. Hence, before things can become gifts—I leave aside their later debasement into commodities—they first become symbols. What initially counts for early preliterate peoples is not a thing's usefulness in the economy of organic society but its symbolism as the physical embodiment of reciprocity, of a willingness to enter into mutual obligation. These are the treaties that extend beyond the blood oath into social oaths: the early elaboration of the biological community into human society, the first glimmerings of a universal *humanitas* that lies beyond the horizon of a universal *animalitas*.

As preliterate communities extended their range of acquired "relatives," the traditional kinship nexus was probably increasingly permeated by the social. Marriage, reciprocity, the ritualistic adoption of strangers as blood relatives, and intracommunity institutions like fraternities and totemic societies must have produced a slow consolidation and layering of responsibilities, particularly in more dynamic organic societies, that were to be richly articulated by custom and ritual. From this social substance there began to emerge a new civil sphere parallel to the older domestic sphere.

That this civil sphere was free of coercion and command is indicated by our evidence of "authority" in the few organic societies that have survived European acculturation. What we flippantly call "leadership" in organic societies often turns out to be guidance, lacking the usual accoutrements of command. Its "power" is functional rather than political. Chiefs, where they authentically exist and are not the mere creations of the colonizer's mind, have no true authority in a coercive sense. They are advisors, teachers, and consultants, esteemed for their experience and wisdom. Whatever "power" they do have is usually confined to highly delimited tasks such as the coordination of hunts and war expeditions. It ends with the tasks to be performed. Hence, it is episodic power, not institutional; periodic, not traditional—like the "dominance" traits we encounter among primates.

Our entire language is permeated by historically charged euphemisms that acquire a reified life of their own. Obedience displaces allegiance, command displaces coordination, power displaces wisdom, acquisition displaces giving, commodities displace gifts. While these changes are real enough historically with the rise of hierarchy, class, and property, they become grossly misleading when they extend their sovereignty to language as such and stake out their claim to the totality of social life. When used as tools in ferreting out the memory of humanity, they do not help to contrast present to past and reveal the tentative nature of the existing world and of prevailing patterns of human behavior; to the contrary, they assimilate the past to the present and in the very pretence of illuminating the past, they cunningly conceal it from our eyes. This betrayal by language is crassly ideological and has served authority well. Behind the inextricable web of history, which so often prevents us from viewing a long development from the point of its origins and beclouds us with an ideology of "hindsight," lies the even more obfuscating symbolism of a language nourished by deception. For remembrance to return in all its authenticity, with the harsh challenge it presents to the existing order, it must retain its fidelity to the *arché* of things and attain a consciousness of its own history. In short, memory itself must "remember" its own evolution into ideology as well as the evolution of humanity it professes to reveal.[*]

---

[*] Lest I be misunderstood as contending that any current trends in linguistics, communications theory, and semiology have created the tools for the renewal of remembrance, I would like to emphasize that this work will be done by anthropologists and historians, insofar as they remain sufficiently self-critical of their own use of language and its ever-changing historical context.

↻

Anthropological etiquette requires that I occasionally sprinkle my remarks with the usual caveats about my use of "selective data," my proclivity for "rampant speculation," and my "normative interpretation" of disputable research materials. Accordingly, the reader should realize that by interpreting the same material differently, one could show that organic society was egotistical, competitive, aggressive, hierarchical, and beleaguered by all the anxieties that plague "civilized" humanity. Having made this obeisance to convention, let me now argue the contrary. A careful review of the anthropological data at hand will show that communities like the Hopi, Wintu, Ihalmiut, and others cited here and in the following pages were not culturally unique; indeed, where we find an organic society in which our modern values and traits prevail, this usually can be explained by unsettling technological changes, invasions, problems of dealing with a particularly difficult environment, and, above all, by contacts with whites.

Paul Radin, summing up decades of anthropological experience, research, and fieldwork, once observed:

> If I were asked to state briefly and succinctly what are the outstanding features of aboriginal civilizations, I, for one, would have no hesitation in answering that there are three: the respect for the individual, irrespective of age or sex; the amazing degree of social and political integration achieved by them; and the existence of a concept of personal security which transcends all governmental forms and all tribal and group interests and conflicts.

These features can be summarized as complete parity or equality between individuals, age-groups and sexes; usufruct and later reciprocity; the avoidance of coercion in dealing with internal affairs; and finally, what Radin calls the "irreducible minimum"—the "inalienable right" (in Radin's words) of every individual in the community "to food, shelter and clothing" irrespective of the amount of work contributed by the individual to the acquisition of the means of life. "To deny anyone this irreducible minimum was equivalent to saying that a man no longer existed, that he was dead"—in short, to cut across the grain of the world conceived as a universe of life.

I do not mean to imply that any existing "primitive" communities can be regarded as models for early periods of human social development. They are the remnant bands of a long history that has always towed them along ways far removed from an ancestral world that separated humanity from animality. More likely than not, the solidarity that existed in Radin's "aboriginal civilizations," their high respect for the natural world and the members of their communities, may have been far more intense in prehistory, when there were none of the divisive political and commercial relations of modern capitalism that have so grossly distorted existing organic societies.

But culture traits do not exist in a vacuum. Although they may be integrated in many different and unexpected ways, certain characteristic patterns tend to emerge that yield broadly similar institutions and sensibilities, despite differences in time and location. The cultural facts of dress, technics, and environment that link prehistoric peoples with existing "primitives" is so striking that it is difficult to believe that Siberian mammoth hunters of yesteryear, with their fur parkas, bone tool kit, and glaciated surroundings were so dissimilar from the Arctic seal hunters of de Poncins' day. The physical pattern that has fallen together here has a unity that justifies a number of related cultural inferences.

Thus, the presence of female figurines, obviously laden with magical or religious significance, in the debris of a prehistoric hunting camp or a Neolithic horticultural village suggests the reasonable probability that the community accorded women a social prestige that would be difficult to find in the patriarchal societies of pastoral nomads. Indeed, such a community may even have traced its lineage system through the mother's name (matrilineal descent). If paleolithic bone implements are etched with cult-like drawings of animals, we have adequate reason to believe that the community had an animistic outlook toward the natural world. If the size of prehistoric house foundations is noteworthy for the absence of large individual dwellings and the adornments in burial sites exhibit no conspicuous wealth, we can believe that social equality existed in the community and that it had an egalitarian outlook toward its own members. Each trait, found singly, may not be convincing support for such general conclusions. But if they are all found together and if they are sufficiently widespread to be characteristic of an entire social era, it would certainly require a hard-nosed empirical outlook and an almost perverse fear of generalization not to accept these conclusions.

◌ʒ

In any case, some ten thousand years ago, in an area between the Caspian Sea and the Mediterranean, nomadic bands of hunter-gatherers began to develop a crude system of horticulture and settle down in small villages, where they engaged in mixed farming. They were followed quite independently some four or five thousand years later in a similar development by Indians of central Mexico. The development of horticulture, or gardening, was probably initiated by women. Evidence for this belief comes from studies of mythology and from existing preliterate communities based on a hoe-gardening technology. In this remote period of transition, when a sense of belonging to a relatively fixed soil community increasingly replaced a nomadic outlook, social life began to acquire entirely new unitary qualities that (to borrow a term devised by Erich Fromm) can best be called *matricentric*. By using this term, I do not wish to imply that women exercised any form of institutional sovereignty over men or achieved a commanding status in the management of society. I merely mean that the community, in separating itself from a certain degree of dependence on game and migratory animals, began to shift its social imagery from the male hunter to the female food-gatherer, from the predator to the procreator, from the camp fire to the domestic hearth, from cultural traits associated with the father to those associated with the mother.* The change

---

* Since these lines were first penned (1970), a number of works have been published that push back certain features of this image to the Paleolithic hunting-gathering period of human development and even earlier, to a more remote hominid foraging stage. Allowing for a number of differences between them, these writers generally view hunting-gathering communities as truly pacific, egalitarian, and probably matricentric societies. This image is sharply contrasted to the modern farmer's world (in my view, patently colored by the traits of more modern tight-fisted peasants) centered around a calculating, stolid, and sullen male, to borrow Paul Shepard's imagery, who presides over a large, obedient family that has been lured from a more carefree life based on hunting to a hardworking, day-long discipline based on food cultivation. Marshall Sahlins has even described the hunting-gathering "stone-age economy" as the "original affluent society" inasmuch as needs were so few, the tool-kit so simple, and the accoutrements of life so portable that men, at least, enjoyed very leisurely lives and considerable personal autonomy. Elizabeth Fisher has carried this pristine image of hunting-gathering to a point where she argues that matriarchy really existed only when men did not associate coitus with conception, an association that first occurred when seeds were planted in the soil and animals bred—more accurately, in my view, *selected*—for their docility.

I do not share these views. Indeed, I not only find them simplistic but regressive. Leaving aside the significance of such crucial social developments as writing, urbanity, fairly advanced crafts and technics, and even the rudiments of science—none of which could have been developed by Paleolithic nomads—I hold that the case for hunting-gathering as humanity's "golden age" is totally lacking in evolutionary promise. But an analytical excursus into the issues raised by Shepard, Sahlins, and Fisher does not belong in a general work of this kind. However, it cannot be ignored at a time when the need for a new civilization threatens to evoke atavistic feelings against any kind of civilization, indeed, to foster a new "survivalist" movement that is antisocial, if not fascistic, in character. Let me note that this trend is not a "return" to the supposed self-sufficiency of the Paleolithic hunter, with all his alleged virtues, but a descent into the depths of bourgeois egotism with its savage ideology of the

in emphasis is primarily cultural. "Certainly 'home and mother' are written over every phase of neolithic agriculture," observes Lewis Mumford, "and not least over the new village centers, at least identifiable in the foundations of houses and graves." One can agree with Mumford that it was woman who probably

> tended the garden crops and accomplished those masterpieces of selection and cross-fertilization which turned raw wild species into the prolific and richly nutritious domestic varieties; it was woman who made the first containers, weaving baskets and coiling the first clay pots.... Without this long period of agricultural and domestic development, the surplus of food and manpower that made urban life possible would not have been forthcoming.*

Today, one would want to replace some of Mumford's words, such as his sweeping use of "agriculture," which men were to extend beyond woman's discovery of gardening into the mass production of food and animals. We would want to confine "home and mother" to early phases of the Neolithic rather than "every phase." Similarly, where the selection of edible plant varieties ends and cross-fertilization for new ones begins is a highly blurred interface in the prehistory of food cultivation. But the spirit of Mumford's remarks is even more valid today than it was two decades ago, when a heavy-handed, male-oriented anthropology would have rejected it as sentimental.

"lifeboat ethic." As for the more readable and well-argued accounts of the hunting-gathering case, the reader should consult Marshall Sahlins's *Stone-Age Economics* (New York: Adine-Atherton, Inc., 1972), Paul Shepard's *The Tender Carnivore and the Sacred Game* (New York: Charles Scribner's Sons, 1973), and Elizabeth Fisher's *Woman's Creation* (New York: Anchor Books/Doubleday, 1979).

* Whether many edible plant varieties were consciously selected or developed spontaneously under conditions of cultivation is arguable. Erich Isaac and C. D. Darlington incline toward the view that spontaneous selection accounted for the early development of cereals and other plant varieties. Levi-Strauss, on the other hand, contends that most of the technological advances achieved by neolithic agriculturists (including transforming "a weed into a cultivated plant") "required a genuinely scientific attitude, sustained and watchful interest and a desire for knowledge for its own sake." That preliterate communities achieve a remarkably sensitive and knowledgeable adaptation to their environments is certainly true, but a "watchful interest" nourished by grim need is a far cry from "a genuinely scientific attitude," which even an Archimedes lacked during the heights of the Hellenistic era. See Erich Isaac, *The Geography of Domestication* (Englewood Cliffs, N. J.: Prentice-Hall, Inc., 1970); C. D. Darlington, "The Origins of Agriculture," *Natural History*, Vol. LXXIX, No. 5; Claude Levi-Strauss, *The Savage Mind* (Chicago: University of Chicago Press, 1966).

If anything, woman's stature in inscribing her sensibilities and her hands on the beginnings of human history has grown rather than diminished. It was she who, unlike any other living creature, made the sharing of food a consistent communal activity and even a hospitable one that embraced the stranger, hence fostering sharing as a uniquely human desideratum. Birds and mammals, to be sure, feed their young and exhibit extraordinary protectiveness on their behalf. Among mammals, females provide the produce of their bodies in the form of milk and warmth. But only woman was to make sharing a universally social phenomenon to the point where her young—as siblings, then male and female adults, and finally parents—became sharers irrespective of their sex and age. It is she who turned sharing into a hallowed communal imperative, not merely an episodic or marginal feature.

Finally, we cannot ignore the fact that woman's foraging activities helped awaken in humanity an acute sense of place, of *oikos*. Her nurturing sensibility helped create not only the origins of society but literally the *roots* of civilization—a terrain the male has arrogantly claimed for himself. Here "stake in civilization" was different from that of the predatory male: it was more domestic, more pacifying, and more caring. Her sensibility ran deeper and was laden with more hope than the male's, for she embodied in her very physical being mythology's ancient message of a lost "golden age" and a fecund nature. Yet ironically she has been with us all the time with a special genius and mystery—one whose potentialities have been brutally diminished but ever present as a voice of conscience in the bloody cauldron that men have claimed for their "civilization."

The benign qualities nurtured in this Neolithic village world are perhaps no less significant than its material achievements. A close association exists between communal management of land and matrilineal descent in surviving gardening cultures. Clan society, perhaps a slow reworking of totemic cults in hunting bands, may have reached its apogee in this period and, with it, a communal disposition of the land and its products. "To live with" had probably become "to share," if the two expressions were ever different in their meaning. In the remains of early Neolithic villages, we often sense the existence of what was once a clearly peaceful society, strewn with symbols of the fecundity of life and the bounty of nature. Although there is evidence of weapons, defensive palisades, and protective ditches, early horticulturists seem to have emphasized peaceful arts and sedentary pursuits. Judging from the building sites and graves, there is little evidence, if any, that social inequality existed within these communities or that warfare marked the relationships between them.

Presiding over this remote world was the figure and symbolism of the Mother Goddess, a fertility principle so old in time that its stone remains have even been found in Paleolithic caves and encampments. Hunter-gatherers, early horticulturists, advanced agriculturists, and the priests of "high civilizations" have imparted utterly contradictory traits to her—some deliciously benign, others darkly demonic. But it is more than fair to assume that in the early Neolithic, the priests had not yet sculpted the cruel, Kali-like image into her figure. Apparently, like Demeter, she was more of a feminine principle, latent with loving and mourning, not the mere fertility symbol—the magic thing that endeared her to hunter-gatherers. That she could not remain untainted by patriarchy is obvious from a reading of the *Odyssey*, in which the island-hopping seafarers debase woman and her domain to cruel chthonic enchantresses who devour the trusting warriors in distress.

What strongly reinforces interpretations of the goddess as a more giving principle is the unqualified nature of mother-love itself in contrast to the conditional love associated with patriarchy. Erich Fromm, in the provocative essays he prepared for the Institute for Social Research, noted that woman's love, compared with that of the judgmental patriarch who provides love as a reward for the child's performance and fulfillment of its duties, "is not dependent on any moral or social obligation to be carried out by the child; there is not even an obligation to return her love." This unconditional love, without expectation of any filial reward, yields the total deobjectification of person that makes humanness its own end rather than a tool of hierarchy and classes. To assume that the goddess did not symbolize this untainted sense of identification is to question her association with the feminine—in short, to turn her into a god, which priestly corporations were to do later with extraordinary deftness. Odysseus, in degrading Demeter to Circe, also reveals how the lovely sirens might have charmed humans and beasts into a sense of commonality with each other. Homer's epic, however, will forever hide from us the intriguing possibility that their song originally gave to humanity the music of life rather than the luring melody of death.

❧

How close the early Neolithic village world may have been to that of the early Pueblo Indians, which the most hardened white invaders were to describe in such glowing terms, may never be known.

Yet the thought lingers that, at the dawn of history, a village society had emerged in which life seemed to be unified by a communal disposition of work and its products; by a procreative relationship with the natural world, one that found overt expression in fertility rites; by a pacification of the relationships between humans and the world around them. The hunter-gatherers may have left the world virtually untouched aside from the grasslands they cleared for the great herds, but such an achievement is safely marked by its absence of activity. There is a want of environmental artistry, of a landscape that has been left the better for humanity's presence, one that has the breath of mind as well as spirit bestowed upon it. Today, when the hunter-gatherer's mere parasitism of the environment has emerged as a virtue in juxtaposition to contemporary man's insane exploitation, we tend to fetishize restraint to the point of passivity and nondoing. Yet the matricentric horticulturists managed to touch the earth and change it, but with a grace, delicacy, and feeling that may be regarded as evolution's own harvest. Their archaeology is an expression of human artfulness and natural fulfillment. Neolithic artifacts seem to reflect a communion of humanity and nature that patently expressed the communion of humans with each other: a solidarity of the community with the world of life that articulated an intense solidarity within the community itself. As long as this internal solidarity persisted, nature was its beneficiary. When it began to decay, the surrounding world began to decay with it—and thence came the long wintertime of domination and oppression we normally call "civilization."

3 ❧ THE EMERGENCE OF HIERARCHY

The breakdown of early Neolithic village society marks a decisive turning point in the development of humanity. In the millennia-long era that separates the earliest horticultural communities from the "high civilizations" of antiquity, we witness the emergence of towns, cities, and finally empires—of a qualitatively new social arena in which the collective control of production was supplanted by elitist control, kinship relations by territorial and class relations, and popular assemblies or councils of elders by state bureaucracies.

This development occurred very unevenly. Where settled agricultural communities were invaded by pastoral nomads, the shift from one social arena to another may have occurred so explosively that it acquired apocalyptic proportions. Languages, customs, and religions seemed to replace each other with bewildering rapidity; old institutions (both heavenly and earthly) were effaced by new ones. But such sweeping changes were rare. More often than not, past and present were subtly melded together into a striking variety of social forms. In such cases, we witness a slow assimilation of traditional forms to new ends, a repeated use of old relationships for new purposes. In the complex interpenetration of old by new, early social forms may have lingered on through the entire span of post-Neolithic history. Not until the emergence of capitalism did the peasant village and its cultural repertory disappear as the locus of rural life—a fact that will be of considerable importance when we consider humanity's legacy of freedom.

Actually, the most complete shift occurred in the psychic apparatus of the individual. Even as the Mother Goddess continued to occupy a foremost place in mythology (but often adorned with the demonic traits required by patriarchy), women began to lose whatever parity they had with men—a change that occurred not only in their social status but in the very view they held of themselves. Both in home and economy, the social division of labor shed its traditional egalitarian features and acquired an increasingly hierarchical form. Man staked out a claim for the superiority of his work over woman's; later, the craftsman asserted his superiority over the food cultivator; finally, the thinker affirmed his sovereignty over the workers. Hierarchy established itself not only objectively, in the real, workaday world, but also subjectively, in the individual unconscious. Percolating into virtually every realm of experience, it has assimilated the syntax of everyday discourse—the very relationship between subject and object, humanity and nature. Difference was recast from its traditional status as unity in diversity into a linear system of separate, increasingly antagonistic powers—a system validated by all the resources of religion, morality, and philosophy.

⚭

What accounts for these vast changes in humanity's development, aside from the meteoric impact of the great historical invasions? And were their darker, often bloody aspects the unavoidable penalties we had to pay for social progress? Our answers to these questions touch on one of the major social problematics of our time—the role of scarcity, reason, labor, and technics in wrenching humanity from its "brutal" animal world into the glittering light of "civilization," or in Marxian terminology, from a world dominated by "necessity" to one dominated by "freedom." My use here of the word dominated is not to be taken lightly; its implications for Marxian theory will be examined later in this work. For the present, let me note that Enlightenment and, more pointedly, Victorian ideologies—the ideologies that Marx shared in their broad contours with liberal economists explained "man's ascent" from Neolithic "barbarism" to capitalism in strikingly similar ways. These explanations are worth reexamining—not so much to refute them but to place them in a larger perspective than nineteenth-century social theory could possibly attain.

According to these views, history's onward march from the stone age to the modern occurred primarily for reasons related to technological development: the development of advanced agricultural techniques, increasing material surpluses, and the rapid growth of human populations. Without the increases in material surpluses and labor "resources" that Neolithic society first began to make possible, humanity could never have developed a complex economy and political structure. We owe the advent of "civilization" to the early arts of systematic food cultivation and increasingly sophisticated tools like the wheel, kiln, smelter, and loom. All these provided an increasing abundance of food, clothing, shelter, tools, and transportation. With this basic reserve of food and technics, humanity acquired the leisure time to gain a greater insight into natural processes and settled into sedentary life-ways from which emerged our towns and cities, a large-scale agriculture based on grains, the plow, and animal power, and finally a rudimentary, machine technology.

But this development, presumably so rich in promise for humanity's self-fulfillment, has not been free of a Janus-faced ambiguity, of its dark side and treacherous aspects. The stream of human progress has been a divided one: The development toward material security and social complexity has generated contrapuntal forces that yield material insecurity and social conflict unique to "civilization" as such. On the one side, without the agrarian economy that the early Neolithic introduced, society would have been mired indefinitely in a brute subsistence economy living chronically on the edge of survival. Nature, so the social theorists of the past century held, is normally "stingy," an ungiving and deceptive "mother." She has favored humanity with her bounty only in a few remote areas of the world. Rarely has she been the giving nurturer created in distant times by mythopoeic thought. The "savage" of Victorian ethnography must always struggle (or "wrestle," to use Marx's term) with her to perpetuate life—which is ordinarily miserable and mercifully brief, tolerable at times but never secure, and only marginally plentiful and idyllic. Humanity's emergence from the constrictive world of natural scarcity has thus been perceived as a largely technical problem of placing the ungiving forces of nature under social command, creating and increasing surpluses, dividing labor (notably, separating crafts from agriculture), and sustaining intellectually productive urban elites. Thus, given the leisure time to think and administer society, these elites could create science, enlarge the entire sphere of human knowledge, and sophisticate human culture.* As Proudhon plaintively declared, echoing the prevailing spirit of the time:

> Yes, life is a struggle. But this struggle is not between man and man—it is between man and Nature; and it is each one's duty to share it.

Marx assumed the same view toward the "burden of nature." But he placed considerable emphasis on human domination as an unavoidable

---

* How much this entire ideological complex of rescuing "savages" from the trials of nature, of paganism, and of the ignorance of modern technology, not to speak of profligate values, accorded with the colonialist mentality of Europe and America is difficult to emphasize. Economistic interpretations of human social development, whether liberal or Marxian, provided a superb ideological rationale for bringing "savages" into history by placing them under Euro-American sovereignty, not only to "civilize" them culturally but to "industrialize" them technically. For Marx this consideration was all-important in his treatment of the colonial world, but it was no less important for such rugged imperialists as Kipling, H. Rider Haggard, and Leopold of Belgium.

feature of humanity's domination of the natural world. Until the development of modern industry (both Marx and Engels argued), the new surpluses produced by precapitalist technics may vary quantitatively, but rarely are they sufficient to provide abundance and leisure for more than a fortunate minority. Given the relatively low level of preindustrial technics, enough surpluses can be produced to sustain a privileged class of rulers, perhaps even a substantial one under exceptionally favorable geographic and climatic conditions. But these surpluses are not sufficient to free society as a whole from the pressures of want, material insecurity, and toil. If such limited surpluses were equitably divided among the multitudes who produce them, a social condition would emerge in which "*want* is made general," as Marx observed, "and with want the struggle for necessities and all the old shit would necessarily be reproduced." An egalitarian division of the surpluses would merely yield a society based on equality in poverty, an equality that would simply perpetuate the latent conditions for the restoration of class rule. Ultimately, the abolition of classes presupposes the "development of the productive forces," the advance of technology to a point where everyone can be free from the burdens of "want," material insecurity, and toil. As long as surpluses are merely marginal, social development occurs in a gray zone between a remote past in which productivity is too low to support classes and a distant future in which it is sufficiently high to abolish class rule.

Hence emerges the other side of humanity's drama: the negative side of its development, which conveys the real meaning of the "social problem" as used by Marxian theorists. Technical progress exacts a penalty for the benefits it ultimately confers on humanity. To resolve the problem of natural scarcity, the development of technics entails the reduction of humanity to a technical force. People become instruments of production, just like the tools and machines they create. They, in turn, are subject to the same forms of coordination, rationalization, and control that society tries to impose on nature and inanimate technical instruments. Labor is both the medium whereby humanity forges its own self-formation and the object of social manipulation. It involves not only the projection of human powers into free expression and selfhood but their repression by the performance principle of toil into obedience and self-renunciation. Self-repression and social repression form the indispensable counterpoint to personal emancipation and social emancipation.

For the present, it is important to ask if the problematic I have so summarily presented is quite as autonomous as earlier social theorists have claimed. Is it an inescapable drama—a dialectic that is woven into the human condition as the very substance of history? Does our "disembeddedness" from nature, our "ascent to civilization," and our human fulfillment involve a penalty—the domination of human by human as a precondition for the domination of nature by humanity— that may well turn the "success" of this historic project into a grim mockery by yielding the dehumanization of humanity and the immolation of society?

◌ℛ

In trying to answer these questions, we are again burdened by all the paradoxes created by hindsight. The drama that Victorian thought presents would seem irrefutable if we were to look backward from a history layered by stages in which the last stage imparts functions to the first such that every stage is a logical social descendant of previous ones. There is a certain wisdom in the view that the present enlarges the meaning of the past, which does not yet know itself fully in the light of its "destiny." But the notion of "destiny" must never be simplified to mean predestiny. History might well have followed different paths of development that could have yielded "destinies" quite different from those confronting us. And if so, it is important to ask what factors favored one constellation of possibilities over others. For the factors that have shaped our own history are deeply embedded in our sensibilities as the bad habits of the past—habits that we will have to cope with if we are to avoid the dark side of the future that lies before us.

Let us consider a factor that has played an important ideological role in shaping contemporary society: the "stinginess" of nature. Is it a given that nature is "stingy" and that labor is humanity's principal means of redemption from animality? In what ways are scarcity, abundance, and post-scarcity distinguishable from each other? Following the thrust of Victorian ideology, do class societies emerge because enough technics, labor, and "manpower" exist so that society can plunder nature effectively and render exploitation possible, or even inevitable? Or do economic strata usurp the fruits of technics and labor, later to consolidate themselves into clearly definable ruling classes?

In asking these questions, I am deliberately reversing the way in which Victorian social theorists have typically oriented such inquiries. And I am asking not if the notion of dominating nature gave rise to the domination of human by human but rather if the domination of human by human gave rise to the notion of dominating nature. In short, did *culture* rather than technics, *consciousness* rather than labor, or *hierarchies* rather than classes either open or foreclose social possibilities that might have profoundly altered the present human condition with its diminishing prospects of human survival?

Our contemporary commitment to the "logic of history" in its typically economistic form has made it difficult to provide a serious and meaningful account of the explosive clashes between tradition and innovation that must have occurred throughout history. Instead of looking at the past from the standpoint of its origins, we have made both past and future captive to the same belief in economic and technical inexorability that we have imposed on the present. Hence we have been serving up the present as the history of the past—a typically economistic history that slights the need for far-reaching changes in lifestyle, wants, sexual status, definitions of freedom, and communal relations. Accordingly, the stance we take with respect to human social development has a relevance that goes beyond our consciousness of the past. Recast in a more open and intellectually unconstrained manner, it may well provide us with a vision that significantly alters our image of a liberated future.

‰

How easily we can slip into a conventional historical stance can be seen from recent fervent controversies around the meaning given to the concept of scarcity. It has become rather fashionable to describe scarcity simply as a function of needs so that the fewer our needs and the smaller our tool-kit, the more "abundant," even "affluent," nature becomes. In its divine simplicity, this contention removes the need to strike a balance between humanity's obvious potentialities for producing a rich literary tradition, science, a sense of place, and a broad concept of shared humanity on the one side, and, on the other, the limits that an oral tradition, magic, a nomadic way of life, and a parochial sense of folkdom based on kinship place on these potentialities. Actually, by emphasizing material affluence per se in terms of needs and resources, this functional approach to scarcity subtly capitulates to the very economistic stance it is meant to correct. It merely recreates from a hunter-gatherer viewpoint a calculus of resources and wants that a bourgeois viewpoint imparted to social theory during the last century.

At the risk of an excursus, which may try the reader's patience, I would like to discuss the issue of scarcity in somewhat general terms and then return to my more concrete account of the emergence of hierarchy. Scarcity is not merely a functional phenomenon that can be described primarily in terms of needs or wants. Obviously, without a sufficiency in the means of life, life itself is impossible, and without a certain excess in these means, life is degraded to a cruel struggle for survival, irrespective of the level of needs. Leisure time, under these conditions, is not *free* time that fosters intellectual advances beyond the magical, artistic, and mythopoeic. To a large extent, the "time" of a community on the edge of survival is "suffering time." It is a time when hunger is the all-encompassing fear that persistently lives with the community, a time when the diminution of hunger is the community's constant preoccupation. Clearly, a balance must be struck between a sufficiency of the means of life, a relative freedom of time to fulfill one's abilities on the most advanced levels of human achievement, and ultimately, a degree of self-consciousness, complementarity, and reciprocity that can be called truly human in full recognition of humanity's potentialities. Not only the functional dictates of needs and wants but also a concept of human beings as more than "thinking animals" (to use Paul Shepard's expression) must be introduced to define what we mean by scarcity.

These distinctions raise a second and perhaps more complex problem: scarcity can not only impair human survival but also impede the actualization of human potentialities. Hence, scarcity can be defined in terms of its biological impact and also its *cultural* consequences. There is a point at which society begins to intervene in the formation of needs to produce a very special type of scarcity: a *socially* induced scarcity that expresses social contradictions. Such scarcity may occur even when technical development seems to render material scarcity completely unwarranted. Let me emphasize that I am not referring, here, to new or more exotic wants that social development may turn into needs. A society that has enlarged the cultural goals of human life may generate material scarcity even when the technical conditions exist for achieving outright superfluity in the means of life.

The issue of scarcity is not merely a matter of quantity or even of kind; it can also be a socially contradictory hypostatization of need as such. Just as capitalism leads to production for the sake of production, so too it leads to consumption for the sake of consumption. The great bourgeois maxim, "grow or die," has its counterpart in "buy or die." And just as the production of commodities is no longer related to their function as *use-values*, as objects of real utility, so wants are no longer related to humanity's sense of its real needs. Both commodities and needs acquire a blind life of their own; they assume a fetishized form, an irrational dimension, that seems to determine the destiny of the people who produce and consume them. Marx's famous notion of the "fetishization of commodities" finds its parallel in a "fetishization of needs." Production and consumption, in effect, acquire suprahuman qualities that are no longer related to technical development and the subject's rational control of the conditions of existence. They are governed instead by an ubiquitous market, by a universal competition not only between commodities but also between the creation of needs—a competition that removes commodities and needs from rational cognition and personal control.*

Needs, in effect, become a force of production, not a subjective force. They become blind in the same sense that the production of commodities becomes blind. Orchestrated by forces that are external to the subject, they exist beyond its control like the production of the very commodities that are meant to satisfy them. This autonomy of needs, as we shall see, is developed at the expense of the autonomy of the subject. It reveals a fatal flaw in subjectivity itself, in the autonomy and spontaneity of the individual to control the conditions of his or her own life.

To break the grip of the "fetishization of needs," to dispel it, is to recover the *freedom of choice*, a project that is tied to the freedom of the *self* to choose. The words *freedom* and *choice* must be emphasized: they exist cojointly and are tied to the ideal of the autonomous individual who is possible only in a free society. Although a hunter-gatherer community may be free from the needs that beleaguer us, it must still answer to very strict material imperatives. Such freedom as it has is the product not of choice but of limited means of life. What makes it "free" are the very *limitations* of its tool kit, not an expansive knowledge of the material world. In a truly *free* society, however, needs would be formed by *consciousness* and by *choice*, not simply by environment and tool kits. The affluence of a free society would be transformed from a wealth of things into a wealth of culture and individual creativity. Hence, want would depend not only on technological development but also on the cultural context in which it is formed. Nature's "stinginess" and technology's level of development would be important, but only as secondary factors in defining scarcity and need.

The problems of needs and scarcity, in short, must be seen as a problem of selectivity—of *choice*. A world in which needs compete with needs just as commodities compete with commodities is the warped

---

* Here, I cannot resist Karl Polanyi's priceless observation: "Rational action as such is the relating of ends to means; economic rationality, specifically, assumes means to be scarce. But human society involves more than that. What should be the end of man, and how should he choose his means? Economic rationalism, in the strict sense, has no answer to these questions, for they imply motivations and valuations of a moral and practical order that go beyond the logically irresistible, but otherwise empty exhortation to be 'economical." See Karl Polanyi, *The Livelihood of Man* (New York: Academic Press, 1977), p.13.

realm of a fetishized, limitless world of consumption. This world of limitless needs has been developed by the immense armamentorium of advertising, the mass media, and the grotesque trivialization of daily life, with its steady disengagement of the individual from any authentic contact with history. Although choice presupposes a sufficiency in the means of life, it does not imply the existence of a mindless abundance of goods that smothers the individual's capacity to select use-values rationally, to define his or her needs in terms of *qualitative*, ecological, humanistic, indeed, philosophical criteria. Rational choice presupposes not only a sufficiency in the means of life with minimal labor to acquire them; it presupposes above all a *rational society*.

Freedom from scarcity, or *post-scarcity*, must be seen in this light if it is to have any liberatory meaning. The concept presupposes that individuals have the material possibility of choosing what they need—not only a sufficiency of available goods from which to choose but a transformation of work, both qualitatively and quantitatively. *But none of these achievements is adequate to the idea of post-scarcity if the individual does not have the autonomy, moral insight, and wisdom to choose rationally*. Consumerism and mere abundance are mindless. Choice is vitiated by the association of needs with consumption for the sake of consumption—with the use of advertising and the mass media to render the acquisition of good an *imperative*— to make "need" into "necessity" devoid of rational judgment. What is ultimately at stake for the individual whose needs are rational is the achievement of an autonomous personality and selfhood. Just as work, to use Marx's concepts, defines the subject's identity and provides it with a sense of the ability to transform or alter reality, so needs too define the subject's rationality and provide it with a capacity to transform and alter the nature of the goods produced by work. In both cases, the subject is obliged to form judgments that reflect the extent to which it is rational or irrational, free and autonomous or under the sway of forces beyond its control. Post-scarcity presupposes the former; consumerism, the latter. *If the object of capitalism or socialism is to increase needs, the object of anarchism is to increase choice.* However much the consumer is deluded into the belief that he or she is choosing freely, the consumer is heteronymous and under the sway of a contrived necessity; the free subject, by contrast, is autonomous and spontaneously fulfills his or her rationally conceived wants.

In summary, it is not in the diminution or expansion of needs that the true history of needs is written. Rather, it is in the *selection* of needs as a function of the free and spontaneous development of the subject that needs become qualitative and rational. Needs are inseparable from the subjectivity of the "needer" and the context in which his or her personality is formed. The autonomy that is given to use-values in the formation of needs leaves out the personal quality, human powers, and intellectual coherence of their user. *It is not industrial productivity that creates mutilated use-values but social irrationality that creates mutilated users.*

Scarcity does not mean the same thing when applied to a "savage," peasant, slave, serf, artisan, or proletarian, any more than it means the same thing when it is applied to a chieftain, lord, master, noble, guild-master, or merchant. The *material* needs of a "savage," peasant, slave, serf, artisan, and proletarian are not so decisively different from each other, but the most important differences that do arise derive from the fact that their individual definitions of scarcity have changed significantly as a result of differences between need structures. Often, the needs of these oppressed classes are generated by their ruling-class counterparts. The history of white bread in the anthropology of needs, for example, is a metaphor for the extent to which tastes associated with gentility—not with physical well-being and survival—are turned into the needs of the lowly as compellingly, in the fetishism of needs, as the very means of survival. Similarly, the ascetic rejection by the lowly of their rulers' needs has functioned as a compensating role in imparting to the oppressed a lofty sense of moral and cultural superiority over their betters. In both cases, the fetishism of needs has impeded humanity in using its technics rationally and selecting its needs consciously.

Our own skewed concepts of scarcity and needs are even more compelling evidence of this fetishism. Until comparatively recent times, needs retained some degree of contact with material reality and were tempered by some degree of rationality. For all the cultural differences that surrounded the concept of scarcity and needs in the past, their fetishization was almost minimal by comparison with our own times. But with the emergence of a complete market society, the ideal of both limitless production and limitless needs became thoroughly mystified—no less by socialist ideologues than by their bourgeois counterparts. The restraints that Greek social theorists like Aristotle tried to place on the market, however much they were honored in the breach, were completely removed, and objects or use-values began to infiltrate the lofty human goals that society had elaborated from the days of their conception in the *polis*. The ideals of the past, in effect, had become so thoroughly bewitched by things that they were soon to become things rather than ideals. Honor, today, is more important as a credit rating than a sense of moral probity; personality is the sum of one's possessions and holdings rather than a sense of self-awareness and self-cultivation. One can continue this list of contrasts indefinitely.

Having demolished all the ethical and moral limits that once kept it in hand, market society in turn has demolished almost every historic relationship between nature, technics, and material well-being. No longer is nature's "stinginess" a factor in explaining scarcity, nor is scarcity conceived as a function of technical development that explains the creation or satisfaction of needs. Both the culture and the technics of modern capitalism have united to produce crises not of scarcity but of abundance or, at least, the expectation of abundance, all chit-chat about "diminishing resources" aside. Western society may accept the reality of economic crises, inflation, and unemployment, and popular credulity has not rejected the myth of a "stingy" nature that is running out of raw materials and energy resources. Abundance, all the more because it is being denied for structural economic reasons rather than natural ones, still orchestrates the popular culture of present-day society. To mix solid Victorian metaphors with contemporary ones: if "savages" had to perform heroic technical feats to extricate themselves from the "claw-and-fang" world of the jungle and arrive at a sense of their humanity, then modern consumers of market society will have to perform equally heroic ethical feats to extricate themselves from the shopping malls and recover their own sense of humanity.

To "disembed" themselves from the shopping mall, they may require more powerful agents than ethics. They may well require a superfluity of goods so immense in quantity that the prevailing fetishism of needs will have to be dispelled on its own terms. Hence, the ethical limits that were so redolent with meaning from Hellenic times onward may be inadequate today. We have arrived at a point in history's account of need where the very *capacity* to select needs, which freedom from material scarcity was expected to create, has been subverted by a strictly appetitive sensibility. Society may well have to be overindulged to recover its capacity for selectivity. To lecture society about its "insatiable" appetites, as our resource-conscious environmentalists are wont to do, is precisely what the modern consumer is not prepared to hear. And to impoverish society with contrived shortages, economic dislocations, and material deprivation is certain to shift the mystification of needs over to a more sinister social ethos, the mystification of scarcity. This ethos—already crystallized into the "life-boat ethic," "triage," and a new bourgeois imagery of "claw-and-fang" called *survivalism* marks the first steps toward ecofascism.

ଓ

If terms like scarcity and need are so conditional, once humanity is assured survival and material well-being, why did history betray the rich humanistic ideals it was to create so often in the past—especially when an equitable distribution of resources could have made them achievable? At the threshold of history, as a reading of the ancient texts indicates, an inertial tendency developed in which the attainment of the few to a high estate was inextricably identified with the debasement of the many to a low estate. The bas reliefs of Mesopotamia and Egypt, and later the writings of Plato and Aristotle, leave no doubt that the precondition for the emergence of tribal "big men" involved not only material sufficiency but cultural inferiority. Power, personality, and social immortality are entangled completely with powerlessness, depersonalization, and often genocide. "Big" and "small" have never been differences in size, socially speaking, but differences in *contrast*, just like "needs" and "luxuries" or "scarcity" and "security." Even to a mind as perceptive as Aristotle's, the greatness of the Hellenes was nature's compensation for the deficiencies of the barbarians. This notion, so compelling in all the relationships between ruler and ruled, often favors display over personal wealth, generosity over acquisition, hardiness over comfort, and self-denial over luxury. It is the former traits, rather than the latter, that elevate the "well-born" over the "ill-born." Much that passes for luxury in the precapitalist world was a lavish exhibition of power rather than pleasure. Repression has commonly been the affirmation of authority, not merely of exploitation, and we often misinterpret history when we suppose that the knout has been applied solely to extract labor rather than obedience. Indeed, the ruling classes of the past have dealt with the ruled as children, not merely as toilers—a fit that has its template as much in patriarchy as it does in technics.

But how did these hierarchical values crystallize out of the egalitarian communities I have described up to now? What social substance gave them reality long before classes and states emerged to give them almost unchallenged power? To ignore the increases in productivity and population of the early Neolithic would be as simplistic as to make them the all-important factor that changed early society's complementary values into later society's egocentric ones. Growing surpluses and "manpower" are much too weighty a fact to be ignored in explaining humanity's movement into history.

But here, too, we encounter a paradox that reverses the conventional interpretation surpluses in goods and labor are given in producing "civilization." The Neolithic villagers were more a species of *homo collectivicus* than the *homo economicus* we are today. Their social outlook was shaped by the habits of usufruct and the norms of the irreducible minimum, not by appetites of acquisition and rivalry. Cast into the avaricious and atomized world of capitalism, they would be horrified by the impersonal relationships and grasping egotism of bourgeois society. Thus, the psychological, institutional, and cultural problems these villagers faced in dealing with their new surpluses must have been formidable. How could they dispose of them without transgressing the community's norms of usufruct, complementarity and the irreducible minimum? How could they preserve the harmony and unity of the community in the face of new possibilities for differentials of wealth?

To answer these questions in terms of today's social standards would have been impossible, for these standards had yet to be devised. Many other standards, often totally at odds with our own, were adopted—most notably, disaccumulation rather than accumulation, of which the potlatch ceremonies of the Northwest Coast Indians are an extreme example. Even if we look beyond tribal life to more politically organized societies, we witness an orgy of mortuary construction and the rearing of lavish public buildings of which Egypt's pyramids and Mesopotamia's ziggurats are extreme examples of another kind. Conventional theories based on class analyses to the contrary notwithstanding, rulership rested less on proprietorship, personal possessions, wealth, and acquisition—in short, the *objects* that confer power—than it did on the *symbolic* weight of status, communal representation, religious authority, and the disaccumulation of goods that the Neolithic village had hallowed.

Hence, the moral premises of the early Neolithic village were never totally discarded until millennia later, with the emergence of capitalism. They were manipulated, modified, and often grotesquely distorted. But they persisted like an incubus within the new order of relationships—a menacing force from the past, always lurking within society as the memory of a "golden age." It is difficult to understand how notions of scarcity, emerging surpluses, technical advances, and authoritarian values could have contributed to the formation of classes and the State in the face of the distributive problems surpluses created for these egalitarian societies. The resistance of the Neolithic village to social forms like class, private property, acquisitiveness, and even patriarchy may well have exceeded the difficulties that "free market" capitalism encountered in removing the resistance of English agrarian society to a market economy (to borrow from Karl Polanyi's account).

Just as we must look within the medieval world to find the germinal bourgeois spirit that eventually dissolved the manor and guilds of feudal society, so we must look within the primordial community to find the early embryonic structures that transformed organic society into class society. These structures must be regarded as more fundamental than classes. They were hierarchies rooted in age, sex, and quasi-religious and quasi-political needs that created the power and the material relationships from which classes were formed. Given organic society's emphasis on usufruct, complementarity, and the irreducible minimum, it is difficult to believe that class rule, private property, and the State could have emerged, fully accoutred and omnipresent, largely because surpluses rendered their existence possible.

❧

Organic societies, even the most egalitarian, are not homogeneous social groups. Each member of the community is defined by certain everyday roles based on sex, age, and ancestral lineage. In early organic societies, these roles do not seem to have been structured along hierarchical lines, nor do they seem to have involved the domination of human by human. Generally, they simply define the individual's responsibilities to the community: the raw materials, as it were, for a functional status in the complex nexus of human relationships. Lineage determines who can or cannot marry whom, and families related by marriage are often as obligated to help each other as are kin directly related by blood ties. Age confers the prestige of experience and wisdom. Finally, sexual differences define the community's basic division of labor.

Even before material surpluses began to increase significantly, the roles each individual played began to change from egalitarian relationships into elites based increasingly on systems of obedience and command. To make this assertion raises a number of very provocative questions. Who were these emerging elites? What was the basis of their privileges in early society? How did they rework organic society's forms of community status—forms based on usufruct, a domestic economy, reciprocity, and egalitarianism—into what were later to become class and exploitative societies? These questions are not academic: they deal with emotionally charged notions that still lurk to this very day in the unconscious apparatus of humanity, notably the influence of biological facts, such as sex, age, and ancestry on social relationships. Unless these notions are carefully examined and the truths separated from the untruths, we are likely to carry an archaic legacy of domination into whatever social future awaits us.

Of the three roles cited, the sex-linked and age-linked are the most important and somewhat intertwined in the development of the hierarchies that preceded social classes and economic exploitation. For the purposes of clarity, however, we must explore these roles separately. To argue over whether the socialization of individuals into sex-related roles is based on biological facts would be to belabor the obvious; the physical differences between men and women clearly produce different sex-related capacities, at least in materially undeveloped societies. But the nature of these capacities and the extent to which they are reflected by the status of women in preliterate communities are issues that have been so highly colored by cultural biases that rarely are they adequately examined in the anthropological literature. Melville Jacobs rightly warns us that:

> Anthropologists of Euro-American origins face a problem of examining their projections of ideas and feelings about women's status into another socio-cultural system. To put it badly, judgments by anthropologists about the status of the feminine sex, when the provenience of such scientists is in western civilization whose women occupied a low status throughout the Christian era, are at once suspect if they have not obtained word-for-word native comments and then closely analyzed both them and overt behavior. And this is not a kind of research which can be completed in a day or two.

Such research has yet to be completed for most cultures, despite generations of sharp dispute in modern anthropology.

The fact is that male biases toward women almost consistently color what little research has been done on this touchy subject. Even though they may deny it, men (including the older generation of anthropologists) tend to believe that women are physically "weak" and that they inherently depend on men for their material survival in nature. In more imaginative moments, they regard women as emotionally "fragile" and innately lacking a capacity for "abstract thought."*

---

* How deeply ingrained these notions are in the male mind can be seen by examining the attitudes of male radicals, many of whom earnestly raised the banner of female emancipation as a basic social issue. Marx, for example, in response to personal questions by one of his daughters, remarked that what he liked most in a woman was "weakness." Robert Briffault, a Marxian anthropologist of the 1920s, whose three-volume work, *The Mothers*, was (despite all its deficiencies) a monumental critique of social biases toward women and their historical contributions, nevertheless concluded that "women are constitutionally deficient in the qualities that mark the masculine intellect.... Feminine differs from masculine intelligence in kind; it is concrete, not abstract; particularising, not

These notions find no support from disinterested research. Although women are normally physically weaker and shorter than men of the same ethnic background, the word weaker, here, is a relative term: it is relative to the muscular differences between women and men, not to the survival tasks that are imposed on humanity by the natural world. Male prejudice notwithstanding, women who have engaged in arduous work for most of their lives can match men in most physically demanding tasks, as many anthropological accounts of preliterate communities unwittingly reveal. They can certainly learn to hunt as well as men, given the opportunity to do so; normally, in fact, they catch whatever small animals they can find as part of their food-gathering activities. In many cultures, women not only collect the community's plant food, but they also do most of the fishing. If the family's shelter is a small one, it is usually they who build it, not the men. Women show as much endurance as men on long marches, and they commonly carry the same or heavier burdens.*

Where women haven't been conditioned into abject passivity, their emotional fortitude and mature behavior often make the men seem like spoiled children. As to their capacity for "abstract thought," women probably contributed a sizable number of religious formulators— the true "generalizers" in preliterate communities—to the prehistory of humanity, as the wide prevalence of Celtic and Nordic shamanesses and prophetesses attests. Nor should we forget, here, that the oracular messages at Delphi, on which the leading men of ancient Greece counted for guidance, were delivered by priestesses. If it was priests who interpreted these cryptic messages to suppliants, this may well have been a patriarchal modification of a more archaic practice, when female prophetesses and chtonic "matriarchal" goddesses occupied a preeminent religious position in organic society.

So much for the "innate" limitations that men so often attribute to women. As for their early status, a careful survey of food-gathering and hunting communities reveals that women enjoyed a higher degree of parity with men than we have been commonly led to believe. Both

---

generalising. The critical, analytical, and detached creative powers of the intellect are less developed in women than in men." See Erich Fromm, ed., *Marx's Concept of Man* (New York: Frederick L. Ungar, Inc., 1959), p. 296; Robert Briffault, *The Mothers* (New York: The MacMillan Co., 1927), Vol. III, p. 507.

* To cite only one of many examples: Elizabeth Marshall Thomas, who spent many months with the Bushmen of the Kalahari Desert, describes one of their young women, Tsetchwe, slight-boned and well under five feet, who entered the camp with a sackload of melons and firewood after food-gathering on the plains. With her infant son riding on

sexes occupy a distinctly sovereign role in their respective spheres, and their roles are much too complementary economically to make the domination of women by men the comfortable social norm that biased white observers served up generations ago to allay the guilt-feelings of Victorian patriarchs. In daily life, women withdraw into a sorority based on their domestic and food-gathering activities and men into a fraternity of hunters. There, both sexes are completely autonomous. The sharply etched distinctions between "home" and the "world" that exist in modern society do not exist in organic communities. There, home and world are so closely wedded that a man, shut out from a family, is literally a nonsocial being—a being who is nowhere. Although the male tends, even in many egalitarian communities, to view himself as the "head" of the family, his stance is largely temperamental and accords him no special or domestic power. It is simply a form of boastfulness, for the hard facts of life vitiate his pretenses daily. Woman's food-gathering activities usually provide most of the family's food. She not only collects the food, but prepares it, makes the family's clothing, and produces its containers, such as baskets and coiled pottery. She is more in contact with the young than the male and takes a more "commanding" role in their development. If her husband is too overbearing, she can unceremoniously put him out of the hut or simply return to her own family where she and her children are certain of being provided for no matter what her family thinks of her decision. As she ages, her experience becomes a revered source of wisdom; she becomes a "matriarch" in many cases, the head of the family in fact, if not in form.

What women in preliterate communities distinctly *do* lack is the male's mobility. The human child's protracted development and dependency—a long period of mental plasticity that is vitally necessary for elaborating a cultural continuum—restricts the mother's capacity to move about freely. The primal division of labor that assigned hunting tasks to the male and domestic tasks to the female is based on a hard biological reality: A woman, coupled to a noisy infant, can scarcely be expected to practice the stealth and athleticism needed to hunt large animals. By its very nature, the mother-child relationship limits her to comparatively sedentary lifeways. Moreover, if woman is not weak in terms of her capacity to do hard work, she is certainly the "weaker sex" when pitted against armed, possibly hostile men from an alien community. Women need their men not only as hunters but also as guardians of the family and the group. Men become the community's guardians not by

it, Tsetchwe's load "must have weighed almost a hundred pounds ..."—and this load was not carried by the women for just a few feet or yards. See Elizabeth Marshall Thomas, *The Harmless People* (New York: Vintage Books, 1958), p. 90.

virtue of usurpation, but because they are better equipped muscularly in a materially undeveloped culture to defend their community against hostile marauders.*

Without saying as much, Elizabeth Marshall Thomas recounts an episode that sums up this hard reality in a striking fashion. As she and her party approached a suspicious group of Bushmen, the band "drew back and together, the women behind the men, babies in their arms, and watched us hostilely." This is a very primeval tableau. It must have occurred countless times over the ages—the women, with babies in their arms behind the men, their protectors. And it is also a very revealing tableau, latent with major implications for the future development of the early group. For not only hunting, but also defense and later war are part of the male's division of labor. Insofar as these responsibilities require the conscious administrative coordination of people and resources, they are not merely hard biological facts of life; instead, they are uniquely *social* facts, or what we, in the modern world, are likely to call *political.*

ॐ

As bands began to increase in size and number, as they began to differentiate into clans, tribes, tribal federations and make war on each other, an ever larger social space emerged that was increasingly occupied by men. Men tended to become the clan headsmen or tribal chiefs and fill the councils of tribal federations. For all of this was "men's work," like hunting and herding animals. They had the mobility and physical prowess to defend their own communities, attack hostile communities, and thereby administer an extrabiological, distinctly social sphere of life.

In communities where matrilineal descent carried considerable cultural weight and woman's horticultural activities formed the basis of economic life, she assumed social roles very similar in form to those of the man's. Usually, she occupied these roles on the clan level, rarely on the tribal one. Moreover, she almost invariably shared her social role with males. In a matricentric society, these males were her brothers, not her husband. What woman's social eminence in matricentric communities reveals, however, is that the male's rising position in social affairs results not from any conscious degradation of woman to a domestic

---

* These observations on the male's well-developed muscular capacities are not meant to deny the female's considerable strength. The physical differences between the sexes are relative. Early society made the most of these differences because it had to, but it did not fetishize them or polarize them as we do into "strong men" and "fragile women." Nor did it extend their physical differences to character and personality.

"unworldly" sphere. To the contrary, what it clearly shows is that, in the beginning at least, the male did not have to "usurp" power from the female; indeed, social "power" as such did not exist and had yet to be created. The social sphere and the man's position in it emerged naturally. The primordial balance that assigned complementary economic functions to both sexes on the basis of parity slowly tipped toward the male, favoring his social preeminence.

But here I must introduce a discordant note. Even as the scale tipped slowly toward the male, his increasing preeminence began to alter the temperament of the primeval group. The social sphere emerged not only as an elaboration of the role in the division of labor; it also tended to assimilate his temperament as a hunter, a guardian, and eventually as a warrior. Doubtless, the new development toward a male-oriented culture occurred very slowly and with many lapses, generally modified by the shifting economic roles of the sexes in the course of social development. In largely food-gathering societies, the community seems to be essentially matricentric in culture and temperament; so, too, in early horticultural societies. On the other hand, in predominantly hunting and pastoral societies, a patricentric culture and temperament seems to predominate. Yet, on this obscure shifting ground of prehistory, one senses a slow crystallization of social norms and moods along male-oriented lines, even before elaborate hierarchies and economic exploitation emerge. With the rise of cities, the biological matrix of social life is almost completely shattered. Kinship ties are replaced by civic ties; the natural environment by a man-made environment; the domestic sphere by a political sphere. Not only patricentricity but patriarchy, for which there is no female analogue in organic communities, come into their own completely.*

But this development occurs much later. For the present let us examine the differences in temperament between the two sexes and determine if the shift from a matricentric to a patricentric outlook introduced the elements of domination into preliterate societies.

The male, in a hunting community, is a specialist in violence. From the earliest days of his childhood, he identifies with such "masculine" traits

---

* Here, I must reiterate the point that a "matriarchy," which implies the domination of men by women, never existed in the early world simply because domination itself did not exist. Hence, Levi-Strauss's "proof," so widely cited these days, that men have always "ruled" women because no evidence exists that women ever "ruled" men is simply irrelevant. What is really at issue is whether "rule" existed at all. When Levi-Strauss assumes that "rule" always existed, he merely projects his own social outlook into early society—ironically a typically masculine trait to which even Simone de Beauvoir falls victim in her splendid work, *The Second Sex*.

as courage, strength, self-assertiveness, decisiveness and athleticism—traits necessary for the welfare of the community. The community, in turn, will prize the male for these traits and foster them in him. If he becomes a good hunter, he will be highly regarded by everyone: by envious men and admiring women, by respectful children and emulative youths. In a society preoccupied with the problem of survival and obliged to share its resources, a good hunter is an asset to all.

Similarly, the female is a specialist in child rearing and food-gathering. Her responsibilities focus on nurture and sustenance. From childhood she will be taught to identify with such "feminine" traits as caring and tenderness, and she will be trained in comparatively sedentary occupations. The community, in turn, will prize her for these traits and foster them in her. If she cultivates these traits, she will be highly regarded for her sense of responsibility to her family, her skill and artfulness. In a matricentric society, these traits will be elevated into social norms that could well be described as the temperament of the community. We find this temperament today in many American Indian and Asian villages that practice horticulture, even if the kinship system is patrilineal. Similarly, in a patricentric society, "masculine" traits will be elevated into the norms of a community temperament, although they rarely coexist with matrilineal systems of kinship.

There is no intrinsic reason why a patricentric community, *merely* because it has a "masculine" temperament, must be hierarchical or reduce women to a subjugated position. The economic roles of the two sexes are still complementary; without the support that each sex gives to the other, the community will disintegrate. Moreover, both sexes still enjoy complete autonomy in their respective spheres. In projecting our own social attitudes into preliterate society, we often fail to realize how far removed a primordial domestic community is from a modern political society. Later, in a review of early mythology, I shall show that the concept of power is still highly amorphous and undifferentiated in the primordial world. As long as the growing civil sphere is a pragmatic extension of the male's role in the division of labor, it is merely that and no more. Even while the civil sphere is expanding, it is still rooted in domestic life and, in this sense, enveloped by it; hence, the numinous power that surrounds woman in the most patricentric of primordial societies.

Only when social life itself undergoes hierarchical differentiation and emerges as a separate terrain to be organized on its own terms do we find a conflict between the domestic and civil spheres—one that extends hierarchy into domestic life and results not only in the subjugation of woman, but in her degradation. Then, the distinctively "feminine" traits, which primordial society prizes as a high survival asset, sink to the level of social subordination. The woman's nurturing capacities are degraded to renunciation; her tenderness to obedience. Man's "masculine" traits are also transformed. His courage turns into aggressiveness; his strength is used to dominate; his self-assertiveness is transformed into egotism; his decisiveness into repressive reason. His athleticism is directed increasingly to the arts of war and plunder.

Until these transformations occur, however, it is important to know the raw materials from which hierarchical society will raise its moral and social edifice. The violation of organic society is latent within organic society itself. The primal unity of the early community, both internally and with nature, is weakened merely by the elaboration of the community's social life—its ecological differentiation. Yet, the growing civil space occupied by the male is still enveloped in a natural matrix of blood-ties, family affinities, and work responsibilities based on a sexual division of labor. Not until distinctly social interests emerge that clash directly with this natural matrix and turn the weaknesses, perhaps the growing tensions, of organic society into outright fractures, will the unity between human and human, and between humanity and nature, finally be broken. Then power will emerge, not simply as a social fact, with all its differentiations, but as a concept—and so will the concept of freedom.

ଔ

To find what is perhaps the one primary group that, more than any other in preliterate communities, transects kinship lines and the division of labor that in its own right forms the point of departure for a separate social interest as distinguished from the complementary relations that unite the community into a whole—we must turn to the age group, particularly to the community's elders. To be born, to be young, to mature, and finally to grow old and die is a natural fact—as much as it is to be a woman, a man, or belong to a blood-lineage group. But the older one becomes, the more one acquires distinct interests that are not "natural." These interests are uniquely social. The later years of life are a period of diminishing physical powers; the declining years, a period of outright dependency. The aging and the aged develop interests that are tied neither to their sexual roles nor to their lineage. They depend for their survival ultimately on the fact that the community is social in the fullest sense of the term; that it will provide for them not because they participate in the process of production and reproduction, but because of the *institutional* roles they can create for themselves in the social realm.

The sexes complement each other economically; the old and the young do not. In preliterate communities, the old are vital repositories of knowledge and wisdom, but this very function merely underscores the fact that their capacities belong largely to the cultural and social sphere. Hence, even more than the boasting self-assertive male who may be slowly gaining a sense of social power, the aging and the aged tend to be socially conscious as such—as a matter of survival. They share a common interest independent of their sex and lineage. They have the most to gain by the institutionalization of society and the emergence of hierarchy, for it is within this realm and as a result of this process that they can retain powers that are denied to them by physical weakness and infirmity. Their need for social power, and for hierarchical social power at that, is a function of their loss of biological power. The social sphere is the only realm in which this power can be created and, concomitantly, the only sphere that can cushion their vulnerability to natural forces. Thus, they are the architects *par excellence* of social life, of social power, and of its institutionalization along hierarchical lines.

The old can also perform many functions that relieve young adults of certain responsibilities. Old women can care for the children and undertake sedentary productive tasks that would otherwise be performed by their daughters. Similarly, old men can make weapons and teach their sons and grandsons to use them more effectively. But these tasks, while they lighten the burdens of the young, do not make the old indispensable to the community. And in a world that is often harsh and insecure, a world ruled by natural necessity, the old are the most dispensable members of the community. Under conditions where food may be in short supply and the life of the community occasionally endangered, they are the first to be disposed of. The anthropological literature is replete with examples in which the old are killed or expelled during periods of hunger, a practice that changes from the episodic into the customary in the case of communities that normally leave their aged members behind to perish whenever the group breaks camp and moves to a different locale.

Thus, the lives of the old are always clouded by a sense of insecurity. This sense is incremental to the insecurity that people of all ages may feel in materially undeveloped communities. The ambiguity that permeates the outlook of the primordial world toward nature— a shifting outlook that mixes reverence or ecological adaptation with fear—is accented among the aged with a measure of hatred, for insofar as fear is concerned they have more to fear from nature's vicissitudes than do the young. The nascent ambiguities of the aged toward nature later give rise to Western "civilization's" mode of repressive reason. This exploitative rationality pits civil society against domestic society and launches social elites on a quest for domination that, in a later historical context, transforms insecurity into egotism, acquisitiveness, and a craze for rule-in short, the social principle graduated by its own inner dialectic into the asocial principle. Here, too, are the seeds for the hatred of eros and the body, a hatred, in turn, that forms the archetypal matrix for willful aggression and the Thanatic death wish.

Initially, the medium by which the old create a modicum of power for themselves is through their control of the socialization process. Fathers teach their sons the arts of getting food; mothers, their daughters. The adults, in turn, consult their parents on virtually every detail of life, from the workaday pragmatic to the ritual. In a preliterate community, the most comprehensive compendium of knowledge is inscribed on the brains of the elders. However much this knowledge is proffered with concern and love, it is not always completely disinterested; it is often permeated, even if unconsciously, by a certain amount of cunning and self-interest. Not only is the young mind shaped by the adults, as must necessarily be the case in all societies, but it is shaped to respect the wisdom of the adults, if not their authority. The harsh initiation ceremonies that many preliterate communities inflict on adolescent boys may well have the purpose of using pain to "brand" the elders' wisdom on young minds, as a number of anthropologists contend; but I would also suggest that it "brands" a sense of their authority as well. The aged; who abhor natural necessity, become the embodiment of social necessity; the dumb "cruelty" that the natural world inflicts on them is transmitted by social catalysis into the conscious cruelty they inflict on the young. Nature begins to take her revenge on the earliest attempts of primordial society to control her. But this is nature internalized, the nature in humanity itself. The attempt to dominate external nature will come later, when humanity is conceptually equipped to transfer its social antagonisms to the natural world outside. By drinking at the magic fountain of wisdom, however, the educators are educated into the temperament of repressive rationality. The toll demanded by nature in the Norse cosmography is already being claimed: the wounded eye of Odin begins to lose its vision.

ᘓ

In fairness to primordial society, we must note that hierarchy founded merely on age is not institutionalized hierarchy. Rather, it is hierarchy in its most nascent form: hierarchy embedded in the matrix of equality. For age is the fate of everyone who does not die prematurely. To the extent that privileges accrue to the elders, everyone in the community is heir to them. Inasmuch as these privileges vary with the fortunes of the community, they are still too tenuous to be regarded as more than compensations for the infirmities that elders must suffer with the aging process. The primordial balance that accords parity to all members of the community, women as well as men, is thereby perpetuated in the privileges accorded to the old. In this sense they cannot be regarded simply as privileges.

What is problematical in the future development of hierarchy is *how* the elders tried to institutionalize their privileges and *what* they finally achieved. Radin, in a perceptive if overly ruthless discussion of age-linked hierarchy, notes that the elders in food-gathering communities "almost always functioned as medicine-men of some kind or another," and, with the development of clan-agricultural societies, acquired their "main strength" from the "rituals and ritualistic societies which they largely controlled." Social power begins to crystallize as the fetishization of magical power over certain forces of nature. In trying to deal with this dialectical twist, we must refocus our perspective to include an entirely unique mode of social sensibility and experience, one that is strikingly modern: the sensibility and experience of the elder *cum* shaman.

The shaman is a strategic figure in any discussion of social hierarchy because he (and, at times, she, although males predominate in time) solidifies the privileges of the elders—a general stratum in the primordial community—into the particularized privileges of a special segment of that stratum. He professionalizes power. He makes power the privilege of an elect few, a group that only carefully chosen apprentices can hope to enter, not the community as a whole. His vatic personality essentially expresses the insecurity of the individual on the scale of a social neurosis. If the male hunter is a specialist in violence, and the woman food-gatherer a specialist in nurture, the shaman is a specialist in fear. As magician and divinator combined in one, he mediates between the suprahuman power of the environment and the fears of the community. Weston La Barre observes that in contrast to the priest, who "implores the Omnipotent," the shaman is "psychologically and socially the more primitive of the two .... External powers invade and leave his body with practiced ease, so feeble are his ego boundaries and so false his fantasies." Perhaps more significant than this distinction is the fact that the shaman is the incipient State personified. As distinguished from other members of the primordial community, who participate coequally in the affairs of social life, the shaman and his associates are professionals in political manipulation. They tend to subvert the innocence and amateurism that distinguishes domestic society from political society. Shamans "banded informally [together] even in the simplest food-gathering civilizations," notes Radin. "As soon as the clan political patterns emerged we find them formally united together, either in one group or separately." Bluntly stated, the shamanistic groups to which Radin alludes were incipient political institutions.

Their political role is given greater emphasis by Weston La Barre in his massive study of shamanism and crisis cults:

> Every cultist ingroup is incipiently an autonomous entity, a closed society, a political unit, and therefore every Church is a potential State. Overemphasized in explaining crisis cults, the political has been curiously neglected in most studies of shamanism. Both North American and Siberian shamans ... were often leaders as well as protectors of their groups; and South American shaman-messiahs commonly combined political and magical power over men and cosmos alike. Paul Roux has studied the power equally over the elements and political events among the shamans of Genghis Khan; and Rene de Nebesky-Wojkowitz has shown that the state oracle or ceremonial divination in Tibet is a prophetic trance of distinctly shamanistic character. The ancient Chinese *wu* were political shamans too. Clearly the Asiatic and American shaman has the same traditional roots, and his intrinsic political aspect reappears strikingly in the messianic ghost dance prophets of North America and in the god-kings and shaman-chiefs of South America, Amazonian and Andean alike.

For several pages thereafter, La Barre adduces data of a similar character for almost every area of the world and nearly every early civilization, including the Greco-Roman.

But the shaman's position in primordial society is notoriously insecure. Often highly remunerated for his magical services, he might be as vindictively attacked, perhaps assassinated outright, if his techniques fail. Thus, he must always seek alliances and, more significantly, foster the creation of mutually advantageous power centers for his protection from the community at large. As a quasi-religious formulator, a primitive cosmologist, he literally creates the ideological mythos that crystallizes incipient power into actual power. He may do this in concert with the elders, enhancing their authority over the young, or with the younger but more prominent warriors, who tend to form military societies of their own. From them, in turn, he receives the support he so direly needs to cushion the ill-effects that follow from his fallibility. That he may compete with these powers and attempt to usurp their authority is irrelevant at this period of development. The point is that the shaman is the demiurge of political institutions and coalitions. He not only validates the authority of the elders with a magico-political aura but, in his need for political power, he tends to heighten the "masculine" temperament of a patricentric community. He exaggerates the aggressive and violent elements of that temperament, feeding it with mystical sustenance and supernatural power.

❧

Domination, hierarchy, and the subordination of woman to man now begin to emerge. But it is difficult to delineate in this development the emergence of organized economic classes and the systematic exploitation of a dominated social stratum. The young, to be sure, are placed under the rule of a clan or tribal gerontocracy; the elders, shamans, and warrior chiefs, in turn, acquire distinct social privileges. But so ingrained in society are the primordial rules of usufruct, complementarity and the irreducible minimum that the economy of this early world proves to be surprisingly impervious to these sociopolitical changes. "The majority of aboriginal tribes," observes Radin, "possessed no grouping of individuals based on true class distinctions." He adds that "Slaves not a few of them had, but, while their lives were insecure because they had no status, they were never systematically forced to do menial work or regarded as an inferior and degraded class in our sense of the term." Men of wealth there were, too, in time, but as Manning Nash observes, "in primitive and peasant economies leveling mechanisms play a crucial role in inhibiting aggrandizement by individuals or by special groups." These leveling mechanisms assume a variety of forms:

> forced loans to relatives or co-residents; a large feast following economic success; a rivalry of expenditures like the potlatch of the Northwest Coast Indians in which large amounts of valuable goods were destroyed; the ritual levies consequent on holding office in civil and religious hierarchies in Meso-America; or the giveaways of horses and goods of the Plains Indians. Most small-scale economies have a way of scrambling wealth to inhibit reinvestment in technical advance, and this prevents crystallization of class lines on an economic base.

In fact, independent wealth, the most precious of personal goals in bourgeois society, tends to be highly suspect in preliterate societies.

Often, it is taken as evidence that the wealthy individual is a sorcerer who has acquired his riches by a sinister compact with demonic powers. Wealth so acquired is "treasure," bewitched power concretized, the stuff from which mythology weaves its Faustian legends. The very "independence" of this wealth—its freedom from direct social control—implies a breach with the most basic of all primordial rules: the mutual obligations imposed by blood ties. The prevalence of the lineage system, as distinguished from "civilization's" territorial system, implies that, even if hierarchy and differentials in status exist, the community consists of kin; its wealth, as Patrick Malloy observes, must be "used to reinforce or expand social relations," not weaken or constrict them. Wealth can be acquired only within the parameters of the lineage system, and it effectively filters down to the community through the workings of the "leveling system." As Malloy astutely observes: the "richest man" in the community will frequently "be the worst off because he has given all of his material wealth away." He has definite obligations "to provide gifts when requested, take care of bride-wealth, and other important functions critical to the survival of the community."

Thus, nature still binds society to herself with the primal blood oath. This oath validates not only kinship as the basic fact of primordial social life, but its complex network of rights and duties. Before hierarchy and domination can be consolidated into social classes and economic exploitation; before reciprocity can give way to the "free exchange" of commodities; before usufruct can be replaced by private property, and the "irreducible minimum" by toil as the norm for distributing the means of life—before this immensely vast complex can be dissolved and replaced by a class, exchange, and propertied one, the blood oath with all its claims must be broken.

Hierarchy and domination remain captive to the blood oath until an entirely new social terrain can be established to support class relations and the systematic exploitation of human by human. We must fix this *pre*class, indeed, *pre*economic, period in social development clearly in our minds because the vast ideological corpus of "modernity"—capitalism, particularly in its western form—has been designed in large part to veil it from our vision. Even such notions as primitive communism, matriarchy, and social equality, so widely celebrated by radical anthropologists and theorists, play a mystifying role in perpetuating this veil instead of removing it. Lurking within the notion of primitive communism is the insidious concept of a "stingy nature," of a "natural scarcity" that dictates communal relations—as though a communal sharing of things is exogenous to humanity and must be imposed by survival needs to overcome an "innate" human egoism that "modernity" so often identifies with "selfhood." Primitive communism also contains the concept of property, however "communal" in character, that identifies selfhood with ownership. Usufruct, as the transgression of proprietary claims in any form, is concealed by property as a public institution. Indeed, "communal property" is not so far removed conceptually and institutionally from "public property," "nationalized property," or "collectivized property" that the incubus of proprietorship can be said to be removed completely from sensibility and practices of a "communist" society. Finally, "matriarchy," the rule of society by women instead of men, merely alters the nature of rule; it does not lead to its abolition. "Matriarchy" merely changes the gender of domination and thereby perpetuates domination as such.

"Natural scarcity," "property," and "rule" thus persist in the very name of the critique of class society, exploitation, private property, and the acquisition of wealth. By veiling the primordial blood oath that constrains the development of hierarchy and domination into class society, economic exploitation, and property, the class critique merely replaces the constraints of kinship with the constraints of economics instead of transcending *both* to a higher realm of freedom. It reconstitutes bourgeois right by leaving property unchallenged by usufruct, rule unchallenged by nonhierarchical relationships, and scarcity unchallenged by an abundance from which an ethical selectivity of needs can be derived. The more critical substrate of usufruct, reciprocity, and the irreducible minimum is papered over *by a less fundamental* critique: the critique of private property, of injustice in the distribution of the means of life, and of an unfair return for labor. Marx's own critique of justice in his remarks on the Gotha Program remains one of the most important contributions he made to radical social theory, but its economistic limitations are evident in the tenor of the work as a whole.

These limitations acquire an almost stark character in the European centricity of his sense of history, particularly as revealed in his emphasis on the "progressive role of capitalism" and his harsh metaphors for the noncapitalist world. Is it true, as Marx emphasized, that "human progress," after mastering "the results of the bourgeois epoch, the market of the world and the modern powers of production" by placing them "under the common control of the most advanced peoples" (notably, Europeans) will "cease to resemble that hideous pagan idol, who would not drink the nectar but from the skulls of the slain"? These remarks reveal Victorian arrogance at its worst and patently neglect the vital "prehistory" that the nonwestern world had elaborated over many millennia of development.

It is important to remember that class society is not the creation of humanity as a whole. In its most ruthless form, it is the "achievement" of that numerically small proportion of "advanced peoples" who were largely confined to Europe. By far, the great mass of human beings who occupied the planet before the Age of Exploration had developed alternatives of their own to capitalism, even to class society. By no means do we have the right to regard them as arrested societies that awaited the gentle caress of "civilization" and the sculpting of the crucifix. That their social forms, technologies, cultural works, and values have been degraded to mere "anthropologies" rather than histories in their own right is testimony to an intellectual atavism that views anything but its own social creations as mere "remains" of its "prehistory" and the "archaeology" of its own social development.

What we so arrogantly call the "stagnation" of many non-European societies may well have been a different, often highly sensitive, elaboration and enrichment of cultural traits that were ethically and morally incompatible with the *predatory* dynamism Europeans so flippantly identify with "progress" and "history." To fault these societies as stagnant for elaborating qualities and values that Europeans were to sacrifice to quantity and egoistic acquisition tells us more about European conceptions of history and morality than non-European conceptions of social life.

Only now, after our own "pagan idols" such as nucleonics, biological warfare, and mass culture have humiliated us sufficiently, can we begin to see that non-European cultures may have followed complex social paths that were often more elegant and knowledgeable than our own. Our claims to world cultural hegemony by right of conquest has boomeranged against us. We have been obliged to turn to other cultures not only for more humane values, more delicate sensibilities, and richer ecological insights, but also for *technical* alternatives to our highly mystified "powers of production"—powers that have already begun to overpower us and threaten the integrity of life on the planet. But until recently, our prevailing system of domination not only blinded us to the full history of our own social development; it also prevented a clear understanding of alternative social developments—some vastly better than our own, others as bad but rarely worse. If these developments are to provide us with alternative ethical and technical pathways to a better future, we must first reexamine the vast legacy of domination that has so far blocked our vision.

4 ∝ EPISTEMOLOGIES OF RULE

The shift from hierarchical to class societies occurred on two levels; the material and the subjective. A clearly material shift was embodied in the emergence of the city, the State, an authoritarian technics, and a highly organized market economy. The subjective shifts found expression in the emergence of a repressive sensibility and body of values—in various ways of mentalizing the entire realm of experience along lines of command and obedience. Such mentalities could very well be called *epistemologies of rule*, to use a broad philosophical term. As much as any material development, these epistemologies of rule fostered the development of patriarchy and an egoistic morality in the rulers of society; in the ruled, they fostered a psychic apparatus rooted in guilt and renunciation. Just as aggression flexes our bodies for fight or flight, so class societies organize our psychic structures for command or obedience.

A repressive rationality, not to be confused with reason as such, rendered the social change from organic society to class society highly ambiguous in character. Reason has always identified human fulfillment with a consciousness of self, with logical clarity, and with salvation from humanity's complete absorption into the misty world of the mythopoeic. Even matters of faith and religion have been interpreted rationally—as highly systematic theologies rationally derived from a few fundamental beliefs. But this vast project of humanization—from organic to class society—occurred without a clear ethical basis for human fulfillment, one that had a definite rational content. Hence the emergence of class society was to be burdened from its outset by a paradox: how can reason, conceived as a *tool* or method for achieving ethical goals, be integrated with reason conceived as the inherent feature or *meaning* of these ethical goals?

Tragically, it was not left to reason alone, as the great thinkers of the Enlightenment so optimistically believed, to resolve this paradox. Crises have riddled class society from its inception. In the western world, at least, they have produced a legacy of domination so formidable that it threatens to push us into an abyss that may engulf social life itself. The result has been the emergence of a misplaced antirationalism so blistering and introverted in its hostility to mind that it has literally lost sight of the legacy of domination itself. In surrendering mind to intuition, rationality to mere impulse, coherence to eclecticism, and wholeness to a mystical "oneness," we may very well reinforce this legacy if only because we refuse to dispel it with the means of rational analyses.

In our reaction to Enlightenment thought, we must rescue reason without becoming "rationalistic," without reducing reason to mere technique. Rarely has society been so direly in need of a clear understanding of the way we mentalize rule and of the history of domination than today, when the very survival of humanity is at stake. In any case, it is only in the *use* of reason rather than in rationalizing about reason that mind reveals its promises and pitfalls. It would be better to use our rational faculties and reflect on them later than to lose them altogether to a dark heritage that may obliterate mind itself.

∞

The material and subjective levels on which hierarchical societies crystallized into class societies are not sharply separable. Or to use the language of Victorian social thought, we cannot comfortably speak of one level as the "base" for the other; both, in fact, are inextricably intertwined. The city, which from the beginnings of history appears as the "effect" of basic changes from kinship to territorialism, is so crucially important as the arena for dissolving the blood oath that it can only be regarded as a "cause," however ancillary it seems to important changes in technics and ideology. In fact, urban life from its inception occupies such an ambiguous place in the commonsense logic of cause and effect that we would do well to use these concepts gingerly.

This much is clear: the blood oath which, more than any single factor, held together primordial values and institutions with a certain degree of integrity, could only be surmounted after the claims of blood ties could be replaced by those of civic ties. Only after the territorial system began to dissolve the kinship system or, at least, attenuate its nexus of responsibilities, could hallowed terms like brother and sister cease to be compelling natural realities.* Thereafter, "brotherhood" increasingly came to

---

* This is not to say that the emergence of cities immediately conferred citizenship on its occupants, irrespective of their ethnic or social status. Quite to the contrary: ethnicity, whether real or fictive, still formed the juridical basis for urban consociation; only gradually

mean a commonality of material and political interests rather than those of kinship, and "sisters" were to become the means for establishing alliances—for uniting males into social fraternities based on military, political, and economic needs.

The social and cultural impact of these material and subjective factors, so clearly rooted in the development of the city and State, can hardly be overstated. Humanity was to cling to the primal blood oath with such tenacity that primordial social forms often remained intact even after they had been divested of their content. In many cases, the clans were not immediately destroyed; often they were retained and like the extended family persisted as mere shadows of the past. In fact, they were subtly reworked in certain societies into instrumentalities of the newly emerging State—first, in the service of early priestly corporations, later, in vestigial form, in the service of the military chieftains and kings.

Here, we sense the ideological activities of the early priesthood that had emerged from a reworking of shamanism. By freeing itself from the social vulnerabilities of the shaman, whose body constituted a mere vessel for spirits, the priestly corporation had acquired the role of a cosmic brokerage firm between humanity and its increasingly anthropomorphic deities—deities no longer to be confused with the nature spirits that peopled the environment of organic society. Theology began to gain ascendancy over divination. Seemingly rational accounts of the origins, workings, and destiny of the cosmos—laden with an epistemology of rule—tended to replace magic. By emphasizing the "guilt" of the human "wrong-doer" and the "displeasure" of the deities, the priestly corporation could acquire an immunity to failure that the shaman had always lacked. The *technical* failures of the shaman, which typically rendered his social status so insecure in primordial society, could be reinterpreted by the emerging priesthood as evidence of the *moral* failure of the community itself. Drought, diseases, floods, locust infestations, and defeats in warfare—to cite the Biblical afflictions of ancient humanity—were reinterpreted as the retribution of wrathful deities for communal wrong-doing, not merely as the dark work of malevolent spirits. Technical failure, in effect, was shifted from the priestly corporation to

did the city wean its dwellers from the realities or myths of a common ancestry. The most vulnerable victim of urban society was the clan or, perhaps more generally, corporate ties and responsibilities based on kinship. Until Roman times, when the exigencies of empire required loyalty from widely disparate ethnic groups, cities accorded privileges of one kind or another and in varying gradations to members, who shared claims to a common ancestry, rather 'than to strangers, who were often confined to separate quarters of the city as were Jews in the ghettoes of the medieval world.

a fallen humanity that had to atone for its moral frailties. And only priestly supplications, visibly reinforced by generous sacrifices in the form of goods and services, could redeem humanity, temper the punitive actions of the deities, and restore the earlier harmony that existed between humanity and its gods. In time, sacrifice and supplication became a constant effort in which neither the community nor its priestly corporation could relent. When this effort was institutionalized to the extent that the episodic became chronic, it created the early theocracies that go hand-in-hand with early cities, whose foci were always the temple, its priestly quarters, its storehouses, craft shops, and the dwellings of its artisans and bureaucracies. Urban life began with an altar, not simply a marketplace, and probably with walls that were meant to define sacred space from the natural, not simply as defensive palisades.

It is breathtaking to reflect on the intricate variety of ideological threads in this new tapestry, with its stark insignias of class and material exploitation. By converting mundane nature spirits and demons into humanlike supernatural deities and devils, the priestly corporation had cunningly created a radically new social and ideological dispensation— indeed, a new way of *mentalizing* rule. The guardian deity of the community increasingly became a surrogate for the community as a whole— literally, a personification and materialization of a primal solidarity that gradually acquired the trappings of outright social sovereignty. Ludwig Feuerbach was to unwittingly mislead us when he declared that our humanlike gods and goddesses were the projections of humanity itself into a larger-than-life religious world; actually, they were the projection of the priestly corporation into an all-too-real pantheon of social domination and material exploitation.

In any case, the communal lands and their produce, once available to all by virtue of the practice of usufruct, were now seen as the endowment of a supernatural deity whose earthly brokers voiced its wishes, needs, and commandments. Ultimately, they acquired theocratic sovereignty over the community, its labor, and its produce. Communal property, to toy with a contradiction in terms, had emerged with a vengeance as the communism of the godhead and its earthly administrators. The communal whole, which had once been at the disposition of the community *as a whole*, was now placed at the disposition of the deified "One," if only a patron deity in a supernatural pantheon, who in the very role of personifying the community and its unity had turned it into an obedient congregation ruled by a priestly elite. The nature spirits who had peopled the primordial world were absorbed into tutelary deities. The Mother Goddess who represented the fecundity of nature in all its diversity, with its rich variety of subdeities, was trampled down by the "Lord of Hosts," whose harsh moral codes were formulated in the abstract realm of his heavenly Supernature.

The clan, too, like the priestly corporation, was transformed into an economic corporation. Community, once conceived as the vital *activity* of communizing, became the source of passive communal labor, a mere instrument of production. Communal traits were valued insofar as they lent themselves to technical coordination, exploitation, and rationalization—a very ancient commentary on the exploitative nature of a communism structured around hierarchy. Hence clan society, far from being initially effaced, was used against itself to produce a wealth of material objects. The priestly corporation, in effect, had become a clan unto itself that raised itself like the Hebrew Levites above all clans. It had become something quite new: a *class*.

Accumulated wealth, now conceived as the sum of humanity's material sacrifices to the deities, was divested of the demonic traits that organic society had imputed to treasure. The wealthy temples that emerged in the Old World and New are testimony to a sacralization of accumulated wealth; later, of booty as the reward of valor; and finally, tribute as the result of political sovereignty. Gifts, which once symbolized alliance between people in mutual support systems, were now transformed into tithes and taxes for supernatural and political security. This steady reworking of the communal clans into labor forces, of communal lands into proprietary sacerdotal estates, of conciliatory myths into repressive religious dramas, of kinship responsibilities into class interests, of hierarchical command into class exploitation—all were to appear more like shifts of emphasis in traditional systems of right rather than marked ruptures with hallowed customs. Leaving the catastrophic effects of invasions aside, primordial society seems to have been seduced into the new social disposition of class society without clearly departing from the outlines of organic society.

But it was not within the temple precincts alone that these changes occurred. Fairly recent data from Mesopotamia and Robert McAdams's admirable comparisons of Mesoamerica with Mesopotamia reveal that the civil sphere of the male warrior was as deeply implicated in transforming organic society into class society as the sacerdotal sphere of the priestly corporation. The priesthood has the power of ideology— by no means insignificant, but a power that relies on persuasion and conviction. The warrior has the power of coercion—one that relies on the more compelling effects of physical prowess, weaponry, and violence.

While the interests of the priestly corporation and the military society intertwine, at times quite intimately, they often unravel and oppose each other. The warrior who confronts his opponent tends to be more demanding and certainly more thoroughgoing in the exercise of his interests than the priest who stands between the community and its deities as a sacerdotal agent or broker. Neither the ideologies nor the institutions these different historical figures create are identical or even calculated to produce the same social effects. The warrior societies that emerged within organic society were more thoroughgoing in uprooting it than the priestly corporations that emerged outside it—after it had already undergone considerable modification by hierarchical institutions and relegated shamanistic practices to a folk magic and medicine. The warriors supplanted their theocratic predecessors, actually leaning to all appearances on the very ideological changes that the theocracies had produced. Hence, it was the warrior chieftain and his military companions from whom history recruited its classical nobility and its manorial lords, who produced the political State, and later, the centralized monarchy with priestly vestiges of its own. This largely military fraternity cut across the lineage system of clan society with the power of a battle-ax and eventually all but destroyed its hold on social life. And again, the clans persisted, like the *capulli* of the Aztecs and the ascriptive family units of Sumerian society, although they were steadily divested of social power.

Theocracies are not incompatible with certain democratic features of tribal life, such as popular assemblies and councils of elders. Insofar as the privileges of the priestly corporation are respected, tribal democracy and theocracy may actually reinforce each other institutionally—the one, dealing with the material concerns of the body politic, the other dealing with the material concerns of the temple and the sacred. Between them, an active division of functions may emerge that the fraternal military societies can only regard as a humiliating restriction of their hunger for civil power. The earliest conflicts between Church and State were initially, in fact, three-way conflicts that involved the democratic claims of the clans—and, ultimately, their complete removal from the conflict.

☙

As I have argued for years, the State is not merely a constellation of bureaucratic and coercive institutions. It is also a state of mind, an instilled mentality for ordering reality. Accordingly, the State has a long history—not only institutionally but also psychologically. Apart from dramatic invasions in which conquering peoples either completely subdue or virtually annihilate the conquered, the State evolves in gradations, often coming to rest during its overall historical development in such highly incomplete or hybridized forms that its boundaries are almost impossible to fix in strictly political terms.

Its capacity to rule by brute force has always been limited. The myth of a purely coercive, omnipresent State is a fiction that has served the state machinery all too well by creating a sense of awe and powerlessness in the oppressed that ends in social quietism. Without a high degree of cooperation from even the most victimized classes of society such as chattel slaves and serfs, its authority would eventually dissipate. Awe and apathy in the face of State power are the products of social conditioning that renders this very power possible. Hence, neither spontaneous or immanent explanations of the State's origins, economic accounts of its emergence, or theories based on conquest (short of conquests that yield near-extermination) explain how societies could have leaped from a stateless condition to a State and how political society could have exploded upon the world.

Nor was there ever a single leap that could account for the immense variety of states and quasi-states that appeared in the past. The early Sumerian state, in which the governing *ensi,* or military overlords, were repeatedly checked by popular assemblies; the Aztec state, which was faced with a tug-of-war between the *capulli* and the nobility; the Hebrew monarchies, which were repeatedly unsettled by prophets who invoked the democratic customs of the "Bedouin compact" (to use Ernst Bloch's term); and the Athenian state, institutionally rooted in direct democracy—all of these, however much they differ from each other and conflict with the centralized bureaucratic states of modern times, constitute very incomplete developments of the State. Even the highly bureaucratic Pharaonic State of the Ptolemies left much of Egyptian village life untouched, despite its demands for taxes and corvee labor. The centralized states that emerged in the Near East and Asia were not as invasive of community life at the base of society as is the modern State, with its mass media, highly sophisticated surveillance systems, and its authority to supervise almost every aspect of personal life. The State, in the authentically finished, historically complete form we find today, could have emerged only after traditional societies, customs, and sensibilities were so thoroughly reworked to accord with domination that humanity lost all sense of contact with the organic society from which it originated.

Clan society was not effaced in a single or dramatic stroke, any more than the State was to be established in a single historical leap. Until they were neutralized as a social force, the clans still retained large areas of land during the early urban phase of society. The warrior societies, for their part, reinforced their military power with economic power by claiming the lands of conquered peoples, not of their own folk, as private booty. Extratribal conquest, in effect, was to lead to the war chieftain's aggrandizement with large private estates, often worked by their aboriginal inhabitants as serfs. As for the warrior societies that clustered around the chieftains, the most permanent spoils of battle and victory were the lands they carved out as their own demesnes—estates, in effect—which they then elaborated into an internal manorial hierarchy of villeins, tenants, serfs, and slaves. Judging from Mesoamerican data, the manorial economy eventually began to outweigh the *capulli* economy in sheer acreage and produce. Indeed, Sumerian records and Spanish accounts of Aztec society tell a woeful tale of the gradual sale of the clan lands to the manors and the reduction of the food cultivators, free or captive, to a serf-like or tenant status.* Beyond the city walls, in the more remote areas of the society, village life still retained much of its vitality. The old ways were to remain, however faintly and vestigially, into modern times. But the blood oath, with its highly variegated customs and rituals, became more symbolic than real. Class society had supplanted hierarchical society, just as hierarchical society had supplanted the egalitarian features of organic society.

This sweeping shift from social ties based on kinship, usufruct, and complementarity to classes, proprietorship, and exploitation could not have occurred without concomitant changes in technics. Without the large-scale, animal-powered plow agriculture, now generally managed by males, that replaced woman's digging stick and hoe, it is difficult to conceive that surpluses would have arisen in sufficient quantity to support professional priests, craftsmen, scribes, courts, kings, armies, and bureaucracies—in short, the vast paraphernalia of the State. Yet several cultural paradoxes confront us. Aztec society, despite its obvious class structure, exhibited no technological advances beyond the simplest pueblo communities. Among American Indian societies we find no plows that furrow the earth, no wheels for transportation although

---

* The sale of the clan lands should not be regarded as evidence for the right to freely alienate traditional community lands. The new feudal dispensation that normally followed the rise and later the weakening of military kingships still viewed land as the locus for a nearly sacred sense of place, not as mere "real estate." Most likely, the clan lands that were sold to the emerging nobility were viewed as a transfer of title *within* the community, and between the clan-folk and their military leaders. Even Aristotle could not buy land in Athens because he was not a native Athenian, however renowned his fame and influential his teachings. Greek though he was, in Athens he was still a stranger, not a citizen.

they appear in Aztec toys, no domestication of animals for agricultural purposes. Despite their great engineering feats, there was no reduction of food cultivation from a craft to an industry. Conversely, in societies where plows, animals, grains, and great irrigation systems formed the bases for agriculture, primordial communal institutions were still retained together with their communal distributive norms. These societies and their values persisted either without developing classes or by coexisting, often ignominiously, with feudal or monarchical institutions that exploited them ruthlessly—but rarely changed them structurally and normatively.

More commonly than not, humanity either did not "advance" into class society or did so only in varying degrees. Plow agriculture, grains, and the elaboration of crafts may have provided the necessary condition for the emergence of cities, classes, and exploitation in many areas of the world, but they never provided sufficient conditions. What renders European society, particularly in its capitalist form, so historically and morally unique is that it surpassed by far *every* society, including the Near Eastern ones in which it was rooted, in the extent to which economic classes and economic exploitation—indeed, economics as we know it today—colonized the most intimate aspects of personal and social life.

The centrality of the city in achieving this transformation can hardly be overemphasized. For it was the city that provided the territory for territorialism, the civic institutions for citizenship, the marketplace for elaborate forms of exchange, the exclusivity of quarters and neighborhoods for classes, and monumental structures for the State. Its timbers, stones, bricks, and mortar gave enduring tangibility to social, cultural, institutional, and even moral changes that might have otherwise retained the fugitive quality of mere episodes in humanity's convoluted history or simply been absorbed back into nature, like an abandoned field reclaimed by forest. By virtue of its endurance and growth, the city crystallized the claims of society over biology, of craft over nature, of politics over community. Like the cutting edge of class society's battleaxe, it fought back the ever-invasive claims of kinship, usufruct, and complementarity, affirming the sovereignty of interest and domination over sharing and equality. For a conquering army to obliterate a culture's city was to annihilate the culture itself; to reclaim the city, be it a Jerusalem or a Rome, was to restore the culture and the people who had created it. On the very urban altars of the blood oath, the city drained kinship of its content while exalting its form, until the husk could be discarded for a mere reproductive unit we euphemistically call the "nuclear family."

❧

However sweeping these objective changes toward class society may have been, they are not nearly as challenging as the changes that had to be achieved in the *subjective* realm before classes, exploitation, acquisition, and the competitive mentality of bourgeois rivalry could become part of humanity's psychic equipment. We gravely misjudge human nature if we see it only through an epistemology of rule and domination, or worse, class relationships and exploitation. Howard Press has observed that "separation is the archetypal tragedy." But there are different ways to separate. Although this "tragedy" may be necessary to allow the individual to discover his or her uniqueness and identity, it should not have to assume the socially explosive form of rivalry and competition between individuals.

A phenomenology of the self has yet to be written that takes into account the conciliatory and participatory aspects of self-formation. The "I" that emerges from the welter of "its," the magic boundary that the infant must cross to distinguish itself from the undifferentiated experiences that flood its sensorimotor apparatus, is not the product of antagonism. Fear has to be learned; it is a *social* experience—as is hatred. The commonly accepted ideology that the *enlargement* of egocentricity is the authentic medium in which selfhood and individuality come into their own is a bourgeois trick, *the rationale for bourgeois egotism*. This notion is contradicted by Piaget's life-long researches into the early years of childhood. As he observes,

> Through an apparently paradoxical mechanism whose parallel we have described apropos of the egocentrism of thought of the older child, it is precisely when the subject is most self-centered that he knows himself the least, and it is to the extent that he discovers himself that he places himself in the universe.

Accordingly, Piaget finds that language, reflective thought, and the organization of a spatial, causal, and temporal universe become possible "to the extent that the self is freed of itself by finding itself and so assigns itself a place as a thing among things, an event among events."

Early humanity could never have survived without being (in Piaget's sense) "a thing among things, an event among events." Social Darwinism aside, creatures specialized in the powerful neurophysical capacity to mentalize and conceptualize, to plan and calculate would have destroyed themselves in a Hobbesian war of all against all. Had reason, with its capacity for calculation, been used to divide and destroy rather than unite and create, the very human quality of humanity would have turned upon itself and the species immolated itself ages ago, long before it devised its armamentarium of modern weaponry.

Organic society's conciliatory sensibility finds expression in its outlook in dealing with the external world—notably in animism and magic. Basically, animism is a spiritual universe of conciliation rather than an aggressive form of conceptualization. That all entities have "souls"—a simple "identity of spirit and being," to use Hegel's words—is actually lived and felt. This outlook pervades the practice of simple preliterate peoples. When Edward B. Tylor, in his classic discussion of animism, notes that an American Indian "will reason with a horse as if rational," he tells us that the boundaries between things are functional. The Indian and the horse are both *subjects*—hierarchy and domination are totally absent from their relationship. "The sense of an absolute psychical distinction between man and beast, so prevalent in the civilized world, is hardly to be found among lower (sic) races." The very epistemology of these "lower races" is qualitatively different from our own.

Preliterate epistemology tends to unify rather than divide: it personifies animals, plants, even natural forces and perfectly inanimate things as well as human beings. What are often mere abstractions in our minds acquire life and substance in the preliterate animistic mind. To the animist, man's soul, for example, is his breath, his hand, his heart, or other such clearly substantial entities.

This animistic outlook in its many modifications will pervade the mind long after the passing of organic society. Our difficulty in dealing with the seemingly paradoxical qualities of Greek philosophy stems from the tension between its animistic outlook and secular reason. Thales and the Ionian thinkers, although apparently rationalistic in the sense that their outlook was secular and based on logical causality, nevertheless saw the world as alive, as an *organism*, "in fact," as Collingwood observes, "as an animal." It is something "ensouled ... within which are lesser organisms having souls of their own; so that a single tree or a single soul, is according to [Thales], both a living organism in itself and also a part of the great living organism which is the world." This animistic outlook lingers on in Greek philosophy well into Aristotle's time; hence the difficulty we encounter in neatly classifying Hellenic thought into "idealist" and "materialist" compartments.

Magic, the technique that the animist employs to manipulate the world, seems to violate the conciliatory epistemology of this sensibility.

Anthropologists tend to describe magical procedures as "primitive man's" fictive techniques for "coercion," for making things obey his will. A closer view, however, suggests that it is we who read this coercive mentality into the primordial world. By magically imitating nature, its forces, or the actions of animals and people, preliterate communities project their own needs into external nature; it is essential to emphasize that external nature is conceptualized at the very outset as a mutualistic community. Prior to the manipulative act is the ceremonious supplicatory word, the appeal to a rational being—to a *subject*—for cooperation and understanding. Rites always precede action and signify that there must be communication between equal participants, not mere coercion. The consent of an animal, say a bear, is an essential part of the hunt in which it will be killed. When its carcass is returned to the camp, Indians will put a peace pipe in its mouth and blow down it as a conciliatory gesture. Simple mimesis, an integral feature of magic and ritual, implies by its very nature unity with the "object," a recognition of the "object's" subjectivity. Later, to be sure, the word was to be separated from the deed and become the authoritarian Word of a patriarchal deity. Mimesis, in turn, was to be reduced to a strategy for producing social conformity and homogeneity. But the ritual of the word in the form of incantations and work songs reminds us of a more primordial sensibility based on mutual recognition and shared rationality.

I do not mean that organic society lacked a sense of particularity in the manifold of this experiential unity. To the animist, bears were bears and not bisons or human beings. The animist discriminated between individuals and species as carefully as we do—often exhibiting a remarkable attention to detail as revealed in late Paleolithic cave paintings. The *repressive* abstraction of the individual bear into a bear spirit, a universalizing of the spirit of bears that denies their specificity, is, I suspect, a later development in the elaboration of the animistic spirit. In rendering the individual bear subject to *manipulative* forms of human predation, generalization in this form marks the first steps toward the objectification of the external world. Before there were bear spirits there were probably only individual bears, as Tylor suggests, when he tells us that if "an Indian is attacked and torn by a bear, it is that the beast fell upon him intentionally in anger, perhaps to revenge the hurt done to another bear." A bear that has will, intentionality, and knows anger is not a mere epiphenomenon of a bear spirit; it is a being in its own right and autonomy.

By abstracting a bear spirit from individual bears, by generalizing from the particular to the universal, and further, by infusing this process of abstraction with magical content, we are developing a new epistemology for explaining the external world. If the individual bear is *merely* an epiphenomenon of an animal spirit, it is now possible to objectify nature by completely subsuming the particular by the general and denying the uniqueness of the specific and concrete. The emphasis of the animistic outlook thereby shifts from accommodation and communication to domination and coercion.

This intellectual process probably occurred in gradual steps. The Orpheus legend, one of the most archaic in mythology, is still based on the notion of a *guardian spirit* rather than a master of animals. Orpheus charms the animal universe into reconciliation and harmony. He is a pacifier in a brute world of "claw and fang." From the Orpheus legend, we sense the existence of a time when pacification and abstraction were not mutually exclusive processes. But effect a slight shift in the emphasis of the legend and we pass from the imagery of a guardian of animals into that of a master of animals. This shift is probably the work of the shaman who, as Ivar Paulson suggests, concomitantly embodies the protector of game—the *master* of their spirits—and the helper of the hunter. The shaman magically delivers the hunted animal into the hands of the hunter: he is the master implied in mastery. As both elder and professional magician, he establishes the new, quasi-hierarchical boundaries that subvert the old animistic outlook.

That hallowed process called Reason, of generalization and classification, appears very early in an involuted and contradictory form: the *fictive* manipulation of nature begins with the *real* manipulation of humanity. Although the shaman's efforts to give greater coherence to the world will become social power that confers upon humanity greater control over the external world, the shaman and, more precisely, his successor—the priest—initially divides this world to manipulate it. Women, as shamannesses or priestesses, are no more immune to this phenomenon than men. In either case, Weston La Barre is certainly correct in saying that early hunter-gatherers projected the social structure of secular power onto the supernatural just as other groups do: "The fit of myth to the social structure of a hunting band is exact. Myth anticipated no later social dispensation, for religion reflected only the then contemporary social structure."

Moreover, as we can suspect, the shamans and priests are always at work. They not only generalize and formulate, but they regeneralize and reformulate. The early coalitions they form with the elders and warrior-chiefs, later the conflicting issues they face with the emergence of increasingly complex agricultural societies, place new demands upon their ideological ingenuity which, in turn, lead to new generalizations and formulations. After their death, the more renowned shamans and priests become the raw materials for producing godheads. A compromise is struck between animism and religion, one that phases shamanism into the priestly corporation. The early deities reveal this new melding by combining an animal face with a human body or vice versa, as in the cases of the Sphinx and the Minotaur. Inexorably, this process of continual substitution yields a pantheon of deities that are entirely human, even in their capricious behavior.

As society slowly develops toward hierarchy and then into class structures, so too do the deities. In a hierarchical society that is still saturated with matricentric traditions, the foremost deity is the Mother Goddess, who personifies fertility and soil, the cojoined domains of sexuality and horticulture. In a well-entrenched patricentric society—one that introduces the male, his beasts, and the plow into food cultivation—the Mother Goddess acquires a male consort, to whom she gradually yields her eminence as patriarchy becomes prevalent. This process continues onward across the threshold of "civilization" into urban societies until the socialization of the deities leads to political theogonies. If the community confers in assemblies, so too do the deities; if the impact of war on primitive urban democracies leads to the establishment of a supreme ruler, a supreme deity also tends to emerge. As long as the world is under the sway of shamanistic and, more significantly, priestly mediation, it tends to remain embedded in a religious matrix. Nor does it ever free itself of the mythopoeic and religious as long as human dominates human. Social divisions are obscured by myth and mythology: even the warrior-chieftain tries to validate his social status by becoming a priest or a deity. Authoritarian social forces are made to appear as natural forces, like the deities that personify or seem to manipulate them.

∞

Where nature is touched by the works of the food cultivator, humanity had no difficulty in devising deities that are part of the earth and domestic hearth: folk gods and folk goddesses whose behavior was often determined by seasonal cycles or human supplication. Wars, catastrophes, famines, and great misfortunes occurred, to be sure, but they occurred against the background of natural order. The deities of Mesopotamia, for example, may seem more unruly and harsher than those that presided over the destiny of Egypt; the behavior of the river in the former land was less predictable and more destructive than that of the latter. Significant as they may be, however, the differences between the deities in the two great alluvial civilizations were differences in degree rather than in kind. Nature was still a nurturing mother who provided care and solicitude. She bestowed lush harvests and security to the community who revered her and never failed to provide her with a ceremonial bounty of its own.

But contrast these well-tilled lands with the arid steppes and the parched desert of the Bedouin. Here, insecurity and conflict between patriarchal warrior-shepherds over water rights and herds are a chronic human condition, and it is easy to see why new deities begin to emerge who assume a more terrible visage than that of the agriculturalists' nature spirits, gods, and goddesses. Here, nature seems very much like a clenched fist that capriciously stamps out man and his herds. No domestic hearth exists from which he can warm his soul after the labors of the day; only the nomad's camp with its ambience of impermanence. Nor are there lush fields, crisscrossed by cool streams. For the Bedouin, only the heavens are blue, presided over by a scorching sun. The wide horizon, broken by stark mountains and plateaus, instills a sense of the infinity of space, of the transcendental and other-worldly. Woman, the embodiment of fecundity and a relatively benign nature to the agriculturist, has no symbolic place in this stark universe—except perhaps as a mere vessel to produce sons, herdsmen, and warriors. She is not so much exploited as simply degraded.*

These pastoral nomads, separated from agriculture by climatic changes or by population pressures on the land, are an expelled, ever-wandering, and restless people. They are accursed by the very chtonic deities that still linger among them as ghosts of a lost Eden. As herdsmen, they are a people who live mainly among domestic beasts, each of which is an alienable quantum; the mere *number* of animals the patriarch owns is a measure of his wealth and prestige. Power and fortune can be determined with numerical exactness: by the size of one's herds and the number of one's sons. From these people—historically the

---

* This description is admittedly a Weberian "ideal type." It does not take into account the many variations and complexities that enter into Bedouin or, more generally, pastoral ecology. There is now general agreement that pastoralism represents a late development, in fact, a spin-off from agricultural society, not the intermediate "stage" between hunting and agricultural "stages" to which it was assigned by nineteenth-century anthropologists. Hence the later patriarchal structure and values are mixed with matricentric traditions from earlier ways of life. This fact may explain the equivocal position of women in the Hebrew Bible and in many existing pastoral communities today. Nor do all pastoral communities confine themselves to shepherding. They will cultivate food when they can and have peacefully interacted with farming communities at all levels of development throughout history, both trading with them or grazing their flocks on the stubble of harvested farmland. My concern, here, is primarily with what is *unique* to the pastoral world, not what it shares with the many horticultural and agricultural communities that were to become objects of pastoral invasions.

Hebrews, who articulate the pastoral sensibility *par excellence*—a new epistemology of rule and a new deity will emerge, based on the infinite, the harsh expression of male will, and the often cruel negation of nature. As noted by H. and H. A. Frankfort,

> The dominant tenet of Hebrew thought is the absolute transcendence of God. Yahweh is not in nature. Neither earth nor sun nor heaven is divine; even the most potent natural phenomena are but reflections of God's greatness. It is not even possible to name God .... He is *holy*. That means he is *sui generis* .... It has been rightly pointed out that the monotheism of the Hebrews is a correlate of their insistence on the unconditioned nature of God. Only a God who transcends every phenomenon, who is not conditioned by any mode of manifestation—only an unqualified God can be the one and only ground of *all* existence.

Behind such cosmogonies lies the dialectic of a contradictory rationality, at once liberating and repressive—as reason embedded in myth. Doubtlessly, real intellectual powers are being exercised; they are actualizing themselves with mythopoeic materials. The graduation of animistic thought from the individual to the species, from bears to the "bear spirits," is an obvious preliminary to a conception of natural forces as humanly divine. The deities are subtle evidence of humanity's presence in nature as a natural force in its own right.

It is tempting, here, to see the steppe lands and particularly the desert as domineering environments that brought humanity into subjugation to nature and to view the Bedouin as involved in a bitter "struggle" with nature. Yet such an image would be very simplistic. To the Bedouin, the starkness of the nomad's arid world was often seen as a source of purification, indeed of moral and personal freedom. To the great Hebrew prophets, most notably figures like Amos, the desert was above all the land to which one returned to find the strength of character and moral probity to fight injustice. Hence the nobility that was imputed to the herdsman, who, wandering with his flocks and left to his own thoughts, came closer to the deity than the food cultivator. His contact with the desert imbued him with a sense of righteousness. The significance of the Semitic contribution to our western sensibility lies not simply in the patriarchal edge it gave to the already existing hierarchies of agricultural societies—a contribution I have emphasized here for heuristic purposes. It also lies in the moral probity and transcendental mentality that generalized the concrete image of nature so prevalent among peasant peoples into a Supernature that was as strikingly intellectual as it was willful in its abstractness.

Hence with the Hebrews, religion exhibits a growing tendency to abstract, to classify, and to systematize. For all its obvious contradictions, the Hebrew Bible is a remarkably coherent account of humanity's evolution into society. Even in the Hebrews' devaluation of natural phenomena we have a break with mythopoeic thought as such, a rupture with phenomena as fantasy, a willingness to deal with life on realistic and historical terms. Social history, as the will of God, replaces natural history as the cosmogony of spirits, demons, and divine beings. The Hebrews, as the Frankforts emphasized,

> propounded not a speculative theory, but revolutionary and dynamic teaching. The doctrine of a single, unconditional, transcendent God rejected time-honored values, proclaimed new ones, and postulated a metaphysical significance for history and for man's actions.

The destiny of man moves to the center of the intellectual stage: it is *his* fate and that of his species, albeit in the form of the "chosen people," that forms a central theme in the Hebrew Bible.

But an antithetical rationality permeates this "revolutionary and dynamic teaching." With the Hebrews, the epistemology of rule comes into its own as a *transcendental conception of order*. Domination becomes *sui generis*: it divides the indivisible by fiat. Merely to relegate the Hebrew Yahweh to a *monotheistic* preemption of a multifarious nature or even the human deities who peopled the pagan world is a simplification. Indeed, such efforts had been in the air for centuries before Judaism had acquired eminence by turning, in its Christian form, into a world religion. Nor were the Hebrews the only people to regard themselves as chosen; this is a tribal archaism that most preliterate and later literate people symbolize in their ethnic nomenclature when they describe themselves as "The People" and others as "strangers" or "barbarians."

What renders the Hebrew Bible unique is that it is self-derivative: God's will, as it were, *is* God. No cosmogony, morality, or rationality is necessary to explain it, and man's duty is to obey unquestioningly. When Moses first encounters Yahweh and asks for his name, the reply is a damning intonation: "I am that I am." And further: "I Am hath sent me unto you." What Moses confronts is not merely an *only* God or a jealous one; he confronts a *nameless* God whose transcendence closes Him to all being beyond His own existence and will. The concrete now *completely* becomes the mere *product* of the universal; the principle, by which animism and early cosmogonies are to evolve from the particular to the general, has been totally reversed. The order of things emerges not from nature to Supernature, but from Supernature to nature.

Characteristically, the biblical notion of creation "is not a speculative cosmogony," Rudolph Bultmann observes, "but a confession of faith in God as Lord. The world belongs to him and he upholds it by his power." This world is now pervaded by hierarchy, by ruler and ruled, over whom presides that nameless abstraction, the Lord. Man, viewed from the Lord's eyes, is an utterly abject creature, yet, viewed from ours, a hierarch in his own right. For the Lord ordains that Noah will be "feared" by "every beast of the earth," by "every fowl in the air," and by "all that moveth upon the earth and ... all the fishes of the sea." The communication that the animist magically achieves with the hunted animal, first as an individuated being and later as an epiphenomenon of a species-spirit, is not transformed into "fear." That animals can feel "fear" still acknowledges their subjectivity—a feeling, ironically, they share with people who are inspired by the "fear of God"—but it is a subjectivity that is placed under human domination.

Equally as significant, people too are caught in a nexus of human domination. Biblical power is the *mana* that all masters can use against their slaves: ruler against ruled, man against woman, the elders against the young. Hence we need have no difficulty in understanding why the Hebrew Bible becomes a universalized document: the supreme code of the State, school, workshop, body politic, and family. It is *mana* that has acquired metaphysical trappings which make it virtually invulnerable to the incredulity an increasingly secularized world brings to the *mana* of the warrior chieftain, divine king, and domestic patriarch. "Hebrew thought did not entirely overcome mythopoeic thought," observe the Frankforts. "It created, in fact, a new myth—the myth of the Will of God." Yet more than myth is involved in Yahweh's injunctions. Behind the stories, episodes, and history that the Hebrew Bible contains is a nascent philosophical apriorism that links human sovereignty with aggressive behavior. The perpetuation of hierarchy, in effect, appears as a matter of human survival in the face of inexorable forces.

Yahweh's will completes the growing separation between subject and object. More significantly, His will divided the two not simply as particulars that make for a richer wholeness, but antagonistically: the object is subjugated to the subject. They are divided as opposites that involve a denial of the concrete, of facticity, and of the body by the abstract, the universal, and the mind. Spirit can now be opposed to reality, intellect to feeling, society to nature, man to woman, and person to person, because the order of things as expressed by Yahweh's "I Am" has so ordained it. One does not have to invoke custom, law, or theory to explain this order; the transcendental Will of God—a god who is *sui generis*—has ordered this dispensation. It is not for man to question His omnipotence.

This religious separation of the world's order in terms of sovereignty rather than complementarity was to serve its acolytes well. For the emerging ruling classes and the State, it provided an ideology of unreasoned obedience, of rule by fiat and the powers of supernatural retribution. And it had achieved this sweeping transformation not by invoking nature and her deities—the "bear spirit," the part-human and part-animal deities typified by Egyptian religio-animism, or by the irascible anthropomorphic deities of Sumer and Greece—but by invoking a completely disembodied, abstract, and nameless Supernature that allowed for the codification of pure belief without the constraints of empirical reality. The desert landscape of the Bedouin merely sharpened this ideology but did not form it, for the "Bedouin compact" tends to belie its political claims of unrestricted sovereignty. Indeed, it is doubtful that an ideology so demanding of subservience and obedience by patriarchs as well as their wives, children, and retainers could have come from simple Bedouins who were soon to settle down to an agricultural way of life. This ideology was patently fashioned by priests and military commanders, by stern lawgivers and Spartan-like soldiers so clearly embodied in the figure of a Moses. That the Lord demands from Moses a tent of goat's hair for his earthly dwelling suggests that the ideology, in its early parts in the Hebrew Bible, was formulated when the confederated Hebrew tribes were pushing their way into Canaan. Later it was elaborated, after their conquest of the land, into a richly humanistic and highly idealistic ethical document.*

---

* Ironically, the morally demanding and antinaturalistic Bedouin values of the Hebrew Bible played a more formative role in the New Testament than the Old, despite Christianity's gospel of love. In the period directly preceding the emergence of the Roman Empire, Judaism acquired a highly ethical character. The Hebrew prophets, particularly Amos, imbued Judaism with a commitment to justice and a hatred of tyranny so intense that the ancient Jews revolted incessantly against the Roman imperium—leading finally to the destruction of Judea as a national entity. By Jesus's time, the Pharisees had reworked the Deuteronomic Code into one of the most humane in the ancient world. The Mosaic *lex talionis*, with its demand for "an eye for an eye," had been replaced by monetary compensation; corporal punishment was greatly restricted; the use of ordeal to determine female adultery was abolished; finally, both debtors and slaves were treated with a degree of consideration that was virtually unprecedented for the time. As Hyam Maccoby's *Revolution in Judea* (New York: Taplinger Publishing Co., 1980) indicates, the interface between Judaism and Christianity was crassly, almost cynically rewritten by the Hellenistic authors of the existing gospels. According to Maccoby these authors distorted beyond all recognition Jesus's nationalistic goals, the ethical ideas of his Nazarene followers, and the activist message of the Jerusalem Church led by Jesus's brother, James.

෬

With the Greeks, the epistemology of rule is transformed from a moral principle, based on faith, into an ethical principle, based on reason. Although mythopoeic thought is never absent from the Hellenic cultural legacy, it either takes on a highly intellectualized form or is preempted by mind, or *nous*. The Greek realm of reason is not focused on Supernature; its authentic locus is the *polis*, or the so-called city-state.

Like the Semitic patriarchal clan, the *polis*, too, is partly shaped by a compelling natural environment: mountains that wrinkle the Greek promontory and foster a high degree of communal autonomy and personal virtuosity in nearly all tasks from agriculture to metallurgy and war. The word amateur is Latin in origin, but it accurately reflects the Hellenic predisposition to a modest degree of competence in all fields, for balance and self-sufficiency *(autarkeia)*, that has so characteristically marked mountain-dwelling communities in the past and placed the imprint of self-reliance, character, hardiness, and a freedom-loving spirit on their inhabitants. For such peoples, independence of spirit tended to become an end in itself, although their isolation could also yield a narrow parochialism that militated against any real breadth of vision.

Hellenic intellectualism was centered primarily in the coastal and island *poleis* of antiquity, where a rare balance was struck between the free-ranging spirit of their mountain origins and the cosmopolitan spirit of their maritime contacts. Within these *poleis*, specifically the Athenian, a new dualism emerged: Home, or *oikos*, and the *agora* (a marketplace which, in time, was transformed into a highly variegated civic center) were counterposed to each other. The *agora*, more broadly, the *polis* itself "was the sphere of freedom," as Hannah Arendt has noted, echoing the motif of Aristotle's *Politics*. To the extent that home and *polis* were related to each other,

> it was a matter of course that the mastering of the necessities of life in the household was the condition for freedom of the *polis*. What all Greek philosophers, no matter how opposed to *polis* life, took for granted is that freedom is exclusively located in the political realm, that necessity is primarily a prepolitical phenomenon, characteristic of the private household organization, and that force and violence are justified in this sphere because they are the only means to master necessity—for instance, by ruling over slaves—and to become free. Because all human beings are subject to necessity, they are entitled to violence toward others; violence is the prepolitical act of liberating oneself from the necessity of life for the freedom of the world.

This epistemological dualism between necessity and freedom, a dualism utterly alien to Hebrew monistic thought, rested on such sweeping assumptions about nature, work, individuality, reason, woman, freedom, and technics that it would require a separate work to deal with them adequately. Here, I offer a cursory examination of some of these assumptions, with particular reference to the western legacy of domination, and leave their implications to a later study.

To begin with, Greek rationality did not quite foster a rejection of nature. A nature *tamed* by man, notably the orderly fields of the agriculturalist and the sacred groves of the deities, was a pleasing desideratum. They were refreshing to the eye and to the spirit. Nature, in this form, was infused with reason and sculpted by human creativity. What the Greeks thoroughly feared and resisted was wild, untamed nature (as Havelock Ellis was to emphasize)—a *barbarian* nature, as it were. Wild nature was not merely prepolitical; it was beyond the realm of order. Neither reason nor necessity could find a home in the tangle of the unbridled forest and its perils. The Greek notion of man's domination of nature—a notion that was no less real than the modern—could not find fixity and meaningfulness there. In the Greek mind, the *polis*, which included its well-tilled environs, waged a constant battle against the encroachment of the unruly natural world and its barbarian denizens. Within its confines, the *polis* created a space not only for discourse, rationality, and the "good life," but even for the *oikos*, which at least had its own realm of order, however prepolitical in character. Underpinning the supremacy of the *polis* over the *oikos* was a more universal dualism, the supremacy of order or *kosmos* over meaningless dissolution or *chaos*. All of Greek nature philosophy took these intellectual coordinates—particularly as they referred to the coherence of the *polis* against the forces for incoherence—as their basic reference points. The love of wild nature was to come later, with the European Middle Ages.

By the same token, Greek rationalism did not denigrate work and materiality. Indeed, the Athenian yeoman, the *hoplite* who as farmer-citizen formed the military backbone of the classical democracy, worked hand-in-hand with his hired help and such slaves as he could afford to own. Often, this small labor force shared the same fare and material conditions of life. The Greek love of the human body, of athleticism, and respect for physical form is proverbial. What Greek rationalism thoroughly denigrated—and we speak of its elites—was the toil associated with trade and the pursuit of gain. For in the marketplace lay the forces that threatened to undermine the Hellenic ideal of self-sufficiency, balance, and limit—that is, of the *kosmos* that could be undermined so easily by chaos when the vigilance of reason was relaxed.

In a widely quoted passage, Aristotle articulated this fear with a clarity that is characteristically Hellenic. There are some people who

> believe that getting wealth is the object of household management and the whole idea of their lives is that they ought either to increase their money without limit, at any rate not to lose it. The origin of this disposition in men is that they are intent upon living only, and not upon living well; and, as their desires are unlimited, they also desire that the means of gratifying them should be without limit.

For Aristotle, the threat of the unlimited lies not only in imbalance and dependence; it also lies in the subversion of form—without which identity itself dissolves and the meaningful is supplanted by the meaningless.

Hence, even more than the equipoise provided by balance, the Greeks sought an orderly arrangement of the dualities they had introduced into the western intellectual tradition: the duality between nature and society, work and free time, sensuousness and intellect, individual and community. The dualities existed and acquired meaning only because they existed contrapuntally, each in opposition to and in conjunction with the other. The genius of reason was to recognize and adjust the tension between them by giving both epistemological and social priority to the second term in the duality over the first. Even the *polis*, conceived as the realm of freedom, was continually beleaguered by the problem of whether the community would be capable of maintaining an identity between the collective interest and the individual. "In Athenian ideology the state was both superior and antecedent to its citizens," observes Max Horkheimer. As it turned out, at least for a brief period of time:

> This predominance of the *polis* facilitated rather than hindered the rise of the individual: it effected a balance between the state and its members, between individual freedom and communal welfare, as nowhere more eloquently depicted than in the Funeral Oration of Pericles.

But in the Hellenic mind, order always had to resist disorder— *kosmos* to resist *chaos*. This imagery is essential in achieving any understanding of how the Greeks—and every European ruling class that was to follow the decline of the *polis*—were to think about the human condition. Its accolades to balance and equipoise notwithstanding, the predominant note in Hellenic thought was always a hierarchical organization of reality. It was always stated in rational and secular terms, but we cannot forget that *chaos* had a very mundane and earthy substantiality in the form of a large population of slaves, foreigners, women and potentially unruly freedmen who were placed in an inferior status within the *polis* or had no status at all.

❧

The principal architects of Greece's hierarchical epistemology— Plato and Aristotle—had a long philosophical pedigree rooted in pre-Socratic nature philosophy. How to account for domination of literally half of the *polis*, its women, and a very substantial number of slaves? How to deny civil and political rights to the alien residents and freedmen who literally infested the *polis* and provided for its most essential day-to-day services? These questions had to be resolved on rational terms, without recourse to myths that opened the door to *chaos* and its dark past.

For both Plato and Aristotle, a rational answer required intellectual objectivity, not the divine revelation and deified Will of early Hebrew social thought. The notion of human equality (which the Bible does not exclude and which its greatest prophets, in fact, emphasized) had to be impugned on *naturalistic* grounds—an ordered rational nature that the Greek mind could accept. Here, both Plato and Aristotle agreed. But they were divided on the locus of this nature, the actual cauldron in which differences between people could be stratified in systems of command and obedience.

Plato's strategy was, in many ways, the more atavistic: Differences in individual capacities and performances stem from differences in souls. The few who are equipped to rule—the guardians in Plato's idealized society (mistitled *The Republic*)—are born with "gold" and "silver" souls. Those with "gold" souls are destined by their inborn spiritual qualities to be the philosopher-rulers of the *polis*; those with "silver" souls, its warriors. The two are trained alike in a rigorous regimen that fosters athleticism, communal sharing of all possessions and means of life— a family-like solidarity that essentially turns the entire stratum into a large *oikos*—and a Spartan-like denial of luxuries and comfort. Later, the visibly "gold" and "silver" souls are functionally separated—the former, to develop their intellectual and theoretical qualities, the latter to elaborate their capacity to fulfill practical, generally military, responsibilities.

The remainder of the population—its farmers, craftsmen, and merchants, who have "bronze" or "iron" souls—are hardly mentioned. Apparently, they will enjoy more secure lives sculpted by their guardians. But their lifeways do not appear to be very different from that of the commoners in Plato's day. *The Republic* is thus essentially authoritarian—in some respects, totalitarian. The philosopher-rulers are free to blatantly (or "nobly," in Plato's words) lie to the entire populace in the interests of social unity and purge the *polis* of "ignoble" ideas and literature. Here, Plato notoriously includes Homeric poetry and probably the contemporary drama in his day that he viewed as degrading to humanity's image of the gods.

On the other hand, women in the guardian stratum enjoy complete, indeed unrestricted, equality with men. Plato, having removed the *oikos* from the life of the ruling class and replaced it with a form of domestic communism, has shifted the realm of necessity, of the prepolitical, to the shoulders of the commoners. With inexorable logic, he sees no reason why women in the guardian stratum should now be treated any differently from the men. Hence, all that is to limit their activities—be it war, athletics, education, or philosophical pursuits—are their physical abilities. They may be philosopher-rulers no less than men of comparable intellectual stature. Nor are the "gold" or "silver" souls that "mutate," as it were, among the commoners to be kept from entering the guardian stratum. Similarly, "bronze" or "iron" souls that appear among the children of the guardians are to be plucked from the ruling stratum and placed among the commoners.*

Despite all the accolades *The Republic* was to receive over the centuries after it was composed, it is not a utopia, a vision of a communist society, or in any sense of the term a democracy. It is an ideal form, an *eidos*, in Plato's metaphysical world of forms. What must be emphasized, here, is that Plato's rationality is ruthlessly, even cynically or playfully, hierarchical. The *polis*, if it was to survive from Plato's viewpoint, had to yield to the "cruelty of reason," so to speak, and follow the full logic of domination. Without hierarchy and domination, there can be no *kosmos*, no order. The Greeks—and they alone are of concern to Plato—must drastically alter the *polis* along the lines dictated by a repressive epistemology.

For Aristotle, *The Republic*'s rationalistic ideality is misplaced. Its theoretical purity removes it from his category of practical reason to which the formulation of a rational *polis* and its administration belong. Hence Aristotle stands at odds with Plato's "cruelty of reason," which dematerializes the pragmatic problems of ordering the *polis* along workable lines. His *Politics* undertakes a severe critique of the ideal *polis* as such, including Plato's and those proposed by his predecessors. Perhaps no work was to exercise a more profound influence on western social thought. What counts for our purposes is Aristotle's intensely critical

* Plato's tripartite theory of souls was not laid to rest in *The Republic*. It surfaced again in very radical Gnostic theories of late antiquity and in embattled Christian heresies of the Middle Ages and the Reformation. See Chapters 7 and 8.

strategy and concerns. Reason must exorcise its own myths, notably Plato's attempt at ideality and its proclivity to remove itself from the practical problems of social administration and reconstruction.

Aristotle's principal concerns in the *Politics* are distinctly those of his time: slavery, the nature of citizenship, and the rational classification of *poleis* that validates the choice of one type over another. Throughout, reason must be informed by ethics and by the desire of rational man to lead the "good life," which by no means is confined to the material. The work clearly establishes a rational basis for slavery and patriarchy, and a political meritocracy as the authentic arenas for citizenship. For Aristotle, the Greeks have been endowed by geography, climate, and their innate intellectual qualities to rule not only the barbarians, but also slaves and women—both of whom are "prepolitical" and benefit profoundly by the "higher" mental faculties of their male masters. Given the woman's and slave's "inferior" rationality, their inability to formulate policies and meaningful courses of behavior, they, no less than their masters, benefit from his "superior" rationality and his capacity to give them direction and govern their nonrational behavior. Slavery and patriarchy, in effect, are seen as the gifts of reason, not its chains.

Despite their differences, Plato and Aristotle elaborated social theories with a consistency and logic that must have seemed impeccable to many of their successors. And both laid not only the foundations for a rational social philosophy but established a repressive epistemological tradition that spans entire ages of western thought. Various sociobiologies were to draw their inspiration from Platonistic and neo-Platonic theories. Aristotelian theory was to acquire an incredible composite legacy that reaches into Thomistic theology and, despite its severe class orientation, into "scientific socialism."

Most important of all, the two thinkers, indeed Hellenic thought as a whole, universalized hierarchy as rational—perhaps democratic when possible, often totalitarian when necessary. By its very existence, the *polis* created a new tradition in western notions of citizenship and imparted to them an unprecedented secularity that gave modern social thought its authentic foundations. It also created the issues that were to beleaguer the western mind and praxis for centuries to come— and a thoroughly repressive mentality for dealing with them. For better or worse, we are in no sense free of this legacy's worldliness, candor, and logic. Cross-fertilized with Hebrew thought, European intellectuality was born in classical Athens and wound its way through the centuries until, like it or not, we still remain its heirs.

❧

The Hebrew and Hellenic mentalities were similar in their firm commitment to hierarchical relations structured around faith or rationality. Objectively, we have come a long way from the cunning of the priestly corporation in turning clan values against organic society; from the rise and commanding role of the warrior-chieftains and their entourages in the expansion of the male's civil sphere; from the disintegration of a communal economy into a manorial one; and finally, from the emergence of the city as the arena for dissolution of kinship relationships and the blood oath by citizenship, class interests, and the State. We have seen how the transcendental will of Yahweh and the rational elements of Hellenic epistemology have structured differentia along antagonistic lines, violating the animist's sense of complementarity and interpretation of concrete reality along conciliatory lines.

The legacy of domination thus develops as a manipulation of primordial institutions and sensibilities against each other, often by mere shifts of emphases in social reality and personal sensibility. Abstraction and generalization, whether as faith or reason, are used not to achieve wholeness or completeness but to produce a divisive antagonism in the objective and subjective realms. Other possible epistemologies, which might have favored a more "relaxed opening of the self to insight," to use Alvin Gouldner's words, have been ignored in favor of "values centering on mastery and control." This needlessly divisive development can be seen as a betrayal of society and sensibility to what the western mind has claimed for itself as *the* "history of mankind." Now that we are beginning to reap the terrible harvest of this betrayal, we must challenge the claims of that history to sovereignty.

But the story of this betrayal does not end with these institutional and subjective changes. It reaches further into the core of the psyche by internalizing hierarchy and domination as eternal traits of human nature. More than Yahweh's will and classical antiquity's rationality are needed to secure rule as an integral feature of selfhood. This feature entails not only humanity's commitment to its own self-repression through faith and reason; it must also *police* itself internally by acquiring a self-regulating "reality principle" (to use Freud's terms) based on guilt and renunciation. Only then can the ruled be brought into full complicity with their oppression and exploitation, forging within themselves the State that commands more by the power of the "inner voice" of repentance than the power of mobilized physical violence.

Neither Freud nor Marx have helped us fully understand this process. Each in his own way has absolved "civilization," specifically its western form, from its very real guilt in formulating a reality principle based on rule. By making self-repression (Freud) and self-discipline (Marx) the historic knout for achieving mastery over nature—and ultimately Freud's view, no less than Marx's, comes down to *precisely* this Victorian social project—they have made domination an indispensable phase or moment in the dialectic of civilization. Whether as sublimation or production, the self-mastery of humanity persists as a precondition for social development.

Terms like repression, renunciation, and discipline, used in their typical psychological sense, have all too often been euphemisms for oppression, exploitation, and powerlessness. And they have been shrewdly linked to "historic purposes" that have never served the ends of "civilization," whatever these may be, but simply the aggrandizement and power of elites and ruling classes. To a large extent, the theoretical corpus of Marx and Freud blur and conceal the extent to which such attempts to manipulate the self are actually extensions of class interests into selfhood. But it is now becoming patently clear that these interests are forging an apathetic, guilt-ridden, will-less psyche that serves not to foster social development but to subvert it. The mastery of human by human, both internally and externally, has actually begun to erode selfhood itself. By rendering personality increasingly inorganic, it has been pulverizing the very self that presumably lends itself to repression and discipline. In terms of contemporary selfhood, there is simply very little left to shape or form. "Civilization" is "advancing" not so much on the back of humanity but, eerily enough, without it.

More recently, sociobiology has provided its own reinforcement to this Freudo-Marxian "paradigm." The notion that the human brain, as a product of biological evolution, contains primal autonomic, "animalistic," and, capping them both, "higher," more complex cerebral components that must modify, repress, or discipline the raw impulses of the "lower" "animalistic" brain to avoid behavioral and social disorder is patently ideological. Its genesis in Hellenic dualism is obvious. That we have layered brains that perform many functions unthinkingly is doubtlessly neurologically sound. But to impute to specific layers *social* functions that are distinctly biased by hierarchical and class interests; to create an all-embracing term like "civilization" that incorporates these interests into a biology of the mind; and, finally, to foster a Victorian hypostatization of work, renunciation, guilt, sublimation, and discipline in the service of industrial production and profitable surpluses—all of this is to anchor the shibboleths of Yahweh's will and Hellenic repressive rationality in evolution and anatomy.

◌ৎ

To render this ideological development more clearly, let us return to certain assumptions that are built into psychoanalytic categories and see how well they hold up anthropologically. When speaking of organic societies, is it meaningful to say that social life creates a repressive "reality principle"? That the need for productive activity requires the deferral of immediate satisfaction and pleasure? That play must give way to work and complete freedom to social restrictions that make for security? Or, in more fundamental terms, that renunciation is an *inherent* feature of societal life and guilt is the constraint that society instills in the individual to prevent the transgression of its rules and mores?

I admit that these questions greatly simplify the role that the Freudians and Freudo-Marxians assign to a repressive rationality. Yet it is precisely at levels where psychoanalytic arguments are most simplified that we find the most important differences between organic and hierarchical societies. Perhaps the best general answer that might be given to all of these questions is this: there is very little to renounce or repress when very little has been formed. The sharply etched instincts that psychologists of the past imputed to human nature are now known to be rubbish. A human nature *does* exist, but it seems to consist of proclivities and potentialities that become increasingly defined by the instillation of social needs. The sexual instinct becomes an object of repression when society overstimulates it and concomitantly frustrates what it has exaggerated in the first place— or, of course, when society just blocks the adequate satisfaction of minimal biosexual needs. Even pleasure, conceived as the fulfillment of desire or as a broad "principle" (to follow Freudian nomenclature), is socially conditioned. If immediate gratification is frustrated by the natural world itself, no renunciatory apparatus is required to "repress" this "need." The "need," if it exists at all, simply cannot be fulfilled, and what is most human about human nature is that human beings can know this harsh fact.

In organic societies, social life more or less approximates this state of affairs. Nature generally imposes such restrictive conditions on human behavior that the social limits encountered by the individual are almost congruent with those created by the natural world. The "superego" and "ego," to use Freudian categories, formed by the child seem to be (as they so often are in fact) the products of natural limitations transmuted into social relationships. The sharp tension between the child and its parents and between the individual and society, which repression presupposes, is attenuated by the fact that the natural world forms the matrix for the social world and places limits on its development. Stated in Freudian terms, the "pleasure principle" is *formed* by the "reality principle." The two are *simply not distinguishable from each other to the extent that they are in hierarchical and class societies.* Hence, they barely exist as separate principles, and the antagonism between them is virtually meaningless. The receptive sensibility, so characteristic of organic society, has yet to be subverted by the demanding, aggressive attitude that provides "civilization" with its rationale for repressive reason and institutions.

Accordingly, organic societies do not make the moral judgments we continually generate against transgressions of our social rules. In the preliterate world, cultures are normally concerned with the *objective* effects of a crime and whether they are suitably rectified, *not* with its subjective status on a scale of right and wrong. "Viewed from certain African data, a crime is always a wrong done to society which has been detected," notes Paul Radin. "A wrong committed in full knowledge that it was such but which has not been detected is simply a fact that has no social consequences." While there may be a "spiritual" dimension to a "wrongdoer's state of mind," there is "no feeling of sin in the Hebrew-Christian meaning of the term." All that society asks of the wrongdoer is that he or she merely recognize that an offense has been committed against the harmony of the community. If the offense is redressed, no stigma is attached to the action. "This serves, as a matter of fact, as the best and most effective deterrent to wrongdoing," Radin emphasizes with characteristic utilitarian fervor. He goes on to note that when a Bantu was asked

> whether he was penitent at the time he committed a certain crime and the native answered, "No, it had not been found out then," there was no cynicism implied nor was this a sign of moral depravity. No disturbance in the harmony of the communal life had occurred.

The native may feel *shame* if the transgression is discovered or may lose face as a result of public disapproval, but he or she does not feel *guilt*, notably, an internalized sense of self-blame and anxiety that evokes repentance and a desire for atonement.*

---

* My quotations are drawn from Paul Radin's excellent work, *The World of Primitive Man* (New York: Henry Schuman, Inc., 1953). Apparently independently of Radin, E. R. Dodds made the distinction between a shame-culture and a guilt-culture around the same time, based largely on early Hellenic materials. See E. R. Dodds: *The Greeks and the Irrational* (Berkeley: University of California Press, 1951). That I have not drawn extensively on Dodds' work is due merely to oversight. His work was not known to me when these lines were written.

Guilt and repentance, as distinguished from shame and the practical need to redress the effects of a social transgression, become character traits with the emergence of morality. Historically, the formulation of moral precepts is initially the work of the prophet and priest; later, in its more sophisticated forms, as ethics, it is the realm of the philosopher and political thinker. These precepts reflect an entirely different mental state than what occurs in organic society. To say that social transgressions are "bad" and that obedience to society's mores is "good" is quite different from saying that one behavior upholds the harmony of the group and that another disrupts it. "Good" and "bad" are moral and later ethical judgments. They are not delimited exclusively to acts. What makes "good" and "bad" particularly significant is that they are evidence of the subtle introjections of social codes into the individual's psyche: the judgments individuals make when they take counsel with their consciences—that enormously powerful product of socialization. We shall later see that morality, particularly as it phases into its *rational* form as ethics, fosters the development of selfhood, individuality, and a new cognizance of the good and the virtuous. Here, I am primarily concerned with those highly opaque emotional sanctions called *customs*. Viewed from this perspective, morality was devised to mystify and conceal a once-unified, egalitarian system of *behavior*. The seemingly moral standards of that community were centered not around the "sinfulness" of behavior or the unquestioning commands of a patriarchal deity and a despotic State, but around the *functional* effects of behavior on the integrity and viability of the community.*

With the breakdown of the organic community, privilege began to replace parity, and hierarchical or class society began to replace egalitarian relationships. Moral precepts could now be used to obscure the mutilation of organic society by making social values the subject-matter of ideological rather than practical criteria. Once acts were transferable from the real world to this mystified realm, society's rules were free to mystify reality itself and obscure the contradictions that now emerged in the social realm.

---

* This distinction is worth elaborating further with two examples. What the Bantu people blame "is not cheating, nor stealing," observes W. C. Willoughby, "but a clumsiness of operation that leads to detection." This "amoral" attitude was to linger on into historical times as a behavioral norm in Sparta, the least developed of the Greek city-states. As part of their military training, Spartan youth were sent out to rob citizens of their own community and kill serfs or *helots* who were suspected of aggressive attitudes toward their masters. What was shameful, not evil, was the fact that they were caught. To the Hebrews and Athenians, by contrast, cheating and stealing were regarded as *intrinsically* reprehensible, not merely as social acts but as violations of divine commandment or rational behavior.

But, as yet, this process was merely the *ideological* side of a more crucial restructuring of the psyche itself. For morality not only staked out its sovereignty over overt behavior as restraints on "immoral" acts; it went further and assumed guardianship against the "evil" thoughts that beleaguered the individual's mind. Morality demands not only behavioral "virtue" but spiritual, psychic, and mental as well. The rational evaluation of right and wrong is ignored. That was to be left to ethics. Hierarchy, class, and ultimately the State penetrate the very integument of the human psyche and establish within it unreflective internal powers of coercion and constraint. In this respect, they achieve a "sanitizing" authority that no institution or ideology can hope to command. By using guilt and self-blame, the inner State can control behavior long before fear of the coercive powers of the State have to be invoked. Self-blame, in effect, becomes self-*fear*—the introjection of social coercion in the form of insecurity, anxiety and guilt.

Renunciation now becomes socially meaningful and "morally" invaluable to history's ruling elites because there really *is* something to renounce: the privileges of status, the appropriation of material surpluses, even the lingering memory of an egalitarian order in which work was pleasurable and playful and when usufruct and the irreducible minimum still determined the allocation of the means of life. Under the conditions of class rule, a "pleasure principle" *does*, in fact, emerge. And it stands sharply at odds with a "reality principle" whose limits were once congruent with those imposed by nature. To the extent that the ruling few are freed from these limits by the toiling many, the tension between the two principles is increasingly exacerbated; it assumes the form not only of a social trauma, notably, as class conflict, but also of psychic trauma in the form of guilt, renunciation, and insecurity.

But here the Freudian drama completely deceives us—and reveals an extraordinary reactionary content. The fact that nature's limits constitute the only "reality principle" of organic society is ignored; indeed, it is displaced by a mythic "pleasure principle" that must be constrained by guilt and renunciation. Cooperative nature is turned into predatory nature, riddled by egoism, rivalry, cruelty, and the pursuit of immediate gratification. But "civilization," formed by rationality, labor, and an epistemology of *self*-repression, produces a "reality principle" that holds unruly nature under its sovereignty and provides humanity with the matrix for culture, cooperation, and creativity. Freud's transposition of nature and "civilization" involves a gross misreading of anthropology and history. A "reality principle" that, in fact, originates in nature's limits, is transmuted into an egoistic pursuit for immediate gratification—in short, the very "pleasure principle" that social domination has *yet* to create historically and render meaningful. The natural home of humanity, to borrow Block's terminology, which promotes usufruct, complementarity, and sharing, is degraded into a Hobbesian world of all against all, while the "civilized" home of humanity, which fosters rivalry, egotism, and possessiveness, is viewed as a Judeo-Hellenic world of morality, intellect, and creativity. Freud's drastic reshuffling of the "pleasure principle" and "reality principle" thus consistently validates the triumph of domination, elitism, and an epistemology of rule. Divested of what Freud calls "civilization," with its luxuriant traits of domination, repressive reason, and renunciation, humanity is reduced to the "state of nature" that Hobbes was to regard as brutish animality.

Shame has no place in this Freudian universe—only guilt. "Civilization," whose ends this specious "reality principle" is meant to serve, turns out to be precisely the class and exploitative society unique to western capitalism—a "civilization" of unadorned domination and social privilege.[*] Freud's congruence of views with Marx is often remarkable in their common orientation toward "civilization." For Freud, work "has a greater effect than any other technique of living in the direction of binding the individual more closely to reality; in his work he is at least securely attached to a part of reality, the human community."

Ultimately, it is not the ends of "civilization" that are served by the Freudian "reality principle" but the ends of the "pleasure principle" that the ruling elites have preempted for themselves. It is not nature that fosters an unruly psychic animality with its appetite for immediate gratification, but a hierarchical "reality principle"—an epistemology of rule—one that rests on domination and exploitation. The truly brutish "mob" that Freud fearfully associated with the ascendency of aggressive instincts over sweet reason exists on the summits of "civilization," not at its base. Freud's pessimism over the fate of "civilization" may have been justified, but not for the reasons he advanced. It is not a repressed humanity whose aggressiveness threatens to extinguish "civilization" today but the very architects of its superego: the bureaucratic institutions and their "father-figures" that rule society from above.

---

* The similarity of the Freudian drama with the Hobbesian has not received the attention it deserves. Perhaps no one more than Hobbes would agree with Freud's view that individual liberty "is not a benefit to culture. It was greatest before any culture, though indeed it had little value at that time, because the individual was hardly in a position to defend it." Further: "The desire for freedom that makes itself felt in a human community may be a revolt against some existing injustice and so may prove favourable to a further development of civilization and remain compatible with it. But it may also have its origin in the primitive roots of the personality, still unfettered by civilizing influences, and so become a source of antagonism to culture." See Sigmund Freud, *Civilization and its Discontents* (London: The Hogarth Press Ltd., 1930), p. 60.

5 ⚬₹ THE LEGACY OF DOMINATION

The hierarchical origins of morality occur in the early and classical forms of family organization—in the moral authority claimed by its male head. The Bible provides ample evidence of the sovereignty enjoyed by the patriarch in dealing with his wives and children. To put it bluntly, they were his chattels, like the animals that made up his herds. His power over them lacked all restraint but that evoked by compassion and by the feeling of immortality he derived from the living products of his loins. Whether or not the son be cast in the image of the father, both are nevertheless made in the image of the deity who thereby unites them by covenant and blood. The demanding characteristics of father-love, in contrast to the selfless characteristics of mother-love, represent the male's resolution of his quarrel with eternity. The Hebrew patriarchs required no heaven or immortal soul, for both of them existed in the physical reality of their sons.

More intriguing, however, is the paternal authority claimed by the Greeks, whose philosophers tried to give moral precepts a rational or ethical—not a divine—sanction. Initially, the head of the household occupied an almost regal position with respect to other members of the family. Despite the rational dimension Hellenic philosophy tried to impart to social relationships, however, its capacity to invade the family was initially limited. As E. R. Dodds was to observe in a fascinating study of the issue:

> Over his children his authority is in early times unlimited: he is free to expose them in infancy [that is, engage in infanticide] and in manhood to expel an erring or rebellious son from the community, as Theseus expelled Hippolytus, as Oeneus expelled Tyedeus, as Trophios expelled Pylades, as Zeus himself cast out Hephaestos from Olympus for siding with his Mother.

Until well into the sixth century B.C., the son "had duties but no rights; while his father lived, he was a perpetual minor." In its classical form, patriarchy implied male gerontocracy, not only the rule of males over females. The young, irrespective of their sex, were placed rigorously under the moral and social authority of the oldest members of the family.

The Greek patriarch's commanding position over the private lives of his wards was to be sharply attenuated by the State, which was to stake out its own claims over young males whom it needed for bureaucrats and soldiers. But in that shadowy period of transition when the late Neolithic phased into Bronze-Age and Iron-Age "civilizations," when strongly patriarchal invaders were to overwhelm settled, often matricentric, cultures, male-oriented family structures formed the basic social elements of the community and starkly imprinted wide-ranging values on social life. Indeed, they helped to prepare the moral underpinnings of political institutions and the State—ironically, the very structures by which they were to be ultimately absorbed.

Even before social classes emerged and the priesthood established quasi-political temple despotisms over society, the patriarch embodied in a social form the very system of authority that the State later embodied in a political form. In the next chapter, we shall examine the curious dialectical tension between the patriarchal family and the State that gave rise to ideas of justice and ethics—a dialectic in which the father was transformed from a tyrant into a judge and later from a judge into a teacher. But until patriarchal power was attenuated by political forces, it was the father who embodied not only a prepolitical morality of social domination, but more specifically, a morality that entailed visions of the domination of nature.

The earliest victim of this domineering relationship was *human* nature, notably, the human nature of woman. Although patriarchy represents a highly authoritarian form of gerontocracy in which the elders initially began to rule society as a collective whole, woman increasingly lost her parity with man as the latter gained social ascendency over the domestic sphere of life with the expansion of his civil sphere. Patricentricity and finally patriarchy came completely into their own. By the same token, woman became the archetypal Other of morality, ultimately the human embodiment of its warped image of evil. That the male still opposes his society to woman's nature, his capacity to produce commodities to her ability to reproduce life, his rationalism to her "instinctual" drives has already received enough emphasis in the anthropological and feminist literature. Accordingly, woman enters into man's moral development as its antipode—the antithetical and contrasting factor *par excellence*—in shaping its tenets. Personally, she has no part "in the efficiency on which [the male's] civilization is based," observe Horkheimer and Adorno in their superb discussion of her status:

> It is man who has to go out into an unfriendly world, who has to struggle and produce. Woman is not a being in her own right, a subject. She produces nothing but looks after those who do; she is a living monument to a long-vanished era when the domestic economy was self-contained.

In a civilization that devalues nature, she is the "image of nature," the "weaker and smaller," and the differences imposed by nature between the sexes become "the most humiliating that can exist in a male-dominated society ... a key stimulus to aggression."*

Yet woman haunts this male "civilization" with a power that is more than archaic or atavistic. Every male-oriented society must persistently exorcise her ancient powers, which abide in her ability to reproduce the species, to rear it, to provide it with a loving refuge from the "unfriendly world," indeed, to accomplish those material achievements—food cultivation, pottery, and weaving, to cite the most assured of woman's technical inventions—that rendered that world possible, albeit on terms quite different from those formulated by the male.

Even before man embarks on his conquest of man—of class by class—patriarchal morality obliges him to affirm his conquest of woman. The subjugation of her nature and its absorption into the nexus of patriarchal morality forms the archetypal act of domination that ultimately gives rise to man's imagery of a subjugated nature. It is perhaps not accidental that nature and earth retain the female gender into our own time. What may seem to us like a linguistic atavism that reflects a long-gone era when social life was matricentric and nature was its domestic abode may well be an on-going and subtly viable expression of man's continual violation of woman as nature and of nature as woman.

The symbolism of this violation already appears early in primordial ceremonies, almost as though the wish is father to the act and its ritualistic affirmation in mere drama is a harbinger of its later reality. From the depths

---

* The principal weakness of this moving statement is the extent to which the authors ignore woman's productive role in the very economy the male preempts. Unwittingly, they reinforce the image, so current in their own time, that woman is always confined to a domestic world—one that is *literally* conceived as a shelter—and her functions in the world of labor are minimal. In fact, the primordial domestic economy, which Horkheimer and Adorno exile to prehistory, was one in which woman was far from "sheltered," indeed, one in which she was *of* the world no less than the man, but a world whose environment was largely domestic rather than civil.

of the Ituri forest to the gilded confines of the Church, woman is raised up to her appropriate eminence all the more to cast her down in subjugation to man. Even the central African pygmies, Turnbull's *Forest People*, have the equivalent of Eve or Pandora, who alternately seduces and succors the male, but in the end must never be permitted to "dominate" him. Her association with the arts of "civilization" is permeated by an envious negativity. Eve seduces Adam into eating the fruit of the tree of right and wrong, only to afflict him with the curse of knowledge. Her Hellenic sister, Pandora, exposes man to the ills that follow the loss of all innocence. And the Sumerian "harlot" who sleeps with Enkidu in the Gilgamesh Epic irrevocably denatures him by separating him from his friends, the beasts of the plains and forest. The *Odyssey* is a spiteful expedition through history in which the epic exorcises the ancient female deities by ridiculing them as perverse harridans.

But patriarchal morality reduces woman not merely to a generalized Hegelian Other who must be opposed, negated, and contained, as Simone de Beauvoir emphasized a generation ago; it particularizes this otherness into a specific hatred of her inquisitiveness, of her probing subjectivity and curiosity. Even in denying woman's "being in her own right," man affirms it by damning Eve for responding to the serpent, Pandora for daring to open the box of afflictions, and Circe for her power of prevision. A gnawing sense of inferiority and incompleteness stamps every aspect of the newly emergent male morality: evil abounds everywhere, pleasure and the senses are deceptive, and the *chaos* that always threatens to engulf the *kosmos* must be constantly warded off lest nature reclaim "civilization." Ironically, there is no denial, here, of woman's subjectivity but a shrieking fear of her latent powers and the possibility that they may be stirred back into life again.

Hence, patriarchal morality must bring her into complicity with the male's ever-tremulous image of her inferiority. She must be taught to view her posture of renunciation, modesty, and obedience as the intrinsic attributes of her subjectivity, in short, her total negation as a personality. It is utterly impossible to understand why meaningless wars, male boastfulness, exaggerated political rituals, and a preposterous elaboration of civil institutions engulf so many different, even tribal, societies without recognizing how much these phenomena are affirmations of male activity and expressions of his "supremacy." From the mindless and incessant conflicts that New Guinean peoples wage between themselves to the overly meticulous institutionalization of political forms, the male is ever-active and "overburdened" by his responsibilities—often because there is so little for him to do in primordial communities and even in many historical societies. But his increasing denigration of woman and his transposition of otherness from a conciliatory to antagonistic relationship generates a hostile ambience in society—a meanness of spirit, a craving for recognition, an aggressive appetite, and a terrifying exaggeration of cruelty—that is to render man increasingly prone to the victimization of his own kind. The slave is the male incarnation of the long-enslaved woman: a mere object to be possessed and used by the canons of patriarchal morality. The structuring of otherness antagonistically, which Hegel celebrated as the first steps toward self-identity, becomes an epistemology that devaluates humanity into an aggregate of mere objects, a psychological regression that ultimately leads to the arrogant conception of human beings as the mere embodiment of labor.

As victim and aggressor, woman and man are thus brought into blind complicity with a moral system that denies their human nature and ultimately the integrity of external nature as well. But latent forever in the repressive morality that emerges with patriarchy is a smoldering potentiality for revolt with its explosive rejection of the roles that socialization has instilled in all but the deepest recesses of human subjectivity. The moral constraints imposed by patriarchy and finally by class rule remain a constant affront to human rationality. From the ashes of morality arises the program of a new approach to right and wrong—a *rational* discipline called ethics—that is free of hierarchically instilled patterns of behavior. From ethics will emerge rational criteria for evaluating virtue, evil, and freedom, not merely blame, sin, and their penalties. Ethics may try to encompass morality and justify its epistemologies of rule, but it is always vulnerable to the very rational standards it has created to justify domination.

Self-denial and the increasingly heightened contradictions of rule create tensions so inherently destabilizing to "civilization" that class society must always be armored—not only psychologically by the State it cultivates within the individual, but physically by the State it institutionalizes. As Plato reminded the Athenians, the slave's nature is an unruly one, a philosophical formulation for a condition that could periodically become an explosive social reality. Where morality and psychic introjection fail to contain mounting social and personal contradictions, class society must have recourse to outright coercion— to the institutionalized system of force we call the political State.

⍥

Between society and the fully developed political State there is ultimately a historical point where the psychic constraints created by repressive socialization and morality begin to deteriorate. No longer can social and personal contradictions be resolved by means of discourse. All that remains is recourse to the threat of brute violence. Precapitalist society never shunned this possibility or cloaked it with sanctimonious homilies about the sacredness of life. It candidly admitted that coercion was its ultimate defence against social and popular unrest.

One might conjecture that the State as an instrument of organized violence evolved from the open exercise of violence. This has been the thesis of many radical theorists such as Proudhon. Yet there is much that so reductionist a view leaves unanswered historically, as both Marx and Kropotkin implied in a number of their writings.* The State did not simply explode on the social horizon like a volcanic eruption. Pastoral invasions may have accelerated its development dramatically, but a leap from stateless to State forms is probably a fiction.

The fact that the State is a hybridization of political with social institutions, of coercive with distributive functions, of highly punitive with regulatory procedures, and finally of class with administrative needs—this melding process has produced very real ideological and practical paradoxes that persist as major issues today. How easily, for example, can we separate State from society on the municipal, economic, national, and international levels? Is it possible to do so completely? Have State and society become so inextricably interwoven that a free society is impossible without certain State features such as the delegation of authority? In short, is freedom possible without the "depoliticized" State Marx was to proffer, or a "minimum" State, as some of his "libertarian" acolytes have contended? An attempt to answer these questions must be deferred to the closing chapters of this book. For the present, what concerns us are those attributes of the State that have meshed it with society to a point where our ability to distinguish between the two is completely blurred.

---

* In Marx's case, I refer to the very curious formulation in *The Civil War in France* that freedom "consists in converting the State from an organ superimposed upon society into one completely subordinated to it"—a formulation that calls not for the ultimate abolition of the State but suggests that it will continue to exist (however differently it is reconstituted by the proletariat) as a "nonpolitical" (i.e., administrative) source of authority. In Kropotkin's case, I refer to the belief he shared with Bakunin that the State was a "historically necessary evil" and his elaboration of the virtues of the medieval commune as a quasi-libertarian form of social life with only limited regard for its political trappings. There is a much larger question that anarchism, particularly its syndicalist variant, has not clearly faced: exactly what forms of the State's administrative organ would disappear if the pyramidal structure advanced by syndicalist theory were actually realized? Martin Buber, in his *Paths in Utopia*, exploited such paradoxes in his criticism of Kropotkin and his snide reference to Bakunin's notion of the regenerative effects of revolution.

Clearly, a distinction must first be made between social coercion and social influence. Despite their similarities, the two are not identical: Weber's charismatic leader at the beginnings of history is hardly the same as an impersonal bureaucracy near its end. The first is personal; the second, institutional. To take this distinction still further, hierarchical relationships that are based on personality are notoriously loose, ad hoc, and easily disassembled, like the "dominance-submission hierarchies" ethologists so readily impute to primates. Bureaucratic relationships, by contrast, are notoriously rigid, sclerotic, and intentionally divested of all personality. They tend to be self-perpetuating and self-expansive. As mere instruments of rule, bureaucratic structures are quintessentially hierarchical; indeed, they are the political expression of *objective* power, of power that "merely" happens to be executed by people who, as bureaucrats, are totally divested of personality and uniqueness. Accordingly, for many areas of the modern world, such people have been turned almost literally into a State technology, one in which each bureaucrat is interchangeable with another including, more recently, with mechanical devices.*

The difference between social coercion and social influence is clearly seen in seemingly hierarchical societies that are still politically undeveloped. The fairly stratified Northwest Coast Indians provide a good example that could easily be extended to include the more sophisticated cultures of Polynesia. These Indian societies had slaves, and presumably the very "last and lowliest citizen knew his precise hereditary position with an [exactly] defined distance from the chief," observes Peter Farb. But, in point of fact, they could hardly be called State-structured communities. The chief "had no political power and no way to back up his decisions." His social influence was based on prestige. He lacked any "monopoly of force." If he failed to perform his duties to the satisfaction of the community, he could be removed. Indeed, despite the highly stratified structure of these communities, they were not a "class society" in any modern sense of the term. Stratification was based on whether one was more closely related by blood ties to the chief or less related—literally, to use Farb's term, a matter of "distance from the chief." In short, lineage determined status, not economic position or institutional gradations. "To insist upon the use of the term 'class

---

* The great Stalinist purges of the last generation attest to the loss of any human dimension in bureaucratic rule. The nearly genocidal proportions which these purges were to assume among the Stalinist bureaucrats themselves are vivid evidence that virtually everyone in the system was seen to be expendable and easily liquidated, to use the barbarous official term for mass arrests and murders.

system' for Northwest Coast society," observes P. Drucker, "means that each individual was in a class by himself"—a situation that more closely resembles primate "hierarchies" than the institutionalized stratification we associate with a class society.

What initially characterizes the emergence of the State is the gradual politicization of important social *functions*. From Indian American to the most distant reaches of Asia, we find considerable evidence that personal status roles, very similar in principle to the chieftainships of the Northwest Coast Indians, were slowly transformed into political *institutions*, a transformation that involved not only coercion but the satisfaction of genuine social needs. One of the principal needs these institutions satisfied was the redistribution of goods among ecologically and culturally disparate areas. In the absence of local markets, the kingly figures who rose to prominence in the Nile valley, on the Mesopotamian plains, in the Peruvian mountains, and in the river valleys of India and China made it possible for the produce of food cultivators, hunters, animal herders, and fishermen to reach communities, including administrative cities, that might otherwise have had access to only a limited variety of goods. Although similar functions had been performed earlier by temple storehouses on a local scale, the monarchs of ancient civilizations graduated these functions to an imperial scale.

Moreover, they also served to buffer periods of "feast" and "famine." The story of Joseph is more than a Biblical parable on consanguineal responsibilities and allegiances. It exemplifies autocratic ideology that intermingles the social with the political principle in the mystified world of prophetic dreams. Joseph embodies the combined roles of the clairvoyant with the vizier, the mythopoeic figures with the calculating rational functionary. If Gilgamesh reminds us of the warrior who must be socialized from deity into king, Joseph reminds us of a still earlier change: the tribal shaman who is to become an explicitly *political* figure before society and the State are clearly distinguishable. His story, in fact, confronts us with one of the paradoxes of the past that remains with us today: where does the political seer (from the charismatic leader to the constitutional theorist) end and the social administrator, pure and simple, begin? Indeed, where can the State be distinguished from the socially pragmatic functions it begins to absorb? These are no idle questions, as we shall see, for they haunt us continually in our attempts to reconstruct a vision of a free and human social future.

Joseph is also one of the earliest political professionals, and professionalism is a hallmark of statism—the abolition of social management as an "amateur" activity.* Canons of efficiency become a political morality in themselves, thereby replacing the still unarticulated notion of informal, presumably inefficient forms of freedom. Even more than Yahweh, the State is a jealous god. It must preempt, absorb, and concentrate power as a nutritive principle of self-preservation. This form of political imperialism over all other prerogatives of society produces a rank jungle of metaphysical statist ideologies: the Enlightenment's identification of the State with society, Hegel's concept of the State as the realization of society's ethical idea, Spencer's notion of the State as a "biological organism," Bluntschli's vision of the State as the institutionalization of a "collective will," Meyer's idealization of the State as an organizing principle of society. One can go on indefinitely and selectively piece together a corporative vision of the State that easily lends itself to Fascist ideology.

Historically, the State obliterates the distinction between governance and administration. The so-called primitive peoples in organic societies were acutely conscious of this difference. The closer we come to cultures organized in bands and comparatively simple tribes, the more "rule" is an ad hoc, non-institutionalized system of administration. Even the Crow Indian military and religious societies (actually, club-like fraternities) are examples not of government but of administration. In contrast to the permanent institutionalized structures based on obedience and command that government presupposes even on the most rudimentary levels, Crow societies were marked by a rotation of functions and by episodic sovereignty for very limited and well-defined ends. Such sovereignty as these societies enjoyed over the community as a whole was largely functional: they primarily policed the bison hunts, a project whose success involved a high degree of coordination and discipline.

To call these activities "governmental" rather than "administrative" and to see in them evidence of a fully developed State rather than political functions of the most rudimentary kind is not mere word-play. It reflects conceptual confusion at its worst. In political ideologies of all types, the abuse of terms like government and administration turn the State into the template for a free society, however much its functions are reduced to a "minimum." Ultimately, this confusion provides the State with

---

* The ritualistic side of Joseph's acquisition of power, which is later to be secularized into the electoral ritual, is one of the most compelling passages in the drama: "And Pharaoh took off his signet ring from his hand, and put it upon Joseph's hand, and arrayed him in vestures of fine linen, and put a gold chain about his neck. And he made him to ride in the second chariot which he had; and they cried before him: 'Abrech'; and he set him all over the land of Egypt." (Genesis 41: 52–41, Masoretic Text)

the ideological rationale for its maximum development, notably the Soviet-type regimes of Eastern Europe. Like the market, the State knows no limits; it can easily become a self-generating and self-expanding force for its own sake, the institutional form in which domination for the sake of domination acquires palpability.

The State's capacity to absorb social functions provides it not only with an ideological rationale for its existence; it physically and psychologically rearranges social life so that it seems indispensable as an *organizing principle* for human consociation. In other words, the State has an epistemology of its own, a *political* one that is imprinted upon the psyche and mind. A centralized State gives rise to a centralized society; a bureaucratic State to a bureaucratic society; a militaristic State to a militaristic society—and all develop the outlooks and psyches with the appropriate "therapeutic" techniques for adapting the individual to each.

In restructuring society around itself, the State acquires superadded social functions that now appear as political functions. It not only *manages* the economy but *politicizes* it; it not only *colonizes* social life but *absorbs* it. Social forms thus appear as State forms and social values as political values. Society is reorganized in such a way that it becomes indistinguishable from the State. Revolution is thus confronted not only with the task of smashing the State and reconstructing *administration* along libertarian lines; it must also smash society, as it were, and reconstruct human *consociation* itself along new communal lines. The problem that now faces revolutionary movements is not merely one of reappropriating society but literally reconstituting it.*

❧

But this melding of State and society, as we shall see, is a fairly recent development. Initially, what often passes for the State in the sociological literature of our time is a very loose, unstable, indeed, even a fairly democratic ensemble of institutions that have very shallow roots in society. Popular assemblies of citizens are rarely complete State forms, even when their membership is resolutely restricted. Nor are chieftainships and rudimentary kingships easily resolvable

---

* By this I mean creating a qualitatively new society, not merely establishing "work democracy," an "equitable distribution of goods," or even "expropriating the expropriators"—i.e., retaining capitalism without its capitalists. Lenin's assertion that "socialism is state capitalism for the benefit of the people" reveals the bankruptcy of the socialist project of appropriating the present society while unthinkingly perpetuating its old perverse traits within the "new" one. Nor do economistic libertarian movements offer us a qualitatively new alternative, however anti-authoritarian their goals.

into authentic political institutions. During early stages of antiquity, when councils and centralized institutions begin to assume State-like forms, they are easily unravelled and governance returns again to society. We would do well to call the tenuous political institutions of Athens *quasi*-State forms, and the so-called Oriental despotisms of antiquity are often so far-removed from village life that their control of traditional communities is tenuous and unsystematic.

The medieval commune is marked by equally striking ambiguities in the relationships between State and society. What renders Kropotkin's discussion of the commune so fascinating in *Mutual Aid* is his very loose use of the term State to describe its system of self-governance. As he emphasizes,

> Self-jurisdiction was the essential point, and self-jurisdiction meant self-administration. But the commune was not simply an autonomous part of the State—such ambiguous words had yet to be invented by that time—*it was a State in itself.* It had the right of war and peace, of federation and alliance with its neighbors. It was sovereign in its own affairs, and mixed with no others. The supreme political power could be vested in a democratic forum, as was the case in Pskov, whose *vyeche* sent and received ambassadors, concluded treaties, accepted and sent away princes, or went on without them for dozens of years; or it was vested in, or usurped by, an aristocracy of merchants or even nobles as was the case in hundreds of Italian and middle European cities. The principle, nevertheless, remained the same: *The city was a State* and—what is perhaps more remarkable—when the power in the city was usurped by an aristocracy of merchants or even nobles, the inner life of the city and the democratism of its daily life did not disappear: they depended but little upon what could be called the *political form* of the State.

Given Kropotkin's highly sophisticated anarchist views, these lines are remarkable—and they actually cast considerable light on the formation of the State as a graded phenomenon. The State acquires stability, form, and identity only when personal loyalties are transmuted into depersonalized institutions, power becomes centralized and professionalized, custom gives way to law, and governance absorbs administration. But the decisive shift from society to the State occurs with the most supreme political act of all: the delegation of power. It is not insignificant that heated disputes, both theoretically and historically, have revolved about this crucially important act. Social contract theory, from Hobbes to Rousseau, recognized in the delegation of power an almost metaphysical centrality. The social contract itself was seen as an act of personal disempowerment, a conscious surrender by the self of control over the social conditions of life. To Hobbes and Locke, to be sure, the delegation of power was restricted by the security of life (Hobbes) and its extension through labor into the sanctity of property (Locke).

Rousseau's views were sterner and more candid than those of his British predecessors. In a widely quoted passage in *The Social Contract*, he declared:

> Sovereignty, for the same reason as it makes it inalienable, cannot be represented. It lies essentially in the general will and will does not admit of representation: it is either the same, or other; there is no intermediate possibility. The deputies of the people, therefore, are not and cannot be its representative: they are merely its stewards, and can carry through no definitive acts. Every law the people has not ratified in person is null and void—is, in fact, not a law. The people of England regards itself as free: but it is grossly mistaken: it is free only during the election of members of parliament. As soon as they are elected, slavery overtakes it, and it is nothing.

Removed from the general context of *The Social Contract*, this passage can be easily misunderstood. But what is important is Rousseau's clear distinction between deputation and delegation, direct democracy and representation. To delegate power is to divest personality of its most integral traits; it denies the very notion that the individual is *competent* to deal not only with the management of his or her personal life but with its most important context: the *social* context. Certainly early societies did not deal with the issue of delegated power in terms of selfhood and its integrity, but the historical record suggests that they functioned as though these issues profoundly influenced their behavior.

The problem of delegated power emerged most clearly in the affairs of the "city-state." Indeed, beyond localized social areas, the problem itself becomes elusive and obscure if only because it loses its human scale and comprehensibility. In Sumerian history according to Henri Frankfort, the earliest "city-states" were managed by "equalitarian assemblies," which possessed "freedom to an uncommon degree." Even subjection to the will of the majority, as expressed in a vote, was unknown. The delegation of power to a numerical majority, in effect, was apparently viewed as a transgression of primal integrity, at least in its tribal form. "The assembly continued deliberation under the guidance of the elders until practical unanimity was reached." As the city-states began to expand and quarrel over land and water-rights, the power to wage war was conferred on an *ensi* or "great man." But this delegation of power would revert to the assembly once a conflict between the "city-states" came to an end. As Frankfort notes, however,

> The threat of an emergency was never absent once the cities flourished and increased in number. Contiguous fields, questions of drainage and irrigation, the safe-guarding of supplies by procuring safety in transit— all these might become matters of dispute between neighboring cities. We can follow through five or six generations a futile and destructive war between Umma and Lagash with a few fields of arable land as the stakes. Under such conditions the kingship [*bala*] seems to have become permanent.

Even so, there is evidence of popular revolts, possibly to restore the old social dispensation or to diminish the authority of the *bala*. The records are too dim to give us a clear idea of all the issues that may have produced internal conflicts within Sumerian cities, but a leap from tribalism to despotism is obvious myth.

The issue of delegating power while affirming the competency of the body politic achieves an extraordinary degree of consciousness and clarity in classical Athens. Perikles' Funeral Oration is one of the most remarkable vestiges we have of *polis* democracy, as reconstructed by one of its opponents, Thukydides. The oration celebrates not only civic duty and freedom; it strongly affirms the claims of personality and private freedom. Athens' laws "afford equal justice to all in their private differences," Perikles is reported to have declared, and "class considerations" do not "interfere with merit; nor again does poverty bar the way. If a man is able to serve the *polis*, he is not hindered by the obscurity of his position." Political freedom

> extends also to our ordinary life. There, far from exercising a jealous surveillance over each other, we do not feel called upon to be angry with our neighbour for doing what he likes, or even indulge in those injurious looks which cannot fail to be offensive, although they inflict no positive penalty. But all this ease in our private relations does not make us lawless as citizens.

From these personally exhilarating observations, for which there is no available precedent in the classical literature, the oration builds up to a keen worldly sense of Athens as a *polis* that transcends the confines of a tradition-bound community:

> We throw open our city to the world, and never by alien acts exclude
> foreigners from any opportunity of learning or observing, although the
> eyes of an enemy may occasionally profit by our liberality, trusting less
> in system and policy than to the native spirit of our citizens; while in
> education, where our rivals from their very cradles by a painful discipline
> seek after manliness, at Athens we live exactly as we please and yet are
> just as ready to encounter every legitimate danger.

Perikles' confidence in the integrity of the *polis* is built upon his
expansive confidence in the integrity of its citizens. Here, the Athenian
ideal of citizenship as the physical reality of the body politic—indeed, as
society incarnated into an assembled community of free individuals
who directly formulate and administer policy—finds a conscious
expression that it does not achieve again until very recent times. To
Perikles, all Athenians are to be viewed as competent individuals, as selves
that are capable of self-management, hence their right to claim unmediated
sovereignty over public affairs. The genius of Athens lies not only in
the completeness of the *polis* but in the completeness of its citizens,
for while Athens may be "the school of Hellas," Perikles doubts
"if the world can produce a man, who where he has only himself
to depend upon, is equal to so many emergencies and graced by so happy
a versatility, as the Athenian." The Greek concept of *autarkeia*, of
individual self-sufficiency graced by an all-roundedness of selfhood, forms
the authentic basis of Athenian democracy. Not surprisingly, this famous
passage, which begins with a paean to the community, Athens, ends
with its warmest tribute to the individual—the Athenian.

We have very few statements, including the declarations of human
rights produced by the great revolutions, that bear comparison with
Perikles'. The great oration exhibits a sensitive balance between community
and individual, and an association of social administration with
competence that rarely achieves comparable centrality in later statements
on freedom. It is not in "god" that the Athenian *polis* placed its "trust,"
but in itself. The practice of a direct democracy was an affirmation of
citizenship as a process of direct action. Athens was institutionally
organized to convert its potentially monadic citizenry from free-
floating atoms into a cohesive body politic. Its regular citizen assemblies
(*Ecclesia*), its rotating Council of Five Hundred (*Boule*), and its court
juries that replicated in the hundreds the *polis* in miniature, were the *conscious*
creations of a public realm that had largely been fostered intuitively in tribal
societies and were rarely to rise to the level of rational practice in the

centuries to follow. The entire Athenian system was organized to obstruct political professionalism, to prevent the emergence of bureaucracy, and to perpetuate an active citizenry *as a matter of design*. We may rightly fault this democracy for denying power to slaves, women, and resident aliens, who formed the great majority of the population. But these traits were not unique to Athens; they existed throughout the Mediterranean world in the fifth century B.C. What was uniquely Athenian were the institutional forms it developed for a minority of its population—forms that more traditional "civilizations" rendered into the privilege of only a very small ruling class.

Conflicts over delegation and deputation of power, bureaucracy, and the citizen's claims to competence appear throughout history. They recur in the medieval commune, in the English, American, and French revolutions, in the Paris Commune of 1871, and even recently in the form of popular demands for municipal and neighborhood autonomy. Like a strange talisman, these conflicts serve almost electrically to dissociate the social claims of the State from the political claims of society. The issue of public competence penetrates the ideological armor that conceals State functions from social to separate governance from administration, professionalism from amateurism, institutionalized relations from functional ones, and the monopoly of violence from the citizens in arms. Athenian institutions were unique not merely because of their practices, but because they were the products of *conscious intent* rather than the accidents of political intuition or custom. The very practice of the Athenians in creating their democratic institutions was *itself* an end; it was equivalent to the *polis* conceived as a social process.

A very thin line separates the practice of direct democracy from direct action.* The former is institutionalized and self-disciplined; the latter is episodic and often highly spontaneous. Yet a relationship between an assembled populace that formulates policies in a face-to-face manner and such actions as strikes, civil disobedience, and even insurrection can be established around the right of a people to assume unmediated control over

---

* The most common definitions of direct action are usually exemplary rather than theoretical. They consist of citing strikes, demonstrations, "mob violence," sit-ins of all kinds and in all places, Ghandian civil disobedience, and even vigilantism. In all such cases, our attention is directed to *events* rather than goals and theoretical generalizations. What unites this behavior under the term "direct action" is the unmediated intervention of people into affairs that are usually resolved by parliamentary debates and legislation. People take over the streets; they may even occupy the parliamentary structures and rely on their own action rather than on political surrogates to achieve certain ends.

public life. Representation has been validated by an elitist belief that the only select individuals (at best, selected by virtue of experience and ability, at worst, by birth) are qualified to understand public affairs. Today, representation is validated by instrumental reasons, such as the complexity of modern society and its maze of logistical intricacies.

Hellenic democracy acquired a particularly onerous—actually, fearsome—reputation as a "mobocracy," which is a modern translation of its opponents' views in the fifth century B.C., perhaps because it revealed that direct action could be institutionalized without being bureaucratized. Hence, direct action could be turned into a permanent process—a permanent revolution—not merely a series of episodic acts. If it could be shown that direct action as a form of self-administration serves to stabilize society, not reduce it to chaotic shambles, the State would be placed in the dock of history as a force for violence and domination.

A few important questions remain. Under what social conditions can direct action be institutionalized as a direct democracy? And what are the institutional forms that could be expected to produce this change? The answers to these questions, like others we have raised, must be deferred to the closing portions of the work. What we can reasonably ask at this point is what kind of citizen or public self—what principle of citizenship and selfhood—forms the true basis for a direct democracy? The common principle that legitimates direct action and direct democracy is a body politic's commitment to the belief that an assembled public, united as free and autonomous individuals, can deal in a competent, face-to-face manner with the direction of public affairs.

No concept of politics has been the target of greater derision and ideological denunciation by the State, for it impugns every rationale for statehood. It substitutes the ideal of personal competency for elitism, amateurism for professionalism, a body politic in the protoplasmic sense of a face-to-face democracy for the delegation and bureaucratization of decision-making and its execution, the re-empowerment of the individual and the attempt to achieve agreement by dialogue and reason for the monopoly of power and violence. From the State's viewpoint, the public "usurpation" of social affairs represents the triumph of *chaos* over *kosmos*. And if the legacy of domination has had any broader purpose than the support of hierarchical and class interests, it has been the attempt to exorcise the belief in public competence from social discourse itself. Although direct democracy has received more gentle treatment as an archaism that is incompatible with the needs of a "complex" and "sophisticated" society, direct action as the training ground for the selfhood, self-assertiveness, and sensibility for direct democracy has been consistently denounced as anarchy, or equivalently, the degradation of social life to chaos.*

○઼

One society—capitalism, in both its democratic and totalitarian forms—has succeeded to a remarkable degree in achieving this exorcism—and only in very recent times. The extraordinary extent to which bourgeois society has discredited popular demands for public control of the social process is the result of sweeping structural changes in society itself. Appeals for local autonomy suggest politically naive and atavistic social demands only because domination has become far more than a mere legacy. It has sedimented over every aspect of social life. Indeed, the increasingly vociferous demands for local control may reflect the extent to which community itself, be it a municipality or a neighborhood, is faced with extinction.

What makes capitalism so unique is the sweeping power it gives to economics: the supremacy it imparts to *homo economicus*. As Marx, who celebrated this triumph as an economic historian with the same vigor he was to condemn it as a social critic, observed:

> The great civilizing influence of capital [lies in] its production of a stage of society in comparison to which all earlier ones appear as mere *local* developments of humanity and as *nature-idolatry*. For the first time, nature becomes purely an object of humankind, purely a matter of utility; ceases to be recognized as a power for itself; and the theoretical discovery of its autonomous laws appears merely as a ruse so as to subjugate it under human needs, whether as an object of consumption or as a means of production.

Much of this quotation was written in bad faith, for no one was more mindful in his day that the fear of capital and attempts to contain it on ethical grounds reach back to Aristotle's time and even earlier. But the effects of capitalism and its historical uniqueness are accurately represented. In every precapitalist society, countervailing forces (all "nature-idolatry" aside) existed to restrict

---

* Unfortunately, the cause of direct democracy and direct action has not always been well served by its acolytes. On the whole, the most mischievous example of this disservice is the very common view that direct action is merely a "tactic" or "strategy," not a sensibility that yields the selfhood necessary for self-management and direct democracy. Nor is elitism alien to self-styled "libertarians" who use high-minded ideals and gullible followers as stepping stones to personal careers and social recognition.

the market economy. No less significantly, many precapitalist societies raised what they thought were insuperable obstacles to the penetration of the State into social life. Ironically, Marx, more so than the major social theorists of his day, recognized the power of village communities to resist the invasion of trade and despotic political forms into society's abiding communal substrate.

In *Capital*, Marx meticulously explored the remarkable capacity of India's traditional village society to retain its archetypal identity against the corrosive effects of the State. As he observed:

> Those small and extremely ancient Indian communities, for example, some of which continue to exist to this day, are based on the possession of the land in common, on the blending of agriculture and handicrafts and on an unalterable division of labor, which serves as a fixed plan and basis for action whenever a new community is started. ... The law which regulates the division of labor in the community acts with the irresistible authority of a law of nature, while each individual craftsman, the smith, the carpenter and so on, conducts in his workshop all the operations of his handicraft in the traditional way, but independently; without recognizing any authority. The simplicity of the productive organism in these self-sufficing communities which constantly reproduce themselves in the same form and, when accidentally destroyed, spring up again on the same spot and with the same name—this simplicity supplies the key to the riddle of the unchangeability of Asiatic societies, which is in such striking contrast with the constant dissolution and refounding of Asiatic states, and their never-ceasing changes of dynasty. The structure of the fundamental economic elements of society remains untouched by the storms which blow up in the cloudy regions of politics.

Again, one could wish for a less economistic and perhaps less technical interpretation of the Asian village whose elaborate culture seems to completely elude Marx's attention in these passages. So overwhelming was this cultural "inertia" that nothing short of genocidal annihilation could overcome its capacity to resist invasive economic and political forces.*

---

* Most notably the massive uprooting of village populations and the engineered "famines" carried out by the British more than a century ago in India and the wholesale slaughter of country people by the Americans in Indochina. Perhaps it will seem uncharitable, but I must add that the Americans inadvertently performed a great service for the cause of "socialism" when they destroyed the Vietnamese village society. Whatever

A similar role was played by the guilds of medieval Europe, the yeomanry of Reformation England, and the peasantry of western Europe. Well into the twentieth century, farmers in townships (or comparatively isolated farmsteads) and urban dwellers were locked into clearly definable neighborhoods, extended families, strong cultural traditions and small, family-owned retail trade. These systems coexisted with the burgeoning industrial and commercial apparatus of capitalist America and Europe. Although a market economy and an industrial technology had clearly established their sovereignty over these areas, the self retained its own nonbourgeois refuge from the demands of a purely capitalistic society. In home and family (admittedly patricentric and parochial), in town or neighborhood, in a personalized retail trade and a relatively human scale, and in a socialization process that instilled traditional verities of decency, hospitality, and service, society still preserved a communal refuge of its own from the atomizing forces of the market economy.

By the middle of the present century, however, large-scale market operations had colonized every aspect of social and personal life. The buyer-seller relationship—a relationship that lies at the very core of the market—became the all-pervasive substitute for human relationships at the most molecular level of social, indeed, personal life. To "buy cheaply" and "sell dearly" places the parties involved in the exchange process in an inherently antagonistic posture; they are potential rivals for each other's goods. The commodity—as distinguished from the gift, which is meant to create alliances, foster association, and consolidate sociality—leads to rivalry, dissociation, and asociality.

Aside from the fears that philosophers from Aristotle to Hegel have articulated in their concern for the dissociative role of a commerce and industry organized for exchange, society itself had long buffered exchange with a social etiquette of its own—one that still lingers on in the vestigial face-to-face archaic marketplace of the bazaar. Here, one does not voice a demand for goods, compare prices, and engage in the market's universal duel called "bargaining." Rather, etiquette requires that the exchange process begin gracefully and retain its communal dimension. It opens with the serving of beverages, an exchange of news and gossip, some personal chit-chat, and, in time, expressions of

the future of southeast Asia may hold, I am convinced that this service will coincide admirably with the schemes of the North Vietnamese Communists for establishing collective farms and fostering industrial development—just as the genocidal destruction of the Russian village by Stalin in the 1930s paved the way for "socialism" in the Soviet Union.

admiration for the wares at hand. One leads to the exchange process tangentially. The bargain, if struck, is a bond, a compact sealed by time-honored ethical imperatives.

The apparently noncommercial ambience of this exchange process should not be viewed as mere canniness or hypocrisy. It reflects the limits that precapitalist society imposed on exchange to avoid the latent impersonality of trade, as well as its potential meanness of spirit, its insatiable appetite for gain, its capacity to subvert all social limits to private material interest, to dissolve all traditional standards of community and consociation, to subordinate the needs of the body politic to egoistic concerns.

But it was not only for these reasons that trade was viewed warily. Precapitalist society may well have seen in the exchange of commodities a return of the inorganic, of the substitution of things for living human relationships. These objects could certainly be viewed symbolically as tokens of consociation, alliance and mutuality—which is precisely what the gift was meant to represent. But divested of this symbolic meaning, these mere things or commodities could acquire socially corrosive traits. Left unchecked and unbuffered, they might well vitiate all forms of human consociation and ultimately dissolve society itself. The transition from gift to commodity, in effect, could yield the disintegration of the community into a market place, the consanguinal or ethical union between people into rivalry and aggressive egotism.

That the triumph of the commodity over the gift was possible only after vast changes in human social relationships has been superbly explored in the closing portion of *Capital*. I need not summarize Marx's devastating narration and analysis of capitalist accumulation, its "general law," and particularly the sweeping dislocation of the English peasantry from the fifteenth century onward. The gift itself virtually disappeared as the objectification of association. It lingered on merely as a byproduct of ceremonial functions. The traditional etiquette that buffered the exchange process was replaced by a completely impersonal, predatory—and today, an increasingly electronic—process. Price came first, quality came later; and the very things that were once symbols rather than mere objects for use and exchange were to become fetishized, together with the "needs" they were meant to satisfy. Suprahuman forces now seemed to take command over the ego itself. Even self-interest, which Greek social theory viewed as the most serious threat to the unity of the *polis*, seemed to be governed by a market system that divested the subject of its very capacity to move freely through the exchange process as an autonomous buyer and seller.

Ironically, modern industry, having derived from archaic systems of commerce and retailing, has returned to its commercial origins with a vengeful self-hatred marked by a demeaning rationalization of trade itself. The shopping mall with its extravagant areas delivered over to parked motor vehicles, its sparcity of sales personnel, its cooing "muzak," its dazzling array of shelved goods, its elaborate surveillance system, its lack of all warmth and human intercourse, its cruelly deceptive packaging, and its long check-out counters which indifferently and impersonally record the exchange process—all speak to a denaturing of consociation at levels of life that deeply affront every human sensibility and the sacredness of the very goods that are meant to support life itself.

What is crucially important here is that this world penetrates personal as well as economic life. The shopping mall is the *agora* of modern society, the civic center of a totally economic and inorganic world. It works its way into every personal haven from capitalist relations and imposes its centricity on every aspect of domestic life. The highways that lead to its parking lots and its production centers devour communities and neighborhoods; its massive command of retail trade devours the family-owned store; the subdivisions that cluster around it devour farmland; the motor vehicles that carry worshippers to its temples are self-enclosed capsules that preclude all human contact. The inorganic returns not only to industry and the marketplace; it calcifies and dehumanizes the most intimate relationships between people in the presumably invulnerable world of the bedroom and nursery. The massive dissolution of personal and social ties that comes with the return of the inorganic transforms the extended family into the nuclear family and finally delivers the individual over to the purveyors of the singles' bars.

With the hollowing out of community by the market system, with its loss of structure, articulation, and form, we witness the concomitant hollowing out of personality itself. Just as the spiritual and institutional ties that linked human beings together into vibrant social relations are eroded by the mass market, so the sinews that make for subjectivity, character, and self-definition are divested of form and meaning. The isolated, seemingly autonomous ego that bourgeois society celebrated as the highest achievement of "modernity" turns out to be the mere husk of a once fairly rounded individual whose very completeness as an ego was possible because he or she was rooted in a fairly rounded and complete community.

As the inorganic replaces the organic in nature, so the inorganic replaces the organic in society and personality. The simplification of the natural world has its uncanny parallel in the simplification of society and subjectivity. The homogenization of ecosystems goes hand in hand with the homogenization of the social environment and the so-called individuals who people it. The intimate association of the domination of human by human with the notion of the domination of nature terminates not only in the notion of domination as such; its most striking feature is the *kind* of prevailing nature—an *inorganic* nature—that replaces the organic nature that humans once viewed so reverently.

We can never disembed ourselves from nature—any more than we can disembed ourselves from our own viscera. The technocratic "utopia" of personalized automata remains a hollow myth. The therapies that seek to adjust organic beings to inorganic conditions merely produce lifeless, inorganic, and depersonalized automata. Hence, nature always affirms its existence as the matrix for social and personal life, a matrix in which life is always embedded by definition. By rationalizing and simplifying society and personality, we do not divest it of its natural attributes; rather, we brutally destroy its organic attributes. Thus nature never simply coexists with us; it is part of every aspect of our structure and being. To turn back natural evolution from more complex forms of organic beings to simpler ones, from the organic to the inorganic, entails the turning back of society and social development from more complex to simpler forms.

The myth that *our* society is more complex than earlier cultures requires short shrift; our complexity is strictly technical, not cultural; our effluvium of "individuality" is more neurotic and psychopathic, not more unique or more intricate. "Modernity" reached its apogee between the decades preceding the French Revolution and the 1840s, after which industrial capitalism fastened its grip on social life. Its career, with a modest number of exceptions, has yielded a grim denaturing of humanity and society. Since the middle of the present century, even the vestiges of its greatness—apart from dramatic explosions like the 1960s—have all but disappeared from virtually every realm of experience.

What has largely replaced the sinews that held community and personality together is an all-encompassing, coldly depersonalizing bureaucracy. The agency and the bureaucrat have become the substitutes for the family, the town and neighborhood, the personal support structures of peoples in crisis, and the supernatural and mythic figures that afforded power and tutelary surveillance over the destiny of the individual. With no other structure to speak of but the bureaucratic agency, society has not merely been riddled by bureaucracy; it has all but become a bureaucracy in which everyone, as Camus was wont to say, has been reduced to a functionary. Personality as such has become congruent with the various documents, licenses, and records that define one's place in the world. More sacred than such documents as passports, which are the archaic tokens of citizenship, a motor vehicle license literally validates one's identity, and a credit card becomes the worldwide coinage of exchange.

The legacy of domination thus culminates in the growing together of the State and society—and with it, a dissolution of the family, community, mutual aid, and social commitment. Even a sense of one's personal destiny disappears into the bureaucrat's office and filing cabinet. History itself will be read in the microfilm records and computer tapes of the agencies that now form the authentic institutions of society. Psychological categories have indeed "become political categories," as Marcuse observed in the opening lines of his *Eros and Civilization*, but in a pedestrian form that exceeds his most doleful visions. The Superego is no longer formed by the father or even by domineering social institutions; it is formed by the faceless people who preside over the records of birth and death, of religious affiliation and educational pedigree, of "mental health" and psychological proclivities, of vocational training and job acquisition, of marriage and divorce certificates, of credit ratings and bank accounts; in short, of the endless array of licenses, tests, contracts, grades, and personality traits that define the status of the individual in society. Political categories have replaced psychological categories in much the same sense that an electrocardiograph has replaced the heart. Under state capitalism, even economic categories become political categories. Domination fulfills its destiny in the ubiquitous, all-pervasive State; its legacy reaches its denouement in the dissolution, indeed, the complete disintegration, of a richly organic society into an inorganic one—a terrifying destiny that the natural world shares with the social.

Reason, which was expected to dispel the dark historic forces to which a presumably unknowing humanity had been captive, now threatens to become one of these very forces in the form of rationalization. It now enhances the efficiency of domination. The great project of western speculative thought—to render humanity self-conscious—stands before a huge abyss: a yawning chasm into which the self and consciousness threaten to disappear. How can we define the historical subject—a role Marx imputed to the proletariat—that will create a society guided by selfhood and consciousness? What is the *context* in which that subject is formed? Is it the workplace, specifically, the factory? Or a new emancipated *polis*? Or the domestic arena? Or the university? Or the countercultural community?

With these questions, we begin to depart from the legacy of domination and turn to countervailing traditions and ideals that may provide some point of departure for a solution. We must turn to the legacy of freedom that has always cut across the legacy of domination. Perhaps it holds some clue to a resolution of these problems—problems which, more than ever, leave our era suspended in uncertainty and riddled by the ambiguities of rationalization and technocratic power.

6 ⬧ JUSTICE—EQUAL AND EXACT

The notion of "freedom" does not seem to exist in organic society. As we saw earlier, the word is simply meaningless to many preliterate peoples. Lacking any institutionalized structure of domination, they have no way of defining a condition that is still intrinsically part of their social lives—a condition into which they grow without the elaborate hierarchical and later class structures of the late Neolithic and of "civilization." As "freedom" and "domination" are not in tension with each other, they lack contrast and definition.

But the very lack of distinction between "freedom" and "domination" leaves organic society unguarded against hierarchy and class rule. Innocence exposes the community to manipulation on the most elementary levels of social experience. The elders, shamans, later the patriarchs, priestly corporations, and warrior chieftains, who are to corrode organic society, need only produce shifts in emphasis from the particular to the general—from specific animals to their spirits; from zoomorphic to anthropomorphic deities; from usufruct to communal property; from demonic treasure to kingly storehouses; from gifts to commodities; finally, from mere barter to elaborate marketplaces.

History may have been bloody and its destiny may be a universal tragedy with heroic efforts and lost possibilities punctuating its long career. But a body of hopeless ideals and a meaningless movement of events it was not. With the loss of innocence appeared new concepts that were to have a highly equivocal effect on social development, a certain ideological armoring, a growth of intellectual powers, an increasing degree of individuality, personal autonomy, and a sense of a universal *humanitas* as distinguished from folk parochialism. To be expelled from the Garden of Eden can be, regarded, as Hegel was to say, as an important condition for its return—but on a level that is informed with a sophistication that can resolve the paradoxes of paradise.

The universalization of ideas acquires its most beguiling intellectual form in the ever-expansive meaning people give to freedom. Once unfreedom emerges to yield the notion of freedom, the notion acquires a remarkable logic of its own that produces, in its various byways and differentia, a richly articulated body of issues and formulations—a veritable garden from which we can learn and from which we can pluck what we want to make an attractive bouquet. From the loss of a society that was once free comes the vision of an admittedly embellished, often extravagantly fanciful golden age—one that may contain norms even more liberatory in their universality than those which existed in organic society. From a "backward-looking" utopianism, commonly based on the image of a bountiful nature and unfettered consumption arises a "forward-looking" utopianism based on the image of a bountiful economy and unfettered production. Between these two extremes, religious and anarchic movements develop a more balanced, although equally generous, vision of utopia that combines sharing with self-discipline, freedom with coordination, and joy with responsibility.

Almost concomitantly with this utopian development, largely "underground" in nature, we witness the open emergence of justice—first, as a surrogate for the freedom that is lost with the decline of organic society, later as the ineffable protagonist of new conceptions of freedom. With justice, we hear the claims of the individual and the ideal of a universal humanity voice their opposition to the limits imposed on personality and society by the folk collective. But freedom, too, will divide and oppose itself as mere "happiness" (Marx) and extravagant "pleasure" (Fourier)—as we shall see in the chapters that follow. So, too, will labor—conceived as the indispensable toil in which every society is anchored or as the free release of human powers and consociation even in the realm of demanding work.

Coherence requires that we try to bring these various components of the legacy of freedom together. Coherence also requires that we try to interlink our project with nature to impart rationality not only to social but also to natural history. We must explore the values, sensibilities, and technics that harmonize our relationship with nature as well as ourselves. Coherence finally requires that we try to bring together the threads of these shared histories—natural and social—into a whole that unites differentia into a *meaningful* ensemble, one that also removes hierarchy from our sense of meaning and releases spontaneity as an informed and creative nisus.

But a strong caveat must here be raised: ideas, values, and institutions are not mere commodities on the shelves of an ideological supermarket; we cannot promiscuously drop them into shopping carts like processed goods. The context we form from ideas, the ways we relate them, and the meanings we impart to them are as important as the components and sources from which our "whole" is composed. Perhaps it is true, as the world of Schiller seemed to believe, that the Greeks said everything. But if so, each thinker and practitioner said it in very specific ways, often rooted in very limited social conditions and for very different purposes. We can never return to the setting in which these ideas were formed—nor should we try. It is enough that we understand the differences between earlier times and our own, earlier ideas and our own. Ultimately, we must create our own context for ideas, if they are to become relevant to the present and future. And we must discern the older contexts from which they emerged—all the more not to repeat them. To put it quite bluntly, freedom has no "founding fathers," only free thinkers and practitioners. If it had such "fathers," it would also be direly in need of morticians to inter it, for that which is "founded" must always answer to the claims of mortality.

⋈

Freedom, conceived as a cluster of ideals and practices, has a very convoluted history, and a large part of this history has simply been unconscious. It has consisted of unstated customs and humanistic impulses that were not articulated in any systematic fashion until they were violated by unfreedom. When the word freedom did come into common usage, its meaning was often consciously confused. For centuries, freedom was identified with justice, morality, and the various perquisites of rule like "free time," or else it was associated with "liberty" as a body of individual, often egoistic, rights. It acquired the traits of property and duties, and was variously cast in negative or positive terms such as "freedom from..." or "freedom for...."

Not until the Middle Ages did this Teutonic word (as we know it) begin to include such metaphysical niceties as freedom from the realm of necessity or freedom from the fortunes of fate, the Ananke and Moira that the Greeks added to its elucidation. The twentieth century has made a mockery of the word and divested it of much of its idealistic content by attaching it to totalitarian ideologies and countries. Thus, to merely "define" so maimed and tortured a word would be utterly naïve. To a large extent, freedom can best be explicated as part of a voyage of discovery that begins with its early practice—and limits—in organic society, its negation by hierarchical and class "civilizations," and its partial realization in early notions of justice.

Freedom, an unstated reality in many preliterate cultures, was still burdened by constraints, but these constraints were closely related to the early community's material conditions of life. It is impossible to quarrel with famine, with the need for coordinating the hunt of large game, with seasonal requirements for food cultivation, and later, with warfare.

To violate the Crow hunting regulations was to endanger every hunter and possibly place the welfare of the entire community in jeopardy. If the violations were serious enough, the violator would be beaten so severely that he might very well not survive. The mild-mannered Eskimo would grimly but collectively select an assassin to kill an unmanageable individual who gravely threatened the well being of the band. But the virtually unbridled "individualism" so characteristic of power brokers in modern society was simply unthinkable in preliterate societies. Were it even conceivable, it would have been totally unacceptable to the community. Constraint, normally guided by public opinion, custom, and shame, was inevitable in the early social development of humanity—not as a matter of will, authority, or the exercise of power, but because it was unavoidable.

Personal freedom is thus clearly restricted from a modern viewpoint. Choice, will, and individual proclivities could be exercised or expressed within confines permitted by the environment. Under benign circumstances, behavior might enjoy an extraordinary degree of latitude until it was restricted by the emergence of blatant social domination. But where domination did appear, it was a thankless phenomenon which, more often than not, yielded very little of that much-revered western shibboleth, "dynamism," in the social development of a community. Polynesia, with its superb climate and rich natural largesse of produce, was never the better for the emergence of hierarchy, and its way of life was brought to the edge of sheer catastrophe by European colonizers. "Where nature is too lavish, she keeps [man] in hand, like a child in leading strings," Marx was to disdainfully observe of cultures in benign environments that were often more devoted to internal elaboration than "social progress." "It is not the tropics with their luxuriant vegetation, but the temperate zone, that is the mother country of capital."

But organic society, despite the physical limitations it faced (from a modern viewpoint), nevertheless functioned unconsciously with an implicit commitment to freedom that social theorists were not to attain until fairly recent times. Radin's concept of the irreducible minimum rests on an unarticulated principle of freedom. To be assured of the material means of life irrespective of one's productive contribution to the community implies that, wherever possible, society will compensate for the infirmities of the ill, handicapped, and old, just as it will for the limited powers of the very young and their dependency on adults. Even though their productive powers are limited or failing, people will not be denied the means of life that are available to individuals who are well-endowed physically and mentally. Indeed, even individuals who are perfectly capable of meeting all their material needs cannot be denied access to the community's common produce, although deliberate shirkers in organic society are virtually unknown. The principle of the irreducible minimum thus affirms the existence of *inequality* within the group—inequality of physical and mental powers, of skills and virtuosity, of psyches and proclivities. It does so not to ignore these inequalities or denigrate them, but on the contrary, to *compensate* for them. Equity, here, is the recognition of inequities that are not the fault of anyone and that must be adjusted as a matter of unspoken social responsibility. To assume that everyone is "equal" is patently preposterous if they are regarded as "equal" in strength, intellect, training, experience, talent, disposition, and opportunities. Such "equality" scoffs at reality and denies the commonality and solidarity of the community by subverting its responsibilities to compensate for differences between individuals. It is a heartless "equality," a mean-spirited one that is simply alien to the very nature of organic society. As long as the means exist, they must be shared as much as possible according to needs—and needs are unequal insofar as they are gauged according to individual abilities and responsibilities.

Hence, organic society tends to operate unconsciously according to the *equality of unequals*—that is, a freely given, unreflective form of social behavior and distribution that compensates inequalities and does not yield to the fictive claim, yet to be articulated, that everyone is equal. Marx was to put this well when, in opposition to "bourgeois right" with its claim of the "equality of all," freedom abandons the very notion of "right" *as such* and "inscribes on its banners: from each according to his ability, to each according to his needs." Equality is inextricably tied to freedom as the recognition of inequality and transcends necessity by establishing a culture and distributive system based on compensation for the stigma of natural "privilege."

The subversion of organic society drastically undermined this principle of authentic freedom. Compensation was restructured into rewards, just as gifts were replaced by commodities. Cuneiform writing, the basis of our alphabetic script, had its origins in the meticulous records the temple clerks kept of products received and products dispersed, in short, the precise accounting of goods, possibly even when the land was "communally owned" and worked in Mesopotamia. Only afterwards were these ticks on clay tablets to become narrative forms of script. The early cuneiform accounting records of the Near East prefigure the moral literature of a less giving' and more despotic world in which the equality of unequals was to give way to mere charity. Thereafter "right" was to supplant freedom. No longer was it the primary responsibility for society to care for its young, elderly, infirm, or unfortunates; their care became a "private matter" for family and friends—albeit very slowly and through various subtly shaded phases. On the village level, to be sure, the old customs still lingered on in their own shadowy world, but this world was not part of "civilization" merely an indispensable but concealed archaism.

∞

With the coming of the warriors and their manorial economy, a new social disposition arose: the warrior code of might. But mere coercion alone could not have created the relatively stable society, largely feudal in structure and values, that is described for us in such detail by the Homeric poets. Rather, it was the *ethos* of coercion—the mystification of courage, physical prowess, and a "healthy" lust for combat and adventure. It was not might as such but the *belief* in the status, indeed, the *mana*, that might conferred on the individual that led to an ideology of coercion, which the victor and his victim mutually acknowledged and celebrated. Accordingly, fortune itself—a derivative of the goddess of chance Tyche (Greek), or Fortuna (Latin)—acquired the form of a metaphysical principle. Very few expressions, possibly incantations, are older than the "casting of the die" and the "fortunes of war." Tyche and Fortuna now emerged as the distinct correlates of bronze-age warrior athleticism.

These bronze-age societies were clearly class societies, and wealth in the form of booty garnered by raids abroad and surpluses at home figured profoundly in their notions of fortune. "The world of Agamemnon and Achilles and Odysseus was one of petty kings and nobles," observes M.I. Finley, "who possessed the best land and considerable flocks, and lived a seigniorial existence, in which raids and local wars were frequent." Power and social activity centered around the noble's household, which was in fact a fortress. Power in this society "depended upon wealth, personal prowess, connexions by marriage and alliance, and retainers." Wealth was indeed a crucial factor: its accumulation and acquisition determined the capacity of a noble to acquire retainers, who were often little less than mercenaries, to acquire arms, and to wage war. Marriage was less an instrument of clan alliances than of dynastic power; the Homeric noble acquired land and wealth, not merely kinsmen, with a favorable match. In fact, the "alliances" he established were marked by a great deal of treachery and faithlessness, features that are characteristic of a political society rather than a tribal one. Tribal society was clearly waning:

> There is no role assigned to tribes or other large kinship groups. In the twenty years Odysseus was away from Ithaca, the nobles [suitors of

Penelope, Odysseus' wife] behaved scandalously toward his family and his possessions; yet his son Telemachus had no body of kinsmen to whom to turn for help, nor was the community fully integrated. Telemachus' claims as Odysseus' heir were acknowledged in principle, but he lacked the [material and physical] power to enforce them. The assassination of Agamemnon by his wife Clytaemnestra and her paramour Aegisthus placed an obligation of vengeance on his son Orestes, but otherwise life in Mycenae went on unchanged, except that Aegisthus ruled in Agamemnon's place.

Apparently, these dynastic quarrels, assassinations, and usurpations were not of special concern to the "masses," who lived an unchronicled inner life in their obscure communities. They simply went about their own business, working their own parcels of land or the "best land" explicitly owned by the nobles. They herded the nobles' "considerable flocks." As a class apart, theirs was also an interest apart. Nowhere in the Homeric narratives do they seem to have intervened in the conflicts of the heroes. So considerably weakened were the powers of the democratic tribal institutions and so extensively had kinship ties been replaced by territorial ties and class relationships that when Telemachus pleaded his case against the suitors to the assembly of Ithaca, the assembly "took no action, which is what the assembly always did in the two [Homeric] poems." Homer's nobles, to be sure, still lived by an aristocratic code of honor, "including table fellowship, gift-exchange, sacrifice to the gods and appropriate burial rites," but this aristocratic code and its obvious roots in early society were now continually violated by greed, acquisitiveness, and egotism.

The nobles of the *Odyssey* were an exploitative class—not only materially but psychologically, not only objectively but subjectively. The analysis of Odysseus (developed by Horkheimer and Adorno) as the nascent bourgeois man is unerring in its ruthless clarity and dialectical insight. Artifice, trickery, cunning, deception, debasement in the pursuit of gain—all marked the new "discipline" that the emerging rulers imposed on themselves to discipline and rule their anonymous underlings. "To be called a merchant was a grave insult to Odysseus," Finley observes; "men of his class exchanged goods ceremoniously or they took it by plunder." Thus was the primordial code of behavior honored formally. But "valor" became the excuse for plunder, which turned into the aristocratic mode of "trade." Honor had in fact acquired its commodity equivalent. Preceding the prosaic merchant with goods and gold in hand was the colorful hero with shield and sword.

Indeed, the commodity continued to make its pedestrian way against all codes. In Homeric times there is "seafaring and a vital concern for trade, more exactly for the import of copper, iron, gold and silver, fine cloths and other luxuries," notes Finley. "Even chieftains are permitted to go on expeditions for such purposes, but generally trade and merchandising seem to be the business of foreigners." Thus is status adorned, affirmed, and its appetite for accoutrements and luxuries (the material substance of privilege) satisfied by the statusless.

Here, we witness a radically new social dispensation. When chieftains, however few in number, are prepared to intermingle with foreigners, indeed pedestrian traders, and truck with them, even the warrior code is in the balance. Might as right can no longer enjoy its high prestige in society's distribution of goods. A new ethos had to emerge if the integrity of trade and the security of traders was to be preserved and port cities were to become viable commercial centers. Piracy and looting could only be episodic: their rewards were indeed the mere bounty and spoils of war. And the nobles of bronze-age Greece were by no means ossified creatures of custom and tradition. Like their peers in England, millennia later (as the enclosure movements of the fifteenth century onward were to show), they were governed by naked self-interest and by an increasing desire for the better things of life.

The new code that was now to supplant valor and coercion also had a very old pedigree, notably in a reciprocity that had become standardized and lost its "accidental form" (to use Marx's terminology) as a mode of exchange; indeed, one that was built on a clear and codifiable notion of equivalents. The notion of *equivalence*, as distinguished from usufruct, the irreducible minimum, and the equality of unequals, was not without its cosmic grandeur in the literal sense of a formal, quantifiable, even geometric order. Tyche and Fortuna are too irascible to support the spirit of calculation, foresight, and rationality required by systematic commerce. Chance is in the "lap of the gods," and in Homeric Greece, these deities were hardly the most stable and predictable of cosmic agents. Until capitalism completed its hold on social life, merchants were the pariahs of society. Their insecurities were the most conspicuous neuroses of antiquity and the medieval world, hence their need for power was not merely a lust but a compelling necessity. Despised by all, disdained even by the ancient lowly, they had to find firm and stable coordinates by which to fix their destinies in a precarious world. Whether as chieftain or as statusless trader, he who would venture on the stormy waves of commerce needed more than Tyche or Fortuna by which to navigate.

The new code that edged its way into those preceding it picked up the principle of an exact, quantifiable equivalence from advanced forms of reciprocity, but without absorbing their sense of service and solidarity. Might was brought to the support of fair-dealings and contract, not merely to violent acquisition and plunder. The cosmic nature of equivalence could be validated by the most dramatic features of life. "Heaven and hell ... hang together," declare Horkheimer and Adorno—and not merely in the commerce of the Olympian gods with the chthonic deities, of good with evil, of salvation with disaster, of subject with object. Indeed, equivalence is as ancient as the very notions of heaven and hell, and is to have its own involuted dialectic as the substitution of Dike for Tyche and Justitia for Fortuna.

In the heroic age that celebrated Odysseus' long journey from Troy to Ithaca, men still traced equivalence back to its "natural" origins:

> Just as the Gemini—the constellation of Castor and Pollux—and all other symbols of duality refer to the inevitable cycle of nature, which itself has its ancient sign in the symbol of the egg from which they came, so the balance held by Zeus, which symbolizes the justice of the entire patriarchal world, refers back to mere nature. The step from chaos to civilization, in which natural conditions exert their power no longer directly but through the medium of human consciousness, has not changed the principle of equivalence. Indeed, men paid for this very step by worshipping what they were once in thrall to only in the same way as all other creatures. Before, the fetishes were subject to the law of equivalence. Now equivalence has itself become a fetish. The blindfold over Justitia's eyes does not only mean that there should be no assault upon justice, but that justice does not result in freedom.[*]

Justitia, in fact, presides over a new ideological dispensation of equality. Not only is she blindfolded; she also holds a scale by which to measure exchange fairly—"equal and exact." Guilt and innocence are juridical surrogates for the equitable allotments of things that appear in the marketplace. Indeed, all scales can *ever* do is to reduce

---

[*] These sparkling remarks were written by Horkheimer and Adorno. But they err seriously on one account: "the fetishes" were not "subject to the law of equivalence," although there can be no doubt that "equivalence itself has become a fetish." Similarly, both men accept a commonplace fallacy (prevalent when they composed their book) that the "shaman wards off danger by means of ... equivalence [which] regulates punishment and reward in civilization." Here, too, the writers impute to the primordial world, even to the shaman, the sensibility of exchange—or a cosmic marketplace that had yet to be established. See Max Horkheimer and Theodor Adorno, *Dialectic of Enlightenment* (New York: Herder and Herder, 1972), pp. 16–17.

qualitative differences to quantitative ones. Accordingly, everyone must be equal before Justitia; her blindfold prevents her from drawing any distinctions between her supplicants. But persons are very different indeed, as the primordial equality of unequals had recognized. Justitia's rule of equality—of equivalence—thus completely reverses the old principle. Inasmuch as all are theoretically "equal" in her unseeing eyes, although often grossly unequal in fact, she turns the equality of unequals into the *inequality of equals*. The ancient words are all there, but like the many changes in emphasis that placed the imprint of domination on traditional values and sensibilities, they undergo a seemingly minor shift.

Accordingly, the rule of equivalence, as symbolized by the scales in Justitia's hand, calls for *balance*, not compensation. The blindfold prevents her from making any changes of measure due to differences among her supplicants. Her specious "equality" thus yields a very real inequality. To be right is to be "just" or "straight," and both, in turn, negate equality on its own terms. Her "just" or "straight" judgment yields a very unbalanced and crooked disposition that will remain concealed to much of humanity for thousands of years—even as the oppressed invoke her name as their guardian and guide.

Rarely has it been possible to distinguish the cry for Justice with its inequality of equals from the cry for Freedom with its equality of unequals. Every ideal of emancipation has been tainted by this confusion, which still lives on in the literature of the oppressed. Usufruct has been confused with public property, direct democracy with representative democracy, individual competence with populist elites, the irreducible minimum with equal opportunity. The demand of the oppressed for equality acquires, as Engels put it, "a double meaning." In one instance, it is the "spontaneous reaction against the social inequalities, against the contrast of rich and poor ... surfeit and starvation; as such it is the expression of the revolutionary instinct and finds its justification in that, and indeed only in that." In the other instance, the demand for equality becomes a reaction against justice as the rule of "equivalence" (which Engels sees simply as the "bourgeois demand for equality"), and "in this case it stands and falls with bourgeois equality itself." Engels goes on to emphasize that the demand of the oppressed for equality ("the proletarian demand for equality") is "the demand for the abolition of classes." But more than the abolition of classes is involved in freedom. In more general terms, "the proletarian demand for equality" is a demand for the "injustice" of an egalitarian society. It rejects the rule of equivalence for the irreducible minimum, the equalization by compensation of inescapable inequalities, in short, the equality of unequals. This demand has been repeatedly thrown out of focus, often for centuries at a time, by stormy battles for Justice, for the rule of equivalence.

◌ʒ

The realm of justice, however, also prepares the ground for freedom by removing the archaisms that linger on from the folk world of equality. Primordial freedom with its rule of the irreducible minimum and its equality of unequals was strikingly parochial. Aside from its lavish code of hospitality, organic society made no real provisions for the rights of the stranger, the outsider, who was not linked by marriage or ritual to the kin group. The larger world beyond the perimeter of "The People" was "inorganic," to use Marx's appropriate term. Loyalties extended in varying degrees of obligation to those who shared the common blood oath of the community and to allies united by material systems of gift reciprocity. The notion of a humanity in which all human beings are considered united by a common genesis was still largely alien. Primordial peoples may be inquisitive, shy, or cordial toward strangers—or they may kill them for the most whimsical reasons. But they owe the stranger no obligation and are bound by no code that requires respect or security for the unpredictable new being that is in their midst—hence, the unpredictability of their own behavior. Even Hellenic society, despite its high claims to rationality, did not advance to a point where the resident alien enjoyed authentic social, much less political, rights beyond the security and protection the *polis* owed to everyone who lived within its precincts. For much of the ancient world, this dubious status of the stranger was a distinctly widespread condition, despite the crucial services such aliens performed for the community and its citizens.

Breaking the barriers raised by primordial and archaic parochialism was the work of Justitia and the rule of equivalence. And far from constituting an authentic "break," the changes came very slowly. Nor were these changes the work of abstract theorists or the fruits of an intellectual awakening. The agents for the new juridical disposition in the rights of city dwellers were the strangers, who often serviced the city with craft or commercial skills. They were helped by the oppressed generally, who could hope to escape the whimsies and insults of arbitrary rule only by inscribing their rights and duties in an inviolable, codified form. Justitia, Dike, or whatever name she acquires in the "civilizations" of antiquity, is in large part the goddess of the social and ethnic outsider.

Her rule of equivalence honors the plea for equity, which must be clearly defined in a written legal code if her scale and sword can redress the inequities that the "outsider" and the oppressed suffer under arbitrary rule. Thus, Justitia must be armed not only with a sword but with the "legal tablets" that unequivocally define rights and duties, security and safety, rewards and punishments.

The earliest of these legal tablets, the Babylonian Code of Hammurabi (ca. 1790 B.C.), still contains distinct class biases and the instrumentalities of class oppression. Like the Mosaic *lex talionis*, the rule of equivalence is enforced with all the fury of class vengeance. The price for social infractions is paid with eyes, ears, limbs, and tongues, not to speak of life itself. But the Code does not try to conceal the "unequal" class nature of this vengeance: nobles get the better of commoners, men of women, and freemen of slaves. Here, the appropriation of primordial society's equality of "unequals," however perverted its form, still claims its penalty. But the Code also weights privilege with a *greater* burden of social responsibility. Although the nobles of Hammurabi's time "possessed a great many perquisites of rank," as Howard Becker and Harry Elmer Barnes tell us, "including the right to exact heavily disproportionate retaliation for personal injuries ... [they] could also be more severely punished for their offenses and, guilty or not, had higher fees to pay."

The later code's were to free themselves from most of these inequitable "archaisms." From the eighth century B.C. onward, we can observe in Hebrew Palestine and in Greece a steady unfolding of the dialectic of justice: the slow transformation of organic society's equality of unequals into class society's inequality of equals. The Mosaic *lex talionis* was fully established as the law of the land, despite such token concessions to the poor in the Deuteronomic Code as mortgage restrictions, the release every seventh year of Hebrew bondsmen from debt slavery, and the hallowing of the fiftieth year as a "jubilee" in which everyone reacquires their possessions. Like the injunction in Leviticus that every debt slave be treated as a "hired servant and as a sojourner," these gestures were largely symbolic. Debt slavery alone, with its humiliating status of craven service, violated the very soul of the ancient desert democracy—the "Bedouin compact"—around which the Hebrew tribes were united during their invasion of Canaan. That it could have entered into the juridical life of the community at all was a cruel acknowledgement of the compact's dissolution.

In Athens, the reforms initiated by Solon opened the way to juridical equality based on political equality, or what has been called Hellenic democracy. Justice now openly functioned as the rule of equivalence, the rule of commodity equivalence, which produced new classes and inequities in personal power and wealth even as it guarded the *demos*, the people of Athenian ancestry, from the exercise of arbitrary social power. Yet within the framework of a society presumably governed by law instead of persons, it was *only* the *demos* that had complete custody of the political system. Perikles' funeral oration may mark a secular and rational ascent in the direction of recognizing the existence of a *humanitas*, but it provides us with no reason to believe that the "barbarian" world and, by definition, the "outsider," were on a par with the Hellene and, juridically, the ancestral Athenian.

In fact, Athenian alien residents not only lacked the right to participate in assemblies like the *Ecclesia* and the *Boule* or in the jury system; they had no explicit juridical rights of their own beyond the security of their property and lives. As we know, they could buy no land in the *polis*. Even more strikingly, they had no direct recourse to the judicial system. Their cases could only be pleaded by citizens in Athenian courts. That their rights were thoroughly respected by the *polis* may speak well for its ethical standards, but it also attests to the exclusivity of the ruling elite whose intentions, rather than laws, were the guarantors of the alien's rights.

Aristotle, an alien resident of Athens, does not equivocate on the superiority of the Hellenes over all other peoples. In citing the failure of the highly spirited "barbarians" of the north to organize into *poleis* that could "rule their neighbors," he reveals the extent to which he, together with Plato, identified the *polis* with social domination. Moreover, he rooted the capacity of the Hellenes to form *poleis*, to "be free," and to be "capable of ruling all mankind" in their ethnic origins and their existence as the Hellenic *genos*.* Blood, as well as geography, confers the capacity to rule. Aristotle sees the Hellenes as diversified such that "some have a one-sided nature" and "others are happily blended" in spiritedness and intelligence. But to him the ability to form *poleis*, to "rule," is a "natural quality" that allows for no social qualifications.

The formal disappearance of the blood group into a universal *humanitas* that sees a common genesis for every free individual was not to

---

* Hannah Arendt reminds us that the word *humanitas*, with its generous implications of a universal human commonality, is Latin, not Greek. In Attic Greek, the term for "mankind" is *pan to anthropinon*, which is often misleadingly translated as the word "humanity." Certainly, to Aristotle (unless I misread his *Politics*), the phrase refers to "man" as a biological datum, not a social one. In itself, the word has no distinctive qualities aside from the obvious differences that separate human beings from animals. Hence, in Aristotle's eyes, there would always be "men" innately destined to rule and others innately destined to obey.

receive juridical recognition until late in antiquity, when the Emperor Caracalla conferred citizenship on the entire nonslave male population of the Roman Empire. It may well be that Caracalla was as eager to enlarge the tax base of the Empire as he was to prop up its sagging sense of commonality. But the act was historically unprecedented. For the first time in humanity's evolution from animality to society, an immense population of highly disparate strangers ranging throughout the Mediterranean basin were brought together under a common political rubric and granted equal access to laws that had once been the privilege of only a small ethnic group of Latins. Juridically, at least, the empire had dissolved the exclusivity of the folk, the kin group, that had already devolved from tribal egalitarianism into an aristocratic fraternity of birth. According to the strictures of late Roman law, genealogy was dissolved into meritocracy and the blood relationship into a territorial one, thereby vastly enlarging the horizons of the human political community.

Caracalla's edict on citizenship was reinforced by a growing, centuries-long evolution of Roman law away from traditional patriarchal absolutism and the legal subordination of married women to their husbands. In theory, at least, the notion of the equality of persons was very much in the air during late imperial times. By the third century A.D., Roman "natural law"—that combined body of jurisprudence variously called the *ius naturale* and the *ius gentium*—acknowledged that men were equal in nature even if they fell short of this condition in society. The departure this idea represented from Aristotle's concept of "mankind" was nothing less than monumental. Even slavery, so basic to Roman economic life, had been placed at odds with the Hellenic notion of the slave's inborn inferiority. To Roman jurists of the imperial period, servitude now derived not from the natural inferiority of the slave but, as Henry Maine has observed, "from a supposed agreement between victor and vanquished in which the first stipulated for the perpetual services of his foe; and the other gained in consideration the life which he had legitimately forfeited." Chattel slavery, in effect, was increasingly viewed as contractual slavery. Although Roman society never ceased to view the slave as more than a "talking instrument," its legal machinery for dealing with slaves was to belie this degradation by the restrictions imposed in late imperial times on the appallingly inhuman practices of the republican period.

෬

The notion of a universal humanity would probably not have remained more than a political strategy for fiscal and ideological ends were it not for the emergence of a new credo of individuality. The word humanity is a barren abstraction if it is not given existential reality by self-assertive personalities who enjoy a visible degree of autonomy. Such beings could hardly be created by an imperial edict. To the extent that organic society declined, so too did the intense sense of collectivity it had fostered. A new context had to be created for the individual that would render it functional in an increasingly atomized world. Not that classical antiquity or the medieval world ever produced the random, isolated, socially starved monads who people modern capitalist society. But the waning of primordial society placed a high premium on a new type of individual: a resourceful, comparatively self-sufficient, and self-reliant ego that could readily adapt itself to—if not "command"—a society that was losing its human scale and developing more complex political institutions and commercial ties than any human community had known in the past.

Such individuals had always existed on the margins of the early collective. They were ordinarily given a certain degree of institutional expression if only to provide a safety valve for marked personal idiosyncrasies. Tribal society has always made allowances for aberrant sexual behavior, exotic psychological traits, and personal ambition (the "big man" syndrome)—allowances that find expression in a high degree of sexual freedom, shamanistic roles, and an exaltation of courage and skill. From this marginal area, society recruited its priests and warrior-chieftains for commanding positions in later, more hierarchical institutions.

But this development is not simply one of breakdown and recomposition. It occurs on a personal level and a social level—egocentric and sociocentric. Viewed on the personal level, the individual accompanies the emergence of "civilization" like a brash, unruly child whose cries literally pierce the air of history and panic the more composed, tradition-bound collectivity that continues to exist after the decline of organic society. The ego's presence is stridently announced by the warrior, whose own "ego boundaries" are established by transgressing the boundaries of all traditional societies. The Sumerian hero Gilgamesh, for example, befriends the stranger, Enkidu, who shares his various feats as a companion, not a kinsman. Valor, rather than lineage, marks their myth-beclouded personal traits.

But misty, almost stereotyped figures like Gilgamesh seem like metaphors for individuality rather than the real thing. More clearly etched personalities like Achilles, Agamemnon, and the Homeric warriors are often cited as the best candidates for western conceptions of the newly born ego. "The model of the emerging individual is the Greek hero," observes Max Horkheimer in his fascinating discussion of the rise and decline of individuality. "Daring and self-reliant, he triumphs in the struggle for survival and emancipates himself from tradition as well as from the tribe." That these qualities of daring and self-reliance were to be prized in the Greco-Roman world is accurate enough, but it is doubtful if the model is properly placed. In fact, the most striking egos of the archaic world were not the bronze-age heroes celebrated by Homer but the iron-age antiheroes so cynically described by Archilochus. Indeed, Archilochus himself was the embodiment of this highly unique personality. He links a hidden tradition of the ego's self-assertion in organic society with the calculating individual of emerging "civilization."

Unlike a quasi-mythical despot like Gilgamesh or a newly-arrived aristocrat like Achilles, Archilochus speaks for a remarkable breed: the displaced, wandering band of mercenaries who must live by their wits and cunning. He is no Homeric hero but rather something of an armed bohemian of the seventh century B.C. His self-possession and libertarian spirit stand in marked contrast to the disciplined lifeways that are congealing around the manorial society of his day. His very existence almost seems improbable, even an affront to the heroic posture of his era. His occupation as the itinerant soldier reflects the sweeping decomposition of society; his arrogant disdain for tradition exudes the negativity of the menacing rebel. What cares he for the shield he has abandoned in battle? "Myself I saved from death; why should I worry about my shield? Let it be gone: I shall buy another equally good." Such sentiments could never have been expressed by a Homeric hero with his aristocratic code of arms and honor. Nor does Archilochus judge his commanders by their mien and status. He dislikes a "tall general, striding forth on his long legs; who prides himself on his locks, and shaves his chin like a fop. Let him be a small man," he declares, "perhaps even bow-legged, as long as he stands firm on his feet, full of heart."

Archilochus and his wandering band of companions are the earliest record we have of that long line of "masterless men" who surface repeatedly during periods of social decomposition and unrest—men, and later women, who have no roots in *any* community or tradition, who colonize the world's future rather than its past. Their characters are literally structured to defy custom, to satirize and shatter established mores, to play the game of life by their own rules. Marginal as they may be, they are the harbingers of the intensely individuated rebel who is destined to "turn the world upside down." They have broad shoulders, not puny neuroses, and express themselves in a wild, expletive-riddled poetry or oratory. Society must henceforth always warily step aside when they appear on the horizon and silently pray that they will pass by unnoticed by its restive commoners—or else it must simply destroy them.

But these are the few sharply etched personalities of history, the handful of marginal rebels whose significance varies with the stability of social life. Their fortunes depend upon the reception they receive by much larger, often inert, masses of people. On another, more broadly based level of history, the notion of individuality begins to percolate into these seemingly inert "masses," and their personalities are emancipated not by Archilochus and his type but by society itself, which has a need for autonomous egos who are free to undertake the varied functions of citizenship. The development of the individual on this social level, in short, is not an isolated, idiosyncratic personal phenomenon; it is a change in the temper, outlook, and destiny of millions who are to people civilization for centuries to come and initiate the history of the modern ego up to the present day. Just as the contemporary proletariat was first formed by severing a traditional peasantry from an archaic manorial economy, so the relatively free citizen of the classical city-state, the medieval commune, and the modern nation-state was initially formed by severing the young male from an archaic body of kinship relationships.

⊂⊅

Like the blood oath, the patriarchal family constituted a highly cohesive moral obstacle to political authority—not because it opposed authority as such (as was the case with organic society) but rather because it formed the nexus for the authority of the father. Ironically, patriarchy represented, in its kinship claims, the most warped traits of organic society in an already distorted and changing social world.* Here, to put it simply, gerontocracy is writ large. It answers not to the needs of the organic society's principle of sharing and solidarity but to the needs of the oldest among the elders. No system of age hierarchy has a more overbearing content, a more repressive mode of operation. In the earliest form of the patriarchal family, as we have seen, the patriarch was answerable to no one for the rule he exercised over the members of his family. He was the incarnation, perhaps the historical source, of arbitrary power, of domination that could be sanctioned by no principle, moral

---

* Here I must again guard the reader against confusing patriarchy with patricentricity. Even the term patriarchal state can be misused if we fail to see the perpetual antagonism between the State and *any* kind of autonomous family unit.

or ethical, other than tradition and the ideological tricks provided by the shaman. Like Yahweh, he was the primal "I" in a community based on the "we." To a certain extent, this implosion of individuation into a single being, almost archetypal in nature, is a portent of widespread individuality and egotism, but in a form so warped that it was to become the quasi-magical personification of Will before a multitude of individual wills were to appear.

Justice slowly transformed the patriarch's status, first by turning the feared father into the righteous father, just as it transformed Yahweh from a domineering, jealous God into a just God. Patriarchy, in effect, ceased to be mere arbitrary authority. It became juridical authority that was answerable to certain precepts of right and wrong. By turning the crude, warrior morality of "might is right" into the rule of equivalence and the *lex talionis* of equity, justice produced the transition from mere arbitrary coercion to coercion that must be justified. Coercion now had to be explained according to concepts of equity and inequity, right and wrong. Justice, in effect, provided the transition from arbitrary and even supernatural power to juridical power. From a tyrant, the patriarch became a judge and relied on guilt, not merely fear, to assert his authority.

This transformation of the patriarch's status occurred as a result of genuine tensions in the objective world. The elaboration of hierarchy, the development of incipient classes, and the early appearance of the city and State combined as social forces to invade the family and stake out a secular claim on the role of the patriarch in the socialization and destiny of the young. Organized religions, too, staked out their own claim. Women were largely excluded from this process of secularization and politicization; they remained the chattels of the male community. But the young men were increasingly called upon to take on social responsibilities as soldiers, citizens, bureaucrats, craftsmen, food cultivators—in short, a host of duties that could no longer be restricted by familial forms.

As society shifted still further from kinship to territorial forms, from broadly hierarchical to specifically class and political forms, the nature of patriarchy continued to change. Although patriarchy retained many of its coercive and juridical traits, it became increasingly a mode of rational authority. Young men were granted their birthright as citizens. No longer were they merely sons; the father was obliged to guide his family according to the ways of reason. He was not simply the just father, but also the wise father. In varying degrees, conditions now emerged for devaluing the patriarchal clan-family and for its substitution by the patricentric nuclear family, the realm of a highly privatized monogamous relationship between two parents and their offspring. Under the aegis of justice, the State acquired increasing control over the highly insulated domestic world—initially, by dissolving the internal forces that held the patriarchal family together with its own juridical claims.*

❧

   The dissolution of the all-encompassing patriarchal "I" into fairly sovereign individuals with "ego-boundaries" of their own gained greater impetus with the expansion of the *polis* into the *cosmopolis*—with the small, self-enclosed "city-state" into the large, open "world city" of the Hellenistic era. With the growing role of the stranger as craftsman, trader, and sea-faring merchant, the notion of the *demos* united by blood and ethical ties into a supreme collective entity gave way to the claims of the individual. Now, not merely citizenship but the private interests of the wayfaring ego, partly shaped by the problems of economic interest, became the goals of individuality. The *cosmopolis* is a tremendous commercial emporium and, for its time, a merchant's playground. We can closely trace the individual's fortunes from the kinship group and from the enclave of the patriarch, into the "city-state," particularly the Athenian *polis*, where individuality assumes richly articulated civic qualities and a vibrant commitment to political competence. From the "brother" or "sister" of organic society, the individual is transformed into the "citizen" of political society, notably the small civic fraternity.**

   But as the civic fraternity expands in scope beyond a humanly comprehensible scale, the ego does not disappear; it acquires highly privatized, often neurotic, traits that center around the problems of a new inwardness. It retreats into the depths of subjectivity and self-

---

* At various times, it should be added, this was done to politicize the family and turn it into an instrument for the State or, for that matter, the Church. The Puritan family comes to mind when we speak of extreme examples of religious zealotry, but by no means were Anabaptists and utopistically oriented religious tendencies in the Reformation immune to theocratic types of family structures. The most damning examples of this development were the family relations fostered by the Nazi regime in Germany and the Stalinist regime in Russia. Neither men nor women were to benefit by these totalitarian family entities, which only superficially restored the role of the *paterfamilias* in all its atavistic splendor in order to colonize his children in the Hitler Youth and the Young Pioneers.

** For the wary reader, I wish to note that I use the term "political society" here, in the Hellenic sense of the *polis* as a *society*, not in the modern sense of a State. The *polis* was not quite a State, the views of many radical theorists notwithstanding. Institutionally, in fact, it was a direct democracy whose equivalent, at least along formal lines, we have rarely seen since the dissolution of organic society.

preoccupation. The *cosmopolis* does not offer the social rewards of the *polis*—a highly charged civicism, an emphasis on the ethical union of competent citizens, or firm bonds of solidarity or *philia*.

Nor does it offer a new sense of community. Hence, the ego must fall back on itself, almost cannibalistically as we shall see in our own era, to find a sense of meaning in the universe. Epicurus, the privatized philosopher of retreat *par excellence*, offers it a garden in which to cultivate its thoughts and tastes—with a wall, to be sure, to block it off from the bustle of a social world it can no longer control. Indeed, the State itself takes its revenge on the very insolent creature it helps to create: the "world citizen," who is now helpless under the overbearing power of a centralized imperial apparatus and its bureaucratic minions.

Nevertheless, the ego requires more than a place, however well-cultivated in which to find its bearings. Divested of its niche in the *polis*, it must find a new niche in the *cosmopolis*—or, as any *cosmopolis* literally suggests, in the *kosmos*. *Humanitas* now becomes a *kosmos*, a new *principle* for ordering experience; and the "city-state," like the folk world before it, becomes an object of ideological derision. Initially, this derisive outlook takes the form of the politically quietistic philosophy of Stoicism that the educated classes embrace in late antiquity.

The Stoics, whose ideas were to nourish the Christian clergy for centuries to come, brought the fruits of justice—the individuated ego and the ideal of "universal citizenship"—into convergence with each other during the age of the *cosmopolis* and Empire. Epictetus, whose writings appeared during one of the most stable periods of the Imperial Age, radically clears the ground for this new, rather modern, type of ego. From the outset, he harshly derides the *polis's* sense of exclusivity as atavistic:

> Plainly you call yourself Athenian or Corinthian after that more sovereign realm which includes not only the very spot where you were born, and all your *household*, but also that region from which the race of your *forebears* has come down to you.

But this is patently absurd, he declares, and shallow:

> When a man has learned to understand the government of the *universe* and has realized that there is nothing so great or sovereign or *all-inclusive* as this frame of things wherein men and God are united, and that from it comes the seeds from which are sprung not only my father or grandfather, but all things that are begotten and that grow upon the earth, and rational creatures

in particular—for these alone are by nature fitted to share in the society of God, being connected with Him by the bond of reason—why should he not call himself a citizen of the universe and a son of God?

In its universality and sweep, this statement voiced nearly two thousand years ago matches the most fervent internationalism of our own era. But here Epictetus was formulating not a program for institutional change but rather an ethical stance. Politically, the Stoics were utterly quietistic. Freedom, to Epictetus, consists exclusively of internal serenity, of a moral insulation from the real world—one that is so all-inclusive that it can reject every material need and social entanglement, including life itself. By the very nature of a "freedom" carried to such quietistic lengths, it is impossible for any being

> to be disturbed or hindered by anything but itself. It is a man's own judgment which disturbs him: For when the tyrant says to man, "I will chain your leg," he that values his leg says: "Nay, have mercy," but he that values his will says: "If it seems more profitable to you, chain it."

In his own way, Max Stirner, the so-called individualistic anarchist of the early nineteenth century, was to turn this Stoic notion of the utterly self-contained ego on its feet and infuse it with a militancy—indeed, an arrogance—that would appall the Stoics. But in principle, both Epictetus and Stirner created a *utopistic vision of individuality* that marked a new point of departure for the affirmation of personality in an increasingly impersonal world.

ᘯ

Had this doctrine of worldly disenchantment and personal withdrawal drifted off into history with the empire that nourished it, later periods might have seen it merely as the passionless voice of a dying era, like the exotic cults and world-weary poems that intoned the end of antiquity. But Christianity was to rework Stoicism's quietistic doctrine of personal will into a new sensibility of heightened subjectivity and personal involvement, inadvertently opening new directions for social change. It is easy—and largely accurate—to say that the Church has been a prop for the State. Certainly Paul's interpretation of Jesus' message to "render unto Caesar what is Caesar's" leaves the troubled world unblemished by any political and social challenges. Early Christianity had no quarrel with slavery, if we interpret Paul's injunctions correctly. Yet when Paul persuades Onesimus, the runaway Christian slave, to return to his Christian master, Onesimus is described as "that dear and faithful brother who is a fellow citizen of yours," for slave, master, and Paul are themselves "slaves" to a higher "Master in heaven." "Citizen" and "slave," here, are used interchangeably. Accordingly, Christianity entered into a deep involvement with the fortunes of the individual slave. Between Christian priest and human chattel there was a confessional bond that was literally sanctified by a personal deity and by the intimate relationship of a sacred congregation.

This existential quality reflects a feature of Christianity that has survived every epoch since its appearance: Universal citizenship is meaningless in the absence of real, unique, concrete citizens. The concept that humanity is a "flock" under a single Shepherd attests to the equality of *all* persons under a single loving God. They are equal not because they share a political recognition of their commonality but rather a spiritual recognition by their Father. In Jesus, social rank and hierarchy dissolve before the leveling power of faith and love. On this spiritual terrain, worldly masters can be less than their slaves in the eyes of God, the wealthiest less than the poorest, and the greatest of kings less than their lowliest subjects. An all-pervasive egalitarianism liberates the subject from all ranks, hierarchies, and classes that are defined by social norms. Not merely citizenship but the principle of equality of all individuals and the absolute value of every soul unites the citizens of the Heavenly City into a "holy brotherhood."

The worldly implications of this message are stated far more compellingly in the exegetical literature of Augustine than in the holy writ of Paul. Like Epictetus and Paul, Augustine completely dissolves the *genos* into a "Heavenly City" that invites humanity as a whole to become its citizens. No folk ideology can admit this kind of conceptual framework into its outlook of the world. By contrast, the Heavenly City—for Augustine, its early voice is the universal Church—melds all diversity among peoples,

> all citizens from all nations and tongues [into] a single pilgrim band. She takes no issue with that diversity of customs, laws, and traditions whereby human peace is sought and maintained. Instead of nullifying or tearing down, she preserves and appropriates whatever in the diversities of divers races is aimed at one and the same objective of human peace, provided only that they do not stand in the way of faith and worship of the one supreme and true God.

Lest this be dismissed merely as Stoic and Pauline quietism—or worse, clerical opportunism that renders the Church infinitely adaptable— Augustine adds that the

> Heavenly City, so long as it is wayfaring on earth, not only makes use of earthly peace but *fosters* and *actively pursues* along with other human beings a common platform in regard to all that concerns our pure human life and does not interfere with faith and worship.

The Church does not merely render unto Caesar what is Caesar's; it replaces his claims to *dominus* by a clerical dominion and his claims to *deus* by a heavenly deity:

> This peace the pilgrim City already possesses by faith and it lives holily and according to this faith as long as, to attain its heavenly competition, it refers every good act done for God or for his fellow man. I say "fellow man" because, of course, any community life must emphasize *social* relationships.

Augustine's ambiguities are more explosive and implicitly more radical than his certainties. Latent in these remarks is the potential quarrel of Church with State that erupts with Pope Gregory VII and the investiture crisis of the eleventh century. The ecumenicalism of the remarks opens the way to outrageous compromises not only with paganism and its overt naturalistic proclivities but to anarchic tendencies that demand the rights of the individual and the immediate establishment of a Heavenly City on earth. The "peace of the pilgrim City" will be reduced to a chimera by unceasing "heresies," including demands for a return to the communistic precepts and egalitarianism of the apostolic Christian congregation. Finally, Augustine's historicism admits not only of the indefinite postponement of Christ's return to earth (so similar to the unfulfilled promise of communism in the Marxian legacy) but also of the eventual *certainty* of Christ's return to right the ills of the world in a distant millennial era. Owing to his ambiguities, Augustine created immense problems that beleaguered western Christianity for centuries and enriched the western conception of the individual with not only a new sense of identity but also a new sense of enchantment.

☙

The secularization of the individual and the disenchantment of personality that came with Machiavelli's emphasis on the amorality of political life and Locke's notion of the proprietary individual divested the self and humanity of their utopian content. Tragically, both were reduced to objects of political and economic manipulation. Christianity had made the self a wayfaring soul, resplendent with the promise of creative faith and infused with the spell of a great ethical adventure. Bourgeois notions of selfhood were now to make it a mean-spirited, egoistic, and neurotic thing, riddled by cunning and insecurity. The new gospel of secular individuality conceived the self in the form *homo economicus*, a wriggling and struggling monad, literally possessed by egotism and an amoral commitment to survival.

From the sixteenth century onward, western thought cast the relationship between the ego and the external world, notably nature, in largely oppositional terms. Progress was identified not with spiritual redemption but with the technical capacity of humanity to bend nature to the service of the marketplace. Human destiny was conceived not as the realization of its intellectual and spiritual potentialities, but as the mastery of "natural forces" and the redemption of society from a "demonic" natural world. The outlook of organic society toward nature and treasure was completely reversed. It was *nature* that now became demonic and *treasure* that now became fecund. The subjugation of human by human, which the Greeks had fatalistically accepted as the basis for a cultivated leisure class, was now celebrated as a common human enterprise to bring nature under human control.

This fascinating reworking of Christian eschatology from a spiritual project into an economic one is fundamental to an understanding of liberal ideology in all its variants—and, as we shall see, to Marxian socialism. So thoroughly does it permeate the "individualistic" philosophies of Hobbes, Locke, and the classical economists that it often remains the unspoken assumption for more debatable social issues. With Hobbes, the "state of nature" is a state of disorder, of the "war of all against all." The material stinginess of physical nature reappears as the ethical stinginess of human nature in the isolated ego's ruthless struggle for survival, power, and felicity. The chaotic consequences that the "state of nature" must inevitably yield can only be contained by the ordered universe of the State.

What is more important than Hobbes' notion of the State is the extent to which he divests nature of all ethical content. Even more unerringly than Kepler, who marveled at the mathematical symmetry of the universe, Hobbes is the mechanical materialist *par excellence*. Nature is mere matter and motion, blind in its restless changes and permutations, without goal or spiritual promise. Society, specifically the State, is the realm of order precisely because it improves the individual's chances to survive and pursue his private aims. It is not far-fetched to say that Hobbes' ruthless denial of all ethical meaning to the universe, including society, creates the intellectual setting for a strictly utilitarian interpretation of justice. To the degree that liberal ideology was influenced by Hobbes' work, it was forced to deal with justice exclusively as a means to secure survival, felicity, and the pragmatics of material achievement.

Locke, who tried to soften this Hobbesian legacy with a benign concept of human nature, deals more explicitly with external nature. But, ironically, he does so only to degrade it further as the mere object of human labor. Nature is the source of proprietorship, the common pool of resources from which labor removes the individual's means of life and wealth. Whatsoever man "removes out of the State that Nature hath provided, and left it in, he hath mixed his *Labour* with, and joyned to it something that is his own, and thereby makes it his *property*." Lest it be thought that nature and labor join people together, Locke assures us that the very opposite is the case:

> It being by him removed from the common state nature placed it in, hath by this *labour* something annexed to it, that excludes the common right of other Men. For this *Labour* being the unquestionable Property of the Labourer, no man but he can have a right to what that is once joyned to, at least where there is enough, and as good left in common for others.

What raises Locke beyond mere proprietary platitudes is the pronounced function he imparts to labor. The isolated ego, which Hobbes rescued from the hazards of mechanical nature by a political covenant, Locke strikingly rescues by an economic one. So far, Hobbes and Locke are as one in the extent to which they filter any spiritual qualities out of their social philosophies. Where Hobbes is arrested by the problem of human survival in a basically chaotic or meaningless world, Locke advances the higher claims of property and person, and perhaps more strikingly for our age, the crucial role of labor in shaping that most fascinating piece of property—the individual itself. For it is "Labour, in the Beginning, [that] *gave a Right of Property*, where-ever any one was pleased to imploy it, upon what was common," and it was property "which Labour and industry began" that underpinned the "*Compact* and Agreement" that created civil society. The individual achieves its identity as the "*Proprietor of his own Person*, and the actions or Labour of it." Human activity, in effect, is human labor. How profoundly Locke opened a gulf between Greco-Christian thought and liberal ideology can best be seen when we recall that for Aristotle, human activity is basically thinking, and for Christian theology, spirituality.

This reduction of social thought to political economy proceeded almost unabashedly into the late nineteenth century, clearly reflecting the debasement of all social ties to economic ones. Even before modern science denuded nature of all ethical content, the burgeoning market economy of the late Middle Ages had divested it of all sanctity. The division within the medieval guilds between wealthy members and poor ultimately dispelled all sense of solidarity that had united people beyond a commonality of craft. Naked self-interest established its eminence over public interest; indeed, the destiny of the latter was reduced to that of the former. The objectification of people as mere instruments of production fostered the objectification of nature as mere "natural resources."

Work too had lost its sanctity as a redemptive means for rescuing a fallen humanity. It was now reduced to a discipline for bringing external nature under social control and human nature under industrial control. Even the apparent chaos that market society introduced into the guild, village, and family structure that formed the bases of the pre-industrial world was seen as the surface effects of a hidden lawfulness in which individual self-interest, by seeking its own ends, served the common good. This "liberal" ideology persisted into the latter part of the twentieth century, where it is celebrated not merely within the confines of church and academy, but by the most sophisticated devices of the mass media.

But what, after all, was this common good in a society that celebrated the claims of self-interest and naked egotism? And what redemption did onerous toil provide for a humanity that had been summoned to surrender its spiritual ideals for material gain? If liberalism could add nothing to the concept of justice other than Locke's hypostatization of proprietorship, and if progress meant nothing more than the right to unlimited acquisition, then most of humanity had to be excluded from the pale of the "good life" by patently self-serving class criteria of justice and progress. By the end of the eighteenth century, liberal theory had not only been debased to political economy, but to a totally asocial doctrine of interest. That human beings acted in society at all could be explained only by the compulsion of needs and the pursuit of personal gain. In a mechanical world of matter and motion, egotism had become for isolated human monads what gravitation was for material bodies.

The most important single effort to provide liberalism with an ethical credo beyond mere proprietorship and acquisition was made in the same year that the French *sans culottes* toppled the most luminous stronghold of traditional society. In 1789, Jeremy Bentham published his *Introduction to the Principles of Morals and Legislation*, advancing the most coherent justification for private interest as an ethical good. In a majestic opening that compares with Rousseau's *Social Contract* and Marx's *Communist Manifesto*, Bentham intoned the great law of utilitarian ethics:

> Nature has placed mankind under the governance of two sovereign masters, *pain* and *pleasure*. It is for them alone to point out what we ought to do, as well as determine what we should do.

In any case, they "govern us in all we do, in all we say, in all we think." Thus caught up in the universal principles that predetermine our behavior irrespective of our wishes—a formula that lies at the heart of scientism, whether liberal or socialist—Bentham abandoned "metaphor and declamation" for a calculus of pain and pleasure, a system of moral bookkeeping that identifies evil with the former and good with the latter. This utilitarian calculus is explicitly quantifiable: Social happiness is seen as the greatest good for the greatest number. Here, social good comprises the sum of pleasures derived by the individuals who make up the community. To the sensory atomism of Locke, Bentham added an ethical atomism of his own, both of which seem to form exact fits to a monadic age of free-floating egos in a free-falling marketplace:*

> Sum up all the values of all the *pleasures* on the one side, and those of all the *pains* on the other. The balance, if it is on the side of the pleasure, will give the *good* tendency of the act upon the whole and if on the side of pain, the *bad* tendency of it upon the whole.

What applies to the individual, in Bentham's view, can be extended to the community as the sum of all good and bad tendencies to which each of its members is exposed.

———

* In contrast to the philosophical radicalism that sees in atomic theories as far back as those of Democritus and Epicurus evidence of an ascendant individualism, I would argue that they are evidence of the dissolution of the self into a *decadent* individualism. Atomic or atomistic theories, I suspect, do not achieve general acceptance when the self is well-formed and well-rooted, but when its form and its roots have begun to wither and the community base by which it is truly nourished has begun to disappear. The great individuals of history like Perikles, Aeschylus, the Gracchi, Augustine, Rabelais, Diderot, Danton, and the like are rooted psychologically in viable and vibrant communities, not neurotically confined to gloomy attics and mummified by isolation like Dostoyevsky's Raskolnikov in *Crime and Punishment*.

Rarely do we encounter in Justitia's checkered career a more unadorned attunement of her scale to ethical quanta. Even acts that yield a calculable predominance of pleasure or pain are atomized and lend themselves, in Bentham's view, to clearly delineable episodes, just like chapters in a Richardson novel. What is striking about Bentham's ethical atomism is the kind of rationality it employs. Aristotle's ethics, too, was built on the idea of happiness. But happiness in the Greek view was a goal we pursued as an "an *end* in itself," not as a "*means* to something else." It was derived from the very nature of human beings as distinguished from all other living things, a nature that could never be formulated with the precision of mathematics. If happiness was a rational and virtuous way of life, as Aristotle argued, it attained its full realization in the contemplative mind and in an ethical mean that rose above excess of any kind.

Bentham, by contrast, offered his readers no ethics in any traditional sense of the term but rather a scientistic methodology based on a digital calculation of pleasurable and painful units. The qualitative intangibles of human sentiments were coded into arithmetic values of pleasure and pain that could be cancelled or diminished to yield "surpluses" of either happiness or misery. But to dismiss Bentham merely as an ethical bookkeeper is to miss the point of his entire approach. It is not the ethical calculus that comprises the most vulnerable features of utilitarian ethics but the fact that *liberalism had denatured reason itself into a mere methodology for calculating sentiments*—with the same operational techniques that bankers and industrialists use to administer their enterprises. Nearly two centuries later, this kind of rationality was to horrify a less credulous public as a form of thermonuclear ethics in which varying sums of bomb shelters were to yield more or less casualties in the event of nuclear war.

That a later generation of liberals represented by John Stuart Mill rebelled against the crude reduction of ethics to mere problems of functional utility did not rescue liberalism from a patent loss of normative concepts of justice and progress. Indeed, if interests alone determine social and ethical norms, what could prevent *any* ideal of justice, individuality, and social progress from gaining public acceptance? The inability of liberal theory to answer this question in any terms other than practical utility left it morally bankrupt. Henceforth, it was to preach a strictly opportunistic message of expediency rather than ethics, of meliorism rather than emancipation, of adaptation rather than change.

But we are concerned, for the moment, with liberalism not as a cause or ideology, but rather as the embodiment of justice. Anarchism and revolutionary socialism profess to be concerned with freedom. Fascism is concerned neither with justice nor freedom but merely with the instrumentalities of naked domination; its various ideologies are purely opportunistic. Hence the fate of justice reposes with the fate of the ideas of such serious thinkers as John Stuart Mill and his followers. Their failure to elicit an ethics from justice that could rest on its rule of equivalence leaves only Bentham's utilitarian ethics—a crude, quantitative theory of pains and pleasures—as justice's denouement.

Let us not deceive ourselves that Bentham's methodology or, for that matter, his ethics have dropped below the current ideological horizon. It still rises at dawn and sets at dusk, resplendent with the multitude of colors produced by its polluted atmosphere. Terms like "pleasure" and "pain" have not disappeared as moral homilies; they merely compete with terms like "benefits" and "risks," "gains" and "losses," the "tragedy of the commons," "triage," and the "lifeboat ethic." The inequality of equals still prevails over the equality of unequals. What is so stunning to the careful observer is that if justice never came to compensate but merely to reward, its spirit has finally become mean and its coinage small. Like every limited ideal, its history has always been greater than its present. But the future of justice threatens to betray even its claims to have upheld the "rights" of the individual and humanity. For as human inequality increases in fact, if not in theory, its ideology of equivalence assails the ideal of freedom with its cynical opportunism and a sleazy meliorism.

7☙ THE LEGACY OF FREEDOM

The most triumphant moment of Justitia does not occur in her apotheosis as "bourgeois right," when the marketplace gives materiality to the rule of equivalence. Rather, it occurs in those times of transition when justice is extricating itself from the parochial world of organic society. This is the heroic moment of innocence, before the materiality of equivalence in the form of the commodity reclaims an early idealism. At this time, justice is emergent, creative, and fresh with promise—not worn down by history and the musty logic of its premises. The rule of equivalence is still loosening the grip of the blood oath, patriarchy, and the civic parochialism that denies recognition to individualism and a common humanity. It is opening society's door to personality with all its wild eccentricities and to the stranger as the shadowy figure of the "outsider." But by the bourgeois era, particularly its nineteenth-century cultural apogee, individual fulfillment reveals itself as naked egotism, and the dream of a common humanity becomes the threadbare cloak for harsh social inequalities. Penalty for reward is inscribed all over the face of the century and measured out unrelentingly in the cruel dialectic of the inequality of equals. Heaven and hell indeed hang together, as Horkheimer and Adorno observe.

What, then, of freedom—of the equality of unequals? Where does it begin to separate from the liberatory achievements of justice and pick up its own thread of development? I do not mean a return to organic society; instead, I mean a new advance that will include the individuality fostered by justice's maxim of equals and the shared participation of the individual in a common humanity.

The word "freedom" initially appears in a Sumerian cuneiform tablet that gives an account of a successful popular revolt against a highly oppressive regal tyranny, thousands of years ago. In *The Sumerians,* Samuel Noah Kramer tells us that "in this document . . . we find the word 'freedom' used for the first time in man's recorded history; the word is *amargi* which ... means literally 'return to the mother.'" Alas, Kramer wonders, "we still do not know why this figure of speech came to be used for 'freedom.'" Thereafter, "freedom" retains its features as a longing to "return to the mother," whether to organic society's matricentric ambience or to nature perceived as a bountiful mother. The classical world is preoccupied with justice, fair dealings, individual liberty, and enfranchisement of the outsider in the world city, rather than with freedom's equality of unequals. Freedom is viewed as utopistic and fanciful, and relegated to the underworld of repressed dreams, mystical visions, and Dionysian "excesses" like the Saturnalia and other ecstatic mystical rituals.

As theory and an explicit ideal, freedom again rises to the surface of consciousness with Christianity. When Augustine places the wayfaring "Heavenly City" into the world as a force for social change, he also locates it in a meaningful, purposeful historical drama that leads to humanity's redemption. Hence humankind is removed from the meaningless recurring cycles of ancient social thought. Here we encounter the radical face of history's "double meaning" as it was developed by the Christian fathers. According to Augustine, creation initiates a distinctly linear, time-laden evolution analogous to the individual's own stages of life. The period from Adam to Noah is humanity's childhood, Noah to Abraham its boyhood, Abraham to David its youth, and David to the Babylonian captivity its manhood. After this, history passes into two concluding periods beginning with the birth of Jesus and ending with the Last Judgment. Within this history, the heavenly and earthly cities are engaged in an irreconcilable series of conflicts in which each achieves episodic triumphs over the other. However, a dialectic of corruption and germination assures the triumph of the heavenly city over the earthly. Redemption thus ceases to be the arbitrary whim of a deity; it ceases, in effect, to be exclusively transcendental and becomes anthropological. History imparts to faith a logic and intelligibility that inspires hope, meaning, and *action*. Augustine's view of redemption is prospective rather than retrospective; the "golden age" of the pagan now lies in a historically conditioned future, one that is to be attained in a battle with evil, rather than a long-lost natural past. In Augustine's time, this vision served to diffuse the millenarian hopes of the emerging Christian world for an imminent Second Coming of Christ. But it later haunted the Church like a postponed debt, whose claims must be honored by its clerical creditors sooner or later.

The decisive idea in Augustine's work, observes Ernst Bloch, is that

> for the first time a political utopia appears in history. In fact, it produces history; history comes to be as *saving history in the direction of the kingdom*, as a single unbroken process extending from Adam to Jesus on the basis of the Stoic unity of mankind and the Christian salvation it is destined for.

By placing Christian eschatology in a historical context, Augustine initiates a concept of utopia that is earthbound and future-oriented. History has a goal that extends beyond cyclic return to a final culmination in the practical affairs of humanity. Biblical narrative parallels personal development; hence it ceases to be an inventory of miracles, rewards, and punishments. The "world order," in turn, ceases to be the consequence of a transcendental world that exists beyond it, however much Augustine permeates it with the will of God. It is an order in which that Will is immanent in the earthly world as well, an order that includes *causally* related events as well as *miraculous* ones.

But Augustine not only provides us with the first notion of a political utopia; he emphatically denigrates political authority. To be sure, early Christianity had always viewed political entanglements as tainted. Like the Stoics before them, the Church fathers of the late Roman world articulated the individual's feelings of increasing separation from all levels of political power and social control. Gone were the popular assemblies of the *polis*, the *hoplites* or militias of citizen-farmers, the citizen-amateurs chosen by lot to administer the day-to-day affairs of the community. The Roman republic and, more markedly, the empire had long replaced them with senatorial and imperial rulers, professional armies, and an elaborate, far-flung bureaucracy. For Stoicism and Christianity to preach a gospel of abstinence from political activism merely expressed in spiritual and ethical terms a situation that had become firmly established as fact. It neither challenged the political order of the time nor acquiesced to it, but merely acknowledged existing realities.

By contrast, Augustine did more than counsel indifference to political authority; he denounced it. Franz Neumann, describing what he calls the "Augustinian position," acutely notes the dual nature of this denunciation. Augustine viewed politics as evil: "Political power is coercion, even in origins and purpose." For human to dominate human is "unnatural":

> Only at the end of history with the advent of the Kingdom of God can and will coercion be dispensed with. From this philosophy derive two

radically different, yet inherently related, attitudes: that of total conformism and that of total opposition to political power. If politics is evil, withdrawal is mandatory. Forms of government and objectives of political power become irrelevant. Salvation can be attained through faith, and early life should be a mere preparation for it. Monasticism is the first consequence. By the same token, however, the demand for the immediate destruction of politics and the establishment of a Kingdom of God may equally be supported by the Augustinian premise. The Anabaptist movement [of the Reformation era] was perhaps the most striking manifestation of the total rejection of society.

More accurately, the Anabaptists rejected the political world represented by the State.

The conflict latent in this dual message of political quietism and messianic activism could hardly be suppressed once the Christian doctrine became increasingly secularized. The Church was the major factor behind its own transformation from an other-worldly into a worldly power—notably by its growing conflict with the temporal power to which Pauline Christianity had entrusted humanity's worldly destiny. The most explosive of these conflicts developed in the eleventh century, when Pope Gregory VII forbade the lay investiture of bishops and claimed this authority exclusively for the Papacy. The dispute reached its culmination when the Holy See excommunicated the Holy Roman Emperor, Henry IV, for contumaciously resisting the Church's claims, and called upon Henry's subjects to deny him fealty.

This was more than an extension of ecclesiastical power. Gregory was asserting the higher authority of spiritual over political power. In so doing, he challenged political power and placed it in a tainted ethical light. Accordingly, the Pope traced political authority as such back to evil and sin in a fashion that makes the Augustinian position seem tepid by comparison. Thus, declaimed Gregory,

> Who does not know that kings and rulers took their beginning from those who, being ignorant of God, have assumed, because of blind greed and intolerable presumption, to make themselves masters of their equals, namely men, by means of pride, violence, bad faith, murder, and nearly every kind of crime, being incited thereto by the prince of the world, the Devil?

Taken by themselves, these heady words match the most stinging attacks that were to be leveled against political authority by the revolutionary chiliastic leaders of the Reformation period.

Thereafter, Christian doctrine became increasingly social and secular until religious disputes barely concealed harsh clashes over the implications of the Augustinian position. The eventual submission of sacerdotal to secular power did not terminate these conflicts. To the contrary, it made them outrageously worldly in character. In the twelfth century, John of Salisbury bluntly turned his back on the feudal hierarchy of his day, a hierarchy based on the unquestioning obedience of ruled to ruler, and proceeded to explore the validity of governance by law. Tyranny—by which John meant the disregard of law as dictated by the people—was beyond legitimation and could be overthrown by force. This far-reaching, avowedly revolutionary position was drawn not from the Christian father Augustine, but from the republican theorist Cicero. Its medievalistic references to "princes" and "kings" aside, it had a distinctly republican ring.

While Christian doctrine drifted into Thomistic scholasticism, with its explicit justification of hierarchy and its designation of political power as natural, Joachim of Fiore, almost a contemporary of John of Salisbury, brought the radical eschatology of Christianity completely into the open. Joachim's goal was not to "cleanse the Church and State of their horrors," observes Bloch. "They were abolished instead, or rather a *lux nova* was kindled in it—the 'Third Kingdom,' as the Joachimites called it," The Third Kingdom—the coming historical stage illumined by the Holy Spirit—was to succeed the Old Testament stage based on the Father and the New Testament stage based on the Son. With the illumination provided by the Holy Spirit, all masters, both spiritual and temporal, would disappear, and "wheat" would replace the "grass" brought by the Old Testament era and the "sheaves" brought by the New.

Joachimism fed directly into the great chiliastic movements that swept through the medieval world in the fourteenth century and surfaced again during the Reformation. Bloch's assessment of Joachim's influence is worth noting:

> For centuries, genuine and forged writings of Joachim's remained in circulation. They appeared in Bohemia and in Germany, even in Russia, where sects aspiring to original Christianity were clearly influenced by the Calabrian preaching. The Hussites' "kingdom of God in Bohemia"—repeated a hundred years later in Germany by the Anabaptists—meant Joachim's *civitas Christi*. Behind it lay the misery that had come long since; in it lay the millennium whose coming was due, so men struck a blow of welcome. Special attention was paid to the abolition of wealth and poverty; the preaching of those

seeming romantics took brotherly love literally and interpreted it financially. "During its journey on earth," Augustine had written, "the City of God attracts citizens and gathers friendly pilgrims from all nations, regardless of differences due to customs, laws, and institutions that serve material gain and assure earthly peace." The Joachimites' coming *civitas Dei*, on the other hand, kept a sharp eye on institutions that served material gain and exploitation, and the tolerance it practiced—namely, toward Jews and heathens—could not but be alien to international ecclesiasticism. Its criterion for citizenship was not whether a man had been baptized, but whether he heard the fraternal spirit in himself.

The Joachimite "financial" interpretation of brotherly love carried Christian eschatology beyond the confines of the Augustinian position into a distinctly secular social philosophy and movement. The social theories of Machiavelli, Hobbes, and Locke owe their secular quality to the assimilation of "other-worldliness" to "this-worldliness," a process that begins with John of Salisbury and Joachim of Fiore. Christian social theory, particularly its radical wing, had overcome the duality between heaven and earth on which Pauline Christianity had been nourished. Once the split was transcended, heavenly questions were superseded by practical problems of law, power, authority, equality, and freedom. Pope Gregory VII had opened sluice gates that his era could never again close. Once the Church itself became the plaything of the temporal powers and the papacy an instrument of Rome's local patriciate, heaven too began to lose its hypnotic power over the human mind, and hope ceased to find refuge in the spiritual dispensation of an otherworldly King. When the Puritans of 1649 removed the head of Charles I in the name of a new religious credo, they effectively removed the head of their heavenly Father as well. In the following century, the Parisian *sans culottes* were to remove kingly and queenly heads with invocations to no higher authority than reason.

❧

Christian historicism, with its promise of an early utopistic future, taken together with the Church's appeals for direct popular support against anticlerical abuses by lay authority, had a strong influence on radical social movements of medieval and early modern times. Until Marxian socialism acquired the status of official dogma in nearly half the world, Christianity was to play a predominant role in the spiritual and intellectual life of western society. No doctrine could kindle more fervent hopes among the oppressed, only to dash them to the ground when the clerical and civil powers periodically combined to repress subversive sects and radical popular movements. Contradictions within Christian religious precepts were to provide the grindstone for sharpening the knives of social criticism, which, in turn, gave rise to new ideas for social reconstruction. Despite its patently conflicting messages, Christianity offered the principles, examples, social metaphors, ethical norms, and above all a spiritual emphasis on the virtuous life that were to foster an unprecedented zealotry in periods of social rebellion. Its ethical impact on medieval movements for change contrasts sharply with economistic and materialistic explanations of human behavior. Such a tremendous movement as Anabaptism—a movement that enlisted nobles and learned sectarians as well as poor townspeople and peasants in support of apostolic communism and love—could not have emerged without anchoring its varied ideals in Christian ethical imperatives. These ideals outweighed life itself in the eyes of its acolytes.

To describe religion, particularly Christianity, as the "heart of a heartless world," as Marx does, is not to dismiss religion but to acknowledge its autonomous existence as an ethical dimension of society. From the late Roman world to the Enlightenment, every significant radical ideal was cast in terms of Christian doctrine. Even when people looked backward toward a lost golden age or forward to a Last Kingdom, they often also looked upward to a "heavenly" dispensation for inspiration, if not validation. Christian doctrine was a stellar body in the world's firmament of belief—a source of illumination that would not be discarded as a guiding force in human affairs until the eighteenth or nineteenth century.

Freedom's equality of unequals had never totally disappeared as a principle of "compensation," if only because this principle could be used to provide credibility for privilege as well as equality. Where justice assailed the inequities of class rule or its claims to status as a matter of birth, the notion of "compensation" reinforced these inequities by according to "unequals" a greater "compensatory" increment in power, wealth, and authority. "Compensation" acknowledged the "superiority" of the slave master and feudal lord over their slaves and serfs; it accorded the ruler the authority and means to live according to the norms of rulership. Ironically, the nobles of imperial Rome and feudal Europe claimed the "freedom" to live on very *unequal* terms with the oppressed and exploited beneath them. Normally, it was to Caesar and the feudal monarchs, not to local satraps and lords, that the oppressed turned for justice. Neither freedom nor justice were prevalent as principles in European manorial society; rather, a fairly precise system of rights and duties was established between ruling and ruled classes, based on highly modified customs and traditions that derived from tribal times. Territorial lords were to be compensated for their military prowess in defending their lands and subjects from "barbarian" raiders—and from the dynastic conflicts generated by feudal society itself. Villeins, peasants, and serfs were also to be compensated for the material support they gave to secure safety and peace in a very troubled era.* In effect, compensation for inequalities had been denatured into *privilege*.

Wherever this system of rights and duties broke down, the oppressed often returned to the egalitarian premises that had nourished the principle of compensation. To the oppressed, what held for the territorial lords could easily hold for them; they too could claim the privileges conferred by "inequality." Hence the "backward look" to a golden age was not always evidence of nostalgia or of an ethical drama in which authority and oppression were unavoidable penalties for original sin and the loss of innocence. Often, the "backward look" involved an attempt by the oppressed to restore freedom's equality of unequals—to recover the very premises from which ruling classes had reworked ancient traditions to support their own "compensatory" privileges.

But with Christianity, this "backward look" acquired a vibrant sense of futurity—and not only because of Augustinian or Joachimite historicism. To the pagan world, the memory of a golden age elicited basically quietistic and nostalgic responses. Even in the ancient cycles of eternal recurrence, it was doomed to be succeeded by faulted epochs. From Plato to the Stoics, social theory contains a quietistic core, a sense of fatalism and resignation, in which "ideal" *poleis* are frozen in their ideality and their distance from the real world, or else reduced to private gardens as loci for an ethical retreat. Within any given social cycle, the golden age could no longer be expected to return; there was no point in striving for it. All epochs in the cycle were as predetermined as the

---

* To undo this specious principle of "compensation" as the warped form of freedom was the *radical* function of justice. The "freedom" of the feudal nobility to be "unequal" took a highly concrete form. Juridically, class differences "were manifested by differences in the extent of penance," observe Georg Rusche and Otto Kirchheimer. "Penance was carefully graded according to the social status of the evildoer and of the wronged party. Although this class differentiation only affected the degree of penance at first, it was at the same time one of the principal factors in the evolution of corporal punishment. The inability of lower-class evildoers to pay fines in money led to the substitution of corporal punishment." Rusche and Kirchheimer contend that this development "can be traced in every European country." G. Rusche and O. Kirchheimer, *Punishment and Social Structure* (New York: Columbia University Press, 1939), p. 9.

inexorable cycles of nature. To be sure, the oppressed or the morally inspired did not always heed this fate that the ruling classes of antiquity imparted to history; plebeians and slaves could rise in great insurrectionary conflicts. But rarely were domination and slavery brought into question. The slave's dream of freedom, as some short-lived but successful rebellions suggest, was to turn the slave-master into a slave. Vengeance, not hope, was the poor man's notion of settling his accounts with his oppressor.

Christianity, by contrast, offered a different vision. Authority, laws, domination, and servitude were explained by the need to restrain a "fallen humanity." Sin, like the afflictions in Pandora's box, had been released by woman's "accursed curiosity," but redemption and its abolition of authority, laws, domination, and servitude lay in the offing. The Christian clergy retained an activistic stance toward absolution and brought the flock into motion to fight sin, Moslem infidels, and the territorial lords as the needs of the Church hierarchy required. Hence, to look back to the Garden of Eden was actually to look forward to its recovery, not to bemoan its disappearance. The ethical drama that eventually would yield its recovery was an *active* struggle with the powers of evil and wrong: humanity made its own history. Yahweh, as the transcendental expression of Will, had been transmuted into the many existential wills of the Christian congregation. With the Christian emphasis on individuality and a universal humanity, Fortuna now returned in a more spiritual light to remove any notion of predetermination of one's personal fate—a feeling that Calvin was to challenge during the Reformation. The Christian ethical drama became a *battleground*—not a stage—that was occupied by free-willing combatants, not stylized, carefully rehearsed actors. The masks used in classical drama to express an actor's sentiments were removed to show the real face of the medieval and modern individual. If there was any script, it was the Bible—with all its wrenching ambiguities—not the cold and carefully wrought hexameters of ancient tragedy.

❧

This battleground was marked by several striking features that greatly influenced European struggles for freedom. Its paradisiacal gardens were located not only in time but also in place.[*] Consigned as they might be to the past, they nevertheless occupied a geographic

* This point was made a generation ago by A. L. Morton in *The English Utopia* (London: Lawrence & Wishart, 1952) and recently emphasized by Frank E. and Fritzie P. Manuel in their *Utopian Thought in the Western World* (Cambridge: Harvard University Press, 1979)

area on earth. As such, they posed a constant subversive affront to the class and priestly emphasis on the supernatural, with its afterlife rewards for obedience and virtue. This implicit opposition of nature to Supernature—of earthly rewards to heavenly—is crucial. It flouts the authority of heaven and tests the ingenuity of humanity to find its haven of freedom and abundance within life itself and on the earth. Hence, such visions were not a *utopos*, or "no place," but a distinct "some place" with definite boundaries. Historically, attempts to locate the Garden of Eden were made repeatedly—not only symbolically but also geographically. Ponce de Leon's pursuit of the "Fountain of Youth" is merely one of innumerable explorations that for centuries occupied the lives and claimed the fortunes of explorers.

Certainly, the oppressed believed that the Garden of Eden was still on earth, not in heaven—in *nature*, not in Supernature. In the outrageously heretical medieval image of such a garden, the "Land of Cokaygne," this place was the creation of a bountiful maternal natural world—an *amargi*—not an austere paternal deity. The utterly anarchic fourteenth-century version of this "some place" broadly satirizes the Christian heaven, against which it opposes an almost Dionysian, sensuously earthy world of nature—a world that, like maternal love, gives freely of its fruits to a denied and deserving humanity:

> Though paradise be merry and bright, Cokaygne is a fairer sight.
> What is there in Paradise but grass and flowers and green boughs?

By contrast, Cokaygne has "rivers great and fine of oil, milk, honey, and wine." Food is bountiful, cooked and baked by nature's own hand; eternal day replaces night, peace replaces strife, and "all is common to young and old, to stought and stern, meek and bold."

Cokaygne, merely by virtue of its location, openly flouts clerical sensibilities. "Far in the sea, to the West of Spain, is a land called Cokaygne." In his analysis of the poem, A. L. Morton adds:

> This westward placing clearly connects Cokaygne with the earthly paradise of Celtic mythology. Throughout the Middle Ages the existence of such a paradise was firmly believed in, but the church always placed its paradise in the East and strongly opposed the belief in a western paradise as a heathen superstition. In spite of this ecclesiastical opposition the belief persisted.... So strong were these beliefs that in the form of St. Branden's Isle the western paradise had to be christianised and adopted by the Church itself, and a number

of expeditions were sent out from Ireland and elsewhere in search of the Isle. Nevertheless, the fact that Cokaygne is a *western* island is an indication that the Cokaygne theme is of popular and pre-Christian character, and the western placing may in itself be taken as one of the specifically anti-clerical features.

The heretical insouciance of the poem is revealed most clearly in its flagrantly "common" tastes, if not in its *déclassé* and bohemian tone. To the modern mind, it is notable for its lack of any technological means to achieve its bounty; such a technology, in any case, was hopelessly beyond human achievement at the time. More importantly, there is no toil in Cokaygne, no compulsory exertion, no need to master oneself or others for labor. Cokaygne is created not by humanity, its arts, or its institutions but by nature, which gives freely of its wealth and pleasures. The notion of nature as a realm of "scarce resources," which is articulated clearly in Aristotle's *Politics*, has yielded to the notion of nature as a realm of plenty and abundance; hence, no need exists for institutions and restrictions of any kind, or for hierarchy and domination. Indeed, Cokaygne is not a society at all but a fecund land, and its human inhabitants may live in it without placing any constraints on their desires. It is libertarian—indeed, deliciously libertine—because nature is no longer the product of a stern, demanding Creator; it is instead an *emancipated* nature that goes hand in hand with an emancipated humanity and an emancipation of human fantasy.

The premises on which the entire vision of Cokaygne rests are strangely modern. Peace, harmony, and freedom in the most absolute sense are predicated on material superfluity. People require no protection or rule; their every desire can be satisfied without technics or the need to bring other human beings into personal or institutional subjugation. No war, conflict, or violence mars Cokaygne's landscape. In the sheer splendor of this plenty and the givingness of nature, the "pleasure principle" and "reality principle" are in perfect congruence. Hence no conceivable tensions need disturb the security and peace of Cokaygne. Pleasure is the rule, abundance enables *desire* to replace mere need, because every wish can be fulfilled without exertion or technical strategies.

Cokaygne further implies a view of human nature that is benign rather than conceived in sin. Humanity is afflicted not because it has eaten of the fruit of the tree of knowledge but because it has eaten of the bitter root of scarcity. Scarcity is not the penalty of sin but rather its cause. Given a level of abundance that removes this bitter root, individuals have no need to dominate, manipulate, or empower themselves at the expense of others. The appetite for power and the desire to inflict harm are removed by nature's sheer fecundity.

❧

The land of Cokaygne appears again, as a sanctuary of privilege in Rabelais's Abbey of Theleme. But for the present, I wish to emphasize that Cokaygne is a *consumerist* concept of freedom, involving no labor, technics, or canons of productivity. This concept is woven through the broad popular movements of history for centuries. And even where it ebbs briefly, Cokaygne is recovered by heretical elites, by the "elect" who acknowledge no authority or denial of pleasure other than that dictated by their own "inner light." Allowing unrestrained freedom to consume, to take from life its proffered riches, this vision of freedom acquires a distinctly utopian form. It passes from imagery and geography into a cerebral sensibility—a philosophy, as it were—and a way of life that is represented by the Brethren of the Free Spirit. During the Reformation, it degenerates into the "military communism" of the Adamite plunderers. In our own time, it acquires distinctly esthetic qualities among the Symbolist and Surrealist artists whose demand for the fulfillment of desire are inscribed as slogans on the walls of Paris during the May–June events of 1968. Charles Fourier's utopian visions incorporate the problematic of scarcity, need, and labor that this tradition of freedom seeks to resolve by natural, elitist, or esthetic means; but his phalansteries, the basic units of his utopia, are *technically* oriented and involve a recourse to strategies that root it only partly in the Cokaygne imagery.

In contrast to these consumerist concepts, we also witness the emergence of *productivist* concepts of freedom. These notions of humanity's ability to create a communistic, sharing, and nonauthoritarian society have their material roots in science, technics, and the rational use of labor. In this vision, the means that will yield the reconciliation of human with human are supplied not by nature but by "man" himself. Utopias of plenty will be created by his labor and consciousness, by his capacity to organize society for the attainment of producer-oriented ends. Freedom thus is seen as the technical rationalization of the means of production, a project often associated with the concept of reason itself. The means, as it were, tend to become the ends of the utopian project and human emancipation. Nature is perceived as neither fecund nor even generous but, in varying degrees, ungiving and intractable to human goals.

Initially, this tendency in the realm of freedom is highly ascetic. Inequality will be overcome by a humane, loving denial of the means of life by fortunate individuals for the less fortunate. Everyone works as best as he or she can to create a common fund of goods that is parcelled out according to authentically valid needs. Radical Christian sects like the Hutterites emphasized the ethical rather than material desiderata that come with this simple communistic way of life. Communism to them was a spiritual discipline, not an economy. Later, the concept of a free, productive, communistic community draws its primary, although by no means exclusive, inspiration from economic motives that involve the fostering of self-interest ("class interest") and technical innovation. A distinctly bourgeois spirit infuses, if not totally replaces, an ethical ideal. In contrast to visions of a golden age and the Last Kingdom, the realm of freedom is seen not as a backward-looking world of the past but a forward-looking world of the future in which humanity must fashion itself—often in conflict with internal as well as external nature.

But to sharply polarize earlier visions of freedom around categories such as consumerist or productivist, hedonistic or ascetic, and naturalistic or antinaturalistic is grossly artificial and one-sided. Insofar as they aspired to freedom, the sects and movements that commonly are grouped in these categories were opposed to hierarchy as they understood it in their day (particularly in its exaggerated ecclesiastical form) and intuitively favored a dispensation of the means of life based on the equality of unequals. Beyond these two attributes, however, difficulties arise. Ordinarily, many of the medieval and Reformation visions of freedom were highly eclectic and, like the concept of justice, pregnant with double meanings. Moreover, whether these visionaries regarded themselves as rebels or conformists in regard to Christianity's "true" meaning, their ideas were guided by Christian precept. The Bible provided the common realm of discourse and dispute among all parties. Until the Reformation, when the breakdown of feudal society led to an explosion of community experiments, the individuals and groups who held to various libertarian ideals were small in number, often widely scattered, and lived extremely precarious lives. Their ideals were largely formed in the crucible of social transition—in periods of tumultuous change from one historic era to another.

Thus, groups that, during the breakdown of the ancient world and the years of early Christianity, might have emphasized a productivist and ascetic outlook sometimes shifted their perspectives during more stable periods to a consumerist and hedonistic interpretation of freedom. Comparatively large popular movements from the late imperial Roman era became highly elitist sects during medieval times and developed a harshly predatory view of their rights and their freedoms. Naturalistic folk visions of freedom like the Land of Cokaygne underwent a strange shifting of meanings, acquiring a rabidly anticlerical character at one time, becoming a visceral, earthly, and attainable "paradise" at another time, and providing a source of ribald satire at still a third. The Reformation and the English Revolution of the late 1640s brought virtually all these tendencies to the surface in the form of rebellions and significant practical experiments. After that they faded away and were supplanted by secular utopias, more systematically wrought ideals, and major social movements such as anarchism and socialism. Hence, when speaking of consumerist or productivist visions of freedom, one must bear in mind that they often merged and changed over time, being embodied either as ideals of small sects or as social movements that gripped the imagination of sizable segments of the population.

ⳤ

Although Biblical interpretation and exegesis formed the arena for the eschatological debates and conflicts of the late imperial and medieval worlds, the sources for nearly all versions of the Last Kingdom or Last Days were highly eclectic. Ideologically, the opening centuries of the Christian era were no less tumultuous than the Reformation some thirteen hundred years later. The very consolidation of Christianity as an organized body of canon and dogma hung in the balance—less because of its conflicts with entrenched pagan religions than because of its own internal divisions. At the outset, the Pauline Church in Rome (from which Catholicism was to emerge) stood sharply at odds with its Jamesian counterpart in Jerusalem. The two centers of the new faith were divided not only by geography but also by conflicting views of Christianity as a world religion. Pauline Christianity stood for accommodation to the Roman State and for an ideologically ecumenical orientation toward the gentiles. Jamesian Christianity centered around a nationalistic resistance to the "whore" Rome and around the preservation of a largely Judaic body of traditions. Christianity's problem of distancing itself from its Judaic origins was tragically resolved by the fall of Jerusalem in 70 A.D. Thereafter, the Jamesian Church disappeared with the destruction of Judea and the uncompromising Zealots who had produced the Christian Messiah.

But the Church's drift toward reconciliation with the State now encountered a crisis. The "gnostic revolt," as it has been so broadly depicted, formed a radically unique reinterpretation of the Judeo-

Christian doctrine and of the early Church's conciliatory attitude toward political authority. Viewed from a religious aspect, *gnosis* is literally "illuminated" by its Hellenic definition as "knowledge." Its emphasis on religion tends to be avowedly intellectual and esoteric. But more so than the Greek ideals of wisdom (*sophia*) and reason (*nous*), its emphasis on revelation is consistently otherworldly. And its eschatological orientation draws amply on the archaic cosmogonies of Zoroastrianism, Buddhism, Christianity itself, and a wide variety of pagan cults that invaded Roman society during its decline. Neither Judaism nor Pauline Christianity were immune to any of these far-reaching syncretic melds of religious and quasi-religious belief. But Judaic nationalism aside, their battlegrounds were narrower than those of the gnostic religions that began to emerge in the second and third centuries A.D.

Gnosticism must be dealt with very prudently before any of its tendencies are described as a Christian "heresy." In its Manichaean form, it is simply a different religion, like Islam or Buddhism. In its Ophite form, it is a total, utterly anarchistic, inversion of Christian canon and dogma. And in its Marcionite form, its point of contact with Christianity is both too intimate and too challenging to be regarded as either Christian or non-Christian. In virtually all its forms (and they are too numerous to elucidate here), gnosticism slowly percolated through the Christian world, affecting later radical sects and movements that were to open startling new visions of personal and social freedom. Gnosticism matured as a rival of Christian doctrine in the medieval Cathari, and it circuitously and indirectly influenced deviations from Christianity such as the Brethren of the Free Spirit, certain creeds of apostolic Christianity, and early historical schisms in Protestantism. It finally reappeared as an increasingly worldly pantheism among revolutionary radicals in the English Revolution, such as Gerrard Winstanley, the Digger leader. In these five major trends that were to destabilize almost every form of entrenched or emerging orthodoxy, gnosticism either anticipated or influenced the religio-social conflicts that were to profoundly expand the legacy of freedom—a legacy conceived as a history of not only doctrines but also of social movements.

The "gnostic religion," as Hans Jonas has called it in his matchless account of the subject, is much too complex to discuss in detail here. Our proper concerns are those common features that give a remarkably emancipatory quality to doctrines loosely described as "gnostic Christianity." Christian gnostics shared with other gnostics a dramatic dualism, a Platonistic doctrine of the "three-souls" and an "ethics" (if such it can be called) that exhibits very challenging, indeed modern concepts of human freedom and the meaning of the human condition.

What unified the "gnostic religion" is a cosmogonic drama and an eschatology as compelling as the Judeo-Christian. Basically, the human condition is shaped by a conflict between two principles: the "good" and its "other," which commonly is interpreted as an evil, malevolent, or even "Satanic" principle. These principles ordinarily were personified as deities by the gnostics, but it would be a crucial error to identify them with the Judeo-Christian drama of a heavenly deity and his demonic alter ego. To be sure, Manichaeanism, which became Pauline Christianity's most important rival in the third and fourth centuries, patently absorbed the image of a God who is literally represented by light and a Satan who is conceived as darkness and materiality. Valentinus (c. 125–160), whose gnostic theology exercised considerable influence in Rome and North Africa, developed a highly exotic cosmogony of "Aeons" that terminate in the person of Jesus, who provides humanity with the *gnosis* for divining the conflict between the Demiurge, the creator of the material world, and the Mother or Sophia, who can be represented for our purposes as a banished spiritual principle. Salvation occurs when the cosmos is restored to a universal "fullness" of spirit by the marriage of Sophia to Jesus. With few exceptions, the Christian gnostics grouped human souls into the spiritually pure and illuminated *pneumatics*, the imperfect *psychics* who could be illuminated, and the hopelessly material *hylics*, who are incapable by their very constitution of redemption and illumination. These distinctions played a significant role in the imagery of an "elect" or "chosen" elite whose claims upon society are virtually limitless, owing to their own perfect and pure nature. Similar distinctions were to mark some of the most radical heresies of the Middle Ages and Reformation.

In terms of gnosticism's ethical consequences, the doctrine closest to Christianity itself, and perhaps more accessible to a Christological interpretation of personal and social behavior, is the Gospel of Marcion (c. 144), who precedes Valentinus. A Christian bishop who was later excommunicated from the Roman Church, Marcion started from a highly selective reinterpretation of the New Testament. He does not burden us with the mythological material that often preoccupied the gnostic teachers, nor does he resort to the dubious allegorical interpretations central to the Catholic theologians of his day and ours. He claims to interpret the meaning of the gospel and the passion of Jesus literally—indeed, to single out in Paul's writings the truly authentic Christian creed. Hence, not only do his views seem to retain a clear Christian identity (a fact that vexed the Church fathers enormously), but also his work became their most disquieting doctrinal "heresy." Nevertheless, at its core Marcionism remained irremediably gnostic and opened the most dramatic cleavage in Christian doctrine, a cleavage in which later "heresies" were to find refuge. His gnosticism has a simplicity that is not encountered in other gnostic teachers. Its very directness gave his "heresy" far-reaching ethical consequences that were later echoed by such cultic groups as the Ophites in Marcion's own era, the Free Spirit conventicles in the Middle Ages, and the Puritan "Saints" in the English Revolution.

Like the gnostic doctrines generally, Marcion's doctrines are rigorously dualistic. The world, including humanity, has been created by a Demiurge, an oppressive creator. In marked contrast is a superior, unknown God, an "alien" acosmic deity who embodies "goodness" and is the father of the Christ person. The "good" God is the alien, even to the people whose salvation Jesus is to achieve. By the same token, this deity is alien to the cosmos that has been created entirely by the Demiurge. Each divinity is separate from and antithetical to the other. The Demiurge is "just"; his antithesis, the alien God, is "good." Here, Marcion uncannily opposes "justness" or justice to "goodness"— which, by a mere fraction of a step forward, could yield the concept of "freeness." This remarkable antithesis between a calculating, petty "justness" and a generous, overflowing "goodness" expresses one of the most remarkable insights in the legacy of freedom. Marcion does not equivocate about the moral contrast created by these two deities. Like the petty, weak, mean-spirited world he has created, the Demiurge is worthy of his own product, as the Church father Tertullian complained: "Turning up their noses, the utterly shameless Marcionites take to tearing down the work of the Creator"—and, one could add, the Creator himself. As to the "good" God of Marcion, Tertullian tells us that he is "naturally unknown and never except in the Gospel revealed." He is as alien to humanity as he is to everything the Demiurge has created, but his overflowing goodness induces him to send his Son into the Demiurge's world and redeem its human habitants.

Examining Marcion's ethical conclusions raises the question whether he advances any ethics at all. Disapproval, aversion, distaste for the "just" Demiurge and his world are apparent, but there is no evidence that Marcion has any other ethical stance. In a cosmos that is tainted but blameless and burdened by justice rather than goodness, it is fair to ask whether Marcion believes in the existence of evil—even whether "goodness" can have meaning beyond its antithetical and polarized relationship to justice. Humanity's redemption seems to involve a *transcendence* rather than an act of ethical hygiene. Insofar as human behavior is concerned, Marcion preaches a gospel of uncompromising asceticism—not as a matter of ethics, as Hans Jonas observes, "but of metaphysical alignment." By refusing to participate in sensual pleasures and worldly events, the Marcionites functioned as obstructionists to the Demiurge's creation; the reproduction of the species, for example, merely reproduces the world from which humanity must be rescued.

Marcion's amoral asceticism not only provides a sweeping inversion of the ascetic ideal but also unintentionally lends itself to an utterly libertine approach.* The Ophites, a gnostic cult that surfaced in North Africa, extended Marcion's "amoral" stance and his interpretation of the Old Testament to the point of an overt nihilistic "morality." Granting Marcion's view of the Old Testament and most of the New Testament as tainted documents of the "just" God, the Ophites concluded that a correct interpretation of the Garden of Eden allegory ennobles the serpent and Eve. By persuading Eve and, through her, Adam to eat of the fruit of the tree of knowledge, the serpent introduces *gnosis* into the world. It is not accidental that the "just" deity views this seduction as "original sin," for with *gnosis* humanity acquires the means to discover the truly despicable nature of the Creator and unmask him and his narrowness of spirit. Hippolytus, in his account of the Peratal, an Ophic cult, extends this dramatic inversion to include the murder of Abel by Cain:

> This general Serpent is also the wise Word of Eve. This is the mystery of Eden; this is the river that flows out of Eden. This is also the mark that was set upon Cain, whose sacrifice the god of this world did not accept whereas he accepted the bloody sacrifice of Abel: for the lord of this world delights in blood. This Serpent is he who appeared in the latter days in human form at the time of Herod.

---

* Here, as in Augustine's work, is another of those ambiguities that foster either complete social quietism or a fiery social activism. Although Marcion's denigration of the Judaic "just deity" as mean-spirited forms a marked advance over the limited notion of justice, his asceticism marks a decided regression in ancient political life. Marcion's doctrines spread widely after the Jews had failed in one of the most heroic and selfless revolts against the Roman Empire—a revolt that led to the extermination of Judea as a nation. Marcion, like Paul before him, thus appealed to some of the most quiescent political tendencies in the Empire. His image of Jesus fostered a totally distorted version of a Hebrew nationalist who, as Hyam Maccoby puts it, "was a good man who fell among Gentiles.... As a Jew, he fought not against some metaphysical evil but against Rome." (Hyam Maccoby, *Revolution in Judea*, p.195). Fortunately, the radical Christian "heretics" who later emerged and unsettled the medieval world were men and women who were just as earthily oriented as the original founder of their religion. Like Jesus, they too fought "not against some metaphysical evil" but against the Papacy and the territorial lords of their day. Marcion formulated a body of ideas that, in the real world at least, were used in the pursuit of ends he never intended to achieve.

Radical "amorality" thus turns upon asceticism to encourage unrestrained freedom and the open defiance of the Demiurge's moral tenets. In contrast to Marcion, the Ophites accept the three-soul classification of gnosticism, with its pneumatics, psychics, and hylics. Marcion would not have accepted this prototypic notion of the "elect," which infected not only official Christianity but also many of the radical "heresies" that were ideologically related to gnosticism. In fact, here we reach the limits of gnosticism as a "gospel" of freedom. Things being what they are, only the few—an elite by nature modeled partly on Plato's "guardians" (albeit without their "asceticism" and "communism")—are free to indulge their every appetite. If gnosticism had been left at this point, it would have retreated back to a questionable libertinism that could no longer be identified with Marcion's generous libertarian message.

What matters is not so much the elitist conclusions that the gnostic cults adopted but the eschatological strategy they used—a strategy that could easily be divested of its elitist sequelae. Based on this strategy, the claim of cults such as the Ophites to "forbidden things" (including orgiastic ones) could also be viewed as a "metaphysical alignment." *All* "moral" judgment, not only that of the orthodox Christian, is tainted. The "moral" code is merely the "complement of the physical law, and as such the internal aspect of the all-pervading cosmic rule," observes Jonas. "Both emanate from the lord of the world as agencies of his rule, unified in the double aspect of the Jewish God as creator and legislator." Human will in normative law is appropriated "by the same powers that control his body. He who obeys it has abdicated the authority of his self." To defy the authority of the Creator and his juridical minions was turned from a "merely permissive privilege of freedom" into "a positive metaphysical interest in repudiating allegiance to all objective norms...."

Jonas sees in gnostic libertinism more than mere defiance; it is "a positive obligation to perform every kind of action, with the idea of rendering to nature its own and thereby exhausting its powers." Accordingly, "sinning" becomes "something like a program." Its completion is a "due rendered as the price of ultimate freedom." Jonas concludes that it is doubtful whether

> the preachers of these views lived up to their own professions. To scandalize has always been the pride of rebels, but much of it may satisfy itself in provocativeness of doctrine rather than of deeds. Yet we must not underrate the extremes to which revolutionary defiance and the vertigo of freedom

could go in the value-vacuum created by the spiritual crisis. The very discovery of a new vista invalidating all former norms constituted an anarchical condition, and excess in thought and life was the first response to the import and dimensions of that vista.

❧

But can this exploration of the gnostics end with a discipline of indiscipline? A wild compulsion to be free? Gnosticism's commitment to "goodness" and physical indulgence implies the latent existence of more creative impulses than a "moral nihilism." We hear the message of Rabelais's Abbey of Theleme, whose devotees are no longer spiritual pneumatics but earthly rationalists; we also hear the message of Fourier's "phalanstery," which resonates with a radically new social, cultural, and technical dispensation: its psychological cosmos of personal affines, its gastronomic delights, its artistic and variegated organization of labor, its concept of work as play, and its generous (for Fourier's time) commitment to the emancipation of women. No hierarchy or system of domination infects this message. Fourier can be placed at least partly in the gnostic tradition by virtue of his emphasis on human spontaneity, personal freedom, and a refusal to deny the claims of the flesh. This is even more true for Rabelais, perhaps *because* of his elitist Renaissance proclivities and his clerical background. Ultimately, the denial of justice for "goodness" and of repression for freedom provide a more secure common ground for the humanistic utopians of the modern world and the gnostics of the ancient world than their dizzying idiosyncracies would lead us to believe.

We also hear another message. Where imagination is permitted to outstrip all the constraints that ideology, morality, and "law" place on human creative powers, what emerges is the voice of art, not merely of theology. Religion has always been a ritualized drama that appeals to aesthetic needs as well as to faith. And gnosticism shared with the cultic mysteries of the ancient world, as well as with Christianity, a need to achieve a derangement of the senses, an ecstatic union of spirit with body that theology described as a union of worshipper with deity. *A world that is rendered askew is a world that can be seen anew*—and changed according to the dictates of art as well as reason. Herein lies the great power of imagination that has vitalized radical movements for centuries: a "world turned upside down" that has been the goal of great anarchic movements, from the ancient world to the French student radicals of 1968.

Gnosticism, by giving desire an unyielding claim on the entire universe of experience, does not seem to limit its credo of "illumination" to a limited place in personal life. Its appeal to defiance as an "obligation" is a program for everyday life. The gnostic experience, if such it can be called, is not locked into episodic rituals and ceremonies; it is an ongoing, unrelieved calling. *Gnosis* is expected to transfigure every detail of one's encounter with reality—to create a transmundane reality of "goodness" that is close to a communion with the true God. To use the language of Surrealism, it places a "halo" over the ordinary things and events that normally drift by us unperceived. The very spontaneity it fosters in the self is the correlate of a permanent state of desire rather than mere need, of a passionate perception of the world rather than one deadened by custom, routine, and predictability.

If these creative, indeed, esthetic, aspects of the radical gnostic "programs" are depicted accurately, then the closing centuries of antiquity anticipated a more universal secular impulse to freedom than a strictly religious interpretation of gnosticism would lead us to believe. What gnosticism seems to imply is a colonization of *every* aspect of human experience by desire. Schiller's dream of an esthetically enchanted world and Breton's hypostatization of "the marvelous" as the explosive grenades that unsort the world of given reality would be coterminous with the gnostic experience of "ecstatic illumination." But the gnostics were not "political animals" in Aristotle's sense of the term. They were not citizens of the *polis* or *cosmopolis* but ultimately of a highly spiritual world. They emphasized inward-oriented experiences, not an active contact with the social world. The Cathari, a gnostic sect that flourished during the Middle Ages, had a program for self-extinction. Their extreme rejection of the "hylic" or material—from reproduction to food—would have guaranteed a retreat from the Demiurge's cosmos into an utterly ineffable one had the Albigensian "crusade" of the thirteenth century not led to their virtual extermination.

Communism, which cannot easily be reduced to cultic conventicles, drew its inspiration from *Acts* in the New Testament and other "Judaic" writings that Marcion would have banished from Christian canon and dogma. Because it was apostolic in its efforts to establish its ethical legitimacy and superiority against the Church's self-interest and greed, communism has no discernible roots in ancient gnosticism. But Christianity's ample history—be it the account of its wayward hierarchy or of their "heretical" opponents—is not a story of doctrinal consistency. Just as the Church was to bend before the onslaught of changing events, so too did the devout congregations outside its fold. By the time of Luther and Calvin—and perhaps most markedly during the English Revolution of the seventeenth century—heretical and recalcitrant congregations of revolutionary heretical "Saints" (as they called themselves) were to surface from their hidden folds in Christian society and move to the center of political life. We shall investigate the activities of these "Saints," their various tendencies, their politics, and their growing secularity in the following chapter. Particularly in the British Isles, the Puritan radicals ceased to be mere spiritual conventicles; from religious "Saints" they became "God's Englishmen." Once-hidden heretical congregations and religious pulpits now occupied the seats of rebellious parliaments, parliamentary rostrums, and (perhaps more compellingly) the tents, barracks, and military councils of Oliver Cromwell's New Model army.

What is significant about this sweeping entry of Christian heretics into political institutions is not merely the secularity of the development. At heart, most of the erstwhile heretics were theocrats—and not very tolerant ones at that, particularly in matters of religious dogma. The various Puritan sects of the late sixteenth and early seventeenth centuries had no love for their enemies and no charity toward "Papists," however uneasily they lived with one another within a common Protestant fold. But they were nonconformists. Their hatred of authority often greatly exceeded their hatred of official religious dogma. The attempt of official English Protestantism (that is, the Anglican Church's attempt to contain its Presbyterian dissidents, and the dissidents' attempt, once they became ascendant, to contain the Puritans) was nearly as fierce as the efforts of the English Church as a whole to exorcise its Catholic past. Nonconformity thus introduced a millennia-long tradition of fiery disputes over ecclesiastical structure *as such*. The Church policy raised stormy questions and, finally, rebellions around the right of the king to head the English Church, the right of bishops to control congregations, and the freedom of the congregation—indeed, of each member—to answer to no authority whatever beyond the claims of his or her "inner voice."

Christianity, in effect, had inadvertently spawned a remarkably new "politics": a politics distinctly libertarian in its orientation, often anarchic in its structure, and remarkably unfettered in the restrictions it placed on individual freedom. It had created an ethical arena for a godly citizenship whose libertarian scope was even broader than that of the Athenian concept of citizenship. Unlike the citizen of the *polis*, the Christian "heretic" had to recognize that one was answerable *only* to God, and hence had to be in a higher estate of citizenship in the New Jerusalem than in the earthly city. By visualizing themselves as God's "elect," the "Saints" may have been elitists, especially when they were forced by persecution into the medieval and early Reformation underground of damned heretics. But as the Reformation provided a sweeping impetus for social activism, and as theocracies appeared in Geneva under Calvin, in Scotland under Knox, and finally in England under Cromwell, questions of authoritarian versus libertarian structure ceased to be merely ecclesiastical issues. They became political and social issues as well. The Puritan New Model army that brought English royalty to its knees and placed King Charles on the scaffold was itself a richly articulated, often raging body of radical congregations—the arena of fiery heretical sermonizers—that was represented by rank-and-file "agitators" (as the soldiers' representatives were actually called) who sat on the Army Council together with major-generals. Together they formulated and furiously argued over issues of not only military policy but also social and political policy. On at least two occasions, Cromwell nearly lost control of his own military "Saints" in near or outright mutinies.

By spawning nonconformity, heretical conventicles, and issues of authority over person and belief, Christianity created not merely a centralized authoritarian Papacy but also its very antithesis: a quasi-religious anarchism. Up to the seventeenth century and for several generations later, particularly in America, the political and social structures of freedom were as central to Christian discourse as were issues of religious ideology.

◌ℛ

From the eighteenth-century Enlightenment until our own time, the waning of this realm of discourse on the structures of freedom was to have the same tragic consequences as the secularization of the individual and the disenchantment of personality to which I have already alluded. The moral issues of freedom were to suffer a decline with the secularism introduced by Machiavelli, Hobbes, Locke, Bentham, and the Victorian liberals. In addition, the very notion that freedom—that is, *active* citizenship in the Periklean and Hellenic sense—presupposes the existence and development of certain distinct libertarian institutions was to be eclipsed by debates and analyses on the subjects of property ownership, the mystique of nationhood (and the nation-state), and the tendency to equate institutional centralization with social rationalism. Hobbes, Locke, and Marx were obviously concerned with security and property when they did not discourse on the nature and need of centralized authority. The active revolutionaries of the modern era—Cromwell, Robespierre, Babeuf, Blanqui, and Lenin, to cite the most familiar of the lot—were dogmatic centralists who often moved beyond the limits of liberal republicanism in order to foster highly authoritarian political forms. Except for rejoinders by the anarchists and certain utopian socialists who had emerged from the French Revolution, Christian heretics faded out of the revolutionary tradition into a historical limbo, at least until comparatively recent times. The nation-state was now equated with community; the notion of a representative republic, with the direct democracy of the *polis*. The very terms of the debate over authority had become so distorted that the debate itself virtually ceased to be intelligible to later generations.

The imagery of a recurring history, largely cyclic in character, often replaced Christianity's eschatological vision of the Last Days, with its populist reward of a Land of Cokaygne or at least an earthly Jerusalem. The republican ideal that permeated the Great French Revolution was always haunted by a Caesarist shadow, a republican Bonapartism, that its own contemporary historians justified as a stabilizing factor in Europe's march toward freedom, specifically toward freedom of trade. The Jacobins read Plutarch not only as a guide to Roman virtue but also as a revolutionary handbook; perhaps it was more germane as a source of social forecasts than Rousseau's *Social Contract*, which was read as a source of social theory. They awaited their Napoleon as surely as the Roman plebes awaited their Caesar. Seeing the world with the new sense of recurrence that had replaced the Christian emphasis on a linear history, they viewed their cards as stacked and accepted the fall of the republic itself fatalistically—indeed, in almost a dreamlike trance, if Robespierre's personal passivity between his overthrow and his execution is any indication.

With the exception of the Paris Commune of 1871, which exploded as an anarchic confederal image of a France administered by a Commune composed of decentralized communes, European socialism had decorated itself with republican trappings at best and dictatorial ones at worst. By the autumn of 1917, Lenin had combined Brutus and Caesar in one person. Despite his slogan of "All Power to the Soviets!"—and even earlier in the summer of the same year, "All Power to the Shop Committees!" (a strictly anarchosyndicalist demand)—Lenin readily dispensed with both forms and replaced them by the Party as a State organ.

The Party, as such, was the unique structural innovation of the post-Reformation era. Its contemporaneity and its impact on political life have rarely been fully appreciated. From the twelfth century onward, Christian heretics found their home in the small, highly decentralized, personally intimate conventicle—an almost cellular type of association that fostered an intense form of intimacy and support that was sorely lacking in the larger Christian congregations of the time. These family-like units lent themselves uniquely to a confederal form of interaction among groups from which, cell by cell, a truly organic body politic could be constructed. With the onset of the Reformation, as such groups became increasingly involved in secular affairs, they functioned more like *social* organisms than like State or political institutions. Brotherhoods such as the Hutterites even became alternative communistic societies, self-sufficient and complete unto themselves. Perhaps even more striking is the fact that the conventicle form of association never disappeared, despite the ascendancy of the Party. Completely secular in character but no less small, intimate, and decentralized, it persisted within the Spanish anarchist movement as the "affinity group." From Spain it spread throughout the world with the recent growth of libertarian organizations, acquiring the names of "collective," "commune," and "cooperative" with the emergence of the New Left in the 1960s.

By contrast, the Party was simply a mirror image of the nation-state, and its fortunes were completely tied to the State's development. The Party was meant to be very large, often embracing sizable masses of people who were knitted together bureaucratically in depersonalized, centralized organs. When the Party was *not* "in power," it was merely the disinherited twin of the State apparatus, often replicating it in every detail. When the Party *was* "in power," it became the State itself. Rarely has it been understood that the Bolshevik Party and the Nazi Party were themselves complete State apparatuses that completely supplanted the preexisting State structures they "seized." Hitler, no less than Lenin, was to follow Marx's famous maxim that the State must not be merely occupied but "smashed" and replaced by a new one.

But Marx was stating a fact about parties in general that, after the French Revolution, had already ceased to be a novelty. The modern State could more properly be called a "*party*-state" than a "nation-state." Organized from the top downward with a bureaucratic infrastructure fleshed out by a membership, the Party possesses an institutional flexibility that is much greater than that of the official State. Structurally, its repertory of forms ranges from the loosely constructed republic to highly totalitarian regimes. As a source of institutional innovation, the Party can be sculpted and molded to produce organizational, authoritarian forms with an ease that any State official would envy. And once in power, the Party can make these forms part of the political machinery itself. Our own era has given the Party an autonomy unequaled by any State institution, from the ancient pharaohs to the modern republics. As the history of Russian Bolshevism and German fascism dramatically demonstrated, parties have shaped European states more readily than states have shaped their parties.

Yet the ascendancy of the nation-state, the party, and, in more recent years, the highly centralized bureaucratic State did not lack ideological reactions against them. The English "Saints" who carried Cromwell to power never encountered the highly coordinated institutions or even the centralized bureaucracies that the absolute monarchs of the European continent and, perhaps, more significantly, the Jacobin "despotism of freedom" had fashioned in the seventeenth and eighteenth centuries. Only the Papacy, a feeble institution by the time of the English Revolution, had anticipated any state-like apparatus like the French Revolution was to produce. The Tudor and Stuart monarchies, while more centralized than English royal houses of the past, were still too inept to anticipate the world of nation-states that would follow.

The French Revolution—first under Robespierre and later under Bonaparte—had fashioned the centralized nation-state with a vengeance. For the first time in Europe, the word "Saint" was replaced by the word "patriot." While Marx exulted in the willful ruthlessness of the nation-state, lesser-known revolutionaries drew less favorable, icily clear antiauthoritarian lessons of their own. One such was Jean Varlet, a popular street orator (or *Enragé*) of 1793 who managed to survive Robespierre's murderous purge of the Parisian radicals. Varlet decided (flatly contradicting his more celebrated contemporary, Gracchus Babeuf) that "Government and Revolution are incompatible." This statement, in its sweep and generality, was more unequivocal than any conclusion voiced by the radical "Saints" about the State or even authority. It was anarchist. Indeed, Varlet had been the target of this very epithet by his liberal opponents in the feverish days of 1793—as, in fact, the Levellers, had been in the English Revolution more than a century earlier, when a paper favorable to Cromwell described them as "Switzerizing Anarchists."

The term was to stick and to acquire an ever-richer meaning on the margins of European and American society. Both Thomas Paine and Jefferson drew conclusions somewhat similar to those of Varlet from the quasi-dictatorship of the Jacobins and its Bonapartist sequelae. Even more significant than Paine's derogatory remarks about government were the essentially reconstructive confederal notions that Jefferson advanced to Destutt de Tracy in 1811. Concerned with the need for relatively federalist institutional forms at the base of society, Jefferson astutely diagnosed the reasons why republican France so easily slipped into imperial France with Napoleon's *coup d'état:*

The republican government of France was lost without a struggle because the party of "un et indivisible" had prevailed. No provincial [and one could easily add, local] organizations existed to which the people might rally under the laws, the seats of the Directory were virtually vacant, and a small force sufficed to turn the legislature out of their chamber, and salute its leader chief of the nation.

Having concentrated all political authority in the national State, the Jacobins and their successors, the Directory, had denuded the country of all local, decentralized foci of power from which the revolution could mount an effective resistance to the Bonapartist monarchy.

That Jefferson imputed a greater wisdom to the American Revolution for its confederal orientation raises issues that must be deferred to a later discussion. Jefferson himself was no "Switzerizing Anarchist," and the American Revolution did not reproduce Switzerland's cantonal form of confederation.* But a confederalist orientation was to linger on—in the writings of Proudhon, who provocatively declared himself to be an "*anarchiste*"; in Bakunin, who was to help make anarchism into a movement; and in Kropotkin, who was to vastly enrich anarchism with a wealth of historical traditions, a strikingly pragmatic vision of the technological and social alternatives it offered, and a creative vision drawn largely from the writings of Robert Owen and Charles Fourier.

---

* Jefferson, in fact, was more of a liberal whig than a radical democrat, and more of a classical republican than a decentralist. Here, I am exclusively concerned with intellectual aspects of Jefferson's political philosophy rather than his vexing, often opportunistic practice. For a useful correction of the "Jefferson myth," see Elisha P. Douglas, *Rebels and Democrats* (New York: Quadrangle Books, 1955), pp. 287–316.

8 ∞ FROM SAINTS TO SELLERS

But what of the social movements that these expanding notions of freedom were meant to influence? What of the ancient tribes who crossed the threshold into "civilization," the plebes and slaves to whom Christianity appealed, the discontented congregations of the "elect" and the unruly conventicles of the radical "Saints," the mystics and realists, the ascetics and hedonists, the pacifists and warriors of Christ who were to "turn the world upside down"? Up to now, I have explored the legacy of freedom in terms of its development as a theory. But how did the legacy function as a social movement, and how did the social movement react back upon the legacy, raising problems not only of faith and "Sainthood" but in our own time problems of economics, technics, and the impact of a marketplace of sellers? To understand the legacy of freedom as it was *lived*, not only thought, we must immerse our ideas in the rich flux of reality and sort out their authenticity in the earthy experiences of the oppressed.

Historically, the earliest expression of freedom within the realm of unfreedom consists of popular attempts to restore the irreducible minimum and the circulation of wealth frozen in the temples, manors, and palaces of the ruling elites. The "big men"—initially, the tribal warrior-chieftains, later the nobles and monarchs of the secular realm and their priestly counterparts—were the custodians of society's use-values. They collected them in storehouses (an action partly justified by the Biblical story of Joseph) and redistributed them according to a hierarchy of values that increasingly reinforced their authority. The early history of "civilization" is largely an account of the custodians' expanding grip on the productive process: their deployment and rationalization of labor, their control over its fruits, and their personal appropriation of an increasingly larger fraction of the labor process and its social product.

But this history is also an account of the mystification of the social wealth they siphoned off to reinforce their power. Treasure—in the form of large ornate structures, costly furnishings and attire, jewels, art works, storehouses of products, even intangibles such as writing and knowledge—looms over the "masses" as the materialization of an all-pervasive malevolent force. The shamans and priests did their work well by transforming mundane things into transmundane things, objects into symbols; they thereby restructured the very process of *generalization*—which must itself be emancipated from hierarchy—into the supernatural imagery of *transubstantiation*. The ancient mysteries invaded the mental processes of humanity and changed them epistemologically from *gnosis* into the warped form of a *sacrament*: real bread was turned into the "body" of Christ and real wine into his "blood." Even in the distant, pre-Christian era of antiquity, the real things that the primordial world generously recycled within the community to satisfy real needs were turned into sacramental things consecrating power and hierarchy. The "fetishization" of use-values long preceded the "fetishization" of exchange-values and market-generated "needs."

Consolidated as mystified power and authority, the treasure of the ruling elites had to be exorcised. It had to be removed from the hands of the hierarchical strata who guarded it. It also had to be stripped of its mystified traits by a two-fold process of dissolution: firstly, by restoring this treasure to the natural, comprehensible forms of mundane use-values in order to render authority itself mundane and controllable; secondly, by recirculating wealth within the community in order to restore the principle of usufruct. Accordingly, by plundering, redistributing, or even "purifying" property with the torch of the incendiary, the "masses" were not merely oriented toward a consumerist disposition of wealth, but were also demystifying its institutional function as a force for domination—as well as restoring the primordial principles of the irreducible minimum and the equality of unequals. In this tradition-laden version of the "black redistribution," we find a rational attempt to subvert the hold of objects as the incarnation of hierarchy and domination over the lives of human beings. These expropriative explosions of the people, which so often are dismissed as the "plundering" expeditions of "primitive rebels" (to use Eric Hobsbawn's fatuous characterization), were surprisingly sophisticated in their intentions. They recur throughout history. Even the most unadorned consumerist visions of freedom have a broader social dimension than we normally suppose; they are concerned not only with the satisfaction of human needs but with the *desymbolization* of power and property.

But two epistemologies are in conflict here. The ruling classes react to the "black redistribution" not only with personal fear and a savage lust for vengeance, but with horror toward the desecration of their hierarchical vision of "order." The "black redistribution" affronts not only their own proprietary claim to the social product but also their view of the social product as a *kosmos* of proprietary claims. Perhaps the earliest record we have of these reactions is a lamentation by a member of the privileged classes, recounting a peasant rebellion that apparently swept over the Nile Valley at the beginning of ancient Egypt's "feudal" period (c. 2500 B.C.):

> Behold the palaces thereof, their walls are dismantled.... Behold, all the craftsmen, they do no work; the enemies of the land impoverish its crafts. [Behold, he who reaped] the harvest knows naught of it; he who has not plowed [fills his granaries].... Civil war pays no taxes.... For what is a treasure without its revenues? ... Behold, he who has no yoke of oxen is [now] possessor of a herd; and he who found no plow-oxen for himself is [now] owner of a herd. Behold, he who had no grain is [now] owner of granaries; and he who used to fetch grain for himself [now] has it issued [from his own granary].

Not only had the *kosmos* fallen apart, but with it the State: "[The] laws of the judgment-hall are cast forth, men walk upon [them] in the public places, the poor break them open in the midst of the streets. James Breasted, from whom this account is drawn, astutely observes that this despoliation of the records, archives, and written laws was "particularly heinous from the orderly Egyptian's point of view; the withdrawing of writings and records from the public offices for purposes of evidence or consultation was carefully regulated." In this sacrilegious act of destruction, the blood oath took its revenge on written legal ties; parity, on status sanctified by codes; usufruct, on the titles that confer ownership of property; and the irreducible minimum, on the accounts of taxes and grain deliveries to the State, nobility, and priesthood.

Thereafter, almost every peasant war was marked not only by the redistribution of property but also by the burning of archives. The impulse for such actions came from the revolutionary impulse, not from the memory of previous revolts, whose history had been largely suppressed. In that distant period related by the Egyptian scribe, the memory of tribal life may still have permeated the reality of "civilization," and the Word, with its moral, legal, and mystical nuances, had not completely replaced the deed. Contract and moral precept still floated on a primordial quicksand that required many centuries of "civilization" before it could fully harden into class rule and become solidly internalized as guilt, renunciation, and a fear of the "chaotic" impulses that raged in the unconscious of the oppressed.

The memory of later uprisings (which are probably very similar in nature to the one we already have explored) was so completely appropriated by the ruling classes that the historical record is sketchy at best and venal in the accounts it does contain. We know that about the same time the ancient Egyptian peasantry rose against the entrenched class system of the Old Kingdom or possibly the nobility of the Middle Kingdom, a similar uprising occurred in the Sumerian city of Lagash (for which Kramer, puzzled by the literal meaning of the word *amargi*, provides a fairly complete account). Judging from Athenian references, Sparta's serf-like helots revolted with disconcerting frequency. So troubling was this history of underclass unrest that even the fairly benign Athenian *polis* lived in uncertainty about its own slave population. Rome, particularly toward the end of its republican era, was apparently destabilized by a series of slave and gladiatorial revolts, among which Spartakus's historic rebellion (73 8.c.) was apparently the most far-reaching and dramatic. This army of slaves and gladiators, later joined by impoverished free people, engaged in a series of major looting expeditions that swept over the Campania and southern Italy until it was crushed by Crassus and Pompey.

However, Greece and Rome's class conflicts were largely confined to disputes between commoners and nobles over demands for a fair redistribution of the land, the cancellation of mortgages, and greater juridical equality within the prevailing system of ownership and political authority. Quasi-nationalist uprisings afflicted both city-states after they were drawn into the pursuit of imperial ends. But these conflicts rarely involved deep-seated internal social changes either at home or abroad.

CR

Only with the advent of Christianity did the libidinal, instinctive movement for freedom resurge—not only as gnosticism but also as a radical interpretation of canonical ideals. Even seemingly "orthodox" Christian communities exhibited these communistic and fervently millenarian qualities, which were to unsettle western society for centuries. Apostolic deeds were used against the ecclesiastical Word—the one as bluntly secular, the other as cunningly divine. The covenant of justice—Old Testament law—was transmuted into the covenant of freedom as practiced by the early Christian congregations that apparently existed in ancient Judea before the fall of Jerusalem.

Christianity's mixed message can be grouped into two broad and highly conflicting systems of belief. On one side there was a radical, activistic, communistic, and libertarian vision of the Christian life largely drawn from the Jamesian Church in Jerusalem; on the other side there was a conservative, quietistic, materially unworldly, and hierarchical vision that seems to derive from the Pauline Church in Rome. The radical interpretation of a devout life and Christian eschatology may have had even more canonical support than the conservative, despite the Roman Church's apparent purging of the New Testament to remove the radical ideals of its Jamesian progenitors. Apostolic Christianity advances a vision of the earliest community of believers that stands sharply at odds with the surrounding Roman world. Communal sharing—communism—is one of its most outstanding features. According to *Acts*, "all that believed were together, and had all things in common, and they sold their possessions and goods, and parted them all, according as every man had need." As if to reinforce this view of the Christian life, the gospel intones: "And the multitude of them that believed were of one heart and of one soul, not one of them said that all of the things which he possessed was his own; but they had all things in common." If we take this description of the early Christian community literally (and there is no reason why we shouldn't), the first believers practiced not merely communism but usufruct.

The Pauline Church in Rome reinforced this apostolic account. Barnabas (c. 130), in his "Epistle to the Christians," made the gospel message a practical injunction: the true believer should "communicate in all things with thy neighbor" and "shall not call things thine own." Justin the Martyr (c.100–165) urged that the redeemed "who loveth the path to riches and possessions above any other now produce what we have in common and give to everyone who needs." Tertullian (c.160–230), already faced with radical "heresies" that were to rend the Church of his day, nevertheless emphasized that "We acknowledge one all-embracing commonwealth—the world." Having cited the Christian doctrine of a universal *humanitas*, as distinguished from a parochial folk or a selected elite (a distinction he apparently found it still necessary to make), Tertullian then declared that Christians were "one in mind and soul, we do not hesitate to share all our earthly goods with one another. All things are common among us but our wives." Although the Church dealt with such descriptions, possibly such admonitions, very warily, these it probably could not expunge. Apparently, the *Acts* and the writings of the Church fathers cited here were too well-known to be suppressed or reduced to apocryphal writings. The Church encountered similar problems in dealing with the gospel of Matthew, in ritual and language the most Judaic of the New Testament writings, and with the gospels of Mark and Luke, both of which reveal strong biases against wealth and proprietary proclivities.

No less important are the apocalyptic visions advanced in *Matthew* and particularly in *Revelation*. These visions of the Last Days, together with similar prophecies in the Old Testament, attained immense popularity among the early Christian congregations and surged up as an explosive program for "heretical" tendencies and movements during the Reformation. Matthew's gospel is wrenched by anger. Jesus comes not to "abolish the Law or the Prophets ... but to complete them." Pacific though Jesus may be, he warns the disciples: "Do not suppose I have come to bring peace to the earth. It is not peace I have to bring, but the sword." "Vipers," the "wrath" of the "Kingdom to come," "vengeance"—all these terms rise up angrily in the text, as much from the mouth of Jesus as from that of John the Baptizer (a figure apparently modeled on Amos whose god is a "barn burner," to use Bloch's expression). *Revelation* or *Apocalypse* (the original Greek title) is chiliastic to the core; its fiery symbolism aside, it predicts the Last Days in terms of the total annihilation of the Roman Empire, to be followed by the Second Coming of Jesus, the raising of the devout from the dead, and a utopian heaven on earth in the form of a New Jerusalem.

To the early Christians, the Apocalypse and the Second Coming, with its ensuing millennium, were not spiritual metaphors or remote events. They were earthly and imminent. The all-encompassing renunciation that Jesus demands of his disciples would be meaningless if the "throne of glory," with its promise of repayment "a hundred times over" and its reward of "eternal life," were not close at hand. The huge stakes advanced by both parties in this cosmic bargain—on one side, the heart-wrenching humiliation and crucifixion; on the other, the loss of "houses, brothers, sisters, father, mother, children or land"— could hardly be expected to end in a paltry and remote dispensation.

Nor could the early Christian congregations be asked to look forward to less. Norman Cohn has pieced together the various apocalyptic fantasies of the Christian congregations during the first few centuries of persecution into a "paradigm" that was to haunt the Church and guide the revolutionary eschatological movements of the oppressed for centuries to come. According to this vision:

> The world is dominated by an evil, tyrannous power of boundless destructiveness—a power moreover which is imagined not as simply human but as demonic. The tyranny of that power will become more and more outrageous, the suffering of its victims more and more intolerable—

until suddenly the hour will strike when the Saints of God are able to rise up and overthrow it. Then the Saints themselves, the chosen, holy people, who hitherto have groaned under the oppressor's heel, shall in their turn inherit dominion over the whole earth. This will be the culmination of history; the Kingdom of the Saints will not only surpass in glory all previous kingdoms, but it will have no successors.

To this "paradigm" must be added a number of vital eschatological visions that are essentially utopian. The "Saints of God" are a devout, earthly people, not necessarily divine otherworldly personages, and they will be led by a holy messiah with miraculous powers. The earthly "Kingdom of God" will be a world of plenty in which, according to the vision of Lactantius (a Christian proselytizer of the fourth century):

The earth shall bear all fruits without man's labor. Honey in abundance shall drip from the rocks, fountains of milk and wine shall burst forth. The beasts of the forests shall put away their wildness and become tame...no longer shall any animal live by bloodshed. For God shall supply all with abundant and guiltless food.

Thus Christianity, during many of its wayward pagan accretions, was to acquire not only a large calendar of saints and miraculous achievements but also, in terms of folk appeal, the ancient land of Cokaygne.

Yet by no means does this "paradigm" yield more than an ascetic social quietism—one that initially recruits martyrs for the Church rather than warriors. The oppressed who joined the early Christian congregations shaped their fantasies in the form of miracles, not muscular conflicts. The mentality of the ancient slave and of impoverished country and city folk left an indelible mark of resignation on the new religion. Unsettling as the early Christian imagery of a vengeful Second Coming may have been to the masters of the Roman world, these Christians lived in a world of portents and omens. Tertullian, for example, tells us of a wondrous vision that had been reported: every morning for forty days a walled city was seen in the sky of Judea, clearly signifying that the heavenly Jerusalem would shortly descend to the earth. Patently, the Second Coming was clearly at hand—indeed, imminent.

After two centuries of passive waiting, however, such miraculous notions of the Apocalypse had been worn to shreds. A new note began to appear in the chiliastic literature. The Latin poet Commodianus advanced a more militant, activistic concept of the Apocalypse based upon violence and crusading zealotry. To Commodianus, the "Saints" were warriors, not mere penitents; they were free, with the Deity's consent, to loot and devastate wantonly. After much battling back and forth between the heavenly hosts and the forces of Antichrist, the holy folk would win over the evil ones and enjoy the rewards of immortality in their New Jerusalem. These consolingly material rewards included not only eternal life but also freedom from the burdens of age, inclement weather, and the ascetic life. The "Saints" could marry and have children; the earth would be rejuvenated, and the "Holy Ones" would enjoy its rich material bounty.

The "double meaning" of these chiliastic visions did not escape the eyes of the Church fathers. Augustinian Christianity ruthlessly purged the now-established religion of its millenarian fantasies by turning them into spiritual allegories—the device *par excellence* that the Church was to use repeatedly against any undesirable literal interpretations of the Bible. To Augustine, the Second Coming had essentially arrived with the establishment of the Church. Official Christianity elevated the vision of an earthly paradise to heaven and suppressed as "heresies" any departure from its otherworldly focus. Not that the earthly world could be left to its own ways—Christ, as well as the Church, would intercede to transform it—but the Second Coming was off in the distant future, when the Church's custody of the earth and its task of sorting out the holy from the irredeemable ones had been completed.

❧

The chiliastic visions of a New Jerusalem, however, did not disappear. They were driven underground, only to surface again with the changing social conditions that layered the Middle Ages, often acquiring increasingly radical traits. During their long history, these visions branched off into two types of social movements—the ascetic and the hedonistic—that later intersected very visibly during the Reformation. After this era, they entered into the more worldly revolutionary movements of the capitalist era.

The ascetic movements were austere and messianic, like the early Christian sects; but they were far from quietistic. Their methods were almost maniacally violent and their hatred was directed principally against the clergy. The New Jerusalem they sought to bring to earth has been called "anarcho-communistic" by several scholars, a term not always used very felicitously here, but one with a truthful core to it. By far the largest of the medieval "heresies" were polarized around these Spartan apocalyptic ideals, which found their ideological roots in apostolic descriptions of the early Christian community.

The hedonistic movements veered sharply toward worldly interests. Even their chiliasm tended to lapse into an amoral worldliness that probably scandalized the more austere messianic "heresies" of the time. It seems unlikely that medieval hedonistic tendencies were directly influenced by ancient gnostic ideologies, however close the Brethren of the Free Spirit seem to the Ophites of an earlier era. But the reasoning by which the former arrived at their involuted notion of Christian virtue and unfettered sexuality is more pantheistic than dualistic. The mystical distinction made by Meister Eckhart (c. 1260–1328) between a lofty, unreachable, and unknowable "Godhead" and a God who is overflowing, omnipresent, and close to humanity approximates a gnostic dualism that allows for a transcendental "alien" deity on the one hand and an immanent deity on the other. But Eckhart's immanent deity is a warm, highly Christianized God who appears in each human soul as a "divine spark." Although Eckhart and his disciples surely did not regard themselves as departing from the Church, his mystical theology does seem to encourage an autonomy of action that could have served the ideological needs of hedonistic conventicles well.

The earliest example of a large-scale ascetic "heresy" is the Crusade of the Shepherds (or *Pastoureaux*), which emerged in the middle of the thirteenth century, when crusades were still largely movements of the oppressed rather than of errant military adventurers and the ruling classes. The *Pastoureaux*, composed mainly of zealous young people, began to march through the towns of France, at first attacking Jews and then the clergy, whom they accused of being "false shepherds" of their flocks. The movement enjoyed immense popular support and turned into a chronic, century-long assault upon the established institutions of the Church. Cities were taken by force, churches and monasteries were sacked, the homes of wealthy burghers were plundered, and even the Papal residence at Avignon was menaced by one of the *Pastoureaux* columns. They finally were excommunicated by Pope John XXII (who also later condemned Eckhart) and ruthlessly hunted down by the territorial lords. Few popular movements in the medieval world seem to have inspired greater fear among the ruling classes of this era or more seriously challenged the very basis of the social order than this "shepherds' crusade."

The *Pastoureaux* had their German parallel in the Flagellants— the large bands of self-afflicting penitents who scourged themselves and one another with whips and branches. Here, asceticism was carried to the point of ecstatic self-torture; in its own way, it was perhaps more a doctrine of the flesh than a denial of it. Like the *Pastoureaux*, their focus became increasingly worldly; starting as a spiritually redemptive movement, they soon became a social movement and launched violent attacks upon the clergy—and, implicitly, upon the ruling classes as a whole. Their repudiation of institutional Christianity extended not only to the clergy's claims to divine authority but even to the validity of the sacrament of the Eucharist. It is questionable whether they accepted any need for priestly intervention between humanity and the deity; they patently anticipated the Reformation by claiming that they were *directly* instructed and guided by the Holy Spirit, a notion that lies at the core of virtually all radical Reformation ideologies. Accordingly, they did not hesitate to violently disrupt Church services and angrily orate against the sovereignty of the Papacy.

To confine the anticlerical features of the *Pastoureaux*, Flagellants, and the later Reformation movements merely to doctrinal disputes or attempts by underclass elements to plunder Church properties would be to gravely misread a deeper constellation of radical motives that often guided such movements. The Church was more than a large property-owner in the Middle Ages, and its wealth was not simply an affront to the Christian commitment to poverty. The Church was also a massive *hierarchical* structure—the reality and symbol of overbearing authority. To the shepherds and penitents of the thirteenth century—indeed, to the intellectuals in the new universities, the burghers in the new towns, and even the newly emerging proletariat of the Lowlands and northern Italy—the Church's claim that it would bridge the chasm it had opened between the ordinary individual and the Deity was an affront to Christianity's gospel of inwardness, selfhood, and its implicit recognition of the accessibility of each soul to God. Christian clerics, no less than the pagan priests before them, viewed themselves as brokers between humanity and the Deity—the surrogates for the congregation's contact with God.

However spiritual the anticlerical rebellions of the time may seem to the modern mind, the fact remains that anticlericalism had a grossly underrated anarchic dimension. In trying to remove the clergy from its function as humanity's delegate to the spiritual kingdom, all the anticlerical movements of the time were striking a blow against the notion of representation itself and its denial of the individual's competence to manage his or her spiritual affairs. That the Church's wealth was an extraordinarily magnetic lodestone and its moral hypocrisy a source of popular fury are indubitable social facts that surfaced repeatedly. But the Church was also a *political* challenge. Its hierarchy was offensive to the pre-industrial mind because it challenged—indeed, obstructed—the individual's freedom to participate directly in the spiritual kingdom, to relate to the Deity without mediation, to participate in a direct democracy concerning matters of faith (a free "nation of prophets" as Christopher Hill was to call the radical communities of the English Revolution).

The Church, in effect, gave no recognition to the congregation's claims to competence; it had a kingdom, not a community; a State, not a *polis*. Both clerical and temporal lords sensed that anticlerical movements could easily turn into civil insurrections—and such insurrections often followed religious unrest. The *Pastoureaux* movement was shortly followed by the repeated insurrections of Flemish workers against the commercial aristocracies of the Lowland cities. The Lollard "heresy" in England and the Lutheran "heresy" in Germany preceded peasant revolts in both countries. Until fairly recent times, religious unrest was often the prelude to social unrest. Widespread religious dissidence fed directly into the English Revolution of the 1640s and the "Great Awakening" influenced the American Revolution of the 1770s.

Accordingly, both the *Pastoureaux* and the Flagellants were continental precursors of the English Peasants' Revolt of 1381 and the exhortations of John Ball, one of its leaders (albeit a rather minor one). Economically, the revolt itself had limited goals the peasants were resisting enserfment and the rigid ceilings that had been imposed on their earnings. But socially, people of the fourteenth century had ceased to think of equality and freedom as the distant practice of a golden age, buried irretrievably in the past. Instead, they began to perceive these ideals as preordained rights that humanity could hope to achieve in the near future.

The fortunes of the English Peasants' Revolt—its temporary successes and its defeat at the treacherous hands of the monarchy—are matters of historical detail. What counts, here, is the tenor of the sermons that Ball and possibly many of his compatriots delivered to the peasants before and during the uprising. According to Froissart, who chronicled the revolt from an aristocratic viewpoint, Ball staked out the right of all people to social equality and to the means of life. If everyone is "descended from one father and one mother, Adam and Eve, how can the lords say or prove that they are more lords than we—save that they make us dig and till the ground so that they can squander what we produce?" This was a fiery question that must have permeated the entire land, as well as the spirit (if not the goals), of the English Peasants' Revolt and the continental rebellions that would later follow. Ball's attack upon the injustices inflicted on the English peasantry was not limited to an appeal for the already ritualized looting expedition that marked many earlier movements. He demanded a more radical and far-reaching "black redistribution": a state of affairs in which "all things are in common and there is neither villein nor noble, but all of us are of one condition."

These social ideals were to find their culmination in the Taborites of Bohemia, a movement that appeared a century or so after the defeat of the English Peasants' Revolt. The Taborites were an offshoot of the quasi-Protestant Hussites who, in 1419, rebelled in Prague against German and Papal sovereignty. For nearly two decades, the Hussites successfully resisted the Catholic armies of the Emperor Sigismund and the combined forces of the Holy Roman Empire.

But the more extreme Taborites were avowedly communistic in their social ideals. Sending forth their appeals and their armies from their newly founded city of Tabor (named after the mountain of Christ's transfiguration), they demanded the abolition not only of taxes, dues, rent, and imposts, but also of all private property. Kenneth Rexroth, in his perceptive account of the communal movements of the past, describes them as

> extreme millenarians, the most militant so far in the history of dissent. They believed that Christ's Second Coming (disguised as a brigand) and the universal destruction of the evil world would occur almost immediately, at first in 1420; and when that date passed, it was never postponed more than a few years.

The new dispensation was to be very bloody: "In preparation for the coming of the kingdom it was the duty of the brotherhood of saints to drench their swords in the blood of evildoers, indeed to wash their hands in it." Following upon this macabre baptism (an imagery that was not entirely alien to John Ball and other millenarians), "Christ would appear on a mountain top and celebrate the coming of the kingdom with a great messianic banquet of all the faithful."

Despite their orgiastic commitment to blood and public festivals, the Taborites were largely ascetics. But like many Reformation radicals, they were ecumenically intermixed with hedonistic millenarians. The hedonists were later to be expelled from Tabor and formed the notorious Adamite sect, which actually reflected a very different chiliastic disposition. Both tendencies, in fact, were almost avowedly anarchic: laws were to be abolished, the elect would enjoy immortality, and the Second Coming would create a world of material abundance free from toil and pain, even in childbirth. All human authority would be replaced by a community of free people in which "none shall be subject to another."

In appraising the Taborite commune, Rexroth astutely notes:

> If socialism in one country is doomed to become deformed and crippled, communism in one city is impossible for any length of time. Sooner or later the garrison society will weaken but the outside world does not. It is always there waiting, strongest perhaps in times of peace. Tabor was never able to balance its popular communism of consumption with an organized and planned communism of production, nor the exchange of goods between city communes and peasant communes.

As it turned out, when Tabor and the entire Bohemian national movement were crushed by Sigismund, "it was the peasant communism of the Hutterites and Brethren which survived." They linger on with us as parochial colonies that still preserved their Reformation traditions and language as the archeological remains of a long-lost world.

But the Christian communal movement did not disappear with the Reformation. It surfaced again in the English Revolution of the late 1640s and early 1650s, particularly in the north and west of England—the "dark corners of the land," according to the Parliamentary party. A modern breed of "masterless men" like Archilochus millennia earlier, they lived largely uprooted and wayfaring lives. With their emphasis on private interpretations of Scripture, their hatred of civil and ecclesiastical authority, and their social "democracy of prophets," they fostered a strong sense of spiritual community in regions that the Parliamentarians had virtually abandoned. Here we find the early Quakers, The Familialists, the Seekers, and the Fifth Monarchy men, some of whom actually rose in armed revolt against Cromwell's conservative custodianship of a revolution he had never started. Only when the world, "turned upside down" by the revolution, had been restored to its normal philistine concerns, did eschatological movements disappear completely or take the form of tractable sects and societies. The wide-ranging definitions of freedom raised by the Marcionite gnostics and practiced by ascetic communists such as the Taborites were thoroughly transmuted (often with considerable attrition) into rationally disciplined and highly secular ideologies. Today, we fervently debate their tenets under very different names, hardly mindful of their pedigree or the extent to which they anticipated our theories and practices. The most well-known of these radical movements reached their apogee in the English Revolution, then drastically narrowed their millenarian scope. They became amiable service organizations, such as the Society of Friends (Quakers), with very little awareness of their own fiery, often violent, chiliastic origins.

By the Reformation, most ascetic millenarian movements were grouped under the broad rubric of "Anabaptism," a simple doctrine that rejected infant baptism for adult baptism on the rather sound basis that only mature people could understand the subtleties of the Christian calling. But to the ruling classes of the time, including many staid Protestants, the word Anabaptism, like the word anarchist today, was used more as a pejorative symbol of public opprobrium than as an authentic body of ideas. The term was used promiscuously to include such widely disparate social and religious movements as the Bohemian nationalists in Prague, the manic Taborite millenarians, and even their frenzied offshoots such as the Adamite sects or the pacifist Hutterites. It is fair to say that hardly any founders or early acolytes of Anabaptism were spared the beatitudes of martyrdom. Insofar as they were real millenarians, all the Anabaptists, real and imaginary, are utterly separated from our own time by the ideological chasm of religion: the "Second Coming," the miraculous powers of Christ, and the theocratic proclivities that often substituted a "messianic" hierarchy for an ecclesiastical one. Actually, many of these millenarians were not communists at all; at best their communism was marginal.

But from this highly mixed welter of independent, often conflicting or intersecting beliefs, there emerges one figure who bridges the chasm from religious to secular communism. Gerrard Winstanley is perhaps best known as the leader and theorist of the Diggers, a miniscule group of agrarian communists who in 1649 tried to cultivate the "free" or waste lands on St. George's Hill near London. Actually, these experiments, which were conceived as an "exemplary" effort to promote communal ideals, were ignored in their day. What really swept the Digger movement into historical accounts of radical movements was Winstanley's own pamphlets, and these received most recognition long after Winstanley himself had passed into history.

As Rexroth accurately emphasizes, "All the tendencies of the radical Reformation"—and, we may add, the most important millenarian movements of earlier times—"seem to flow together in Winstanley, to be blended and secularized, and become an ideology rather than a theology." Winstanley was not a military communist like the Taborites; he was a committed pacifist, and so far as we know, he remained one throughout his life. Nor was he a hedonist like the Adamites; he adhered to a strictly ascetic concept of the righteous life. But his views became markedly pantheistic, even hostile to any notion of an anthropomorphic deity. His naturalism brings him very close to Enlightenment social theory: "To know the secrets of nature is to know the works of God." His denial of a supernatural heaven and hell as a "strange conceit" would have brought him to the stake a few centuries earlier. He emphasizes the need not only for "communal property" but perhaps even for usufruct. "The earth with all her fruits of Corn, Cattle, and such like was made to be a common Store-House of Livelihood," he declares, "to all mankind friend and foe, without exception." These words are not merely brave but also deeply felt. Reason is the "great creator" that "made the earth a common treasury" and anarchy (in the literal sense of "no-rule") was its earliest disposition—for "not one word was spoken in the beginning that one branch, of mankind should rule over another."

In time, these libertarian and communistic ideals suffered from Winstanley's bitter encounters with the counter-revolutionary moods following the collapse of the Leveller movement in 1649 and the Cromwell reaction that succeeded it. His *Law of Freedom in a Platform or, True Magistracy Restored*, written in 1652, reveals a disenchantment with the outcome of the revolution. The failure of the Digger experiments—more precisely, the popular indifference the Diggers encountered—had altered Winstanley's high expectations. His "True Magistracy" is a representative democracy, not a direct one; it is more punitive than loving, and more centralized and perhaps needlessly structured than libertarian. Perhaps this vision had been with him from the beginning, but it stands at odds with some of his earlier, more general views. Nor does his work end in hope. Few lines are more memorable and touching than the poem that concludes the pamphlet:

> Truth appears in Light, Falsehood rules in Power,
> To see these things to be, is cause of grief each hour.
> Knowledge, why didst thou come, to wound, and not to cure?
> I sent not for thee, thou didst me inlure.
> Where knowledge does increase, there sorrows multiply,
> To see the great deceit which in the World doth lie....
> O death where art thou? wilt thou not tidings send?
> I fear thee not, thou art my loving friend.
> Come take this body, and scatter it in the Four,
> That I may dwell in One, and rest in peace once more.

Thereafter, Winstanley faded into the oblivion that ultimately devoured the revolution itself. But more than many proponents of like views, he has received from posterity "the roses of rebels failed."

☙

The hedonistic trend in medieval chiliasm, like the gnostic Ophites, is redolent with aspirations for personal autonomy. Medieval hedonistic conventicles were compellingly individualistic and almost completely free of patricentric values. Christianity's powerful message of the individual's sanctity in the eyes of God, its high valuation of personality and the soul, and its emphasis on a universal humanity bred a sense of individuality and freedom that could easily turn against clerical hierarchy and dogma. During the twelfth and thirteenth centuries, a variety of highly radical sects surfaced from the depths of Christianity's fascinating cauldron of ideas. Some, like the Free Spirit, were quite explicitly radical; others, like the Beghards and Beguines, were less so. Crystallized into conventicular networks and secular orders, these sects produced ideas that severely vexed the Church and brought it into sharp conflict with its own doctrinal offspring.

Perhaps the most important theological issue the Church had to face was the rise of a broadly philosophical pantheistic movement. A thousand years earlier gnosticism had raised the question of how a truly "good" God could have created a woefully sinful world. Its theorists answered this puzzling problem not by anchoring their reply in "original sin", and a fallen humanity but by creating two deities: a "good," transcendental, "alien" God whose son Jesus had come to redeem the world, and a faulty, "just," petty deity who had created the material world from which the spiritually pure "pneumatics" enjoyed immunity. If sin and anything "fallen" existed in the gnostic orbit of ideas, it was imputed primarily to the Creator, not to humanity. And the genius of gnosticism was to locate this concept of the defective within the petty realm of "justice," where the rule of equivalence and the *lex talionis* prevailed, rather than within the realm of ethics, where "goodness" was the norm.

Medieval pantheism, by contrast, tried to raise a dualistic vision of virtue into a unified outlook by seeking to achieve a mystical personal union with the supreme "One," the embodiment of goodness. This outlook stands in marked contrast to both gnostic and Christian dualism and, in fact, leads to Spinoza's later, more Judaic concept of a unifying, "godly" substance. By the thirteenth century, mystics such as David of Dinant and Amaury claimed that matter and mind were identical with God— indeed, that everything could be unified *as* God. The spread of these pantheistic ideas to the ordinary people of Paris and Strasbourg produced a number of sects such as the New Spirit, the sisterhood of the

Beguines and the brotherhood of the Beghards, and most notoriously, the Brethren of the Free Spirit. To these sects, humanity was composed of the same divine substance as God, hence it could enter into direct communion with the deity. Such a view not only challenged the need for ecclesiastical intervention between humanity and God, but also gave its acolytes an exhilarating sense of personal freedom that could easily justify the removal of all worldly restrictions on human behavior and open the way to unrestrained moral license.

The secular "convents" and "monasteries" that now began to proliferate throughout the Lowlands, France, Germany, and northern Italy quickly staked out coexisting claims to the duties of their ecclesiastical counterparts. Perhaps the earliest of these new lay institutions, the sisterhood of the Beguines and the brotherhood of the Beghards, presented the most serious threat to the Church's authority. Wars and plagues had created a very large number of "masterless" people, most of whom were forced into lives of beggary and crime. Whether as a charitable act or from a desire to enlist them in the performance of "good works," a little-known ecclesiastic named Lambert began to collect the women into lay, nun-like groups—the Beguines—who were expected to dedicate themselves to charitable activities. They were soon emulated by many displaced and footloose men—the Beghards— who formed a corresponding male network that collaborated with the women. The accounts of the two lay orders, largely derived from hostile clerics, are harshly derogatory. Church and lay groups were rivals for the same charitable sources of income, and inevitably they entered into sharp conflict with each other. Finally, the Church began to take action against the orders. In 1311, the lay orders were condemned by the Council of Vienne and were later partly scattered by the ecclesiastical and territorial lords, although some Beguine hostels lingered on as charitable almshouses.

But many Beguines and Beghards were absorbed into a new "heresy"—the Brethren of the Free Spirit. In their account of western mysticism, Thomas Katsaros and Nathaniel Kaplan discuss how this "heresy" grew at a "tremendous rate" and was primarily responsible for the convening of the Council of Vienne. To the Church, the acolytes of the Free Spirit may have seemed like the ultimate of "heresies," if not the very incarnation of Satanism. In any case, the Free Spirit stood at irredeemable odds with Christian orthodoxy.

According to Jeffrey B. Russell's definitive summary, the Brethren of the Free Spirit "formed a loosely constructed group of sects during the thirteenth and fourteenth century, especially in the Rhineland and central

Germany." Russell places the "heresy" primarily in the towns "in which bourgeois patricians had gained control and in which the artisans were in the process of asserting their rights against the patricians." The period in which the "heresy" flourished was one of widespread class conflict between the merchant princes and the artisan class, particularly in Flanders. But Russell rightly notes that "It is not possible to generalize about the social class of the Brethren." According to one chronicler, "they include monks, priests, and married people; another describes them as laborers, charcoal burners, blacksmiths, and swineherds; and yet another indicates that they were rough and illiterate men." However, Russell warns us that Marxist historians may tend to exaggerate

> the elements of class warfare here, but the doctrines of the Brethren do clearly indicate that social protest was involved. For instance, they believed that a handmaiden or serf could take and sell his master's goods without his permission. That tithes need not be paid to the Church is also a doctrine indicative of more than strictly theological discontent.

But a radical ethical doctrine—or an "amoral" one in the gnostic sense—there surely was. It was based on the "belief that the individual Christian is justified by the Holy Spirit dwelling within him and that it is from within, rather than from the institutional Church, that all grace proceeds." Accordingly, acolytes of the Free Spirit are in a state of grace, very much like the gnostic "pneumatics," irrespective of their behavior. "A man [and certainly a woman] can perform a sinful act without being in sin, and as long as he acts with the intention of following the will of the Spirit, his action is good."

Norman Cohn was to impart an almost legendary quality to the Free Spirit among young countercultural radicals of the 1960s by linking it with the mystical anarchism of Heinrich Suso. This Dominican follower of Eckhart, like the master himself, was a highly educated ascetic, and he wrote vigorous denunciations of the more plebian hedonistic sects of the period. Cohn describes a

> sketch written about 1330 in the chief stronghold of the heresy, Cologne, [in which] the Catholic mystic Suso evokes with admirable terseness those qualities in the Free Spirit which made it essentially anarchic. He describes how on a bright Sunday, as we were sitting lost in meditation, an incorporeal image appeared to his spirit. Suso addresses the image.
> "Whence have you come?"

The image answers: "I come from nowhere."

"Tell me, what are you?"

"I am not."

"What do you wish?"

"I do not wish."

"This is a miracle! Tell me, what is your name?"

"I am called Nameless Wildness."

"Where does your insight lead to?"

"Into untrammeled freedom."

"Tell me, what do you call untrammeled freedom?"

"When a man lives according to all his caprices without distinguishing between God and himself, and without before or after."

Suso's dialogue would be tantalizingly incomplete if we did not have other pronouncements by the Brethren of the Free Spirit that clarify its meaning. The dialogue is definitely libertine in its implications and involves the divine in human motivation. Thus, according to some of these pronouncements: "He who recognizes that God does all things in him, he shall not sin. For he must not attribute to himself, but to God, all that he does." A man with a conscience, then, "is himself a Devil, and hell and purgatory, tormenting himself," for "Nothing is sin except what is thought of as sin." As Cohn notes,

> Every act performed by a member of this elite was felt to be performed "not in time but in eternity"; it possessed a vast mystical significance and its value was infinite. This was the secret wisdom which one adept revealed to a somewhat perplexed inquisitor with the assurance that it was "drawn from the innermost depths of the Divine Abyss" and worth far more than all the gold in the municipal treasure of Erfurt. "It would be better," he added, "that the whole world should be destroyed and perish utterly than that, a 'free man' should refrain from one act to which his nature moves him."

Accordingly, adepts of the Free Spirit gave up all penitential and ascetic behavior for a life of pure pleasure, not merely one of happiness. More than "red," or fiery, their outlook on life was "purple," or sensuous. We have no vocabulary within the framework of ordinary life to describe this remarkable epistemology. It sought more than the physically orgiastic but rather the conversion of reality into a *surreality* of experience and a divination of the nature of things. The halo later discerned by Andre Breton's Nadja in the world around her, even in the most commonplace objects, was here made into a metaphysical principle. But it was a practical principle, not merely an ideological one. Vigils, fasting, and all sensuous denial were brought to an end; the body was to be indulged with the choicest wines and meats and clothed in the most sensuous garments. At times, the adepts would even dress as nobles which, as Cohn notes, was "a social affront and source of confusion in the Middle Ages, when differences in dress denoted differences in status."

But the acolytes of this extraordinary movement did not stop with such pleasures as food and dress; they proceeded to practice a promiscuous "mystically colored eroticism." Sexual promiscuity was seen not as an act of defilement but rather as one of purification. A woman was all the more "chaste" for partaking of uninhibited sexual intercourse, as, of course, was a man. Indeed, "one of the surest marks of the 'subtle in spirit' was, precisely, the ability to indulge in promiscuity without fear of God or qualms of conscience," observes Cohn.

> Some adepts attributed a transcendental, quasi-mystical value to the sexual act itself, when it was performed by such as they. The *Homines intelligentiae* called the act "the delight of Paradise" and "the acclivity" (which was the term used for the ascent to mystical ecstasy); and the Thuringian "Blood Friends of 1550 regarded it as a sacrament, which they called "Christerie." For all alike, adultery possessed a symbolic value as an affirmation of emancipation.

Hence, freedom to the Free Spirit meant even more than the right to orgiastic pleasure, an ecstasy of the senses; it meant total spontaneity of behavior and a cosmic reattunement to nature, the embodiment of God. Perhaps unknown to its acolytes, the Free Spirit restored Supernature to nature, and nature, in turn, to an almost enchanted mythopoeic status in the spiritual balance of things. Such ideas or intuitions were not to die easily; they spoke too deeply to the inner, libidinal recesses of human desire. Hence the Free Spirit, or its doctrines, remained a persistent "heresy" for centuries—one that has recurred right up to the present day as independent rediscoveries by the Symbolists in the late nineteenth century, the Surrealists in the 1920s, and in the counterculture of the 1960s. It constituted an indispensable dimension of freedom as a release from the internal regimentation of feeling and bodily movements—the subjective aspect of the existentially liberated individual. Without this aspect the notion of freedom remains an externalized social abstraction that has no space for its "heretics," its creative artists, and its intellectual innovators.

During the Hussite upheaval, the doctrines of the Free Spirit appeared among the Adamites—the most anarchistic wing of the normally ascetic Taborites. Subjected to harsh persecution within labor itself, this group was driven from the city and chased down by the Hussite military commander, Jan Ziska. Those who escaped Ziska's troops fortified themselves on an island in the River Nezarka and established a free, quasi-military community that combined the hedonistic lifeways of the Free Spirit with the most radical communistic practices of the laborites. The Adamites were not a quiescent enclave of devoutly religious adepts like the Anabaptists: small as they were in numbers, they were a harsh, demanding social movement that developed its own "amoral" morality and a crusading zealousness that often degenerated into sheer rapine. Their bloodthirsty expeditions into the surrounding countryside and the butchery they practiced makes it difficult to unravel the problems inherent in "military" or "warrior" communism—problems that I will examine shortly.

The Free Spirit acquired its most idiosyncratic expression during the English Revolution, when a new, albeit harmless, sect—the Ranters—scandalized the Puritan revolutionaries with their own brand of hedonism. A. L. Morton, who has written one of the most comprehensive accounts of their activities and beliefs, emphasizes that both theologically and politically, the Ranters constituted the "extreme left wing of the sects" that abounded at the time. The Ranters pushed all the radical implications of Puritanism and its offshoot sects "to their furthest logical conclusions" and "even a little beyond." This trend soon culminated in open conflict with the law. As Morton observes,

> The conviction that God existed in, and only in, material objects and men led them at once to a pantheistic mysticism and a crudely plebian materialism, often incongruously combined in the same person. Their rejection of scripture literalism led sometimes to an entirely symbolic interpretation of the Bible and at others to a blunt and contemptuous rejection. Their belief that the moral law no longer had authority for the people of a new age enjoying the liberty of the sons of God led to a conviction that for them no act was sinful, a conviction that some hastened to put into practice.

To speak of the Ranters as an organized movement or even as a sect in any organized sense is to understate the highly individualistic focus of their ideas. It could be easily argued that there were almost as many Ranter ideologies as there were Ranters. What stands out clearly amid the medley of their ideas is not only their hedonistic proclivities, which were often expressed with wild abandon, but also their scorn for all authority, both civil and religious. Not even the Bible was immune to denigration. *The Ranters Last Sermon* depicts the Scriptures, perhaps the most sacred single document of the English Revolution, as

> but meer Romance, and contradictory to itself; only invented by the Witts of Former Ages, to keep People in subjection, and in Egyptian slavery; likewise, That there was as much truth in the History of Tom Thumb, or The Knights of the Sun, as there was in that Book.

Unlike earlier "heretics," the writer makes no appeal to authority; authority itself is completely dissolved in mockery and sarcasm.

Nor could the Ranters claim a monopoly on outwardly sensuous behavior during the revolutionary period. Nudity and probably a mystical belief in the power of uninhibited sexuality to achieve a communion with God filtered through many sectarian movements of the time. Quite respectable Quakers, Christopher Hill tells us, made forays beyond the boundaries of asceticism and went "'naked for a sign,' with only a loin cloth around their middles." Indeed, the

> Quaker doctrine of perfectibility continued to testify against the hatred of the body.... [They] thought lace-making an unsuitable occupation for members of their Society, but they had no objection to brewing or keeping an ale-house.

Other sectarians were probably prepared to go much further along the road of hedonism or the respect for the flesh than moderate Ranters, but the ecumenical use of the word "Ranter" subsumed their doctrines and practices.

ᘒ

Even more than early antiquity's "black redistribution," the medieval folk utopias, Christianity's apocalyptic doctrines, gnosticism's concept of a "good" God who is alien to a petty "just" Creator, and finally the long line of sectaries that culminated in the overtly secular Ranters—all increasingly distinguished freedom from justice, the equality of unequals from the inequality of equals. All their doctrines or practices were based on compensation and complementarity. The more hedonistic of these sects and movements ventured even further: the concept of freedom was expanded from a limited ideal of happiness based on the constraints of shared needs into an ideal of pleasure based on the satisfaction of desire.

But the realization of any of these ideals clearly presupposed the transformation of the individual and of humanity from a condition of sin to one of "grace," which, in turn, had presuppositions of its own. Grace could be achieved only by an internal—indeed, a psychological or spiritual—transformation of one's very sense of being. As conceived by the Christian world, this change had to be so far-reaching in its depth and scope that it led into the very notion of transubstantiation itself—a radical change in the very substance of selfhood. Christianity, in its official form, imposed the overt discipline of the law, of the Deuteronomic Code, on the faithful; humanity, after all, was unruly and predisposed to evil by original sin. Freedom was to be reserved for heaven—if, indeed, freedom it could be truly called, beyond the moral plentitude voiced by the Sermon on the Mount. On earth, humanity was expected to live by conventional codes of justice, both ecclesiastical and temporal. Luther made heavenly freedom an affair of the inner life, of a deeply subjective faith that had relatively little to do with the earthly world's works; Calvin, by placing a stronger emphasis on works, provided the doctrinal basis for the social activism so congenial to the emerging bourgeoisie and the revolutionary English Puritans. But whether Catholic or Protestant, official Christianity quickly lost its power as a transcendental force. It had always been predisposed to adaptation. Initially, it accommodated itself to Caesar; later (although grudgingly), to feudalism's territorial lords; and finally, to capitalism (for which it provided an image of an entrepreneurial Jesus, who trades in souls and markets the gospel).

The gnostics, by contrast, appealed to the mind and to the power of knowledge in bringing humanity into their unique conception of grace. This lofty endeavor could hardly hope to succeed on doctrinal grounds alone—hence the socially withdrawn nature of gnosticism during late antiquity. "Civilization" had created a new character-structure, a new internal discipline for containing the spirit: a "reality principle" that denied the integrity of the passions, spontaneity, and desire. Society's fear of the Hobbesian "natural man" has antedated by centuries Freud's commitment to "civilization" and its inherently repressive strategies. If *gnosis*, or knowledge, was to guide human behavior and bring heaven to earth, it had to be reinforced by a psychic "battering ram" that could demolish the individual's "civilized" (that is, carefully policed) character structure. A hallucinogenic strategy had to be devised to derange the Statist, later economistic, epistemology that class society had instilled in the human personality.*

One heretical Christian tendency was to choose asceticism as its hallucinogen, thereby totally inverting pleasure, even happiness, in an ecstatic denial of the senses and elementary bodily needs. This "poor man's" pleasure, so to speak, fully recognized the powers of the flesh and acceded to them more by mistreating the body and its urges than by denying them. Ironically, Heinrich Suso is one of the most extraordinary exemplars of this doctrine. The psychotic self-torture he inflicted on his body to achieve a hallucinogenic and ecstatic communion with his gnostic-type deity goes far beyond the outermost limits of asceticism. It reveals a masochistic involvement with the flesh that beggars the martyrdom of the saints.

The hedonistic Ophites, the Free Spirit, Adamites, and Ranters, on the other hand, evoked the rich man's pleasures as a battering ram for deranging "civilization's" "reality principle" and character structure. Their hallucinogenic strategy for producing a personality (not merely a mind) that was receptive to *gnosis* centered around the uninhibited, spontaneous claims of the body—a "discipline" of indiscipline that deployed the "pleasure principle" to dissolve the "reality principle." Choice foods and garments, sexual promiscuity, the right to steal and even kill were all combined into a program for redemption that had lost all its otherworldly status. What could conceivably be more ecstatic than the orgiastic delirium of uninhibited sexuality that the "good" God surely mandated for the acolyte in his or her rejection of the "just" Creator—the fount of sinful world? Indeed, crime made one an "outlaw" in the literal, almost *holy* sense of the term: it pitted the acolyte against the Creator's mean-spirited realm of justice and opened the way to a duel between the "divine spark" in the individual and the mundane

---

* Significantly, this was precisely the strategy that guided the counterculture of the 1960s, not the use of drugs to provide the "highs" and "lows" for adapting the individual to an utterly insane society. By the 1970s and 1980s, people were employing a bewildering variety of drugs to render them either functional or indifferent to the system—not to discover alternatives to it. The sixties' "drug culture," whatever its faults, was concerned with "blowing" consciousness, and it provided living alternatives—however unsatisfactory many of them proved to be—in the form of communes, personal support systems, a credo of sharing, and a gospel of love to sustain the "heretics" of its day. The present "drug culture" is entirely sinister; it is a strategy for attuning one's flow of adrenalin to meet the demands of the society or simply to render the individual insensate. And, of course, it offers no alternative or support system whatever except the psychoanalyst's office or the so-called "mental" institution.

integument that concealed it. With a few changes in words this gospel can be suddenly transformed into Bakunin's hypostatization of the bandit and folk attitudes toward banditry.

Moreover, a new world constructed around the rich man's pleasures was a desideratum in itself. It actualized the promise of the folk utopias like Cokaygne, and gave them contemporaneity and an identifiable place, notably in the conventicle of the hedonistic heretics. But here, the hedonistic heretics encountered a dilemma: unrestrained and undiscriminating desire presupposes a plenitude of goods to satisfy the holy community. However, neither nature nor the technological armamentarium of the time could possibly be so all-providing. Asceticism encountered a dilemma of its own: it not only demanded immense material sacrifices for very tenuous ethical rewards, but it also abandoned the very hope of attaining them in a future utopia. The ascetic radicals stood at odds with the time-honored "black redistribution" that insurgent peoples have always invoked indeed, pleasure itself had ceased to be a desideratum. Neither of the two disciplines could be expected to enlist humanity as a whole (although asceticism—as we shall see—held much greater promise as a popular morality than hedonism).

Hence the hedonists and many of the ascetics turned to an elitist, neo-Platonist doctrine of souls. Only the elect—a small group of "pneumatics" or "Saints"—could hope to achieve grace; their retainers, the "psychics," might aspire to elevate their status to "sainthood" by making contact with the elect, servicing their needs, and heeding their wisdom. The rest of humanity, whether rich or poor, was simply doomed. These unfortunates were the irredeemable minions of the "just" Creator, and they lived in a hopelessly fallen state. They could be plundered and killed; indeed, it became a discipline among the elect to use them for its own ends.

ଔ

From a theoretical viewpoint, freedom had acquired a scope and—particularly in its gnostic and late medieval forms—a degree of sophistication unprecedented in the history of ideas. The distinction between justice and freedom has yet to make its way through the maze of present-day radical ideologies; apart from a few individual theorists, the two ideals are still victims of considerable confusion. The dual functions of pleasure and asceticism—indeed, of desire and need—have yet to be clarified in contemporary radical thought. So, too, do the notions of scarcity and post-scarcity. The distinction between "freedom from" and "freedom for"—that is, between negative and positive freedom—has been carefully analyzed in categories and juridical tenets; but we still await a full discussion of a *reconstructive* utopianism that can clarify in practice the broader distinctions between authority and an informed spontaneity.

But what is the historical subject that will create a free society? What is the context within which that subject is formed? The Christian and gnostic radicals faced both these questions more resolutely than they faced the logic of their own premises. They wavered and divided on such issues as the full logic of asceticism and pleasure—a logic which only the ascetic Cathari and the hedonistic Adamites followed to the end but they were generally clear about which agents would achieve a holy estate. In both cases, the answers were elitist, reflecting a Manichaean image of the world composed of "Saints" and "sinners." Christians were expected to accept a divine disposition that favored the "Saints" over the "sinners"; indeed, in the case of the hedonists, they were to accept the exploitation of the "sinners" by the "Saints."

But even in the late Middle Ages such elitist conclusions were hardly the inevitable consequences of Christian or gnostic radicalism. Marcion had never accepted them at the beginnings of the gnostic "heresy," nor had Winstanley at the end of the Christian Reformation. Significantly, both men were ascetic in their outlook. An ascetic social disposition could have enjoyed considerable popular appeal if it was suitably moderated by ethical arguments for a balanced restriction of needs, as opposed to Cathari fasts to the death or Suso's orgy of self-torture. The fourteenth and fifteenth centuries may well have marked a unique watershed for western humanity. History seemed to be poised at a juncture: society could still choose to follow a course that yielded a modest satisfaction of needs based on complementarity and the equality of unequals. Or it could catapult into capitalism with its rule of equivalence and the inequality of equals, both reinforced by commodity exchange and a canon of "unlimited needs" that confront "scarce resources."

Many concrete factors favored the choice of the latter over the former: Perhaps, as orthodox Marxists seem to believe, capitalism was the "inevitable" outcome of European feudalism. Perhaps—but Christianity and its various "heresies" had opened *a transcendental level of discourse* that embraced not only the intellectuals, ecclesiastics, and educated nobles of medieval society, but also reached out to multitudes of the oppressed, particularly its town dwellers. For all its shortcomings, medieval society was not only pre-industrial but also ethically oriented. It lived not only on a mundane level of self-interest and material gain but also on an idealistic level of personal redemption and grace. One cannot explain the early crusades of the poor, on the one hand, and the extent to which many nobles converted to radical Anabaptist sects, on the other, without recognizing the enormous importance of the ethical sphere for people of the Middle Ages.

Hence, the ascetic Christian radicals had a *transclass* constituency at their disposal: a historical subject who was neither plebian nor patrician but *Christian* (in a mutilated but deeply sensitive meaning of the term). This Christian could be motivated by ethical ideals to an extent that would puzzle modern individuals. Plunder, exploitation, and the pleasures of the flesh certainly never lost their hold on the Christian's Janus-faced outlook. Hierarchy, class rule, and "'civilization" had left their deep-seated wounds on Christian society from the days of its inception. But the medieval outlook was more schizophrenic and sometimes more apocalyptic, in an ethical sense, than contemporary individuals can ever understand.

This ethical world, to be sure, did not hang freely suspended in the ethereal air of idealism, nor did it arise from high-minded inspiration alone. It emerged from a richly textured social context of human-scaled towns, vibrant and highly variegated neighborhoods, and closely-knit villages. The "masterless" men and women who provided the leavening for the emancipatory intuitions that abounded were rootless outsiders or footloose wanderers whose functional lineage goes back to archetypal figures such as Archilochus. But this also was true of the Biblical prophets, of Jesus and his disciples, and of the Church's great missionaries. The ideal of a universal humanity included both the isolated village and the worldwide Christian congregation. The sole passport of the Middle Ages was evidence of baptism and a testament of common faith.

Accordingly, the congregation's view of society was more integrated and expansive than it is today, despite our rhetoric of "one world" and the "global village." Important as material interests were in the past, even the most oppressed strata in Christian society would have found it difficult to reduce social problems to economic ones. So richly textured and articulated a society assumed as a matter of course that material need could not be separated from ethical precept. To attain a "Christian" society, however broadly such words were interpreted, not only did systems of ownership and the distribution of goods have to be changed, but even as late as Reformation times, "matters of the soul"—the accepted mores, beliefs, institutions, and, in a more personal vein, one's character and sexual life—required alteration. These broader needs—indeed, this view of need itself—cannot be reduced to mere "superstructural" ideologies without forcing the mentality of a market society on a largely manorial one, high technology on artisanship, an industrial world on a domestic one, an atomized labor force on a highly communal system of production based on guilds and an atomized society on a richly associative body of human relations.

Was capitalism a more "sophisticated" substitute for medieval society? To say "yes" would be arrogant presumption and an insult to the highly complex civilizations, both past and present, that have resisted "modernization." To emphasize the preeminence of contemporary society in history is, subtly, to elevate a deadening, homogenizing mass media over the spiritual yearning elicited by religious ceremonies, a mechanistic scientism over a colorful mythopoeic sensibility, and an icy indifference to the fate of one's immediate neighbors over a richly intertwined system of mutual aid. Now that torture has returned to the modern world as a rationalized technique for interrogation and punishment, the medieval rack has become picayune by comparison. And while modern society no longer drags its heretics to the stake, it incinerates millions of utterly innocent people in gas chambers and nuclear infernos.

Much that we would call the ideological, moral, cultural, and institutional "superstructure" of medieval society was deeply intertwined with its economic and technical "base." Both "superstructure" and "base" were enriched and broadened by the wealth each brought to the other. Economic life and technical development existed within a wide-ranging orbit of cultural restraints as well as cultural creativity. Freedom could be defined not merely in material terms but in ethical terms as well. That capitalism was to distort this wide-ranging orbit and virtually destroy it has already been emphasized but can bear some repetition. The era that separates the Middle Ages from the Industrial Revolution was to be marked by a terrifying deterioration of community life, by a reduction of highly cherished popular ideals to brazen economic interests, and by a disintegration of individuality into egotism. Freedom and the revolutionary subject who had upheld its ideals suffered the denaturing, rationalization, and economization that have become the fate of the human community and the individual. Indeed, capitalism has redefined the terms by which to discuss the nature and prospects of freedom, and in some respects it has expanded the concept of freedom itself. But its economistic focus is very real. Capitalism reflects the authentic economization of society, and of the "social question" itself, by an economy that has absorbed every cultural, ethical, and psychological issue into a material system of needs and technics.

Such economistic interpretations of present-day society are not mere ideological distortions; they accurately depict the dominant reality of our time. What is so troubling about this image is that it makes no attempt to *transcend* the very level of life it describes. Almost every critique of the "bourgeois traits" of modern society, technics, and individuality is itself tainted by the very substance it criticizes. By emphasizing economics, class interest, and the "material substrate" of society as such, such critiques are the bearers of the very "bourgeois traits" they purport to oppose. They are in perilous default of their commitment to transcend the economic conditions of capitalist society and to recover the ethical level of discourse and ideals capitalism so savagely degraded. In the parlance of many radical theorists, a "rational society" often means little more than a highly rationalized society, and "freedom" often means little more than the effective coordination of humanity in the achievement of economic ends.

By "economizing" the totality of life, capitalism "economized" the "social question," the structures of freedom, and the revolutionary subject. The communal context for this subject has been largely dissolved. The English Revolution imposed a new imperative on the legacy of freedom: to discuss human emancipation meaningfully, one now had to exorcize the demons of material denial, a new system of "scarcity" largely created by the market system, and the nature of technological development. Freedom is now completely entangled with economics, a liberated life with the notion of "scarce resources," utopia with technics, and the ethical revolutionary subject with the proletariat.

But has the "economization" of freedom been a total regression in our level of discourse? Actually, economics, too, has an ecological dimension. I refer not to "Buddhist," "convivial," "steady-state" or "Third Wave" economics but to the character of work, technics, and needs that a free society must confront. Having uprooted community and dissolved the traditional revolutionary subject of European society, capitalism has forced us to define the relationship of the ethical life to the material. It matters very little, now, whether or not this development is "desirable"; the fact is that it has happened, and we are obliged to deal with its reality. Whether as wound or scar tissue, the "social question" now includes the question of our technical interaction with nature—what Marx called humanity's "metabolism" with nature—not just our attitude toward nature and our ethical interaction with each other.

I do not mean that technical issues can henceforth be substitutes for ethical discourse and relations. But placed in their proper context, they can actually help to reverse the "economization" of social life. Every appeal of human consciousness, be it "class consciousness" or "personal consciousness," is an appeal to the creativity of mind and an expression of belief in human virtue. Marx the "materialist," Hegel "the idealist," Kropotkin the "ecologist," and Fourier the "utopian" have all embarked on the same voyage of hope: a belief in the powers of human reason to attain a free society. None has had a court of appeal more supreme than the sovereignty of thought and insight. The material dispensation that capitalism has created for the future is *itself* a "freedom"—one that has arisen, ironically, from the very context of bourgeois social relations. It is a freedom not merely to choose the kinds of goods society should produce (the freedom of a productivist utopia), but to choose from among the extravagant, often irrational array of needs that capitalism has created (the freedom of a consumerist utopia). When these two freedoms are melded into a still higher one, the utopian dream that lies ahead can be neither strictly productivist nor consumerist. In light of the freedom to choose products and needs, both as producer *and* consumer, one can envision a higher ideal of freedom—one that removes the taint of economism and restores the ethical basis of past times, and that is infused with the options opened by technical achievement. Potentially, at least, we are faced with the broadest conception of freedom known thus far: *the autonomous individual's freedom to shape material life in a form that is neither ascetic nor hedonistic, but a blend of the best in both—one that is ecological, rational, and artistic.*

The emergence of a possibility, to be sure, is not a guarantee that it will become an actuality. To draw upon Pottier's lines in his inspired revolutionary hymn, "The Internationale," how will a new society "rise on new foundations"? Under what "banner" can humanity "be all" again? In view of the stark alternatives that faced the Adamites and "military" or "war" communism in modern, authoritarian contexts, how can human society now produce a sufficiency of goods for everyone (rather than an elite) and provide the individual the freedom to choose among needs as well as products? Within the material realm of life, this is the most complete form of human autonomy that we can ever hope to achieve—both as an expression of rational criteria for making choices and of the rational *competence* of the individual to do so. Indeed, if we can believe in the competence of free individuals to determine policy in the civil realm, we can also believe in the competence of free individuals to determine their needs in the material realm as well. The Saints who had found their inspiration in Christianity and its belief in a 'New Jerusalem' were to become the sellers who bought and sold in the emerging capitalist market, thereby leaving the belief in a new golden age in the hands of secular rebels and revolutionaries.

In any case, the backward look toward a golden age has itself been absorbed by the very past into which it tried to peer. Once capitalism came into the world and tainted it with a "sense of scarcity," one now had to look forward—not only upward toward the heavens but also downward toward the earth—to the material world of technology and production.

9 ❧   TWO IMAGES OF TECHNOLOGY

In trying to examine technology and production, we encounter a curious paradox. We are deeply riven by a great sense of promise about technical innovation, on the one hand, and by a thorough sense of disenchantment with its results, on the other. This dual attitude not only reflects a conflict in the popular ideologies concerning technology but also expresses strong doubts about the nature of the modern technological imagination itself. We are puzzled that the very instruments our minds have conceived and our hands have created can be so easily turned against us, with disastrous results for our well-being—indeed, for our very survival as a species.

It is difficult for young people today to realize how anomalous such a conflict in technical orientation and imagery would have seemed only a few decades ago. Even such a wayward cult hero as Woody Guthrie once celebrated the huge dams and giant mills that have now earned so much opprobrium. The people whom Guthrie and his radical companions of the 1930s addressed had a deep reverence for technology, specifically those skills and devices that we place under the rubric of "technics." New machines, like artistic works, were objects of display that radiantly enraptured not only the connoisseur of futurism, the manufacturer, and the specialist, but the general public in all walks of life. Popular American utopias were unreeled in monumental technocratic images; they embodied power, a preening mastery of nature, physical gigantism, and dazzling mobility. The largely technical "New World of Tomorrow," celebrated in the last of the truly great fairs—New York World's Fair of 1939—fascinated millions of visitors with its message of human achievement and hope. In fact, technics had become as much a cultural artifact as a mechanical one. The early part of the century witnessed the emergence of an intensely social and messianic art (Futurism, Expressionism, the Bauhaus, to cite the most celebrated ones) that was overwhelmingly technological in its exhortations and in its derogation of more leisurely, reflective, craft-oriented, and organic traditions.

The hold of technics on the social imagery of that time was more fetishistic than rational. Even the First World War, which witnessed a massive use of the new technological armamentarium to slaughter millions of people, did not dispel this technical mythos. Only in the sequelae of the second of these worldwide conflicts, with all its terrifying results, did we begin to witness chilling doubts in the popular mind over the wisdom of technical innovation. Nuclear weaponry, perhaps more than any single factor, has created a popular fear of a "technics-run-wild." The 1960s began to exhibit a pronouncedly anti-technical bias of its own that has since turned into a complex duel between the "high" or "hard" technologies (those associated with fossil and nuclear fuels, industrial agriculture, and synthetics) and the so-called "appropriate" or "soft" technologies (those structured around solar, wind, and hydraulic sources of energy, organically grown food, and human-scale, craft-like industries).

What clearly renders "appropriate" technology increasingly attractive today is not any popular celebration of its achievements or promise; rather, it is a growing fear that we are irretrievably committing ourselves to destructive systems of mass production and widespread problems of environmental pollution. The artistic messiahs of a technocratic society are gone. Humanity now seems to feel that technology has ensnared it; it has the mien of a victim rather than a beneficiary. If the first half of the century witnessed the emergence of "high" technology as a popular "art-form" because the great majority of the industrialized world's population still lived in small communities with almost antique technical artifacts, the end of the century is witnessing the emergence of "appropriate" technology as a popular "art-form" precisely because "high" technology has placed a gilded cage over the suffocating millions who now clutter the cities and highways of the western world.

⌘

The grim fatalism slowly permeating western humanity's response to technics derives in large part from its ethical ambivalence toward technical innovation. The modern mind has been taught to identify technical sophistication with a "good life" and, to a large extent, with a social progressivism that culminates in human freedom. But none of these images has been suitably clarified, at least not from a historical perspective. Today, by far the great majority of people view the "good life" or "living well" (terms that date back to Aristotle) as a materially secure, indeed highly affluent life. Reasonable as this conclusion may seem in our own time, it contrasts sharply with its Hellenic origins. Aristotle's classic distinction between "living only" (a life in which people are insensately driven to the limitless acquisition of wealth) and "living well" or within "limit" epitomizes classical antiquity's notion of the ideal life, however much its values were honored in the breach. To "live well" or live the "good life" implied an ethical life in which one was committed not only to the well-being of one's family and friends but also to the *polis* and its social institutions. In living the "good life" within limit, one sought to achieve balance and self-sufficiency—a controlled, rounded, and all-sided life. But self-sufficiency, which for Aristotle seems to embody this conceptual constellation of ideals, does "not mean that which is self-sufficient for a man himself, for one who lives a solitary life, but also for parents, children, wife, and in general for his friends and fellow citizens, since man is born for citizenship."

The dichotomy between the modern image of a materially affluent life and the classical ideal of a life based on limit parallels the dichotomy between modern and classical concepts of technics. To the modern mind, technics is simply the ensemble of raw materials, tools, machines, and related devices that are needed to produce a usable object. The ultimate judgment of a technique's value and desirability is operational: it is based on efficiency, skill, and cost. Indeed, cost largely summarizes virtually all the factors that prove out the validity of a technical achievement. But to the classical mind, by contrast, "technique" (or *techné*) had a far more ample meaning. It existed in a social and ethical context in which, to invoke Aristotle's terms, one asked not only "how" a use-value was produced but also "why." From process to product, *techné* provided both the framework and the ethical light by which to form a metaphysical judgment about the "why" as well as the "how" of technical activity. Within this ethical, rational, and social framework, Aristotle distinguished between the "master workers in each craft" who are "more honourable, and know in a truer sense and are wiser than the manual workers." In contrast to their strictly operational subordinates, "who act without knowledge of what they do, as fire burns," master workers act with an insight and ethical responsibility that renders their craft rational.

Techné, moreover, covered a wider scope of experience than the modern word technics. As Aristotle explains in *Nichomachean Ethics*, "All art [*techné*] is concerned with coming into being, that is, with contriving and considering how something may come into being which is capable of either being or not being, and whose origin is in the maker and not in the thing made." Here he distinguishes the crafted product—even artistic works such as architectural masterpieces and sculpture—from natural phenomena, which "have their origins in themselves." Accordingly, *techné* is a "state concerned with making, involving a true course of reasoning...." It is "potency," an essential that *techné* shares with the ethical "good." All "arts, i.e., productive forms of knowledge, are potencies; they are originative sources of change in another thing or in the artist himself considered as other."

These far-reaching ethical and metaphysical remarks indicate how much the classical image of *techné* contrasts with the modern image of technics. The goal of *techné* is not restricted to merely "living well" or living within limit. *Techné* includes living an ethical life according to an originative and ordering principle conceived as "potency." Viewed even in an instrumental sense, *techné* thus encompasses not merely raw materials, tools, machines, and products but also the producer—in short, a highly sophisticated subject from which all else originates.* To Aristotle, the "master-craftsman" is distinguished subjectively from his apprentices or assistants by virtue of honor, a sense of "why" products are created, and generally a wisdom of things and phenomena. By starting with the rationality of the subject, Aristotle establishes a point of departure for bringing rationalization to the production of the object.

Modern industrial production functions in precisely the opposite way. Not only is the modern image of *techné* limited to mere technics in the instrumental sense of the term, but also its goals are inextricably tied to unlimited production. "Living well" is conceived as limitless consumption within the framework of a totally unethical, privatized level of self-interest. Technics, moreover, includes not the producer and his or her ethical standards (proletarians, after all, service the modern industrial apparatus in total anonymity) but the *product* and its constituents. The technical focus shifts from the subject to the object, from the producer to the product, from the creator to the created. Honor, a sense of "why," and any general wisdom of things and phenomena have no place in the world required by modern industry. What really counts in technics is efficiency, quantity, and an intensification of

---

* The extent to which Aristotle's image of *techné* influenced Marx is hard to judge, particularly in terms of Marx's own image of technology and design. But these classical insights appear in most of the Marxian problematics we group under the category of "alienation," the distinction between human labor and animal activity, and the notion of the "humanization of nature" in Marx's early writings. Aristotle, far from being a "primitive" in economics and technics, was in fact highly sophisticated; his views, far from "preceding" Marx's, actually anticipated them.

the labor process. The specious rationality involved in producing the object is foisted on the rationalization of the subject to a point where the producer's subjectivity is totally atrophied and reduced to an object among objects.

In fact, the objectification of subjectivity is the *sine qua non* of mass production. Here, "thought or word becomes a tool [and] one can dispense with actually 'thinking' it, that is, with going through the logical acts involved in verbal formulation of it," notes Horkheimer. He also observes:

> As has been pointed out, often and correctly, the advantage of mathematics—the model of all neo-positivistic thinking—lies in just this "intellectual economy." Complicated logical operations are carried out without actual performance of all the intellectual acts upon which the mathematical and logical symbols are based. Such mechanization is indeed essential to the expansion of industry; but if it becomes the characteristic feature of mind, if reason itself is instrumentalized, it takes on a kind of materiality and blindness, becomes a fetish, a magic entity that is accepted rather than intellectually experienced.

Horkheimer's remarks, while seemingly occupied with the impact of a new technics on a waning, traditional subjectivity, might easily be read as an account of the effects of a new subjectivity on a waning traditional technics. I do not mean to say that the technics that emerged from this subjectivity did not reinforce it. But if I read the historical record correctly, it is fair to say that long before mass manufacture came into existence, there had already been widespread destruction of community life and the emergence of uprooted, displaced, atomized, and propertyless "masses"—the precursors of the modern proletariat. This development was paralleled by science's evocation of a new image of the world—a lifeless physical world composed of matter and motion that preceded the technical feats of the Industrial Revolution.

Technics does not exist in a vacuum, nor does it have an autonomous life of its own. Hellenic thought, which appropriately linked craft and art under the rubric of *techné*, also linked both with the value system and institutions of its society. From this standpoint, a given body of sensibilities, social relations, and political structures were no less the components of technics than the material intentions of the producer and the material needs of society. In effect, *techné* was conceived holistically, in the sense that we today describe an ecosystem. Skills, devices, and raw materials were interlinked in varying degrees with the rational, ethical, and institutional ensemble that underpins a society;

insofar as *techné* was concerned, all were regarded as an integrated whole. Today, if such "extratechnical" aspects like rationality, ethics, and social institutions seem barren and more inorganic by comparison with those of earlier times, it is because technology in the modern sense of the term *is* more inorganic. And not because modern technics now determines the "supratechnical," but rather because society has devolved toward the inorganic in terms of its own "social tissue" and structural forms.

For the present, we need a clearer image of what is meant by "technics": the problems of sensibility it raises, the functions it performs, and, of course, the dangers and promises latent in technical innovation. To confine the discussion merely to advances in skills, implements, and the discovery of raw materials is to commit ourselves to a very shallow account of all these issues. Without examining the changes in society that variously opened or closed it to technical innovation, we would have great trouble explaining why a vast body of newly discovered technical knowledge failed to influence one body of social relations, yet seemingly "determined" their form elsewhere or at another time. To say that one society was "ready" for the compass, movable type, or the steam engine, while another was not, blatantly ignores the question of the relationship of society to technology. In the following chapter I shall show more thoroughly that it is neither technical change nor Marx's "production relations" that changed society, but rather an immanent dialectic within given societies themselves, where organized coercion was not directly involved.

○

Let me begin my exploration of technics and the contrasting images that shape its form and destiny by examining the ideologies that exist around labor—that most human of all technical categories. Short of sexuality, no subject has been more intractable to a reasonably unprejudiced analysis and more encrusted by highly embattled ideologies. Labor, perhaps even more than any single human activity, underpins contemporary relationships among people on every level of experience—whether in terms of the rewards it brings, the privileges it confers, the discipline it demands, the repressions it produces, or the social conflicts it generates. To critically examine these encrustations in their most sophisticated ideological form (notably, Marx's remarkable analysis of labor) is perhaps the most authentic point of departure for approaching the subject.

Here, in contrast to the procedure I have honored so far, the past does not illuminate the present nearly as much as the present illuminates the past and gives it often startling relevance to the future.

Owing to our weighty emphasis on the "domination of nature," our economization of social life, our proclivities for technical innovation, and our image of labor as homogeneous "labor-time," modern society may be more acutely conscious of itself as a world based on labor than any society before it. Hence we may occasionally look backward but only to penetrate the mists that obscure our vision.

To the modern mind, labor is viewed as a rarefied, abstract activity, a process extrinsic to human notions of genuine self-actualization. One usually "goes to work" the way a condemned person "goes" to a place of confinement: the workplace is little more than a penal institution in which mere existence must pay a penalty in the form of mindless labor. Expressions like a "nine-to-five job" are highly revealing; they tell us that work, labor, or toil (today one can use any of these words as equivalents) is external to "real life," whatever that may mean. We "measure" labor in hours, products, and efficiency, but rarely do we understand it as a concrete human activity. Aside from the earnings it generates, labor is normally alien to human fulfillment. It can be described in terms of that new suprahuman world of "energetics"—be it psychic, social, "cosmic," or even ecological (if the systems-theorists are correct)—that is comprehensible in the form of the rewards one acquires by submitting to a work discipline. By definition, these rewards are viewed as incentives for submission, rather than for the freedom that should accompany creativity and self-fulfillment. We commonly are "paid" for supinely working on our knees, not for heroically standing on our feet.

Even Marx, who first articulated the abstract character of labor, tends to mystify it as a precondition for "freedom" rather than submission— ironically, by tinting labor with humanistic metaphors that it no longer possesses. *Capital* has a famous comparison between the unconscious activity of the animal and the conscious activity of human beings. Here Marx opposes the worker

> to Nature as one of her own forces, setting in motion arms and legs, head and hands, the natural forces of his body, in order to appropriate Nature's productions in a form adapted to his own wants. By thus acting on the external world and changing it, he at the same time changes his own nature.

Marx then adduces the illustration of the spider and the bee, which can put to shame many a weaver and architect, but he notes that

> what distinguishes the worst architect from the best of bees is this, that the architect raises his structure in imagination before he erects it in reality. At

the end of every labour-process, we get a result that already existed in the imagination of the labourer at its commencement. He not only effects a change in form of the material on which he works but he also realizes a purpose of his own that gives the law to his *modus operandi*, and to which he must subordinate his will.

The apparent "innocence" of this description is highly deceptive. It is riddled by ideology—an ideology that is all the more deceptive because Marx himself is unaware of the trap into which he has fallen. The trap lies precisely in the *abstraction* that Marx imparts to the labor process, its ahistorical autonomy and character as a strictly technical process. From the outset, one may reasonably ask whether it is meaningful any longer to say that, at the "commencement" of "every labour process," the laborer is permitted to have an imagination, much less to bring it to bear on the production of use-values. Even the process of design by today's architects and other professionals has become a stereotyped process of rational techniques. Moreover, "mindless labor" is not merely a result of mechanization; as I shall reveal, it is the calculated and deliberate product of subordination and control. Finally, is it correct to believe that a multitude of spontaneous creations of human "labour," from cathedrals to shoes, were often guided more by cerebral designs than by esthetic, often undefinable impulses in which art was conjoined with craft?* As I also shall note, the vocabulary of technics is a good deal more than cerebral.

Marx's largely technical interpretation of labor clearly reveals itself when he describes the interaction between labor and its materials with the most "organic" metaphors at his command:

> Iron rusts and wood rots. Yarn with which we neither weave nor knit, is *wasted*. *Living* labour must *seize* upon these things and rouse them from their *death-sleep*, change them from mere possible use-values into *real* and *effective* ones. Bathed in the *fire* of labour, they are *appropriated* as part and parcel of labour's organism, and, as it were, made *alive* for the *performance* of

---

* One wonders, in fact, how fully the Surrealists understood Marx—or perhaps even their own program for the sovereignty of fantasy—when they entered Marxist movements in such large numbers. By the same token, one cannot help but ask how the Parisian students of 1968 could have emblazoned such slogans as "Imagination to Power!" on the red flags of socialism. Today, when the liberation of imagination involves the recovery of the productive process itself as an ecological mediation of humanity with nature, the inconsistencies that cling to ostensibly "sophisticated" minds (particularly those which have lost their very materiality in the corridors of the academy) boggles human intelligence.

their functions in the process, as elementary constituents of new use-values, of new products, ever ready as means of subsistence for individual consumption, or as means of production for some new labour-process.

The terms I have emphasized in this passage reveal the extent to which Marx's own imagination is completely tainted by Promethean, often crassly bourgeois, design images that seemingly prefigure the "use-values" he seeks to "liberate" from the "death-sleep" of nature. Like the island of the Lotus-eaters in the *Odyssey*, the dreamlike world of nature is presumably a "wasted" one until a Homeric hero, empowered by a Fichtean "Ego," fires nature from within itself into the "non-Ego" or "otherness" of a challenging antagonist. Hence, despite Marx's fervent references to William Petty's concept of a "marriage" between nature and labor, there is no authentic marriage other than a coercive patriarchy that sees the wedding compact as a license from Yahweh to place all of reality under the iron will of the male elders.

The concepts reared by the human imagination in productive activity, as distinguished from the instinctive drives of the spider and bee, are *never* socially neutral. Nor can they *ever* be cast in strictly technical terms. From the very outset of the design process, the technical imagination is potentially problematical in even the best of social circumstances. To leave it unquestioned is to ignore the most fundamental problems of humanity's interaction with nature. I say this not from any conviction that the mind is necessarily fixed by any innate, neo-Kantian structures that define the imaginative process as such. Rather, I contend that the mind and certainly the technical imagination, short of attaining the self-consciousness that western philosophy has established as its most abiding ideal, remain highly vulnerable not only to society's ongoing barrage of cultural stimuli, but also to the very imagery that forms the language of the imagination itself.

To Marx, both the labor process and the cerebral design that guides it are essentially utilitarian: they have an irreducible technical ground, a *modus operandi*, that acquires the neutrality and rigor of scientific lawfulness. While their effectiveness may be enhanced or diminished by history, the design and the labor processes that execute it are to him ultimately a physical interaction. Indeed, without such an underlying, socially neutral interaction, Marx's theory of "historical materialism"—with its *deus ex machina* called the "means of production"—would be as meaningless in Marxian social theory as Hegel's ruthless teleological system would be without the Hegelian notion of "Spirit." Both systems must be moved by something that is not itself bogged down in the contingent. Hence the design process and the labor process are necessarily equipped with a suprahistorical refuge from which they can preside over history—and into which Marx retreats from time to time with all the second thoughts that riddle so much of his theoretical corpus.

That Marx and many of his Victorian contemporaries disparaged "nature idolatry" in extremely harsh terms is not accidental. The Romantic movement of the nineteenth century echoed a much broader and ancient sensibility: the view that production should be a symbiotic, not an antagonistic, process. Although the movement was primarily aesthetic, it combined with anarchist theories of mutualism—notably Kropotkin's extraordinarily prescient writings—to ferret out a much broader "natural design": a "marriage" between labor and nature that was conceived not as a patriarchal domination of "man" over nature but as a productive relationship based on harmony, fertility, and creativity. Libertarian and aesthetic movements in the nineteenth century were still heir to the image of a fecund interaction between humanity's craft and nature's potentialities. But labor was seen not as "fire," or industry as a "furnace." The imagery of these movements was drastically different. Labor was viewed as the midwife, and tools as the aids, in delivering nature's offspring: use-values.

Such a view implied that the very "imagination" in which the "architect raises his structure" is socially and ethically derivative. Perceived reality involves an epistemology of domination—or liberation—that cannot be reduced to technical grounds alone. Hence the design images of production, the very figures reared in the minds of engineers, architects, artisans, or laborers, are not socially or ethically neutral. There is no irreducible technical ground from which to formulate a value-free theory of technics and of labor. The images of labor as "fire" and of natural phenomena as enshrouded by a "death-sleep" are formed from the visual reservoir of a highly domineering sensibility. The imagery of modern technical design has its origins in the epistemologies of rule; it has been formed over a long period of time by our very specific way of "knowing" the world—both one another and nature—a way that finds its ultimate apotheosis in industrial agriculture, mass production, and bureaucracy.

෬

Implicit in virtually every contemporary image of labor is a unique image of *matter*—the material on which labor presumably exercises its "fiery" powers to transform the world. To the modern mind, matter essentially constitutes the fundament of an irreducible "being," whether we choose to make it interchangeable with energy, particles, a mathematical principle, or simply a convenient functional premise. Whatever our choice, we see matter as the base level of substance, the substrate of reality. Indeed, once matter achieves specificity by virtue of its interactions, it ceases by definition to be "matter" and acquires the form of a "something," a reducible particular.

Conceived in this sense, matter completely accords with a quantitative interpretation of reality. It may be fragmented but it remains undifferentiated. Hence, it can be weighed and counted, but without regard to any differences that vitiate its homogeneity for the purposes of enumeration. It may be kinetic but it is not developmental. Hence it poses no problems that demand qualitative interpretation. From a philosophical viewpoint, matter may interact internally, but it lacks immanence or self-formation. Thus, it has reality but lacks subjectivity. Matter, in the modern mind, is not merely despiritized; it constitutes the very antithesis of spirit. Its objectivity is the source of contrast that illuminates our concept of subjectivity. The conventional definition of matter betrays this utterly spiritless conception in a generally despiritized world. It is the stuff that occupies space—the homogeneous material whose presence can be quantitatively determined by its weight and volume.

Our image of labor, in turn, is the despiritized counterpart of matter, located within the dimension of time. Perhaps no view expresses this metaphysical fugue of labor and matter more incisively than Marx's discussion of abstract labor in the opening portions of *Capital*. Here, abstract labor, measurable by the mere flow of time, becomes the polar conception of an abstract matter, measurable by its density and the volume of space it occupies. Descartes' *res extensa*, in effect, is complemented by Marx's *res temporalis*—a conceptual framework that shapes his analysis not only of value but of freedom, whose "fundamental premise" is the "shortening of the working day." Indeed, there is as much Cartesian dualism in Marx's work as there is Hegelian dialectic.

To follow Marx's discussion further, if we strip away the qualitative features of commodities—features which satisfy concrete human wants—then

> they have only one common property left, that of being products of labor. But even the product of labor itself has undergone a change in our hands. If we make abstraction from its use-value, we make abstraction at the same time from the material elements and shapes that make the product a use-value; we see in it no longer a table, a house, yarn, or any other useful things. Its

existence as a material thing is put out of sight. Neither can it any longer be regarded as the product of the labor of the joiner, the mason, the spinner, or of any other definite kind of productive labour.... A use-value, or useful article ... has value only because human labour in the abstract has been embodied or materialized in it. How, then, is the magnitude of this value to be measured? Plainly, by the quantity of the value-creating substance, the labour contained in the article. The quantity of labour, however, is measured by its duration, and labour-time in its turn finds its standard in weeks, days, and hours.

Leaving aside their functions as part of the critique of political economy, these lines are a mouthful in terms of Marx's analytical procedure, his philosophical antecedents, and his ideological purposes. There is nothing "plainly" conclusive about Marx's results because he is neither analyzing a commodity nor strictly generalizing about it. Actually, he is *idealizing* it—possibly beyond the degree of "ideality" that every generalization requires to transcend its clinging welter of particulars.

The degree of "abstraction" that Marx makes from a commodity's "use value"—from the "material elements and shapes that turn the product into a use-value"—is so far-reaching in terms of what we know about the anthropology of use-values that this very theoretical process must itself be socially justified. In effect, Marx has removed the commodity from a much richer social context than he may have realized, given the scientistic prejudices of this time. Not only is he dealing with the commodity form of use-values, but he also is dealing *unreflectively* with socially constituted and historically developed traditions and fact—more precisely, presuppositions about technics, labor, nature, and needs that may very well render his analytical procedure and conclusions specious. We do not know whether we get to the "essence" of a commodity—of a use-value produced for the purposes of exchange—if we divest it of its concrete attributes so that its "existence as a material thing" can really be "put out of sight." Perhaps even more fundamental to a commodity are precisely those concrete attributes—its form as a "use-value"—that provide the *utopian* dimension, the "principle of hope," inherent within every desirable product of nature and technics (its dimension of the "marvelous," as Andre Breton might have put it). Herein may lie the ultimate contradiction within the commodity—the contradiction between its abstract nature as an exchange-value and its "fecundity" as a use-value in satisfying desire—from which the most basic historical contradictions of capitalism have been spawned.

In any case, Marx's process of idealization yields a more far-reaching result than he could have anticipated clearly. Abstract labor can only produce abstract matter—matter that is totally divested of the "material elements and shapes that make the product a use-value." Neither Marx nor the political economists of his time were in any position to realize that abstract matter, like abstract labor, is a denial of the utopian features—indeed, the sensuous attributes—of concrete matter and concrete labor. Hence "use-value" as the materialization of desire and "concrete labor" as the materialization of play were excluded from the realm of economic discourse; they were left to the utopian imagination (particularly the anarchic realm of fantasy as typified by Fourier) for elaboration. Political economy had lost its artfulness. Its adepts became a body of "worldly thinkers" whose world, in fact, was defined by the parameters of bourgeois ideology.

For Marx, this development toward a disenchanting "science" was theoretically and historically progressive. Adorno may have said more than he realized when he sardonically accused Marx of wanting to turn the whole world into a factory. For Marxian theory, the reduction of concrete labor into abstract labor is a historical as well as theoretical desideratum. Abstract labor may be a creature of capitalism but, like capitalism itself, it is a necessary "moment" in the dialectic of history. Not only is it a medium for rendering exchange ratios possible on an extensive scale, but, from an even larger perspective, it becomes part of the technical substrate of freedom. By its very plasticity, abstract labor renders human activity interchangeable, the rotation of industrial tasks possible, and the use of machinery flexible. Its capacity to flow through the veins of industry as mere undifferentiated human energy renders the manipulation and reduction of the working day possible and, concurrently, the expansion of the "realm of freedom" at the expense of the "realm of necessity." If Marx's communism was meant to be a "society of artists," he was not prepared to recognize that the colors on their canvases might be limited to varying tints of gray.

ଔ

To compare the outlook of organic society to this ensemble of ideas is literally to enter a qualitatively different realm of imagery and a richly sensuous form of sensibility. Organic society's image of the world contrasts radically in almost every detail with Marxian, scientistic, and frankly bourgeois notions of matter, labor, nature, and technics—indeed, with the very structure of the technical imagination it brings to bear upon experience. To speak of organic society's "outlook" toward these issues or even its "sensibility" rarely does justice to the polymorphous sensitivity of its epistemological apparatus. As my discussion of animism has shown, this sensory apparatus elevated the inorganic to the organic, the nonliving to the living. Even before nature was spiritized, it was personified. But not only was the natural "object" (living or not) a subject in its own right; so, too, were the *tools* that mediated the relationship between the workers and the material on which they worked. The "labor process" itself assumed the organic character of a unified activity in which work appeared as an element in a gestative process—literally an act of reproduction, of birth.

To be more specific, the technical imagination of organic society—its very mode of conceptualization—far from being strictly utilitarian, exhibited an enchanted synthesis of creative activity. No subject and object were placed in opposition to each other, nor did a linear sequence of events follow one upon the other. Rather, the materials, work process, and transformed result became an organic whole, an ecotechnic synthesis, which more closely approximated a gestative, reproductive activity than the abstract exercise of human powers we denote as "labor" or "work." Like a medium that encompassed both "producer" and "materials," the labor process flowed between the two and annealed them into a common result in which neither the craftsperson nor the materials preempted the other. Labor-*time*, much less "abstract labor," would have been conceptually unformulatable. Time, like Bergson's *durée*, was physiological and could not be anchored in notions of linearity. Labor, now wedded to the specificity of its activity and the concreteness of its "product," had no meaning beyond its concreteness as a sensuous activity—hence the vast world of phenomena, like land, which were "priceless" (to use our limping terminology) and beyond the equations of exchange.

Accordingly, it would have been meaningless to use the word "product" in its modern sense when, instead of a result existing apart from craftsperson and material, organic society actually meant a new fusion of human and natural powers. Aristotle's notions of "material cause," "privation," and "formal cause"—actually, a causal *pattern* that involves the participation of the material itself in an immanent striving to achieve its potentiality for a specific form—are redolent with the characteristics of this earlier organic epistemology of production. In effect, the labor process was not a form of production but rather of reproduction, not an act of fabrication but rather of procreation.

How much this orientation toward the labor process permeated the sensuous outlook of preliterate communities is fully revealed by anthropological and mythological data. No less than agriculture, other productive activities (most notably metallurgy, which yields the most dramatic transformation of materials) were viewed as sacrosanct activities that involved a highly sexualized activity between the human workers and a feminine earth. As Mircea Eliade observes:

> Very early we are confronted with the notion that ores "grow" in the belly of the earth after the manner of embryos. Metallurgy thus takes on the character of obstetrics. Miner and metal-worker intervene in the unfolding of subterranean embryology: they accelerate, the rhythm of the growth of ores, they collaborate in the work of Nature and assist it to give birth more rapidly. In a word, man, with his various techniques, gradually takes the place of Time: his labours replace the work of Time.

Eliade's emphasis on "time," here, is grossly misplaced. In fact, as he himself notes, what is really at issue in this imagery of embryonic ores is a notion of "matter" that is held "to be alive and sacred...." In effect, "matter" is *active*. It strives to realize itself, its latent potentialities, through a nisus that finds fulfillment in wholeness. To use a more organic terminology, the self-realization of matter finds its very exact analogy in the processes of gestation and birth.

To speak, as Marx does, of the worker's "appropriation" of "Nature's productions in a form adapted to his own wants" is to assume that there is no developmental synchronicity between human "wants" and natural "wants." A sharp disjunction is thereby created between society, humanity, and "needs" on the one side, and nature, the nonhuman living world, and ecological ends on the other. By contrast, organic society contains the conceptual means for functionally distinguishing the differences between society and nature without polarizing them. Insofar as production is also reproduction, insofar as creation is also gestation and the product is the child of this entire process rather than an "appropriated" thing, a "marriage" does indeed exist between nature and humanity that does not dissolve the identity of the partners into a universal, ethereal "Oneness."

Labor fully participates in this development by pursuing "the transformation of matter, its perfection and its transmutation," to use Eliade's formulation. It would be as if labor were a causal principle inherent in gestating matter, not a "force" external to it. Accordingly, labor is more than a "midwife" of "Nature's productions": it *is* one of "Nature's productions" in its own right and coterminous with nature's fecundity. If society flows out of nature with the result that it, like mind, has its own natural history, so labor flows out of nature and also has its own natural history.

Accordingly, labor's destiny is irrevocably tied to the primordial vision of the earth as a living being. Nonhuman life labors together with humanity just as bears are believed to cooperate with hunters; hence both are drawn into a magic sphere of cooperation that daily nourishes primordial mores of usufruct and complementarity. In organic society, it would seem that no one could fully "possess" a material bounty that had been *bestowed* as much as created. Thus, nature itself was the grand "leveller" that provided the compensatory rationale for adjusting the equality of unequals in the material world, like "natural law" and "natural man" were to be for adjusting the inequality of equals in the juridical and political worlds. A providing nature was one whose "labor" was manifestly expressed in the rich variety of phenomena that clothed the natural landscape.

So strongly did this animistic sensibility fasten itself upon the human mind that, as late as the fifth century B.C., at the high tide of classical Hellenic philosophy, Anaxagoras could seriously reject the "four-element" and atomic theories of nature on the ground that hair could not "come from what is not hair" nor "flesh from what is not flesh." In this theory of *homeomeries*, as Aristotle tells us,

> Anaxagoras says the opposite to Empedocles [theory of four elements], for he calls the *homeomeries* elements (I mean flesh and bone and each of these things), and air and fire he calls mixtures of these and of all other "seeds"; for each of these things is made of the invisible *homeomeries* all heaped together.

The *homeomeries*, in fact, comprise a philosophical sophistication of a more primordial view that the substance *of* the earth *is* the earth itself with all its variegated minerals, flora, and fauna.

Concrete labor thus confronted concrete substance, and labor merely participated in fashioning a reality that was either present or latent in natural phenomena. Both labor and the materials on which it "worked" were *coequally* creative, innovative, and most assuredly artistic. The notion that labor "appropriates" nature in any way whatever—a notion intrinsic to both Locke's and Marx's conceptual framework— would have been utterly alien to the technical imagination of organic society and inconsistent with its compensatory and distributive principles. So crucial was the coequality of substance with labor, in any understanding of this early technical imagination, that work was distinguished by its capacity to discover the "voice" of substance, not simply to fashion an inert "natural resource" into desired objects. Among the old Anvilik Eskimo, ivory carvers "rarely tried to impose a pattern on nature, or their own personalities on matter," observes Rene Dubos. Holding the "raw ivory" in his hand, the craftsman

> turned it gently this way and that way, whispering to it, "Who are you? Who hides in you?" The carver rarely set out consciously to shape a particular form. Instead of compelling the fragment of ivory to become a man, a child, a wolf, a seal, a baby walrus, or some other preconceived object, he tried subconsciously to discover the structural characteristics and patterns inherent in the material itself. He continuously let his hand be guided by the inner structure of the ivory as it revealed itself to the knife. The form of the human being or animal did not have to be created; it was there from the beginning and only had to be released.

Work was thus revelation as well as realization, a synchronicity of subject and object. Only later was it to bifurcate into a tyranny of subject over object—initially, by reducing human beings to objects themselves. Absorbed within the totality of organic society, the tool was part of the "Way" of the craftsperson, not a frozen instrumental component of a vocational "tool-kit." The term "Way," universal to the language of all early communities, united ethos, ritual, sensibility, duty, and lifestyle with cosmogony and with the substances that made up the world. To set one apart from the other was simply incomprehensible to the extraordinary sensibility of that remote era. Work, in turn, had an almost choral quality: it was incantative and evocative, and it soothed and coaxed the substance that the tool had organically conjoined with the craftsperson.

Rarely, to this day, do preliterate people work silently. They whisper, hum, sing, or quietly chant; they nurse and nurture the material by gently rocking and undulating their bodies, by stroking it as though it were a child. The imagery of the mother with a nursing child is perhaps more evocative of the true process of early crafthood than is the smith striking the glowing iron between hammer and anvil. Even later, at the village level, food cultivators were buoyed by choral songs and festivities, however arduous may have been their labor in sowing and harvesting grain. The "work song," a genre that still lived a century ago in nearly all pre-industrial occupations, is the historic echo of the primal chant, itself a technics, that elicited spirit from substance and inspirited the artisans and their tools.

✃

We know quite well that ores do not reproduce themselves in exhausted mines, that ivory does not conceal an animate being, and that animals do not obligingly respond to hunting ceremonies. But these fancies may serve to inculcate a human respect for nature and cause people to cherish its bounty as more than exploitable "natural resources." Ceremony and myth may enhance that respect and foster a rich sensitivity for the artistic and functional integrity of a crafted object. Group ceremonies, in fact, deepen group solidarity and make a community more effective in the pursuit of its ends. But the modern mind is unlikely to believe that mythopoeic notions of hunting and crafting are solidly rooted in natural phenomena. Function should not be mistaken for fact. And however effective mythopoeic functions may be in achieving certain practical, often aesthetic ends, their success does not validate their claims to intrinsic truth.

But experience has thoroughly deflated scientistic images of matter as a merely passive substrate of reality, technics as strictly "technical," and abstract labor as a social desideratum. The fact that the natural world is orderly (at least on a scale that renders modern science and engineering possible) has long suggested the intellectually captivating possibility that there is a logic—a rationality if you will—to reality that may well be latent with meaning. For some three centuries now, a scientific vision of reality has been solidly structured around the presupposition that we can interpret reality's orderliness in the form of a scientific logic, rigorously answerable to such rationally demanding systems as mathematics. But no assumption or even suggestion has been made that logic and reason inheres in the world itself. Science, in effect, has been permitted to live a lie. It has presupposed, with astonishing success, that nature is orderly, and that this order lends itself to rational interpretation by the human mind, but that reason is *exclusively* the subjective attribute of the human observer, not of the phenomena observed. Ultimately, science has lived this lie primarily to avoid the most unavoidable "pitfalls" of metaphysics—that an orderly world that is also rational may be regarded as a meaningful world.

The term meaning, of course, is redolent with animism. It is suggestive of purpose, consciousness, intentionality, subjectivity—in short, the qualities we impart to humanity as *distinguished* from nature, not to humanity as an expression of nature whose mind is deeply rooted in natural history. The logical consequences of the very logic of scientism threaten to subvert the distance science has carefully created between itself and the wealth of phenomena it subjects to its analytic strategies. Science, in effect, has become a temple built on the foundation of seemingly animistic and metaphysical "ruins," without which it would sink into the watery morass of its own contradictions.

Science's defense against this kind of critique is that order may imply a rational arrangement of phenomena that lends itself to rational comprehension, but that none of this implies subjectivity, the capacity to *comprehend* a rational arrangement. To all appearances, nature is mute, unthinking, and blind, however orderly it may be; hence it exhibits neither subjectivity nor rationality in the human sense of self-directive and self-expressive phenomena. It may be sufficiently orderly to be thinkable, but *it* does not think. Nevertheless, subjectivity, even in its human sense, is not a newly born result, a terminally given condition. Subjectivity can be traced back through a natural history of its own to its most rudimentary forms as mere sensitivity in all animate beings and, in the view of philosophers such as Diderot, in the very reactivity (*sensibilité*) of the inorganic world itself. Although the human mind may be the expression of subjectivity in its most complex and articulate form, it has been increasingly approximated in graded forms throughout the course of organic evolution in organisms that were able to deal on very active terms with highly demanding environments. What we today call "mind" in all its human uniqueness, self-possession, and imaginative possibilities is coterminous with a long *evolution* of mind. Subjectivity has not always been absent from the course of organic and inorganic development until the emergence of humanity. To the contrary, it has always been present, in varying degrees, throughout natural history, but as increasingly close approximations of the human mind as we know it today. To deny the existence of subjectivity in nonhuman nature is to deny that it can exist either in its given human form or in any form at all.

Moreover, human subjectivity itself can be defined as the very *history* of natural subjectivity, not merely as its product—in much the same sense that Hegel defined philosophy as its own history. Every layer of the human brain, every phase in the evolution of the human nervous system, every organ, cell, and even mineral component of the human body "speaks," as it were, from its given level of organization and in the graded subjectivity of its development, to the external habitat in organic evolution from whence it came and to the internal habitat into which it has been integrated. The "wisdom of the body," like the wisdom of the mind, speaks in a variety of languages. We may never adequately decipher these languages, but we know they exist in the varied pulsations of our bodies, in the beat of our hearts, in the radiant energy of our musculatures, in the electrical impulses emitted by our brains, and in the emotional responses generated by complexes of nerve and hormonal interactions. A veritable "music of the spheres" resonates within each living form and between it and other living forms.

We are also haunted by the possibility that a different order of subjectivity permeates our own. This subjectivity inheres in the *wholeness* of phenomena and their interrelationships. Is it farfetched to ask whether an *organic* subjectivity that stems from the fullness, complexity, and self-regulating relationships of ecosystems exhibits a "mentality" in nature similar in principle to the *cerebral* subjectivity of human beings? When we speak of the "wisdom of the body"—or, for that matter, the "fecundity of life" and the "revenge of nature"—we speak a language that often goes beyond strictly metaphoric terms. We enter into a realm of "knowingness" from which our strictly cerebral processes have deliberately exiled themselves. In any case, to bring together the natural history of mind with the history of natural mind is to raise a host of questions that can probably be answered only by presuppositions. Here, we stand at a juncture in the long career of knowledge itself. We may choose to confine mentality strictly to the human cerebrum as a Galileo and Descartes would have done, in which case we have committed mentality completely to the vaults of our skulls. Or we may choose to include the natural history of mind and expand our vision of mind to include nature in its wholeness, a tradition that includes the era of philosophic speculation from the Hellenic to the early Renaissance. But let us not deceive ourselves that science has chosen its way on the basis of presuppositions that are stronger or more certain than those of other ways of knowing.

Unless human mentality validates its claim to "superiority" by acquiring a better sense of meaning than it has today, like it or not, we are little more than crickets in a field, chirping to one another. Certainly, our words have no sense of coherence and destiny other than a preening claim to "superiority" that totally ignores our responsibilities to other human beings, to society, and to nature. Potentially, as Hans Jonas has beautifully put it, we may well make up in depth and insight what we lack in cosmic scope and the finality of achievement. But just as function must not be mistaken for fact, neither must potentiality be mistaken for actuality. The great bulk of humanity is not even remotely near an understanding of its potentialities, much less an intuitive grasp of the elements and forms of their realization. A humanity unfulfilled is not a humanity at all except in the narrowest biosocial sense of the term. Indeed, in this condition, a humanity unfulfilled is more fearsome than any living being, for it has enough of that mentality called mere "intelligence" to assemble all the conditions for the destruction of life on the planet.

Hence, it is not in the innocent metaphors, the magical techniques, the myths, and the ceremonies they generate that the animistic imagination has earned the right to a more rational review than it has received up to now. Rather, it is its hints of a more complete logic—a logic possibly complementary to that of science, but certainly a more organic logic—that render the animistic imagination invaluable to the modern mind. Anvilik Eskimos who believe that ivory conceals a vocal subject are in error, just as are Plains Indians if they believe that they can engage in a verbal dialogue with a horse. But both the Eskimo and Indian, by assuming subjectivity in the ivory and horse, establish contact with a truth about reality that mythic behavior obscures but does not negate. They correctly assume that there is a "Way" about ivory and horses, which they must try to understand and to whose claims they must respond with insight and awareness. They assume that this "Way" is an ensemble of qualitative features—indeed, as Pythagoras was to see, of form that every object uniquely possesses. Lastly, they assume that this form and these qualities comprise a "Way" that exists in a larger constellation of interrelationships—one that a strictly cerebral mentalism commonly overlooks. Perhaps most essentially, the Anvilik Eskimo and Plains Indian place themselves in an *order* of phenomena, an organized *organic* habitat, that never merely "falls" together as an accumulation of "objects," but always—perhaps even by definition—*forms* an organism or an organic totality that derives from the nisus of "matter." Whether God plays dice with the world or not, to use Einstein's pithy phrase, the world never "hangs loose." This intuition is priceless even when we consider the least of things. Ivory *does* have its "grain," its internal structure and form; good craftspeople must know *where* to carve and to shape if they are to bring a material to the height of its aesthetic perfection. Any result that is less and less perfect than it could be is a violation of that "grain" and an insult to its integrity. A horse, too, has its "grain" or its "Way"—its prickly nerves, its need for attention, its capacity to fear, its delight in play. Behind its verbal muteness lies a wealth of sensibility that the rider must explore if the horse is to achieve its own capacity for perfection—if its potentialities are to be realized.

Humanity's habitat is thus latent with phenomena that "are," others that are "becoming," and still others that "will be." Our imagery of technics cannot evade the highly fluid nature of the world in which we live and the highly fluid nature of humanity itself. The design imagination of our times must be capable of encompassing this flow, this dialectic (to use a grossly abused term), not to cut across it with wanton arrogance and dogmatic self-confidence. To subserve our already fragile environment only to what humanity alone "can be"—and definitely still is not!—is to immerse the world in a darkness that is largely of our own making, to taint the clarity that its own age-old evolution of wisdom has produced. We are still a curse on natural evolution, not its fulfillment. Until we become what we *should* be in the constellation of life, we would do well to live with a fear of what we *can* be.

෬

From order to reason to meaning; from the graded natural history of mind to the emergence of human mind; from the organic subjectivity of the whole to the cerebral subjectivity of some of its parts; from the mythic "Way" to the knowledgeable "Way"—all these developments, with their various presuppositions about knowledge and their insights into reality, do not negate the presuppositions and insights of conventional science. They simply question science's claims to universality.[*]

Greek thought too had its visions of knowledge and truth. Moira, the so-called goddess of destiny, who antedated the Olympian deities, combined Necessity and Right. She was the meaning that mere explanation lacked, the ethical point toward which a seemingly blind causality converged. There is nothing "primitive" or merely mythopoeic about this vision of causality. On the contrary, it may be too sophisticated and demanding for the mechanically oriented mind to comprehend.

To put the issue quite directly, the "how" of things is inadequate unless it can be illuminated by the "why." Events that lack the coherence of ethical meaning are merely random. They are alien not only to science but also to nature, for even more than the proverbial "vacuum," nature abhors the incoherence of disorganization, the lack of meaning that comes with disorder. And it is hardly demeaning for science, in reconsidering its metaphysical presuppositions, to make room for other

---

[*] Lest there be any misunderstanding about this statement, I repeat that I am not questioning scientific insight and method as such but rather its preemptive, often metaphysical claims over the entire cosmos of knowledge. In this view I would stand with Hegel, whose distinction between "reason" and "understanding" has never been more valid than today. Speculative thought—imagination, art, and intuition—is no less a source of knowledge than are inductive-deductive reasoning, empirical verification, and scientific canons of proof. Wholeness should apply as much in our methods as it does in the evolution of reality.

metaphysical presuppositions that can illuminate areas of subjectivity to which a strictly scientistic outlook has proven to be blind.

These remarks are no more than a guidepost to a larger project—a philosophy of nature—that can hope to resolve the issues I have raised. Taken together, however, their bearing on technology is immense. To be sure, the industrial machine seems to have taken off on its own without the driver (to rephrase Horkheimer), but this metaphor tends to be an excuse to impute too much autonomy to the machine. The driver is still there. Even more than nature, we who have created this machine must be awakened from our own slumber. Before we fully developed the machine, we began to organize our sensibilities, relationships, values, and goals around a cosmic enterprise to mechanize the world. What we forgot in the process is that we too occupy the very world we have sought to mechanize.

Just as serious as the extent to which we have mechanized the world is the fact that we cannot distinguish what is *social* in our lives from what is technical. In our inability to distinguish the two, we are losing the ability to determine which is meant to subserve the other. Herein lies the core of our difficulties in controlling the machine. We lack a sense of the social *matrix* in which all technics should be embedded—of the social meaning in which technology should be clothed. Instead, we encounter the Hellenic conception of *techné* in the form of a grotesque caricature of itself: a *techné* that is no longer governed by a sense of limit. Our own, thoroughly market-generated conception of *techné* has become so limitless, so unbounded, and so broadly defined that we use its vocabulary ("input," "output," "feedback," *ad nauseam*) to explain our deepest interrelationships—which consequently are rendered shallow and trite. In its massive tendency to colonize the entire terrain of human experience, technics now raises the apocalyptic need to arrest its advance, to redefine its goals, to reorganize its forms, to rescale its dimensions— above all, to reabsorb it back into organic forms of social life and organic forms of human subjectivity.

The historic problem of technics lies not in its size or scale, its "softness" or "hardness," much less the productivity or efficiency that earned it the naïve reverence of earlier generations; the problem lies in how we can *contain* (that is, absorb) technics within an emancipatory society. In itself, "small" is neither beautiful nor ugly; it is merely small. Some of the most dehumanizing and centralized social systems were fashioned out of very "small" technologies; but bureaucracies, monarchies, and military forces turned these systems into brutalizing cudgels to subdue humankind and, later, to try to subdue nature. To be sure, a large-scale technics will foster the development of an oppressively large-scale society; but every warped society follows the dialectic of its own pathology of domination, irrespective of the scale of its technics. It can organize the "small" into the repellent as surely as it can imprint an arrogant sneer on the faces of the elites who administer it. Terms like "large," "small," or "intermediate," and "hard," "soft," or "mellow" are simply externals—the attributes of phenomena or things rather than their essentials. They may help us determine their dimensions and weights, but they do not *explain* the immanent qualities of technics, particularly as they relate to society.

Unfortunately, a preoccupation with technical size, scale, and even artistry deflects our attention away from the most significant problems of technics—notably, its ties with the ideals and social structures of freedom. The choice between a libertarian and an authoritarian technics was posed by Fourier and Kropotkin generations ago, long before Mumford denatured the word libertarian into the more socially respectable and amorphous term, democratic.* But this choice is not peculiar to our times; it has a long, highly complex pedigree. The exquisitely designed pottery of a vanishing artisan world, the beautifully crafted furnishings, the colorful and subtly intricate patterns of textiles, the carefully wrought ornaments, the beautifully sculpted tools and weapons—all attest to a wealth of skills, to a care for product, to a desire for self-expression, and to a creative concern for detail and uniqueness that has faded almost completely from the productive activity of our day. Our admiration for these artisan works unconsciously extends into a sense of inferiority or loss of the artisan world in which they were formed—a world that is all the more impressive because we recognize the high degree of subjectivity expressed by the objects. We feel that identifiable human beings imprinted their personalities on these goods; that they possessed a highly attuned sensitivity to the materials they handled, the tools they used, and to the age-old artistic norms their culture established over countless generations. Ultimately, what arouses us emotionally is the fact that these objects attest to a fecund human spirit, a creative subjectivity that articulated its cultural heritage and its wealth in materials that might otherwise seem pedestrian and beyond artistic merit in our own society. Here, the surreal halo around everyday things—the reconquest of everyday life by a pulsating integration of hands, tools, mind, and materials—was actually achieved not merely as part of the metaphysical program of European intellectuals but also by the common folk who lived that life.

---

* I would add that the phrase "libertarian technics," as distinguished from "democratic technics," has become all the more necessary today. "Workplace democracy" has come to mean little more than a participatory approach to productive activity, not an emancipatory one. A "democratic technics" is not necessarily a nonhierarchical or ecological one.

But in our preoccupation with the skill, care, and sensibilities of traditional artisans, we all too easily forget the nature of the culture that produced the craftsperson and the craft. Here, I refer not to its human scale, its sensitivity of values, and its humanistic thrust, but to the more solid facts of the social structure and its rich forms. That Eskimos crafted their equipment with considerable care because they had a high sense of care for each other is obvious enough, and that the animate quality of their crafts revealed an internal sense of animation and subjectivity need hardly be emphasized. But in the last analysis, all these desiderata flowed from the libertarian structure of the Eskimo community. Nor was this any less the case in the late Paleolithic and early Neolithic communities (or of organic society generally), whose artifacts still enchant us and whose traditions later formed the communal and aesthetic base of the "high civilizations" of antiquity. To the degree that its social traditions retain their vitality, even in a vestigial form, its skills, tools, and artifacts retain the all-important imprint of the artisan conceived as a self-creative being, a self-productive subject.

Initially, a libertarian is distinguished from an authoritarian technics by more than just the scale of production, the kind or size of implements, or even the way in which labor is organized, important as those may be. Perhaps the most crucial reason for what produces this distinction is the emergence of an *institutional* technics: the priestly corporation; the slowly emerging bureaucracies that surround it; later the monarchies and the military forces that preempt it; indeed, the very belief systems that validate the entire hierarchical structure and provide the authoritarian core of an authoritarian technics. Lavish material surpluses did not produce hierarchies and ruling classes; rather, hierarchies and ruling classes produced lavish material surpluses. Mumford may be perfectly correct in observing that one of the earliest machines to appear in history was not an inanimate ensemble of technical components but a highly animate "megamachine" of massed human beings whose large-scale, coordinated labor reared the huge public works and mortuaries of early "civilizations." But the growing religious and secular *bureaucracies* were even more technically authoritarian. Indeed, they were the *earliest* "machines" that eventually made the "megamachine" possible—that mobilized it and directed its energies toward authoritarian ends.

However, these bureaucracies' most signal achievement was not the coordination and rationalization of this newly developed human machine; it was the effectiveness with which they reduced their animate subjects, their vast armies of peasants and slaves, to utterly inanimate objects. The "megamachine" could be disbanded as easily as it could be mobilized; its human components lived out the greater part of their lives in the organic matrix of a village society. More important than the "megamachine" was the extent to which institutional technologies objectified the labor it generated and, above all, the laborers who formed it. Labor and the laborer suffered not merely under the whip of material exploitation but even more under the whip of spiritual degradation. As I have already noted, early hierarchies and ruling classes staked out their claims to sovereignty not only by a process of elevation but also by a process of debasement. The vast armies of corvee labor that dragged huge stone blocks along the banks of the Nile to build pyramids provided an image not just of an oppressed humanity, but of dehumanized beasts— ultimately, of inanimate objects upon whom their foremen and rulers could exercise their sense of power.* Their sweat formed the balm of rule; the stench from their bodies, an incense to tyranny; their corpses, a throne for mortal men to live by the heady norms of deities. For the many to become less was to make the few become more.

It is difficult for us to understand that political structures can be no less technical than tools and machines. In part, this difficulty arises because our minds have been imprinted by a dualistic metaphysics of "structures" and "superstructures." To dissect social experience into the economic and political, technical and cultural, has become a matter of second nature that resists any melding of one with the other. But this tendency is also partly due to an opportunistic political prudence that is wary of confronting the stark realities of power in a period of social accommodation. Better and safer to deal with technics as tools, machines, labor, and design than as coercive political institutions that organize the very implements, work, and imagination involved in the modern technical ensemble. Better to deal with how these means achieve certain destructive or constructive forms on the natural landscape than to explore the deformations they produce within subjectivity itself.

A liberatory technology presupposes liberatory institutions; a liberatory sensibility requires a liberatory society. By the same token, artistic crafts are difficult to conceive without an artistically crafted society, and the

---

* This curse of the crowned dwarf lingers on, from the pyramid of Cheops to the concentration camps of Hitler and Stalin—indeed, from the silver mines of Laurium to the textile factories of Manchester. Far more repellent than the material hedonism of tyranny is its greatest single luxury: its pleasure principle of pain. To delight in the spectacle of degradation and suffering, rulers have created huge mortuaries and palaces whose construction consumed the lives of thousands merely to provide a cosmic shelter for the few. Not for nothing did the Pharaohs of Egypt complete their tombs long before their deaths: the loathsome pleasure in witnessing the construction of these strictly human-made edifices was as great as the contemplation of their own grandeur.

"inversion of tools" is impossible without a radical inversion of all social and productive relationships. To speak of "appropriate technologies," "convivial tools," and "voluntary simplicity" without *radically* challenging the political "technologies," the media "tools," and the bureaucratic "complexities" that have turned these concepts into elitist "art forms" is to completely betray their revolutionary promise as a challenge to the existing social structure. What renders Buckminster Fuller's "spaceship" mentality and the design mentality of the "how-to-do-it" catalogues, periodicals, and impresarios of the "appropriate technology movement" particularly unsavory is their readiness to make "pragmatic" compromises with the political technologies of governmental and quasigovernmental agencies that nourish the very technologies they profess to oppose.

෬

Once we grant that the term "technics" must also include political, managerial, and bureaucratic institutions, we are obliged to seek the nontechnical spheres—the *social* spheres—that have resisted the technical control of social life. More precisely, how can the social sphere absorb the machines that foster the mechanization of society? I have already noted that the great majority of humankind often resisted technical development. Historically, Europeans stood almost alone in their willingness to accept and foster technical innovation uncritically. And even this proclivity occurred fairly late, with the emergence of modern capitalism. The historical puzzle of what renders some cultures more amenable to technical developments than others can only be resolved concretely—by exploring various cultures internally and revealing, if possible, the nature of their development.

The most important feature of technics in a pre-industrial societal complex is the extent to which it ordinarily is *adaptive* rather than *innovative*. Where a culture is rich in social structure, where it enjoys a wealth of human relationships, communal responsibilities, and a shared body of mutual concerns, it tends to *elaborate* a new technical ensemble rather than "develop" it. Controlled by the constraints of usufruct, complementarity, the irreducible minimum, and disaccumulation, early societies tended to elaborate technics with considerable prudence and with a keen sensitivity for the extent to which it could be integrated into existing social institutions. Ordinarily, the ability of technics to alter a societal structure significantly was the exception. Technical innovation occurred in response to major climatic changes or to violent invasions that often transformed the invader as much as the invaded.

Even when the "superstructure" of a society changed considerably or acquired a highly dynamic character, the "structure" of the society changed little or not at all. The "riddle of the unchangeability of Asian societies," as Marx was to call it, is in fact the solution to the entire puzzle of the interaction of society with technics. Where technics—bureaucratic, priestly, and dynastic as well as tools, machines, and new forms of labor—encroached upon the social life of tribes and villages, the latter tended to bifurcate from the former and stolidly develop a life and dynamic of its own. The real powers of the Asian village to resist technical invasions or to assimilate them to their social forms lay not in a fixed "systematic division of labor," as Marx believed. Its powers of resistance lay in the intensity of Indian family life, in the high degree of care, mutualism, courtesy, and human amenities that villagers shared as cultural norms, in the rituals that surrounded personal and social life, in the profound sense of rootedness in a communal group, and in the deep sense of meaning these cultural elaborations imparted to the community.

It is surprising to learn how technical innovation left vast aspects of social life untouched and often contributed very little to an explanation of major historical developments. Despite the extraordinary technical ensemble it created, the Neolithic Revolution changed relatively little in the societies that fostered it or adopted its technics. Within the same community, hunting coexisted with newly developed systems of horticulture up to the threshold of "civilization," and often well into antiquity in many areas. Village settlements, often highly mobile in Central Europe, retained strong tribalistic features in the Near East. James Mellaart's work on Çätal Hüyük, a Neolithic city in central Turkey, presents a very sizable community of thousands—well-equipped with a fairly sophisticated technology—that apparently was distinguished for its matricentricity, its egalitarian character, and its pacific qualities. As recently as 350 A.D., Indians of the Nazca culture in the coastal regions of Peru provided "the general picture [of] a sedentary democratic people without marked class distinctions or authoritarianism, possibly without an established religion," observes J. Alden Mason. Unlike the nearby Moche culture of the same period, the Nazca culture exhibits

> less difference in the "richness" or poverty of the graves, and women seem to be on an equality with men in this respect. The apparent absence of great public works, of extensive engineering features, and of temple pyramids implies a lack of authoritarian leadership. Instead, the leisure time of the people seems to have been spent in individual production, especially in the making of perfect, exquisite textiles and pottery vessels.

By no means is it clear that such Neolithic techniques as pottery, weaving, metallurgy, food cultivation, and new means of transportation altered in any qualitative sense the values of usufruct, complementarity, and the irreducible minimum that prevailed in hunting-gathering societies. In many cases, they may have reinforced them. At a time when the words "Neolithic Revolution" are meant to convey sweeping societal changes that technical innovations are believed to have induced, it may be wise to restore some balance by emphasizing the continuity in values, outlook, and community responsibilities the new villages preserved and possibly enhanced.

New World prehistory is a mine of data, provocative issues, and imaginative possibilities so heavily biased by neo-Marxist interpretations that its cultures seem to be mere reactions to climatic and technical factors. Yet after we have categorized Indian communities according to inventories of their "tool kits" and environmental surroundings, we are often surprised to find how markedly they resemble one another attitudinally, in their basic cultural substance, even ceremonially. Among bands, tribes, chiefdoms, and states we find an extraordinary commonality of outlook, basic human conventions, communal solidarity, and mutual care that tends to override their different economic activities as food gatherers, hunters, food cultivators, and the various combinations thereof. These similarities are strongest on the community level of the society, not its political or quasipolitical summits.

Technics, in the narrow, instrumental meaning of the term, does not fully or even adequately account for the institutional differences between a fairly democratic federation such as the Iroquois and a highly despotic empire such as the Inca. From a strictly instrumental viewpoint, the two structures were supported by almost identical "tool kits." Both engaged in horticultural practices that were organized around primitive implements and wooden hoes. Their weaving and metalworking techniques were very similar; their containers were equally functional. Like all New World societies, they both lacked large domestic animals for agricultural purposes, plows, wheeled vehicles, pottery wheels, mechanical spinning and weaving machines, a knowledge of smelting, bellows, and modestly advanced carpentry tools—in short, virtually all the techniques that mark the most significant advances of the Neolithic. When we look at the Iroquois and Inca "tool kits," we seem closer to the late Paleolithic than to the high Neolithic. Nor do we find marked differences between them in their orientation toward sharing, communal aid, and internal solidarity. At the *community* level of social life, Iroquois and Inca populations were immensely similar—and richly articulated in their social and cultural qualities.

Yet at the *political* level of social life, a democratic confederal structure of five woodland Indian tribes obviously differs decisively from a centralized, despotic structure of mountain Indian chiefdoms. The former, a highly libertarian confederation, was cemented by elected but recallable chiefs (in some cases chosen by women), popular assemblies, a consensual decision-making procedure in the united tribal council in matters of war, the prevalence of matrilineal descent, and a considerable degree of personal freedom. The latter, a massively authoritarian state, was centered around the person of a deified "emperor" with theoretically unlimited power; it was marked by a far-flung bureaucratic infrastructure, by patrilineal descent and by a totally subservient peasantry. Communal management of resources and produce among the Iroquois tribes occurred at the clan level. By contrast, Inca resources were largely state-owned, and much of the empire's produce was simply confiscation of food and textile materials and their redistribution from central and local storehouses. The Iroquois worked together freely, more by inclination than by compulsion; the Inca peasantry provided corvee labor to a patently exploitive priesthood and state apparatus under a nearly industrial system of management.

Doubtless, climatic and geographic factors helped sculpt the structure developed by the two systems of association. A highly forested area would tend to yield looser political units than would fairly open geographic areas, where visibility between communities was high. The variegated physiography of the Andes, from the lush Amazon valley to the virtually barren Pacific slopes, would have placed a high premium on mobilized labor, a pooling of resources from different ecosystems, and a more secure and diversified redistribution of goods. But the very mountainous terrain that fostered decentralization among the Greek *poleis* did not seem to inhibit centralization among the Inca, and the temperate forest land that fostered a hierarchical society in medieval Europe did not obstruct the superb elaboration of an egalitarian democracy in pre-Columbian America.

Hindsight and a highly selective choice of "tool kits" may help us describe *how* a band developed into a tribe, a tribe into a chiefdom, and a chiefdom into a state, but they do not explain *why* these developments occurred. From time immemorial, hierarchies and classes have used shifts in emphasis to reverse social relations from systems of freedom to those of rule, without dropping a single term from the vocabulary of organic society. Ironically, this cunning on the part of the rulers indicates the extent to which the community valued its egalitarian and complementarian traditions.

∞

Quite apart from New World prehistory, a vast social development began much earlier in the Near East, from which it radiated outward over the entire Eurasian continent. The "Neolithic Revolution" of the Old World was technically more dramatic and more ancient than that of the New. But technics, in a strictly instrumental sense, explains surprisingly little about the sweeping developments that carried society into semi-industrialized—indeed, relatively mechanized—systems of agriculture, pottery, metallurgy, weaving, and above all a highly coordinated system of mobilizing labor.

None of the great empires of antiquity developed substantially beyond a late Neolithic or early Iron Age technics. From a strictly instrumental viewpoint, their technical ensemble was notable for its smallness of scale. As Henry Hodges oberves in his broad assessment of classical technics:

> The ancient world under the domination of Rome had in fact reached a kind of climax in the technological field. By the end of the Roman period many technologies had advanced as far as possible with the equipment then available, and for further progress to be made, a bigger or more complex plant was required. Despite the fact that the Romans were quite capable of indulging in gigantic undertakings, their technologies remained at the small-equipment level. Thus, for example, if it was required to increase the output of iron the number of furnaces was multiplied, but the furnaces themselves remained the same size. Whatever the cause, the idea of building a larger furnace and devising machinery to work it seems to have been beyond the Roman mind. As a result; the last few centuries of Roman domination produced very little that was technologically new. No new raw materials were discovered, no new processes invented, and one can indeed say that long before Rome fell all technological innovation had ceased.

But innovation there surely was—not in the instruments of production but in the instruments of administration. In terms of its far-reaching bureaucracy, legal system, military forces, mobilization of labor, and centralization of power, the Roman Empire at its peak was the heir, if not the equal, of the authoritarian apparatus of preceding empires.

Probably no imperial system in the Old World ever achieved the totalitarian attributes of Egypt or the brutality of Assyria. Corvee labor gave the Near East its public buildings, temples, mortuaries, megalithic sculptures and symbols, and its highly coordinated irrigation works. Egypt and Mesopotamia led the way by enlisting hundreds of thousands to raise the structures that still monumentalize their existence. But the early commandeering of labor by the Near Eastern despotisms established no distinctions of class or status: artisans as well as peasants, city folk as well as rural folk, wealthy as well as poor, scribes as well as laborers, even Egyptian priests as well as their congregations—all were subject to the labor demands of the State. Later this "democracy" of toil was to be honored in only the breach, until it gave way to a visibly onerous burden on the agrarian and urban poor.

In regions with small farmers, it was difficult to establish totalitarian states. Where their position was weakened, or where large labor surpluses were readily available, centralized states were much more possible and often developed. Carthage and Rome cultivated the *latifundia* system: a plantation economy worked by gang (largely slave) labor. Sparta introduced a communistic warrior-elite system in which each citizen at birth was given a small, state-owned landed competence, worked by serf-like helots, that reverted to the *polis* after his death. In contrast, Athens and Hebrew Palestine developed a yeoman farming class that worked the land with family labor and often with two or three slaves.

But apart from a few states that were based on the individual farmer, the authentic hallmark of early "civilizations" was an extensive system of mobilized labor—either partly or wholly devoted to food cultivation and monumental works. Where elaborate irrigation systems were necessary, the underclass of riverine societies indubitably gained greater material security from these totalitarian systems of labor organization and redistribution than they would have enjoyed on their own. Egyptian mortuary records celebrate the success with which the Pharaohs alleviated local famines. But what the peasantry acquired in the form of buffers to nature's uncertainties they may have more than lost in the onerous toil that was exacted from them for often frivolous monumental works. Nor can we be very sure, unlike archaeologists of a generation ago, that the highly centralized regimes of the Old World (and New) greatly enhanced the coordination and effectiveness of alluvial irrigation systems. A carefully tended network of trenches, canals, and pools had appeared in arid areas long before the "high civilizations" of antiquity surfaced. That the "hydraulic" communities of the pre-dynastic world were sorely afflicted by conflicts over water and land rights was clearly a serious problem, but centralization often served merely to escalate the level of conflict to an even more destructive one between kingdoms and empires.

From the New World to the Old, the stupendous elaboration of centralized states and the proliferation of courts, nobles, priesthoods, and military elites was supported by a highly parasitic institutional technology of domination composed of armies, bureaucrats, tax farmers, juridical agencies and a septic, often brutal belief system based on sacrifice and self-abnegation. Without this political technology, the mobilization of labor, the collection of vast material surpluses, and the deployment of a surprisingly simple "tool-kit" for monumental technical tasks would have been inconceivable. Beyond the responsibility of massing huge numbers of human beings into regimented tasks, this system had three essential goals: to intensify the labor process, to abstract it, and to objectify it. A carefully planned effort was undertaken to piece work together so that the State could extract every bit of labor from the "masses," reduce labor to undifferentiated labor-time, and transmute human beings into mere instruments of production. Historically, this unholy trinity of intensification, abstraction, and objectification weighed more heavily on humanity as a malignant verdict of social development than did theology's myth of original sin. No "revolution" in tools and machines was needed to produce this affliction. It stemmed primarily from the elaboration of hierarchy into crystallized warrior elites, and from the genesis of an institutional technics of administration largely embodied in the State, particularly in the bureaucracy that managed the economy. Later, this technics of administration was to acquire a highly industrial character and find its most striking expression in the modern factory system.

○ℜ

The manorial economy of the Middle Ages, like the guild system of its towns, never came to social terms with ancient concepts of labor and technics. Infused by Roman concepts of justice, Germanic tribalistic traditions existed for centuries in unresolved tension with the centralistic claims of materially weak monarchies and an ideologically suspect Papacy. Forced back from its inland sea, Europe was buried in its huge forests, bogs, and mountains—a victim of its own accursed invaders from the north and the east. Here, the manor became the social interregnum that cleared the ground for a new historic point of departure. From the eleventh century onward, technics bolted forward with an energy that had not been seen since the Neolithic Revolution. In successive order, the use of windmills was followed by the horse-collar (which made it possible to pull heavy plows and transport inland goods cheaply), striking advances in metallurgy and metallic tools, an imposing system of highly developed agriculture, a complex machine technics based largely on wooden components, and a sophisticated version of the ancient water-wheel that would have surprised the most informed Roman engineers.

Yet none of these technical innovations produced any decisive changes in medieval social relations. Except for the Greek *polis*, the medieval towns were usually more democratic than the urban centers of antiquity, the agrarian system less mobilized and rationalized, the craft occupations more individualistic and democratically structured. We cannot account for this favorable constellation of socio-technical circumstances without noting that the State and its bureaucracies had reached a nadir in the history of political centralization and bureaucratization. Until the emergence of nation-states in England, France, and Spain between the fifteenth and seventeenth centuries, Europe was comparatively free of the despotisms and bureaucracies that coated the social life of North Africa, the Near East, and Asia.

The one class to benefit most from the rising nation-state was the European bourgeoisie. Increasingly centralized monarchies and their growing bureaucratic minions imposed the king's peace on the inland trade routes of Europe, the king's courts on local arbitrary systems of justice, the king's mint on the erratic metallic currency distributed by financial robber barons, the king's navy on nests of maritime pirates, and the king's armies on newly colonized markets. This structure, even more than any appreciable "advances" in instrumental technics, provided the basis for the next great system of labor mobilization: the factory. The modern origins of abstract labor are found not only in the market economy and its clearly defined monetary system of exchange ratios, but also in the English countryside. There, the "factors" who carted raw materials and semi-finished fabrics to cottage workers eventually brought them together under a single roof (a "factory") to rationalize and intensify a fairly traditional body of technics under the watchful eye of foremen and the icy stare of mean-spirited, heartless, and cunning industrial entrepreneurs.

The early factory introduced no sweeping technical dispensation other than the abstraction, rationalization, and objectification of labor and its embodiment in human beings. Spinning, weaving, and dyeing were still performed with all the machines that cottagers had used in their own homes for generations. No engines or prime movers were added to this old ensemble until the machinery for spinning, weaving, and dyeing yarn were invented a century or so later. But a new technics had supplanted the old: the technics of supervision, with its heartless intensification of the labor-process, its conscienceless introduction of fear and insecurity, and its debasing forms of supervisory behavior. Where the "factors" had bought products, not people, the factory bought people, not products. This reduction of labor from its embodiment in products into a capacity of people was decisive; it turned fairly autonomous individuals into totally administered products and gave products an autonomy that made them seem like people. The animate quality that things acquired—qualities which Marx aptly called the "fetishism of commodities"—was purchased at the expense of the animate qualities of people. An underclass was being produced that was almost as inorganic as the factory in which it worked and the tools it used—a transubstantiation of humanity itself that was to have profound consequences for the legacy of domination and the future of human freedom.

Leaving aside the stupendous array of devices and prime movers that the factory was to commandeer in its service, its most important technical achievement has occurred in the technics of administration. No less important than its evolving technical armamentarium was the evolution of the joint-stock company into the multinational corporation, and of the feisty, muscular foreman into the suave, multilingual corporate executive. Nor was the State to be spared its own change from a royal court, with circuit judges and ink-sputtered scribes, into a stupendous bureaucratic population that, together with its military strong-arm, formed a nation-state in its own right within the confines of the nation. The bureaucratic apparatus that underpinned overtly totalitarian monarchies such as the Incas of Peru and Pharaohs of Egypt is dwarfed by the managerial, civil, and corporate bureaucracies of a single American, European, or Japanese commercial city.

But no mere description of this development can pass for an explanation. Bureaucracy, conceived as an institutionalized technics in its own right, may well have its origins in the primordial world. I refer not merely to the internal dialectic of hierarchy that yields a legacy of domination in the forms of gerontocracies, priestly corporations, patriarchy, and warrior chieftains. I am equally concerned with the civil sphere of the male, who produces rationalized ceremonial and military systems as compensatory mechanisms for his own ambivalent status in organic society. He is necessarily less fulfilled in a domestic society, where woman forms the core of authentic social activity, than in a civil society— but one that he must elaborate into a fully articulated and structured sphere of life. His very identity is at stake in a world where production and reproduction are centered around woman, where the "magic" of life inheres in her own personal life-processes, where the rearing of the young, the organization of the home, and the fecundity of nature seem to be functions of her sexuality and personality. Whether he "envies" matricentricity or not is irrelevant; he must evolve an identity of his own which may reach its most warped expression in warfare, arrogance, and subjugation.

The male's identity does not *have* to find fulfillment in an orbit of domination, but where this does occur on a significant scale, it is fatal to the entire social environment. Not only is the community itself transformed by the elaboration of this civil sphere into a political, often militaristic, one; the surrounding communities must also respond—either protectively or aggressively—to the rot developing within the social ecosystem. An apparently democratic, egalitarian, possibly matricentric culture such as the Andean Nazca would have been obliged to react aggressively to an authoritarian, hierarchical, patricentric—and militaristic—culture such as the nearby Moche. Sooner or later, both would have had to confront each other as tyrannical chiefdoms, or the Nazca would have been compelled to defer to the Moche. Given sufficient exposure to external forces, a process of negative selection on the level of political life has always been at work to favor the expansion of ruthless cultures at the expense of the more equable ones. What is surprising about social development is not the emergence of New and Old World despotisms, but their *absence* in large areas of the world generally. It is testimony to the benign power inherent in organic society that so many cultures did *not* follow the social route to Statehood, mobilized labor, class distinctions, and professional warfare—indeed, that they often retreated into remoter areas to spare themselves this destiny.

Perhaps the most important ideological factor to foster the development of capitalism in European society was Christianity, with its strong emphasis on individuation, its high regard for the redemptive role of labor, its elevation of an abstract Supernature over a concrete nature, and its denial of the importance of community as distinguished from the universal Papal congregation. That individual initiative, even more than a high sense of individuality, promoted human will and inventiveness hardly requires elaboration. The Thomas Edisons and Henry Fords of the world are not great individuals, but they are surely grasping egos—vulgar caricatures of the Biblical "angry men." The transformation of Yahweh's Will into man's will is too obvious a temptation to be evaded. Even the Church's ecclesiastics and missionaries, driven by their zealous fanaticism, are more transparently bourgeois men than mere Homeric heroes who lived by the canons of a shame culture.

This emphasis on the personal ego, with its voyaging sense of enterprise, was reinforced by Christianity's obsession with labor. Historically, the Church placed its highest stakes on faith rather than works, on contemplation rather than labor. But in practice, the medieval Christian orders were mundane working establishments which left a heavy imprint on the technologically undeveloped peasantry around them. Monasteries played a major role in innovating technics and in rationalizing labor; indeed, they pioneered as missions, not only in the dissemination of faith but in the dissemination of technical knowledge and planned, orderly systems of work. Here, they found a welcome response, for there was no need to preach a gospel of work to highly impoverished agrarian communities that desperately needed the technical wisdom of knowledgeable and disciplined monastic orders.

The work ethic, despite its ill-repute today as a Calvinist trick, was not invented by the bourgeoisie or, for that matter, by preindustrial ruling classes. Ironically, it can be traced back to the socially underprivileged themselves. The work ethic appears for the first time in Hesiod's *Works and Days*, a peasant *Iliad* of the seventh century before Christ, whose antiheroic workaday title and tenor reflect the tribute the poor man pays to his poor life. For the first time in a written legacy, work—in contrast to valor—appears as an attribute of personal nobility and responsibility. The virtuous man who bends his neck to the yoke of toil occupies the center of the poetic stage and enviously elbows out the aristocrat who lives off his labor. Thus do poor men assemble their virtues as the attributes of toil, renunciation, and husbandry, all the more to affirm their superiority over the privileged who enjoy lives of ease, gratification, and pleasure. Later, the ruling classes will recognize how rich an ideological treasure trove the Hesiods have bestowed upon them. They too will extol the virtues of poverty for the meek, who will find treasure in heaven while the arrogant will pay in hell for their sinful "heaven" on earth.

Hence, toil has its rewards for the Christian congregation, just as contemplation has its rewards for the Christian elect. These rewards, to be sure, remain rather vague: an ethereal, everlasting life that may well be more boring than the earthly one, an unceasing reverence for God, a world abstracted of the luscious concretes that render Cokaygne so superior to Paradise. In its abstract Supernature, Christianity already begins to spawn the vagaries of abstract matter and abstract labor. Yahweh is a nameless God, nature is merely the epiphenomenon of his Word, and even good works are in themselves less virtuous than the activity of working.

The dissociation of working from works—of the abstract process of laboring from the concrete use-values work produces—is savagely dystopian. The lingering concrete use-values of things in a world that has largely reduced them to exchange-values is the hidden romance buried within the warped life of the commodity. To deny them is to deny humanity's claim to the satisfactions and pleasures they are meant to bestow. An overly ascetic and rationalistic outlook is the counterpart of an overly hedonistic and instinctive one. But this denial is precisely the function of a theology that places the Word before the deed, Supernature before nature, and working before works.

As to broad ideological matters, Christianity had fewer differences with Galileo than either of them realized. The Galilean universe of lifeless matter and perpetual motion differs very little in principle from the Christian view of nature as inherently meaningless without the illumination of a heavenly Supernature. By Newton's time, one could read (even write) the *Principia* without feeling any sense of conflict between the Church and the Royal Society. It was naïveté and distrust that separated for so long such kindred outlooks as the Christian and the scientific. The true smoke of peace between them was finally inhaled not from the bowls of ritual Indian pipes but from the belching smokestacks of modern industry.

Finally, no religion assailed more earnestly the authenticity, intensity, and meaningfulness of community affiliation than Christianity. The Stoic plea for a recognition of a universal *humanitas* entailed not a denial of one's loyalty to the community but merely the individual's recognition of mystical affinity to the "city of Man." The Christian plea for a universal *humanitas* was actually more cunning. It shrewdly acknowledged the claims of the State but tried to replace the community's claims with those of the "city of God," notably the Church. The Church's jealousy toward the Christian's community loyalties was lethal; the religion demanded strict obedience to its clerical infrastructure. The notion of Congregation implied that the clergy had priority over all communal claims upon persons—indeed, over all relationships among persons other than those ordained by God—and over all codes of solidarity other than the laws of Deuteronomy and Christ's strictures to his disciples. Thus the Church lived in covert hostility with the community—just as the State could find no peace with the blood oath, even in its patriarchal form. Here, industrial capitalism, like science before it, found a perfect fit between the bourgeois concept of citizenship and the Christian. The free-floating ego, divested of all community roots, became its ideal of individuality and personality. The "masterless men" that all previous societies had feared so intensely became the new image of the untrammeled, self-reliant entrepreneur—and his counterpart in the uprooted, propertyless proletariat.

We must recognize what this attempt to divest technics of its community matrix imparted to the spirit of technical innovation. If the true meaning of *techné* includes an ethical emphasis on limit, then this emphasis was valid only if there was a social agency to nourish and enforce the conception. To the extent that *techné* was thrown into opposition to community, the word began to lose its original ethical connotations and become strictly instrumental. Once societal constraints based on ethics and communal institutions were demolished ideologically and physically, technics could be released to follow no dictates other than private self-interest, profit, accumulation, and the needs of a predatory market economy. The time-honored limits that had contained technics in a societal matrix disappeared, and for the first time in history technics was free to follow its own development without any goals except those dictated by the market.

⅋

The Romans replicated their small iron furnaces instead of enlarging them not because they were technologically obtuse but largely because the communities from which the Roman imperium was formed held its instrumental and institutional technics in check. To say that the Roman mind could not conceive of larger furnaces is simply to reveal that its technical imagination was formed by an artisan conception of the world, however grandiose its political imagination. This bifurcation of State and society, of the central political power and the community, is crucial to an understanding of the nature of a libertarian technology and the relationship of technology to freedom.

Organic society, while institutionally warped and tainted by pre-industrial "civilizations," retained a high degree of vitality in the everyday lives of so-called ordinary people. The extended family still functioned as an attenuated form of the traditional clan and often provided a highly viable substitute for it. Elders still enjoyed considerable social prestige even after their political standing had diminished, and kinship ties were still fairly strong, if not decisive, in defining many strategic human relationships. Communal labor formed a conspicuous part of village enterprise, particularly in agriculture, where it was cemented by the need to share tools and cattle, to pool resources in periods of difficulty, and to foster a technical reciprocity without which many communities could not have survived major crises. One does not have to look for, as Marx put it, "the possession of land in common" or an "unalterable division of labor" that served as "a fixed plan and basis for action" in India's villages in order to know that under the tightly woven political carpet of the State was an active, subterranean social world based on consensus, ideological agreement, shared customs, and a commonality of religious beliefs.

These traits are found even where political despotisms tend to be highly invasive. And they often are highly marked by peasant attitudes toward labor. Their most striking feature is the extent to which any kind of communal toil, however onerous, can be transformed by the workers themselves into festive occasions that serve to reinforce community ties. In a hypothetical account of the work habits of Inca peasants, Mason surmises that:

> Like all cooperative labour, it must have been a jovial and not an onerous occasion, with plenty of chicha beer, singing, and bantering. The songs, perhaps in honor of the gods when working the church lands, or in praise of the emperor while engaged in the state fields, were appropriate to the occasion. As soon as the fields of the gods were finished, the work was repeated on the government lands, and then the people were free to cultivate their own fields. There was a communal spirit of helpfulness, and if a man was called away on state business such as military service his neighbours quietly attended to his agricultural needs.

To the extent that recent archeological discoveries and research into current Andean labor customs throw any light on their work habits, Mason's account seems reasonably accurate. Beneath the massive structure of a highly despotic State that closely supervised its underclasses, the peasantry lived a distinctly separate and socially organic life of its own. Indeed, the Inca State implicitly acknowledged this covert immunity to its controls by punishing the community as a whole if its individual members were guilty of certain infractions of State regulations. This practice is so universal and ancient that it recurs repeatedly throughout history.

One of the most vivid accounts of how communal labor traditions and forms linger on into modern times, often transforming grueling toil into festive work, appears in Tolstoy's *Anna Karenina*. Levin (Tolstoy's typical fictional counterpart) observes peasants haying on his sister's estate. Sitting transfixed on a haycock, he is "fascinated" while teeming peasants in the meadow buoyantly cut the hay, stack it, and pitch it with hayforks on wooden carts.

> Before him in the bend of the river behind the marsh, moved a gaily colored line of peasant women, chattering loudly and merrily, while the scattered hay was rapidly rising into gray, zig-zag ridges on the pale-green stubble.

The men follow the women with their hayforks until the haying is almost complete. The dialogue that ensues is inimitable:

> "Make hay while the sun shines and the hay you'll get will be lovely," said the old beekeeper, squatting down beside Levin. "What lovely hay, sir! Tea, not hay. Look, sir, at the way they pick 'em up! Like scattering grain to the ducks," he added, pointing to the growing haycocks.

The work, in fact, is nearly done and the beekeeper calls out to his son, who responds:

> "The last one, Dad!" shouted the young man, reining in the horse and, smiling, looked around at a cheerful, rosy-cheeked peasant woman, who was driving by, standing on the front part of a cart, flicking the ends of his hempen reins.*

It is tempting to focus our descriptions of technology and our accounts of technological innovation on the large-scale works of mobilized labor favored by early states and ruling elites. The achievements of power—its temples, mortuaries, and palaces—evoke our ingrained awe of power. The hydraulic systems of great alluvial empires like the Egyptian, Mesopotamian, and Asian, and the cities, roads, and megalithic structures of pre-Columbian America cast a long shadow

---

* Lest a reader remind me that Czarist Russia was not an agrarian paradise, I would add that this is precisely my point. Such scenes reflect not Czarist Russia but an earlier time that was to persist in Russian peasant life despite the landlordism of the old regime and the industrialism of the new. Long before I read Tolstoy's account, I heard even more vivid stories of the same nature from my plebian parents who were born in Russian towns and villages near the turn of the century, for there was not only chatter, laughter, and an all-embracing sense of communal warmth, but also eating, drinking, singing, and often dancing. To make toil truly onerous, the people had to be cheated of their own buoyancy, rhythms, natural environment, and communal spirit. Early in time, when the pounding of a drum and the lash of a whip replaced the spontaneous pleasure of physical activity, labor degenerated into the tyranny of toil and the penalty for belonging to the wrong social class.

over history. Tragically, this shadow has largely obscured the technics of peasants and artisans at the "base" of society: their widespread networks of villages and small towns, their patchwork farms and household gardens; their small enterprises; their markets organized around barter; their highly mutualistic work systems; their keen sense of sociality; and their delightfully individuated crafts, mixed gardens, and local resources that provided the real sustenance and artwork of ordinary people. A complete history of technology, food cultivation, and art has yet to be written from the standpoint of the so-called commoners, just as has a complete history of women, ethnic minorities, and the oppressed generally.

In some cases, as we now know, even large political empires like the Hittite Empire were based overwhelmingly on small farms. Typically, these were worked by five or six people, using perhaps two oxen, and the cultivable land was divided into mixed croplands, vineyards, orchards, and pastures that rarely supported more than small flocks of goats and sheep. In imperial Roman times, yeoman farms that had lingered on from the early republican era coexisted with immense *latifundia* worked by thousands of slaves. The beautifully terraced slopes that marked agricultural belts from Indonesia to Peru were worked not merely for the State but (often segregated from State-owned lands) for the needs of the extended family and local community. If Chinese corvee labor in the Sui dynasty (c. 600 A.D.) may have exceeded five million commoners (who were under a guard of 50,000 troops), the great majority of the peasantry continued to work its own plots, cultivating mixed crops and orchards, and raising domestic animals. Even Aztec agriculture, despite the highly despotic militaristic state that governed central Mexico, was organized primarily around clan-type horticulture, notably the lovely floating or *chinampa* gardens that lined and infiltrated the shallows of the Lake of Mexico.

⳧

Viewed at its agrarian "base," medieval Europe may well represent the apotheosis of the small, agriculturally mixed farm within the social framework of a class society. The famous "open field system," with its rotation of fallow and cultivated croplands, was organized around individually farmed narrow strips. But strip farming necessarily involved such close coordination of planting and harvesting between cultivators of adjacent strips that the peasantry normally shared its plows, draft animals, and implements. Not uncommonly, periodic redistributions of the strips were made to meet the material needs of larger families. Carried to the village level, these farming techniques fostered free peasant assemblies, a lively sense of reciprocity, and the reinforcement of archaic communal traditions such as the use of uncultivable land for "commons" to pasture animals and collect wood for fuel and construction materials. The manorial economy of the territorial lords by no means dominated this increasingly libertarian village society; rather, it retained only a loosening hold over the artisan and commercial towns nearby. In later years, the villages and towns in many areas of Europe, thoroughly schooled in the practice of self-management, gained supremacy over the local barons and ecclesiastics. Particularly in Switzerland and the Lowlands, but to a very great extent throughout western Europe, villages and towns established fairly powerful, often long-lived peasant federal republics and strong urban confederations.

The new, comparatively libertarian "institutional technics" spawned by this fascinating world yielded, in turn, an equally remarkable elaboration of a human-scale, comparatively libertarian instrumental technics. Aside from the watermills already in abundance throughout Europe (William the Conqueror's *Domesday Book* lists some 5,500 in about 3,000 English villages in 1086 A.D.), there were also windmills. Apparently derived from the ritual Tibetan prayerwheels, they had become so numerous by the thirteenth century that the Belgian town of Ypres alone could celebrate the fact that it had reared 120 windmills in its environs. Even more striking is the extraordinary, unprecedented variety of uses to which European waterwheels and windmills were put. This multipurpose character of medieval prime movers stunningly illustrates the extent to which unity in diversity is a correlate of ecological technics. Watermills, known as early as Greek times, had been used almost exclusively to mill grain; windmills, already in use in Persia as early as the eighth century, had probably been confined to the same limited uses. By contrast, the lively, alert, and increasingly individuated town and country people of the high and late Middle Ages deployed these new prime movers not only for restricted agricultural purposes but also to raise and trip ensembles of heavy hammers in forges, to operate lathes, to work bellows in blast furnaces, and to turn grindstones for polishing metals as well as grinding grains. The new interest in machinery, as yet small in scale and fairly simple in design, led to a highly variegated use of cams, cranks, and pumps, and of an ingenious combination of gears, levers, and pulleys. It also fostered the triumphal invention of the mechanical clock, which lessened the need for arduous toil and greatly increased the effectiveness of craft production.

What is highly attractive about the new vitality that appeared in medieval technics is not simply the sense of innovation characterizing its development; rather, it is the sense of elaboration that marked the adaptation of the new to the social conditions of the old. Contrary to popular images that read our own values back into the medieval world, the technical "utopians" of that time were far removed in spirit and outlook from the technocratic "utopians" or futurists of the present era. Roger Bacon, the thirteenth-century Franciscan, predicted large, highly powered ships steered by a single operator, flying machines, and wagons that would travel at considerable speed by their own motive power. Figures like Bacon were not prescient engineers of an era to come; they were primarily theologians rather than technicians, alchemists rather than scientists, and scholastics rather than craftsmen. They bore witness more to supernatural powers than to human ingenuity. Some three centuries were to pass before authentic inventors like Leonardo da Vinci secretly sketched their cryptic designs and wrote their notes in a script that could only be read by using a mirror.

Technics in Bacon's time was deeply embedded in (and its development constrained by) a richly communal social matrix that fostered an organic epistemology of design, an aesthetic use of materials, an elaboration of an adaptive technics, a deep respect for diversity, and a strong emphasis on quality, skill, and artfulness. These instrumental norms reflected the social norms of the time. Town and country were much too close to each other to render socially and intellectually acceptable the geometric temples, the urban gigantism, the inorganic social relations, and the deadening images of a mechanical world. However much the Church emphasized heavenly Supernature over earthly nature, the world of nature came increasingly to be seen as gift of a heavenly dispensation—a sensibility that found its theological voice in the ideas of Saint Francis. Work and the high premium placed on skills were much too individuated to make large masses of peasants and "masterless men" amenable to the mobilized labor systems of earlier eras. To the extent that we can think in terms of sizable masses of people, we must think more in terms of ideological crusades rather than of highly controlled labor forces. Owing to its decentralized character and its Christian sense of individual worth, medieval society was simply not capable of utilizing, much less mobilizing, huge numbers of "commoners" to monumentalize itself in public works. For all the abuses of feudal society, corvee labor was confined to the maintenance of public roads and tenant-type systems of food cultivation for the manorial lords, to defensive structures that were needed by the community as well as the barons, and to miscellaneous "gifts" of labor to the nobility and Church.

Technics itself tended to follow an age-old tradition of nestling closely into a local ecosystem, of adapting itself sensitively to local resources and their unique capacity to sustain life. Accordingly, it functioned as a highly specific catalyst between the people of an area and their environment. The rich knowledge of habitat—of region, local flora and fauna, soil conditions, even geology—that enabled people like the Bushmen or San to provision themselves in (as it seemed to Victorian Europe) an utter desert wasteland survived well beyond primordial times into the European Middle Ages. This high sense of the hidden natural wealth of a habitat—a knowledge that has been so completely lost to modern humanity—kept the latent exploitative powers of technics well within the institutional, moral, and mutualistic boundaries of the local community. People did more than just live within the biotic potentialities of their ecosystem and remake it with an extraordinary sensitivity that fostered ecological diversity and fecundity. They also (often artistically) absorbed technically unique devices into this broad biosocial matrix and brought them into the service of their locality.

Only modern capitalism could seriously subvert this ancient sensibility and system of technical integration. And it did so not simply by replacing one instrumental ensemble by another. We gravely mistake capitalism's historically destructive role if we fail to see that it subverted a more fundamental dimension of the traditional social ensemble: the integrity of the human community. Once the market relationship—and its reduction of individual relationships to those of buyers and sellers—replaced the extended family, the guild, and its highly mutualistic network of consociation; once home and the place of production became separate, even antagonistic, arenas, dividing agriculture against craft and craft against factory; finally once town and country were thrown into harsh opposition to each other; then every organic and humanistic refuge from a highly mechanized and rationalized world became colonized by a monadic, impersonal, and alienated nexus of relationships. Community as such began to disappear. Capitalism invaded and undermined areas of social life that none of the great empires of the past could ever penetrate or even hope to absorb. Not only was the technical imagination savagely dismembered but also the human imagination. The cry "Imagination to Power!" became a plea not only for a free-play of fancy but also for a rediscovery of the very *power* to fantasize. Whether its advocates recognized it or not, the urge to bring imagination to power implied a restoration of the power of imagination itself.

❧

The recent emphasis on "limits to growth" and "appropriate technology" is riddled by the same ambiguities that have imparted a conflicting sense of promise and fear to "high technology." I have said enough about the danger of dissociating instrumental technics, "soft" or "hard," from institutional technics; I leave the elaboration of their integration to the closing, more reconstructive chapter of this book, where I shall explore the possible structures of freedom, of human relationships, and of personal subjectivity that delineate an "appropriate" social matrix for a libertarian technics. For the present, however, I must emphasize again that terms like "small," "soft," "intermediate," "convivial," and "appropriate" remain utterly vacuous adjectives unless they are radically integrated with emancipatory social structures and communitarian goals. Technology and freedom do not "coexist" with each other as two separate "realms" of life. Either technics is used to reinforce the larger social tendencies that render human consociation technocratic and authoritarian, or else a libertarian society must be created that can absorb technics into a constellation of emancipatory human and ecological relationships. A "small," "soft," "intermediate," "convivial," or "appropriate" technical design will no more transform an authoritarian society into an ecological one than will a reduction in the "realm of necessity," of the "working week," enhance or enlarge the "realm of freedom."

In addition to subverting the integrity of the human community, capitalism has tainted the classical notion of "living well" by fostering an irrational dread of material scarcity. By establishing quantitative criteria for the "good life," it has dissolved the ethical implications of "limit." This ethical lacuna raises a specifically technical problematic for our time. In equating "living well" with living affluently, capitalism has made it extremely difficult to demonstrate that freedom is more closely identified with personal *autonomy* than with affluence, with empowerment over life than with empowerment over things, with the emotional security that derives from a nourishing community life than with a material security that derives from the myth of a nature dominated by an all-mastering technology.

A radical social ecology cannot close its eyes to this new technological problematic. Over the past two centuries, almost every serious movement for social change has been confronted with the need to demonstrate that technics, "hard" or "soft," can more than meet the material needs of humanity without placing arbitrary limits upon a modestly sensible consumption of goods. The terms of the "black redistribution" have been historically altered: we are faced with problems not of disaccumulation but of rational systems of production. Post-scarcity, as I have emphasized in earlier works, does not mean mindless affluence; rather, it means a sufficiency of technical development that leaves individuals free to select their needs autonomously and to obtain the means to satisfy them. The existing technics of the western world—in principle, a technics that can be applied to the world at large—can render more than a sufficiency of goods to meet everyone's *reasonable* needs. Fortunately, an ample literature has already appeared to demonstrate that no one need be denied adequate food, clothing, shelter, and all the amenities of life.* The astringent arguments for "limits to growth" and the "life-boat ethic" so prevalent today have been reared largely on specious data and a cunning adaptation of resource problems to the "institutional technics" of an increasingly authoritarian State.

It is social ecology's crucial responsibility to demystify the tradition of a "stingy nature," as well as the more recent image of "high" technology as an unrelieved evil. Even more emphatically, social ecology must demonstrate that modern systems of production, distribution, and promotion of goods and needs are grossly irrational as well as antiecological. Whosoever sidesteps the conflicting alternatives between a potentially bountiful nature and an exploitive use of technics serves merely as an apologist for the prevailing irrationality. Certainly, no ethical argument in itself will ever persuade the denied and underprivileged that they must abdicate any claim to the relative affluence of capitalism. What must be demonstrated—and not merely on theoretical or statistical grounds alone—is that this affluence can ultimately be made available to all—but *should* be desirable to none.

---

* See "Toward a Liberatory Technology" in my *Post-Scarcity Anarchism* (Oakland: AK Press, 2004). On the actual availability of food and the politics of demography, see Frances Lappé and Joseph Collins, *Food First* (Boston: Houghton, Mifflin & Co., 1977); Richard Merrill, ed., *Radical Agriculture* (New York: Harper & Row, 1976); and Richard J. Barnett, *The Lean Years* (New York: Simon and Schuster, 1980). The Lappé-Collins book is the best of its kind on the "food problem" and compellingly refutes the myth that there is a "natural scarcity" of food and arable land, even in areas with rising populations. Although Barnett lines himself "up with the Cassandras," this is primarily because he believes that "timing" may lead to an excess of demand for petroleum and certain minerals over supply, not that nature is "stingy." Whether or not this is plausible as a viewpoint, I do not know. But his data reveal that we are faced not with an absolute shortage of materials but with an irrational society.

It is a betrayal of the entire message of social ecology to ask the world's poor to deny themselves access to the necessities of life on grounds that involve long-range problems of ecological dislocation, the shortcomings of "high" technology, and very specious claims of natural shortages in materials, while saying nothing at all about the artificial scarcity engineered by corporate capitalism.

Anything that is not renewable is exhaustible—this is a philistine truism. But confronted by such truisms, one may reasonably ask: When will it be exhausted? How? By whom? And for what reason? For the present there can be no serious claim that any major, irreplaceable resource will be exhausted until humanity can choose new alternatives— "new" referring not simply to material or technical alternatives but above all to institutional and social ones. The task of advancing humanity's right to choose from among alternatives, particularly institutional ones, that may yet offer us a rational, humanistic, and ecological trajectory has not yet been fulfilled by "high" or by "low" technology. In sum, "high" technology must be used by serious social ecologists to demonstrate that, on rational grounds, it is less desirable than ecological technologies. "High" technology must be permitted to exhaust its specious claims as the token of social "progress" and human well-being—all the more to render the development of ecological alternatives a matter of *choice* rather than the product of a cynical "necessity."

Still another issue that may well be regarded as a new technological problematic is the association of the "realm of freedom" with "free time," the political counterpart of Marx's "abstract labor" or "labor time." Here, too, we encounter a tyrannical abstraction: the notion that freedom itself is a *res temporalis*, a temporal thing. The *res temporalis* of free time, like the *res extensa* of irreducible matter, is dead—the "dead time" from which the Parisian students of May– June, 1968 sought freedom by translating time itself into the process of being free. Viewed from this standpoint, "free time" is very *concrete* time—indeed, a very active, socially articulated form of time. It entails not only freedom from the constraints of labor-time, from the time-clock imposed by abstract labor on the "realm of necessity" (or what we so felicitously call "mindless production"); it also entails the use of time to *be* free.

If only in reaction to the deadening time-constraints of abstract labor, the ideal of "free time" is still tainted by a wayward utopianism that exaggerates the power of use-values over the tyranny of exchange-values. Free time is still seen as inactivity on the one hand and material plenitude on the other. Hence, "freedom" is still conceived as freedom *from* labor, not freedom *for* work. Here we encounter the aimless interests of the isolated ego, the rootless "libertarian" monad who wanders waywardly through life as the counterpart of the wayward, rootless bourgeois monad. The workers in *À Nous la Liberté*, Rene Clair's playful French "utopia" of the early 1930s, achieve their freedom in a highly industrialized land of Cokaygne: their functions are taken over completely by machines while they do nothing but frolic in nearby fields and fish en masse along river banks that have an uncanny resemblence to their assembly lines. This is characteristically very *moderne*. Clair's hoboes, the principal characters of the motion picture, leave the tramp's version of freedom imprinted on the conclusion of the cinematic "utopia." They are the "masterless men" of the twentieth century who have yet to be formed into citizens of a community, like the rootless, wandering radicals of the New Left who carried their "community" in their knapsacks or under the roofs of their trucks. The "utopia" is charming but aimless, spontaneous but unformed, easy-going but structureless, poetic but irresponsible. One may live *long* in such a "utopia" but not "live well."

The Hellenic ideal of freedom—an ideal confined to the citizen—was different. Freedom existed *for* activity, not *from* activity. It was not a realm but a practice—the practice of being free by participating in free institutions, by daily recreating, elaborating, and *fostering* the activity of being free. One was not merely "free" in the passive sense of freedom from constraint, but in the active sense of "free*ing*," both of oneself and one's fellow citizens. An authentic community is not merely a structural constellation of human beings but rather the practice of *communizing*. Hence, freedom in the *polis* was a constellation of relationships that was continually in the process of reproduction. According to Fustel de Coulange,

> We are astonished ... at the amount of labor which this democracy required of men. It was a very laborious government. See how the life of an Athenian is passed. One day he is called to the assembly of his deme, and has to deliberate on the religious and political interests of this little association. Another day he must go to the assembly of his tribe; a religious festival is to be arranged, or expenses are to be examined, or decrees passed, or chiefs and judges named. Three times a month, regularly, he takes part in the general assembly of the people; and he is not permitted to be absent. The session is long. He does not go there simply to vote; having arrived in the morning, he must remain till a late hour, and listen to the orators. He cannot vote unless he has been present from the opening of the session, and has heard all the

speeches. For him this vote is one of the most serious affairs. At one time political and military chiefs are to be elected—that is to say, those to whom his interests and his life are to be confided for a year; at another a tax is to be imposed, or a law to be changed. Again, he has to vote on questions of war, knowing well that, in case of war, he must give his own blood or that of a son. Individual interests are inseparably united with those of the state [read *polis*]. A man cannot be indifferent or inconsiderate. If he is mistaken, he knows that he shall soon suffer for it, and that in each vote he pledges his fortune and his life.*

To recover the substantive, richly articulated attributes of "freedom *for*" rather than merely "freedom *from*," I am obliged to speculate about the attributes of a new society that would transmute "busyness" into the process of reproducing freedom on an ever enlarging scale. Yet we may reasonably ask whether technics as a form of social metabolism has certain formal attributes (its social matrix aside, for the present) that can nourish social freedom as a daily activity. How can the design imagination foster a revitalization of human relationships and humanity's relationship with nature? How can it help lift the "muteness" of nature—a problematical concept that we, in fact, have imposed on ourselves—by opening our own ears to its voice? How can it add a sense of haunting symbiosis to the common productive activity of human and natural beings, a sense of participation in the archetypal animateness of nature?

We share a common organic ancestry with all that lives on this planet. It infiltrates those levels of our bodies that somehow make contact with the existing primordial forms from which we may originally have derived. Beyond any structural considerations, we are faced with the need to give an ecological *meaning* to these buried sensibilities. In the case of our design strategies, we may well want to enhance natural diversity, integration, and function, if only to reach more deeply into a world that has been systematically educated out of our bodies and innate experiences. Today, even in alternate technology, our design imagination is often utilitarian, economistic, and blind to a vast area of experience

---

* Experience has taught me to add a caveat. Fustel de Coulange's account of the Athenian's lived freedom is not a "burden" that I would expect the modern individual to bear at this point in history. But that it *could* be so—but it is not. Hence, I am merely providing an illustration of freedom as distinguished from "free time," "recreation," and that empty word "leisure." Nor is it "busyness" or "business"—the "business" of "occupying" or "entertaining" oneself. In any case, I am offering an example of freedom, not a recipe for it.

that surrounds us. A solar house that symbolizes a designer's ability to diminish energy costs may be a monument to financial cunning, but it is as blind and deadened ecologically as cheap plumbing. It may be a sound investment, even an environmental desideratum because of its capacity to use "renewable resources," but it still deals with nature merely as natural resources and exhibits the sensitivity of a concerned engineer—not an ecologically sensitive individual. An attractive organic garden may well be a wise nutritional "investment" over the quality of food obtainable in a shopping mall. But insofar as the food cultivator is preoccupied only with the nutritional value of food on the dinner table, organic gardening becomes a mere technical strategem for "foodwise" consumption, not a testament to a once-hallowed intercourse with nature. All too often, we are flippantly prepared to use hydroponic trays as substitutes for actual gardens and gravel for soil. Since the object is to fill the domestic larder with vegetation, it often seems to make no difference whether our gardening techniques produce soil or not.

Such commonplace attitudes are very revealing. They indicate that we have forgotten how to be organisms—and that we have lost any sense of belonging to the natural community around us, however much it has been modified by society. In the modern design imagination, this loss is revealed in the fact that we tend to design "sculptures" instead of ensembles—an isolated solar house here, a windmill there, an organic garden elsewhere. The boundaries between the "organic" world we have contrived and the real one that may exist beyond them are strict and precise. If our works tend to define our identity, as Marx claimed, perhaps the first step in acquiring an ecological identity would be to design our "sculptures" *as part* of ensembles—as technical *ecosystems* that interpenetrate with the natural ones in which they are located, not merely as agglomerations of "small," "soft," "intermediate," or "convivial" gadgets. The principal message of an ecological technics is that it is integrated to create a highly interactive, animate and inanimate constellation in which every component forms a supportive part of the whole. The fish tanks, "sun tubes," and ponds that use fish wastes to nourish the plant nutriment on which they live are merely the simplest examples of a wide-ranging ecological system composed of a large variety of biota—from the simplest plants to sizable mammals—that have been sensitively integrated into a biotechnical ecosystem. To this system, humanity owes not only its labor, imagination, and tools but its wastes as well.

No less important than the ensemble is the technical imagination that assembles it. To think ecologically for design purposes is to think of technics as an *ecosystem*, not merely as cost effective devices based on "renewable resources." Indeed, to think ecologically is to include *nature's* "labor" in the technical process, not only humanity's. The use of organic systems to replace machines wherever possible—say, in producing fertilizer, filtering out sewage, heating greenhouses, providing shade, recycling wastes, and the like—is a desideratum in itself. But their economic wisdom aside, these systems also sensitize the mind and spirit to nature's own powers of generation. We become aware that nature, too, has its own complex "economy" and its own thrust toward ever-greater diversity and complexity. We regain a new sense of communication with an entire biotic world that inorganic machines have blocked from our vision. As production itself has often been compared with a drama, we should remember that nature's role is more than that of a mere chorus. Nature is one of its principal players and at times, perhaps, the greater part of the cast.

Hence, an ecologically oriented technical imagination must seek to discover the "Way" of things as ensembles, to sense the subjectivity of what we so icily call "natural resources," to respect the attunement that should exist between the human community and the ecosystem in which it is rooted. This imagination must seek not merely a means for resolving the contradictions between town and country, a machine and its materials, or the functional utility of a device and its impact on its natural environment. It must try to achieve their artistic, richly colored, and highly articulated integration. Labor, perhaps even more than technics, must recover its own creative voice. Its abstract form, its deployment in the framework of linear time as a *res temporalis*, its cruel objectification as mere, homogeneous energy, must yield to the concreteness of skill, to the festiveness of communal activity, to a recognition of its own subjectivity. In this broad revitalization of the natural environment, of work, and of technics, it would be impossible for the technical imagination to confine itself to the traditional imagery of a lifeless, irreducible, and passive material substrate. We must close the disjunction between an orderly world that lends itself to rational interpretation and the subjectivity that is needed to give it meaning. The technical imagination must see matter not as a passive substance in random motion but as an active substance that is forever developing—a striving "substrate" (to use an unsatisfactory word) that repeatedly interacts with itself and its more complex forms to yield variegated, "sensitive," and meaningful patterns.

Only when our technical imagination begins to take this appropriate form will we even begin to attain the rudiments of a more "appropriate"—or better, a *liberatory*—technology. The best designs of solar collectors, windmills and watermills, gardens, greenhouses, bioshelters, "biological" machines, tree culture, and "solar villages" will be little more than new designs rather than new meanings, however well-intentioned their designers. They will be admirable artifacts rather than artistic works. Like framed portraits, they will be set off from the rest of the world—indeed, set off from the very bodies from which they have been beheaded. Nor will they challenge in any significant way the systems of hierarchy and domination that originally reared the mythology of a nature "dominated" by one of its own creations. Like flowers in a dreary wasteland, they will provide the colors and scents that obscure a clear and honest vision of the ugliness around us, the putrescent regression to an increasingly elemental and inorganic world that will no longer be habitable for complex forms of life and ecological ensembles.

11 ⊂⊃ THE AMBIGUITIES OF FREEDOM

The technics and the technical imagination that can nourish the development of a free, ecological society are beset by ambiguities. Tools and machines can be used either to foster a totally domineering attitude toward nature or to promote natural variety and nonhierarchical social relationships. Although what is "big" in technics may be very ugly, what is "small" is not necessarily beautiful. Great despotisms have been based on a technology that is Neolithic in scale and form. The criticism of "industrial society" and "technological man" which erupted in the 1970s is testimony to popular disenchantment with the hopes of earlier generations for growing technological development and the freedom it was expected to yield—a freedom based on material plenty and the absence of debasing toil.

Perhaps less obviously, the same ambiguities also becloud our attitudes toward reason and science. To Enlightenment thinkers two centuries ago, reason and science (as embodied in mathematics and Newtonian physics) were latent with the hope of a human mind freed of superstition and of a nature freed of scholastic metaphysics. Voltaire's famous cry against the Church, "*Ecrasez l'infame!*," was evidence of the Enlightenment's belief in the triumph of human mind as much as it was an attack upon clerical dogmatism; Alexander Pope's luminescent panegyric to Newton was as much evidence of a new belief in the intellectual clarity that science would impart to humanity's understanding of the cosmos as it was a tribute to the genius of Newton himself.

These three great pathways or "tools" (to use the language of modern instrumentalism) for achieving human freedom—reason, science, and technics—that seemed so assured merely a generation ago no longer enjoy their high status. Since the middle of the twentieth century, we have seen reason become rationalism, a cold logic for the sophisticated manipulation of human beings and nature; science become scientism, an ideology for viewing the world as an ethically neutral, essentially mechanical body to be manipulated; and technics become modern technology, an armamentarium of vastly powerful instruments for asserting the authority of a technically trained, largely bureaucratic elite. These "means" for rescuing freedom from the clutches of a clerical and mystified world have revealed a dark side that now threatens to *impede* freedom—indeed, to eliminate the very prospects that reason, science, and technics once advanced for a free society and for free human minds.

The ambiguity created by this Janus-faced development of reason, science, and technics leads to an all-pervasive sense that this triune is meaningless as such unless the three are reevaluated and restructured so that each one's latent liberatory side is rescued and its oppressive side clearly revealed. To return to irrationality, superstition, and material primitivism is no more desirable than to defer to the value-free and elitist rationalism, scientism, and technocratic sensibilities that prevail today. The need to rescue reason as an ethically charged *logos* of the world does not conflict with its use as a logic for dealing with that world. The need to rescue science as a systematic interpretation of that *logos* does not conflict with a recognition of the need for analytic techniques and empirical evidence. Finally, the need to rescue technics as a means of mediating our relationship with nature—including human nature—does not conflict with humanity's own right to intervene in the natural world, to do even better than "blind" nature in fostering variety and natural fecundity. All these seemingly contradictory, ambiguous pathways for attaining freedom are essential to our very definition of freedom. Our ability to resolve these ambiguities of freedom depends as much on how we define reason, science, and technics as it does on how we use them.

Ultimately, the paradoxes we encounter in defining reason, science and technics cannot be resolved by a mystical formula that merely vaporizes the issues they raise. Their resolution depends upon a supreme act of human consciousness. We need to surmount the evil that lies in every good, to redeem the gain that inheres in every loss—be it the sociality latent in the solidarity of kinship, the rationality in primal innocence, the ideals in social conflict, the willfulness in patriarchy, the personality in individualism, the sense of humanity in the parochial tribal community, the ecological sensibility in nature idolatry, or the technics in shamanistic manipulation. To redeem these desiderata without completely shedding certain features of the context that gave them viability—solidarity, innocence, tradition, community, and nature—will require all the wisdom and artfulness we possess. Nor can they be adequately redeemed within the present social order. Rather, we need a new kind of imagination—a new sense of social fantasy—to transmute these often oppressive archaic contexts into emancipatory ones.[*]

ଓଃ

In dealing with the ambiguities of freedom; I shall begin with reason, for reason has always formed the secular hallmark of every specifically human achievement. Presumably, it is by virtue of our rationality that we are unique in the "mute" world around us and can achieve our "mastery" over it. The Enlightenment's generous commitment to reason—its vast faith in the human enterprise as the outcome of thought and education—has never been lost even on its most severe critics, nearly all of whom have deployed reason in the very act of denigrating it. William Blake's assault on the "meddling intellect" is a brilliantly conceived intellectual *tour de force*, as was Rousseau's a generation or so earlier. My own arguments in defense of reason's integrity are not meant to be *ad hominem*; like a mocking incubus, "linear thought" abides within the most mystical experiences and the most inspired forms of "illumination." The role assigned to reason and the destiny imparted to it—whether as blessing or as curse—depends crucially on how we define it in the various lives or "stages" of society. Its role also depends on what, in our sensitivity to the world that surrounds and infuses us, reason is permitted to displace.

Every serious critique of reason has focused on its historic instrumentalization into technics—its deployment as a tool or formal device for classification, analysis, and manipulation. In this sense, formal reason has never really been absent from the human enterprise. To anyone who has even an elementary familiarity with the tribal world, formal reason was simply a subdued presence in a larger sensibility justly called *subjectivity*. But subjectivity is not congruent with consciousness; it speaks to a wider and deeper level of interaction with the world than to the mere capacity to classify, analyze, manipulate, or even develop an awareness of self that is distinguishable from that of "otherness."

Critics of "irrationality do not clarify these distinctions by wantonly banishing every subjective experience other than "linear thought" to the

---

* Lest these remarks in support of consciousness seem a bit idealistic to acolytes of "scientific socialism," it is worth noting that Marx too based his ultimate hopes for a new society on consciousness—that is, on class consciousness. To speak of class consciousness as the result of material or economic factors does not shift the balance of the case in Marx's behalf; ecological breakdown, the destruction of human community, and the threat of nuclear extinction are no less material challenges than economic breakdown, alienation, and imperialism. What is lacking in "scientific socialism," however, is the ethical orientation and ecological sensibility that could vitiate its crude scientism—a scientism that reduces the "principle of hope" to mere egotism and self-satisfaction.

realm of the "irrational" or "antirational." Fantasy, art, imagination, illumination, intuition, and inspiration—all are realities in their own right that may well involve bodily responses at levels that have been meticulously closed off to human sensibility by formal canons of thought. This blindness to large areas of experience is not merely the product of formal education; it is the result of an unrelenting training that begins at infancy and carries through the entire length of a lifetime. To polarize one area of sensibility against another may well be evidence of a repressive "irrationality" that is masked by reason, just as "linear thought" appears in the mystical literature under the mask of "irrationality." Freud, in his ineptness in dealing with these issues from his bastion of Victorian biases, is perhaps the most obvious example of a long line of self-appointed inquisitors whose rigid notions of subjectivity reveal a hatred of sensibility as such. This has long ceased to be a light matter. If the Freuds of the late nineteenth century threatened to destroy our dreams, the Kahns, Tofflers, and similar corporate "rationalists" threaten to destroy our futures.

The most incisive critiques of reason—I think particularly of Horkheimer and Adorno's *Dialectic of Enlightenment* and Horkheimer's *Eclipse of Reason*—may well have foundered on their failure to keep such distinctions in mind. Both thinkers clearly recognized a crucial ambiguity in reason, and they were unerring in their interpretation of the problems it raised. To speak of reason today is to address a process that has two entirely different orientations. One involves high ideals, binding values, and lofty goals for humanity as a whole that derive from supra-individual, almost transcendental, canons of right and wrong, of virtue and evil. Reason, in this sense, is not a matter of personal opinion or taste. It seems to inhere in objective reality itself—in a sturdy belief in a rational and meaningful universe that is independent of our needs and proclivities as individuals. This mode of reason—which Horkheimer called "objective reason"—expresses the *logos* of the world and retains its integrity and validity apart from the interplay of human volition and interests.

By contrast, what we commonly regard as reason—more properly, as "reasonable"—is a strictly functional mentality guided by operational standards of logical consistency and pragmatic success. We formulate "reasonable" strategies for enhancing our well-being and chances of survival. Reason, in this sense, is merely a technique for advancing our personal opinions and interests. It is an instrument to efficiently *achieve* our individual ends, not to *define* them in the broader light of ethics and the social good. This *instrumental* reason—or, to use Horkheimer's terms, "subjective reason" (in my view, a very unhappy selection of words)—is validated exclusively by its effectiveness in satisfying the ego's pursuits and responsibilities. It makes no appeal to values, ideals, and goals that are larger than the requirements for effective adaptation to conditions as they exist. Carried beyond the individual to the social realm, instrumental reason "serves any particular endeavor, good or bad," Horkheimer observes. "It is the tool of all actions of society, but it must not try to set the patterns of social and individual life," which are really established or discarded by the mere preferences of society and the individual. In short, instrumental reason pays tribute not to the speculative mind but merely to pragmatic technique.

If reason is now faced with a crisis that challenges its credibility and validity, this challenge no longer stems from the traditional assaults of irrationality and mysticism from which the Enlightenment tried to defend it. That battleground has been dissolved by history. Indeed, what today passes for irrationality and mysticism has become a fragile refuge from the assaults of instrumentalism and the crisis it has produced in reason. The contradictions besetting reason have their origins in the historic reduction of objective reason to instrumental reason—in the disquieting devolution of rationality as an inherent feature of reality to a "reasonableness" that is merely an unthinking efficient technique. If we mistrust reason today, it is because reason has enhanced our technical powers to alter the world drastically without providing us with the goals and values that give these powers direction and meaning. Like Captain Ahab in Melville's *Moby Dick*, we can cry out forlornly: "All my means are sane; my motives and objects mad."

To the most astute critics of instrumental reason, this devolution of objective reason into a logic of manipulation is viewed as a dialectic of rationality itself, an inversion of ends into means. According to these critics, the high ideals formulated by objective reason that were meant to sophisticate rationality as a technique have betrayed themselves to the very instrumentalism that was meant to be in their service. Thus the ethical goals of the "good," viewed existentially as social freedom and individual autonomy, are presumed to have presuppositions of their own. Freedom entails not only the social structure of freedom, we are told, but also a sufficiency in the means of life to practice freedom. Individual autonomy, in turn, entails not only the untrammeled opportunity for self-expression, but also the self-discipline to restrain the unruly commands of the ego. Freedom and individual autonomy, according to this critique, exact a historic toll: the historic deployment of instrumental reason to fulfill the goals reared by objective reason.

Accordingly, to achieve these goals, humanity must attain sufficient control over nature (both external and internal nature) to transmute an ideal into a material and psychological reality. The precondition for freedom is domination—specifically, the domination of the external natural world by man; the precondition for personal autonomy is also domination—the domination of internal psychic nature by a rational apparatus of repression.

This critique of instrumental reason and the crisis of reason thickens further when we are asked to bear in mind that freedom and individual autonomy presuppose not only the rational control of nature but also the reduction of humanity to a well-regulated, efficient means of production. Class society and the State have always been validated—even in certain radical theories—by the role they play in rationalizing labor to a point where material production can ultimately be brought into the service of liberation. The toil of class society in extricating humanity from the domination of nature and myth is inextricably entangled with the toil of humanity in extricating itself from the domination of class society and instrumental reason. Indeed, the instrumentalization of nature as raw materials is thoroughly wedded to the instrumentalization of human beings as means of production. The devolution of reason from an inherent feature of reality into an efficient technique of control yields the dissolution of objective reason itself. The very *source* of objective reason, notably objective reality itself, is degraded into the mere materials upon which instrumental reason exercises its powers. Science, cojoined with technics, renders the entire cosmos into a devitalized arena for technical colonization and control. In objectifying humanity and nature alike, instrumental reason becomes the object of its own triumph over a reality that was once laden with meaning. Not only do means become ends, but the ends themselves are reduced to machines. Domination and freedom become interchangeable terms in a common project of subjugating nature *and* humanity—each of which is used as the excuse to validate the control of one by the other. The reasoning involved is strictly circular. The machine has not only run away without the driver, but the driver has become a mere part of the machine.

The entire critique of reason, at least in the form I have elaborated it so far, is itself actually laden with biases that it unknowingly transmutes into a dialectic of rationality. In fact, the *Dialectic of Enlightenment* is actually no dialectic at all—at least not in its attempt to explain the negation of reason through its own self-development. The entire work assumes that we hold a body of Victorian prejudices—many of them specifically

Marxian and Freudian—that identify "progress" with *increasing control of external and internal nature*. Historical development is cast within an image of an increasingly disciplined humanity that is extricating itself from a brutish, unruly, mute natural history. The image of a humanity that has achieved the degree of productivity and administration that enables it to be free is modeled strictly on an industrial "paradigm of mastery and discipline. But looking back from our own time, the critique dissolves into despair. Far from extricating itself from a seemingly brutish natural history, humanity has enmeshed itself in a ubiquitous system of domination that has no parallel in nature. Nowhere has history redeemed its promise of freedom and autonomy. To the contrary, it almost seems that history must begin anew—not as a split between humanity and its natural matrix, but rather as an elaboration of ecological ties by an instrumentalism that remains in the service of objective reason.

Here is the nub of the problem: the Victorian veil (to which Marx and Freud gave a radical dimension) that obscures the function of *ecology* as a source of values and ideals. If objective reason has increasingly dissolved into instrumentalism, we must recover the rational dimension of reality that always validated reason itself as an interpretation of the world. As long as the world is conceived scientistically, the preeminence of instrumentalism remains ideologically secure. As a "value-free," presumably ethically "neutral" methodology, science not only fosters instrumentalism but also makes of instrumental reason an ideology whose claims of comprehending reality are as universal as those of science itself. Here, social ecology opens a breach in these claims that potentially, at least, may redeem the function of objective reason to once again define our goals and values.

Neither Horkheimer nor Adorno were prepared to invoke the claims of nature against the failures of society. Like the Victorians of the century before, their attitude toward nature was ambiguous. The story of "civilization," in their eyes, had never ceased to be a struggle by reason and freedom to transcend the trammels of unthinking myth and blind natural law. In the post-revolutionary world of the 1920s and 1930s, myth had atavistically raised its head in the fascist appeal to "blood and soil"—the "naturalism" of the modern despotic State. "Objective reason," rooted in a lawful natural world, had atavistically raised its head in the Stalinist appeal for a dialectics of nature. In both cases, nature had served as the ideological vehicle for regression; the one to place humanity under the tyranny of race and irrationality; the other to place the free play and spontaneity of an emancipated society under the tyranny of "inexorable" natural laws. Not that the latent antinaturalism of Marxism had not cast a dark shadow over nature's role in humanity's project of emancipation. Homer's island of the Lotus-eaters is a denial of memory, history, culture, and "progress" that forever haunts Europe's emphasis on human activity with the image of an atavistically immobilized and pacified dream world. But even as their Marxism subsided, Horkheimer and Adorno revealed an unforgiving hatred of the warped history that fascism and Stalinism had inflicted on the human enterprise.

The current ecological crisis, however, reminds us that the preemptive claims of instrumental reason *are failures on their own terms.* Instrumentalism, particularly in its scientific form, has not only failed to live up to its historic claim of emancipating humanity, but it has even failed to approximate its more traditional claim of illuminating mind. Science, immersed in its impersonal gadgetry and its imperious quest for innovation, has lost all contact with the culture of its time. Worse yet, its quest for innovation threatens to tear down the planet itself. Far more than any moral or ideological verdict, these failures are tangible features of everyday life. They are verified by the foul air and water, the rising cancer rates, the automotive accidents, and the chemical wastelands that assault the entire world of a scientistic "civilization." By reducing ethics to little more than matters of opinion and taste, instrumentalism has dissolved every moral and ethical constraint over the impending catastrophe that seems to await humanity. Judgments no longer are formed in terms of their intrinsic merits; they are merely matters of public consensus that fluctuate with changing particularistic interests and needs. Having divested the world of its ethical objectivity and reduced reality to an inventory of industrial objects, instrumentalism threatens to keep us from formulating a critical stance toward its own role in the problems it has created. If Odin paid for wisdom with the loss of one eye, we have paid for our powers of control with the loss of both eyes.

❧

But we can no more divest ourselves of instrumental reason than we can divest ourselves of technics. Both are indispensable to expanded notions of freedom; indeed, their emancipatory role long antedates the emergence of capitalism with its images of a "stingy" nature and "unlimited" needs. Humanity does not live by ethics alone; herein lies one of freedom's most crucial ambiguities. In the face of an increasingly technocratic society and sensibility, on what grounds can we speak of an objective world that provides the needed constraints to instrumentalism? From what source can we derive the values and goals that will subserve instrumentalism to an objective ethics?

To evoke nature as the source for an objectively grounded ethics, as I propose to do, requires careful qualification. A nature conceived as the matrix of "blood and soil," or as the domain of a blind "dialectical" lawfulness that imbues tyranny with the suprahuman qualities of inexorable destiny, would justly be regarded as atavistic. The racial ethos of fascism and the scientistic "dialectics" of Stalinism, both based on very particularistic images of nature, have claimed a toll in life and suffering that beggars the most barbarous eras of human history. We no longer need a "nature" (that is, an authoritarian sociobiology) that advances an ideological rationale for ethnic arrogance and concentration camps under the aegis of "inevitability" or "blind law." But nature is not a homogeneous fabric that is woven from a single thread. The nature to which we can now address ourselves is neither bloody nor blind; it provides no ideological refuge for a mythos of irrationality, race, or, like Marxism, a contrived mechanism that passes itself off as a "social science" concealed under the shroud of Hegel.

The matrix from which objective reason may yet derive its ethics for a balanced and harmonized world is the nature conceived by a radical social ecology—a nature that is interpreted nonhierarchically, in terms of unity in diversity and spontaneity. Here, nature is conceived not merely as a constellation of ecosystems but also as a meaningful natural *history*, a developing, creative, and fecund nature that yields an increasing complexity of forms and interrelationships. And what makes this complexity so significant is not just the stability it fosters (an obvious desideratum in its own right, needed for both the biotic and social worlds). Nature's evolution toward ever more complex forms is uniquely important in that *it enters into the history of subjectivity itself.* From the transition of the inorganic to the organic and through the various phases of evolution that crystallized into human forms of rationality, we witness an increasingly expansive history of molecular interactivity—not only of neurological responses but of an ineffable *sensibilité* that is a function of increasingly complex patterns of integration. Subjectivity expresses itself in various gradations, not only as the mentalism of reason but also as the interactivity, reactivity, and the *growing purposive activity of forms*. Hence, subjectivity emphatically does *not* exclude reason; in part, it is the history of reason—or, more precisely, of a slowly forming mentality that exists on a wider terrain of reality than human cerebral activity. The term subjectivity expresses the fact that substance—at each level of its organization and in all its concrete forms—*actively* functions to maintain its identity, equilibrium, fecundity, and place in a given constellation of phenomena.

Normally, we think of substance in its various forms as passive objects, as yielding phenomena that are "molded" or "selected" by their "environments." External "forces" seem to determine the "traits" that enable material forms (particularly life-forms) to retain their integrity and "survive." Science's passion for reducing all changes within these forms to mere products of accident—the capacity of these forms to "mutate" by mere chance—fatally denies the high degree of nisus, of self-organization and self-creation, inherent in nonhuman phenomena. Science comes perilously close to the very metaphysics and mysticism it has opposed so militantly since the Enlightenment when it ignores the extent to which phenomena play an *active* role in their own evolutionary processes. The traditional image of biological evolution as a series of random point mutations that are "selected" in the interests of survival essentially lies in debris. It would be difficult to explain the elegant organization of living beings—indeed of organs like the eye or ear—without viewing their developmental traits as immanently and creatively constituted, as organized ensembles that emerge together in the organism's interaction with the world around it. The jig-saw puzzle's fit, so to speak, involves the parts as well as the whole—not just the player who is the mechanical *deus ex machina* that seems to be the exclusive "intelligible" factor in the entire puzzle. It is arguable whether the "preference" of carbon atoms to be linked with four other atoms is related by a long evolution of subjectivity to a chimpanzee's use of sticks to probe anthills. But the very strong possibility of such a continuum, gradually mediated by increasingly complex forms of material organization, can no longer be dismissed as mystical. Almost every contemporary vision of nature (apart from the most entrenched bunkers of Victorian science) has increasingly assigned to substance itself more a *creative* role in the evolution of subjectivity than at any time since the demise of classical philosophy.

Accordingly, whether or not we decide to select reason as the most complex expression of subjectivity, the graded emergence of mind in the natural history of life is part of the larger landscape of subjectivity itself. From the biochemical responses of a plant to its environment to the most willful actions of a scientist in the laboratory, a common bond of primal subjectivity inheres in the very organization of "matter" itself. In this sense, the human mind has never been alone, even in the most inorganic of surroundings. Art has expressed this message more poignantly than science, particularly in those abstract paintings evacuated of virtually all sensory experience beyond color and form; for here we recognize *the primal affinity of mind with form itself.* Even those pirates of space travel, the astronauts, are awed by the activity of astral masses, of the cosmic dust and objects swirling around them in a world that seems devoid of matter—in a space that generations of scientists once regarded as a virtual vacuum. "Mind" reaches beyond our cerebral mentalism to a concept of subjectivity in these very broad terms, and ceases to be trapped exclusively within the human brain. Instead, it seems to inhere in the human body as a whole and the natural history it embodies.

Which specific ethical imperatives we draw from an ecological interpretation of nature (as distinguished from the abstract, meaningless, desubjectivized nature that chilled the Victorian mind by its "stinginess" and "brutality") depend ultimately on our exploration of a future ecological society. Here is a *problematic* whose answers can be supplied only by a society capable of rendering them into a living *praxis*. An ecological nature—and the objective ethics following from it—can spring to life, as it were, only in a society whose sensibilities and interrelationships have become ecological to their very core. The nature we normally "create" today is highly conditioned by the social imperatives of our time. This nature may be science's highly quantified nature; the Marxian "abstract matter" that is formed by "abstract labor"; the mystic's cosmos dissolved into an unrelieved, universal "Oneness"; sociobiology's hierarchical nature organized around primal instincts and drives; the Hobbesian-Freudian nature, impudently unruly and invasive; or the vulgarized Darwinian nature, governed by "fang and claw." I have not even alluded to the animistic, Hellenic, Judeo-Christian, medieval, and Renaissance images of nature that still ideologically marble those which I have cited above.

None of the modern images of nature offers a compelling vision of a wholeness that is permeated—as a result of its wholeness—by a larger sense of subjectivity, which we normally identify with human rationality. Each illustrates not so much the need to "resurrect" nature as the need to "resurrect" human subjectivity itself. The flaw in Horkheimer and Adorno's works on reason stems from their failure to integrate rationality with subjectivity in order to bring nature within the compass of *sensibilité*. To do so, they would have had to understand the message of social ecology, a realm that was completely outside their intellectual tradition.

Here, their subdued adherence to Marxism became a major obstacle to what otherwise could have been a superbly comprehensive critique of instrumental reason. They were too afraid to cement their view of nature to subjectivity—a commitment they identified with mythic and classical archaisms. Hence they never provided a meaningful objective matrix for reason. The wish to make this commitment haunts their entire work on reason and enlightenment, but it is a wish they were too prudent to satisfy.

But how can we, who are more familiar with the possibilities of ecology, avoid the invasion of instrumentalism into an ecological approach to ethics? How can we prevent it from turning nature into a mere object for manipulation in the very name of respecting its subjectivity? None of these questions can be answered satisfactorily without recreating our existing sensibilities, technics, and communities along ecological lines. Once this occurred, then an ecological community might well recover its sense of place in its specific ecosystem by allying itself with its natural environment in *a creatively reproductive form*—a form that spawns a human symbiotic sensibility, a human technics that *enriches* nature's complexity, and a human rationality that enlarges nature's subjectivity. Here, humanity would neither give nor take; it would actually *participate* with nature in creating the new levels of diversity and form that are part of a more heightened sense of humanness and naturalness. Our ethical claim to rationality would derive from the participation of human mind in the larger subjectivity of nature, a subjectivity that is a function of form, integration, and complexity. The use of nature as "natural resources"—a usage that seems unavoidable to the "purposive-rational mind" (to use Jürgen Habermas' jargon) would be diminished, indeed eliminated, by an ecological technics that would not only enrich the flow between nature and humanity, but also sensitize humanity to the creativity of nature.

Lest these good intentions seem like just another case of the simplistic sentimentality so characteristic of nature philosophies as a whole, let me emphasize that an ecological ethics is not patterned on a naïve vision of the natural world—either as it exists today or as it might exist in a "pacified" social future. A wolf has no business lying down with a lamb. The imagery is trite and in its own way repellent. The "pacification" of nature does not consist in its domestication. Very much is lost when "wildness" (a stupid word if there ever was one) is removed so completely from nature that it ceases to be a "token of scarcity, suffering, and want," to use Herbert Marcuse's absurd notion of a nature that has not been "recreated by the power of Reason." Marcuse's language, here, is anthropomorphic in its myopia, Marxist in its intent, and preposterous in its claim that "pacification presupposes the mastery of Nature, which is and remains the object opposed to the developing subject." If there are "two kinds of mastery, a repressive and a liberatory one," one might also claim with equal absurdity that there are two kinds of nature: an "evil" one and a "virtuous" one.

Leaving this muddled logic aside, there is no "cruelty" in nature, only the predation (and mutualism) around which natural history has evolved its structures for sustaining life and ecological balance. There is no "suffering" in nature, only the unavoidable physical pain that comes with injury. There is no "scarcity" and "want" in nature, only needs that must be satisfied if life itself is to be maintained. Indeed, the material fecundity of nature, prior to history's "negation of Nature" (to use Marcuse's language again), might have completely stunned its earliest hominid offspring, had they even been mindful of "scarcity" as a social category. I cannot emphasize too strongly that *nature itself is not an ethics*; it is the *matrix* for an ethics, the source of ethical meaning that can be rooted in objective reality. Hence nature, even as the matrix and source of ethical meaning, does not have to assume such delightfully human attributes as kindness, virtue, goodness and gentleness; nature need merely be *fecund* and *creative*—a *source* rather than a "paradigm."

The function of an ethical philosophy does not entail a mimetic reduction of ethics to its source. Rather, it requires a *ground* from which to creatively develop ethical ideals. The child is not the parent, but both are united by the objective continuity of genetic ancestry, gestation, birth, and socialization. The two never completely separate; they coexist, and their lives overlap under normal conditions until the child grows to adulthood and becomes a parent. The two may retain a loving relationship or become antagonists, and the child may become more human, or possibly less human, than the parent. In either case, we are obliged to understand *why* one course of development unfolded, not merely *how* it occurred—and to give it meaning, coherence, and ethical interpretation. In any case the development is real, and we cannot suppress our responsibility to interpret it in ethical terms by claiming that it is merely a series of random events.

To transmute "pacification" into "domestication" is to deal with nature as a model of ethical behavior rather than to accept it for what it really is—a source of ethical meaning that reestablishes our sense of ecological *wholeness*, the underlying dialectic of unity in diversity. It is this lack of wholeness in our relationship with nature that really explains the unfinished social cosmos in which we live, the sense of incompleteness that exists around us. Not only does a truly "pacified" and domesticated natural world arrogantly model nature on society (rational or not) but it also fails to recognize that human rationality is a phase or aspect of natural subjectivity. It is no accident that Marcuse's "pacified" nature is in fact a "rational" nature. Paul Shepard, in a superb refutation of the self-styled "peacemakers" of nature, observes that:

> Each gene in an individual organism acts in the context of many other genes. Hence the genetic changes resulting from domestication may affect the whole creature, its appearance, behavior, and physiology. The temperament and personality of domestic animals are not only more placid than their wild counterparts, but also more flaccid—that is, there is somehow less definition. Of course there is nothing placid about an angry bull or a mean watchdog, but their mothers were tractable, and once an organism has been stripped of its wildness it can be freaked in any direction the breeder wishes. It may be made fierce without being truly wild. The latter implies an ecological niche from which the domesticated animal has been removed. Niches are hard taskmasters. *Escape from them is not freedom but loss of direction.* Man substitutes controlled breeding for natural selection; animals are selected for special traits like milk production or passivity, at the expense of overall fitness and nature-wide relationships.

There is an important moral to be drawn from these remarks that applies not just to animals but human beings as well. The freedom of all organisms is a function of direction—of meaningful "niches" in nature and meaningful communities in society. To be sure, the two are not completely congruent, but there is every reason to regard them as derivative: community from "niche," human being from wild animal. In its own way, our loss of community has been a form of domestication—a condition that lacks meaning and direction—as surely as is the wild animal's loss of its niche. Like our cattle, poultry, pets, and even crops, we too have lost our wildness in a "pacified" world that is overly administered and highly rationalized. The private world we created in our prepolitical communities, the "niches" we occupied in the hidden spaces of social life, are quickly disappearing. Like the genetic structure of domesticated animals, the psychic structures of domesticated humans are undergoing perilous degradation. More than ever we must recover the continuum between our "first nature" and our "second nature," our natural world and our social world, our biological being and our rationality. Latent within us are ancestral memories that only an ecological society and sensibility can "resurrect." The history of human reason has not yet reached its culmination, much less its end. Once we can "resurrect" our subjectivity and restore it to its heights of sensibility, then in all likelihood that history will have just begun.

In summary, human rationality must be seen as a form and a derivative of a broader "mentality," or subjectivity, that inheres in nature as a whole—specifically, in the long development of increasingly complex forms of substance over the course of natural history. We must be very clear about what this means. Natural history includes a history of mind as well as of physical structures—a history of mind that develops from the seemingly "passive" interactivity of the inorganic to the highly active cerebral processes of human intellect and volition. This history of what we call "mind" is cumulatively present not only in the human mind but also in our bodies as a whole, which largely recapitulate the expansive development of life-forms at various neurophysical levels of evolution. What we tragically lack today—primarily because instrumentalism tyrannizes our bodily apparatus—is the ability to sense the wealth of subjectivity inherent in ourselves and in the nonhuman world around us. To some extent, this wealth reaches us through art, fantasy, play, intuition, creativity, sexuality and, early in our lives, in those sensibilities of childhood and youth from which adulthood and the norms of "maturity" wean us in the years that follow.

The landscape of nature—its *formal organization*, from the astral level of our universe to the least noticeable ecosystems around us—has messages of its own to impart. It too has a voice to which Bruno and Kepler in the Renaissance and a growing number of life scientists today have tried to respond. Indeed, from the time of Pythagoras onward, the classical tradition in philosophy found subjectivity in the evolution of form *as such*, not only in the morphology of individual beings. Conceived as an *active process of ever-growing, interrelated complexity*, the "balance of nature" can be viewed as more than just a formal ensemble that life presupposes for its own stability and survival. It can also be viewed as a formal ensemble whose very organization into integrated wholes exhibits varying levels of "mentalism," a subjectivity to which we will respond only if we free our sensorium from its instrumentalist inhibitions and conventions.

        CR

Our interpretation of science is not far removed from our interpretation of reason. Viewed as the methodical application of reason to the concrete world, science has acquired the bad name that instrumentalism and technics have earned over the past few decades.

Its overstated claims as a strategy for observation, experimentation, and the generalization of data into "inexorable" natural laws—and its highly vaunted assertions of "objectivity" and intellectual universality—have exposed it to charges of an unfeeling arrogance toward sentiment, ethics, and the growing crisis in the human condition. Once regarded as the herald of enlightenment in all spheres of knowledge, science is now increasingly seen as a strictly instrumental system of control. Its use as a means of social manipulation and its role in restricting human freedom now parallel in every detail its use as a means of natural manipulation. Most of its discoveries in physics, chemistry, and biology are justly viewed with suspicion by its once most fervent adepts, as the controversies over nuclear power and recombinant DNA so vividly reveal. Accordingly, science no longer enjoys a reputation as a means of "knowing," of *Wissenschaft* (to use the language of the German Enlightenment), but as a means of domination—or what Max Scheler, in a later, more disenchanted time, called *Herrschaftswissen*. It has become, in effect, a cold, unfeeling, metaphysically grounded technics that has imperialistically expanded beyond its limited realm as a *form* of "knowing" to claim the entire realm of knowledge as such.

We are thus confronted with the paradox that science, an indispensable tool for human well-being, is now a means for subverting its traditional humanistic function. The ethical neutrality of the nuclear physicist, the food chemist, and the bacteriologist involved in developing lethal pathogens for military purposes is a numbing symbol of a "science-run-wild" that compares in even more frightening detail to the image of a "technics-run-wild." The heated controversies over the hazards of nuclear power and recombinant DNA are evidence that science is thoroughly entangled in debates that deal with its claims not just to technical competence but to moral maturity as well.

Like reason and technics, science too has a history and, broadly conceived beyond its instrumentalist definition, it can also be regarded as that history. What we so glibly call "Greek science" was largely a nature philosophy that imparted to speculative reason the capacity to comprehend the natural world. To understand and impart coherence to nature was an activity of the contemplative mind, not merely of experimental technique. Viewed from the standpoint of this rational framework, Plato and Aristotle's considerable corpus of writings on nature were not "wrong" in their accounts of the natural world. Within this large body of nature philosophy, we find insights and a breadth of grasp and scope that the physical and life sciences are now trying to recover.* Their varying emphases on substance, form, and development—what normally are depicted as a "qualitative" orientation, as distinguished from modern science's "quantitative" orientation—exhibit a range of thought that may well be regarded as broader, or at least more organic, than science's traditional emphases on matter and motion. The classical tradition stressed activity, organization, and process; the Enlightenment tradition stressed matter's passivity, random features, and mechanical movement. That the Enlightenment tradition has yielded slowly to the classical—a development forced upon it by a growing sense of nature's historicity, contextual qualities, and the importance of form—has not led to a clear understanding of the differences separating them and the way in which they share a historical continuity that could yield their integration without any loss of their specific identities.

To call classical, mechanistic, evolutionary, and relativistic forms of science "complementary" may very well miss a crucial point. They do not simply supplement one another nor are they "stages" in humanity's increasing knowledge of nature, a knowledge that presumably "culminates" in modern science. This kind of thinking about the history of science is still very popular and often highly presumptuous in its elevation of all things modern and presumably free of speculation and "theology." Actually, these different forms of science encompass different levels of natural development and differ in their avowed scope. They are not simply different "paradigms," as Thomas Kuhn has argued, that radically replace one another. To assume that there is a "science" *as such* in which the classical tradition is largely "erroneous," in which the Renaissance tradition is partly "correct," and in which the modern tradition is more "true" in its understanding of nature than any of its predecessors is to assume that nature is cut from a single cloth and differs only in its forms of tailoring. Ironically, Kuhn's views have been attacked most harshly not so much by critics who reject the history of science as a displacement of one prevailing scientific "paradigm" by a different one. Rather, he has been most sharply criticized for his tendency to view the logic of "scientific revolutions" as being guided by "techniques of persuasion" rather than by proof, by psychological

---

* The extensive literature on these issues began in the early part of this century, with the decline of mechanism and the emergence of relativity. Leaving the pioneering work of late nineteenth-century thinkers aside, one thinks of the influence of Whitehead's *Science and the Modern World*, the synoptic vision of Collingwood's *The Idea of Nature*, and the discussions generated by Kuhn's *The Structure of Scientific Revolutions*, Bertalanffy's *Problems of Life*, Herrick's *The Evolution of Human Nature*, and particularly Hans Jonas' admirable *The Phenomenon of Life*, which is perhaps only now receiving the appreciation it deserves.

and social factors rather than by the test of objective studies of reality.

Ignoring Kuhn's later attempt to backtrack upon his more challenging conclusions about the structure of the scientific community itself, what is most striking about his views of the "paradigmatic" revolutions in science is the *way* in which they have been contrasted with one another. I speak less of Kuhn, here, than of the conventional wisdom of scientism, which tends to focus on the methodological differences between classical nature philosophy and modern science. The common notion that modern science really embarked upon its unique voyage when it consciously adopted Francis Bacon's program of controlled empirical observation and experimental verification is a trite myth that more accurately reflects the intellectual conflicts in Bacon's time than it does the authentic differences between classical and Renaissance notions of nature. Without necessarily articulating it, classical nature philosophers had been working with Bacon's program of observation and experimentation for centuries. Perhaps more appropriately, Bacon, with his "Great Instauration," gave science a function that classical theory had never fully accepted: "man's" *recovery* of his mastery over the natural world, a view that was pitted against the medieval Schoolman's (actually, Christianity's) contemplative orientation toward nature.

Yet, even here, it is still misleading to assume that the classical tradition, like the medieval, was strictly contemplative and that the modern was overwhelmingly pragmatic. The idea of domination had been an *on-going practice* in the form of *human* domination—of a humanity conceived by its rulers as "natural resources" or "means of production"—from the inception of "civilization" itself. Bacon's Great Instauration had been a functioning reality for thousands of years, not merely in class society's attempts to subjugate nature for the purposes of control, but to subjugate humanity itself. Its temple was not Bacon's utopian laboratory, the House of Salomon, but the State, with its bureaucracies, armies, and the knouts of its foremen. We do a grave injustice to the authentic history of "scientific method" when we forget that before science established its laboratory to control nature, the State had established its palaces and barracks to control humanity. The Great Instauration drew its inspiration from the domination of human by human before it made the domination of nature central to its ideals and functions.*

---

* Here, Horkheimer and Adorno (and the Frankfurt School generally) do us a great disservice by imputing domination to the emergence of reason as such. The way in which Horkheimer develops this argument is highly instructive and reveals the basic difference between his theoretical strategy and the one advanced in this book. "If one

The most fundamental difference between classical nature philosophy and modern science lies in their radically different concepts of causality. Here is the real ontological issue—not the turgid chatter about "methodology"—that separates knowledge itself from mere matters of technique, that clarifies the all-important problem of the relationship of means to ends, which is so vital to any critique of instrumental reason and an authoritarian technics. To Aristotle, who never ceased to be a keen observer, a sophisticated generalizer, and committed experimenter (like Archimedes after him), natural causality was not exhausted by mechanical motion. Causation involved the very material, the potentiality for form, the formative agent, and the most advanced form toward which a phenomenon could develop. His concept of causality, in effect, was *entelechial*. It assumed that a phenomenon was "drawn" to actualize its full potentiality for achieving the highest form specific to it—to develop intrinsically and extrinsically toward the formal self-realization of its potentialities.

Hence, causation to Aristotle is not merely motion that involves change of place—like the change of place produced by one billiard

should speak of a disease affecting reason," Horkheimer observes, "this disease should be understood not as having stricken reason at some historical moment, but as being inseparable from the nature of reason in civilization as we have known it so far. The disease of reason is that reason was born from man's urge to dominate nature, and the 'recovery' depends on insight into the nature of the original disease, not on a cure of the latest symptoms. The true critique of reason will necessarily uncover the deepest layers of civilization and explore its earliest history. From the time when reason became the instrument for domination of human and extrahuman nature by man—that is to say, from its very beginnings—it has been frustrated in its own intention of discovering the truth. This is due to the very fact that it made nature a mere object, and that it failed to discover the trace of itself in such objectivization, in the concepts of matter and things not less than in those of gods and spirit. One might say that the collective madness that ranges today, from the concentration camps to the seemingly most harmless mass culture reactions, was already present in germ in primitive objectivization, in the first man's calculating contemplation of the world as a prey." See Max Horkheimer, *The Eclipse of Reason* (New York: Oxford University Press, 1947), p.176.

If our discussion of organic society is correct, then this is a libel on early animism and predation. But more significantly, this quasi-Marxian image of the human project of conquering nature starts on the wrong foot; it was not nature that was the earliest object of domination, but humanity itself—particularly the young and women. Indeed, even after the emergence of hierarchy, reason's objectification of phenomena was largely centered on the domination of "man by man," long before "nature idolatry" succumbed to secular philosophy and science. Marcuse in no way resolves the error of his colleagues by advancing a "New Science" that will be structured around a "mastery" that is "liberatory" instead of "repressive" or a nature that "will always remain the object opposed [!] to the developing subject." Where Horkheimer will never be faulted for his consistency, Marcuse's remarks are riddled by such contradictions.

ball striking another. While it may certainly be mechanical, causation is more meaningfully and significantly *developmental*. It should be seen more as a graded process, as an emerging process of self-realization, than as a series of physical displacements. Accordingly, matter, which always has varying degrees of form, is latent with potentiality—indeed, it is imbued by a nisus to elaborate its potentiality for greater form. Hence it enters into Aristotle's notion of causation as a "material cause." The form that is latent in matter and strives toward its full actualization is a "formal cause." The intrinsic and the extrinsic forces that sculpt the development—here, in the latter case, Aristotle refers to external agents, like the sculptor who fashions a bronze horse—are the "efficient cause." And lastly, the form that all these aspects of causality are meant to actualize represents the "final cause."

Aristotelian causality, in effect, is not only developmental but also directive and purposive. It has also been called "teleological" because the final form toward which substance strives is latent in the beginning of the development. The term, however, is redolent with notions of a predetermined, inexorable end—a notion that Aristotle takes great pains to eschew. In *On Interpretation*, he is careful to point out that

> it cannot be said without qualification that all existence and non-existence is the outcome of necessity. For there is a difference between saying that that which is, when it is, must needs be, and simply saying that all that is must needs be, and similarly in the case of that which is not. In the case, also, of two contradictory propositions this holds good. Everything must either be or not be, whether in the present or in the future, but it is not always possible to distinguish and state determinately which of these alternatives must necessarily come about.

What characterizes the "teleological dimension" of Aristotelian causality is that it has *meaning*, not predetermination; causality is oriented toward achieving wholeness, the fulfillment and completeness of all the potentialities for form latent in substance at different levels of its development. This sense of meaning is permeated by ethics: "For in all things, as we affirm, nature always strives after 'the better.'" Here, the word *strive* requires emphasis, for Aristotle rarely imputes thought, in our cerebral meaning of the term, to nature; rather, nature is an organized *oikos*, a good household, and "like every good householder, is not in the habit of throwing away anything from which it is possible to make anything useful." The extent to which this brilliant insight, so integral to Aristotle's overall philosophy, has been confirmed by ecology and paleontology can hardly be emphasized too much.

Within the framework of Aristotelian causality, Hegel's concept of dialectic (a grossly abused term, these days) is virtually congruent with Aristotle's causal orientation. Like Aristotle, Hegel's entire goal is to comprehend the notion of wholeness, not a specious "synthesis" that is formed from the transformation of a thesis into its antithesis. Such a methodological formula for dialectic not only divests it of all organic content but reduces dialectic to a method—an instrumental technique in the high tradition of Marxian orthodoxy, rather than an ontological causality. As Hegel observes in one of his most trenchant accounts of the dialectic,

> Because that which is implicit comes into existence, it certainly passes into change, yet it remains one and the same, for the whole process is dominated by it. The plant, for example, does not lose itself in mere indefinite change. From the germ much is produced when at first nothing was to be seen; but the whole of what is brought forth, if not developed, is yet hidden and ideally contained within itself. The principle of this projection into existence is that the germ cannot remain merely implicit, but it is impelled toward development, since it presents the contradiction of being only implicit and yet not desiring so to be. But this coming without itself has an end in view; its completion is fully reached, and its previously determined end is the fruit or produce of the germ, which causes a return to the first condition.

Mind carries this movement further, for Hegel, and rather than "doubling" back to its germinal form goes forth to the full realization of "coming to itself."*

What is crucial for both Hegel and Aristotle is their common notion of "final cause," their commitment to wholeness and meaning in phenomena. More than any aspect of Aristotle's ideas, this one was to become a veritable battleground between science and Schoolman theology; indeed, to the extent that mechanism became the prevalent "paradigm" of Renaissance and Enlightenment science, the notion of "final cause" became the gristmill on which science sharpened its scalpel of "objectivity," scientistic "disinterestedness," and the total rejection of values in the

---

* To the reader who knows Aristotelian philosophy, one cannot help but note how much Hegel has borrowed from the Greek thinker. The passage contains Aristotle's notions of substance (*ousia*), privation, causation, and teleology—which, for Aristotle, is simply a doctrine that each thing has itself as its own end and must be studied from a comprehension of its own form.

scientific organon. To imply a sense of direction in causality—a "why" rather than merely a "how" in nature—was redolent of theology. Medieval scholasticism had so thoroughly Christianized Aristotelian nature philosophy and causality that the Renaissance mechanicians viewed them as little more than a system of Catholic apologetics; even Hobbes's vision of a "social mechanics" veered sharply into a critique of Aristotle's final cause. To be sure, this conflict was unavoidable and even freed Aristotle's own thought from the inquisitorial grip of the Church. But opposition and persecution (Bruno and Servetus were to go to the stake and Galileo to confinement as science's principal martyrs in this conflict) led to an exaggerated rejection of all organicism—indeed, to an astringent Cartesian dualism between a "soulful" subjectivity exclusively confined to "man" and a strictly mechanical, quantitative view of physical nature.

But this battle was not won without a severe penalty. To free the human mind from the trammels of religion, humanity itself was enslaved to the powers of science. A new organon replaced the old. The Baconian ideal of humanity's recovery of its mastery over nature did not cleanse it of the taint of "original sin" and restore it to the plentitude of the Garden of Eden. Science joined hands with technics to *reinforce* the mastery of human over human by enslaving humanity to the same dark, mythic world of domination that it once had ideologically opposed. Science itself had now become a theology. Beginning with the nineteenth century, humanity has become increasingly instrumentalized, objectivized, and economized—even more than the very controlled nature that Bacon's Great Instauration was intended to create. Rationalization has combined with science to produce a technocracy that now threatens to divest humanity itself—and its natural environment—of the subjectivity by which the Enlightenment had intended to illuminate the world.

ᚲ

Philosophical orientations that replace one "paradigm" by another in the course of intellectual "revolutions" produce a serious breakdown of continuity, integration, and wholeness in the realm of knowledge. They disrupt the ecology and history of knowledge itself—in social theory as much as in scientific theory. We have lost a tremendous wealth of exciting traditions by substituting a Hobbesian project of "social science" for an Aristotelian project of social ethics (not that the Aristotelian provides the "highest" point we could hope to attain in social theory). The all-pervasive sweep of Christianity over the European world, followed more recently by Marxism, has interred an invaluable body of social ideals and insights. In our own time, one is reminded of the loss of the intensely libertarian hopes fostered by radical groups in the English, American, and French revolutions, all of which have been blanketed by the Leninist "revolutions" of the present century or consigned (to use Trotsky's noxious phrase) to the "dust-bin of history." One is also reminded of the wealth of utopian ideas from which Marx pilfered before replacing them with the myth of a "scientific socialism." Like Christianity before it, socialism has fostered a dogmatic fanaticism that closed off countless new possibilities—not only to human action but also to human thought and imagination. Science, while less demanding in its attacks upon its own heretics, exhibits an equal degree of fanaticism in its intellectual claims. To defy science's metaphysical, often mystical, presuppositions that are rooted in an eerily passive "matter" and a physical concept of motion is to expose oneself to accusations of metaphysics and mysticism, and to an intellectual persecution that science itself once suffered at the hands of its theological inquisitors.

There is a strong tendency within new scientific "paradigms" to view various forms of different "natures"—inorganic and organic, kinetic and developmental, random and meaningful—as inherently antagonistic to one another rather than as different in scope, as levels of development, and as components of a larger whole. Only recently have we begun to escape from a mechanistic reductionism of all natural phenomena to a "paradigm" based on mathematical physics. The widely touted "unity of science" which theorists of the last century advanced during the triumphant heights of the Newtonian cosmic image, was often little more than an intellectual nightmare—a "Oneness," rather than a "unity of science," which theorists of the last century advanced during the most unreconstructed mysticism that western thought had ever achieved. Nothing could be more riddled by metaphysical and mystical notions than a causality reduced almost entirely to a universe based on a kinetics of interacting forces at a distance and of motion that (to explain chemical bonding) yielded mere interlocking arrangements between atoms.

By Laplace's time, nature was seen as a kinetic agglomeration of irreducible "atoms" from which the cosmos was constructed, like a solid Victorian bank. The conception of atoms as the "building blocks" of the universe was taken literally, and even the Deity was seen less as a "Creator" or parent of the world than as an architect. This image designated a passive nature sculpted by intrinsic, often random, forces—which qualified ruling elites could manipulate according to their interests once science had "unlocked" the "secrets" of an enchanted and cryptic nature. Efficient cause, removed from the larger ethical matrix of Aristotelian causality, was now conceived as the sole description for natural phenomena in kinetic interaction. The image of nature as a "construction-site," which even Bloch borrowed, produced its own technological cant. Terms like "building blocks," "mortar," and "cement" that are still commonplace in works on physics replaced classical philosophy's images of "love" and "hate," "justice" and "injustice," "entelechy" and "kinesis" that, for all their anthropomorphic qualities, implied not only an enchanted nature or even an ethical nature but a passionate nature. What remained from the past to "explain" the ultimate Newtonian mystery of action at a distance and the troubling facts of gravitation were the terms "attraction" and "repulsion," terms that still survive in electromagnetism.

It is difficult to explain how much this technological cant and the imagery it reflected served the interests of domination in an industrial market society. For this cant was not merely philosophical but eminently social in its character, just as the language of present-day systems theory—with its extension of terms like "input," "output," and "feedback" into everyday discourse—reflects the corporatization of daily life, its reduction to a "flow diagram." To conceive of all phenomena as constructed from a homogeneous, lifeless, passive, and malleable "matter" was to place humanity itself within the orbit of all these attributes. Flesh, no less than stone and steel, was merely matter that had been accidentally structured into a more elaborate agglomeration of the same irreducible material. Even thought had lost its high estate, and was instead conceived as a "fluid" that formed an exudate of the brain and the nervous system. Labor, as mere energy, was considered to be rooted not merely in political economy but also in the "economy of nature." This opened a direct tie between the radical critique developed by Marx and accommodative strategies formulated in a later period by Social Darwinism. The Enlightenment ideal of human reeducation according to the canons of reason was interpreted to mean training according to canons of efficient performance.

Science, seen in terms of a history that wantonly discarded its past by a radical succession of "paradigms," stands alone in the world because it has marched through this succession apart from nature. Having divested itself of antecedents that once addressed themselves to the different emerging levels of natural history, science now lacks the continuity that relates these levels intelligibly. It lacks a sense of limit that confirms what is or is not valid in various ways of knowing reality; it lacks an awareness of new forms of reality that linger on the boundaries of "established data." In short, modern science has not developed in relation to nature but in relation to its own "paradigms." The pursuit of the "unity of science" should in no sense be understood as a pursuit of the unity of nature. The former is an intellectual enterprise between scientific contestants and collaborators, not an enterprise that authentically involves the natural world.

The rediscovery of nature is more important at this point in the development of human knowledge than are such trite enterprises as the "reenchantment of the world" (a phrase that tends to dissolve into mere metaphor when it lacks the flesh of social insight and a naturalistic elaboration). If science is to resolve the dilemma of its rationalization in the social world, it must learn to balance the need for self-interpretation with the insights furnished by different levels of natural development. Science must turn to nature itself for nutriment. It must be thoroughly mindful of the presuppositions—the biases—that continually enter into its epistemological structures. The debates between supporters of one "paradigm" and another must be infused with a sense of history—both natural and intellectual—rather than to rest on dynastic ideological successions and exclusions. Science must candidly ask itself questions shaped by natural reality, not by a self-enclosed intellectualism that separates its ideological history from the history of the natural world. Hence science must overcome its ambiguities by recognizing that it is both its own history as a whole—not one or another phase of that history—and natural history as well. In this sense, neither Aristotle nor Galileo were wrong *per se*, however much the latter detested the former; they observed different aspects of realities imparted to them by nature and by different levels of natural development.

Underlying any project for rediscovering nature is a body of key questions. If there is any unity of nature to be discovered, what message does it have to offer? What is its essential meaning? And if we are to talk of meaning in nature—of the "why" as well as the "how" of natural phenomena—how are we to develop graded forms of causality (whether they are Hellenic or modern, for example, or the phasing of one into the other) so that we do not completely exclude one or the other? And if we grant that meaning does exist, how are we to interpret its direction, its teleology? Must we foreclose the possibility that ends may be latent in beginnings by speaking of "teleology" as if the end must necessarily follow from its beginning as a totally preordained "final cause"? Can we loosen up our current narrow, ironclad notions of teleology to see it more as a graded, emergent, and *creative* development rather than an overly deterministic form of causality?

These questions, so crucial for developing an ecological ethics and an ecologically oriented science, cannot stay frozen in the forms used by crude scientistic ideologues for centuries. If nothing else, we must reclaim the right to think freely about ideas and reality without having restrictions imposed upon us by ideologues who merely answer each other's errors with errors of their own. Science, in effect, must cease to be a Church. It must tear down the ecclesiastical barriers that separate it from the free air of nature and from the garden which nourished its intellectual development.

☙

Technics, the skills and instruments for humanity's metabolism with nature, formed the crucible in which the modern concepts of reason and science were actually forged. In the sphere of production (in Marx's "realm of necessity") the ambiguities of freedom emerged with unadorned clarity. During the modern industrial era and even earlier, during certain preindustrial periods, reason finally became mere rationalization and science was visibly transmuted from a pursuit of knowledge into mere technique and instrumentalism. Hence it should not seem surprising that technics exhibits the ambiguities of freedom in their most striking form. The notion that technology is intrinsically morally neutral, that the proverbial "knife" cuts either way—as weapon to kill or as tool to cut, depending upon the user or the society in which it is used—was not a widely accepted viewpoint until the rise of industrialism. To be sure knives, like other hand tools, can be viewed in such ethically neutral terms. But in the larger context of technics—notably, tools, machines, skills, forms of labor, and "natural resources"—the means of production rarely were regarded as value-free, nor was their impact contingent merely on individual or social intentions.

Although pre-industrial societies may not have explicitly distinguished between libertarian and authoritarian technics (a distinction that probably forced itself upon the modern mind with the massive supremacy of highly centralized industrial technologies over traditional crafts), they apparently were more aware than we of the ecological implications of technique. If Stephan Toulmin and June Goodfield are correct in their appraisal, pre-industrial communities distinguished very early in history between "natural arts" and "artificial crafts"—a distinction that expressed ethical outlooks basically different from our own toward technological development. The "natural arts," such as farming, husbandry, and medicine, were patently necessary for human survival, and their place in the preservation of the individual and the community was of central importance. But they were "natural" not just for pragmatic reasons; their very success in satisfying basic human needs required that they be subtly in rhythm with "natural change." The artisan's insight melded human craft and nature together into not only the natural materials required by the Anvilik Eskimos for their soapstone artistry but also the larger natural processes that determined the success of an enterprise.

Toulmin and Goodfield, in effect, refer to a cosmic tableau in which the person engaged in a "natural art" was situated in order to "steer [these natural processes] in a favorable direction" and to utilize "certain natural powers" stronger than those possessed by the individual to remedy the disasters that afflicted agriculture or health. Accordingly, all efforts were valueless if one failed to act at the "correct time" in synchrony with "natural cycles." Ritual became as much a part of production as seasonal changes, climatic variations, drought, and predation, or, in the case of medicine, the periodic onset of certain illnesses. It is fair to say that we are reclaiming these remote, apparently lost sensibilities today with our growing awareness that sound food cultivation and good health presuppose the attunement of life—and crafts—with biological cycles that foster soil fertility and physical well-being. Both the organic farmer and the serious practitioner of holistic health, for example, have been obliged to cultivate insights that extend far beyond the conventional wisdom of the agronomist and the physician. Certain all-important notions—that nutriment and health are not merely industrial products, artifacts ("magic bullets") that can be engineered into existence; that our modern pharmacopias for agriculture and physical well-being cannot function as substitutes for a wisely "crafted" way of life; that life itself is a "calling," which rests on that rare combination of craft and nature we designate as "art"—have their roots in ancient notions of a sense of craft that is "in step with the ruling cycles of natural change."

By contrast, the "artificial crafts played a much smaller part in men's lives than the natural arts," Toulmin and Goodfield observe. "Given flint tools and weapons, and some pottery, life was supportable at a primitive level without metal, glass or perfume, even in an English winter." These remarks belabor the obvious and render the distinction between "natural arts" and "artificial crafts" merely pragmatic. We must not ignore the essentially metaphysical aspects that distinguish them. Artificial or not, early crafts such as metalworking, glass-making, and dyeing alike had the task of imitating Nature, and of creating products which were indistinguishable from the best natural materials. The earliest glass objects known are certain Egyptian beads which were used as personal ornaments in place of precious stones; even then they were known as "sparklers." Glass-making thus began as the production of artificial jewels, and since gold and jewels were always in short supply men continued to think of the crafts in this light as late as classical times. The metal-workers of Alexandria, for instance, produced silver and copper alloys having the appearance and properties of gold; and they developed for this purpose a whole range of techniques for depositing a durable golden colour on a relatively cheap alloy. There was nothing necessarily fraudulent about these techniques. Men were paying for the appearance, not the "atomic weights," so the craftsmen and customers alike were entitled to be satisfied with the results.

Hence the "natural" rather than the valuable, the useful and beautiful rather than the costly and the rare still retained their primordial hold even on "artificially" crafted products. Use-value, as it were, held its predominant position over exchange-value and the glitter of the utopian held sway over the dross of self-interest.

To the degree that the craftsperson "imitated" nature, he or she had entered into a quasi-mystical communion that authenticated the natural qualities of human-made products. Skill was permeated by the imagery of a natural endowment, of gifts bestowed upon the craftsperson by natural forces—gifts that, in some sense, had to be reciprocated. The naturalistic "law of return" reflects a distinctly ecological sensibility—indeed, a sense of responsibility that involves compensation for what is withdrawn or even simulated in the natural world. Hence, as Toulmin and Goodfield tell us:

> A ritual element can be found also in the artificial crafts of the ancient world, where at first sight the recipes (for producing the product) looked so much more direct. For example, in the Mesopotamian recipes for glass and glazes ... instructions for the necessary technical procedures are accompanied by other injunctions of a ritual kind. The recipes from the library of Assurbanipal (seventh century B.C.) begin by explaining that the glass-furnace must be built at the auspicious time: a shrine to the appropriate Gods must be installed, and care must be taken to keep the good will of the deities in the daily operations of the workshop.

In laying the plans for the glass-furnace, the builder was warned to set a censer of pine incense as an offer to the "embryo-gods," a reference that, as Toulmin and Goodfield observe,

> has a history. In the earlier set of recipes, dating from 1600 B.C., there is a very obscure passage in which some scholars have seen evidence that actual human embryos—possibly still-born infants—were buried in the furnace. What could have been the point of this? There is little contemporary evidence, but perhaps we may read back into this association beliefs which are quite explicit later on. For, if one contrasts the brilliancy and cohesion of new-poured glass or metal ingots with the dirty and chaotic pile of ore, ash and sand from which they are made, the change is most striking: it is as though one had transformed a dull, lifeless agglomeration into a living unity. The sparkle of gold and glass had something of the vital spark visible in the human eye, so that it was not mere fancy to see, in the artificial production of these materials, the creation of something superior—if not actually alive.

Production, in effect, implied not only reproduction, as Eliade has observed for metallurgy, but also animation—not as "raw materials" bathed in the "fire of labor," but as nature actively imbuing its own substance with a "vital spark." The spiritized nature of technics is reflected in a highly suggestive body of possibilities that only recently have entered into our accounts of the history of technology.

The original "magic" of gold, in fact, may justify a more literal interpretation of the metal than we have previously given. Its original attraction is perhaps less a function of its monetary value and rarity than of the fact that it is untarnishable. The metal seems to present a mystical eternality to the flux and change that afflict more mundane objects. Alchemy may have drawn its inspiration from these attributes; well before gold became coinage or the ornamental evidence of wealth and power, it may have been sacred substance that defied the assault of time and the perishability of things. If these speculations are valid, the division of labor between "natural arts" and "artificial crafts"—indeed, the historic division of labor between food cultivation and crafts that underpins the separation of town and country—is haunted by ideological ghosts: the rearing of temples, the fabrication of sacred objects and altars, the ornamentation of deities, the artistry applied to priestly vestments and artifacts. Only later do artificial crafts begin to apply to personal products that satisfy the appetites of ruling classes.

After all has been said about the classical world's disdain for labor, I wish to add a qualifying note. In many respects, Hellenic and Roman ideas about work score a profound ethical advance over preliterate and early ancient mystical attitudes toward technics. Claude Mossé reminds us that Odysseus built his own boat, and that Hephaestus, the deity of crafts, spent his life "in the red glow of his forge." The ancient world did not despise work as such. The origins of the Greek ideal of free time derive not only from an ideological disdain for the slave and for enslavement but also from a profound respect for freedom as an *activity*. Aristotle pointedly observes that "the best ordered *poleis* will not make an artisan a citizen." Citizenship will "only belong to those who are released from manual occupations" and, in effect, are thereby engaged in the work of managing the *polis*. It is this latter concept of active citizenship based on individual autonomy and freedom of judgment that is central to the Hellenic notion of citizenship. As Mossé correctly observes, "It is not the manual activity of work which makes labour despised, but the *ties of dependence* which it creates between the artisan and the person who uses the product which he manufactures." The Hellenic attitude toward labor is conditioned as much by the autonomy of the worker as it is by an association of active citizenship with free time. The ethical principle of autonomy is no less significant than the social and psychological factors that shaped the attitude of the *polis*.

Mossé's elaboration of this Greek view toward work is worth citing in more detail.

> To build one's own house, one's own ship, or to spin and and weave the material which is used to clothe the members of one's own household is in no way shameful. But to work for another man, in return for a wage of any kind, is degrading. It is this which distinguishes the ancient mentality from a modern which would have no hesitation in placing the independent artisan above the wage-earner. But, for the ancients, there is really no difference between the artisan who sells his own products and the workman who hires out his services. Both work to satisfy the needs of others, not their own. They depend on others for their livelihood. For that reason they are no longer free. This perhaps above all is what distinguishes the artisan from the peasant. The peasant is so much closer to the ideal of self-sufficiency (*autarkeia*) which was the essential basis for man's freedom in the ancient world. Needless to say, in the classical age, in both Greece and Rome, this ideal of self-sufficiency had long since given way to a system of organized trade. However,

the archaic mentality endured, and this explains not only the scorn felt for the artisan, labouring in his smithy, or beneath the scorching sun on building sites, but also the scarcely veiled disdain felt for merchants or for the rich entrepreneurs who live off the labour of their slaves.

By contrast, the farmer earned not only the material independence requisite for a free man, but also the sense of security requisite for a free spirit. He was no client. The classical mind read clientage into vocations that would surprise us today—for example, the dependence of wealthy usurers on their debtors, of traders on their buyers, of craftsmen on their customers, and of artists on their admirers. Even though the usurer, trader, and artisan began to preempt the farmer in social power, the tension between reality and ideal, while it finally destroyed the traditional reality, did not destroy the traditional ideal. In fact, agriculture enjoyed cultural eminence in the classical world not only because it conferred self-sufficiency on its practitioners but also because it was seen as an *ethical* activity, hence not only a *techne*. "Life in the fields strengthened both the body and soul," Mossé observes.

> Love for the soil was an essential ingredient of patriotism.... The earth was just and gave her fruits to those who understood how to tend her, and who obeyed the injunctions of the gods. Whatever magical practices they resorted to, in order to gain good harvests, they certainly never took the place of the day-to-day care the earth needed, and experience was the basis of this knowledge which was handed down from father to son. But the science of agriculture went no further than an attempt to find better ways of organising labor.

Food cultivation as a spiritual—indeed religious—activity had not been changed basically by the emergence of the *polis* and the republican city-state. But it had also been given a moral dimension that was more in accord with the rationalism of the classical world.

The secularization of technics occurred within a context that, while rational and pragmatic, was not strictly rationalistic and scientistic. Initially, religion—and later, ethics—defined the very function of technology within society. The use of tools and machines called for a series of explanations that were not only mystical but also ethical and ecological explanations rather than strictly pragmatic. Were arts authentically "natural" or not? Were crafts "artificial"? If so, in what sense? Did they accord with the structure, solidarity, and ideology of the community? At a later time, when the *polis* and the republican city-state emerged, more sophisticated parameters for technical change emerged as well. Did technical changes foster the personal autonomy that became so integral to the Hellenic ideal of citizenship and a palpable body politic? Did they foster personal independence and republican virtue? Viewed from an ecological viewpoint, did they accord with a "just" earth who "gave her fruits to those who understood how to tend her"? Here, the concept of an "appropriate" technology was formulated not in terms of logistics and physical dimensions but in terms of an ecological ethics that visualized an active nature as "just," comprehending, and generous. Nature abundantly rewarded the food cultivator (or the artisan) who was prepared to function symbiotically in relation to her power of fecundity and her injunctions.

❧

    Despite the morass of slavery into which the classical world descended, only to be followed by feudal forms of servitude, these ethical distinctions did not disappear. A close association between ethics and technics persisted throughout medieval society, the Renaissance, and the Enlightenment. Feudal custom and the Protestant ethic dictated a sense of moral responsibility and theological "calling" toward work and technical change, all other social and doctrinal limitations aside. The medieval guilds were not merely occupational associations; they regulated the quality of goods according to very distinct canons of fairness and justice in which Biblical precept played as much of a role as economic considerations. Until the enclosure movements of the sixteenth century turned the English nobility into mere agricultural entrepreneurs, the manorial society over which it presided had an avowedly patronal character. When the nobility began to betray its traditional yeoman clients by replacing them with sheep, the Tudor monarchs from Henry to Elizabeth vigorously sought to arrest this development and became the objects of sharp opprobrium by the landlord and merchant classes of the time.

    By the late eighteenth century, England had plummeted recklessly into a brutalizing industrial society that advanced terribly meager ethical criteria for mechanization. Bentham, as noted earlier, identified the "good" quantitatively rather than in terms of an abiding sense of right and wrong. Adam Smith, in many ways more of a moralist than an economist, saw "good" in terms of self-interest governed by a vague "rule of justice." From an ethical viewpoint, the displaced yeomanry and the new working classes were simply abandoned to their fate. If the emerging factory system stunted its human "operatives" (to use the language of the day)—if it shortened their lives appallingly, fostering pandemics like tuberculosis and cholera—the new English manufacturing class advanced no weighty ethical imperatives for the human disasters it produced, beyond some hazy commitment to "progress." The British ruling elite may have been sanctimonious, but it was often blissfully lacking in hypocrisy, as the writings of one of its greatest theorists, David Ricardo, has revealed. "Progress" was unabashedly identified with egotism; the classical ideal of autonomy and independence, with "free competition." English industrialists were never infused with a spirit of "republican virtue"—nor, for that matter, were the ideologists of the French Revolution, despite all their mimicking of Roman postures and phraseology. Neither Adam Smith on one side of the Channel nor Robespierre on the other identified their ethical views with the existence of an independent yeoman class whose capacity for citizenship was a function of their autonomy. Both spokesmen were oriented ideologically toward vague notions of "natural liberty" that found their expression in freedom from government (Smith) or a "tyranny of freedom" (Rousseau) that took the form of a highly centralized State.

It was actually in America—and perhaps there alone—that republican virtue most closely approximated the classical ideal. A living federalism, which was not significantly diluted until the latter half of the nineteenth century, provided the soil for a stunning variety of political institutions and economic relationships. To be sure, this rich galaxy of forms included the slavocracy of the southern states, institutions (and ideologies) for the genocidal occupation of Indian lands, and a barely concealed system of peonage involving not only indentured servitude during the colonial period but the plantation economy that came with the expropriation of Mexican territories. But New England political life was organized around the face-to-face democracy of the town meeting and around considerable county and statewide autonomy. An incredibly loose democracy and mutualism prevailed along a frontier that was often beyond the reach of the comparatively weak national government.

Permeating this relatively democratic world was an intense republican ideology that provided the ethical context of American technical development for generations after the Revolution. Although it is commonplace to cite Jefferson as this ideology's most articulate spokesman, we must often be reminded how closely his views approximated the classical ideal and how deeply they affected American technical development. In the famous *Notes on the State of*

Virginia of 1785, Jefferson's association of republican virtue with the "natural arts" of agriculture and an autonomous yeoman class reads like a strident passage from Cicero's *De Officiis*:

> Those who labour in the earth are the chosen people of God, if ever he had a chosen people, whose breasts he has made his peculiar deposit for substantial and genuine virtue. It is the focus in which he keeps alive that sacred fire, which otherwise might escape from the face of the earth. Corruption of morals in the mass of cultivators is a phaenomenon of which no age nor nation has furnished an example. It is the mark set on those, who not looking up to heaven, to their own soil and industry, as does the husbandman, for their subsistence, depend for it on the casualties and caprice of customers. Dependence begets subservience and venality, suffocates the germ of virtue and prepares fit tools for the designs of ambition.

Jefferson's concern for the independence of a republican body politic renders this passage strikingly unique. Eighteenth-century European political economists like the Physiocrats had also given primacy to the "natural arts," notably to agriculture over manufactures. But they had done so more as a source of wealth rather than because of social morality. Jefferson's emphasis on agriculture is largely ethical; it is anchored not only in the virtues of husbandry as a technical calling but in the farmer as an independent citizen. By contrast, the "mobs of the great cities" are corrupted by their clientage, self-interest, and lascivious appetites. They lack the industry, virtue, and moral cohesion that is necessary for freedom and stable republican institutions.

Nor was Jefferson alone in this ethical stance. Similar views were echoed (although far less fervently) by John Adams as early as the 1780s, and even by Benjamin Franklin, whose favorable view of the "artificial crafts" was that of a highly urbanized republican artisan—of a printer turned propagandist. For our purposes, what makes Jefferson's views unique is the extent to which he exalted the virtues of nature as such. He speaks to us not only in the traditional language of "natural law," but in a more aesthetic vernacular that reveals his appreciation of the mutual enhancement of the natural world and labor. The Biblical injunction of hard labor in the fields as penance is replaced by an ecological vision of virtuous labor as freedom. The husbandman "looking up to heaven" or down to his "own soil" is the imagery of ecology, not of political economy.

But we soon encounter a remarkable paradox. Once this fervently republican tradition is extended beyond an agricultural society peopled by self-sufficient farmers, it contains the seeds for its own negation. Perhaps even more striking, this tradition provides a basis not only for the absorption of the "natural arts" by the "artificial crafts" but also for the total mechanization of personal and social life. Neither Jefferson nor the agrarian populists of his day could have prevented the growth of manufactures in the New World, nor could they present a strong ideological case against the increase of nonagricultural pursuits. Indeed, Jefferson the president was significantly different from Jefferson the author of the *Declaration of Independence*. If the vitality of the republic, conceived as a *body politic*, depended upon the independence and autonomy of its yeomanry, then the vitality of the republic, conceived as a *nation*, depended upon the independence and autonomy of its economy. An agrarian America that required industrial goods could hardly hope to retain its republican integrity if it remained a mere client of European industry. It followed logically that America had to develop its own industrial base in order to maintain its own sense of republican virtue.

Here lay the conditions for a supremely ironical development in the relation of ethics to technics. To preserve its secular ethics, American republican ideology had to accept a course of technical development that threatened to vitiate its own classical premises. The nation could not become autonomous without rendering its own body politic of self-sufficient yeomen increasingly heteronomous. To cease to be a client of English industry, America required an industry of its own with its consequent rationalization of labor and its use of scientific principles to devise sophisticated instruments of production. Jefferson had never seen English factory towns and the squalor they produced; his unruly urban "mobs" were largely artisans and small retailers. Yet even this modest level of economic development sufficed to disquiet him. The emergence of the factory raised even more thundering problems. Visitors to England during the first half of the nineteenth century returned to their respective homelands with horrendous accounts of the filth, the disease, and the demoralization of the working classes that accompanied the new industrial system. In the 1830s, De Tocqueville told the French about Manchester, this "new Hades," with its "heaps of dung, rubble from buildings, putrid stagnant pools ... the noise of furnaces, the whistle of steam" and the "vast structures" enshrouded in "black smoke" that "keep air and light out of the human habitations which they dominate." A decade later, Engels gave the Germans an even more detailed, vivid account of England's chief industrial city. Still another decade later, Dickens described the situation to his more fortunate countrymen in the well-to-do parts of the country.

To build a large factory complex in the new United States meant little more than to place classical republican ethics on the rack. How could Yankee merchant-entrepreneurs, whose parents and grandparents had presumably risked their lives and fortunes for the republican ideal, hope to decorate a relatively sophisticated industrial system with the garlands of republican virtue? The ideal itself had to be modified without overly abusing its form, which itself had to be significantly altered without seeming to lose its surface attributes. Accordingly, the concern for the autonomy of the body politic with its world of free farmers had to be transferred to a concern for the autonomy of the nation with its world of free entrepreneurs. This problem was to become a central theme of American social life for more than a century after Jefferson's death. It recurs to this day as a cultural reflex against an increasingly centralized and bureaucratic society.

Republican virtue viewed as a *human* good had to be depersonalized, generalized, and finally objectified into republican virtue viewed as an *institutional* good. This change in emphasis was decisive. Where Jefferson had placed the locus of his ethics in a family-worked farm, independent and strong in its commitment to independence, the new merchant-entrepreneurs placed the locus of their ethics in an industrial community worked by hired, robotized hands. The autonomy of The Republic, in effect, was purchased at the expense of its republicans. This shrewd dehumanization of ethics into a mere stratagem for material gain assumed a highly sinister form. If The Republic now began to supplant its republicans, its sense of "virtue" persisted—but now as a *discipline* rather than as an ideal.

As John F. Kasson has noted in an excellent study of technology and American republican values, a decisive step in achieving this shift in emphasis occurred in the 1820s, when a group of Boston merchant-entrepreneurs built the earliest American industrial complex at what was to be called Lowell, Massachusetts. Francis Cabot Lowell, who conceived this textile manufacturing complex and provided it posthumously with his name, also furnished it with its ethical rationale, its initial design, and its ubiquitous criteria of discipline. As Kasson observes,

> Previous American factory settlements had retained the English system of hiring whole families, often including school-age children. Lowell and his associates opposed the idea of a long-term residential force that might lead to an entrenched proletariat. They planned to hire as their main working force young single women from the surrounding area for a few years apiece. For

a rotating force such as this, women were an obvious choice. Able-bodied men could be attracted from farming only with difficulty, and their hiring would raise fears that the nation might lose her agrarian character and promote resistance to manufactures. Women, on the other hand, had traditionally served as spinners and weavers when textiles had been produced in the home, and they constituted an important part of the family economy.

Here, piety and pastoralism formed a perfect fit with profit and productivity. The women were expected to be docile. Raised in a Puritan tradition that preached a message of self-discipline, hard work, obedience, and salvation, their sense of virtue was home-bred and merely required paternal surveillance. On this score, the Lowell mill-owners used their concept of republican ideals in an unprecedentedly expansive manner: the factory system's demands for order and hierarchy were introduced into every aspect of the employee's living situation.

The first manufacturing complex, which opened in September, 1823, consisted of six factory buildings "grouped in a spacious quadrangle bordering the river and landscaped with flowers, trees, and shrubs." The greenery that surrounded Lowell and its buildings not only imparted the appropriate pastoral setting for a classical republican community but also insulated its employees from large towns with their unruly "mobs" and insidious political ideas. The factory buildings, in turn, were

> dominated by a central mill, crowned with a Georgian cupola. Made of brick, with flat, plain walls, and white granite lintels above each window space, the factories presented a neat, orderly, and efficient appearance, which symbolized the institution's goals and would be emulated by many of the penitentiaries, insane asylums, orphanages, and reformatories of the period. Beyond the counting house at the entrance to the mill yard stretched the company dormitories. Their arrangement reflected a Federalist image of proper social structure. The factory population of Lowell was rigidly defined into four groups and their hierarchy was immutably preserved in the town's architecture.

A Georgian mansion directly below the original factory in Lowell symbolized the authority of the complex's manager. Beneath the company's agent

> stood the overseers, who lived in simple yet substantial quarters at the ends of the rows of boardinghouses where the operatives resided, thus

providing a secondary measure of surveillance. In the boardinghouses themselves lived the female workers who outnumbered male employees three to one. Originally these apartments were constructed in rows of double houses, at least thirty girls to a unit, with intervening strips of lawn.

Later, as the company expanded, the apartments were strung together, "blocking both light and air. These quarters were intended to serve intentionally as dormitories and offered few amenities beyond dining rooms and bedrooms, each of the latter shared by as many as six or eight girls, two to a bed."

Although Lowell's textile technology belongs to the beginnings of the industrial system, its obsessive concern with surveillance and discipline was eerily in advance of its time. It reveals with startling clarity the implications of the factory as a unique form of *social* organization—an issue that only recently has come to the foreground of institutional discourse. Lowell did not merely exploit its workers; it sought to totally recondition them. Its surveillance system may seem particularly crude today, but at the time it was highly effective in reshaping the very outlook of naïve country folk:

> The factory as a whole was governed by the superintendent, his office strategically placed between the boardinghouses and the mills at the entrance to the mill yard. From this point, as one spokesman enthusiastically reported, his "mind regulates all; his character inspires all; his plans, matured and decided by the directors of the company, who visit him every week, control all." Beneath his watchful eye in each room of the factory, an overseer stood responsible for the work, conduct, and proper management of the operatives therein.... In addition ... corporate authorities relied upon the factory girls to act as moral police over one another. The ideal, as described by an unofficial spokesman of the corporation, represented a tyranny of the majority that would have made De Tocqueville shudder.

Theoretically, at least, the mere suspicion of moral and behavioral improprieties led to ostracism until the suspected operative, shunned by her coworkers on the streets of the town, on the job, and in the boardinghouse, was reduced to an outcast. Eventually, the victim of this unrelenting social pressure would be forced to leave the community.

It would be simplistic to dismiss Lowell as an industrial penitentiary, a blight among many that marked the onset of the Industrial Revolution in America. As with the factory system in England, one of the primary functions of such highly supervised working conditions was to regularize labor, to standardize it, and to govern its rhythms by the tick of the clock and the tempo of the machine. But Lowell was also a uniquely American phenomenon. Ideologically, it had been reared on the basis of a distinct republican ethic that related technics to lofty concepts of citizenship. In practice, however, it dramatically demonstrated how ethics could be dismembered by technology—indeed, absorbed into it. Values that had stemmed from a long tradition of human rationality became not only dehumanized but also rationalized, not only instruments in the service of industrial exploitation but also sources of social regimentation.

Far from being a phase in early industrial development like the unfeeling factory town of Manchester, Lowell was in many ways far ahead of its time. As early as the 1820s, when small-scale agriculture and family-type artisanship were still predominant in American society, an industrial entity had emerged that, in the very name of domestic republican ideals, thoroughly industrialized every detail of a community's personal life. Lowell had created not only a society of "artificial crafts" but also a cosmos of industrial hierarchy and discipline. Nothing was spared from these industrial attributes—not dress, food, entertainment, reading matter, leisure time, sexuality, or demeanor. As Kasson notes, the

> cupolas which crowned Lowell's mills were not simply ornamental; their bells insistently reminded workers that time was money. Operatives worked a six-day week, approximately twelve hours a day, and bells tolled them awake and to their jobs (lateness was severely punished), to and from meals, curfew, and bed.

Although Lowell was to fade away as a model industrial community, its legacy never disappeared. Such a highly regulated world did not reappear in the United States until the 1950s, albeit in the pastel colors favored by social engineers and reinforced less by brute surveillance than by the subtle arts of industrial psychology. But these new techniques were effective because Lowell and its successors had done their job well. The dissociation of traditional republican ethics from technics was complete. By the 1950s, the factory system and market had begun to invade the last bastions of private life and had colonized personality itself. No overseers and superintendents were needed to perform this task. Reinforced by rationality as a mode of instrumentalism and science as a value-free discipline, the Lowells of our own era have ceased to be an extrinsic feature of social mechanization. They arose immanently from the factory system as a way of life and the marketplace as the mode of human consociation. Technics no longer had to pretend that it had an ethical context; it had become the "vital spark" of society itself. In the face of this massive development, no private refuge was available, no town or frontier to which one could flee, no cottage to which one could retreat. Management ceased to be a form of administration and literally became a way of life. Ironically, republican virtue was not completely discarded; it was simply transmuted from an ideal into a technique. Autonomy was reworked to mean competition, individuality to mean egotism, fortitude to mean moral indifference, enterprise to mean the pursuit of profit, and federalism to mean free trade. The ethic spawned by the American Revolution was simply eviscerated, leaving behind a hollow shell for ceremonial exploitation. As it turned out, it was not the hideous squalor of a Manchester that placed a lasting imprint on the industrial age but the clinical sophistication of bureaucratic disempowerment and media manipulation.

⋈

What is most chilling about the ambiguities of freedom—of reason, science, and technics—is that we now take their existence for granted. We have been taught to regard these ambiguities as part of the human condition, with the result that they merely coexist with each other rather than confront each other. We are becoming deadened to the contradictions they pose, their relationship to each other in contemporary life and the history of ideas, and the harsh logic that must eventually assert itself when one element of these ambiguities asserts itself over the other. Our intellectual neutrality toward reason and rationalism, science and scientism, and ethics and technics creates not only confusion about the notion of paradox as such, but also a misbegotten "freedom" to alternate flippantly between both sides of the ambiguity—or worse yet, to mindlessly occupy utterly conflicting positions simultaneously.

The social and ecological problems of our time will not allow us to delay indefinitely in formulating a sound outlook and practice. The individual elements of these ambiguities of freedom have acquired a life of their own, all the more because our neutrality fosters abstention and withdrawal. The continuing substitution of rationalism for reason, of scientism for science, and of technics for ethics threatens to remove our very sense of the problems that exist, not to speak of our ability to resolve them. A look at technics alone reveals that the car is racing at an increasing pace, with nobody in the driver's seat. Accordingly, commitment and insight have never been more needed than they are today. Whether or not the time is too late I will not venture to say neither pessimism nor optimism have any meaning in the face of the commanding imperatives that confront us. What must be understood is that the ambiguities of freedom are not intractable problems—that there *are* ways of resolving them.

The reconstruction of reason as an interpretation of the world must begin with a review of the modem premises of rationalism—its commitment to insight through opposition. This oppositional commitment, common to objective and subjective reason alike, casts all "otherness" in stringently antithetical terms. Understanding *as such* depends upon our ability to control what is to be understood—or, more radically, to conquer it, subjugate it, efface it, or absorb it. Like the Marxian vision of labor, reason is said to establish its very identity through its powers of negativity and sovereignty. An activistic rationalism of the kind so endearing to both German idealism and American pragmatism is a rationalism of conquest, not of reconciliation; of intellectual predation, not of intellectual symbiosis. That there are phenomena in our world that must be conquered, indeed, disgorged— for example, domination, exploitation, rule, cruelty, and indifference to suffering—needs hardly to be emphasized. But that "otherness" *per se* is intrinsically comprehended in oppositional terms also biases that comprehension in the direction of instrumentalism, for hidden within a dialectic of strict negativity are the philosophical tricks for using power as a predominant mode of comprehension.

Just as we can justifiably distinguish between an authoritarian and a libertarian technics, so too can we distinguish between authoritarian and libertarian modes of reason. This distinction is no less decisive for thought and its history than it is for technology. The creatively reproductive form we wish to impart to a new ecological community requires the mediation of a libertarian reason, one that *bears witness* to the symbiotic animism of early preliterate sensibilities without becoming captive to its myths and self-deceptions. Even though animals have not been persuaded by rituals and ceremonials to seek out the hunter, we would do well to respect the animals and plants we consume by using an etiquette, perhaps even ceremonies, that acknowledge their integrity and subjectivity as living beings. For here nature has offered up a sacrifice to us that demands some kind of recompense in turn—even an aesthetic one. Nor are we alone the participants and audience for that ceremonial; life surrounds us everywhere and, in its own way, bears witness to ours. Our habitat, in effect, is not merely a place in which we happen to live; it is also a form of natural conscience.

The symbiotic rationality I have called libertarian is a ubiquitous presence, a sensibility, a state of mind, not merely a cerebral series of thoughts. To harvest life and feed on it unthinkingly is to diminish the sense of life within us as well as the reality of life around us. Denied its aesthetics and ceremonials, an ecological sensibility becomes a mere pretense at what we so flippantly call "ecological thinking," or (to use the sleazy formula of one prominent environmentalism) the notion that there is no "free lunch" in nature. Libertarian rationality does not include "lunches" or "snacks" in its vision of ecological balance. It is a redefinition of "otherness" not simply as a "thou," but as the very *way* by which we relate to beings apart from ourselves. Our approach to all the particulars that constitute nature is as intrinsic to a libertarian rationality as the images we form of them in our minds. Hence it is a practice as well as an outlook. How we till the soil or plant and harvest its produce—indeed, how we walk across a meadow or through a forest—is coextensive with the rationality we bring to the environments we are trying to comprehend.

The "other," to be sure, is never us. It is apart from us just as surely as we are apart from it. In western philosophy, particularly in its Hegelian forms, this fact has inexorably locked "otherness" as such into various concepts of alienation. Leaving Hegelian interpreters aside, however, any serious reading of Hegel's works reveals that he was never fully comfortable with his own notion of the "other." Alienation conceived as *Entäusserung* is not similar to alienation conceived as *Selbstentäusserung*. The former, favored by Marx, views "otherness"— specifically, the products of human labor—as an antagonistic mode of objectification that asserts itself above and against the worker. By no means does Marx confine *Entäusserung* to capitalism; it also emerges in humanity's intercourse with nature since, under natural conditions, even cooperative labor, in Marx's view, "is not voluntary but natural, not as [the workers'] united power, but as an alien force existing outside them ... and which they therefore cannot control, but which on the contrary, passes through its own power series of phases and stages, independent of man, even appearing to govern his will and action." Hence *Entäusserung* in the antagonistic sense of "estrangement" is coextensive with humanity's "embeddedness" in nature—another example of Marx's atrocious misreadings of "savage" society—and can be annulled only by its conquest of nature.

In Hegel's mature ontology, alienation as "otherness" is the *Selbstentäusserung*, or "self-detachment," of Spirit—the unfolding concretization of its potentialities into self-consciousness. Self-detachment is not committed to antagonism as much as it is to wholeness, fullness, and completeness. Although Hegel's emphasis on negativity can never be denied, he repeatedly weakens its asperity—for example, in his vision of "true love." "In love the separate does still remain," he wrote in his youthful years, "but as something united and no longer as something separate; life (in the subject) senses life (in the object)." This sense of detachment as a unity in diversity runs through the entire Hegelian dialectic as certainly as does its sweeping spirit of antithesis. Hegel's concept of transcendence (*aufhebung*) never advances a notion of outright annihilation. Its negativity consists of annulling the "other" in order to absorb it into a movement toward a richly variegated completeness.

But Hegel's notion of alienation is strictly theoretical. If we remain with him too long, we risk trying to explore different forms of reason in purely speculative terms. Reason, as I have emphasized, has its own natural and social history that provides a better means of resolving its paradoxes than does a strictly intellectual strategy. It also has its own anthropology, which reveals an approach to "otherness" that is based more on symbiosis and conciliation than detachment and opposition. The formation of the human mind is inseparable from the socialization of human nature at birth and its early period of development. However significant biology may be in shaping the human nervous system and its acuity, it is ultimately the gradual introduction of the newborn infant to culture that gives reason its specifically human character. We must turn to this early formative process to find the germinal conditions for a new, libertarian mode of rationality and the sensibility that will infuse it.

Biology and socialization, in fact, conjoin precisely at the point where maternal care is the most formative factor in childhood acculturation. Biology is obviously important because the neural equipment of human beings to think symbolically and to generalize well beyond the capacity of most primates is a tangible physical endowment. The newborn infant faces a long period of biological dependency, which not only allows for greater mental plasticity in acquiring knowledge but also provides time in which to develop strong social ties with its parents, siblings, and some kind of rudimentary community. No less important is the *form* of the socialization process itself, which intimately shapes the mentality and sensibility of the young.

Reason comes to the child primarily through the care, support, attention, and instruction provided by the mother. Robert Briffault, in his pioneering work on the "matriarchal" origins of society, accurately depicts this anthropology of reason. He observes that the

> one known factor which establishes a profound distinction between the
> constitution of the most rudimentary human group and all other animal
> groups [is the] association of mother and offspring which is the sole form of
> true social solidarity among animals. Throughout the class of mammals
> there is a continuous increase in the duration of that association, which is the
> consequence of the prolongation of the period of infantile dependence,
> and is correlated with a concomitant protraction of gestation and the
> advance in intelligence and social instincts.

We may reasonably question whether the mother-infant relationship is
the "sole form of true social solidarity among animals"—particularly
in the case of primates, which have a surprisingly large repertoire
of relationships. But had Briffault emphasized that the mother-infant
relationship is the *initial* step in the socialization process—the cradle in
which the need for consociation is created—he would have been accurate.
The role of this relationship in shaping human thought processes and
sensibilities is nothing less than monumental, particularly in matricentric
cultures where it encompasses most of childhood life.

In many respects, "civilization" involves a massive enterprise to
undo the impact of maternal care, nurture, and modes of thought on
the character structure of the offspring. The imagery of growing *up*
has actually come to mean growing *away* from a maternal, domestic
world of mutual support, concern, and love (a venerable and highly
workable society in its own right) into one made shapeless, unfeeling, and
harsh. To accommodate humanity to war, exploitation, political obedience,
and rule involves the undoing not only of human "first nature" as an animal
but also of human "second nature" as a child who lives in dependency
and protective custody under the eyes and in the arms of its mother.

What we so facilely call "maturity" is not ordinarily an ethically
desirable process of growth and humanization. To become an
"autonomous," "perceptive," "experienced," and "competent"
adult involves terms that historically possess very mixed meanings.
These terms become very misleading if they are not explicated in the
light of the social, ethical, economic, and psychological goals we have
in mind. The child's growth away from the values of a caring mother
toward autonomy and independence becomes a cultural travesty and a
psychological disaster when it results in a youth's degrading dependency
upon the caprices of an egotistical and unfeeling taskmaster.

Neither the youth's autonomy nor its character structure benefit
by "maturity" in this form. Dickens's account of Oliver Twist is not

a study of the growth of a child's capacity to cope as he "develops" from life in a nineteenth-century orphanage to survival in the wens of London. Rather, it is a study of a dehumanizing society that tends to destroy whatever sense of sympathy, care, and solidarity is woven into its character structure by maternal love. By contrast, the "primitive" Hopi children are in an immensely enviable position when they find many mothers to succor them and many loving relations to instruct them. They acquire a much greater social gift than "independence," which modern capitalism has redefined to mean "rugged egotism." Indeed, Hopi children acquire the all-important gift of *inter*dependence, in which individual and community support each other without negating the values of kindness, solidarity, and mutual respect that become the child's psychic inheritance and birth right.

This heritage is formed not only by maternal care and nurture but also by a very specific rationality that often is concealed within the maudlin term "mother love." For it is not only love that the mother ordinarily gives her child, but a rationality of "otherness" that stands sharply at odds with its modern arrogant counterpart. This earlier rationality is unabashedly *symbiotic*. Fromm's evocation of "mother love" as a spontaneous, unconditional sentiment of caring, free from any reciprocating obligations by the child, yields more than the total deobjectification of person that I emphasized earlier. "Mother love" also yields a rationality of deobjectification that is almost universal in character, indeed, a resubjectivization of experience that sees the "other" within a logical nexus of mutuality. The "other" becomes the active component that it always has been in natural and social history, not simply the "alien" and alienated that it is in Marxian theory and the "dead matter" that it is in classical physics.

I have deliberately emphasized the word *symbiotic* in describing this libertarian rationality. The dual meaning of this ecological term is important: symbiosis includes not only mutualism but also parasitism. A libertarian rationality is not unconditional in its observations, like "mother-love;" indeed, to deny *any* conditions for judging experience is naïve and myopic. But its *preconditions* for observation differ from an authoritarian rationalism structured around estrangement and ultimately around command and obedience. In a libertarian rationality, observation is always located within an ethical context that defines the "good" and is structured around a self-detachment (to use Hegel's term) that leads toward wholeness, completeness, and fullness (although more in an ecological rather than Hegel's metaphysical sense). A libertarian rationality raises natural ecology's tenet of unity in diversity to the level of reason itself; it evokes a logic of unity between the "I" and the "other" that recognizes the stabilizing and integrative function of diversity—of a cosmos of "others" that can be comprehended and integrated symbiotically. Diversity and unity do not contradict each other as logical antinomies. To the contrary, unity is the *form* of diversity, the *pattern* that gives it intelligibility and meaning, and hence a unifying principle not only of ecology but of reason itself.

A libertarian rationality that emphasizes the unity of "otherness" is not a logic of surrender, passivity, and sentimentality, as Jacob Bachofen, in his work, *Das Mutterrecht* ("Mother Right"), imputed to mother-love and "matriarchy" more than a century ago. Symbiosis, as I have already observed, does not deny the existence of a harmful parasitism that can destroy its host. A libertarian rationality must acknowledge the existence of an "other" that is itself blatantly antagonistic and oppositional. Actually, the ability to manipulate nature and to function actively in natural and social history is a desideratum, not an evil. But human activity is expected to occur within an ethical context of virtue, not a value-free context of utility and efficiency. There is a natural and social history of mentalism that *objectively* validates our concepts of the "good." Our very ability to form such concepts from the vast reservoir of natural development in all its gradations and forms derives from this natural history of subjectivity. Humanity, as part of this natural history, has the intrinsic right to participate in it. As a unique agent of consciousness, humanity can provide the voice of nature's internal rationality in the form of thought and self-reflective action. Libertarian reason seeks to consciously mitigate ecological destruction, in the realms of both social ecology and natural ecology.

Actually, the formal structure of dialectical and analytical reason would require very little alteration to accommodate a libertarian rationality. What would have to change decisively, however, is the overwhelming *orientation* of rational canons toward control, manipulation, domination, and estrangement that collectively bias authoritarian rationalism. Libertarian reason would advance a contrasting view in its orientation toward ecological symbiosis, but doubtless this can be regarded as a bias that is neither more nor less justifiable than the bias of authoritarian rationalism. But biases are not formed from mere air. Not only do they always exist in every orientation we hold, but their impact upon thought is all the more insidious when their existence is denied in the name of "objectivity" and a "value-free" epistemology.

It is not the interplay between abstract intellectual categories to which we must turn in order to validate the assumptions behind all our views. It is to experience itself—to natural and social history—that we must turn to test these assumptions. Not only in nature but also in "maternal care," in the very cradle of human consociation itself, do we find a human "second nature" that is structured around nurture, support, and a deobjectified world of experience rather than a world guided by domination, self-interest, and exploitation. It is in this social cradle that the most fundamental canons of reason are formed. The story of reason in the history of "civilization" is not an account of the sophistication of this germinal rationality along libertarian lines; it is a vast political and psychological enterprise to brutally extirpate this rationality in the interest of domination, to supplant it by the "third nature" of authority and rule. That fetid word "modernity"—and its confusion of personal atomization with "individuality"—may well demarcate an era in which the cradle of reason has finally been demolished.

◌◌

A new science that accords with libertarian reason, in turn, has the responsibility of rediscovering the concrete, which is so important in arresting this enterprise. Ironically, "paradigms" that quarrel with "paradigms," each blissfully remote from the natural history and ecological reality in which they should be immersed, increasingly serve the ends of instrumentalism with its inevitable manipulation of mind and society. Paradoxical as it may seem, the abstraction of science to methodology (which is largely what scientific "paradigms" do) tends to turn the scientific project itself into a problem of method, or more bluntly, a problem of instrumental strategies. The confusion between science as *knowledge*, or *Wissenschaft*, and as "scientific method" has never been adequately unscrambled. Since Francis Bacon's time, the identification of scientific verification with science itself has given a priority to technique over reality and has fostered the tendency to reduce our comprehension of reality to a matter of mere methodology. To recover the supremacy of the concrete—with its rich wealth of qualities, differentia, and solidity—over and beyond a transcendental concept of science as method is to slap the face of an arrogant intellectualism with the ungloved hand of reality. Plagued as we are today by a neo-Kantian dualism and transcendentalism that has given mind "a life of its own"—supplanting the reality of history with a mentalized myth of "historical stages," the reality of society with "flow diagrams," and the reality of communication with "metacommunication"—the recovery of the concrete is an enterprise not simply involving intellectual ventilation but also intellectual detoxification. Whatever we may think of Paul Feyerband's intellectualized version of anarchism, we may well treasure his work; he has opened the windows of modern science to the fresh air of reality.

"Science" must become the many sciences that make up its own history, from animism to nuclear physics; it must therefore respond to the many "voices" emitted by natural history. But these voices speak the language of the *facts* that constitute nature at different levels of its development. They are concrete and detailed; indeed, it is their very diversity as concretes that makes the organization of substance a drama of ever more complex forms, of "molecular self-organization" (to use the language of biochemistry). To recognize the specificity of these facts, their *uniqueness* as forms in enriching the enterprise of knowledge, is not to reduce science to a crude empiricism that replaces the scientist's need to generalize. Generalizations that seek to *elude* these concretes by fettering them to purely intellectual criteria of "truth" and "scientific method"—to garner what is quantitative in reality at the expense of what is qualitative—is to reject as archaic "paradigms" a vast heritage of truth whose value often lies in its richer, more qualitative view of reality.

Even natural ecology has not been immune to this orientation. It is already paying a severe penalty in its once-promising range of scope for its attempts to gain scientific "credibility" by surrendering its respect for the qualitative uniqueness of each ecosystem and instead describing the ecosystem in terms of energy values and flow diagrams. Reductionism and systems theory have scored yet another triumph. Hence, one of the key problems of science still lingers on. The scientist must approach nature for what it really is: active, developmental, emergent, and deliciously variegated in its wealth of specificity and form.

ෆ

Finally, technics must reinfuse its "artificial crafts" with its "natural arts" by bringing natural processes back into *techné* as much as possible. I refer not just to the traditional need to integrate agriculture with industry, but to the need to change our very concept of industry. The use of the Latin term *industria* to mean primarily a contrivance or device rather than diligence is of comparatively recent vintage. Today, the word industry has become almost synonymous with production organized around machines and their products or "manufactures." Industry and its machines, in turn, foster a very special public orientation: we see them as rationally arranged, largely self-operating instruments, conceived and designed by the human mind, that are meant to shape, form, and transform "raw materials" or "natural resources." The steel, glass, rubber, copper, and plastic materials that are turned into motor vehicles; the water and chemical ingredients that are turned into Coca-Cola; even the wood that is turned into mass-produced furnishings and the flesh that is turned into hamburgers—all are regarded merely as manufactures, the products of industry. In their finished form, these products bear no resemblance to the ores, minerals, vegetation, or animals from which they were derived. Assembled or packaged, they are transmuted results of processes that reflect not the sources but the mere background of their constituent materials. The craftsperson of antiquity continually added a natural dimension to the products of his or her "artificial crafts"—say, by carving the legs of couches to look like animal limbs or painting statues with sensuous colors. But what little artistry modern industry adds to its products is explicitly geometric and anti-natural—more precisely, *inorganic* in its passion for the "honesty" of the transmuted materials with which it functions.

This extraordinary, indeed pathological, disjunction of nature from its manufactured results stems from a largely mythic interpretation of technics. The products of modern industry are literally *denatured*. As such, they become mere objects to be consumed or enjoyed. They exhibit no association with the natural world from which they derive. In the public mind, a product is more intimately associated with the company that manufactured it than with the natural world that made its very existence and production possible. A car is a "Datsun" or a "Chevrolet," not a vehicle that comes from ores, minerals, trees, and animal hides; a hamburger is a "Big Mac," not the remains of an animal that once ranged a distant region of grasslands. Packaging obscures the corn and wheat fields of the Midwest behind the labels of the Del Monte, General Foods, and Pepperidge Farm corporations. Indeed, when we say that a product, food, or even therapy is "natural," we usually mean that it is "pure" or "unadulterated," not that it comes from nature.

What this orientation—or lack of orientation—reveals is not merely that advertising and media have imprinted corporate names on our minds with a view toward guiding our preferences and purchasing power. Perhaps more significantly, the actual fabrication of the product—from mine, farm, and forest to factory, mill, and chemical plant—has reduced the entire technical process to a mystery. In the archaic sense, "mystery" was once seen as a mystical, divinely inspired process (for example, metallurgy); but the mystery surrounding modern production is more mundane. We simply do not *know* beyond our own narrow sphere of experience how the most ordinary things we use are produced. So complete is the disjunction between production and consumption, between farm and factory (not to speak of between factory and consumer) that we are literally the unknowing clients of a stupendous industrial apparatus into which we have little insight and over which we have no control.

But this apparatus is itself the "client" of a vastly complex natural world, which it rarely comprehends in terms that are not strictly technical. We think of nature as a nonhuman industrial "apparatus." It "fabricates" products, in some vaguely understood manner, that we treat as an industrial phenomenon—with our extensive use of agricultural chemicals, our whaling and fishing marine factories, our mechanical slaughtering devices, and our denaturing of entire continental regions to mere factory departments. We commonly verbalize this industrial conception of nature in the language of mechanics, electronics, and cybernetics. Our description of the nonhuman or natural processes, as regulated by "negative feedback" or as systems into which we "plug" our "inputs" and "outputs," reflects the way we have "freaked" the natural world (to use Paul Shepard's vivid term) to meet the ends of industrial domination.

What is most important about our denaturing of natural phenomena is that we are its principal victims—we become the "objects" that our industry most effectively controls. We are its victims because we are unconscious of the way, both technically and psychologically, in which industry controls us. *Techné* as mystery has returned again, but not as a process in which the agriculturist or craftperson totally participates in a mystically enchanted process. We do *not* participate in the modern industrial process except as minutely specialized agents. Hence we are unaware of how the process occurs, much less able to exercise any degree of control over it. When we say that modern industry has become too complex, we normally mean that our knowledge, skills, insights, and traditions for growing or fabricating our means of life have been usurped by a stupendous, often meaningless, social machinery that renders us unable to cope with the most elementary imperatives of life. But it is not the complexity of machinery that inhibits our ability to deal with these imperatives; it is the new rules of the game we call an "industrial society" that, by restructuring our very lives, has interposed itself between the powers of human rationality and those of nature's fecundity. Most westerners ordinarily cannot plant and harvest a garden, fell a tree and shape it to meet their needs for shelter, reduce ores and cast metals, kill and dress animals for food and hides or preserve food and other perishables. These elementary vulnerabilities result not from any intrinsic complexity that must exist to provide us with the means of life; but from an ignorance of the means of sustaining life—an ignorance that has been deliberately fostered by a system of industrial clientage.

The factory was not born from a need to integrate labor with modern machinery. On the contrary, this building block of what we call "industrial society" arose from a need to *rationalize* the labor process—to intensify and exploit it more effectively than employers could ever hope to achieve with early cottage industries based on a self-regulated system of artisanship. Sidney Pollard, quoting an observer of the pre-factory era, notes that workers who were free to regulate their own time as domestic craftpersons rarely worked the modern eight-hour day and five-day week. "The weavers were used to 'play frequently all day on Monday and the greater part of Tuesday, and work very late on Thursday night, and frequently all night on Friday'" to ready their cloth for the Saturday market day. This irregularity, or "naturalness," in the rhythm and intensity of traditional systems of work contributed more toward the bourgeoisie's craze for social control and its savagely anti-naturalistic outlook than did the prices or earnings demanded by its employees. More than any single technical factor, this irregularity led to the rationalization of labor under a single ensemble of rule, to a discipline of work and regulation of time that yielded the modern factory, often with none of the technical developments we impute to the "Industrial Revolution." Before the steam engine, power loom, and flying shuttle came into use—indeed, before some of these machines were even invented—the traditional spinning wheel, hand loom, and dyeing vat that once filled the working areas of cottagers were assembled in large sheds primarily to mobilize the workers themselves, to regulate them harshly, and to intensify the exploitation of their labor.

Hence, the initial goal of the factory was to dominate labor and destroy the worker's independence from capital. The loss of this independence included the loss of the worker's contact with food cultivation. English parliamentary legislation in the late seventeenth century acknowledged that "custome hath been retained time out of mind ... that there should be a cessation of weaving every year, in the time of harvest" so that spinners and weavers could use their time "chiefly employed in harvest worke." As recently as the early nineteenth century, this practice was sufficiently widespread to warrant a comment in the *Manchester Chronicle* that many weavers could be expected to help in the late summer and early autumn harvesting operations on farms near the city.

The periodic shifting of workers from factories to fields should hardly be taken as an act of bucolic generosity on the part of England's ruling classes. Until the 1830s, English landlords still held a political edge over the industrial bourgeoisie. Workers who left factories during harvest seasons to work in the countryside were merely transported from one realm of exploitation to another. But it was intrinsically important for them to retain their agrarian skills—skills that their children and grandchildren were later to lose completely. To live in a cottage, whether as an artisan or as a factory worker, often meant to cultivate a family garden, possibly to pasture a cow, to prepare one's own bread, and to have the skills for keeping a home in good repair. To utterly erase these skills and means of livelihood from the worker's life became an industrial imperative.

The worker's complete dependence on the factory and on an industrial labor market was a compelling precondition for the triumph of industrial society. Urban planning, such as it was, together with urban congestion, long working hours, a generous moral disregard for working-class alcoholism, and a highly specialized division of labor melded the needs of exploitation to a deliberate policy of proletarianization. The need to destroy whatever independent means of life the worker could garner from a backyard plot of land, a simple proficiency in the use of tools, a skill that provided shoes, clothing, and furnishings for the family—all involved the issue of reducing the proletariat to a condition of total powerlessness in the face of capital. And with that powerlessness came a supineness, a loss of character and community, and a decline in moral fiber that was to make the hereditary English worker one of the most docile members of an exploited class during the past two centuries of European history. The factory system, with its need for a large corps of unskilled labor, far from giving the workers greater mobility and occupational flexibility (as Marx and Engels were to claim), actually reduced them to aimless social vagabonds.

To reinfuse the "artificial crafts" with the "natural arts is not just a cardinal project for social ecology; it is an ethical enterprise for rehumanizing the psyche and demystifying *techné*. The rounded person in a rounded society, living a total life rather than a fragmented one, is a precondition for the emergence of individuality and its historic social hallmark, autonomy. This vision, far from denying the need for community, has always presupposed it. But it visualizes community as a *free* community in which *inter*dependence, rather than dependence or "independence," provides the many-sided social ingredients for personality and its development. If we (like Frederick Engels in contemptuously dismissing German Proudhonian demands for workers' gardens as "reactionary" and atavistic) hypostatize industrial authority, hierarchy, and discipline as an enduring technological desideratum, we do little more than reduce the worker from a human being to a wage laborer and the "artificial crafts" to a brutalizing factory. Here, Marxism articulated the bourgeois project more consistently and with greater clarity than its most blatant liberal apologists. In treating the factory and technical development as socially autonomous (to use Langdon Winner's excellent term), "scientific socialism" ignored the role that the factory, with its elaborate hierarchical structure, has played in extending the conditioning of workers to obedience, and schooling them in subjugation from childhood through every phase of adult life.

By contrast, a radical social ecology not only raises traditional issues, such as the reunion of agriculture with industry, but also questions the very structure of industry itself. It questions the factory conceived as the all-enduring basis for mechanization—and even mechanization conceived as a substitute for the exquisite biotic "machinery" that we call food chains and food webs. Today, when the assembly line visibly risks the prospect of collapsing under the mass neuroses of its "operatives," the issue of disbanding the factory—indeed, of restoring manufacture in its literal sense as a manual art rather than a muscular "megamachine"—has become a priority of enormous social importance. Taxing as our metaphors may be, nature is a biotic "industry" in its own right. Soil life disassembles, transforms, and reassembles all the "materials" or nutrients that make the existence of terrestrial vegetation possible. The immensely complex food web that supports a blade of grass or a stalk of wheat suggests that biotic processes themselves can replace many strictly mechanical ones. We are already learning to purify polluted water by deploying bacterial and algal organisms to detoxify the pollutants, and we use aquatic plants and animals to absorb them as nutrients. Relatively closed aquacultural systems in translucent solar tubes have been designed to use fish wastes as nutrients to sustain an elaborate food web of small aquatic plants and animals. The fish, in turn, feed upon the very vegetation which their wastes nourish. Thus, natural toxins are recycled through the food web to ultimately provide nutrients for edible animals; the toxic waste products of fish metabolism are reconverted into the "soil" for fish food.

Even simple mechanical processes that involve physical movement—for instance, air masses circulated by pumps—have their nonmechanical analogue in the convection of air by solar heat. Solar greenhouses adjoined to family structures provide not only warmth and food but also humidity control by vegetation. Small, richly variegated vegetable plots, or "French-intensive gardens," not only obviate the need for using industrially produced fertilizers and toxic biocides; they also provide an invaluable and productive rationale for composting domestic kitchen wastes. Nature's proverbial "law of return" can thus be deployed not only to foster natural fecundity but also to provide the basis for ecological husbandry.

One can cite an almost unending variety of biotic alternatives to the costly and brutalizing mechanical systems that drive modern industry. The problem of replacing the latter by the former is far from insurmountable. Once human imagination is focused upon these problems, human ingenuity is likely to be matched only by nature's fecundity. Certainly, the techniques for turning a multitude of these substitutions into realities are very much at hand. The largest single problem we face, however, is not strictly technical; indeed, the problem may well be that we regarded these new biotic techniques as *mere* technologies. What we have not recognized clearly are the social, cultural, and ethical conditions that render our biotic substitutes for industrial technologies ecologically and philosophically *meaningful*. For we must arrest more than just the ravaging and simplification of nature. We must also arrest the ravaging and simplification of the human spirit, of human personality, of human community, of humanity's idea of the "good," and humanity's own fecundity within the natural world. Indeed, we must counteract these trends with a sweeping program of social renewal.

Hence, a crucial caveat must be raised. A purely *technical* orientation toward organic gardening, solar and wind energy devices, aquaculture, holistic health, and the like would still retain the incubus of instrumental rationality that threatens our very capacity to develop an ecological sensibility. An environmentalistic technocracy is hierarchy draped in green garments; hence it is all the more insidious because it is camouflaged in the color of ecology. The most certain test we can devise to distinguish environmental from ecological techniques is not the size, shape, or elegance of our tools and machines, but the social ends that they are meant to serve, the ethics and sensibilities by which they are guided and integrated, and the institutional challenges and changes they involve. Whether their ends, ethics, sensibilities, and institutions are libertarian or merely logistical, emancipatory or merely pragmatic, communitarian or merely efficient—in sum, ecological or merely environmental—will directly determine the rationality that underpins the techniques and the intentions guiding their design. Alternative technologies may bring the sun, wind, and the world of vegetation and animals into our lives as participants in a common ecological project of reunion and symbiosis. But the "smallness" or "appropriateness" of these technologies does not necessarily remove the possibility that we will keep trying to reduce nature to an object of exploitation. We must resolve the ambiguities of freedom *existentially*—by social principles, institutions, and an ethical commonality that renders freedom and harmony a reality.

After some ten millennia of a very ambiguous social evolution, we must reenter natural evolution again—not merely to survive the prospects of ecological catastrophe and nuclear immolation but also to recover our own fecundity in the world of life. I do not mean that we must return to the primitive lifeways of our early ancestors, or surrender activity and *techné* to a pastoral image of passivity and bucolic acquiescence. We slander the natural world when we deny its activity, striving, creativity, and development as well as its subjectivity. Nature is never drugged. Our reentry into natural evolution is no less a humanization of nature than a naturalization of humanity.

The real question is: where have humanity and nature been pitted into antagonism or simply detached from each other? The history of "civilization" has been a steady process of estrangement from nature that has increasingly developed into outright antagonism. Today more than at any time in the past, we have lost sight of the *telos* that renders us an aspect of nature—not merely in relationship to our own "needs" and "interests" but to the meanings within nature itself. No less strident a German idealist philosopher than Fichte reminded us two centuries ago that humanity is nature rendered self-conscious, that we speak for a fullness of mind that can articulate nature's latent capacity to reflect upon itself, to function within itself as its own corrective and guide. But this notion presupposes that we exist sufficiently within nature and are sufficiently part of nature to function on its behalf. Where Fichte patently erred was in his assumption that a possibility is a fact. We are no more nature rendered self-conscious than we are humanity rendered self-conscious. Reason may give us the capacity to play this role, but we and our society are still totally irrational—indeed, we are cunningly dangerous to ourselves and all that lives around us. We do not make the implicit meanings in nature explicit, nor do we act upon nature to enhance its inner striving toward greater variety. We have assumed that social development can occur only at the expense of natural development, not that development conceived as wholeness involves society and nature conjointly.

In this respect we have been our own worst enemies—not only objectively but subjectively as well. Our mental, and later our factual, dissociation of society from nature rests on the barbarous objectification of human beings into means of production and targets of domination— an objectification we have projected upon the entire world of life. To reenter natural evolution merely to rescue our hides from ecological catastrophe would change little, if anything, in our sensibilities and institutions. Nature would still be object (only this time to be feared rather than revered), and people would still be objects instrumentally oriented toward the world (only this time cowed rather than arrogant). The camouflage of green would remain; only its tints would be deeper. Nature would remain denatured in our vision and humanity dehumanized, but rhetoric and palliatives would replace the furnaces of a ruthless industry, and sentimental babble would replace the noise of the assembly line. Let us at least admit, in Voltaire's memorable words, that we cannot drop to the ground on all fours, nor should we do so. We are no less products of natural evolution because we stand erect on our feet and retain the facility of our minds and fingers, whether we regard this heritage as a boon or as a damnation.

Nor can we afford to banish the memory that "civilization" has inscribed on our brains by surrendering our capacity to function self-consciously in society as well as within nature. We would dishonor the countless millions who toiled and perished to provide us with what is worthy in human consociation, not to mention the even larger numbers who were its guileless victims. The soil is no less a cemetery for the innocent dead than it is a source of life. Were we to honor the maxim, "ashes to ashes," earth to earth, society would seem to at least be responding to nature's "law of return." But society has become so irrational and its diet of slaughter so massive that no law—social or ecological—is honored by any of its enterprises. So let there be no more talk about "civilization" and its "fruits," or about "conciliation" with nature for the "good" of humanity. "Civilization" has rarely considered the "good" of humanity, much less that of nature. Until we rid ourselves of the cafeteria imagery that we must repay nature for its "lunches" and "snacks," our relationship with the biosphere will still be contractual and bourgeois to its core. We will still be functioning in a sleazy world of "cost-effective trade-offs" and "deals" for nature's "resources." Only the most spontaneous desire to *be* natural—that is, to be fecund, creative, and intrinsically human, can now justify our very *right* to reenter natural evolution as conscious social beings.

Then what does it mean to be "intrinsically human," to be "natural" in more than a colloquial sense? What, after all, is "human nature" or is natural about human beings? Here, again, it helps to return to the cradle of social life—the extended development of the young and the mother-child relationship—from which we derived our notions of a libertarian rationality. What emerges from Briffault's account and, more recently, from the new anthropology that has happily replaced Victorian studies of "savage society," is the compelling realization that what we call "human nature" is a biologically rooted process of consociation, a process in which cooperation, mutual support, and love are natural as well as cultural attributes. As Briffault emphasizes,

> In the human group by the time that one generation has become sexually mature, new generations have been added to the group. The association between the younger generations, pronounced in all primates, is greatly increased as regards solidarity in the human group. From being a transitory association, it tends to become a permanent one.

The prolonged process of physical maturation in the human species turns individual human nature into a biologically constituted form of consociation. Indeed, the formation not only of individuality but also of personality consists of being *actively* part of a permanent social group. Society involves, above all, a process of *socializing*—of discourse, mutual entertainment, joint work, group ceremonies, and the development of common culture.

Hence, human nature is formed by the workings of an organic process. Initially, to be sure, it is formed by a continuation of nature's cooperative and associative tendencies into the individual's personal life. Culture may elaborate these tendencies and provide them with qualitatively new traits (such as language, art, and politically constituted institutions), thus producing what could authentically be called a society, not merely a community. But nature does not merely phase into society, much less "disappear" in it; nature is there all the time. Without the care, cooperation, and love fostered by the mother-child relationship and family relationships, individuality and personality either are impossible or begin to disintegrate, as the modern crisis of the ego so vividly indicates. Only when social ties begin to decay without offering any substitutes do we become acutely aware that individuality involves not a struggle for separation but a struggle *against* it (albeit in a pursuit of much richer and universal arenas of consociation than the primal kinship group). Society may create these new arenas and extend them beyond the blood oath—that is, when it does not regress in the form of fascism and Stalinism to the most suffocating attributes of the archaic world—but it does not create the *need* to be engrouped, to practice care, cooperation, and love.

To remove any confusion between an "organic society" structured around the blood oath and the utopistic vision of a free society advanced in this chapter, I call the latter an *ecological society*. An ecological society presupposes that the notion of a universal *humanitas*, which "civilization" has imparted to us over the past three millennia, has not been lost. It also assumes that the strong emphasis on individual autonomy, which our contemporary "modernists" so facilely attribute to the Renaissance, will acquire unsurpassed reality—but without the loss of the strong communal ties enjoyed by organic societies in the past. Hierarchy, in effect, would be replaced by interdependence, and consociation would imply the existence of an organic core that meets the deeply felt biological needs for care, cooperation, security, and love. Freedom would no longer be placed in opposition to nature, individuality to society, choice to necessity, or personality to the needs of social coherence.

An ecological society would fully recognize that the human animal is biologically structured to live with its kind, and to care for and love its own kind within a broadly and freely defined social group. These human traits would be conceived as not merely attributes of human nature but also as *constituting* and *forming* it—indeed, as indispensable to the evolution of human subjectivity and personality. Such traits would be regarded not simply as survival mechanisms or social features of the biological human community, but as the very materials that enter into the structure of an ecological society.

℺

If this interpretation of human consociation and its origins is sound, it may provide the basis for a reconstructive approach to an ecological society. Up to now, I have had to define social ecology in largely critical terms—as an anthropology of hierarchy and domination. I have been concerned primarily with authority and the conflict in sensibilities between preliterate societies and the emerging State. I have explored the imposition of rule, acquisitive impulses, and property rights on a recalcitrant archaic world, one that has persistently resisted "civilization"—at times violently, at other times passively. I have chronicled the commitment of traditional societies to usufruct, complementarity, and the irreducible minimum against class society's claims to property, the sanctity of contract, and its adherence to the rule of equivalence. In short, I have tried to rescue the legacy of freedom that the legacy of domination has sought to extirpate from the memory of humanity.

What has relieved this grim account of the rise of hierarchy and domination has been the enduring features of a subterranean libertarian realm that has lived in cunning accommodation with the prevailing order of domination. I have taken note of its technics, forms of association, religious beliefs, conventicles, and institutions. I have tried to pierce through the layered membranes of freedom, from its outward surface as the inequality of equals, probing through its various economic layers of equivalence, to work with its core as a caring personal sensibility, a supportive domestic life; and its own rule of the equality of unequals. I have found residual areas of freedom in communities where the word simply does not exist, in loyalties that are freely given without expectations of recompense, in systems of distribution that know no rules of exchange, and in interpersonal relations that are completely devoid of domination. Indeed, insofar as humanity has been free to voice the subjectivity of nature and meanings latent within it, nature itself has revealed its own voice, subjectivity, and fecundity through humanity. Ultimately, it is in this ecological interplay of social freedom and natural freedom that a true ecology of freedom will be fashioned.

Can we, then, integrate the archaic customs of usufruct; complementarity, and the equality of unequals into a modern vision of freedom? What newer sensibilities, technics, and ethics can we develop, and what newer social institutions can we hope to form? If the freedom of humanity implies the liberation of nature *through* humanity, by what criteria and means can we reenter natural evolution? Our very use of the words "humanity" and "individuality" betrays the fact that our answers must be drawn from a very different context than that of the preliterate social world. In fact, "civilization" has broadened the terrain of freedom well beyond the parochial relationships fostered by the blood oath, the sexual division of labor, and the role of age groups in structuring early communities. On this qualitatively new terrain, we cannot—and should not—rely on the power of custom, much less on traditions that have long faded into the past. We are no longer an inwardly oriented, largely homogeneous group of folk that is untroubled by a long history of internal conflict and unblemished by the mores and practices of domination. Our values and practices now demand a degree of consciousness and intellectual sophistication that early bands, clans, and tribes never required to maintain their freedom as a lived phenomenon.

With this caveat in mind, let us frankly acknowledge that organic societies spontaneously evolved values that we rarely can improve. The crucial distinction in radical theory between the "realm of necessity" and the "realm of freedom"—a distinction that Proudhon and Marx alike brought to radical ideology—is actually a social ideology that emerges along with rule and exploitation. Viewed against the broad tableau of class ideologies, few distinctions have done more than this one to validate authority and domination. "Civilization," with its claim to be the cradle of culture, has rested theoretically on the imagery of a "stingy nature" that could support only elites, whose own "freedom" and "free time" to administer society, to think, write, study, and infuse humanity with the "light of reason," has been possible historically by exploiting the labor of the many.

Preliterate societies never held this view; ordinarily they resisted every attempt to impose it. What we today would call "onerous toil" was then spontaneously adapted to the community's need to *communize* all aspects of life in order to bring a sense of collective involvement and joy to the most physically demanding tasks. Rarely did the "savages" even *try* to "wrestle" with nature; rather, they *coaxed* it along, slowly and patiently, with chants, songs, and ceremonials that we rightly call dances. All this was done in a spirit of cooperation within the community itself, and between the community and nature. "Necessity" was collectivized to foster cooperation and colonized by "freedom" long before preliterate communities verbalized any distinction between the two. The very words "necessity" and "freedom" had yet to be formed by the separation and tensions that "civilization" was to create between them, and by the repressive discipline "civilization" was to impose on nonhuman and human nature alike.

The same is true of usufruct, which stands on a more generous ethical plane than communism, with its maxim of "to each according to his [and her] own needs." What is perhaps most surprising is that classical anarchism, from Proudhon to Kropotkin, cast its notion of consociation in terms of contract with its underlying premise of equivalence—a system of "equity" that reaches its apogee in bourgeois conceptions of right. The notion that equivalence can be the moral coinage of freedom is as alien to freedom itself as is the notion of the State. Nineteenth-century socialisms, whether libertarian or authoritarian, ultimately are still rooted in the concept of property as such and the need to regulate property relationships "socialistically." Proudhon, Bakunin, and Kropotkin's paeans to contracts "freely entered into" between "men" and between communities strangely denies the term "freely" by its limited concept of freedom. Indeed, it is not accidental that this kind of language can be found in the constitutions and legal codes of the most unreconstructed bourgeois republics. Traditional anarchist concepts of contract score no greater advance over our system of justice than Marx's notion of a "proletarian dictatorship" scores any advance over our republican concepts of freedom.

Preliterate societies never adhered to this contractual ideal of association; indeed, they resisted every attempt to impose it. To be sure, there were many treaties between tribes and alliances with strangers. But contractual ties *within* tribes were essentially nonexistent. Not until hierarchy had scored its triumph in the early world and begun its journey into class society did equivalence, "equity," and contract begin to form the context for human social relationships. The *quid pro quo* of exchange and its ethical balance sheets were simply irrelevant to a community guided by the customs of usufruct, complementarity, and the irreducible minimum. The means of life and community support were there to be *had* rather than apportioned, and even where apportionment did exist, it was guided by egalitarian traditions that respected age, acknowledged infirmities, and fostered a loving care for children. Only "civilization" was to put the figure of Justitia on a pedestal and place its purely quantitative weights on her scale. Her blindfold may have very well been a token of her shame rather than her indifference to the realities of inequality.

The treaties that existed between preliterate communities were more procedural than distributive in their intent; they were meant to establish agreement in decision-making processes and ways of coordinating common actions, not to apportion power and things. And under conditions of general reciprocity, personal alliances were simply a way of breaking out of the kinship nexus and broadening support systems beyond the perimeter of the tribe. Hence the "commodities" that were exchanged between people seemingly as "gifts" were actually tokens of mutual loyalty. By no means did they necessarily have an intrinsic "value" of their own beyond a symbolic one, much less ratios or "price tags" that gave them exchange value.

Finally, complementarity is merely our own word for summing up the widely accepted image that organic societies had of themselves as interdependent systems. Ordinarily, in fact, they had no word to articulate this reality—nor any need to formulate one. They *lived* as systems of social ecology and hence were guided more by their sense of respect for personality than by a system of juridical imperatives. Independence in any sense of the free-wheeling bourgeois ego, plunged into social life by an ideology of "sink-or-swim," was not only inconceivable to them; it was altogether frightening, even to such fairly scattered hunting and foraging peoples as the Eskimo. Every preliterate culture had one or several epicenters that, by common understanding, brought scattered families and bands together periodically. Ceremonies were partly an excuse to reiterate traditions of consociation, and partly forms of communizing. To be "exiled" from the group, to be expelled from it, was tantamount to a death sentence. Not that a person so exiled couldn't physically survive, but he or she would *feel* like a "nonperson" as well as be treated like one. Psychologically induced death was not uncommon in preliterate communities.

By contrast, our modern emphasis on "independence" expresses neither the virtues of autonomy nor the claims of individuality; rather, it stridently voices the brute ideology of a pervasive and socially corrosive egotism. It rudely contrasts with the very origins of the spirit of consociation—the selfless, caring love that the human mother ordinarily gives her young—and thoroughly violates our deepest sense of humanity. To be a free-wheeling monad is to lack, as Shepard might say, our very sense of "direction" as living beings, to be bereft of a "niche" or locus in nature and society. It leads to "freaking" society toward the market rather than adapting a generous distributive system to society. Given this orientation (or lack of it), the "realm of necessity" can indeed be rooted in stinginess—but not the "stinginess" of nature. Rather, it is rooted in the stinginess of people—more precisely, of the elites who establish social conventions. When one lives with the continual fear of being "shortchanged," shared by all human monads, one begins to shortchange others routinely—ultimately, maliciously and with an active meanness of spirit. With this resplendent outlook, it is easy for a bourgeois monad to become a "partner" in the buyer-seller relationship and its embodiment as "contract." A society composed of exiles is literally an exiled society—exiled from the roots of human consociation in care and nurture. The "realm of necessity" dominates the "realm of freedom" not because nature itself is jealously possessive of its wealth, but rather because wealth becomes jealously possessive of its hoards and prerogatives.

Domination now enters into history as a social "need"—more precisely, a social imperative—that entangles personality, daily life, economic activity, and even love in its toils. The myth of contractual "trust," with its sanctimonious seals and archaic language, is built on the persistence of contractual mistrust and social estrangement, which the idea of "contract" continually reinforces. That everything has to be "spelled out" is evidence of the ubiquity of moral predation. Every "agreement" reflects a latent antagonism, and (traditional anarchist rhetoric aside) its "mutualistic" ethics lacks any true understanding of care and complementarity. Denied the message of social ecology, the libertarian ideal tends to sink to the level of ideological sectarianism and, even worse, to the level of the hierarchical syndicalism fostered by industrial society.

What "civilization" has given us, in spite of itself, is the recognition that the ancient values of usufruct, complementarity, and the irreducible minimum must be extended from the kin group to humanity as a whole. Beyond the blood oath, society must override the traditional sexual division of labor and the privileges claimed by age groups to embrace the "stranger" and exogenous cultures. Moreover, "civilization" has removed these ancient values from the realm of rigid custom and unthinking tradition by rendering them ideational or conceptual. The tensions and contradictions marking social life beyond the tribal world have added an intellectual acuity to mores that once were accepted unreflectively. The enormous potentialities latent in these developments should not be underestimated. Challenges beyond the imagination of the preliterate community they surely are; for a parochial folk to even conceive of itself as part of humanity involved shattering the bones of deeply embedded customs, traditions, and a sense of biological exceptionalism. The myth of the "chosen people," as I have already noted, is not unique to Judaism; almost every folk, to one degree or another, has this image of itself. To include ethical standards of a shared *humanitas*, of a human community, involved a sweeping change in the process of conceptualizing social relations. A free-flowing realm of ethics, as distinguished from a world of hardened customs (however admirable these may be), is a *creative* realm in which the growth of mind and spirit is possible on a scale that has no precedent in the world of traditional mores. Ethics, values, and with them, social relationships, technics, and self-cultivation can now become self-forming, guided by intellect, sympathy, and love. That "civilization" has usually betrayed its promise of ideational and personal self-creativity does not alter the reality of these potentialities and the many achievements in which they were actualized.

Among the greatest of these achievements were the faltering steps toward individuality that occurred in the Hellenic, late medieval, and modern worlds. Not that preliterate societies lack a sense of and a respect for person, but they place relatively little emphasis on human will, on personal eccentricity or deviance as a value in itself. They are not intolerant when behavior departs from certain standards of etiquette and "normality." Uniqueness is definitely prized, as Dorothy Lee noted, but it is always viewed within a group context. To be overly conspicuous, particularly in the form of self-acclaim, elicits a measure of wariness and may expose the individual to ridicule. One's claims to certain abilities must be proved in reality, to say the least, and are often markedly downplayed. Hence a Hopi child traditionally restrained his or her capacity to perform well lest it vitiate group solidarity. The "big man" syndrome—which probably is a later development in preliterate societies and perhaps is most widely known through Kwakiutl potlatch ceremonies—should be placed side by side with the "humility" syndrome. These are strangely complementary rather than contradictory.

Far more than its claims of achieving rationality, "civilization" certainly did provide the soil for the emergence of the highly willful individual, and placed a high premium on volition as a formative element in social life and culture. Indeed, "civilization" went even further: it identified will with personal freedom. Our individuality consists not only in the uniqueness of our behavior and character structure, but also in our *right* to act in accordance with our sovereign judgment or "freedom of will." In fact, according to the canons of modern individualism, we are free to choose—to formulate our own personal needs, or at least to select from those that are created for us. That the current fetishization of needs reduces this freedom to the level of custom is one of the most subversive factors in the decline of individuality. But the myth of our autonomy is no less real than the reality of its decline. Whether as myth or canon, will—conceived as the personal freedom to choose or to create the constituents of choice—presupposes that there *is* such a phenomenon as the individual, and that he or she is competent and therefore capable of making rational judgments; in short, that the individual is capable of functioning as a self-determined, self-active, and self-governing being.

Tragically, "civilization" has associated volition with control, domination, and authority; hence, it also has associated it with mastery and, in the archaic world, with a godlike superhumanity of the absolute ruler. Figures such as Gilgamesh, Achilles, Joshua, and Julius Caesar were more than just men of action—the supreme egos we associate with the "heroic" cast of personality (the ego as warrior). In several cases they became transcendental figures whose superhumanity carried them beyond the controls of nature itself. This view defiled not only the very notion of a human nature, but also the concrete reality and constraints of the natural world. As late as Hegel's time, they were viewed as metaphysical figures, or "World Spirits," cast from a Napoleonic mold. To this day, in the vulgar imagery of television, they are clothed in the advertising agency's trappings of "charismatic" egos, or what we so appropriately call "personalities" and "stars."

But this commitment of individuality to domination, so compellingly forged by "civilization," is certainly not the sole form of individual creativity. The Renaissance, as Kenneth Clark noted, did not develop a very substantial body of philosophical literature, comparable, say, to that of the late eighteenth and early nineteenth centuries, because it expressed its philosophy in art. For all its understatement of Renaissance thought, this passing observation is arresting. Here, will found expression in the incomparable statuary of Michelangelo's "David" and the ceiling of the Sistine Chapel; in Raphael's "School of Athens"; in Leonardo's "Last Supper"; and in scientific research. Thus heroism acquired another voice from that of the battlefield's clamor. Imagination, stirred to life by the mother's songs and stories, slowly formed around creativity conceived as the expression of beauty.

Hence, it is by no means a given that individuality, autonomy, and willfulness must be expressed in domination; they can just as well be expressed in artistic creativity. Schiller viewed the affirmation of human individuality and power as the expression of joy, play, and fulfillment of the esthetic sensibility; Marx saw it as assertion, Promethean control, and domination—through production, the fire of labor, and the conquest of nature. Yet the poet no more implied a denial of power and individuality than the social thinker. Indeed, the right to imagine a highly individuated life as an art rather than as a conflict has been with us all the time. In contrast to the parochial world of the kin group and its fixity in custom, "civilization" has given us the wider world of the social group and its flexibility in ratiocination. Today, the real issue posed by this historic transcendence is no longer a question of reason, power, and *techné* as such, but the function of *imagination* in giving us direction, hope, and a sense of place in nature and society. The cry "Imagination to Power!" that the Parisian students raised in 1968 was not a recipe for the seizure of power but a glowing vision of the estheticization of personality and society.

ᘓ

We do not normally find these visions in traditional radicalism. The nineteenth-century socialists and anarchists were largely economistic and scientistic in their outlook, often on a scale comparable to the conventional social theorists of their day. Proudhon was no less committed to a "scientific socialism" than was Marx. Kropotkin was often as much of a technological determinist as Engels, although he redeemed this stance by his emphasis on ethics. Both men, like the Victorians of their time, were thoroughly enamored of "progress" as a largely economic achievement. All these principal figures viewed the State as "historically necessary." Bakunin and Kropotkin saw it as an "unavoidable evil"; Marx and Engels saw it as a historically progressive datum. Errico Malatesta, perhaps the most ethically oriented of the anarchists, saw these failings clearly and openly criticized them in Bakunin and Kropotkin. All of them were often dystopian in their outlook. The given reality, with its hypostatization of labor, its reverence for science and technics, its myths of progress, and above all, its commitment to proletarian hegemony, was part of a shared mythology that cements the "libertarian" and "authoritarian" socialisms of the last century into an equally uninhabitable edifice.

Imagination as a socially creative power found its voice not in the prevalent radical social engineers of the nineteenth century but in the rare, luminescent utopian works that flashed annoyingly around "scientific socialists" of all kinds. Occasionally, the iridescence of these works dazzled them, but more often than not, they were embarrassed by these fanciful flights into new realms of possibility and responded with vigorous disclaimers. Utopians—at least, utopians of the vintage of Rabelais and Fourier—had made freedom too lurid and sensuously concrete to be acceptable to the Victorian mind. Even in "good company," a woman may bare her breasts with decorum to feed her infant, but never "wantonly," on a barricade or at a public rally for freedom. The great utopians did precisely that—and more—on their barricades, like the two anonymous "harlots" on the barricades of June, 1848, who insouciantly and defiantly raised their skirts before the attacking National Guardsmen of bourgeois Paris, and were shot down in the act.

What marked the great utopians was not their lack of realism but their sensuousness, their passion for the concrete, their adoration of desire and pleasure. Their utopias were often exemplars of a qualitative "social science" written in seductive prose, a new kind of socialism that defied abstract intellectual conventions with their pedantry and icy practicality. Perhaps even more importantly, they defied the image that human beings were, in the last analysis, machines; that their emotions, pleasures, appetites, and ideals could be cast in terms of a culture that viewed the quantitative as authentic truth. Hence, they stood in flat opposition to a machine-oriented mass society. Their message of fecundity and reproduction thus rescued the image of humanity as an embodiment of the organic that had its place in the richly tinted world of nature, not in the workshop and the factory.

Some of these utopias advance this message with unabashed vulgarity, such as Rabelais' outrageous Abbey of Theleme, a land of Cokaygne dressed in the Renaissance earthiness and sexuality that even the folk utopia lacked. Like nearly all Renaissance utopias, the Abbey is a "monastery" and a "religion," but one that mocks monastic life and reverence for the Deity. It has no walls to contain it, no rules to regulate it. It admits both women and men, all comely and attractive, and accepts no vows of chastity, poverty, or obedience. Lavish dress replaces ecclesiastical black; sumptuous repasts replace gruel and hard bread; magnificent furnishings replace the cold stone walls of the monastic cell; falconries and pools replace somber retreats and work places. The members of the new order spend their lives "not in laws, statutes, and rules, but according to their own free will and pleasure." They arise from bed when it pleases them; dine, drink, labor, and sleep when they have a mind to; and disport themselves as and when they wish. The clock has been abolished, for what is the "greatest loss," in Rabelais' words, than to "count the hours, what good comes of it?"

But what really may have outraged its bourgeois readers were the three Graces who surmount the Abbey's fountain, "with their cornucopias, or horns of abundance," which spurt out water "at their breasts, mouths, ears, eyes, and other open passages of the body. Looking upon this provocative symbol in their courtyard, the women and men of the Abbey are reminded that they must obey one strict rule: "Do as thou wilt." We should not allow the typical Renaissance elitism of Rabelais' Abbey to conceal the intimate association it establishes between pleasure and the total absence of domination. That there are servants, custodians, and laborers who render the vision credible does not alter the fact that it is justifiable as an end in itself. Christian asceticism and the bourgeois work ethic did not aim at the equality of humanity on earth, but rather the repression of every impulse that might remind the body of its sensuous and hedonistic claims. Even if Rabelais can depict the realization of these claims only among the "well-born" and "rich," at least he provides a voice for human individuality, freedom, and a sensuous life that vitiates every form of servitude. Freed from servitude, people possess a natural instinct that "spurs" them to "virtuous actions." If only the few can live honorable lives (I am speaking of views formulated in the sixteenth century), this does not mean that human nature is any the less human or that its virtues cannot be shared by all. The rebellion of free will and the right to choose against "laws, statutes or rules" is thus identified with the claims of earthly pleasure against the life-long penance of denial and toil.

After the Abbey of Theleme, the terrain Rabelais opened was cluttered by sybaritic visions of the "good life." Although the Reformation's sternness muted these privatized hedonistic futuramas, they more or less persisted into our own day as erotic and science-fiction dramas. A few Enlightenment "utopias," if such they can be called, provide notable exceptions. Diderot's superb *Jacques le Fataliste* and his Bougainville dialogue, taken in combination, exude an earthiness and generosity of spirit, a respect for the desires of the flesh and for the cultures of preliterate peoples that have yet to be matched in our own time. But neither work advances a program or even a vision that challenges entrenched values and institutions. They contritely depict a different kind of "fall" from the grace of nature and naturalness of behavior that is more tragic in their hopelessness than redemptive in their idealism.

Perhaps the least understood "utopia" of the period, however, is the Marquis de Sade's plea for a revolutionary emancipation of passion itself from the constraints of convention and Christian morality. The Marquis de Sade has been justly condemned for his rapacious egotism, his objectification of women and sexuality, and the instrumental mentality he exhibits toward the sensuous itself. Yet his *Philosophy of the Bedroom* is perhaps one of the most psychologically disruptive works of its time, although its influence was not felt until a much later period. For de Sade, sexuality is not only a pleasure in its own right; it is a "calling," indeed the "soul's madness"—*l'amour fou*, as Breton and the Surrealists were to call it—that shreds the irrationality of self-constraint and subdued passion. Libertinage becomes libertarian when it opens the most internalized repressions of the psyche to the light of reason and passion, however seemingly miniscule and privatized they may be. In a statement that de Sade regards as "audacious," he declares, "A nation that begins by governing itself as a republic will only be sustained by virtue because, in order to attain the most, one must always start with the least." Heading de Sade's disquisition in the dialogue is the cry: "Yet Another Effort, Frenchmen, If You Would Become Republicans!"

Thereupon de Sade impugns law itself: "Man receives from nature the impressions which allow one to pardon him for this action, while law, on the contrary, being always in opposition to nature and owing nothing to it, cannot be authorized to permit itself the same motives...." Not that de Sade denies the need for laws (which should be as "mild" as possible) or the paraphernalia of a republic; but the libertarian tenor of his position and his passionate hatred of social and psychological restraint are evident. His tenor and position would be more convincing if they applied to the victims of his own sexual tastes. But his orgiastic appeal to a new sensibility, based on a naturalistic reawakening of the senses and the body from the deep sleep of repression, stands sharply at odds with the strong emphasis on "self-discipline" that the emerging industrial bourgeoisie was to impose on the nineteenth century. *L'amour fou*, the indispensable sensory "derangement" that de Sade's "bedroom philosophy" implies, found its resting place in aesthetic movements of the nineteenth-century Symbolists, and our own century's Dadaist and Surrealist movements. In these comparatively exotic forms, it was socially marginal—until the counterculture of the sixties and the "youth revolt" of the eighties in Central Europe swept it from shadowy artistic bohemias into the open light of social activism.

In the early nineteenth century, Rabelais and de Sade enjoyed a brief Indian summer in Charles Fourier's utopian visions, which have received worldwide attention as a seemingly practical system for initiating a "socialist" society. Fourier has been widely heralded for his stunning originality and fertile imagination—but often for the wrong reasons. Despite his vigorous denunciations of liberalism's hypocrisies, he was not a socialist; hence, he was no "precursor" of Marx or Proudhon. Nor was he an egalitarian in the sense that his utopia presumed a radical leveling of the rights and privileges enjoyed by the wealthy. To the extent that such a leveling would occur, it was the work his utopia might hope to achieve gradually, in the fullness of time. Fourier was a rationalist who detested the rationalization of life in bourgeois society; therefore it is a grave error (and one made by many of his critics) to accuse him of "anti-rationalism." Despite his admiration for Newton's mechanical system, his own system yields such a cosmic world of "passionate" intercourse that to regard him as a social "mechanist" (another criticism that has been voiced against him) is simply preposterous.

To be sure, the contradictions in Fourier's "Harmonian" future, which he contrasted with the degrading state of "Civilization," are legion. Women are to be totally liberated from all patriarchal constraints, but this does not prevent Fourier from viewing them as sexual performers—each of whom will cook, later entertain his communities, or *phalansteries*, in singing and other delightful virtuosities, and, in accordance with their feminine proclivities, satisfy the sexual needs of several males. Nonviolent and playful wars will occur in Harmony, and captives, held for several days at most, will be obliged to obey their captors even in performing sexual tasks that may be onerous to them. Secret infidelities will be punished in much the same way. Despite Fourier's basic detestation of authority, however, he toyed with the notion of a world leader at the summit of his vague functional hierarchy, a position he variously offered to Napoleon and Tsar Alexander I.

Yet when such contradictions are placed in the larger perspective of his entire work, Fourier turns out to be the most libertarian, the most original, and certainly the most relevant utopian thinker of his day, if not of the entire tradition. As Mark Poster observes in an excellent review of his work,

> Stamped as a utopian by the pope of socialist orthodoxy [Marx], it has been Fourier's misfortune to be misunderstood by generation after generation of scholars. Seen in his own terms, in the context of his own intellectual problematic, Fourier emerges as a brilliant pioneer of questions that have not been fully examined until the twentieth century. The fate of the passions in bourgeois society, the limitations of the nuclear family, the prospects of communal education, the types of love relations in industrial society, the possibility of attractive labor, the nature of groups and the role of sex in the formation of groups, the dehumanization of market relations, the effects of psychic frustration, the possibility of a non-repressive society— all of these questions, which were dropped by the socialist tradition and never even raised by liberalism have only recently been resurrected from the oblivion fated for all questions relating merely to the "superstructure."

More so than most utopian writers, Fourier left behind pages upon pages of elaborate descriptions of his new Harmonian society, including the most mundane details of everyday life in a phalanstery. His critique of "civilization," notably of capitalism, was utterly devastating; indeed, it is largely for his critical writings that he earned the greatest amount of praise from later socialist writers. But such a one-sided, rather patronizing treatment of Fourier does him a grave injustice. He was above all the advocate of *l'ecart absolu*, the complete rejection of the conventions of his time. *L'ecart absolu* could easily provide a substitute for Maurice Blanchot's plea for an "absolute refusal," an expression that was to acquire special applicability to the social protest voiced by the 1960s. With a fervor and scope that makes him uniquely contemporary, Fourier rejected almost every aspect of the social world in which he lived—its economy, morality, sexuality, family structure, educational system, cultural standards, and personal relations. Virtually nothing in his era or, for that matter, in the deepest psychic recesses of the individuals of his day, was left untouched by his critical scalpel. He even formulated a new conception of the universe that, however fantastic and extravagantly imaginative, is likely to be congenial to the ecological sensibilities of our day.

To Fourier, the physical world is governed not by Newton's law of universal gravitation but by his own "law of passionate attraction"—a law that he exuberantly proclaimed as his greatest contribution to modern knowledge. In place of Newton's mechanical interpretation of the universe, Fourier advances a concept of the cosmos as a vast organism that is suffused by life and growth. A vibrant vitalism so completely replaces the despiritized matter of conventional physics that even the idea of planets copulating is not implausible. Life, as we normally conceive it, and society are merely the offspring of a progressive elaboration of the passions. Fourier, to be sure, is not unique in conceiving of the universe in biological terms. But in contrast to most vitalists, he carries his "law of passionate attraction" from the stars into humanity's innermost psychic recesses.

"Civilization"—the third in seventeen ascending stages that Fourier charts out as humanity's destiny—is perhaps the most psychically repressive phase of all, a phase that brutally distorts the passions and channels them into perverted and destructive forms. The brutalities of the new industrial society, which Fourier recounted with the most powerful prose at his command, are essentially the expression of "civilization's" highly repressive psychic apparatus. Harmony, the culminating stage of society's development, will be marked by the predominance of entirely new social institutions—notably, the phalanstery—that will not only dismantle "civilization's" repressive apparatus but finally provide individuals with the full release of their passions and the full satisfaction of their desires.

Despite the inconsistencies that mar his discussions of women, Fourier was perhaps the most explicit opponent of patriarchalism in the "utopian" tradition. It was he, not Marx, who penned the famous maxim that social progress can be judged by the way a society treats its women. When viewed against the background of the utopian tradition as a whole, with its strong emphasis on paternal authority, this maxim would be enough to single out Fourier as one of the most radical thinkers of his time. But he also distinguished himself from radical social theorists on issues that vex us to this very day. In contrast to the Jacobin creed of republican virtue, he totally rejected an ethic of self-denial, of reason's absolute supremacy over passion, of moderation of desire and restriction of pleasure. Unlike Marx, he denied that work must necessarily be taxing and inherently oppressive. In contrast to Freud, he measured societal advances not in terms of the extent to which eroticism is sublimated into other activities but the extent to which it is released and given full expression. In the Harmonian world, the psychic repressions created by "civilization" will finally be replaced by a full flowering of passion, pleasure, luxury, love, personal release, and joyous work. The "realm of necessity"—the realm of toil and renunciation—will be suffused by the "realm of freedom." Work, however attenuated its role may be in a socialist society, will be transformed from an onerous activity into play. Nature, wounded and perverted by "civilization," will become bountiful and yield abundant harvests for all to enjoy. Indeed, as in the land of Cokaygne, even the salinity of the oceans will give way to a fruit-like, drinkable fluid, and orchards, planted everywhere by Harmonian humanity, will provide a plentitude of fruits and nuts. Monogamy will yield to uninhibited sexual freedom; happiness to pleasure; scarcity to abundance; boredom to a dazzling variety of experiences; dulled senses to a new acuity of vision, hearing, and taste; and competition to highly variegated associations at all levels of personal and social life.

In essence Fourier rehabilitates Rabelais' Abbey of Theleme with his concept of the phalanstery, but his community is to be the shared destiny of humanity rather than of a well-bred elite. Unlike the land of Cokaygne, however, Fourier did not rely on nature alone to provide this material bounty. Abundance, indeed luxury, will be available for all to enjoy because technological development will have removed the economic basis for scarcity and coercion. Work will be rotated, eliminating monotony and one-sidedness in productive activity, because technology will have simplified many physical tasks. Competition, in turn, will be curtailed because the scramble for scarce goods will become meaningless in an affluent society. The phalanstery will be neither a rural village nor a congested city, but rather a balanced community combining the virtues of both. At its full complement, it will contain 1,700 to 1,800 people—which, to Fourier, not only allows for human scale but brings people together in precisely the correct number of "passionate combinations" that are necessary to satisfy each individual's desires.

Fourier, however, stood on a much more advanced and complex social level than Rabelais and de Sade. The monk and the marquis essentially cloistered their views in specific environments. But Fourier boldly stepped up on the social stage for all to see. He furnished it not only with his own presence and his imaginative "license" but also with a fully equipped phalanstery and its luxurious bedrooms, arcades, greenhouses, and work places. His vehicle was not the picaresque novel of the Renaissance or the exotic dialogue of the Enlightenment, but the newspaper article, the treatise, the oral as well as written attack upon injustice, and the compelling pleas for freedom. He was an activist as well as a theorist, a practitioner as well as a visionary.

Fourier's notion of freedom is the most expansive we have yet encountered in the history of liberatory ideals. Even Suso, the Free Spirit, and the Adamites seem lesser in scope, for theirs is still the elitist utopia of Rabelais. They are more like Christian orders than a society, an association of the elect rather than a community for all. Far more than Marx, Fourier linked the destiny of social freedom inextricably with personal freedom: the removal of repression in society must take place concurrently with the removal of repression in the human psyche. Accordingly, there can be no hope of liberating society without self-liberation in the fullest meaning of selfhood, of the ego and all its claims.

Finally, Fourier is in many ways the earliest social ecologist to surface in radical thought. I refer not only to his views of nature but also to his vision of society. His phalanstery can rightly be regarded as a social ecosystem in its explicit endeavor to promote unity in diversity. Fourier painstakingly itemized and analyzed all the possible passions that must find expression within its walls. Although this has been grossly misread as such, it was no pedantic exercise on Fourier's part, however much one may disagree with his conclusions. Fourier seems to have had his own notion of the equality of unequals; the phalanstery must try to compensate in psychic wealth and variety for any inequalities of material wealth existing among its members. Whether its members are well-to-do or not, they all share in the best of wines, the greatest of culinary, sexual, and scholarly pleasures, and the widest conceivable diversity of stimuli. Hence, quantitative variations of income within the community become irrelevant in a feast of diversified, qualitatively superb delights.

For Fourier, an emphasis on variety and complexity was also a matter of principle, a methodological and social critique he leveled at the mechanical outlook of the eighteenth century. The *philosophes* of the French Enlightenment and the Jacobins who followed them "had eulogized sacred simplicity and a mechanical order in which all the parts were virtually interchangeable," observes Frank Manuel in his excellent essay on Fourier. "Fourier rejected the simple as false and evil, and insisted on complexity, variety, contrast, multiplicity." His emphasis on complexity applied not only to the structure of society but also to his assessment of the psyche's own needs. "Fourier's psychology was founded on the premise that in plurality and complexity there was salvation and happiness," Manuel adds; "in multiplicity there was freedom." This is not psychic or social "pluralism" but an intuitive ecological sense of wholeness. What Fourier patently sought was stability through variety and, by virtue of that stability, the freedom to choose and to will—in short, freedom through multiplicity.

The extraordinary decades that led from the Enlightenment to the Romantic Era witnessed a tremendous proliferation of utopias. Many, like Mably's communistic utopia, were utterly authoritarian; others, like Cabet's, were thoroughly ascetic and patriarchal; still others, like Saint-Simon's vision, were largely technocratic and hierarchical. Robert Owen's "utopian" socialism was certainly the most pragmatic and programmatic. A successful textile manufacturer, Owen had organized his famous mill at New Lanark into a paternalistic enterprise in industrial philanthropy that proved highly remunerative financially without maltreating its workers (given the barbarous standards of the early Industrial Revolution). Cleanliness, decent pay, benign discipline, relatively short working hours, cultural events, company schools and nurseries—all tailored to the worker's stamina, sex (most of the operatives were women), and physical condition—demonstrated to a deluge of admiring visitors from all parts of Europe that factory towns could not only be free of demoralization, alcoholism, prostitution, rampant disease, and illiteracy, but they could also yield substantial profits, even in periods of economic depression. Owen ventured far afield in his later years. He devoted most of his fortune to establishing "New Harmony," an American utopia that failed miserably. He later became a revered figure in the English workers' movement, living modestly and writing prolifically in support of his unique version of socialism.

Owen's vision of the "industrial village," which combines factories and workshops with agriculture in human-scaled units, forms the authentic prototype for Kropotkin's communal idea (as developed in his *Fields, Factories, and Workshops*) and Ebenezer Howard's "garden cities." But none of Owen's libertarian and reformist successors added anything that was substantially new to his vision. Like most of the utopians and socialists of his time, he was harshly ascetic and ethically a utilitarian—indeed, he was an avowed admirer of Bentham. As John F. C. Harrison observes, "He did not envisage happiness as the seeking or attainment of pleasure, but rather as some 'rational' form of living." This "rationality" was surprisingly industrial and quantitative. Like many radicals and reformers of the period who "quoted Bentham to the effect that 'the happiness of the greatest number is the only legitimate object of society,'" Owen and the Owenites "added their claim that only in a 'system of general cooperation and community of property' could this greatly desired end be attained."

By the end of the nineteenth century—a time marked by a large number of technocratic, virtually militaristic utopias and syndicalist panaceas—it probably was inevitable that a backward-looking, largely anti-industrial utopia should surface. William Morris, in his *News from Nowhere*, terminated the utopian tradition of the past two centuries with a bucolic recovery of a libertarian but technically medieval evocation of crafts, small-scale agriculture, and a charming commitment to simple living and its values. Amazingly, no utopian thinker spoke more directly to the countercultural values of the 1960s than Morris—and was more thoroughly ignored in favor of a bouquet of flimsy pamphlets and booklets on "simple living."*

CR

Riding the crest of late sixties' sentiments, Herbert Marcuse echoed (and soon abandoned) the deepest impulses of the New Left and counterculture with his cry, "from Marx to Fourier." Reduced to a mere slogan, Fourier was in fact subtly defamed. "Harmonian Society," for all its day-dreaming naïveté, was at least meant to be a *society*—one that Fourier had painstakingly explored (often in meticulous detail) and vigorously championed. Marcuse never undertook this project. If anything, he confused it with his attempts to meld Fourier with Marx.

---

* The radical thrust of utopian thinking, as exemplified by Fourier, has been transmuted by academics, statisticians, and "game theorists" into a thoroughly technocratic, economistic, and aggressive series of futuramas that can be appropriately designated as "futurism." However widely at odds utopias were in their values, institutional conceptions, and visions (whether ascetic or hedonistic, authoritarian or libertarian, privatistic or communistic, utilitarian or ethical), they at least had come to mean a revolutionary change in the status quo and a radical critique of its abuses. Futurism, at its core, holds no such promise at all. In the writings of such people as Herman Kahn, Buckminster Fuller, Alvin Toffler, John O'Neill, and the various seers in Stanford University's "think-tanks," futurism is essentially an extrapolation of the present into the century ahead, of "prophecy" denatured to mere projection. It does not challenge existing social relationships and institutions, but seeks to adapt them to seemingly new technological imperatives and possibilities—thereby redeeming rather than critiquing them. The present does not disappear; it persists and acquires eternality at the expense of the future. Futurism, in effect, does not enlarge the future but annihilates it by absorbing it into the present. What makes this trend so insidious is that it also annihilates the imagination itself by constraining it to the present, thereby reducing our vision— even our prophetic abilities—to mere extrapolation.

Utopistic reconstruction thus remained an uncertain, often unthinking practice. Tragically, this practice tended to narrow in numbers and scope as the sixties expired. Lacking any philosophical direction and respect for mind, it too split in contradictory directions toward a "voluntary simplicity" that denied the need for physical and cultural complexity, a proclivity for gurus that denied the need for nonhierarchical relationships, a self-enclosed asceticism that denied the claims of pleasure, an emphasis on survival that denied the authenticity of desire, and a parochialism that denied the ideal of a free society. Charles Reich's *Greening of America*, which attempted to explain the counterculture to a middle-aged America, has already been supplanted by "The Poisoning of America" (*Time*, September 22, 1980).

If accounts of the "poisoning of America" are even modestly accurate, utopian thinking today requires no apologies. Rarely has it been so crucial to stir the imagination into creating radically new alternatives to every aspect of daily life. Now, when imagination itself is becoming atrophied or is being absorbed by the mass media, the concreteness of utopian thinking may well be its most rejuvenating tonic. Whether as drama, novel, science fiction, poetry, or an evocation of tradition, experience and fantasy must return in all their fullness to stimulate as well as to suggest. Utopian *dialogue* in all its existentiality must infuse the abstractions of social theory. My concern is not with utopistic "blueprints" (which can rigidify thinking as surely as more recent governmental "plans") but with the dialogue itself as a public event.

It is not in this book that the reader should expect to find the "concrete universals" that will stimulate imagination and evoke the details of reconstruction, but rather in the interchange of utopian views that still awaits us. I would like, however, to advance certain basic considerations that no radical utopian vision—particularly an ecological one—can afford to ignore. The distinction between libertarian and authoritarian approaches—in reason, science, technics, and ethics, as well as in society—can be ignored only at grave peril to the utopian vision. This distinction underpins every conceptual aspect of an ecological society. We can ill afford to forget that the two approaches have developed side by side for millennia, and that their contest has affected every aspect of our sensibilities and behavior. Today, when technics has assumed unprecedented powers of control and destructiveness, these approaches can no longer coexist with each other, however uneasily they have done so in the past. The authoritarian technics of the factory—indeed, the factory conceived as a technique for human mobilization—has so completely invaded everyday life (even such domains as the home and neighborhood that once enjoyed a certain degree of immunity to industrial rationalization) that freedom, volition, and spontaneity are losing their physical terrain, however much they are honored rhetorically. We are faced with the desperate necessity of insulating both these arenas from bureaucratic control and the invasion of the media, if individuality itself is to continue.

I speak, here, from a world that once knew community in the form of culturally distinct neighborhoods, even in giant cities; that once communicated personally on tenement stoops, on street corners, and in parks rather than electronically; that once acquired its food and clothing from small, personal retailers who chatted, advised, and gossiped as well as checked prices; that once received most of its staples from small farms existing within a few score miles of the city's center; that once dealt with its affairs leisurely and formed its judgments reflectively. Above all, this world was once more self-regulating in matters of personal and social concern, more human in scale and decency, more firmly formed in its character structure, and more comprehensible as a social entity to its citizenry.

If we take for granted and accept unreflectively that community consists of an aggregate of unrelated, monadic, self-enclosed, and highly privatized egos; that the telephone, radio, television set, and night letter constitute our principal windows to the world; that the shopping mall and its parking lots are our normal terrain for public intercourse; that processed and packaged foods, transported thousands of miles from remote areas of the country, are our major sources of nutriment; that "time is money," fast-talking is a paying skill, and speed-reading is a desideratum; that, above all, bureaucracy comprises the sinews of social life, gigantism is the measure of success, and clientage to professionals and centralized authority is evidence of a public sphere—then we will be irretrievably lost as individuals, will-less as egos, and formless as personalities. Like the natural world around us, we will become the victims of a simplification process that renders us as inorganic and mineral as the ores that feed our foundries and the sand that feeds our glass furnaces.

It is no longer a "New Age" cliché to insist that, wherever possible, we must "unplug" our "inputs" from a depersonalized, mindless system that threatens to absorb us into its circuitry. In little more than a decade, we have been victimized by our electronic and cybernetic society more than the most outspoken critics of everyday life could have anticipated in the sixties. Loss of individuality and personal uniqueness, with its ultimate result in the "liquidation" of personality itself, begins with the loss of our ability to contrast a more human-scaled world that once *was*; another world, approximating complete totalitarianization, that now *is*; and finally a third one, human-scaled, ecological, and rational, that *should be*. Once that sense of contrast disappears, the tension between these worlds also passes away; it is this tension that motivates us to rear up in resistance against our complete defilement. Hence, daily life itself must be viewed as a calling in which we have an ethical responsibility to function in a state of unrelieved opposition to its prevailing norms.

The things we need, how we acquire them, whom we know, and what we say have become the elements of a battleground on a scale we could not have foreseen a generation ago. Today, a food cooperative is unlikely to replace a supermarket; a French-intensive garden to replace agribusiness; barter and mutual aid to replace our banking system; personal intercourse to replace the electronic paraphernalia by which the world "communicates" with itself. But we can still choose the former body of possibilities over the latter "realities." Our choices will keep alive the contrast and tension that technocratic and bureaucratic homogeneity threaten to efface, together with personality itself.

We also must recover the terrain necessary for the personification and the formation of a body politic. To defend society's molecular base— its neighborhoods, public squares, and places of assembly—expresses a demand not only for "freedom from . . ." but also for "freedom for...." The fight for shelter has ceased to be a matter of defending one's private habitat; it has become a fight to autonomously assemble, to spontaneously discuss, to sovereignly decide—in short, to be a public person, to create a public sphere, and to form a body politic against entrenched power and bureaucratic surveillance. What began in the late 1970s as a squatters' movement for more housing in Holland has now turned into a fervent struggle by young people in Switzerland for space free from authority and surveillance. Issues of habitation and logistics have turned into issues of culture, and issues of culture have become issues of politics. What the future of these specific trends in Central Europe may be, I shall not venture to predict. But the trends themselves are crucial; they reflect an intuitive passion for autonomy, individuality, and uniqueness that would win a Fourier's plaudits. Without our "freedom *for*" a public terrain, the phrase "body politic" becomes a mere metaphor; it has no protoplasm, no voices, no faces, and no passions. Hence its potential human components become privatized into their isolated shelters, their purposeless lives, their personal anonymity, and their mindless "pleasures." They become as fleshless as the electronic devices they are obliged to use, as unthinking as the fashionable garments they wear, as mute as the pets with which they console themselves.

To disengage ourselves from the existing social machinery, to create a domain to meet one's needs as a human being, to form a public sphere in which to function as part of a protoplasmic body politic—all can be summed up in a single word: reempowerment. I speak of reempowerment in its fullest personal and public sense, not as a psychic experience in a specious and reductionist form of psychological "energetics" that is fixated on one's own "vibes" and "space." There is no journey "inward" that is not a journey "outward" and no "inner space" that can hope to survive without a very palpable "public space" as well. But public space, like inner space, becomes mere empty space when it is not structured, articulated, and given body. It must be provided with institutional form, no less so than our highly integrated personal bodies, which cannot exist without structure. Without form and articulation, there can be no identity, no definition, and none of the specificity that yields variety. What is actually at issue when one discusses institutions is not whether they should exist at all but what form they should take—libertarian or authoritarian.

Libertarian institutions are *peopled* institutions, a term that should be taken literally, not metaphorically. They are structured around direct, face-to-face, protoplasmic relationships, not around representative, anonymous, mechanical relationships. They are based on participation, involvement, and a sense of citizenship that stresses activity, not on the delegation of power and spectatorial politics. Hence, libertarian institutions are guided by a cardinal principle: all mature individuals can be expected to manage social affairs directly—just as we expect them to manage their private affairs. As in the Athenian *Ecclesia*, the Parisian sections of 1793, and the New England town meetings—all of which were regularly convened public assemblies based on face-to-face democracy—every citizen is free to participate in making far-reaching decisions regarding his or her community. What is decisive, here, is the principle itself: the freedom of the individual to participate, not the compulsion or even need to do so. Freedom does not consist in the *number* of people who elect to participate in decision-making processes, but in the fact that they have the unimpaired opportunity to do so: to *choose* to decide or not to decide public issues. A "mass assembly" is simply an amorphous crowd if it is cajoled to assemble by emoluments, entertainment, the absence of any need to reflect, or the need to make quick decisions with minimal dialogue. Quorums, consensus, and pleas for participation are degrading, not "democratic"; they emphasize quantity as a social goal, not quality as evidence of an ethical community. To limit discussion and reduce problems to their lowest common denominator, lest they tax the intelligence and the attention span of a community, is to foster a people's degradation into a mute, insubstantial aggregate, not to enhance the human spirit. The Athenian *Ecclesia* was a democracy only to the degree that its citizen (alas, all males of Athenian ancestry) *chose* to attend its sessions, not because they were paid to do so or were virtually forced to participate in its deliberations (as occurred in the declining period of the *polis*).

Are these principles and forms of libertarian institutionalization realistic or practical? Can they really work, "human nature" being what it is and "civilization" imprinting its horrendous legacy of domination on the human enterprise? Actually, we will never be *able* to answer these questions unless we try to create a direct democracy that is free of sexual, ethnic, and hierarchical biases. History does provide us with a number of working examples of forms that are largely libertarian. It also provides us with examples of confederations and leagues that made the coordination of self-governing communities feasible without impinging on their autonomy and freedom. Most important is whether or not we accept a radical notion of the individual's competence to be a self-governing citizen.* Depending upon the assumptions one makes, direct democracy is either worth the test of experience or it is inherently excluded from serious social discourse. We cannot interpret the decline of the Athenian *Ecclesia*, the ultimate failure of the Parisian sections, and the waning of the New England town meetings as denying the popular assembly's feasibility for a future society. These forms of direct democracy were riddled by class conflicts and opposing social interests; they were not institutions free of hierarchy, domination, and egotism.

---

* Does this commitment to universal competence yield an "absolute freedom"—to use Hegel's term—that divests a free society of the motivation, meaning, and purpose we so readily ascribe to the effects of conflict and opposition? Charles Taylor, in a recent work, has raised this possibility of a freedom that "has no content," presumably one that will result in the subversion of subjectivity itself. This dilemma of a reconciled world that is boring and lacking in "situations" reflects the agonistic sensibility that pervades the modern mind. What Taylor's concerns express is a larger crisis in western sensibility: the conflict between aggressiveness toward reality and reflectiveness. We may well need a Fichte's aggressiveness to change the insane world in which we live today, but without Goethe's sense of equipoise and reflection as the basis for an ecological sensibility, we will almost certainly slip into a terroristic society—which Taylor, no less than Hegel, is eager to avoid. See Charles Taylor, *Hegel and Modern Society* (New York: Cambridge University Press, 1979), pp. 154–160.

What is extraordinary about them is that they functioned at all, not the weary conclusion that they eventually failed.

A second premise in creating libertarian institutions is a clear distinction between the formulation of policy and its administrative implementation. This distinction has been woefully confused by social theorists like Marx, who celebrated the Paris Commune's fusion of decision-making with administration within the same political bodies and agencies. Perhaps no error could be more serious from a libertarian viewpoint. The danger of delivering policy-making decisions to an administrative body, which normally is a delegated body and often highly technical in character, is redolent with elitism and the usurpation of public power. A direct democracy is face-to-face and unabashedly participatory. A council, committee, agency, or bureau is precisely the opposite: indirect, delegated, and often unabashedly exclusionary. For the latter to *make* policy decisions, as distinguished from coordinating activities, is to remove policy from the public domain—to *depoliticize* the process in the Athenian sense of the term at best, and render policy formulation totally exclusionary at worst. In fact, this subversive range of possibilities, all inimicable to freedom and the ideal of an active citizenry, has been the destiny of the revolutionary council movements since the beginning of the century—notably, the Russian soviets, the German *Räten*, and the Spanish anarcho-syndicalist chain of "committees" that developed early in the Spanish Revolution. Other council movements, such as the Hungarian in 1956, were too short-lived to degenerate as their predecessors had.

Moreover, the council system, conceived as a policy-making structure, is inherently hierarchical. Whether based on factories or communities, it tends to acquire a pyramidal form, however confederal its rhetoric and surface appearance. From factory and village to town, to city, to region, and finally to swollen, infrequently convened, easily manipulated national "congresses," the short-lived German *Räten* and the more long-lived Russian soviets were so far removed from their popular base that they quickly degenerated into decorative instruments for highly centralized workers' parties.

What is obviously at issue is not whether a council has been delegated, chosen by sortition, or formed in an ad hoc manner, but whether or not it can formulate policy. It would matter very little—given a reasonable amount of prudence, public supervision, and the right of the assembly to recall and rotate councilors—if councils were limited to strictly administrative responsibilities. Their narrow functions would thereby define their powers and their limits. It would not be difficult to determine whether these limits, once clearly defined, have been overstepped and the council has engaged in functions that impinge on the assembly's policy-making powers. Nor would it be difficult to determine when certain functions have been discharged and needless administrative bodies can be disbanded. A relentless system of accountability would put administrative groups largely at the mercy of decision-making assemblies, hence reinforcing the limits that confine councils to strictly coordinative functions.

Finally, I must emphasize that direct democracy is ultimately the most advanced form of direct action. There are doubtlessly many ways to express the claims of the individual and community to be autonomous, self-active, and self-managing—today as well as in a future ecological society. To exercise one's powers of sovereignty—by sit-ins, strikes, nuclear-plant occupations—is not merely a "tactic" in bypassing authoritarian institutions. It is a sensibility, a vision of citizenship and selfhood that assumes the free individual has the capacity to manage social affairs in a direct, ethical, and rational manner. This dimension of the self in self-management is a persistent call to personal sovereignty, to roundedness of ego and intellectual perception, which such conjoined terms like "management" and "activity" often overshadow. The continual exercise of this self—its very formation by one's direct intervention in social issues—in asserting its moral claim and right to empowerment stands on a higher level conceptually than Marx's image of self-identity through labor. For direct action is literally a form of ethical character-building in the most important social role that the individual can undertake: active citizenship. To reduce it to a mere means, a "strategy" that can be used or discarded for strictly functional purposes, is instrumentalism in its most insidious, often most cynical form. Direct action is at once the reclamation of the public sphere by the ego, its development toward self-empowerment, and its culmination as an active participant in society.

But direct action can also be degraded, on its own terms, by seeming to honor some of its most dubious characteristics: aggressiveness, arrogance, and terrorism. Inevitably, these characteristics rebound against the individual, and often lead to what Fourier called a malignant "counterpassion"—a spoiled, disappointed adherence to authority, delegated powers, and personal passivity. We are very familiar with the fulminating "anarchist" terrorist who turns into the most reverential supporter of authority, as Paul Brousse's career revealed. Direct action finds its *authentic* expression in the painstaking work of citizenship—such as the building of libertarian forms of organization today and their conscientious administration in routine work with lasting ardor. This unassuming work is all too readily overlooked for dramatic actions and colorful projects.

The high degree of competence individuals have exhibited in managing society, their capacity to distinguish policy-making from administration (consider the Athenian and early Swiss examples), and their awareness of selfhood as a mode of social behavior—all these traits will be heightened by a classless, nonhierarchical society. We have no reason to be disenchanted by history. As barbarous as its most warlike, cruel, exploitive, and authoritarian periods have been, humanity has soared to radiant heights in its great periods of social reconstruction, thought, and art—despite the burdens of domination and egotism. Once these burdens are removed, we have every reason to hope for a degree of personal and social enlightenment for which there are no historical precedents. Through the mother-infant relationship, we regularly plant the seeds of a human nature that can be oriented toward selfless endearment, interdependence, and care. These are not trite words to describe the womb of human renewal, generation after generation, and the love each child receives in virtually every society. They become clichés only when we ignore the possibility that separation can yield an aggressive egotism and sense of rivalry, when material insecurity produces fear toward nature and humanity, and when we "mature" by following the pathways of hierarchical and class societies.

∝

We must try to create a new culture, not merely another movement that attempts to remove the symptoms of our crises without affecting their sources. We must also try to extirpate the hierarchical orientation of our psyches, not merely remove the institutions that embody social domination. But the need for a new culture and new institutions must not be sacrificed to a hazy notion of personal redemption that makes us into lonely "saints" amidst masses of irredeemable "sinners." Changes in culture and personality go hand in hand with our efforts to achieve a society that is ecological—a society based on usufruct, complementarity, and the irreducible minimum—but that also recognizes the existence of a universal humanity and the claims of individuality. Guided as we may be by the principle of the equality of unequals, we can ignore neither the personal arena nor the social, neither the domestic nor the public, in our project to achieve harmony in society and harmony with nature.

Before exploring the general contours of an ecological society, I must first examine the concept of individual competence in managing social affairs. To create a society in which every individual is seen as capable of participating directly in the formulation of social policy is to instantly invalidate social hierarchy and domination. To accept this single concept means that we are committed to dissolving State power, authority, and sovereignty into an inviolate form of personal empowerment. That our commitment to a nonhierarchical society and personal empowerment is still a far cry from the full development of these ideals into a lived sensibility is obvious enough; hence our persistent need to confront the psychic problems of hierarchy as well as social problems of domination. There are already many tendencies that are likely to force this confrontation, even as we try to achieve institutional changes. I refer to radical forms of feminism that encompass the psychological dimensions of male domination, indeed, domination itself; to ecology conceived as a social outlook and personal sensibility; and to community as intimate, human-scaled forms of association and mutual aid. Although these tendencies may wane periodically and retreat for a time to the background of our concerns, they have penetrated deeply into the social substance and ideologies of our era.*

What would further reinforce their impact on contemporary consciousness and practice is the meaning—the function and sense of direction—they impart to our vision of an ecological society. Such a society is considerably more than an ensemble of nonhierarchical social institutions and sensibilities. In a very decisive sense, it expresses the way in which we *socialize* with nature. I use the word "socialize" advisedly: my concern is not merely with those cherished "metabolic" processes of production so central to Marx's idea of labor, nor with the design of an "appropriate" technics so dear to the hearts of our environmental engineers. What concerns me deeply, here, are the functions we impart to our communities as social ecosystems—the role they play in the biological regions in which they are situated. Indeed, whether we merely "situate" our ecocommunities or *root* them in their ecosystems, whether we "design" them merely as part of a "natural site" (like a Frank Lloyd Wright

---

* As Janet Biehl observes in her outstanding book, *Finding Our Way: Rethinking Ecofeminist Politics*: "It is bad enough that we are all less than human today, that the realm of second nature after thousands of years of progress and perversion has reached the cruel impasse that marks the present era. If women have a 'calling,' it is not the particularistic—even elitist—one that ecofeminists assign to them. Rather, it is the challenge to rise to a generous ecological humanism, so underlying to the principles of social ecology, and to an all-embracing sense of solidarity, not only with nonhuman life, but with the men who form an integral part of humanity as a whole." (Montreal: Black Rose Books, 1991; p.157.)

dwelling) or functionally *integrate* them into an ecosystem (like an organ in a living body)—these choices involve very different orientations toward technics, ethics, and the social institutions we so blithely call ecological. Wiser solar technicians have emphasized that a domestic solar energy system is not a component of a home, like a kitchen or bathroom; it is the entire house itself, as an organism interacting with nature. In less mechanical terms, the same principle of organic unity holds true for the ecocommunities and ecotechnologies we seek to integrate into the natural world.

It is a commonplace that every human enterprise necessarily "interferes" with "pure" or "virginal" nature. This notion, which suggests that human beings and their works are intrinsically "unnatural" and, in some sense, antithetical to nature's "purity" and "virginity," is a libel on humanity and nature alike. It unerringly reflects "civilization's" image of "man" as a purely social being and society as an enemy of nature, merely by virtue of the specificity and distinctiveness of social life itself. Worse yet, it grossly distorts the fact that humanity is a manifestation of nature, however unique and destructive—hence the myth that "man" must "disembed" himself from nature (Marx) or "transcend" his primate origins (Sahlins).

We may reasonably question whether human society must be viewed as "unnatural" when it cultivates food, pastures animals, removes trees and plants—in short, "tampers" with an ecosystem. We normally detect a tell-tale pejorative inflection in our discussions on human "interference" in the natural world. But all these seeming acts of "defilement" may enhance nature's fecundity rather than diminish it. The word fecundity, here, is decisive—and we could add other terms, such as variety, wholeness, integration, and even rationality. To render nature more fecund, varied, whole, and integrated may well constitute the hidden desiderata of natural evolution. That human beings become rational agents in this all-expansive natural trend—that they even benefit practically from it in the form of greater and more varied quantities of food—is no more an intrinsic defilement of nature than the fact that deer limit forest growth and preserve grasslands by feeding on the bark of saplings.

For human society to acknowledge that its well-being, perhaps its very survival, may depend upon consciously abetting the thrust of natural evolution toward a more diversified, varied, and fecund biosphere does not necessarily mean that we must reduce nature to a mere object for human manipulation—an ethical degradation of nature as a "something" that merely exists "for us." To the contrary, what is authentically "good" for us may very well not be a purely human desideratum but a natural one as well. As a unique product of natural evolution, humanity brings its powers of reasoning, its creative fingers, its high degree of conscious consociation—all qualitative developments of natural history—to nature, at times as sources of help and at other times as sources of harm. Perhaps the greatest single role an ecological ethics can play is a discriminating one—to help us distinguish which of our actions serve the thrust of natural evolution and which of them impede it. That human interests of one kind or another may be involved in these actions is not always relevant to the ethical judgments we are likely to make. What really counts are the ethical guidelines that determine our judgment.

The concept of an ecological society must begin from a sense of assurance that society and nature are not inherently antithetical. In our characteristic view of difference as a form of opposition and estrangement, we have permitted the unique aspects of human society to obscure our perception of its commonality with nature, as a "niche" in a given bioregion and ecosystem. More pointedly, we have permitted the very failings of "civilization"—its objectification of nature and human beings, its hierarchical, class, domineering, and exploitative relationships—to be interpreted as intrinsic social attributes. Hence, a deformed society has come to represent society as such, with the result that its antihuman and antinatural qualities become visible only when we contract this deformed society with organic society. Without the benefit of this hindsight, we myopically extol the very failings of "civilization" as evidence of the "disembeddedness" of society from nature. Our greatest shortcomings and defaults are turned into grossly unjustifiable "successes"; our most irrational actions and institutions become the "fruits" of human reason and volition. That humanity was expelled from the Garden of Eden does not mean that we must turn an antagonistic face toward nature; rather, it is a metaphor for a new, eminently ecological function: the need to create more fecund gardens than Eden itself.

✿

It is tempting to venture into a utopian description of how an ecological society would look and how it would function, but I have promised to leave such visions to the utopian dialogue that we so direly need today. However, certain biotic and cultural imperatives cannot be ignored if our concept of an ecological society is to have integrative meaning and self-conscious direction. Perhaps the most striking example of how natural evolution phases into social evolution is the fact that we are the heirs of a strong natural thrust toward association. Owing to our prolonged dependency as children and the plasticity of mind that this long period of growth provides, we are destined to live together as a species. Highly privatistic pathologies aside, we have a maternally biased need to associate, to care for our own kind, to collaborate. Whether in village or town, *polis* or city, commune or megalopolis, we seem impelled by the very nature of our child-rearing experiences and attributes to live in a highly associative world.

But what kind of associations could we expect to find in our future ecological society? While the kinship tie or the blood oath is a more strictly biological basis for association than any form we know, it is patently too parochial and restrictive, in view of our modern commitment to a universal *humanitas*. Indeed, it is fair to ask whether the *strictly* biological is necessarily more "natural" than the human social attributes produced by natural evolution. Our very concept of nature may be more fully expressed by the way in which biological facts are *integrated structurally* to give rise to more complex and subtle forms of natural reality. Society itself may be a case in point, at least in terms of its abiding basic elements, and human associations that extend beyond the blood tie may reflect more complex forms of natural evolution than the highly limited biological kinship relations. If human nature is part of nature, the associations that rest on universal human loyalties may well be expressions of a richer, more variegated nature than we hitherto have been prepared to acknowledge.

In any case, it is apparent that we score a much richer ecological advance over the conventional biological wisdom of early humanity when we relate on the basis of a simple affinity of tastes, cultural similarities, emotional compatibilities, sexual preferences, and intellectual interests. Nor are we any the less natural for doing so. Even more preferable than the blood-related family is the commune that unites individuals by what they choose to like in each other rather than what they are obliged by blood ties to like. Conscious cultural affinity is ultimately a more *creative* basis for association than the unthinking demands of kin loyalties. The rudiments of an ecological society will probably be structured around the commune—freely created, human in scale, and intimate in its consciously cultivated relationships—rather than clan or tribal forms that are often fairly sizable and anchored in the imperatives of blood and the notion of a common ancestry. It is not "retribalization" that an ecological society is likely to seek but rather recommunalization with its wealth of creative libertarian traits.

On a still larger scale, the Commune composed of many small communes seems to contain the best features of the *polis*, without the ethnic parochialism and political exclusivity that contributed so significantly to its decline. Such larger or composite Communes, networked confederally through ecosystems, bioregions, and biomes, must be artistically tailored to their natural surroundings. We can envision that their squares will be interlaced by streams, their places of assembly surrounded by groves, their physical contours respected and tastefully landscaped, their soils nurtured caringly to foster plant variety for ourselves, our domestic animals, and wherever possible the wildlife they may support on their fringes. We can hope that the Communes would aspire to live with, nourish, and feed upon the life-forms that indigenously belong to the ecosystems in which they are integrated.

Decentralized and scaled to human dimensions, such ecocommunities would obey nature's "law of return" by recycling their organic wastes into composted nutriment for gardens and such materials as they can rescue for their crafts and industries. We can expect that they would subtly integrate solar, wind, hydraulic, and methane-producing installations into a highly variegated pattern for producing power. Agriculture, aquaculture, stockraising, and hunting would be regarded as crafts—an orientation that we hope would be extended as much as possible to the fabrication of use-values of nearly all kinds. The need to mass-produce goods in highly mechanized installations would be vastly diminished by the communities' overwhelming emphasis on quality and permanence. Vehicles, clothing, furnishings, and utensils would often become heirlooms to be handed down from generation to generation rather than discardable items that are quickly sacrificed to the gods of obsolescence. The past would always live in the present as the treasured arts and works of generations gone by.

We could expect that work, more craftlike than industrial, would be as readily rotated as positions of public responsibility; that members of the communities would be disposed to deal with one another in face-to-face relationships rather than by electronic means. In a world where the fetishization of needs would give way to the freedom to choose needs, quantity to quality, mean-spirited egotism to generosity, and indifference to love, we might reasonably expect that industrialization would be seen as an insult to human physiological rhythms and that physically onerous tasks would be reworked into collective enterprises more festive than laborious in nature. Whether several ecocommunities would want to share and conjointly operate certain industrial entities— such as a small-scale foundry, machine shop, electronic installation, or utility—or whether they would want to return to more traditional but often technically exciting means of producing goods is a decision that belongs to future generations. Certainly, no law of production requires that we retain or expand the gigantic, highly centralized and hierarchically organized plants, mills, and offices that disfigure modern industry. By the same token, it is not for us to describe in any detail how the Communes of the future would confederate themselves and coordinate their common activities. Any institutional relationship of which we could conceive would remain a hollow form until we knew the attitudes, sensibilities, ideals, and values of the people who establish and maintain it. As I have already pointed out, a libertarian institution is a peopled one; hence its purely formal structure will be neither better nor worse than the ethical values of the people who give it reality. Certainly we, who have been saturated with the values of hierarchy and domination, cannot hope to impose our "doubts" upon people who have been totally freed of their trammels.

What humanity can never afford to lose is its sense of ecological direction and the ethical meaning it gives to its projects. As I have already observed, our alternative technologies will have very little social meaning or direction if they are designed with strictly technocratic goals in mind. By the same token, our efforts at cooperation will be actively demoralizing if we come together merely to "survive" the hazards of living in our prevailing social system. Our technics can be either catalysts for our integration with the natural world or the chasms separating us from it. They are never ethically neutral. "Civilization" and its ideologies have fostered the latter orientation; social ecology must promote the former. Modern authoritarian technics have been tested beyond all human endurance by a misbegotten history of natural devastation and chronic genocide, indeed, biocide. The rewards we can glean from the wreckage they have produced will require so much careful sifting that an understandable case can be made for simply turning our backs on the entire heap. But we are already too deeply mired in its wastes to extricate ourselves readily. We have become trapped in its economic logistics, its systems of transportation and distribution, its national division of labor, and its immense industrial apparatus. Lest we be totally submerged and buried in its debris, we must tread cautiously—seeking firm ground where we can in the real attainments of science and engineering, avoiding its lethal quagmire of weaponry and its authoritarian technics of social control.

In the end, however, we must escape from the debris with whatever booty we can rescue, and recast our technics entirely in the light of an ecological ethics whose concept of "good" takes its point of departure from our concepts of diversity, wholeness, and a nature rendered self-conscious—an ethics whose "evil" is rooted in homogeneity, hierarchy, and a society whose sensibilities have been deadened beyond resurrection. Insofar as we hope to resurrect ourselves, we are obliged to use technics to bring the vitality of nature back into our atrophied senses. Having lost sight of our roots in natural history, we must be all the more careful in dealing with the means of life as forms of nature: to discern our roots in the sun and wind, in minerals and gases, as well as in soil, plants, and animals. It is a challenge not to be evaded—notably, to see the sun as part of our umbilical cord to power just as we discern its role in the photosynthetic activities of plants.

Inevitably, I am asked how to go from "here to there," as though reflections on the emergence and dissolution of hierarchy must contain recipes for social change. For social "paradigms" one can turn to such memorable events as the May–June upheaval in France during 1968, or to Portugal a decade later, and possibly to Spain a generation earlier. What should always count in analyzing such events is not why they failed—for they were never expected to occur at all—but how they managed to erupt and persist against massive odds. No movement for freedom can even communicate its goals, much less succeed in attaining them, unless historic forces are at work to alter unconscious hierarchical values and sensibilities. Ideas reach only people who are ready to hear them. No individual, newspaper, or book can undo a character structure shaped by the prevailing society until the society itself is beleaguered by crises. Thus ideas, as Marx shrewdly observed, really make us conscious of what we already know unconsciously. What history can teach us are the forms, strategies, techniques—and failures—in trying to change the world by also trying to change ourselves.

The libertarian technics of change have been discussed and tried extensively. Their capacity for success still must be proven by the situations in which they can really hope to attain their goals. None of the authoritarian technics of change has provided successful "paradigms," unless we are prepared to ignore the harsh fact that the Russian, Chinese, and Cuban "revolutions" were massive counterrevolutions that blight our entire century. Libertarian forms of organization have the enormous responsibility of trying to resemble the society they are seeking to develop. They can tolerate no disjunction between ends and means. Direct action, so integral to the management of a future society, has its parallel in the use of direct action to change society. Communal forms, so integral to the structure of a future society, have their parallel in the use of communal forms—collectives, affinity groups, and the like—to change society. The ecological ethics, confederal relationships, and decentralized structures we would expect to find in a future society, are fostered by the values and networks we try to use in achieving an ecological society.

We know from the Parisian sections that even large cities can be decentralized structurally and institutionally for a lengthy period of time, however centralized they once were logistically and economically. Should a future society, confederally integrated and communally oriented, seek to decentralize itself logistically and economically, it will not lack the existing means and latent talents to do so. Just as New York City has shown that it can effortlessly dismember itself in less than a decade and become a physical ruin, so Germany's cities after World War II have shown that they can rebuild themselves from ruins into thriving (if tasteless) megalopolises in an equal span of time. The means for tearing down the old are available, both as hope and as peril. So, too, are the means for rebuilding. The ruins themselves are mines for recycling the wastes of an immensely perishable world into the structural materials of one that is free as well as new.

ও EPILOGUE

In this book, I have tried to "turn the world upside down" in a form more theoretical than the efforts of the Diggers, Levellers, Ranters and their contemporary descendants. I have tried to shake out our world and explore the conspicuous features of its development. My efforts will succeed if they demonstrate how profoundly the curse of domination has infused almost every human endeavor since the decline of organic society. Hardly any achievement—be it institutional, technical, scientific, ideological, artistic, or the noble claims to rationality—has been spared this curse. In contrast to highly fashionable tendencies to root the origins of this curse in reason as such or in the "savage's" attempts to "wrestle" with nature, I have sought them out in the sinister endeavor of emerging elites to place human beings and human nature in a condition of subjugation. I have emphasized the potentially liberating role of art and imagination in giving expression to what is authentically human, utopistic, and free in human nature.

In contrast to Marx and Freud, who identify "civilization" and "progress" with a repressive self-control, I have argued that anthropology and a clear reading of history present an image entirely antithetical to that of a grasping, Hobbesian type of humanity. Psychological self-abnegation comes with the social conflict and repression that accompany the rise of hierarchy, not of reason and technology. The bas reliefs of Egypt and Mesopotamia reveal a world in which human beings were forced to deny not merely their most human desires and impulses, but also their most rudimentary sense of personality. Eve, the serpent, and the fruit of the tree of knowledge were not the causes of domination but rather its victims. Indeed, society itself, conceived as the work of maternal care with its sequelae in human interdependence, is a standing reminder that the Garden of Eden was in many respects real enough and that the authentic "original sin" closely accords with the radical gnostic image of self-transgression.

I do not profess to believe that we can return to the pristine garden where this violation first occurred. History provides hope for a solution to the problems of hierarchy and domination. Knowledge, or *gnosis*—to know and transcend our primal act of self-transgression—is the first step toward curing our social pathology of rule, just as self-knowledge in psychoanalytic practice is the first step toward curing a personal pathology of repression. But the thought without the act, the theory without the practice, would be an abdication of all social responsibility.

In our own time we have seen domination spread over the social landscape to a point where it is beyond all human control. The trillions of dollars that the nations of the world have spent since the Second World War on means of subjugation and destruction—its "defense budgets" for an utterly terrifying weaponry—are only the most recent evidence of a centuries-long craze for domination that has now reached manic proportions. Compared to this stupendous mobilization of materials, of wealth, of human intellect, and of human labor for the single goal of domination, all other recent human achievements pale to almost trivial significance. Our art, science, medicine, literature, music, and "charitable" acts seem like mere droppings from a table on which gory feasts on the spoils of conquest have engaged the attention of a system whose appetite for rule is utterly unrestrained. We justly mistrust its acts of generosity today, for behind its seemingly worthy projects—its medical technology, cybernetic revolutions, space programs, agricultural projects, and energy innovations—seem to lie the most malignant motives for achieving the subjugation of humanity by means of violence, fear, and surveillance.

This book traces the landscape of domination from its inception in a hidden prehistory of hierarchy that long precedes the rise of economic classes. Hierarchy remains hidden not only in humanity's prehistory but also in the depths of its psychic apparatus. All the rich meaning of the term freedom is easily betrayed during the course of our socialization processes and our most intimate experiences. This betrayal is expressed by our treatment of children and women, by our physical stance and most personal relationships, by our private thoughts and daily lives, by our unconscious ways of ordering our experiences of reality. The betrayal occurs not only in our political and economic institutions but in our bedrooms, kitchens, schools, recreation areas, and centers of moral education such as our churches and psychotherapeutic "conventicles." Hierarchy and domination preside over our self-appointed movements for human emancipation—such as Marxism in its conventional forms, where any self-activity by the "masses" is viewed with suspicion and, more commonly than not, denounced as "anarchistic deviation."

❧

Hierarchy mocks our every claim to have ascended from "animality" to the high estate of "liberty" and "individuality." In the tools we use to save human lives, to sculpt things of beauty, or to decorate the world around us, we remain subtly tainted by an ever-assertive sensibility that reduces our most creative acts to a "triumph" and inscribes the word "masterpiece" with the traits of mastership. The greatness of the Dadaist tradition, from its ancient roots in the gnostic Ophites to its modern expression in Surrealism—a celebration of the right to indiscipline, imagination, play, fancy, innovation, iconoclasm, pleasure, and a creativity of the unconscious—is that it criticizes this "hidden" realm of hierarchy more unrelentingly and brashly than the most sophisticated theoretical games in hermeneutics, structuralism, and semiology so much in vogue on the campuses of contemporary western society.

A world so completely tainted by hierarchy, command, and obedience articulates its sense of authority in the way we have been taught to see ourselves: as objects to be manipulated, as things to be used. From this self-imagery, we have extended our way of visualizing reality into our image of "external" nature. We have mobilized our human nature to embark upon a great social enterprise to "disembed" ourselves from "external" nature, only to discover that we have rendered our own nature and "external" nature increasingly mineralized and inorganic. We have perilously simplified the natural world, society, and personality—so much so that the integrity of complex life forms, the complexity of social forms, and the ideal of a many-sided personality are completely in question.

In an age when mechanical materialism competes with an equally mechanical spiritualism, I have emphasized the need for a sensitivity to diversity that fosters a concept of wholeness as the unifying principle of an ecology of freedom. This emphasis, central to the goals of this book, contrasts markedly with the more common emphasis on "Oneness." In my opposition to current attempts to dissolve variety into mechanical and spiritual common denominators, I have exulted in the richness of variety in natural, social, and personal development. I have presented an account (admittedly somewhat Hegelian) in which the history of a phenomenon—be it subjectivity, science, or technics—constitutes the definition of that phenomenon. In each of these cumulative domains, there are always degrees or aspects of comprehension, insight, and artfulness that we must judiciously reclaim in order to grasp reality in its various gradations and aspects. But western thought has tried to understand experience and act upon reality in terms of only one mode of subjectivity, science, and technics. We tend to root our conceptions of reality in mutually exclusionary bases: economic in one instance, technical in another, cultural in still a third. Hence, profoundly important lines of evolution have been selected as "basic" or "contingent," "structural" or "superstructural" from the standpoint of a limited development in natural and human evolution.

I have tried to show that *each* such "line" or "superstructure" has its own authenticity and historical claim to identity—doubtless interdependent in its relationship with other "lines" of development, but rich in its own integrity. My greatest single concern has been with the interplay between the evolution of domination and that of freedom. By freedom I mean not only the equality of unequals, but also the enlargement of our concepts of subjectivity, technics, science, and ethics, with a concomitant recognition of their history and the insights they provide over different "stages" of their development. I have tried to show not only how these aspects of freedom form a rich, increasingly whole mosaic that only an ecological sensibility can hope to grasp, but also how they interact with one another from organic society onward, without losing their own uniqueness in the rich diversity of the whole. No economic "base" underpins culture any more than a cultural "base" underpins economics. Indeed, the very terms "base" and "superstructure" are alien to the outlook that permeates this book. Reductionist and simplistic, these terms tend to reflect naïve views of a reality whose wealth of interactions defies overly schematic and mechanistic interpretations.

If precapitalist history demonstrates anything, it is the dramatic fact that men and women have made extraordinary sacrifices, including giving up life itself, for beliefs that have centered around virtue, justice, and liberty—beliefs that are not easily explicable in terms of their material interests and social status. The remarkable history of the Jews, an account of almost unrelieved persecution for nearly two millennia; of the Irish in more recent centuries; of sweeping popular revolutionary movements from the time of the Reformation to that of the Paris Commune—all bear witness to the power of religious, national, and social ideals to move hundreds of millions of people to actions of incredible heroism. To say that they were "basically" impelled by "economic factors" of which they were unconscious—by a hidden "economic" dialectic of history—assumes that these economic factors actually prevail when their very existence or authority over human affairs has yet to be proven. Even where economic factors seem to be evident, their significance in guiding human action is often highly obscure. When John Ball or Gerrard Winstanley describe the greed of the ruling classes of their day, one senses that their remarks are guided more by ethical ideals of justice and freedom than by material interest.

The hatred of injustice has seethed all the more in the hearts of the oppressed not simply because social conditions have been particularly onerous but rather because of the searing contrast between prevailing moral precepts of justice and their transgression in practice. Christianity was pervaded by this contrast, hence the highly provocative role it played for so much of human history in generating revolutionary millenarian movements. Not until capitalism tainted history with a "sense of scarcity," making its mean-spirited commitment to rivalry the motive force of social development, did so many of these ideals begin to degenerate into brute economic interests. Even the earliest movements for a "black redistribution" seem to be evidence less of great looting expeditions than of efforts to restore a way of life, a traditional social dispensation, in which sharing and disaccumulation were prevailing social norms. Quite often these movements destroyed not only the legal documents that gave the elites title to the authority and property, but also the palaces, villas, furnishings, even the granaries that seemed to embody their power.

The French Revolution, as Hannah Arendt has pointed out, marks a reversal in the goals of social change from various kinds of ethical desiderata to a conception of the "social question" defined in terms of material need. Actually, this shift in perspective may have occurred much later than Arendt realized, notably in our own century. If Marx exulted in this new sense of economistic "realism" or "materialism," we, in turn, who are afflicted by a conflict between our "fetishization of needs" at one extreme and our yearning for ethical meaning and community at the other, have become the schizoid products of a world frozen into immobility by our sense of personal and social powerlessness. We have invented a mystique of "historical laws" or of "scientific socialisms" that serve more to replace our frustrated drives for meaning and community than to explain the remoteness of these cherished goals in real life.

ᴏ᷍ᴕ

If there is no single generalization of an economic or cultural character in which we can root social development, if no "social laws" exist that underpin an intellectual orientation toward social phenomena, then by what coordinates shall we take our social bearings? I suggest that the most powerful and meaningful context illuminating the human enterprise is the distinction between libertarian and authoritarian. I do not mean to imply that either of these terms expresses any sense of finality about history, or that they are not without ambiguity. Whether there is any terminal point in human history that corresponds to a Hegelian "Absolute" or Marxian "Communism"—indeed, if not to outright extinction—is certainly not for this generation to affirm or deny. It is merely metaphorical to say that humanity's "real history" will begin when its "social question" has been resolved. The Enlightenment's commitment to technological advances is certainly the *least* reliable system of coordinates we possess. Even today, in our most technically oriented of worlds, where ethics itself has acquired the adjective "instrumental," we are being forced to acknowledge that our most alluring designs—for all their "convivial" or "appropriate" attributes—can be deployed to create "alternative" strategies for war.

More than ever before, we must emphasize that the words libertarian and authoritarian refer not only to conflicting forms of institutions, technics, reason, and science, but above all, to conflicting values and sensibilities—in short, to conflicting epistemologies. My definition of the term "libertarian" is guided by my description of the ecosystem: the image of unity in diversity, spontaneity, and complementary relationships, free of all hierarchy and domination. By "authoritarian," I refer to hierarchy and domination as my social guide: the gerontocracies, patriarchies, class relationships, elites of all kinds, and finally the State, particularly in its most socially parasitic form of state capitalism. But without including conflicting sensibilities, sciences, technics, ethics, and forms of reason, the terms "libertarian" and "authoritarian" remain simply institutional terms that have only an implicit character. Their implications must be elicited to the fullest extent to cover the entire range of experience if the conflict between them is to be meaningful and revolutionary.

Reason, placed within this tension between the libertarian and authoritarian, must be permitted to stake out its own claim to a libertarian rationality. Philosophically, we have made far too much of the belief that a libertarian rationality must have canons of truth and consistency, indeed of intuition and contradiction, that completely invalidate the claim of formal and analytical thought to truth. To the extent that intuition and contradiction have more than adequately served the ends of authority in the folk philosophies of fascism and the dialectical materialism of Stalinism—just as analytical reason has served the ends of freedom of thought—we have no certain guide beyond our *ethical* criteria that unconventional modes of thought will necessarily yield emancipatory conclusions. The Buddha and the Christ figures have been used to serve the ends of authority with as much success as they have been used to serve the ends of freedom. Radical mysticism and spiritualism have been as antinaturalistic and antihuman as they have been ecological and millenarian. What is decisive in considering the "canons" of reason—or, more precisely, in shaping a new approach to subjectivity—is the extent to which we raise a biotically variegated ethical standard based on the fecundity of life, on the virtue of complementarity, on the logical image of an ever-richer mosaic of experience, rather than on a hierarchically reared pyramidal view of experience. We need not abandon even Aristotle's Organon, which served western thought as its logical tenets for centuries, or systems theory, whose notion of a circular causality blends the very idea of a point of departure with its conclusion. We have only to sculpt reason into an ethically charged sensibility that is personally and socially emancipatory—whether it is "linear" or "circular." Reason, whose defeat at the hands of Horkheimer and Adorno evoked so much pessimism among their colleagues, can be lifted from its fallen position by a libertarian ethics rooted in a radical social ecology. Such an ethics retains its openness to the richness of human sensibility as the embodiment of sensibility itself at all levels of organic and social evolution.

And there is a ground on which this libertarian ethics can be reared—an area that provides a sense of meaning that does not depend upon the vagaries of opinion, taste, and the icy need for instrumental effectiveness. All nonsense of "folk," "race," "inexorable dialectical laws" aside, there seems to be a kind of intentionality latent in nature, a graded development of self-organization that yields subjectivity and, finally, self-reflexivity in its highly developed human form. Such a vision may well seem like an anthropomorphic presupposition that also lends itself to an arbitrary relativism, no different in character than the "subjective reason" or instrumentalism abhorred by Horkheimer. Yet even the philosophical demand for "presuppositionless" first principles is a presupposition of mind. We have yet to establish why the ancient belief that values inherent in nature provide more reason for doubt than Bertrand Russell's image of life and human consciousness as the product of mere fortuity, a meaningless and accidental freaking of nature into the realm of subjectivity.

Is it too fanciful to suggest that our very being is an epistemology and ontology of its own—indeed, an entire philosophy of organism—that can withstand accusations of anthropomorphism? Form is no less integral to nature than motion and, ultimately, function. Whatever else we choose to call "natural" involves both form and motion as function. To invoke mere fortuity as the *deus ex machina* of a sweeping, superbly organized development that lends itself to concise mathematical explanation is to use the accidental as a tomb for the explanatory. In a deeply sensitive argument for teleology, Hans Jonas has asked whether a strictly physicochemical analysis of the structure of the eye and its stimulation as a source of vision "is meaningful without relating it to seeing." For we will always find

> the purposiveness of organism *as such* and its concern in living: effective already in all vegetative tendency, awakening to primordial awareness in the dim reflexes, the responding irritability of lowly organisms; more so in the urge and effort and anguish of animal life endowed with motility and sense organs; reaching self-transparency in consciousness, will and thought of man: all these being inward aspects of the teleological side in the nature of "matter." ... At all events, the teleological structure and behavior of organism is not just an alternative choice of description: it is, *on the evidence of each one's organic awareness,* the external manifestation of the inwardness of substance. To add the implications: there is no organism without teleology; there is no teleology without inwardness; and: life can be known only by life.

Indeed, one could add that life can be known only as a *result* of life. It can never, by its very nature, be dissociated from its potentiality for knowingness, even as mere sensitivity, need, and the impulse for self-preservation.

෬

Doubtless there is much we can append to Jonas's observations on teleology. We can conceive of teleology as the actualization of potentiality—more precisely, as the end result of a phenomenon's immanent striving toward realization that leaves room for the existence of fortuity and uncertainty. Here, teleology expresses the self-organization of a phenomenon to become what it is without the certainty that it will do so. Our notion of teleology need not be governed by any "iron necessity" or unswerving self-development that "inevitably" summons forth the end of a phenomenon from its nascent beginnings. Although a specific phenomenon may not be randomly self-constituted, fortuity could prevent its self-actualization. Its "telos" would thus appear as the consequence of a prevailing striving rather than as an inevitable necessity.

But what is most fascinating today is that *nature is writing its own nature philosophy and ethics*—not the logicians, positivists, and heirs of

Galilean scientism. As I have noted, we are not alone in the universe, not even in the "emptiness" of space. Owing to what is a fairly recent revolution in astrophysics (possibly comparable only to the achievements of Copernicus and Kepler), the cosmos is opening itself up to us in new ways that call for an exhilarating speculative turn of mind and a more qualitative approach to natural phenomena. It is becoming increasingly tenable to suggest that the entire universe may be the cradle of life—not merely our own planet or a few planets like it. The "Big Bang," whose faint echoes from a time-span of more than fifteen billion years ago can now be detected by the astrophysicist's instruments, may be evidence less of a single accidental "event" than of a form of cosmic "breathing" whose gradual expansions and contractions extend over an infinity of time. If this is so—and we are admittedly on highly speculative grounds—we may be dealing with cosmic *processes* rather than a single episode in the formation of the universe. Obviously, if these processes express an unending form of universal "history," as it were, we, who are irrevocably locked into our own cosmic era, may never be able to fathom their reality or meaning. But it is not completely unreasonable to wonder if we are dealing here with a vast, continuing development of the universe, not simply with a recurring type of cosmic "respiration."

Highly conjectural as these notions may be, the formation of all the elements from hydrogen and helium, their combination into small molecules and later into self-forming macromolecules, and finally the organization of these macromolecules into the constituents of life and possibly mind follow a sequence that challenges Russell's image of humanity as an accidental spark in an empty, meaningless void. Certain phases of this sequence constitute a strong challenge to a view in which the word "accident" becomes a prudent substitute for virtual inevitabilities. A cosmos interspersed with dust composed of hydrogen, carbon, nitrogen, and oxygen molecules seems geared to the unavoidable formation of organic molecules. Radio astronomers have detected cyanogen, carbon monoxide, hydrogen cyanide, formaldehyde, formic acid, methanol, acetaldehyde, and methyl formate in interstellar space. In short, the classical image of space as a void is giving way to the image of space as a restlessly active chemogenetic ground for an astonishing sequence of increasingly complex organic compounds.

From there, it is only a short leap to the self-organization of rudimentary, life-forming molecules. Analysis of carbonaceous chondrites (a group of stony meteorites with small glassy inclusions) yields long-chain aromatic hydrocarbons such as fatty acids, amino acids, and porphyrins—the compounds from which chlorophyll is built. In a series of laboratory studies beginning with the famous Miller-Urey "spark-gap" experiment, simple amino acids were formed by passing electrical discharges through a flask containing gases that presumably composed the earth's early atmosphere. By changing the gases in accordance with later theories of the primal atmosphere, other researchers have been able to produce long-chain amino acids, ribose and glucose sugars, and nucleoside phosphates—the precursors of DNA.

Hypothetically (albeit with an impressive degree of supporting evidence), it is now possible to trace how anaerobic microorganisms might have developed simple membranes and, with increasing complexity, have emerged as distinct life forms capable of highly developed metabolic processes. Few working hypotheses more strikingly reveal the highly graded interface between the inorganic and the organic than speculations on the formation of genetic structures. Such speculations bring us conceptually to the most central feature of life itself: the ability of a complex mosaic of organic macromolecules to *reproduce* itself and yet to do so with changes significant enough to render evolution possible. As early as 1944, Erwin Schrodinger may have provided a clue to organic reproduction and evolution. In *What is Life?* this eminent physicist observed that "the most essential part of a living cell—the chromosome fibre—may suitably be called *an aperiodic crystal.*" The "chromosome fibre" does not merely repeat itself and grow additively, like a "periodic" crystal; instead, it changes significantly to yield new forms—mutations—that initiate and carry on inherited, evolutionary developments.

Graham Cairns-Smith has advanced another hypothesis (one among the many now being proposed and soon forthcoming) that may help clarify the nature of early reproduction processes. DNA is much too unstable chemically, Cairns-Smith emphasizes, to have survived the radiation and heat to which the early earth's surface was exposed. In an analogy that could bear improvement, Cairns-Smith compares DNA with a "magnetic tape: it is very efficient if provided with a suitably protective environment, suitably machined raw materials and suitably complex recording equipment." This machining equipment, he contends, can be found in the inorganic world itself:

> With a number of other considerations, this leads [Cairns-Smith] to the idea of a form of crystallization process as the printing machine, with some kind of crystal defects as the pattern-forming elements. Being as specific as possible, a mica-type clay seemed the most promising possibility.

Minimally, Cairns-Smith's hypothesis suggests that life, in its own ways and following its own genetic evolution, is not miraculously separated from phenomena existing in the inorganic world. I do not mean to imply that biology can be reduced to physics any more than society can be reduced to biology. Insofar as Cairns-Smith suggests that certain clay crystals could possibly be templates of organic reproductive material and thereby launch the evolution of secondary and still more advanced forms of organic hereditary materials, he is also suggesting that nature may be unified by certain common tendencies. Such tendencies would share a like origin in the reality of the cosmos, however differently they function at different levels of self-organization.

My point here is that substance and its properties are not separable from life. Henri Bergson's conception of the biosphere as an "entropy-reduction" factor, in a cosmos that is supposedly moving toward greater entropy or disorder, would seem to provide life with a cosmic rationale for existence. That life forms may have this function need not suggest that the universe has been exogenously "designed" by a supernatural demiurge. But it does suggest that "matter" or substance has inherent self-organizing properties, no less valid than the mass and motion attributed to it by Newtonian physics.

Nor is there so great a lack of data, by comparison with the conventional attributes of "matter," as to render the new properties implausible. At the very least, science must *be* what nature really is; and in nature, life *is* (to use Bergsonian terminology) a counteracting force to the second law of thermodynamics—or an "entropy-reduction" factor. The self-organization of substance into ever-more complex forms—indeed, the importance of form itself as a correlate of function and of function as a correlate of self-organization—implies the unceasing activity to achieve stability. That stability as well as complexity is a "goal" of substance; that complexity, not only inertness, makes for stability; and finally, that complexity is a paramount feature of organic evolution and of an ecological interpretation of biotic interrelationships—all these concepts taken together are ways of understanding nature as such, not mere mystical vagaries. They are supported more by evidence than are the theoretical prejudices that still exist today against a universe charged with meaning, indeed, dare I say, with *ethical* meaning.

This much is clear: we can no longer be satisfied with a passive "dead" matter that fortuitously collects into living substance. The universe bears witness to an ever-striving, *developing*—not merely a "moving"—substance, whose most dynamic and creative attribute is its ceaseless capacity for self-organization into increasingly complex forms.

Natural fecundity originates primarily from growth, not from spatial "changes" of location. Nor can we remove form from its central place in this developmental and growth process, or function as an indispensable correlate of form. The orderly universe that makes science a possible project and its use of a highly concise logic—mathematics—meaningful presupposes the correlation of form with function.* From this perspective, mathematics serves not merely as the "language" of science but also as the *logos* of science. This scientific *logos* is above all a workable project because it grasps a *logos* that inheres in nature—the "object" of scientific investigation.

❧

Once we step beyond the threshold of a purely instrumental attitude toward the "language" of the sciences, we can admit even more attributes into our account of the organic substance we call life. Conceived as substance that is perpetually self-maintaining or metabolic as well as developmental, life more clearly establishes the existence of another attribute: symbiosis. Recent data support the view that Peter Kropotkin's mutualistic naturalism not only applies to relationships within and among species, but also applies morphologically—within and among complex cellular forms. As William Trager observed more than a decade ago:

> The conflict in nature between different kinds of organisms has been popularly expressed in phrases like "struggle for existence" and "survival of the fittest." Yet few people realize that mutual cooperation between different kinds of organisms—symbiosis—is just as important, and that the "fittest" may be the one that most helps another to survive.

Whether intentional or not, Trager's description of the "fittest" is not merely a scientific judgment made by an eminent biologist; it is also an ethical judgment similar to the one Kropotkin derived from his own work as a naturalist and his ideals as an anarchist. Trager emphasized that the "nearly perfect" integration of "symbiotic microorganisms into the economy of the host has led to the hypothesis that certain

---

* The mathematics to which I refer is as much a mathematics of form as it is of quantity—in fact, emphatically more so. In this respect, I follow the Greek tradition, not that of the late Renaissance, and the truth that inheres in the Pythagorean emphasis on form rather than the Galilean on quantity. We have too readily forgotten that mathematics has fallen victim to instrumentalism and the myth of method, no less than have ethics and philosophy.

intracellular organelles might have been originally independent microorganisms." Accordingly, the chloroplasts that are responsible for photosynthetic activity in plants with *eukaryotic*, or nucleated, cells are discrete structures that replicate by division, have their own distinctive DNA very similar to that of circular bacteria, synthesize their own proteins, and are bounded by two-unit membranes.

Much the same is true of the eukaryotic cell's "powerhouse," its mitochondria. The most significant research in this area dates back to the 1960s and has been developed with great elan by Lynn Margulis in her papers and books on cellular evolution. The eukaryotic cells are the morphological units of all complex forms of animal and plant life. The protista and fungi also share these well-nucleated cell structures. Eukaryotes are aerobic and include clearly formed subunits, or organelles. By contrast, the *prokaryotes* lack nuclei; they are anaerobic, less specialized than the eukaryotes, and according to Margulis they constitute the evolutionary predecessors of the eukaryotes. In fact, they are the only lifeforms that could have survived and flourished in the early earth's atmosphere, with its mere traces of free oxygen.

Margulis has argued and largely established that the eukaryotic cells consist of highly functional symbiotic arrangements of prokaryotes that have become totally interdependent with other constituents. Eukaryotic flagella, she hypothesizes, derive from anaerobic spirochetes; mitochondria, from prokaryotic bacteria that were capable of respiration as well as fermentation; and plant chloroplasts, from "blue-green algae," which have recently been reclassified as cyanobacteria. The theory, now almost a biological convention, holds that phagocytic ancestors of what were to become eukaryotes absorbed (without digesting) certain spirochetes, protomitochondria (which, Margulis suggests, might have invaded their hosts), and, in the case of photosynthetic cells, coccoid cyanobacteria and chloroxybacteria. Existing phyla of multicellular aerobic life forms thus had their origins in a symbiotic process that integrated a variety of microorganisms into what can reasonably be called a colonial organism, the eukaryotic cell. *Mutualism*, not predation, seems to have been the guiding principle for the evolution of the highly complex aerobic life forms that are common today.

The prospect that life and all its attributes are *latent* in substance as such, that biological evolution is rooted deeply in symbiosis or mutualism, indicates how important it is to reconceptualize our notion of "matter" as *active* substance. As Manfred Eigen has put it, molecular self-organization suggests that evolution "appears to be an inevitable event, given the presence of certain matter with specified autocatalytic properties and under the maintenance of the finite (free) energy flow [that is, solar energy] necessary to compensate for the steady production of entropy." Indeed, this self-organizing activity extends beyond the emergence and evolution of life to the seemingly inorganic factors that produced and maintain a biotically favorable "environment" for the development of increasingly complex life forms. As Margulis observes, summarizing the Gaia hypothesis that she and James E. Lovelock have developed, the traditional assumption that life has been forced merely to adapt to an independent, geologically and meteorologically determined "environment" is no longer tenable. This dualism between the living and the nonliving world (which is based on accidental point mutations in life-forms that determine what species will evolve or perish) is being replaced by the more challenging notion that life "makes much of its own environment," as Margulis observes. "Certain properties of the atmosphere, sediments, and hydrosphere are controlled by and for the biosphere."

By comparing lifeless planets such as Mars and Venus with the Earth, Margulis notes that the high concentration of oxygen in our atmosphere is anomalous in contrast with the carbon dioxide worlds of the other planets. Moreover, "the concentration of oxygen in the Earth's atmosphere remains constant in the presence of nitrogen, methane, hydrogen, and other potential reactants." Life, in effect, exerts an active role in maintaining free oxygen molecules and their relative constancy in the earth's atmosphere. The same is true of the alkalinity and the remarkable degree of moderate temperature levels of the earth's surface. The uniqueness and anomalies of the Earth's atmosphere

> are far from random. At least the "core," the tropical and temperate regions, surface and atmosphere [temperatures] are skewed from the values deduced by interpolating between values for Mars and Venus, and deviations are in directions favored by most species of organisms. Oxygen is maintained at about 20 percent, the mean temperature of the lower atmosphere is about 22°C, and the pH is just over 8. These planet-wide anomalies have persisted for very long times; the chemically bizarre composition of the Earth's atmosphere has prevailed for millions of years, even though the residence times of the reactive gases can be measured in months and years.

Margulis concludes that it

> is highly unlikely that chance alone accounts for the fact that temperature, pH, and the concentration of nutrient elements have been for immense

periods of time just those optimal for life. It seems especially unlikely when it is obvious that the major perturbers of atmospheric gases are organisms themselves—primarily microbes.... It seems rather more likely that energy is expended by the biota actively to maintain these conditions.

Finally, the Modern Synthesis, to use Julian Huxley's term for the neo-Darwinian model of organic evolution in force since the early 1940s, has also been challenged as too narrow and perhaps mechanistic in its outlook. The image of a slow pace of evolutionary change emerging from the interplay of small variations, which are selected for their adaptability to the environment, is no longer as supportable as it seemed by the actual facts of the fossil record. Evolution seems to be more sporadic, marked by occasional rapid changes, often delayed by long periods of stasis. Highly specialized genera tend to speciate and become extinct because of the very narrow, restricted niches they occupy ecologically, while fairly generalized genera change more slowly and become extinct less frequently because of the more diversified environments in which they can exist. This "Effect Hypothesis," advanced by Elizabeth Vrba, suggests that evolution tends to be an immanent striving rather than the product of external selective forces. Mutations appear more like intentional mosaics than small, scratch-like changes in the structure and function of life forms. As one observer notes, "Whereas species selection puts the forces of change on environmental conditions, the Effect Hypothesis looks to internal parameters that affect the rates of speciation and extinction."

The notion of small, gradual point mutations (a theory that accords with the Victorian mentality of strictly fortuitous evolutionary changes) can be challenged on genetic grounds alone. Not only a gene but a chromosome, both in varying combinations, may be altered chemically and mechanically. Genetic changes may range from "simple" point mutations, through jumping genes and transposable elements, to major chromosomal rearrangements. It is also clear, mainly from experimental work, that permutations of genetically determined morphological shifts are possible. Small genetic changes can give rise to either minor or major morphological modifications; the same holds true for large genetic changes.

Trager's observation that the "fittest" species may well be "the one that most helps another to survive" is an excellent formula for recasting the traditional picture of natural evolution as a meaningless competitive tableau bloodied by the struggle to survive. There is a rich literature, dating back to the late nineteenth century, that emphasizes the role played by intraspecific and interspecific cooperation in fostering the survival of life forms on the planet. Kropotkin's famous *Mutual Aid* summarized the data at the turn of the century, and apparently added the word "mutualism" to the biological vocabulary on symbiosis. The opening chapters of the book summarize the contemporary work on the subject, his own observations in eastern Asia, and a sizable array of data on insects, crabs, birds, the "hunting associations" of mammalian carnivores, rodent "societies," and the like. The material is largely intraspecific; biological "mutualists" of a century ago did not emphasize the interspecific support systems that we now know to be more widespread than Kropotkin could have imagined. Buchner has written a huge volume (1953) on the endosymbiosis of animals with plant microorganisms alone; Henry has compiled a two-volume work, *Symbiosis*, that brings the study of this subject up to the mid-1960s.. The evidence for interspecific symbiosis, particularly mutualism, is nothing less than massive. Even more than Kropotkin's *Mutual Aid*, Henry's work traces the evidence of mutualistic relationships from the interspecific support relationships of rhizobia and legumes, through plant associations, behavior symbiosis in animals, and the great regulatory mechanisms that account for homeostasis in planet-wide biogeochemical relationships.

"Fitness" is rarely biologically meaningful as mere species survival and adaptation. Left on this superficial level, it becomes an almost personal adaptive enterprise that fails to account for the need of all species for life support systems, be they autotrophic or heterotrophic. Traditional evolutionary theory tends to abstract a species from its ecosystem, to isolate it, and to deal with its survival in a remarkably abstract fashion. For example, the mutually supportive interplay between photosynthetic life forms and herbivores, far from providing evidence of the simplest form of "predation" or heterotrophy, is in fact indispensable to soil fertility from animal wastes, seed distribution, and the return (via death) of bulky organisms to an ever-enriched ecosystem. Even large carnivores that prey upon large herbivores have a vital function in selectively controlling large population swings by removing weakened or old animals for whom life would in fact become a form of "suffering."

Ironically, it cheapens the meaning of real suffering and cruelty to reduce them to pain and predation, just as it cheapens the meaning of hierarchy and domination to deinstitutionalize these socially charged terms and dissolve them into the individual transitory links between more or less aggressive individuals within a specific animal aggregation. The fear, pain, and commonly rapid death that a wolf pack brings to a sick or old caribou are evidence not of suffering or cruelty in nature but of a mode of dying that is integrally wedded to organic renewal and ecological stability. Suffering and cruelty properly belong to the realm of personal anguish, needless affliction, and the moral degradation of those who torment the victim. These notions cannot be applied to the removal of an organism that can no longer function on a level that renders its life tolerable. It is sheer distortion to associate all pain with suffering, all predation with cruelty. To suffer the anguish of hunger, psychic injury, insecurity, neglect, loneliness, and death in warfare, as well as of prolonged trauma and terminal illness, cannot be equated with the often-brief pain associated with predation and the unknowing fact of death. The spasms of nature are rarely as cruel as the highly organized and systematic afflictions that human society visits upon healthy, vital beings, animal as well as human—afflictions that only the cunning of the hominid mind can contrive.

Neither pain, cruelty, aggression, nor competition satisfactorily explain the emergence and evolution of life. For a better explanation we should also turn to mutualism and a concept of "fitness" that reinforces the support systems for the seemingly "fittest." If we are prepared to recognize the self-organizing nature of life, the decisive role of mutualism as its evolutionary impetus obliges us to redefine "fitness" in terms of an ecosystem's supportive apparatus. And if we are prepared to view life as a phenomenon that can shape and maintain the very "environment" that is regarded as the "selective" source of its evolution, a crucial question arises: Is it meaningful any longer to speak of "natural selection" as the motive force of biological evolution? Or must we now speak of "natural interaction" to take full account of life's own role in creating and guiding the "forces" that explain its evolution? Contemporary biology leaves us with a picture of organic interdependencies that far and away prove to be more important in shaping life forms than either a Darwin, a Huxley, or the formulators of the Modern Synthesis could ever have anticipated. Life is necessary not only for its own self-maintenance but for its own self-formation. "Gaia" and subjectivity are more than the effects of life; they are its integral attributes.

❧

The grandeur of an authentic ecological sensibility, in contrast to the superficial environmentalism so prevalent today, is that it provides us with the ability to generalize in the most radical way these fecund, supportive interrelationships and their reliance on variety as the foundation of stability. An ecological sensibility gives us a coherent outlook that is explanatory in the most meaningful sense of the term, and almost overtly *ethical.*

From the distant Hellenic era to the early Renaissance, nature was seen primarily as a source of ethical orientation, a means by which human thought found its normative bearings and coherence. Nonhuman nature was not external to human nature and society. To the contrary, the mind was uniquely part of a cosmic *logos* that provided objective criteria for social and personal concepts of good and evil, justice and injustice, beauty and ugliness, love and hatred—indeed, for an interminable number of values by which to guide oneself toward the achievement of virtue and the good life. The words *dike* and *andike*—justice and injustice—permeated the cosmologies of the Greek nature philosophers. They linger on in many terminological variations as part of the jargon of modern natural science—notably in such words as "attraction" and "repulsion."

The fallacies of archaic cosmology generally lie not in its ethical orientation but in its dualistic approach to nature. For all its emphasis on speculation at the expense of experimentation, ancient cosmology erred *most* when it tried to conjoin a self-organizing, fecund nature with a vitalizing force alien to the natural world itself. Parmenides's Dike, like Henri Bergson's *élan vital,* are substitutes for the self-organizing properties of nature, not motivating forces within nature that account for an ordered world. A latent dualism exists in monistic cosmologies that try to bring humanity and nature into ethical commonality—a *deus ex machina* that corrects imbalances either in a disequilibriated cosmos or in an irrational society. Truth wears an unseen crown in the form of God or Spirit, for nature can never be trusted to develop on its own spontaneous grounds, any more than the body politic bequeathed to us by "civilization" can be trusted to manage its own affairs.

These archaisms, with their theological nuances and their tightly formulated teleologies, have been justly viewed as socially reactionary traps. In fact, they tainted the works of Aristotle and Hegel as surely as they mesmerized the minds of the medieval Schoolmen. But the errors of classical nature philosophy lie not in its project of eliciting an ethics from nature, but in the spirit of domination that poisoned it from the start with a presiding, often authoritarian, Supernatural "arbiter" who weighed out and corrected the imbalances or "injustices" that erupted in nature. Hence the ancient gods were there all the time, however rationalistic these early cosmologies may seem; they had to be exorcised in order to render an ethical continuum between nature and humanity more meaningful and democratic. Tragically, late Renaissance thought was hardly more democratic than its antecedents, and neither Galileo in science nor Descartes in philosophy performed this much-needed act of surgery satisfactorily. They and their more recent heirs *separated* the domains of nature and mind, recreating deities of their own in the form of scientistic and epistemological biases that are no less tainted by domination than the classical tradition they demolished.

Today, we are faced with the possibility of permitting nature— not Dike, Justitia, God, Spirit, or an *élan vital*—to open itself to us ethically on its *own* terms. Mutualism is an intrinsic good by virtue of its function in fostering the evolution of natural variety. We require no Dike on the one hand or canons of "scientific objectivity" on the other to affirm the role of community as a desideratum in nature and society. Similarly, *freedom* is an intrinsic good; its claims are validated by what Hans Jonas so perceptively called the "inwardness" of life forms, their "organic identity" and "adventure of form." The clearly visible effort, venture, indeed self-recognition, which every living being exercises in the course of "its precarious metabolic continuity" to preserve itself reveals—even in the most rudimentary of organisms—a sense of identity and selective activity which Jonas has very appropriately called evidence of "germinal freedom."

Finally, from the ever-greater complexity and variety that raises subatomic particles through the course of evolution to those conscious, self-reflexive life forms we call human beings, we cannot help but speculate about the existence of a broadly conceived *telos* and a latent subjectivity in substance itself that eventually yields mind and intellectuality. In the reactivity of substance, in the sensibility of the least-developed microorganisms, in the elaboration of nerves, ganglia, the spinal cord, and the layered development of the brain, one senses an evolution of mind so coherent and compelling that there is a strong temptation to describe it with Manfred Eigen's term, "inevitable." It is hard to believe that mere fortuity accounts for the capacity of life forms to respond neurologically to stimuli; to develop highly organized nervous systems; to be able to foresee, however dimly, the results of their behavior and later conceptualize this foresight clearly and symbolically. A true history of mind may have to begin with the attributes of substance itself; perhaps in the hidden or covert efforts of the simplest crystals to perpetuate themselves, in the evolution of DNA from unknown chemical sources to a point where it shares a principle of replication already present in the inorganic world, and in the speciation of nonliving as well as living molecules as a result of those intrinsic self-organizing features of reality we call their "properties."

Hence our study of nature—all archaic philosophies and epistemological biases aside—exhibits a self-evolving patterning, a "grain," so to speak, that is implicitly ethical. Mutualism, freedom, and subjectivity are not strictly human values or concerns. They appear, however germinally, in larger cosmic and organic processes that require no Aristotelian God to motivate them, no Hegelian Spirit to vitalize them. If social ecology provides little more than a coherent focus to the unity of mutualism, freedom, and subjectivity as aspects of a cooperative society that is free of domination and guided by reflection and reason, it will remove the taints that blemished a naturalistic ethics from its inception; it will provide both humanity and nature with a common ethical voice. No longer would we have need of a Cartesian—and more recently, a neo-Kantian—dualism that leaves nature mute and mind isolated from the larger world of phenomena around it. To vitiate community, to arrest the spontaneity that lies at the core of a self-organizing reality toward ever-greater complexity and rationality, to abridge freedom— these actions would cut across the grain of nature, deny our heritage in its evolutionary processes, and dissolve our legitimacy and function in the world of life. No less than this ethically rooted legitimation would be at stake—all its grim ecological consequences aside—if we fail to achieve an ecological society and articulate an ecological ethics.

Mutualism, self-organization, freedom, and subjectivity, cohered by social ecology's principles of unity in diversity, spontaneity, and nonhierarchical relationships, are thus ends in themselves. Aside from the ecological responsibilities they confer on our species as the self-reflexive voice of nature, they literally define us. Nature does not "exist" for us to use; it simply legitimates us and our uniqueness ecologically. Like the concept of "being," these principles of social ecology require no explanation, merely verification. They are the elements of an ethical *ontology*, not rules of a game that can be changed to suit one's personal needs.

A society that cuts across the grain of this ontology raises the entire question of its very reality as a meaningful and rational entity. "Civilization" has bequeathed us a vision of otherness as "polarization" and "defiance," and of organic "inwardness" as a perpetual "war" for self-identity. This vision threatens to utterly subvert the ecological legitimation of humanity and the reality of society as a potentially rational dimension of the world around us. Trapped by the false perception of a nature that stands in perpetual opposition to our humanity, we have redefined humanity itself to mean strife as a condition for pacification, control as a condition for consciousness, domination as a condition for freedom, and opposition as a condition for reconciliation. Within this implicitly self-destructive context, we are rapidly building the Valhalla that will almost certainly become a trap rather than a fortress against the all-consuming flames of Ragnarok.

Yet an entirely different philosophical and social dispensation can be read from the concept of otherness and inwardness of life—one that, in spirit at least, is not unlike that of the Wintu and Hopi. Given a world that life itself made conducive to evolution—indeed, benign, in view of a larger ecological vision of nature—we can formulate an ethics of complementarity that is nourished by variety rather than one that guards individual inwardness from a threatening, invasive otherness. Indeed, the inwardness of life can be seen as an expression of equilibrium, not as mere resistance to entropy and the terminus of all activity. Entropy itself can be seen as one feature in a larger cosmic metabolism, with life as its anabolic dimension. Finally, selfhood can be viewed as the result of integration, community, support, and sharing without any loss of individual identity and personal spontaneity.

Thus, two alternatives confront us. We can try to calm the antagonistic Bronze Age warrior spirit of Odin, pacify him and his cohorts, and perhaps ventilate Valhalla with the breath of reason and reflection. We can try to mend the tattered treaties that once held the world together so precariously, and work with them as best we can. In the fullness of time, Odin might be persuaded to put aside his spear, cast off his armor, and lend himself to the sweet voice of rational understanding and discourse.

Or our efforts can take a radical turn: to overthrow Odin, whose partial blindness is evidence of a hopelessly aborted society. We can abandon the contractual myths that "harmonized" an inherently divided world, which the Norse epic held together with chains and banishments. It will then be our responsibility to create a new world and a new sensibility based on a self-reflexivity and an ethics to which we are heirs as a result of evolution's relentless thrust toward consciousness. We can try to reclaim our legitimacy as the fullness of mind in the natural world—as the rationality that *abets* natural diversity and integrates the workings of nature with an effectiveness, certainty, and directedness that is essentially incomplete in nonhuman nature.

"Civilization" as we know it today is more mute than the nature for which it professes to speak and more blind than the elemental forces it professes to control. Indeed, "civilization" lives in hatred of the world around it and in grim hatred of itself. Its gutted cities, wasted lands, poisoned air and water, and mean-spirited greed constitute a daily indictment of its odious immorality. A world so demeaned may well be beyond redemption, at least within the terms of its own institutional and ethical framework. The flames of Ragnarok purified the world of the Norsemen. The flames that threaten to engulf our planet may leave it hopelessly hostile to life—a dead witness to cosmic failure. If only because this planet's history, including its human history, has been so full of promise, hope, and creativity, it deserves a better fate than what seems to confront it in the years ahead.

∝ **NOTES**

Except for short, well-known phrases, all direct quotations from other sources are cited in the following notes. In addition, there are frequent sources to provide background material for ideas presented in the text.

The numerals listed to the left of these notes indicate the page or pages of the text where the corresponding source is used or quoted. Only the first occurrence of a particular page number is given; subsequent unnumbered notes refer to the same page. When a source is used or quoted on one (or more) following page(s) in the text, the symbol "f" (or "ff") appears after the page number. When the source is used or quoted in a footnote to the main text, the symbol "n" appears after the page number.

∝ Introduction

65 Lewis Herber (pseud.), "The Problem of Chemicals in Food," in *Contemporary Issues*, Vol. 3, No. 12 (1952), pp. 206–41.

Lewis Herber (pseud.) and Gotz Ohly, *Lebensgefährliche Lebensmittel* (Munich: Hans Georg Mueller Verlag, 1955).

Lewis Herber (pseud.), *Our Synthetic Environment* (New York: Alfred A. Knopf, 1963); republished by Harper & Row (1974) under the author's real name.

Murray Bookchin, *Toward an Ecological Society* (Montreal: Black Rose Books, 1981).

Murray Bookchin, *Post-Scarcity Anarchism* (Palo Alto: Ramparts Press, 1970); also available from AK Press, Oakland (2005).

68 Quote on class struggle from Karl Marx and Frederick Engels, "The Communist Manifesto," in *Selected Works*, Vol. I (Moscow: Progress Publishers, 1969), p. 108.

69 G. W. F. Hegel, *Lectures on the History of Philosophy*, Vol. I (New York: The Humanities Press, 1955), p. 24.

1 ∝ The Concept of Social Ecology

80f Norse account and quotations drawn from P. Grappin, "German Lands: The Mortal Gods," in *Larousse World Mythology* (New York: Hamlyn Publishing Group, Ltd., 1965), pp. 363–83.

86   G. W. F. Hegel, *Phenomenology of Mind* (New York: Humanities Press, 1931 edition), p. 79.

87.   E. A. Gutkind, *Community and Environment* (New York: Philosophical Library, 1954), p. 9.

90   Charles Elton, *The Ecology of Invasions by Plants and Animals* (New York: John W. Wiley, 1953), p. 101.

90f   Allison Jolly, *The Evolution of Primate Behavior* (New York: MacMillan Co., 1972), p. 172.

93   Elise Boulding, *The Underside of History* (Boulder, Colorado: Westview Press, 1976), p. 39.

94f   Jane van Lawick-Goodall, *In the Shadow of Man* (New York: Delta Publishing Co., 1971), p. 123.

95f   See Robert E. Park, *Human Communities* (Glencoe, Illinois: The Free Press, 1952) for the classical statement of the Chicago School's viewpoint.

96   Hegel, *The Phenomenology of the Mind*, p. 81.

97   *Ibid.*, p. 68. The translation by Baille inaccurately renders this famous Hegelian maxim as "The truth is the whole."

98   Marx's observation on "man" and the conditions for historical change appears in "The Eighteenth Brumaire of Louis Napoleon," in *Selected Works*, Vol. I (Moscow: Progress Publishers, 1969), p. 398.

99f   Ernst Bloch, *Das Prinzip Hoffnung*, Band II (Frankfurt am Main: Suhrkamp Verlag, 1967), pp. 806–7.

102   Aristotle, *Metaphysics* (Richard Hope Translation) (Ann Arbor: The University of Michigan Press, 1960), 1036b5–6. " ... or they are materials to be given actualization," which Aristotle describes as *entelechia* or "fulfillment."

103   Benjamin R. Barber, *The Death of Communal Liberty* (Princeton: Princeton University Press, 1974), p. 5.

107   The quotation from Josef Weber appears in "The Ring of the Nibelung," (Wilhelm Lunen, pseud.), in *Contemporary Issues*, Vol. 5, No. 19, pp. 156–99.

2 ଔ The Outlook of Organic Society

110   Dorothy Lee, *Freedom and Culture* (Englewood, New Jersey: Prentice-Hall, Inc., 1959), p. 42.

111   *Ibid.*, p. 8.

112   Dorothy Eggan, "Instruction and Effect in Cultural Continuity," in *From Childhood to Adult*, John Middleton, ed. (New York: The Natural History Press, 1970), p. 117.

113   Lee, *Freedom and Culture*, p. 47.

Hans Jonas, *The Phenomenon of Life* (New York: Dell Publishing Co., 1966), p. 7.

116   Farley Mowatt, *The People of the Deer* (New York: Pyramid Publications, 1968), p. 142.

117   Gontran de Poncins, *Kabloona* (New York: Reynal & Hitchcock, 1941), photo caption.

Lucien Levy-Bruhl, "The Solidarity of the Individual with His Group" in *The Making of Man*, V. F. Calverton, ed. (New York: Modern Library, 1931), pp. 249–78.

123   Paul Radin, *The World of Primitive Man* (New York: Grove Press, 1960), pp. 11,106.

125   Erich Fromm, *The Crisis of Psychoanalysis* (Greenwich, Connecticut: Fawcett Publications, 1961), p. 128.

126   Lewis Mumford, *The City in History* (New York: Harcourt, Brace & World, Inc., 1961), p. 12.

128   Fromm, *The Crisis of Psychoanalysis*, p. 130.

3 ᏸ The Emergence of Hierarchy

132   Pierre-Joseph Proudhon, *What Is Property*, Vol. I (London: Bellamy Library, n.d.), p. 135.

133   Karl Marx and Frederick Engels, *The German Ideology* (Moscow: Progress Publishers, 1964), p. 46. Translation altered to correspond more accurately to Marx's actual terminology.

142   See Karl Polanyi, *The Great Transformation* (Boston: Beacon Press, 1957).

144   Melville Jacobs, *Patterns in Cultural Anthropology* (Homewood, Illinois: The Dorsey Press, 1964), p. 192. Considering the date of this observation, Jacobs' views are perhaps one of the earliest examples of such a criticism by a male anthropologist.

147   Elizabeth Marshall Thomas, *The Harmless People* (New York: Vintage Books, 1958), p. 64.

148n Simone de Beauvoir, *The Second Sex* (New York: Bantam Books, 1961), p. 65.

153   Paul Radin, *The World of Primitive Man* (New York: Grove Press, 1960), p. 212.

Weston La Barre, *The Ghost Dance* (New York: Doubleday & Co., 1970), p. 107.

154　Radin, *The World of Primitive Man*, p. 214.

　　La Barre, *The Ghost Dance*, p. 301.

155　Radin, *The World of Primitive Man*, p. 215.

　　Manning Nash, *Primitive and Peasant Economic Systems* (Scranton, Pennsylvania: Chaldler Publishing Co., 1966), p. 35.

156　Patrick Malloy, personal communication.

157　Karl Marx, "The Future Results of British Rule in India," in *Selected Works*, Vol. I (Moscow: Progress Publishers, 1969), p. 499.

4 ∞ Epistemologies of Rule

163　Robert McAdams, *The Evolution of Urban Society* (Chicago: Aldine Publishing Co., 1966).

168　Howard Press, "Marx, Freud, and the Pleasure Principle," in *The Philosophical Forum*, Vol. 11, No.1 (1970), p. 36.

　　Jean Piaget, *The Construction of Reality in the Child* (New York: Ballantine Books, 1971), pp. x, xi.

169　Edward B. Tylor, "Animism" in *Primitive Culture* (London: Murray, 1873), excerpted in *The Making of Man*, V. F. Calverton, ed. (New York: Modern Library, 1931), p. 646.

　　R. G. Collingwood, *The Idea of Nature* (New York: Oxford University Press, 1960), p. 3–4.

170　Tylor, "Animism," p. 538.

　　*Ibid.*p. 539.

171　Ivar Paulson, quoted in Weston La Barre, *The Ghost Dance* (New York: Doubleday & Co., 1970), p. 163.

　　Ibid., p. 163.

174　H. and H. A. Frankfort, et al, *Before Philosophy* (Baltimore: Penguin Books, 1949), p. 241.

175　*Ibid.*, p. 247.

　　Exodus 3:1(Masoretic Text).

176　Rudolph Bultmann, *Primitive Christianity* (New York: World Publishing Co., 1956), p. 15.

176 Frankfort, *Before Philosophy*, p. 244.

178 Hannah Arendt, *The Human Condition* (Chicago: The University of Chicago Press, 1958), pp. 30–31.

See Havelock Ellis, "The Love of Wild Nature," in *From Rousseau to Proust* (New York: Charles Scribner & Sons, 1935), pp. 58–82.

180 Aristotle, *Politics* (Richard McKeon Translation), in *Basic Works of Aristotle* (New York: Random House, 1941),1257b35–40.

Max Horkheimer, *The Eclipse of Reason*, (New York: Oxford University Press, 1947), pp. 130–31.

184 Alvin Gouldner, *Enter Plato* (New York: Harper & Row, 1971), p. 165.

187 Paul Radin, *The World of Primitive Man* (New York: Grove Press, 1960), p. 249.

188n W. C. Willoughby, *The Soul of the Bantu* (New York: 1928), quoted in *ibid.*, p. 248.

5 ♋ The Legacy of Domination

191 E. R. Dodds, *The Greeks and the Irrational* (Berkeley: The University of California Press, 1968), pp. 45–46.

193 Max Horkheimer and Theodor Adorno, *Dialectic of Enlightenment* (New York: Herder & Herder, 1972), pp. 247–48.

194 Colin M. Turnbull, *The Forest People* (New York: Simon and Schuster, 1962), pp. 154–55.

197 Peter Farb, *Man's Rise to Civilization* (New York: E. P. Dutton & Co., 1968), p. 137.

197f P. Drucker, "Rank, Wealth, and Kinship in Northwest Coast Society," in *American Anthropologist* (1939), p. 58, quoted by Farb, *ibid.*, p. 138.

201 Peter Kropotkin, *Mutual Aid* (Montreal: Black Rose Books; n.d.,1914 edition), pp. 178–79.

202 J-J Rousseau, *Social Contract* (New York: E. P. Dutton, 1950), p. 94.

202f Henri Frankfort, *The Birth of Civilization in the Near East* (New York: Doubleday & Co., 1956), pp. 77–78.

203f Thucydides, *The Peloponnesian War* (New York: Modern Library, 1944), pp. 121–22.

207 Karl Marx, *Grundrisse* (New York: Random House, 1973), pp. 409–10.

208 Karl Marx, *Capital*, Vol. I (New York: Random House, 1977), pp. 477–78.

213 Herbert Marcuse, *Eros and Civilization* (Boston: Beacon Press, 1955), p. xi.

6 ♋ Justice Equal and Exact

218 Karl Marx, *Capital*, Vol. I (New York: Random House, 1977), p. 679.

220 M. I. Finley, *Early Greece* (New York: W. W. Norton & Co., 1970), pp. 84–85.

220f *Ibid.*, p. 85.

221 *Ibid.*, pp. 85–86.

222 Max Horkheimer and Theodor Adorno, *Dialectic of Enlightenment* (New York: Herder & Herder, 1972), p. 14.

223 *Ibid.*, pp. 16–17.

224 Frederick Engels, *Anti-Dühring* (New York: International Publishers, 1939), pp. 157–58.

226 Howard Becker and Harry Elmer Barnes, *Social Thought From Lore to Science*, Vol. I (New York: Dover Publications, 1961), pp. 87–88.

227n Hannah Arendt, *The Human Condition* (Chicago: The University of Chicago Press, 1958), p. 315.

228 Henry Maine, *Ancient Law* (Boston: Beacon Books, 1963), p. 157.

230 Max Horkheimer, *The Eclipse of Reason* (New York: Oxford University Press, 1947), p. 130.

Archilochus quoted in Bruno Snell, *The Discovery of the Mind* (New York: Harper & Row, 1960), p. 49.

234f Epictetus, "Discourses of Epictetus," in *The Stoic and Epicurean Philosophers* (New York: Modern Library, 1940), p. 240. Emphasis added.

235 *Ibid.*, p. 258.

Paul's Letter to Philemon (New Jerusalem Bible).

236f St. Augustine, *The City of God* (New York: Random House, 1950), p. 696.

238 Thomas Hobbes, *Leviathan* (New York: Macmillan Publishing Co., 1962), p. 19ff.

239 John Locke, *The Second Treatise on Civil Government* (New York: New American Library, 1963), p. 332.

Ibid., p. 341.

241 Jeremy Bentham, *An Introduction to the Principle of Morals and Legislation in Ethics,*

in *Writers on Ethics*, Joseph Katz, *et al*, ed. (New York: D. Van Nostrand Co., Inc., 1962), p. 93.

Ibid., p. 106.

7 ❧ The Legacy of Freedom

244f Samuel Noah Kramer, *The Sumerians* (Chicago: The University of Chicago Press, 1963), p. 79.

246 Ernst Bloch, *Man On His Own* (New York: Herder and Herder, 1970), p. 128.

246f Franz Neumann, *The Democratic and Authoritarian State* (New York: The Free Press of Glencoe, 1957), p. 6.

247 Gregory quoted in George H. Sabine, *A History of Political Thought* (Hinsdale, Illinois: Dryden Press, 1973), p. 224.

248 Bloch, *Man On His Own*, p. 133.

248f *Ibid.*, p. 136.

253 Cokaygne verse quoted in A. L. Morton, *The English Utopia* (London: Laurence & Wishart, Ltd., 1952), p. 18.

253f *Ibid.*, p. 13.

260 Tertullian quoted in Hans Jonas, *The Gnostic Religion* (Boston: Beacon Press, 1959), p. 142.

Ibid., p. 144.

261 Hippolytus quoted in *ibid.*, p. 94–95.

262 .*Ibid.*, p. 272ff.

262f *Ibid.*, p. 274.

269 Varlet quoted in George Woodcock, *Anarchism* (New York: The World Publishing Co., 1962), p. 58.

270 Thomas Jefferson, "Letter to Destute Tracy," in *The Portable Thomas Jefferson*, M. D. Peterson, ed. (New York: Penguin Books, 1977), p. 524.

8 ❧ From Saints to Sellers

273 Egyptian scribe quoted in James Breasted, *The Dawn of Conscience* (New York: Charles Scribner's Sons, 1933), p. 195fn.

Ibid., p. 196.

275 Acts 2:44, 45; 4:32 (New Jerusalem Bible).

Barnabas, "Epistle to the Christians," quoted in Max Beer, *The General History of Socialism and Social Struggles*, Vol. I (New York: Russell & Russell, 1957), p. 200.

Justin the Martyr quoted in Max Beer, *The General History of Socialism*, p. 201.

Tertullian quoted in *ibid.*, p. 201–2.

276 Matthew 10:34.

276f Norman Cohn, *The Pursuit of the Millennium* (New York: Harper & Row, 1961), p. 4.

277 Lactantius quoted in *ibid.*, p. 12.

281 Christopher Hill, *The World Turned Upside Down* (New York: Viking Press, 1972).

281f John Ball quoted in Jean Froissart, *Chronicles* (New York: Penguin Books, 1968), p. 212.

282 Kenneth Rexroth, *Communalism* (New York: Seabury Press, 1974), p. 88.

283 *Ibid.*, p. 91.

284 *Ibid.*, p. 138.

285 Gerrard Winstanley, *The Law of Freedom in a Platform or, True Magistracy Restored* (New York: Schocken Books, 1973), pp. 112, 134–42.

288 Jeffrey B. Russell, "The Brethern of the Free Spirit," in *Religious Dissent in the Middle Ages*, J. B. Russell, ed. (New York: John Wiley & Sons, 1971), p. 87–90.

288f Quoted in Norman Cohn, *The Pursuit of the Millennium*, p. 186.

289f *Ibid.*, pp. 186–89.

291 A. L. Morton, *The World of the Ranters* (London: Laurence & Wishart, 1970), p. 70. Quoted in *ibid.*, p. 83.

292 Christopher Hill, *The World Turned Upside Down*, pp. 256, 260.

9 ☙ Two Images of Technology

304 Aristotle, *Metaphysics* (McKeon Translation), in *The Basic Works of Aristotle* (New York: Random House, 1968), 1098b.

Ibid., 981a30.

304f Aristotle, *Nichomachean Ethics*, in *ibid.*, 1140a10–20.

305 Aristotle, *Metaphysics*, in *ibid.*, 1046b.

306 Max Horkheimer, *The Eclipse of Reason* (New York: Oxford University Press, 1947), p. 23.

308f Karl Marx, *Capital*, Vol. I (New York: Random House, 1977), pp. 283–84.

309f *Ibid.*, p. 89. Emphasis added.

312f Karl Marx, *Capital*, Vol. I, p. 128.

316 Mircea Eliade, *The Forge and the Crucible* (New York: Harper & Row, 1971), p. 8.

317 Aristotle, *On the Heavens*, in *Basic Works of Aristotle*, 303a30.

318 Rene Dubos, *A God Within* (New York: Charles Scribner's Sons, 1972), p. 11.

10 ଔ The Social Matrix of Technology

327 See Lewis Mumford, *The Myth of the Machine* (New York: Harcourt, Brace & World, 1966).

330 See James Mellaart, *Çatal Hüyük* (New York: McGraw Hill, 1967).

J. Alden Mason, *The Ancient Civilization of Peru* (New York: Penguin Books, 1957), p. 121.

333 Henry Hodges, *Technology in the Ancient World* (New York: Alfred A. Knopf, 1970), p. 19.

339 See Hesiod, *Works and Days* (Richard Lattimore Translation) (Ann Arbor: The University of Michigan Press, 1973).

342 Mason, *The Ancient Civilization of Peru*, p. 184.

343 Leo Tolstoy, *Anna Karenina* (New York: New American Library, 1961), p. 282ff.

351f Fustel de Coulange, *The Ancient City* (New York: Doubleday, n.d.), p. 334.

11 ଔ The Ambiguities of Freedom

359f Max Horkheimer, *The Eclipse of Reason* (New York: Oxford University Press, 1947), p. 8.

367f Herbert Marcuse, *One-Dimensional Man* (Boston: Beacon Press, 1964), p. 236.

369 Paul Shepard, *The Tender Carnivore and the Sacred Game* (New York: Charles Scribner's Sons, 1973), p. 10. Emphasis added.

371 Max Scheler quoted in William Leiss, *The Domination of Nature* (New York: George Braziller,1972), p. 95.

373   Francis Bacon, "The Great Instauration," in *The English Philosophers*, E. A. Burtt, ed. (New York: Modern Library, 1939), pp. 5–25.

375   Aristotle, *On Interpretation* (McKeon Translation), in *The Basic Works of Aristotle* (New York: Random House, 1968), 19a22–29.

Aristotle, *On Generation and Corruption*, in *ibid.*, 336b27.

Ibid., 744b16.

376   G. W. F. Hegel, *Lectures on the History of Philosophy*, Vol. I (New York: Humanities Press, 1955), p. 22.

382   Stephan Toulmin and June Goodfield, *The Architecture of Matter* (New York: Harper & Row, 1962), p. 28.

Ibid., p. 33.

382f *Ibid.*, p. 32.

383   *Ibid.*, p. 37.

385   Aristotle, *Politics*, in *The Basic Works of Aristotle*, 1278a8.

Claude Mossé, *The Ancient World at Work* (New York: W. W. Norton & Co., 1969), pp. 27–28. Emphasis added.

386   *Ibid.*, p. 27.

389   Thomas Jefferson, *Notes on the State of Virginia* (New York: Harper & Row, 1964), p. 157.

390   Alexis de Tocqueville, *Journey*, quoted in John F. Kasson, *Civilizing the Machine* (New York: Penguin Books, 1976).

391f Kasson, *Civilizing the Machine*, p. 69.

392f *Ibid.*, pp. 73–74, 75.

397   See Joachim Israel, *Alienation* (Boston: Allyn and Bacon, Inc., 1971), pp. 23, 28.

398   G. W. F. Hegel, *Early Theological Writings* (Philadelphia: The University of Pennsylvania Press, 1971), p. 305.

398f Robert Briffault, "The Evolution of the Human Species," in *The Making of Man*, V. F. Calverton, ed. (New York: Modern Library, 1931), pp. 765–66.

406   Quoted in Sidney Pollard, "Factory Discipline in the Industrial Revolution," *Economic History Review*, Vol. 16, No. 2 (1963), p. 256.

Quoted in Dan Clawson, *Bureaucracy and the Labor Process* (New York: Monthly Review Press, 1980), p. 40. See also my "Listen, Marxist!" in *Post-Scarcity Anarchism* and an outstanding work on the subject of labor rationalization by John and Paula Zerzan, *Industrialism and Domestication* (Seattle: Black Eye Press, 1979).

408 Frederick Engels, *The Housing Question* (Moscow: Progress Publishers, 1970).

Langdon Winner, *Autonomous Technology* (Cambridge: MIT Press, 1977).

12 ⊗ An Ecological Society

413 Robert Briffault, "The Evolution of the Human Species," in *The Making of Man*, V. F. Calverton, ed. (New York: Modern Library, 1931), p. 766.

423 Rabelais' account of his utopia must be read as a whole. See especially Francois Rabelais, *Gargantua and Pantagrual* (New York: Penguin Books, 1955), pp. 149–53.

424 Sade's views also require a full reading. See Marquis de Sade: *La Philosophie dans le Boudoir* (The Philosophy of the Bedroom) in *Selected Writings* (New York: British Book Center, n.d.), pp. 235–72.

426 Charles Fourier, *Harmonian Society: Selected Writings*, Mark Poster, ed. (New York: Doubleday & Co., 1971), p. 2. Poster's collection is perhaps the best and most intelligent selection of Fourier's writings in English with a very searching introduction by the editor. See also Frank E. Manuel, *The Prophets of Paris* (New York: Harper & Row, 1962), pp. 197–248.

Maurice Blanchot quoted in Herbert Marcuse, *One-Dimensional Man* (Boston: Beacon Press, 1964), pp. 255–56.

429f Manuel, *The Prophets of Paris*, pp. 229, 239.

430f John F. C. Harrison, *Quest for the New Moral World* (New York: Charles Scribner's Sons, 1969), pp. 48, 49.

431f Herbert Marcuse, *Essay on Liberation* (Boston: Beacon Press, 1969), p. 22.

⊗ Epilogue

452 Hannah Arendt, *On Revolution* (New York: Viking Press, 1965), pp. 36–52.

455 Hans Jonas, *The Phenomenon of Life* (New York: Delta Books, 1966), p. 90. Emphasis added.

457 Erwin Schrodinger, *What is Life? Mind and Matter* (New York: Cambridge University Press, 1944), p. 5. Emphasis added.

Graham Cairns-Smith "Genes Made of Clay," in *The New Scientist*, October 24, 1974, p. 276.

358 William Trager, *Symbiosis* (New York: Van Nostrand Reinhold Co., 1970), p. vii.

460   See Lynn Margulis, *Symbiosis in Cell Evolution* (San Francisco: W. H. Freeman and Co., 1981).

460f Manfred Eigen, "Molecular Self-Organization and the Early Stages of Evolution," in *Quarterly Review of Biophysics*, Vol. 4, No. 2–3 (1971), p. 202.

461f Margulis, *Symbiosis in Cell Evolution*, pp. 348–49.

462   Vrba cited in Robert Lewin, "Evolutionary Theory Under Fire," in *Science*, Vol. 210, No.1(1980), p. 885.

466   Hans Jonas, *The Phenomenon of Life*, p. 82.